FROM MIDSHIPMAN TO FIELD MARSHAL

Mr. E. Wood, R.N.
1852

FROM MIDSHIPMAN TO FIELD MARSHAL

BY

EVELYN WOOD, F.M.
V.C., G.C.B., G.C.M.G.

IN TWO VOLUMES

WITH TWENTY-FOUR ILLUSTRATIONS AND MAPS

VOLUME I

METHUEN & CO.
36 ESSEX STREET W.C.
LONDON

First Published in 1906

TO

MY COMRADES

PAST AND PRESENT

OF ALL RANKS IN BOTH SERVICES

I DEDICATE

THIS STORY OF MY LIFE

CONTENTS

CHAP.		PAGE
	RECORD OF APPOINTMENTS, STAFF APPOINTMENTS, AND WAR SERVICES, EXTRACTED FROM THE OFFICIAL LIST	xi
I.	INTRODUCTION	1
II.	1852—H.M.S. *QUEEN*, 116 GUNS	8
III.	1853-4—LIFE ON BOARD A MAN-OF-WAR	16
IV.	1854—INVASION OF THE CRIMEA	28
V.	1854—THE SIEGE OF SEVASTOPOL	45
VI.	1854-5—A NAKED AND STARVING ARMY	57
VII.	1855—SIEGE OF SEVASTOPOL	69
VIII.	1855—ASSAULT OF THE REDAN	82
IX.	1855—ASSAULT OF THE REDAN—*continued*	92
X.	1856-7—13TH LIGHT DRAGOONS	106
XI.	1858—CENTRAL INDIA	118
XII.	1858—SINDWAHA	131
XIII.	1858-9—A PURSUIT	144
XIV.	1859—THE END OF THE MUTINY	154
XV.	1859—BEATSON'S HORSE	164
XVI.	1859-60—THE SIRONJ JUNGLES	176
XVII.	1860—CENTRAL INDIA HORSE	189
XVIII.	1861-2-3—THE STAFF COLLEGE	202
XIX.	1865-7—"ON THE STAFF"	218
XX.	1867-71—ALDERSHOT	230

CONTENTS

CHAP.		PAGE
XXI.	1871-2-3—90TH LIGHT INFANTRY	247
XXII.	1873—ASHANTI	257
XXIII.	1873-4—AT THE HEAD OF THE ROAD IN ASHANTI	269
XXIV.	1874-8—ALDERSHOT: SOUTH AFRICA	287
XXV.	1878—THE GAIKAS AND PERIE BUSH	304

LIST OF ILLUSTRATIONS AND MAPS

	PAGE
MR. E. WOOD, R.N., 1852 . . . . . *Frontispiece*	
From a Painting by LADY WOOD	
THE BLACK SEA	26
THE CRIMEA, SOUTH-WESTERN PART	34
THE UPLAND	44
PLAN OF THE SIEGE OF SEVASTOPOL	90
CORNET WOOD	100
BISSAEDAR DHOKUL SINGH BAHADUR	138
AN EPISODE AT SINDWAHA	140
SINDWAHA	142
SINDHARA	188
CENTRAL INDIA	200
VAGABOND	220
MAJOR WOOD'S QUARTERS, ALDERSHOT, 1869–71 . . .	246
THE DEATH OF ARTHUR EYRE	280
THE ASHANTI CAMPAIGN	286
MAJOR WOOD'S QUARTERS, 1876–77	292
THE GAIKA REBELLION	302
THE PERIE BUSH	322

NOTE.—The Maps are in most cases placed at the end of the chapter, or chapters, which they are intended to illustrate.

FIELD MARSHAL SIR EVELYN WOOD

V.C., G.C.B., G.C.M.G., p.s.c., BARRISTER-AT-LAW

RECORD OF APPOINTMENTS, STAFF APPOINTMENTS, AND WAR SERVICES EXTRACTED FROM THE OFFICIAL LIST

APPOINTMENTS

ROYAL NAVY, from 15th April 1852 to 6th September 1855.
CORNET, 13TH LIGHT DRAGOONS, 7th September 1855.
LIEUTENANT, 13TH LIGHT DRAGOONS, 1st February 1856.
LIEUTENANT, 17TH LANCERS, 9th October 1857.
CAPTAIN, 17TH LANCERS, 16th April 1861.
BREVET-MAJOR, 17TH LANCERS, 19th August 1862.
BREVET-MAJOR, 73RD FOOT, 21st October 1862.
BREVET-MAJOR, 17TH FOOT, 10th November 1865.
MAJOR, unattached, 22nd June 1870.
MAJOR, 90TH LIGHT INFANTRY, 28th October 1871.
BREVET-LIEUTENANT-COLONEL, 19th January 1873.
BREVET-COLONEL, 1st April 1874.
LIEUTENANT-COLONEL, 90TH LIGHT INFANTRY, 13th November 1878.
    Half-Pay, 15th December 1879.
MAJOR-GENERAL, 12th August 1881.
LIEUTENANT-GENERAL, 1st April 1890.
GENERAL, 26th March 1895.
FIELD MARSHAL, 8th April 1903.

STAFF APPOINTMENTS

NAVAL BRIGADE, ACTING AIDE-DE-CAMP, 1st January to 29th June 1855.

BRIGADE-MAJOR TO FLYING COLUMN, CENTRAL INDIA, 1st November 1858 to 15th April 1859.

AIDE-DE-CAMP IN DUBLIN, 22nd January 1865 to 31st March 1865.

BRIGADE-MAJOR, ALDERSHOT, 31st July 1866 to 13th November 1868.

DEPUTY-ASSISTANT ADJUTANT-GENERAL, ALDERSHOT, 14th November 1868 to 25th November 1871.

SPECIAL SERVICE, GOLD COAST, 12th September 1873 to 25th March 1874.

SUPERINTENDING OFFICER OF GARRISON INSTRUCTION, 10th September 1874 to 27th March 1876.

ASSISTANT QUARTERMASTER-GENERAL AT ALDERSHOT, 28th March 1876 to 1st February 1878.

SPECIAL SERVICE, SOUTH AFRICA, 25th February 1878 to 2nd April 1879.

BRIGADIER-GENERAL, SOUTH AFRICA, 3rd April 1879 to 5th August 1879.

BRIGADIER-GENERAL AT BELFAST AND CHATHAM, 15th December 1879 to 14th January 1881.

LOCAL MAJOR-GENERAL IN SOUTH AFRICA, 15th January 1881 to 27th February 1881.

MAJOR-GENERAL IN SOUTH AFRICA, 28th February 1881 to 16th February 1882.

BRIGADIER-GENERAL AT CHATHAM, 14th February to 3rd August 1882.

MAJOR-GENERAL IN EXPEDITIONARY FORCE, 4th August 1882 to 31st October 1882.

BRIGADIER-GENERAL, CHATHAM, 1st November to 20th December 1882.

SIRDAR, EGYPTIAN ARMY, 21st December 1882 to 31st March 1885.

COMMANDED ON THE LINES OF COMMUNICATION ON THE NILE, 15th September 1884 to 14th June 1885.

MAJOR-GENERAL, EASTERN DISTRICT, 1st April 1886 to 31st December 1888.

LIEUTENANT-GENERAL, COMMANDING AT ALDERSHOT, 1st January 1889 to 8th October 1893.

QUARTERMASTER-GENERAL TO THE FORCES, 9th October 1893 to 30th September 1897.

ADJUTANT-GENERAL TO THE FORCES, 1st October 1897 to 30th September 1901.

GENERAL, COMMANDING 2ND ARMY CORPS, LATER SOUTHERN COMMAND, 1st October 1901 to 31st December 1904.

WAR SERVICES

WOOD, SIR (H.) E., V.C., G.C.B. (FIELD MARSHAL).—

CRIMEAN CAMPAIGN, 1854–5. Served in the Naval Brigade in the battle of Inkerman, and at the bombardments of Sevastopol, in October 1854, April and June 1855, including the assault on the Redan of 18th June (severely wounded). Despatches, *London Gazette*, 2nd and 4th July 1855. Medal, with two Clasps; Knight Legion of Honour; 5th Class, Medjidie; Turkish Medal.

INDIAN MUTINY, 1858–60. Served as Brigade-Major, Beatson's Horse; commanded 1st Regiment of Beatson's Horse; raised and commanded 2nd Regiment of Central India Horse; was present at the action of Rajghur, Sindwaha, Kurai, Barode, and Sindhara. Despatches, *London Gazette*, 24th March and 5th May 1859. Medal and Victoria Cross.

ASHANTI WAR, 1873–4. Raised and commanded Wood's Regiment throughout the campaign; commanded the troops at the engagement of Essaman, Reconnaissance of 27th November 1873; commanded the Right column at the battle of Amoaful (slightly wounded), and was present at the action before Coomassie. Despatches, *London Gazette*, 18th and 25th November 1873; 6th, 7th, and 31st March 1874. Medal with Clasp. Brevet of Colonel; Companion of the Bath.

SOUTH AFRICAN WAR, 1878–9–81. Kafir Campaign, commanded a force in clearing the Buffalo Poort and Perie Bush, and at the attack on the Tutu Bush; at attack on Intaba Ka Udoda Bush, and in the operations on the Buffalo Range. Zulu Campaign, commanded a column at the actions at Zunguin Mountains, and Inhlobane (horse killed), Kambula, and at the battle of Ulundi. Despatches, *London Gazette*, 17th May, 11th and 18th June, 1878; and 21st February, 5th, 15th, 21st, 28th March, 4th, 14th, 21st April, 7th and 16th May, and 21st August, 1879. Medal with Clasp; Knight Commander of the Bath. Transvaal Campaign, conducted negotiations and concluded peace with the Boers. Promoted Major-General; Grand Cross of the Most Distinguished Order of St. Michael and St. George.

EGYPTIAN EXPEDITION, 1882. Commanded 4th Brigade, 2nd Division. Operations near Alexandria, and surrender of Kafr Dowar and Damietta. Despatches, *London Gazette*, November 1882. Thanked by both Houses of Parliament. Medal; Bronze Star; 2nd Class, Medjidie.

OTHER DISTINCTIONS

SUDAN EXPEDITION, 1884–5. Nile. As Major-General on Lines of Communication. Despatches, *London Gazette*, 25th August 1885. Clasp.

GRAND CORDON OF THE MEDJIDIE, 1st Class, 1885.

KNIGHT GRAND CROSS OF THE MOST HONOURABLE ORDER OF THE BATH, 1901.

OTHER DISTINCTIONS

PASSED STAFF COLLEGE, 1864.

BARRISTER-AT-LAW, 1874.

HONORARY COLONEL, 2nd BATTALION ESSEX RIFLE VOLUNTEERS, 1879; and 14th MIDDLESEX (INNS OF COURT), 1900.

JUSTICE OF THE PEACE, 1885.

DEPUTY-LIEUTENANT FOR THE COUNTY OF ESSEX, 1897.

GRAND CROSS IMPERIAL LEOPOLD ORDER, 1904.

FROM MIDSHIPMAN TO FIELD MARSHAL

CHAPTER I

INTRODUCTION

Ancestry—Parentage—The Grammar School and College at Marlborough—I become a Naval Cadet.

THE Woods, from whom I am descended, were for hundreds of years owners of Hareston Manor, Brixton, a small village near Plymouth. There is a record of a John a' Wood living there in the eighth year of the reign of King Edward the Third, and in the north aisle of the church a ledger stone with coat of arms to John Wood, who died A.D. 1724. The Hareston Woods died out, but a younger branch settled at Tiverton, the head of which manufactured lace and serge, and to him was born and duly apprenticed as a lad, Matthew. He soon started in business on his own account, and eventually became a successful hop merchant, being chosen Lord Mayor of London in 1815 and 1816. He represented the City in nine successive Parliaments,[1] and was as fearless in defending the cause of Queen Caroline, which he warmly espoused, as he was in all matters aldermanic and magisterial. When Lord Mayor, he faced, practically alone, a riotous mob, whose leader was exhorting his followers to storm the Bank of England. Mr. Wood running out into the crowd, pulled the ringleader off his horse, and dragged him inside the Bank railings, a prisoner.

In 1820 the Alderman was sitting in his counting-house,

[1] He was created a baronet in 1837.

when an agent of the Duke of Kent, calling late on Saturday afternoon, asked Matthew Wood for the loan of £10,000. The agent explained it was important for reasons of State that the expected baby[1] of the Duchess of Kent, who was then at Ostend, should be born in England, and that His Royal Highness the Duke could not cross over unless he received that sum of money to satisfy his more pressing creditors. Mr. Wood promised to reply on the Monday, after consulting his partners; the agent urged, however, that the state of the Duchess's health admitted of no delay and that she ought to cross immediately, so my grandfather gave him the cheque.

My mother, to whom I owe any good qualities I may possess, came of a race of Cornish squires. John Michell represented Truro in Parliament in the reign of Elizabeth. My uncle, Admiral Sir Frederick Michell, had a lease of a tin mine from the Crown, granted to Thomas Michell, gentleman, dated more than three hundred years ago; and we find Michells of Croft West[2] lending money to a courtier in favour with Charles the Second. The Michells were in comfortable circumstances till Thomas, my mother's grandfather, formed, and maintained, the Four Barrow Hunt. This expense and the investment of £60,000 in tin mines resulted in the sale of the family estate. Sampson Michell, the son of Thomas, entering the Royal Navy, fought under Lord Howe. By permission of our Government, he joined the Portuguese Navy in 1783, and was in 1807 its Commander-in-Chief, his younger children being born at Lisbon. He was very popular with the Portuguese of all classes. The Government promoted him as rapidly as possible, and appointed his eldest son, Frederick, a Second Lieutenant when he was eight years old!

The French having invaded Portugal, the Royal Family embarked for the Brazils in November 1807, but the Portuguese ships were still in the Tagus when Marshal Junot, entering the city with a small escort, himself aimed and fired a gun at the Portuguese men-of-war. The two Michell girls were playing

---

[1] Later Queen Victoria.

[2] Croft West, five miles out of Truro, is now (1906) a farmhouse, the flagged stones of the kennels remaining; and clean cut in a window frame on the ground floor are the names of many Michells, A.D. 1773.

in the garden when the French appeared, and to escape capture were hurried down to the river without a change of clothes and put on board H.M.S. *Lively*, a frigate, which only reached Falmouth after a voyage of twenty-three days!

Sampson Michell, Admiral in the Portuguese Navy, died at the Brazils in 1809, leaving a widow and five children. From savings effected out of his pay he had bought a house at Truro, but Mrs. Michell had only £90 per annum on which to keep herself, two unmarried daughters, and Molly, a lifelong servant. The income tax, then raised as a war tax, was at that time 10d. in the pound; bread sold at 14d. the quartern loaf, so life was difficult for the widow.

The Admiral left to his sons only a fine example, and sound advice: "Never get into debt; do your duty to God and to your country." The elder, Frederick, had joined the Royal Navy six years earlier, and died in 1873, when eighty-four years of age, an Admiral, with eight wounds and eleven decorations; but he appears again in my story. The younger son, Charles, having joined the Royal Artillery from Woolwich, was attached to the Portuguese Army in 1810, and though only a Lieutenant in our Service, commanded a Battery with marked gallantry and ability up to the final engagement, in 1814, at Toulouse. While quartered there he eloped with an attractive but penniless French girl[1] from a convent school, and was soon after, on the reduction of the Army, placed on half pay, his income being a mere pittance. Seven years later, when still in France, with an increasing family, he received from a friend in England a cutting from the *Times*, in which the Government advertised for a teacher of "Fortification and Military Drawing" for Sandhurst College, which had been recently moved to its present position.

[1] In 1887 my friend Dr. Norman Moore, having been summoned to Algiers to see a patient, was on his return seated at dinner in an hotel at Toulouse, and being the only guest, in talking to the waiter asked, "Is there anyone left of the D'Arragon family?" "Oh no," he said; "the last of them, a young lady, eloped with an English officer after the battle, 1814. When you have finished your dinner, if you come to the window, I will show you the bridge on which they met; and she carried her bag with some clothes, to show that she met him of her own accord." Norman Moore, who knew the story, said, "Yes, but the bag was not much bigger than a bonbonnière." He greatly interested the waiter by showing he knew much about the family.

Charles was not only a good draughtsman but an engraver, having studied the art under Bartolozzi, and as specimens of his work he sent an engraving of a plan he had made of Passages, a little seaport in Guipuzcoa, Spain, and a sketch of Nantes, Brittany, where he lived.

Having obtained the appointment in this unconventional manner, he joined the Instructional Staff, at what is now known as Yorktown, Camberley, in 1824, and was promoted later to a similar but better paid post at Woolwich, whence he was sent in 1828 to the Cape of Good Hope as Surveyor-General, and remained there until he was invalided home in 1848. While holding this appointment he made locomotion possible for Europeans, constructing also lighthouses and sea-walls.

I was born at the Vicarage, Cressing, a village near Braintree, Essex, on the 9th of February 1838, the youngest son of John Page Wood, Clerk in Holy Orders, who was also Rector of St. Peter's, Cornhill, in the City of London. My father,[1] educated at Winchester and Cambridge, visited as a lad the Field of Waterloo a few days after the 18th of June 1815, and brought back the small book[2] of a French soldier, killed in the battle. This book, which I still possess, has within its leaves a carnation, and belonged evidently to a Reservist who had been recalled to the Colours in "The Hundred Days." He had served in the campaigns of 1812, 1813, and 1814, and had been discharged on Napoleon's abdication, as is shown by his last pay settlement.

My father took his degree early in 1820, and was immediately appointed Chaplain and Private Secretary to Queen Caroline. In the following year he married Emma Carolina Michell, with whom he had been acquainted for some time; for he frequently accompanied his uncle, Benjamin Wood, to visit copper mines in Cornwall in which the Woods had an interest. Benjamin Wood was later for many years Member for Southwark.

In 1846, owing to monetary troubles, our governess was sent away, and her time having been previously fully occupied

---

[1] He succeeded to the baronetcy in 1843.

[2] An account-book, carried by soldiers of all European armies, showing their service, with statements of pay received, and due.

with the elder children, I had but little instruction, and when I went to the Grammar School, Marlborough, in February 1847, I could only read words of one syllable. This I was ashamed to admit, and was greatly distressed when as a first lesson the master gave me two lines of Latin to learn by heart. My elder brother, understanding my trouble, beckoned me to the bench at his side, and repeated my task until I was word perfect.

After two years at the Grammar School, where boys were sufficiently fed, but caned severely for false quantities, I went to the College at the other end of the town. The food was poor and scanty, yet I preferred the College to the Grammar School, from the greater liberty we enjoyed. I gave no trouble while at the College, or at least escaped adverse notice, till December 1851, when unjust punishment made me anxious to leave the School for any place, or for any profession.

In October our pocket money (mine was 6d. weekly) was collected for providing fireworks, as had been the annual custom, for Guy Fawkes' Day. On the 5th November, after the fireworks had been purchased, and distributed, the Head Master forbade their being displayed. It did not affect me, as boys of our Form, the Lower Fourth, were considered to be too young to let off the crackers and squibs their money had purchased. When night fell, the younger masters endeavoured to enforce the prohibition; several personal acts of violence occurred in which the boys were victorious, for the Upper Fifth and Sixth averaged from seventeen to eighteen years of age, and many were as big as their teachers. Fireworks were let off in the dormitories during the night, and acts of insubordination continued throughout November.

The Head was a learned scholar and kind-hearted man, but not strong enough to master 500 boys, of whom 100 were verging on manhood. I saw him when approaching his desk in the Upper School struck by a swan-shot thrown by a crossbow. The pellet stuck in his forehead, and he allowed it to remain there till school was up. If, as I believe, the feeling of the Lower Fourth was representative of the School, a tactful man might have utilised the shame and remorse we felt, to quell the rebellion; but neither he nor his assistants understood us, and later the masters' desks were burnt, an attempt made to fire some of the out-buildings, and a Translation of the Greek Plays was burnt with the Head's desk. In December the Master expelled three or four boys, and gave the Upper Sixth the choice of being gradually expelled, or of handing up ringleaders for punishment. The low tone of the School was shown by the fact that several selected by the older lads were like myself, under fourteen years of age.

About the middle of December I was reported on a Monday morning for being "Out of bounds, when 'confined to gates,' on the previous Saturday." I pleaded guilty to being out of bounds, but added, "I was not 'confined to gates'; it ended on Friday at sunset." The Head said, "You are so reported, and I mean to flog you." "The punishment for being out of bounds is 2s. 6d. fine; may I not ask the Master (he was sitting at the next desk) if he has not erred?" "No; you are a bad boy, and I'll flog you." "But, sir, for five years of school-life I have never been flogged." "Now you will be:" and I was. The Reverend —— at once expressed regret on paper for his error, and the Head Master said he was sorry for his mistake.

On the Friday of the same week the decisions on the senior boys' investigations were announced, and I heard read out: "Wood, Quartus, to be flogged, to be kept back two days, and until he repeats by heart three hundred lines of any Latin author, and to be fined £2." It would be difficult to imagine greater travesty of justice than to so punish a boy of thirteen, and moreover by fining his parents. I urged my flogging on the Monday should cancel that now ordered, but the Head dissented, adding, "I apologised for that; and you are such a bad boy, I'll flog you before your Form." My twenty-two classmates were marched in to the Sixth Form classroom, and I was ordered to get up. The culprit knelt on a bench, his elbows on a desk. Two prefects held his wrists (nominally) with one hand, and the tail of his shirt with the other. When the Master was about to strike, a noise made him look round: he saw all my classmates looking at the wall. He raged, vowed he would flog them all, but in vain; for when the top boys of the class were forcibly turned about by the prefects they faced round again, and my punishment was inflicted without the additional indignity intended. My class gave me £5. I chose the Fourth Book of the *Æneid*, and next morning repeated the three hundred lines.[1]

I begged my parents to let me leave, offering to go into a London office, Green's Merchant Service, or anywhere, to avoid remaining under the Head Master. My father was negotiating with Green & Co., when shortly after I returned to Marlborough College, in February 1852, I unexpectedly received a nomination for the Royal Navy, being ordered to report for examination at the Royal Naval College, Portsmouth Dockyard, in April. I was placed in charge of Mr. Eastman, a crammer at Portsea, for three weeks, that I might acquire the necessary amount of arithmetic to satisfy the Examiner; for at Marlborough nearly all my school-time was given to Latin and Greek.

Thirty-eight boys faced Captain (later Admiral) Chads on the 15th April. He read out to us half a page from the *Spectator* deliberately, with clear enunciation, and many repetitions, so that no boy could fail to catch the words. While the Examiner was reading, "And this was a very barren spot, barren, barren," he passed up and down the room, and as he turned his back a boy held up a sheet of paper on which he had written "baron" with a big mark of interrogation. I had time only to shake my head when Captain Chads turned, and that boy did not get into the Navy. We were given a short paper on English history, but this presented no difficulties to me, because I had been taught it by my mother at home before I could read.

The examination for soldiers was often at that time even less formidable, certainly in the case of a distinguished officer who has since risen to command the Army, for on joining at Sandhurst a kindly Colonel asked him his name, and continued, "What! a son of my friend Major —— ?" and on receiving an affirmative reply, said, "Go on, boy; you have passed."

---

[1] Doctor Cotton, later Bishop of Calcutta, who came in 1852, reformed the College, which for many years has been, and is now, one of the best in the kingdom.

CHAPTER II

1852—H.M.S. *QUEEN*, 116 GUNS

Drill aloft—A daring but unpopular Captain defies a riotous crew, but is removed—Captain F. T. Michell succeeds him—Disappoints a Patronage Secretary—Officers of H.M.S. *Queen*—Some hard drinkers—Hugh Burgoyne—His stoical endurance.

I JOINED H.M.S. *Victory* on the 15th May, and five days later was transferred to H.M.S. *Queen*, 116 guns (a firstrate, of 3000 tons, launched in 1839, costing about £100,000). She had just returned from the Mediterranean, where she bore the Vice-Admiral's flag, and was by universal consent allowed to be the smartest three-decker in the Fleet. She had "held the record," to employ a term not then in use, for reefing topsails, an operation curtailing the spread of canvas, which was frequently practised every week in the summer in the Vice-Admiral's squadron. The "yard," or spar supporting the canvas, is lowered to the cap, and the sailors crawling out on the yard, take in a reef by passing the reef points, or in other words fasten up the upper part of the sail in a roll on to the yard. The Fleet Orders ordained time was to be recorded from the words "lower away," which was in practice "let go," to "belay," as the reduced canvas was raised again to the required height. No man was supposed to be on the yard while it was being moved down or up, but usually the yardarm men, selected for activity and courage, reached the outer clew before the yard was down, and were seldom in from it till the sail was half-way up. Loss of life occasionally resulted, but the spirit of emulation always produced successors for the dangerous task.

In 1853 I saw this operation, which was not directly useful when completed in such haste, for the greater the speed the more ineffective was the reefing, done many times in 63 seconds; but in 1851 the *Queen's* men did it more than once in 59 seconds. Such almost incredible rapidity was in a measure due to the Captain, a man under whose command I now came for a few weeks. He was a strongly-built, active man, much feared, and still more disliked, by all hands on account of his severity. Nevertheless, he was respected for his activity, indomitable courage, and practical seamanship. His face was scarred by powder marks, a Marine having fired at him close up, when defending a position at Malta, which the Captain attacked at the head of a landing party.

Before H.M.S. *Queen* left the Mediterranean, one morning a treble-reefed topsail broke loose in a gale of wind, and the mass of canvas, flapping with violence, daunted the topsail yardmen, who feared they would be knocked off the yard, on which they hesitated to venture, till the Captain reached them from the deck, and "laying out," passed a rope round the sail and secured it. A few days after I joined, when we were weighing anchor from St. Helen's, Isle of Wight, and had got the stock of our best bower anchor awash, the forecastle man,[1] whose duty it was to shin down the cable and pass a rope through the ring on the stock, to run a hawser in order to "cat" the anchor, twice went half-way down and then climbed back, fearing to be washed off the stock, for the ship's bow rising and falling quickly, gave but little time to pass the rope, and each time the bow fell, the stock went out of sight under water. The Captain, who was as usual dressed in loose frock coat and gold-band cap, cursing the sailor for "a lubberly coward," slid down the chain cable with the rope in his hand on to the stock, and went with it right under water, but when he reappeared he had passed the rope end through the ring.

On the 24th May 1852, H.M.S. *Queen* was lying moored to the Dockyard wall. Now, some fifty years later, attendant tugs are in readiness for outgoing ships, and in those days Captains preferred to have the assistance of a steamer when passing through the narrow exit of the harbour. Our man, however, disdained all such aid. Due honours to the

[1] He was killed at my side in the 21-gun battery before Sevastopol, 19th October 1854.

Sovereign's birthday having been paid, at high tide we set sail, and, casting off, proceeded to Spithead, where, as was then the custom, all the heavy guns, and water for the cruise, were shipped. The *Queen* passed so close to the northern shore that it was necessary to run in our flying-jib boom to save the windows of the "Quebec Hotel," which has since disappeared. Most Captains would have been sufficiently preoccupied with the ship's safety to disregard a small boy. Not so, however, was our Chief. His eye rested on me, standing with hands in both pockets. "What are you doing, sir, with hands in pockets? Aft here, sail-maker's mate, with needle and tar." A big hairy seaman came aft, with his needle and tar bucket. "Sew this young gentleman's hands up in his pockets." I was seized, but as the first stitch was put in the Captain said, "Not this time, but if I see your hands there again, there they'll be for a week." Ten days later, when we were lying inside Plymouth Breakwater, I was ordered to the Captain's cabin. He was writing when the Marine sentry ushered me in, and did not look up. Presently he glanced at me, and said, "Youngster, your uncle, Captain Michell, writes asking me to see after you," and then went on writing. I stood silent, respectful, cap in hand, till raising his head he shouted, "Well, get out of the cabin."

Orders were issued to "pay down" the ship's company, but they had served long enough with their Chief, and the whole crew of Bluejackets, about 770, the 200 Marines standing aloof, came aft in a body, and demanded to be "paid off." When asked for their reasons, they said anything but what they meant, but gained their point, and were by orders of the Admiralty "paid off" on the 2nd July. When nearly all the men had landed, the Captain "called" his gig, and ordered the coxswain to pull for Mutton Cove. Robert Cowling, his coxswain, when the boat was opposite to Drake's Island, said, "Beg your pardon, your honour, but might I be allowed to land you at Mount Wise?"[1] The Captain growled, "Mutton Cove." After another quarter-mile, Cowling began again: "Your honour, might we

---

[1] This place was, and is now reserved for Naval and Military Officers, being close under Government House, while Mutton Cove is the landing-place for private boats and men-of-war's liberty men.

land you this last time at Mount Wise? There are a good many waiting for you at the Cove——" "Curse you, do you hear me?" And the boat went on. There was a large crowd of men just paid off, of wives lawful as well as temporary, whose demeanour and language indicated their hostile intentions. Undaunted, the Captain shouted, as he jumped on to the slimy stone step, "Put the women back, and I'll fight the d——d lot of you, one after the other." Then the Bluejackets, who had been waiting to throw him into the water, ran at him in a body, and raising him shoulder high, carried him, the centre of a cheering mob, to his hotel.

The pennant having been hauled down on the 2nd July, was rehoisted next day by my mother's elder brother, Captain Frederick Michell, a man differing in all characteristics from his predecessor, except that each was courageous, had a strong sense of duty as understood, and possessed a consummate knowledge of seamanship.

My uncle, born A.D. 1788, was in his sixty-fourth year, of middle height, and slight in figure. A courteous, mild manner hid great determination and force of character. In his earlier service he had repeatedly shown brilliant dash, and had been awarded by the Patriotic Fund a Sword of Honour and a grant of a hundred guineas, for gallantry in a boat attack, when he was wounded; and was warmly commended in despatches for the remarkable determination he had shown in the attack on Algiers in 1816. When re-employed in 1852 he had been living at Totnes, Devon, for many years, his last command having been H.M.S. *Inconstant*, paid off in 1843. His influence in the little borough where he lived in an unostentatious manner, befitting his means, was unbounded. He paid his household bills weekly, never owed a penny, was universally respected, and had been twice Mayor.

A vacancy for the Parliamentary representation, impending for some time, occurred within a few weeks of Michell's re-employment. Every voter but the Captain knew, and had told the election agents who solicited the electors, mostly shopkeepers, for their votes and interest, that they "would follow the Captain."

On the morning of the polling-day, Captain Michell called on the Port Admiral and asked for a day's leave to record his vote. The Admiral said somewhat shortly, "I do not like officers asking for leave often; pray when did you have leave last?" "Well, sir, Lord Collingwood gave me six weeks' leave in 1806." This settled the question. My uncle went to Totnes, plumped against the Government candidate, and then returned to his ship. The bulk of the electors had waited for him, and the Government candidate was badly defeated. Within a few days Captain Michell received an indignant letter from a Secretary in Whitehall to the effect, "My Lords were astonished at his ingratitude." My uncle, the most simple-minded of men, was painfully affected. He had imagined that he owed his appointment to his merits, and to the consideration that the troubled Political horizon necessitated the nomination of tried seamen to command. He wrote officially to the Admiralty, stating that unless the Secretary's letter was repudiated, he must resign, and ask for a Court of Inquiry. In replying, "My Lords much regretted the entirely unauthorised and improper letter," etc.

Captain Michell had the reputation of being strict and autocratic with relatives, and my messmates in the gunroom concurred in advising me to ask for a transfer to another ship, so I asked to be sent to H.M.S. *Spartan*, then in the Sound; but another cadet was selected. Later, when two cadets were required for H.M.S. *Melampus*, bound for the Cape of Good Hope, I volunteered; but two boys junior to me were chosen. If I had gone to the Cape, I should have missed the Crimea. My uncle asked me why I had volunteered, and I said frankly mainly to get away from him.

When Michell took command, the crew consisted of a draft of Seamen-gunners and 200 Marines, and his task was to train the large numbers of West Country lads who made up the balance of 970, all told. Very patient, methodical, and precise in all his ways, he always put back every serious case, which might take a prisoner to the gratings,[1] for twenty-four hours' consideration. Some weeks after he joined, overhearing me speak of the third cutter as "My boat," he called me up and rebuked me, saying, "You mean, sir, Her Majesty's boat you have the honour to command."

The Commander of the ship was very different in disposi-

[1] Men when suffering corporal punishment were lashed to gratings.

tion, manners, and temperament. A Scotchman, with a high sense of duty, he was much feared by those inclined to indulge in alcohol.

Drinking to excess was common, and the Midshipmen sent below in the middle watch to mix the tumbler of spirits and water (gin being then the favourite beverage) of the officers in charge of the watch, used to bet who would put in most spirit and least water. In my first year's service two of our officers died from alcoholism.

Our Commander, naturally of a choleric though kindly disposition, was severely tried by some of the older officers in the gunroom, two of whom he often "Proved," when they returned on board from shore leave. He occasionally lost his temper when answered, as he was on many occasions by a hard-drinking officer. One day giving an answer which was deemed to be unsatisfactory, he was greeted by an outburst of passion. "I'll bring your nose to the grindstone; I'll reduce you to a gooseberry." My messmate calmly replied, in the slow, solemn manner of a man who is conscious of having drunk too much, "You cannot, sir, bring my nose to a grindstone, and to reduce me to a gooseberry is a physical impossibility." However, sometimes the Commander won in these wordy contests.

One of our officers, tried in Queenstown Harbour for drunkenness, was defended by a Cork attorney as his "next friend," who thus attempted to trip up the Commander's evidence:—"You say, sir, the prisoner was drunk. I suppose you have had much experience? Yes. Well, kindly define what you mean by being drunk." "A man may be drunk—very drunk—or beastly drunk. Your client was beastly drunk." This settled the case, and the prisoner was dismissed the Service.

The First Lieutenant knew his duty and did it, but amongst men of marked characteristics attracted but little notice. Many of the younger officers were above the average in ability and efficiency, the most striking personality being a Mate, named Hugh (commonly called Billy) Burgoyne, a son of the Field Marshal whose statue stands in Waterloo Place. Mr. Burgoyne was as brave as a lion, as active as a cat, and a very Mark Tapley in difficulties.

We were intimate, for I worked under his orders for some months in the maintop, of which I was Midshipman, and he Mate, and I admired him with boyish enthusiasm for his remarkable courage and endurance of pain, of which I was an eye-witness. In 1852 we were at sea in a half gale of wind increasing in force, and the ship rolling heavily, the topmen of the watch went aloft to send down the topgallant-mast.

I presume that most of my readers are aware that the tall tapering poles which they see in the pictures of sailing ships were not all in one piece, but for the sake of those who are unacquainted with nautical terms I explain that the lower mast has a head which supports the top-mast, which in its turn supports the topgallant-mast, and at the head of the topgallant-mast is similarly fixed a royal-mast. When sailors speak of sending up a topgallant-mast, it means that the mast is placed alongside the top-mast, and pulled up into position by a rope which, passing over a pulley in the top of the topmast, is then fixed in its position by a wedge-shaped piece of iron called a " Fid," which being pushed in a hole in the top of the top-mast, receives and supports the weight of the topgallant-mast.

When it is desired to "house" or send down the topgallant-mast, the man at the top-masthead pulls out the fid on which the topgallant-mast rests. The fid is composed of wood, shod with iron in parts, and for the purpose of extraction is fitted with a "grummet" of rope, or hemp handle. In ordinary weather there is not much difficulty in extracting the fid, and most Able-seamen, holding on with their legs, manage to get both hands on to the grummet and pull out the fid; on this occasion, however, continuous rain had caused the mast to swell, and the fid was embedded tightly; as the ship rolled heavily in the trough of the sea, the man at the top-masthead did not care to trust to his legs, and therefore put only one hand on the fid-grummet. We were losing time, and Burgoyne, with strong language at the man for his want of courage, ran smartly aloft, and pushing him aside, put both hands on to the fid and attempted to withdraw it; at first he failed, for the swollen wood defeated his efforts.

The Marines on deck, who had the weight of the mast on their arms during the several minutes which elapsed while the

Bluejacket was making half-hearted efforts with one hand, had got tired of supporting three-quarters of a ton of dead weight, and thus it happened that just as Burgoyne, getting his fingers inside the hole, had slightly moved the fid, the Marines "coming up"—that is, slacking their hold—let the topgallant-mast down on Burgoyne's hand, which was imprisoned by the tips of the fingers.

He felt his hand could not be extricated until the weight was off it; if he had screamed, the fifty men on the topgallant-fall, *i.e.* the hoisting-rope, would have looked up, and he would have remained with his hand still imprisoned. With extraordinary fortitude and self-command, Burgoyne putting his disengaged hand to his mouth, hailed the deck, making himself heard above the gale. "On deck there." "Ay, ay." "Sway again." The Marines throwing all their weight on the rope, lifted the mast, Burgoyne withdrew his hand, and then becoming unconscious, we sent him down in the bight of a rope.

It is curious that[1] he and two others of our Mess were lost when in command.

[1] Burgoyne was drowned, with all but eighteen of his command, in 1871, in the Bay of Biscay, when H.M.S. *Captain*, struck by a squall, "turned turtle," being overweighted above her water-line. *Eurydice* capsized, 1878; H.M.S. *Atalanta* disappeared, 1880.

CHAPTER III

1853-4—LIFE ON BOARD A MAN OF WAR

Her Majesty Queen Victoria with a steam fleet defeats a squadron of sailing line-of-battle ships — Rough weather in the Channel — Ship nearly wrecked in Grecian Archipelago — My first command — At Sinope—Captain Michell's seamanship—I become a Midshipman—William Peel—Cholera in the Fleet—Reconnaissance of the Crimea.

THE young Bluejackets of H.M.S. *Queen*, trained under zealous and efficient officers, improved rapidly in seamanship, and on the 11th August 1853, did well in a Royal Review off the Isle of Wight.

Her Majesty's ships *Prince Regent* and *Queen* with three steamers represented an enemy cruising off St. Helen's, and Her Majesty the Queen, in the *Victoria and Albert*, led nineteen men-of-war steamers to attack us.

The British fleet advanced in a crescent formation and nearly surrounded their opponents, the Commanders of which, after expending a quantity of blank ammunition, struck their colours in obedience to a signal from the Senior officer, when Her Majesty going on board the tender *Fairy* passed round the captured vessels.

The Fleet dispersed a few days later, and our young crew was severely tested, H.M.S. *Queen* being caught in a heavy gale, which after tossing us about under close-reefed topsails, which were on two occasions blown away, obliged us to run for shelter into Torbay. During the gale the ship's bow and stern rose alternately high out of the water, as she pitched in a choppy sea, and a wave striking the rudder violently, made the wheel revolve with such force as to throw two of the helmsmen right over it, one being severely injured. The wheels on the upper and main deck were then double manned, but it was necessary to control the swaying tiller in the gunroom with steadying tackles, in all thirty-two men being employed for some hours in steering the ship.

The temptations of Plymouth were too much for the probity of our Mess, and Wine caterers, a Clerk, and a Master's Assistant, who misappropriated over £200. Three months later they were tried by Court Martial in the Bosphorus, and dismissed the Service, the one who was the more guilty getting six months' imprisonment; but the money had to be repaid, and in the gunroom our bill of fare up to and including Christmas Day varied only to the extent, say Sundays salt pork and plain duff with sugar, Mondays salt beef and pease pudding, while we had to continue paying our usual Mess bills, those of a Midshipman being limited to 30s. per mensem, and a wine bill not exceeding 7s. 6d.

Tourists who steam past Cape Matapan, the southern point of Greece, in a few hours, may find it difficult to realise that H.M.S. *Queen*, although an unusually good sailer, took seven days to round that promontory. We were nearly wrecked in trying to beat through the Doro Channel. The passage lies between the islands of Negropont and Andros, the most northerly of the Cyclades, there being about six miles from land to land. The wind was north-east, blowing freshly, and dead against us; we were, however, nearly through, but just before dark on the 9th November, when the helm was put down in our last tack, which would have taken us clear, the jib halliards carried away, and the ship missing stays, gathered stern way. We drifted so close to the rocky cliffs of Andros that one might have thrown a biscuit on shore. A staysail brought the ship's head round in time, however, and "wearing," we lay for the night under the lee of the island. Next day the breeze increased to a gale, and the ship was kept under reefed courses, till the mainsail splitting, was replaced by the fore staysail. On the 11th December the Captain bore up, and ran back to Milo, there to remain till the gale blew itself out.

The harbour being landlocked, the sea was calm, as we duly saluted His Excellency the Governor, who came on board. Some hours later he returned to complain that one of the Midshipmen, in practising with his new pistol, had shot the

Governor's donkey. His Excellency was well satisfied with twenty dollars, which my messmate had to pay for his pistol practice.

When we left Milo we had a fair wind up to Constantinople, and from the Golden Horn on to Beicos Bay, where we joined the Allied Fleet. We remained at anchor, amidst lovely scenery, in the Strait, which varying from half a mile to two miles, separates Europe from Asia, for ten days.

On the 3rd January the combined fleets weighed to proceed to Sinope, where five weeks earlier a Turkish squadron of seven frigates had been destroyed by the Russian Fleet. H.M.S. *Queen* and two French line-of-battle ships had reached the northern end of the Strait, when our progress was arrested by signals. The greater part of the fleets had been less prompt in getting under way and making sail, and the wind veering to the N.N.W. and bringing with it a fog, the fleets anchored again in Beicos Bay, the *Queen* remaining just inside the Bosphorus.

Next morning both fleets entered the Black Sea with a southerly wind, and proceeded to Sinope, the Admiral signalling, " The ships and territories of Turkey throughout the Black Sea are to be protected, under any circumstances, from all aggression." We reached the Bay, which is a fine natural harbour on the northern extremity of Asia Minor, on the 6th January. The town had suffered considerably from the Russian shells, two streets being entirely demolished, and amongst the wrecks of the Turkish squadron floated corpses of its indomitable crews. Three Russian men-of-war were off the port on the 4th, forty-eight hours before our arrival, and so narrowly escaped capture, or destruction.

The town of Sinope, then containing about 10,000 inhabitants, is beautifully situated, but perhaps its greatest world-wide interest consists in its being the birthplace of Diogenes. The surrounding country is fertile, with many wooded valleys, which my messmates and I explored to our great pleasure on the Governor's horses, favoured by summer-like weather, though while at sea we had suffered from the intense cold. The fleets were back again in Beicos Bay on the 22nd January, and there remained at anchor for two months.

I got into trouble at the end of February, the result of

obeying orders. A Greek brig drifting down the Bosphorus, flying signals of distress, grounded on the Asiatic side, and our Commander sent the launch with the stream anchor, and the cutter of which I was in charge, to warp her off shore. This was accomplished after a hard day's work. When we were about to return, the Senior officer wanted a glass of grog, and ordered me to put him on board the brig, the grateful Captain of which proffered refreshments.

I took the cutter to the gangway, where my Superior could have ascended on the battens, assisted by a man rope, but he being stout and inactive, preferred the rope ladder suspended from the stern, and ordered me to go there. In vain I urged the swirling stream might cause the cutter's bow to be injured. He insisted on obedience, and my fears being realised, we had to go back in the launch, leaving the cutter with her bow stove in, hauled up on the beach. On returning on board I was severely reprimanded by the Commander. In my defence I submitted I was obliged to obey the order after I had pointed out its risk. He replied, " I don't care, sir; you were in charge of the boat, so you are responsible."

Three months later I was again censured, but this time because I had tried to assert my command. We were lying at the time in Kavarna Bay, and the ship's crew had leave to go on shore by detachments. In the evening two boats were sent to bring them on board, a cutter for the officers, and a barge for the Bluejackets. A Lieutenant ordered me to take into the cutter some of the men. I paid for extra painting of the boat, and wanting to keep her neat and clean, begged that the men might go off in the barge, but was told peremptorily to obey orders. While we were pulling out to the ship, about two and a half miles off, some of the men became noisy, and the Lieutenant ordered me to keep them quiet. I replied to the effect it was useless to talk to drunken men, and when we got on board was reported for hesitating to obey orders. The Commander lectured me severely, predicting I should come to the gallows; nevertheless, I suppose he was generally satisfied with me, for a few days before we left the Bosphorus again, I got, at the age of sixteen, my first independent command. Some links in an adjunct to our chain cable, technically called a "Blake stopper," had become strained, and

I was ordered to take it to the Turkish dockyard at Constantinople, to have them put into a furnace and straightened. This involved absence from the ship for a couple of days, and with the difficulties of language required some tact, but was successfully carried out.

I was possibly chosen for this outing because, before we left England, I had already had some practice in handling a boat, and in the winter of 1852–53 Captain Michell commended me warmly, for him a very unusual act. His daughter, who was staying with him on board the *Queen*, then lying just inside the breakwater which shelters Plymouth Sound, was expecting her son, eight years old, now a distinguished Judge, Sir George Farwell, for a visit. When I left the ship for Mount Wise there was a fresh westerly wind blowing, which before we started to return had increased considerably, and no shore boat ventured to put out to the Sound. We pulled the cutter out to Redding Point, under shelter of Mount Edgcumbe, and then, having close-reefed the sail, stood out till we were under lee of the ship, which was lying head to wind, and got the future Judge up the stern ladder in safety. Indeed, I became so fond of being away in boats, and thus escaping lessons under the Naval Instructor, that he felt bound, as I see by my letters, to get me relieved for a short time, to ensure my passing the two-yearly examination, which I did in due course two years after entering the Service, and thus was enabled to have my jacket adorned with the Midshipman's white patch.

The Allied fleets weighed anchor again on the 24th March to enter the Black Sea, and, as a fleet, there remained for over two years. The start was unfortunate. One of the French men-of-war ran aground. The English flagship collided with two vessels in succession, and this enabled our Captain to prove his seamanship and local knowledge. Fifteen years earlier he had commanded a corvette, and later a frigate, which were often in the Bosphorus, and seeing the misfortunes around him decided to sail up, although the wind was not favourable. He ordered the towing hawser to be let go, and hailing H.M.S. *Furious*, desired the Captain to offer help to the Admiral.

We made all plain sail: the Captain knew the soundings and currents thoroughly, and stood so close in to the shore at Therapia, before he put the ship about, as to startle his crew.

The Admiral, generous in his appreciation of the seamanship shown, signalled "Well done, *Queen*," a signal repeated at least twice within the next few months. No other line-of-battle ship went up the Bosphorus that day under sail, and the *Queen* had to make five tacks ere she entered the Euxine. Our Captain's nerve was as good at sixty-five as it was at Algiers in 1816. We cruised for some days, and then anchored in the Bay opposite to the little town of Baljic, about twenty-five miles north of Varna. Our life on board ship was enlivened by frequent competitions in the Fleet; H.M.S. *Queen*, called a Symondsite, built after the design of Sir William Symonds, was only 247 feet in length, with 50 feet beam. She was the fastest sailer of all the line-of-battle ships, when beating to windward, and was excelled only by H.M.S. *Agamemnon*, when sailing with the wind abaft the beam.

The men were always eager and excited when the signal having been made, "chase to windward," our ship crossed the bows of all other line-of-battle ships. As every foot of canvas the spars and stays would support was spread, the lee guns were always run in, and the watch on deck ordered to lie down up to windward, to counteract the heeling over of the ship caused by the pressure on the sails. The varying speed of ships was found to be inconvenient later, when the Allied fleets cruised off the Crimea coast, and H.M.S. *Queen* was often detached with the fastest French line-of-battle ship, *Marengo*, placed temporarily under Captain Michell's command.

We heard on the 9th April that war was declared, but the French Admiral for some reason did not get the official news for a week later, when three cheers given for war by the English Fleet were repeated by the Allies in unison. On the 17th April we sailed for Odessa, and anchored four miles off the city on the 21st. Next morning the steamers circling round in succession, bombarded the batteries without losing many men, though H.M.S. *Terrible* was hulled eleven times, and the *Vauban* set on fire by a red-hot shot. Indeed, the Russian gunners were not sufficiently well trained to make the contest equal, and after four of their magazines had been exploded their guns were silenced.

H.M.S. *Arethusa*, a 50-gun frigate, engaged a battery five miles off the city in the style of our grandfathers' actions. She was under all plain sail, employed to intercept merchant ships trying to escape along the coast, when the Russians' battery opened fire, and for half an hour an animated fight was maintained by the frigate as she tacked in towards, and out from the land. The Admiral's signal "Recall" was disregarded, until he ordered, "*Arethusa's* Captain, come on board." This brought the frigate out, but having dropped the Captain into his gig the First Lieutenant took the ship back, and recommenced the action, when a more peremptory signal, emphasised by the firing of a gun, ensured obedience.

The young generation of Captains had never been in action, and were naturally eager to smell powder. A steamer bringing despatches arrived during the bombardment, and crossing the Admiral's bows went in to take part with the other steamers in the operations against the batteries, but was soon recalled in terms admitting of no evasion. I was away all day in a boat intercepting small vessels, and as most of them were laden with oranges, our Mess was well supplied for some time.

Three weeks later, while the Allied fleets were cruising off Sevastopol, H.M.S. *Tiger* ran ashore in a dense fog near the spot where H.M.S. *Arethusa* engaged the battery. Captain Giffard behaved with great gallantry, but was severely wounded, and with his crew became prisoners of war. No prisoners could have received kinder treatment from their foes, say at Liverpool. The Governor ensured that all the English were well rationed and lodged; the General's wife sent daily from her own kitchen dishes she had prepared for the wounded officers.

While we were cruising off the Crimea we were enveloped by a fog for six days early in May, and hearing guns signalling as we thought an order to anchor, we let go our stream anchor in 89 fathoms.[1] We rang bells and fired muskets every half-hour, but it was so calm that there was little danger of a collision even to ships under way. The dense fog caused much trouble and perplexity to feathered creatures, and our decks and rigging became for forty-eight hours the resting-place for numbers of pretty horned owlets. They were so exhausted as to allow anyone to pick them up, and many

[1] Probably a record depth.

Midshipmen and sailors tried, though I believe ineffectually, to tame them.

One of my messmates died at this time from erysipelas in the face. Three nights before his death I stopped him going overboard, when he tried in a fit of delirium to drown himself. He had sent for me previously in the middle watch to tell me to make his coffee, which I had been in the habit of doing at two o'clock in the morning. We were friends in spite of a punishment he gave me, the marks of which I carry now, fifty years after the event. When we were on our passage from England to the East, I remarked on one of his unpleasant habits at table, which all the youngsters in the gunroom—about twenty-five in number—resented; I was, I admit, very impertinent. He came round to my side of the table, and lifting me from the seat, put me on the stern-sheets locker; then, sitting on my chest, he took my hand, and bent the tip of the little finger nail down till the nail bled copiously at the root.

On the 6th July, the cutter of which I had charge won a race open to the Fleet. When we were practising for the race, I removed one of the men, a weak oar, replacing him by a spare number. The man resented my action, and a few days later got me severely punished. There was a Fleet Order that officers in charge of boats would, while waiting near the shore, keep the crew in the boat. The intention of the order was to guard against trouble with the inhabitants; but at Baljic, after the first week, it was so universally disregarded that the men were always allowed on shore, and were not ordered back even if we saw a Senior officer approaching. At the appointed hour the crew of the boat returned with exception of the aggrieved sailor, and I found him in a Greek wineshop fighting with some of the inhabitants. Four men carried him down, struggling, to the beach, and put him somewhat roughly into the boat. He jumped out, and started, as he said, to swim to the ship, but was soon sufficiently sobered to shout for help. After we took him in, he was so violent that it became necessary to lash him to the bottom of the boat, and he volunteered the information that his main pleasure in getting drunk was to spite me for taking him out of the boat before the race. When I reported, on going on board, the Captain sentenced the sailor to ten days' imprisonment, and directed the

Commander to give me a severe punishment. He complied conscientiously, and I got "Watch and watch," including confinement to the ship. "Watch and watch" meant four hours on, four off, in the twenty-four hours, and as the culprit's hammock was taken on deck daily at 6.30 a.m. and he was not excused any duties which came round in his turn below, the process resembled that by which the "Lion King,"[1] many years ago, tamed his wild beasts.

The punishment was remitted after three weeks, I believe on the recommendation of the doctor in charge of the ship. If, however, it affected my health, it did not depress my spirits, and I joined every evening in skylarking with my messmates, though I admit now, as I did at the time, I feared doing many of the monkey-tricks which some of us achieved, rather than be deemed to be less courageous than my comrades. The game may be briefly described as that of Follow-my-Leader. Now, I have always been giddy when on a height, and one evening nearly fell from the main truck, which is the flat or slightly round piece of wood crowning the top of the royal-mast, in H.M.S. *Queen* 147 feet in height. The cap or truck is about the size of a dinner-plate, and my shoes being larger than it, protruded over its edges. I held on to the lightning conductor, which reached my waistband, being so nervous as to want to be sick, and at one moment almost let go my hold. It has always puzzled me why some of us are giddy, while others have no nervous apprehension of falling. When Her Majesty the Queen passed through the Fleet off St Helen's, on the 4th August 1853, and the ship's company having "manned yards" were cheering, I saw Private Buckle, Royal Marine Light Infantry, remove the fore royal-mast lightning conductor, and with folded arms balance on his head on the truck.

When we were at anchor in Baljic Bay, I fell overboard one evening when acting as the "Leader" in one of these games. I had come down from the main yardarm, on the brace, and was resting on the brace block, level with the poop, when an officer trying to startle me opened a "quarter gallery" window suddenly, with a shout. He succeeded, for I let go, and falling fortunately immediately between two lower deck

---

[1] Van Amberg, in the forties a celebrated wild-beast tamer, dominated them by breaking their rest.

ports which were open, reached the water after turning over twice in the air. I made my shins bleed by striking the bulging outside of the ship, but was able to swim to the boats made fast astern. Had I fallen on a port—and there was little space between them—I must have been killed.

On the 20th July, General Sir George Brown, who commanded the Light Division, and General Canrobert having embarked in our flagship, H.M.S *Britannia*, the Fleet stood across the Black Sea, heaving to, off Fort Constantine, while we counted the Russian ships in the harbour of Sevastopol, and tried to estimate the value of the defensive works. Our steamers went in close enough to draw fire, but H.M.S. *Fury* was the only one hit. We remained on the coast a week, between Sevastopol and Balaklava. After cruising for some days, H.M.S. *Queen* was detached with the *Marengo*, and our frigates, and Captain Michell as Commodore signalling H.M.S. *Diamond* to take letters into Varna for the English mail, William Peel, her Captain, came on board for orders. All our officers were anxious to see him, for he had already a Service reputation as one of the best, though the youngest Post Captain. He was the third son of that great Minister of whom the Duke of Wellington said, " Of all the men I ever knew he had the greatest regard for truth." Sir Robert had died four years earlier, being mortally injured when his horse fell with him on Constitution Hill.

William entering the Navy in 1838, had seen service on the Syrian Coast and in the China War. He had passed such a brilliant examination after six years' service as to gain promotion at once, and two years later became a Commander. After he became a Post Captain, when in command of H.M.S. *Diamond*, Peel was sitting one day in the stern cabin reading, dressed in frock coat and epaulets, when hearing a shout of " Man overboard," he ran to the stern window in time to see a Bluejacket under the water; without a moment's hesitation the Captain dived, but the man had sunk, and was not recovered.

When I first saw this striking-looking man I had no idea that I was to spend some months with such a highly-strung, nervous, gallant gentleman, and whom I learned to love and esteem more and more daily, as " the bravest of the brave."

In 1855, eight months later, I became his Aide-de-Camp, and we were constantly together until the 18th June, when we were both wounded and invalided to England. I was evidently much struck with Captain Peel's appearance and manners, for I recorded in boyish language, "Captain Peel, very intelligent, sharp as a needle; I never saw a more perfect gentleman."

His looks and bearing were greatly in his favour, for both in face and figure there was an appearance of what sporting men, in describing well-bred horses, call "quality." He was about medium height, with head gracefully set on broad, well-turned shoulders, light in lower body, and with a dignified yet easy carriage; his dark brown wavy hair was generally carefully brushed back, showing an oval face, high square forehead, and deep blue-grey eyes, which flashed when he was talking eagerly, as he did when excited. His face when in repose had a somewhat austere look, with smooth and chiselled outline, a firm-set mouth which was the more noticeable because of his being clean-shaved. I do not know that I have ever met so brave a man and yet one who felt so acutely every shot which passed close to him.

When we returned to Baljic Bay, early in August, cholera had broken out in the British camps near Varna. In addition to the 600 men who died, each Division had a number of men, equal to about a battalion, who required change of air, and these were sent down to the Bosphorus, while the physical efficiency of many of those who remained at duty was seriously impaired, a fact which was not realised by those who criticised the apparent slowness of the advance, and lack of enterprise after the victory, on the Alma, six weeks later.

Cholera soon reached the Fleet.[1] As I showed in *The Crimea in 1854-'94*, the troops were insufficiently supplied with medical equipment, but this could not be alleged as regards the sailors. Indeed, one great advantage in the Naval Service lies in the fact that a crew virtually goes on active service each time a ship leaves harbour. Nevertheless, although we were amply supplied with every requisite, our casualties were greater, because the men were concentrated

[1] In my log, 12.8.54, I read: "H.M.S. *Trafalgar* stood under our stern last night, and asked for medical assistance."

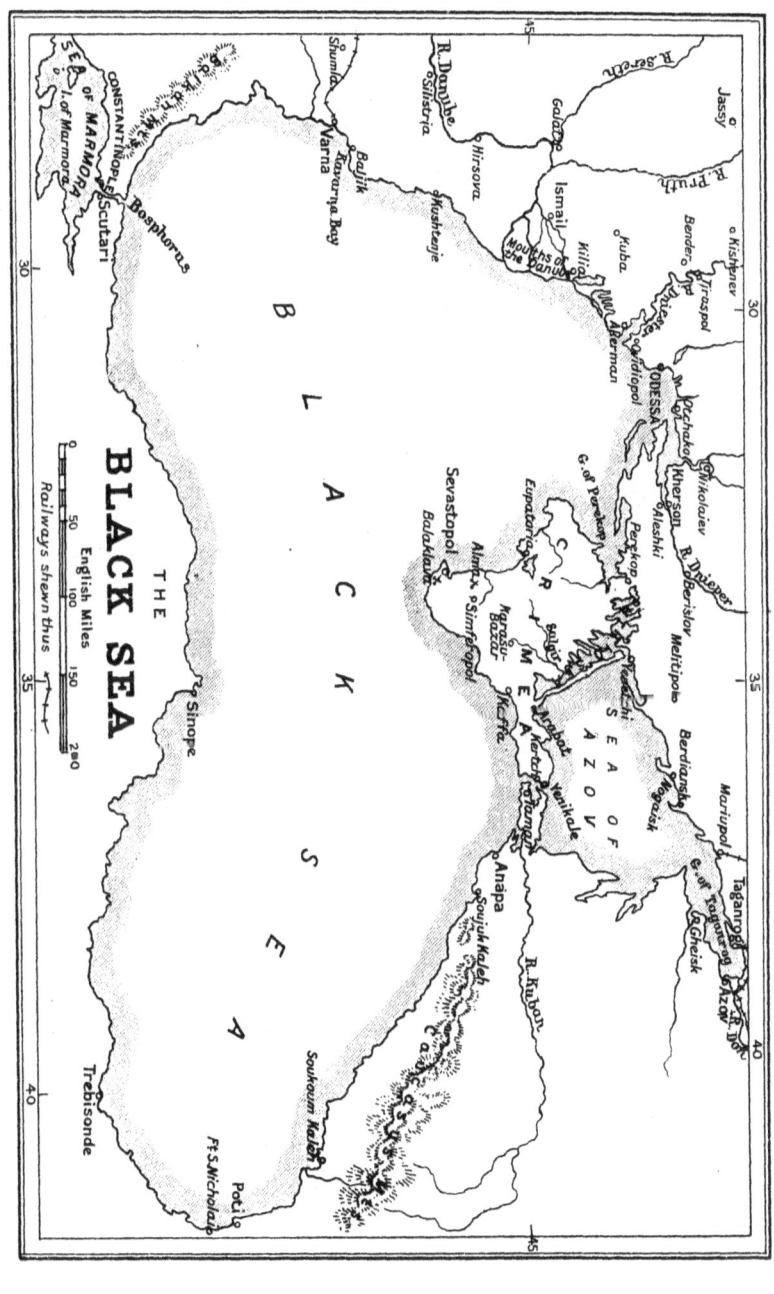

in one place. The French flagship lost 140, of whom 40 died the first night; our flagship lost about one-tenth of the ship's company; and none escaped except H.M. ships *London* and *Queen*.

The screams of a sufferer when seized with cramp often brought on other seizures, and the scenes on a middle or lower deck were trying even to strong nerves. We went to sea to try and shake off the disease. A few days later, so many men were enfeebled by intestinal complaints, that some of the ships, carrying crews of 700 to 1000 men, had not sufficient Effectives to work the sails; and when we returned to our anchorage, and the Admiral wanted his boat, officers had to prepare it. I was sent on board the flagship with a party to furl sails, and while the epidemic lasted we went at sunrise and sunset daily, to bury her dead.

While the fleets were cruising in the Black Sea, the Allied Generals in the *Caradoc*, escorted by H.M.S. *Agamemnon*, reconnoitred the bays and mouths of rivers in the Crimea, from Eupatoria on the north to Balaklava on the south.

Lieutenant-General Sir George Brown wished to land the troops on the Katcha River, but Lord Raglan and his colleagues considered this was undesirable owing to the proximity of the fortress, troops from which might interrupt the disembarkation, and his Lordship chose Kalamita Bay, six miles north of the Bulganac stream.

With one very important exception, the scarcity of potable water, the spot selected was perfect. There was a long, low strip of shingly beach rising gradually 200 yards from the shore, and immediately behind the beach was a lake of brackish water, extending a mile from north to south, and half a mile from west to east.

CHAPTER IV

1854—INVASION OF THE CRIMEA

The Allied Armies re-embarking from Varna, land in the Crimea—The Alma as seen from the masthead of H.M.S. *Queen*—Selecting a Naval Brigade—Balaklava Harbour—The Upland—The English position—First bombardment — Erroneous forecasts of siege —Able-Seaman Elsworthy—A Midshipman's daily prayers.

THE British troops began to re-embark on the 29th August, weakened by cholera not only in numbers, many having been sent to the Bosphorus for change of air, but also by the enfeebled condition of the men, several falling out as they marched down to the Bay. Sailors do not like many passengers on fighting ships, but H.M.S. *Bellerophon* and *Vengeance* were obliged to receive a battalion from a transport on which the epidemic had reappeared, carrying off its Captain with others.

On the 4th September the British transports assembled in Baljic Bay, where the French and Turkish troops embarked. A head wind blew on the 6th, but on the morning of the 7th the Allied fleets sailed for the point of assembly, off the mouth of the Danube. Each British steamer towed two sailing transports, the whole moving in columns, the front and flank covered by men-of-war. There were 37 line-of-battle ships, 100 frigates and smaller men-of-war, 200 steam and sailing transports, making a total of over 600 vessels.

The British ships anchored first off the mouth of the Danube, but though the speed rate had been fixed at 4½ knots, too low to be convenient to our steamers, it was too high for our Allies, whose soldiers were mostly carried in sailing transports, which dropped astern on the afternoon of the 11th, when some squalls rippled the hitherto smooth sea. They were out of sight on the 12th, and reached the point of concentration, forty miles west of Cape Tarkan, on the afternoon of the 13th September, though the distance in a straight line is only 300 miles.

The disembarkation was arranged on the model of that followed by Sir Ralph Abercromby, when he landed in March 1801, in Aboukir Bay. On the 14th September 1854, the men-of-war's boats left their ships, fully armed and provisioned with water and food for three days, and we did not get back until 11.30 that night. All the boats loaded with human freight were drawn up in one long line at 8.15 a.m., when the Captain, superintending from a fast pulling gig in the centre, waved his flag as a signal for the line to advance. In one hour the seven battalions composing the Light Division were on shore, and by 3 p.m. we had landed 14,000 Infantry and two batteries; nor were our Allies less expeditious, for they claimed to have put 6000 on shore in less than 25 minutes.

Our Bluejackets were very careful of their brothers, and where the plank was not long enough to ensure their landing with dry feet, in most cases they were carried ashore in a sailor's arms. We had had an object lesson from a painful loss the French suffered; for in Varna Bay, twenty Zouaves in heavy marching order were stepping on a pontoon, which capsized, and all of them went to the bottom.

The officers landed in full dress, carrying sword, revolver, with greatcoat rolled horseshoe fashion over the shoulder, some spirits in the wooden water-bottle, then called a canteen, three days' boiled salt pork, and three days' biscuit. The Rank and File being weak, many still suffering with intestinal complaints, it was decided to leave their knapsacks on board, and they were sent to Scutari. Each soldier carried fifty rounds of ammunition, three days' rations, greatcoat and blanket in which was rolled a pair of boots, socks and forage cap, of the curious pork-pie shape to which the Army clung until a few years ago. It was a useless article, but not so inconvenient as the handsome head-dress which our Generals liked, but which the men discarded at the first opportunity. In the following winter I saw battalions throwing away their full head-dress as they left Balaklava.

Some horses were hoisted out of the ships into barges,

others were lowered into the sea, and the supporting sling being detached by a tripping line, one or more horses were attached to the stern of a boat, which, being rowed slowly to the shore, was followed by the other horses. All reached land except three of Lord Raglan's, which on being lowered into the water swam out to sea, and were drowned. At sunset a heavy ground swell broke up the rafts, and obliged us to land all articles by passing them from man to man standing in the water; but we continued to work till 11.30 p.m., re-embarking in our boats on the Bluejackets' shoulders some sick soldiers.

It rained dismally that night, and the consequent discomfort and recurrence of cholera induced an order for the tents to be landed, but as we had invaded the Crimea without transport, the sailors had to re-ship the tents again four days later. On the 15th, 16th, and 17th the Bluejackets were at work from daylight till dark, landing Cavalry, Artillery, and ammunition. Before the 19th, we had taken back to the ships 1500 men who were unable to march. Many of these were stricken with cholera and must have suffered acutely, for after they were on board the engines of the ship carrying them to the Bosphorus broke down, and we had to tranship the unfortunate men to another vessel.

The Sister Services saw a great deal of each other in those days, and it was obvious to me then, as it is now, that in similar matters there is much advantage in such association. No sailor would have thought of putting away a part of his kit without a tally or mark on the bag, but there were very few of the soldiers' knapsacks sent to Scutari which could be readily distinguished by any outward sign. While we were landing the troops on the 14th September, H.M.S. *Vesuvius* and *Sampson*, standing in to the mouth of the Bulganac stream, shelled a Russian camp, and obliged the enemy to move it inland. Rain fell steadily in the evening, and, lasting all night, when day broke, came down so heavily as to cause great discomfort, and added considerably to the number of the sick.

On the 19th September the armies moved southwards towards Sevastopol, distant about twenty-five miles. The British force consisted of 1000 sabres, 26,000 Infantry, and 60 guns.

The French had no Cavalry, 28,000 Infantry, and 68 guns, and their Commander, Marshal Arnaud, had 7000 Turks under his orders. The troops, after marching some six miles, bivouacked on the southern bank of the Bulganac stream; next morning the troops "Stood to Arms" early, but did not move till nine o'clock.

In a book published ten years ago, I described the battles of Alma, Balaklava, and Inkerman. The first, on the 20th September, I witnessed from the crosstrees of H.M.S. *Queen*, anchored off the mouth of the river. The two Cavalry actions fought in the Tchernaya Valley, on the 25th October 1854, though within two miles of our camp, being below the plateau on which the Infantry camps were pitched, were out of our sight. Captain Peel rode over and saw the charges, but all those of us who were not in the batteries "Stood to Arms" in camp. I refer to Inkerman farther on, but say no more about the above battles than to show how their results affected the Naval Brigade.

The British casualties at the Alma numbered 2000 of all ranks. That evening I took the Commander and some of the officers on shore in the cutter, and saw as much as I could of the battleground before my superiors returned from it. Before the action was over, we had been ordered by the Admiral to have our surgeons ready for the shore, and carrying parties of sailors had already relieved the soldiers to some extent of the duty of transporting the sick on stretchers to the beach. They had no transport, and therefore could not move their sick or wounded, and it appeared to us it would have been far better for the Army to have marched on the 21st, and have left the entire work of collecting the sick and wounded and burying the dead to the Navy. The troops did not move forward till the 23rd, when we had buried over 700 bodies in and around the breastwork, where the most determined struggle occurred.

The general impression in the Fleet was one of admiration for certain battalions, but the hero of the battle was Lieutenant-General Sir George Brown, then sixty-six years of age. We were told that he rode in front of his Division. He distinguished himself forty years earlier, when leading a section of the "Forlorn Hope" into the great breach at Badajos. Though the Army smiled at his decided conservative views, expressed generally in emphatic language, everyone from Colonels to Buglers admired his courage.

During the night of the 22nd the Russians blocked the entrance to the harbour of Sevastopol by sinking several of their ships in the fairway. We lost sight of the armies when they returned inland on the 25th September, to move round by Mackenzie's farm to Balaklava, which was taken over from the Commandant and a few invalids.

On Sunday, the 1st October, I was Signal Midshipman of the watch, and took over a message, " Line-of-battle ships will send 140 men and proportion of officers for service with land forces." While Captain Michell was discussing the details of the detachment, the Commander sent me on board the ship of the Acting Commodore to ask in what uniform the officers were to land. As I stood on the quarterdeck, bare-headed, the Acting Commodore emerged from his cabin, with a large prayer-book in hand. The ship's company were aft for Divine service, as in respectful tones I delivered my message. He answered my question in emphatic language, which cannot be repeated, but was to the effect that he did not care a ——— if the officers painted their bodies black and went naked. Now, if I had repeated the very words, I should never have got on shore; for the manners of the two captains were as distinct as possible, and yet Michell had great admiration for his Superior, as is evident from one of his letters to his wife I have recently had an opportunity of perusing. It was written after he had returned from a Court Martial, which sat to try the Acting Commodore for having run his ship aground during the bombardment of the forts a month later, and is warm in his expressions of admiration for the way in which the ship was handled, and the courage, skill, and determination of the Captain.

I paraphrased the order: " The Commodore's compliments, and he does not attach any importance to the question of uniform." When I delivered this message, our Captain and the Commander were standing on the poop ladder, and grouped around were some of the fortunate officers who had been chosen—the Commander, the Lieutenant Gunnery Instructor, and another senior Lieutenant, Lieutenant Douglas, and Mr. Sanctuary, a Mate, who was the only gunroom officer then selected. I trembled with excitement as I saw the Commander's eye turn towards me, and then pass on towards the next Midshipman. In those days we generally worked by seniority, but the senior Midshipman had recently been in trouble for having muttered when the Commander vituperated him for some fault, real or imaginary. The next Midshipman, who knew his work, had too high a wine bill to satisfy either the Commander or Captain. They had no proof against him of taking too much alcohol, but their suspicions were not without foundation; indeed, one or more suits of his clothes passed to me in the guise of my wine bill, for though he would not accept money he let me have them for the amount I was allowed to expend on my monthly wine bill. Now the Captain, in spite of his quiet, gentle, dignified manners, was one of the most determined fire-eaters I ever met. He had always been much more severe towards me, his nephew, than to my messmates, and had a month earlier punished me for what was at the worst only an error of judgment. I had received two verbal orders at the same moment; the first man said, "You are to board—and ask——" while the second man said, "You are to wait on the Captain." When I did so, he ordered me "Watch and watch" for not having gone to his cabin before I obeyed the other order. Nevertheless, he was fond of me, and in his letters to his sister, while he admits the propriety of a Senior officer, Captain (afterwards Sir) Stephen Lushington, being sent on shore, he adds, "As I could not go myself, I was determined that our family should be represented;" and turning to the Commander he asked, "Which Midshipman will you take?" "I am thinking, sir." "Then take young Wood." "Oh, but he is too young, sir; it will kill him." "No, I think not; but I will answer for that." And the rugged Commander said, "Well, youngster, you shall go."

The selected detachments went on board H.M.S. *Firebrand* for passage to Balaklava, which is a curious inlet from the sea. When the armies moving round from the north side of Sevastopol, having crossed the Tchernaya Valley, looked down on their objective, they saw below a little pool of water overshadowed east and west by cliffs, from 500 to 600 feet high. The harbour is indeed small,—about 300 yards wide,—but there is anchorage for half a mile, with depth of water for even larger ships than we possessed in 1854, and being land-locked the water is as smooth as an inland lake.

The historian, Mr. Kinglake, aptly named the treeless elevated plateau on which England's Army fought and won, but suffered and starved for months, "The Upland." The highest part of the crest is 500 feet above the Tchernaya Valley, and the plateau extends in a straight line from north to south eight miles, if we reckon in the elevated ground, Balaklava, and Sevastopol harbour. It is also nearly eight miles from west to east, measuring from Kamiesh Bay, to the height overlooking Tractir Bridge, on the Tchernaya River. For practical purposes we may say the extent of ground over which the British Army worked for nine months was in straight lines eight miles by four.

The geological formation is peculiar. The elevated ground, or Upland, being bounded by a cliff-like formation 800 feet high, which runs generally, from the head of Sevastopol harbour on the north, six miles south, and then trends away to the south-west, and passing a mile north-west of Balaklava, joins the cliffs on the sea-coast. The ground falls from this cliff-like formation gradually, northwards towards Sevastopol, north-west to Kamiesh Bay, southwards towards Balaklava, and south-east to the Tchernaya Valley. From the cliffs it rises again slightly about 2000 yards nearer to Sevastopol, thus forming a shallow basin, behind the crest of which the British camps were pitched, generally out of sight of the enemy's batteries, although the camp of the 2nd Division on the north-east corner of the Upland, *i.e.* Inkerman, was partly visible from the harbour, and subject to shell fire from ships in it.

The surface is cut up by many ravines. Those with which we were most concerned in our operations commenced close to the east and southern wall-like boundary, running from south-east to north-west, and they divided the fighting position of the Allies into several different parts. Near the camps they were as obstacles insignificant, but the ravine down which the Woronzow road is carried is, near its mouth, so steep as to be impassable for armed men; and the Careenage ravine is for some distance at its northern end precipitous, and in parts the cliffs overhang a chasm-like gorge.

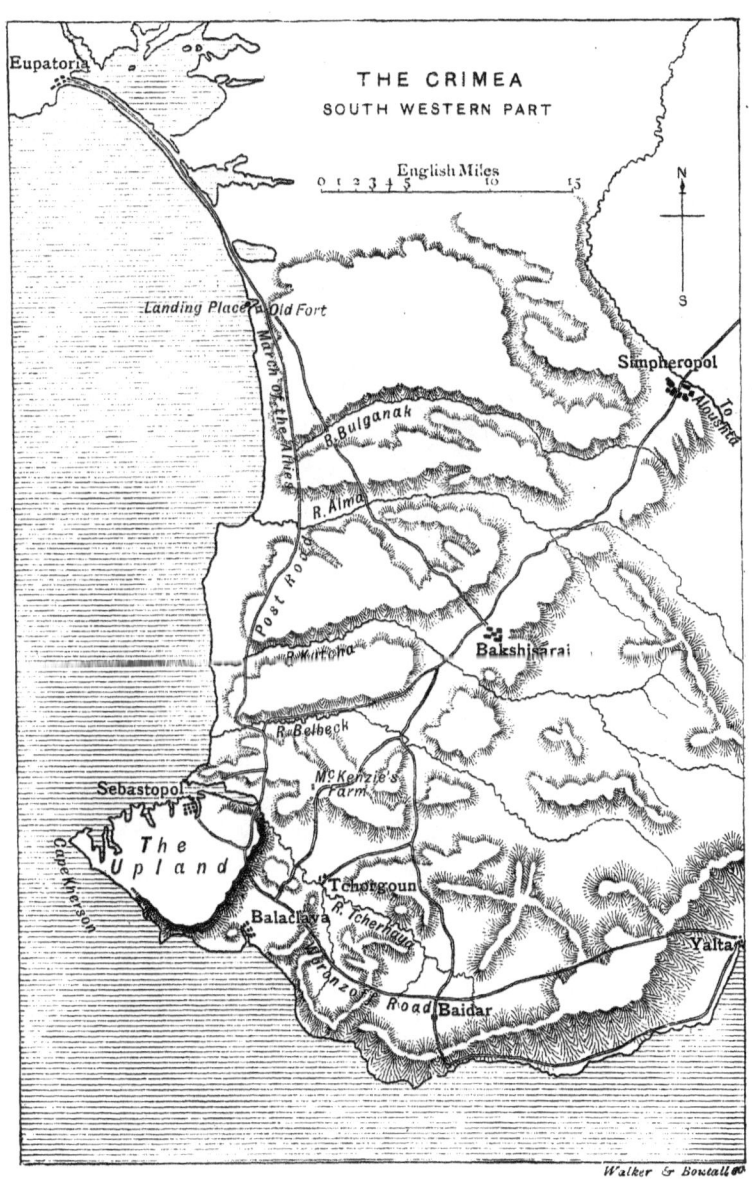

We slept on board H.M.S. *Firebrand*, Captain Moorsom's ship, which took us to Balaklava on the 1st October, but were on shore at four o'clock next morning, when we began to rig up sheers to land our guns. We had got all on shore by sunset, as well as our tents and two blankets each, pitching our camp just under the hamlet of Kadikoi, one and a half miles inland, in immediate proximity to vineyards in which were quantities of ripe grapes. Next morning we were up at three o'clock, when the Commander made me swallow, very much against my will, a dose of quinine. Half an hour later the men were given a similar ration on parade, to make quite sure that no one escaped taking this preventitive against fever. Mr. Sanctuary, our Mate, then took me off to wash in a small ditch, in which we stood stripped to the skin. I was, as I am now, a very chilly individual, and experienced intense discomfort.

We spent the next six days in dragging guns and ammunition up to the top of the rise which overlooks Balaklava Plain. On the 14th October, the so-called Naval Brigade, of 1400 men, was divided, half working from Balaklava to the height, and the other half dragging the guns from the height to the left, or west of, the Light Division camp. The Artillery lent us travelling-carriages for the 68-pounder guns, but they could not lend us enough for the 32-pounders, and nearly all these we hauled up the hill, and later down into battery, on the little solid wooden wheels called "trucks" on which they were worked on board ship. We had fifty men divided between the drag ropes, and a fifer or fiddler on the gun, and if neither was available, a Bluejacket with a voice and ear for music was mounted on the gun to sing the solo of a chorus song, to the tune of which we hauled the guns. I have never seen men work so hard continuously for so many days.

We commenced work at 4.30 a.m., and went on till 7.30 p.m., with one and a half hours off for breakfast and dinner, as our self-imposed task. Later, the men who were going on duty at night rested from 2 p.m. till 8 p.m., working from that hour till daylight. When we got over the wall-like formation I have mentioned, we moved on by detachments, and pitched our tents immediately on the west of the

Woronzow road, to the east side of which the Light Division was encamped.

I describe fully the ground on which our Siege-works and batteries stood, for it was there that the sailors spent their lives, as indeed did the soldiers, the latter dying in some battalions at the rate of 71 in every 100, from starvation, want of clothing, and fatigue. It was in these siege-works that the strength of the Russians was worn down, until they withdrew across the harbour—the battles, glorious as they were, being merely incidents in the struggle.

In the Naval Brigade all casualties were replaced from the Fleet, which is one of the reasons why our sick list showed such satisfactory results in comparison with that of the Army. We had many sick, but as they were continually replaced by Effectives, at the end of nine months, of the fifty officers who landed on the 2nd October, there remained only three who had served throughout the winter. The renewal of our detachments was not the only cause for the Naval Brigade being so much more healthy than were the soldiers. There were many reasons for the remarkable difference, but, stated briefly, the Naval system for messing was good, the cooking arrangements were excellent—the Army had no arrangements for messing or cooking; the sailors had a fair amount of work and sufficient clothing—the soldiers were overworked and in threadbare rags.

The Allies took up their positions to the east, south, and south-west of Sevastopol, and opened trenches about a mile from the enemy's works as they then existed, *i.e.* in the first week of October. These works, speaking generally, were on ridges opposite to those occupied by the Allies, and on the higher points stood the Malakoff, 330 feet; Redan, 300 feet; the Flag Staff battery, 280 feet; and the Central Bastion, 247 feet above the sea. Our engineers were limited in their choice of ground: firstly, from the impossibility of going in to the usual breaching distance unless we included in our works the Victoria ridge, which ran down to the Mamelon, for Russian works erected on it, as they were somewhat later, would have enfiladed our batteries, being able to fire along them, from end to end; secondly, because the hills on which we erected our batteries, sloping down from the crest which covered our camp, with a gentle fall for a mile and a half, at 1800 yards' distance from the Russian works, fell suddenly and steeply, so that if we had gone nearer in, to open our trenches, the enemy in our front would have looked down into them; moreover, from the Inkerman hills in our right rear, they would have taken our batteries in reverse, although at a considerable range. The principal though not the deepest of the ravines mentioned as dividing the Upland, separated the English and French Attacks.

I describe only the English portion of the Position, five ridges sloping down from south-east to north-west, all separated by ravines, the northern part of which had steep sides. Of these ravines the two inner fissures ran through the Russian works; the Careenage ravine, cutting off the Inkerman ridge, terminates in the harbour. The ravine which passed to the westward of the English siege-works joins the largest fissure at the point of connection between the Allied armies, and ends at the head of the Dockyard Creek.

On the crest line of the Upland stood on the Woronzow road a posting-house in which the Light Division placed a picket, and henceforth it was known as the Picket-house, so long as we stayed in the Crimea. It was about 600 yards from it that, on the 8th October, we pitched our camp, out of sight of the enemy. As I mentioned, we stood close to the Light Division, to the left rear of which the 1st Division was encamped, and in sequence the 4th and 3rd Divisions were pitched from one to one and a half miles south-west of the Picket-house, the Cavalry and Horse Artillery being on the plain, between the wall-like cliff and Balaklava. Two French Divisions encamped on and guarded the east and south-east side of the Upland, and two Divisions opened approaches to the left of the English 3rd Division, between it and the sea.

From the 9th to the 16th we helped to dig the batteries, drag down guns and ammunition, amounting to about 500 rounds per gun. On the 16th October the betting in our camp was long odds that the fortress would fall within a few hours. Some of the older and more prudent officers estimated that the Russians might hold out for forty-eight hours, but this was the extreme opinion. A soldier offered me a watch,

Paris made, which he had taken off a Russian officer killed at the Alma, for which he asked 20s. My messmates would not allow me to buy it, saying that gold watches would be cheaper in forty-eight hours.

When Orders came out that evening detailing the Gunnery Lieutenant and Mr. Sanctuary for the first or daylight Relief of the *Queen's* guns, and Lieutenant Douglas and Mr. Wood for the second Relief, Douglas swore, and I cried from vexation, thinking that all the fighting would be over before we had our turn.

THE FIRST BOMBARDMENT

At 2.30 on the 7th October all the officers saw the first detachment of guns' crews march off. It interested me to recall this fact when commanding the Aldershot Division, thirty-five years later, and I had difficulty to ensure that officers examined the soldiers' water-bottles when parading for a long march; for my Diary shows that at 2.30 on the 17th October 1854 the officers felt every wooden canteen which carried water, some with a dash of rum in it. We opened every man's haversack to ensure that he had his salt pork and biscuit, and the Navy owes, to such personal attention to details, much of its success.

At 6.30 a.m. the bombardment opened, and those in camp fidgeted about till nine o'clock, when Lieutenant Douglas having appropriated my pony, cantered up to the Picket-house, whence he could see the Artillery duel, promising to return soon to enable me to have a look at the operations. This pony had been a great convenience to us all, and especially to me; for whenever we stopped work during the first few days after landing, the Commander sent me away on messages, so that I got neither rest nor regular meals.[1] I had given 15s. for the animal. It was stolen from me soon after, but I replaced it early in November by one I bought out of a drove brought by a speculator from Asia Minor. For this I gave £18, but it was a cheap purchase, for it lived until 1883 at my mother's, and later, my sister's residence, in Essex, for the last years of its life.

[1] I read in my Diary that in seven successive days later I spent four on duty in the batteries or elsewhere, and three at Balaklava and Kamiesh.

Lieutenant Douglas had been away half an hour when a Bluejacket ran into the camp from the battery telling us there had been many casualties. He brought an order from Captain Peel for every available man in camp to go down to the battery with powder. I at once loaded up four Maltese carts, with the Relief of the *Queen's* men, and hurried away down the Woronzow ravine, fearing lest my Senior officer might return, and taking the powder himself, order me to remain in camp. When we got to within 500 yards of the 21-gun battery, several shot and shell from the Redan, about 2000 yards distant, passed over our heads on the road which is carried down the ravine. We were lower than the battery, and in a line so as to receive the over-shoot of the Russian guns; a shell bursting immediately over the cart alongside which I was walking, carried away one of the wheel spokes. The men in the shafts and at the drag ropes, dropping their hold, ran for cover. I am constitutionally nervous, but it did not occur to me to run, and thus I was enabled to make a good start with the men, by ordering them peremptorily to return to their duty. I should add that I saw immediately the danger was over. When we got directly behind the battery we were practically in safety, being sheltered by the eastern cliff; for the road there runs deep in the ravine, in some caves on the eastern side of which we stored the powder, and I went into the battery by its left or western end.

The smoke was so dense from the continuous fire as to shut out all objects more than a few yards distant, but I knew the position of the battery well. For a week I had been constantly in it by night and by day; indeed, I had guided Commodore Lushington down on his first visit, thereby gaining a dinner, which was all the more acceptable just then as we were living entirely on salt beef and salt pork. Having placed the men under cover, I went towards the right or eastern end, the guns of which were manned by detachments of the *Diamond* and the *Queen*, that part of the battery being called from Captain Peel's ship, the "Koh-i-noor." About the centre of the battery its two faces met in an obtuse angle, and it was there during the next nine months most of our casualties occurred. The guns on the right face fired at the Malakoff 1740, and the Redan 1400 yards distant. Later, the guns on the right face had the Mamelon also as a target at 1400 yards range. Two guns in the Redan enfiladed the left-hand guns of the right (or eastern) face of the 21-gun battery, and as I passed them a shell close over my head made me stoop, till I felt my foot was on something soft, and another hasty step repeated the sensation. Looking down, I saw I was treading on the stomachs of two dead men, who had been fighting their guns stripped to the waist when killed, and whose bodies had been placed together. I was not only startled but shocked, and the feeling made me hold my head up when in danger for the next eight months.

When I reported my arrival and handed over the men, I was employed carrying powder from caves in the Woronzow road up into the battery, passing in every journey two companies of Infantry, who were lying behind a large heap of loose stones, acting as a covering party for the guns. The soldiers were on the southern slope of the hill, on the crest of which our men in the 21-gun battery were firing northwards. The stones afforded some cover, but the men would have been safer without it, for they were lying exactly where the over-shots from the Malakoff and the Redan crossed. In one of my journeys from the caves to the battery I was passing close to a sergeant as he was cut into two pieces by a round-shot which struck him between the shoulders.

I was glad to get to work, commanding three guns' crews in the battery, for it was less trying to nerves, besides the additional interest. I had taken over from my friend Mr. Sanctuary three 32-pounder guns, and we were discussing the exact elevation for the Malakoff Tower, when he offered to lay a gun for me. While we were checking the aim by looking along the sights, a shell burst on the parapet immediately above us, bringing a great portion of it into our faces. Sanctuary was hit heavily in the face. I got much less of the stones and gravel, but was knocked down by my friend's body. We poured some dirty water over his face, and he soon revived, bravely declining all aid; but either from the wound in his eye, which was destroyed, or possibly from concussion, he could only walk in a circle, and was obliged to accept a man's arm. After he had left the battery, Lieutenant A. King,[1] Horse

---

[1] He commanded the Artillery at Aldershot in 1892.

Artillery, brought three waggons down with powder, and unloaded most of it near the stones where the covering party of Infantry were lying.

It was a peculiarity of our want of system that there was no Commanding officer in the trenches, and it was natural for Lieutenant King to suppose that where the men were lying would be the safest place. He brought one waggon right up to the battery, and having unhooked his horses left it. Although it was in full sight of the Russians, being about three feet above the battery, and was fired on, yet no one was hurt, as it was unloaded by Captain Peel and Lieutenant Douglas. We had more difficulty about the loads left near the stones; they were out of sight of the enemy, but from the fire of two Russian batteries crossing, shot and shell kept tumbling about the boxes in a manner which seemed to threaten destruction to anyone who approached the spot. It was comparatively simple to unload the waggon close to the trenches, for there two brave officers handed out the cases to men who were only momentarily in much danger.

Captain Peel sent me down with some men to bring up the two loads from near the stones. We got up a case or two, when the men, without actually refusing to carry, declared the work was too dangerous, and took cover. I reported this to my own Commander and to Captain Peel, and was ordered to promise any Bluejacket a sum of money who would come down with me. I made the offer in vain. This I reported to my Commander,[1] who said, "Well, I will come," and turning to the captain of the nearest gun he said, "Come on, Daniel Young; we will go to the devil together, if at all." He and the willing, stalwart man shouldered a box between them and carried it up, thus encouraging others, and eventually I got nearly all the boxes up, with only one sailor wounded.

Mr. Daniels, H.M.S. *Diamond*, Aide-de-Camp to Captain Peel, tried with me to carry one up by slinging the box on a fascine.[2] The boxes, holding 112 lbs. net of powder, were lined with interior cases of thick zinc, having over all solid wooden coverings. The weight was too much

[1] He was lost with 200 of the crew in February 1863, when H.M.S. *Orpheus* was wrecked, being in charge of a pilot, on the Mana Kau reef, New Zealand.

[2] An attenuated faggot, used for facing, or revetting earthen walls.

for the fascine, as indeed it was for us, and the case sagged down three times on to my heels, for I was in front, so we agreed that we preferred to accept the chances, and sit on a box to encourage the Bluejackets to return, until the last box had been taken away. Some soldiers helped, one being a man I afterwards knew, Sergeant-Major H. Burke.

We were fortunate in having few casualties, for the Russians aiming high there were more shot striking over the spot than in the battery. While Mr. Daniels and I were sitting on the powder boxes, a mule being led up with two barrels of powder, one on either side, was struck full in the chest by a shell, which exploding scattered the body of the mule, but the powder remained intact. There was another remarkable escape, as the drivers of a waggon we had just emptied were mounting. The wheel driver was swinging his right leg over the horse's back, when its hind quarters were carried away by a round-shot.

Later in the afternoon, another waggon which had been brought to the same place was exploded by a shell, one of the horses being thrown high into the air, on which the Russians, standing up on their parapets, cheered loudly. We did the same, however, when about two o'clock magazines in the Malakoff and in the Redan exploded in rapid succession. The latter battery was wrecked by the explosion: only three guns being able to fire, and later, there were only two guns in the Malakoff in action.

Before the first bombardment, Captain Peel asked Lieutenant Ridge and Midshipman Daniels of H.M.S. *Diamond*, and Lieutenant Douglas and Midshipman Wood of the *Queen*, to disregard fire in the battery, by always walking with head up and shoulders back and without undue haste. He himself was a splendid example. I know he felt acutely every shot which passed over him, but the only visible effect was to make him throw up his head and square his shoulders. His nervous system was so highly strung, however, that eight months later a mere flesh wound incapacitated him for many months. He was a most tender-hearted man towards his fellow-creatures and animals; and in 1851, when he was crossing the Nubian Desert from Korosko to Abu Hamed, he dismounted from his camel in order to give a small dying bird some water.

We opened fire on the 17th with 126 guns. Everyone was certain that the Russian batteries would soon be silenced, and so provision was made for an assault that evening. The troops were kept ready to "fall in," storming columns detailed with Engineer officers as guides, sappers with scaling ladders, and the horses of the Field batteries stood "Hooked in." During the forenoon, however, the French gunners were fairly beaten, two of their magazines blew up, causing great loss of life, and their guns ceased firing at one o'clock, just as the Allied fleets came into action at the harbour's mouth. We were too busy to notice what the effect of the Russian fire was on our men-of-war, but we were all deeply mortified when at sundown we saw them haul out of action.

On the evening of the 17th the British Left Attack ran short of ammunition, and it moreover had the undivided attention of the Russian batteries to the westward of it; for the French still farther west had ceased fire: they had not constructed their magazines with sufficient strength, and in consequence had several explosions. We were better supplied in the 21-gun battery, and, owing to Captain Peel's foresight and determination, his command was the only one which fired unceasingly until the 24th October.

For the opening of the bombardment we sent all our servants into battery, and thus when I got back to camp, just before dark, I had to go with a bucket to the watering-place at the head of the ravine near the 3rd Division, and then to stub up roots in the vineyard for firewood to boil some water. I fried some pork and ship's biscuits, but possibly my efforts as a cook were not approved; at all events, our servant was not allowed to go to battery on the 18th, to my great joy, but he was the only man of the detachment of H.M.S. *Queen* who was kept off duty, and he had to draw rations, cook, and mend clothes of a Commander, four Lieutenants, one Mate, and a Midshipman.

Able-seaman Elsworthy was of that uncommon class of sailors and soldiers who never hesitate on occasion to contradict an officer, but can always remain respectful while doing so. This man had great independence of character, and we became firm friends. I was fond of him because of his care, not only of me, but all my friends, and I respected his determination to always support me, when he thought I was doing my best for the Mess. He generally accompanied me on my foraging expeditions, on which I went daily for the next eight months when not on duty. Once, however, in December, I went down to Kamiesh Bay alone, and gave 58s. for half a large pig. Perhaps I paid too much for it, but I had great difficulty in bringing it home on the pony, and so was mortified when the Commander at dinner found fault with me for my extravagant purchase. Elsworthy, who was waiting on us, interposed, and gravely asserted that the Commander knew nothing about pork, and that not only was the half-pig excellent of its kind, but that it was very cheap. It is only fair to the Commander to add, that I have now, in 1905, read one of his letters at the time to the Captain of the *Queen* eulogising Elsworthy.

That night, before I slept, it occurred to me that I had been very nearly out of this world several times during the day, and that since I had left school I had said very few prayers. A cockpit on board a man-of-war, which for readers who have no nautical knowledge may be described as a cellar lined with wood, to the roof of which, in H.M.S. *Queen*, some twenty-five hammocks were slung, is not a favourable place for devotions. The furniture consisted of some twenty or thirty whitewashed sea-chests, and I cannot recall having seen a man or boy pray there.

I realised in the presence of imminent danger my sins of omission, but like a boy argued it would be cowardly to begin until after the bombardment. When it ceased, my good intentions were forgotten until the next bombardment, with its recurring perils, reminded me. Then the same chain of thought recurred, and similar resolutions were made with identical results. This happened again at the third bombardment, and then I was so ashamed that I have ever since been more mindful of my religious duties.

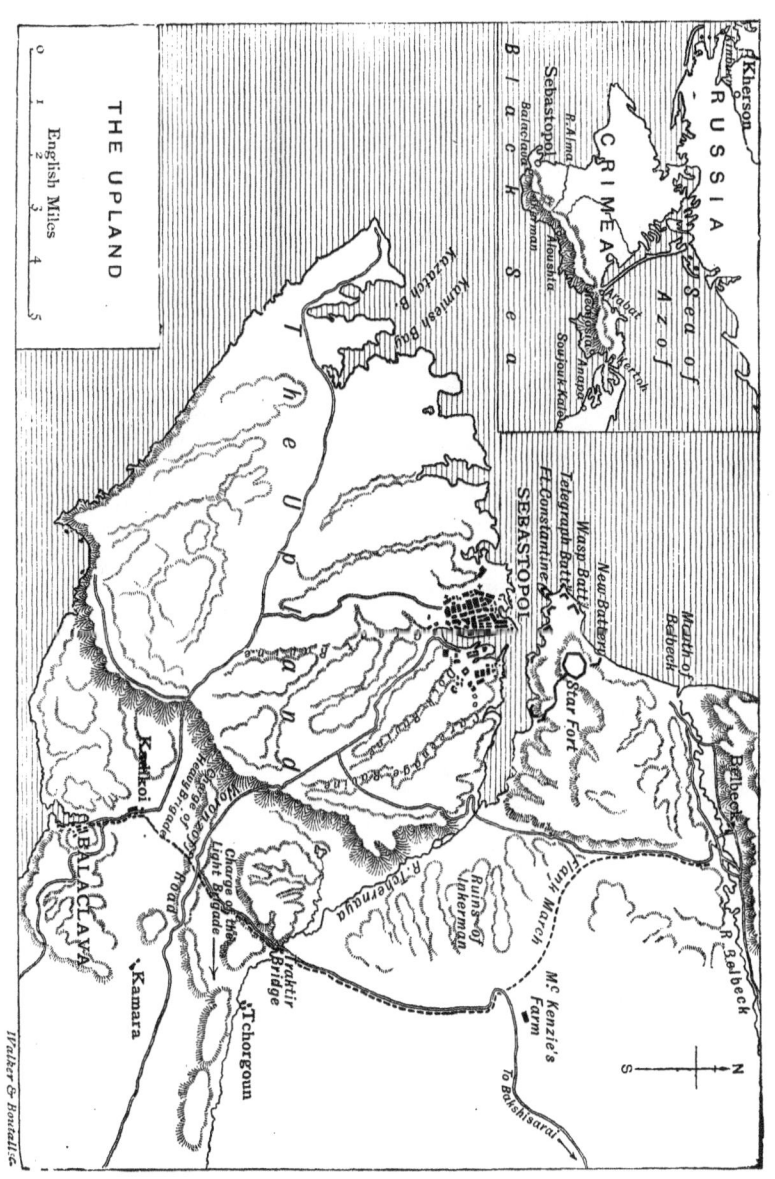

CHAPTER V

1854—THE SIEGE OF SEVASTOPOL

Captain Peel's heroic conduct—My only two pocket-handkerchiefs—Sir William Howard's eulogy of the sailors—Horse Artillery going into action—Battle of Inkerman—Sailors prepare to spike their guns—Foraging at Balaklava—The great gale of the 14th November—" Well done, *Queen*."

THE English batteries, Right and Left Attack, had only eight guns dismounted, and re-opened fire soon after daybreak on the 18th October. The French were sanguine the previous day that they would be ready next morning, but they were not, and asked for twenty-four hours' delay for the assault; but their batteries were not then re-armed, and a further delay became necessary. Indeed, before our Allies were ready, the Russians had repaired their damages, and were in better condition than they had been after a few hours' fire on the 17th October. By the 20th the English batteries had lost the undoubted mastery they had obtained on the first day.

Early on the 18th Captain Peel gave us a proof of remarkable courage. A shell weighing 42 lbs. penetrating the parapet, rolled into the centre of a gun's crew, who threw themselves on the ground. This would not, however, have saved them, for there were several cases of powder being passed into the magazine on the spot, but Peel stooping down lifted the shell, and resting it against his chest carried it back to the parapet, and, stepping on to the ledge of earth termed Banquette, rolled it over the Superior crest, on which it immediately burst.

About noon I had been relieved, and was eating my ration of raw salt pork, a biscuit, and an onion, with some tea without milk or sugar. I was sitting alongside a gun, one of the three

I had been working, on the far side of which there was a magazine built into the parapet, when a shell bursting on the top of the magazine set fire to the roof and sent a shower of sand over my pork. I was more interested in trying to save it than in the effect of the shell, until the flames created some trepidation, and the officer who had relieved me (not belonging to the *Queen*) demoralised the men by his excited demeanour. There was really no danger of the magazine exploding unless another shell struck it in the same spot, but the officer yelled, " Shell burst in the magazine, sir; magazine on fire." Now Ridge, First Lieutenant of H.M.S. *Diamond*, was as cool and unconcerned as if he had been shifting topsails, and responded without the slightest excitement in his tone, " Ay, ay, put it out," suggesting means which might have been used by Smollett, but cannot here be recorded. The shouts were repeated, and eventually, as the men were still flat on the ground, I put down, though unwillingly, my ration, and got up on the magazine, stamping out the burning bags, and kicking earth into the crater made by the explosion. I soon scorched my socks and the lower part of my trousers, and then extinguished the fire by squatting on the sand-bags, which being filled with earth made only a fitful flame.

While I was thus engaged I felt somebody working alongside of me, but I did not pause to look up, for shells and bullets were striking the parapet around us, and thus it was not a spot in which one would stay any longer than was necessary. When the fire was out, a decided voice said, " Jump down," and then I saw it was Captain Peel. He ordered the gun's crew to fall in, sent away the officer who had caused the alarm, and made a speech in praise of my conduct. This was the beginning of a friendship which lasted till his death, in 1858. He was twice my age, and at that period the gulf between a Midshipman and a Post Captain was immense, but as Sir John Robinson, the observant Editor of the *Daily News*, used to contend, " There is a special bond of comradeship between those who have stood together in critical moments of war. Nothing can quite approach it—they have been revealed to each other in a supreme test of moral and physical value. They have been close to God, and have seen each other as He and posterity will appraise them."

THE SIEGE OF SEVASTOPOL

I have often been asked if I was nervous the first time I came under fire, and I have always answered truthfully, "Yes," although I cannot say that my statement has always been credited. Not only was I nervous the first time, but throughout my service the first shot in every action passing near me has been acutely felt, unless I had some duty on hand at the moment. The sense of duty preoccupies a man, and not only from what I felt, but from what I have seen in many actions, the strain on the nerves of a gun detachment is considerably lessened by the fact that the service of a gun being dependent on combined action, compels a Gunner to concentrate his thoughts on his work.

I believe Generals, or any officers in command, who have responsibility, if they are the right sort, lose all sense of personal fear. At the end of the first bombardment, which lasted a week, I was conscious of a decided feeling of exultation in the presence of danger, such as men feel when they do well in manly sports, or women feel when they realise they are pre-eminent among their compeers.

The events which I have related of the carrying up of the powder[1] and the extinguishing of the fired magazine were reported at the time to the Commander-in-Chief, Lord Raglan, and when the Victoria Cross was instituted a year later, with retrospective effect, caused my name to be put forward for the decoration, and eventually obtained for me a Commission without purchase in the Army.

When we opened fire, being very proud of ourselves, we named that part of the 21-gun battery, the guns of which were manned by sailors, the Koh-i-noor Battery, a play on the name of Captain Peel's ship, H.M.S. *Diamond*. "Koh-i-noor" was painted in black letters on a white signboard, and near it was hoisted a Union Jack in the centre of our section of half the battery. Neither the board nor the Union Jack remained after an hour's firing. As wood and paint were scarce, we gave up the board; but the flag-staff was replaced again and again. Captain Peel refixed it twice on the 17th, and in replacing it on the 18th I had a curious escape. The battery

[1] Letter from Captain W. Peel, R.N., to the Rev. Sir John Page Wood: "Your son was only known to me through his gallant behaviour. . . . He volunteered to bring up powder through a fire which daunted others."

was built on a slightly descending slope, about that of St. James's Street, London, S.W., and as the flag stood above the trench or big ditch which formed the battery, shots just missing the top of the parapet, which was about four feet above the surface of the ground, often cut the flag-staff or one of its supports. When the pole had been much reduced in length by its numerous fractures, we fastened the flag on to a spare rammer. This rammer was cut away on the 18th, and as I did not like to remain in sight of the enemy while digging a fresh hole, I collected some trucks or wheels of guns' carriages which had been injured, and in them placed the rammer with the flag, filling up the space with stones and fragments of broken shell. I was just putting the finishing touches to what I thought would give a firm hold, when a shot struck the pile of trucks, and cut them down to the ground.

On the 19th of October our Commander and Lieutenant Douglas were checking the aim of the gun on which my friend Mr. Sanctuary had been wounded: we were not satisfied with our shooting, for it was not till many days later that we realised that two of the Russian guns in the Malakoff Battery which appeared to us to be in the same alignment were not so, one being nearer to us than the other gun standing apparently next to it. The nearer Russian gun required less elevation on our gun for the target, but as we thought the enemy's guns were equidistant from our battery, we believed that the error of "shorts and overs" was due to bad "laying." While the officers were discussing the laying of the gun with the captain of it, the crew of eight men on either side, a 13-inch mortar shell falling immediately in front of the gun close to the carriage, exploded. The result was so strange as to be almost incredible. Our gun was cut in two bits, the charge exploded, and the shot went in the air, the carriage and breech of the gun upsetting, and flying backwards without hurting a man. The following day there was a somewhat similar case. A cart loaded with round-shot had been by error brought in daylight up to the battery, and two men were in the cart throwing out the shot, when a Russian round-shot struck the centre of the load in between the two men without touching either, one man actually having one of our shot in his arms; but the enemy's shot, while it missed them, struck the heap in the cart, scattered the load high in the air, wounding severely three sailors.

That afternoon I gave up a pocket-handkerchief to tie up Able-seaman Simmons, of H.M.S. *Diamond*, who was dangerously wounded by a shell splinter in the thigh. He returned to the battery six months later, bringing back the handkerchief, and thanking me for the loan! On the 20th I gave up my only other handkerchief to save a man's nose. A shell burst immediately over the gun which I was working, striking down several of the crew, amongst others Edward Hallett, of H.M.S. *Queen*. He was injured in several places, and as I helped the doctor to turn him on his back—for all the wounds were in front of his body—we noticed that his nose was nearly off, hanging by a bit of skin. The doctor used my handkerchief to wipe off some of the sand, and then refixed the nose with it. The nose joined satisfactorily, but Hallett died two years later from his other wounds. Sir William H. Russell, *Times* correspondent, wrote the following tribute to the work of the Bluejackets: " The Sailors' Brigade suffered very severely; although they only worked about thirty-five guns in the various batteries, they lost more men than all our siege train, working and covering parties put together."

On the 24th, the firing, which had slackened down daily, ceased. I spent that night in battery, and returned to camp at daylight. Soon after I returned we heard the sound of firing near Balaklava. Captain Peel was the only officer of the Naval Brigade who saw the charges, one of which was immortalised by Tennyson, and as Peel did not return to our camp till evening we had little idea of the world-wide story. One of our officers who had been to Balaklava, in the evening observed, when we were going to sleep, " That was a smart little affair that the Cavalry had this morning." But we " stood to Arms " until the Infantry reinforcements, which moved to the " Col,"[1] returned to their camps.

The difference between the sister Services was noticeable in an incident that day. A Commander was Senior on parade. He had given an order, " Examine arms, draw ramrods," and the Bluejackets having dropped the ramrod to the bottom of

[1] The " Col " was the ascent from Balaklava Plain to the Upland.

the barrel, and removed it, were holding the head an inch from the muzzle. The Inspecting Officers passed round, but the Commander could not remember the next order, "Return ramrods." A soldier would have blundered or asked, but the Commander called, "Go on, men; you know the rest." And they did, without any outward sign of merriment.

I was sent to battery again that night, and having returned to camp at daylight, witnessed at a distance of about a mile and a half the sortie made by the Russians, who, while on the Inkerman crest, were that distance or less from our parade-ground. At one o'clock I was strolling in the camp, when rapid firing commenced near the 2nd Division camp. Bugles sounded all around, and the Naval Brigade fell in, and got out the ammunition. Then I witnessed a most inspiring sight. "E," or "the Black Battery," now the 12th Field Battery, was encamped near Lord Raglan's Headquarters, and after we had "fallen in," passed our camp at top speed, the teams stretched down, and every driver "riding" his horse. I was so much impressed by the set, determined look on the faces of the men, that I have never forgotten it. Not an eye was turned to the right or to the left as the guns swept past us, and nobody seemed to notice the little bank and surface drain on either side of the Woronzow road, which sent the guns jumping up in the air. In silence we watched the battery pass on, until it seemed they came into action in the midst of the Russians, and in a few minutes the enemy fell back.

It was on this day that my friend Hewett[1] gained the Victoria Cross by bravely fighting his battery of two guns, which he had been ordered to spike and retire.

On the morning of the 5th November we breakfasted at 2.30 a.m. as usual, marching to battery at three o'clock. It had rained all night, was drizzling when day broke, and there was a fog, dense in the ravines, but which lifted occasionally on the crest-line of the Upland. At four o'clock we heard plainly the bells ringing in Sevastopol, and the noise of Artillery wheels, but at 5.30 p.m. the pickets reported, "All quiet in Front." I tell nothing of the battle-story now, which I narrated in *The Crimea in 1854-'94*, ten years ago, but it is

[1] Later, Admiral Sir W. M. W. Hewett, V.C., K.C.B.

interesting to recall that when our soldiers were being heavily pressed, the Generals commanding the Light and 4th Divisions declined the aid of Bosquet's Division, which was encamped to the south of the 2nd Division. It came later to help us when invited by Lord Raglan.

The roads from the Upland into the city of Sevastopol follow the ravines or fissures mentioned on p. 37, two of which join the Careenage ravine, passing at the northern end under precipitous cliffs, with gradients of 1 in 4. The Russians therefore sent Reserves and ammunition trains by a track which passes to the east of the Mamelon, and then southward down Gordon's Hill into the middle ravine, whence it turns back northwards to the Careenage ravine. We did not understand at the time how greatly the movements of the Russians were cramped by the ground, and we thought that the columns descending Gordon's Hill were coming to turn the flank of the 21-gun battery. Now the guard of the trenches was so weak that it could not protect them in front and on the flank, and therefore our position appeared precarious.

As the sound of firing on the Inkerman ridges trended farther southwards, six of our guns on the right were run back to fire along the flank, and spikes for disabling all were issued, and the men were shown the line of retreat. The head of a Russian column turned eastwards and disappeared when 1100 yards from our guns, but must have halted, for the tail of it remained for a long time exposed to our fire, at ranges varying from 1100 to 1500 yards, and under its destructive action gradually dissolved. I saw a shell from one of our guns explode in a powder waggon, destroying all the men and horses near it. The enemy endured this heavy fire with resigned courage, their comrades in the Malakoff and the Redan doing all they could to help them by concentrating their fire on the 21-gun battery. The fight was over by one o'clock. If the Russians had not been hampered by the ground, divisions which they intended should ascend by two slopes, getting on to one ridge, the result must have been a disaster for the Allies.

Captain Peel was not in the battery that day, going with Mr. Daniels straight from camp to Inkerman. During the fight, when officers and non-commissioned officers were killed, groups of privates collecting under some natural or self-elected leader of men, charged again and again, and we heard next day that Captain Peel led seven such counter attacks.

When I got back to camp at sunset, I went over to see a shipmate, Captain March, of the Royal Marines, who had been wounded in the fight. We had sent fifty of our two hundred Marines to Eupatoria on the 14th September, and the balance landed at Balaklava, which they garrisoned till a few days before the 5th November, when the Light Division had been so weakened by continuous work as to be unable to relieve their pickets.[1] Captain March was a favourite with everyone on board the *Queen*, and maintained his reputation by his cheery demeanour when badly wounded. He had been struck just behind the mouth by a big bullet, which had made an enormous hole in his jaw, but had left no sign of its exit; he lived, however, for forty years after the battle.

There were mingled feelings in our camps that evening: the officers felt intense pride in their men's enduring courage, but they reflected uneasily that we had narrowly escaped a disaster. I think that with the exception of some night-fighting in the trenches our Infantry never fought during the war with so great, resolute, and sustained determination as on the 5th November.

Three days after the battle I visited the field for motives of business as well as curiosity, for I was nearly barefooted. When on the 1st October we were warned that we must carry everything we took on shore, I limited my load to a shirt, two blankets, two pocket-handkerchiefs, and two pairs of socks. My light sailor's shoes were worn out within a week, in carrying messages for our Commander while he and my shipmates were at meals. I could not have gone on working, but that John Handcock, the Marine who had looked after me on board, and who was stationed on Balaklava Heights, hearing of my shoeless state, sent me down a pair of his own boots. These were also worn out, for although I rode my pony down to Balaklava, it was necessary for me to walk up, as it could not carry me and the things I brought

---

[1] The general officer in charge of the Front at Inkerman had written a week previous to the battle, "I have only the six hundred men on this front position."

for the Mess. I did not like the idea, however, of despoiling a dead man, so I took a Bluejacket with me, to whom I promised half a sovereign for a satisfactory fit. These he soon produced, and I had reason to praise the good workmanship of the Russian boot contractors.

During the last days of October the small quantities of grass remaining in the valleys failed, and it was more and more difficult to keep any flesh on my pony. Elsworthy (*vide* p. 43) and I, in one of our earliest visits to Balaklava, had cast covetous eyes on the stacks of barley laid out on the wharves ready for the ration parties, and later we took the pony down, I carrying ostentatiously the accumulations of my rum ration in a bottle. There was a sentry over the barley, but he perceiving the pony and two men with lashings, one carrying a suggestive bottle of rum, walked to the end of his " beat," and looked steadily towards the mouth of the [harbour until we had balanced a sack on the saddle and lashed it securely. As we departed, the sentry returned and picked up the bottle I had placed between two sacks. This method was followed throughout the winter, and until the month of May, when, being appointed an Aide-de-Camp to Captain Peel, I was able to obtain barley in a legitimate manner, on requisition.[1] I put up a rough shed for the pony, giving it one of my blankets, and had full advantage of its services, as it was never sick or sorry.

The last few days in October were pleasantly warm during the day although cold at night, but after the battle of Inkerman the weather grew daily worse. From the 10th, rain fell heavily, and continued incessantly for many days. That day I had to admit I was sick. I had been suffering from constant diarrhœa, induced by eating salt pork, often uncooked, and now the malady, aggravated by the cold and rainy weather experienced all night in the trenches, had made me seriously ill. The doctor directed me to remain lying down as much as possible, but on the morning of the 14th there befell the troops a great misfortune. It was blowing heavily in gusts at 4 a.m. when the battery Relief marched off, and sheets of rain beating

---

[1] Throughout the winter there was always barley for the taking away, except for ten days, and during that time I fed my pony on biscuits and bread, bought in the French camp, paying 2s. 6d. for a 2-lb. loaf.

on the tent made me congratulate myself I had been excused duty. At about 5 a.m. the tent pole was bending so ominously that the two Lieutenants in the tent with me, having put on all the clothes they possessed, held the pole by turns. At six o'clock, however, while the pole still held intact, a heavier blast of wind, lifting the tent right up in the air, carried it away. I was certainly uncomfortable with the rain beating down on me, and yet my sufferings were as nothing in comparison with hundreds of our soldier-comrades, some of whom wounded, and many sick, lay for hours exposed to the fury of the elements; for the hospital marquees, owing to their great spread of canvas, offered so much resistance to the wind that they were the first to fall. Several men in our Army who were "at duty" were found dead in the morning at their posts. Nearly all our horses broke loose from their picket ropes, and wild with terror careered over the Upland, and sixty of the very few we had, died that night. The force of the gale overturned waggons, and it was impossible for even a strong man to walk upright against the wind. When the tent blew away, my two companions took shelter under a low wall of stones which we had built round the powder magazine about a hundred yards from where our tent had stood, and when the storm moderated a little, more rain falling, I tried to join them; but the wind knocked me down, and I travelled the intervening distance on my hands and knees. Even in this fashion, however, the wind was too much for my remaining strength, and I should not have got to the wall but that our Gunnery Lieutenant and two Bluejackets going down on their knees, and joining hands, stretched out to intercept me. When I got under the shelter of the wall my comrades did all they could to help me, giving me the most sheltered spot.

As we looked around, we could not see more than two or three tents in any of the camps still standing, and these were protected by stone walls. We lay huddled together, thinking what might have happened to the ships, and watching the storm-driven kit which was swept through our camp. During the height of the gale two drums were borne along close to each other, and afforded us much interest. They rolled rapidly until caught by a stone or a tent peg, when the wind would turn them upright for a few seconds, and then a fresh gust carried them on again.

Not far from where we were lying there were two bell-tents still standing, belonging to different ships' detachments. The *Queen's* were on friendly terms with the officers of both, but the Commanders were very different in their nature. When the Senior in one was asked whether he would receive a sick Midshipman, he replied he was not going to have his tent made wet and dirty. About nine o'clock the officers who were in the other tent, belonging to H.M.S. *Bellerophon*, heard of my state, and two of them came over to invite me in. They supported me down, but to open the door would have had the effect of carrying the tent away, so I had to crawl in through a pool of water, which added to the mud already covering my jacket and trousers. My hosts, however, made light of this inconvenience, and regardless of the effect of my dirty state, covered me up in their clean dry blankets. I slept till awakened by the voice of our Commander, on his return from the battery, shouting, " Where, and how, is young Wood ? "

About twelve o'clock the south-west wind veered to the westward, and then sleet fell, followed by snow, which lay on the hills; but from two o'clock the wind, though colder, was moderating, and the Naval Brigade set to work to repitch our camp, and by nightfall had collected, in many cases from afar, what remained of it.

Our losses that day were great both in lives and in stores, twenty-one vessels being wrecked off the mouth of Balaklava Harbour. A magazine ship carrying ten million rounds, and the *Prince*, one of our largest transports, laden with warm clothing and stores of all descriptions, went down. The French lost a line-of-battle ship and the *Pluton* off Eupatoria, where a Turkish line-of-battle ship sank with all hands. Many of the houses in Sevastopol were unroofed in the height of the gale.

The Admiral again made the signal, " Well done, *Queen*." She was anchored off the mouth of the Katcha River, six miles north of Sevastopol, and during a lull in the storm sent boats to rescue men from several Austrian and Greek ships which had gone ashore. It was work of considerable danger, increased by the stupid barbarity of a few Cossacks, who fired on the rescue parties, wounding two of our men. Captain Michell, to whom this rescue was due, was not only brave himself, but possessed the more uncommon courage, that of daring to order others to risk their lives. He had previously offered to break the boom which closed the harbour mouth, by taking his ship at it under all plain sail; but, not unnaturally perhaps, his offer was declined by the Admiral. The rudder-head of the *Queen* was cracked by the action of the waves, and a week later I see by the Captain's letters to his wife, and to the Commander who was with the brigade on shore, when the Admiral wished to send the *Queen* and the other sailing vessels down to the Bosphorus, Michell objected on the ground that if the line-of-battle ships could not physically assist the troops, yet their presence might do something to encourage them. Later he was ordered down, and writing to the Admiral from the Bosphorus in January 1885, mentions he has only 330 men on board out of 970 the establishment, all the others having landed.

CHAPTER VI

1854-5—A NAKED AND STARVING ARMY

Indescribable sufferings of the old soldier—Contrast of naval with military system—Commodore Lushington's work—Lunch with Lord Raglan—*Times* correspondent saves remnant of Army—Christmas Day—Captain Peel's plan for cutting out a Russian ship—A pony's sagacity.

THE storm on the 14th was the commencement of misery so great as to defy adequate description. Some writers have ascribed the loss of lives and of health to the climate. This is inaccurate. The climate of the Crimea, though more variable, is no more inclement than that of the north of England; moreover, we now know that few men or animals, with adequate food and suitable clothing, are killed by bad weather, and as long as they are well fed hard work has little adverse effect on their health. Officers who were able to procure extra food and clothing maintained in comparison their health, while the Rank and File were perishing by hundreds. In eight battalions which served in the immediate Front with the sailors, 73 men out of every 100 died from starvation and want of clothing. The weather was indeed deplorable. I see by my Diary our batteries were flooded on the 27th November, and to add to the trials of the troops, cholera reappeared on the 2nd December.

Some fresh meat was issued in January and February, but the sick were always served first, and as the whole quantity available in sixty days worked out at 14 lbs. a man, with more than half the Army in hospital, the men still " at duty " had practically none. Moreover, if it had been issued, there were no means of cooking it; although an Army Order authorising a ration of fuel was issued in the first week in December, it was nearly a month before effect could be given to the order.

The troops lived practically on salt meat, biscuit, and rum. They preferred pork, because it was more easily cooked than what the sailors call salt-junk, for Chicago beef had not then been canned. Many of the men could eat neither beef nor pork, for their mouths were affected with scurvy.

The War Minister wrote in the spring of 1854 to Lord Raglan: "I cannot help seeing through the calm and noble tone of your announcement of the decision to attack Sevastopol that it has been taken in order to meet the views and desires of the Government, and not in entire accordance with your opinions." The disaster is summed up in the Report of the Sevastopol Inquiry Committee presented to the House of Commons in 1855. The Committee show clearly that "the blame rested on the Ministry, and on the nation." The Administration which ordered the expedition had no adequate information as to the amount of the forces in the Crimea, as to the strength of the fortresses to be attacked, or of the resources of the country to be invaded. They did not foresee the probability of a protracted struggle, and made no provision for a winter campaign.

The *Queen* sailed for the Bosphorus early in December. Many Army officers imagine that the comparative plenty in the Sailors' camp was due to their drawing supplies from the Fleet. This is an error. We got canvas, blankets, carpenters' tools, and such like from our ships, but our food was entirely drawn from Army stores; indeed, the Navy had no storeships on which we could draw, and in the worst of the weather, when snow lay thick on the ground, were occasionally on half rations, and often on the verge of starvation, though there was always food at Balaklava.

In the Naval Brigade, when the men returned at daylight from the battery, they were allowed to rest for three hours, and were then marched down to Balaklava for supplies, each man carrying up from 30 to 50 lbs. in haversacks or bags. The sailors did get their warm clothing a few days earlier than it was available for the Army, our first instalment being issued on the 30th December. It is remarkable that the Naval officers should have been so much more successful in looking after their men than the Army officers, but the fact is undoubted that they were so. The suffering caused to the Army arose from want of transport for nine miles. Nevertheless, even without transport, something might have been done in the winter by organisation, but Army officers had not been trained to think of measures for supplying the men's wants.

Regimental officers could not obtain clothing until they had signed requisitions and forms, it being held of more importance in peace to ensure a soldier not getting a coat a month earlier than he was entitled to it by regulation, than that he should be kept in health.

The losses in the Naval Brigade by disease were small, from all causes only $10\frac{1}{2}$ per cent., of which 7 per cent. were fatal wound cases. The Cavalry lost an average of 15 per cent., and 24 per cent. died in the Infantry battalions, which during the winter were carrying stores from Balaklava. The Infantry in the Front, however, lost on an average 39 men in every 100, and, as stated above, in eight battalions which were most exposed the mortality amounted to 73 per cent.

The Naval Brigade on the 20th November left the high ground near the Picket-house and moved to a new camp, which was pitched at the head of a ravine running between Headquarters and the French camps. Here we were much more sheltered from the wind, and were, moreover, a mile nearer Balaklava. It took us three days, for we had to carry on our backs tents, hospital marquee, and ammunition. About this time, however, our work became lighter, for we sent only half detachments, *i.e.* guns' crews, down to the batteries at night, and thus got more work done, in the way of building and carrying, than previously had been the case. As I have recorded, Captain Peel did much to bring out the grand fighting qualities of the sailors employed in the Right Attack. Commodore (later Sir Stephen) Lushington initiated all the sanitary measures which helped to keep down our sick list; it was he who organised the carrying parties, and got the warm clothing brought up. He insisted on the tents being thoroughly drained, and made shelters, the walls being rough stones, for drying the men's clothing. After he had built a wooden hospital, the next shed, which he got up about the middle of January, was converted into a drying-room. In contrast with the Army arrangements, where the soldier who up to December was supposed to cook in the little tin pot he carried on his back, the sailors had company cooks, who were not sent to the trenches.

We made sufficiently good soup cauldrons out of the big empty powder-cases, one of which proved too heavy for me and my companion on the 17th October. Whenever there was coal or charcoal in Balaklava, some was brought up daily, the Officers in command themselves carrying loads. Commodore Lushington borrowed some well-sinkers from the Army, and thus ensured our men drinking only pure water; and not only was great attention paid to the cleanliness of our camp, but latrines were placed on the far side of the ravine, and to get the men over it with dry feet he built a suspension bridge, the footway of which was made of casks. In December the Commodore got two thousand pairs of drawers, and bought personally three hundred pairs of boots at Constantinople, which were issued to the men on repayment.

Every morning before the Bluejackets marched off, whether at three or six o'clock, they had to drink their cocoa or coffee on parade, to ensure that they did not go down to battery with an empty stomach. Similarly quinine and lime juice were issued, and always drunk in the presence of an officer. When the men returned from the batteries in the evening, they had hot soup, made from salt meat which had been soaked for many hours to extract the saline. Not only had the sailors much more clothing than the soldiers, but the officers saw that every Bluejacket on returning from the trenches hung his wet garments in the drying shed,[1] which was heated with a stove, so that he did not lie down in his wet clothes. Later in the siege, when our men got their pay monthly, there was some drunkenness, and it being detrimental to health, was checked by a Tattoo Roll parade taken by officers, who in those days did much of the work performed by non-commissioned officers in the Army.

When we moved over our camp to the sheltered ravine, the *Queen's* officers made a hut twenty-four feet long, eight feet broad, and seven feet high. Following the Tartar fashion, we sank the hut about four feet, allowing the roof only to show above ground. In it we had our meals, but it was not big enough for use as a dormitory. A day or two after we shifted camp, Commodore Lushington had a visit from the officer

[1] Erected in January 1855.

commanding the French regiment encamped immediately to the westward of our ravine, who said most politely, "We gather that some of your men have indistinct ideas on the ownership of animals. Now, I have given our men strict orders they are not to retaliate, but I had better explain to you that this one-sided arrangement cannot continue, and as I have got in my corps some of the most expert thieves from Paris, unless your men desist, some morning when you wake you will find that half your camp has disappeared." We passed this on to our Bluejackets, and the hint must have been taken, for we remained good friends.

On the 11th December I received a message from the Officer commanding the Infantry detachments in the trenches, asking me to fire on a working party of some twenty Russians, employed under the Malakoff Tower, in extending a trench towards the Mamelon. I trained a Lancaster gun on the party, a range of 1720 yards; but as the gun always carried to the right, I laid a little to the left of the Russian right-hand man. They usually kept a look-out man, who gave warning when our guns fired, when the men disappeared into the trenches: on this occasion, however, at least half of them remained at work, and the shell catching the left-hand man cut him in two.

Next night when I went to sleep, at about eight o'clock, in battery, it was freezing and bitterly cold, so I had crawled into a hole, being more anxious for shelter from wind than rain. The wind dropped about 2 a.m., and rain fell. This awoke me, and I realised that I was getting wet, but was too tired to rise. When I tried to do so at daylight, on the Relief arriving, it was freezing again, for with the coming day the temperature had fallen, and I was unable to move. My comrades carried me back to camp, and with hot bottles to my feet and all around me, I revived. About this time the Naval officers,[1] before returning to camp at daylight, went round to help in soldiers who from the intense cold had become incapable of movement.

At the end of that week I made the acquaintance of Lord

[1] Commodore Lushington's Diary shows he saw a soldier coming out of the trenches towards camp, and ran to help him; but the man fell dead before he got to him, having struggled on till his heart ceased to act.

Raglan. When I was not in battery I went down daily to Balaklava or Kamiesh Bay to buy food for our Mess, and being at the latter place I went on board H.M.S. *Beagle*, to see Hewett.[1] I stayed for the night, appreciating greatly the good food, but still more the unlimited power of ablution, and a new coat and trousers he gave me. Lieutenant Burgoyne,[2] H.M.S. *Swallow*, my former shipmate in H.M.S. *Queen* (*vide* p. 13), dined with us, and next morning asked me to take a letter to his father, Sir John Burgoyne, the Engineer-in-Chief of the Army. I willingly assented, although to deliver it I should have to go a mile or so round. When I left Kamiesh it was raining, and by the time I had walked eight miles to Headquarters, it seemed to me double that distance. I was covered with mud to my knees and wet through, so was anxious not to be seen, for besides being very dirty, Midshipmen were then taught to regard their superiors with awe. I was hurrying away, after handing in my letter, when I was called back and taken to see Lord Raglan, who had lunching with him General Niel, to whom I was presented. My host covered me with confusion by narrating the incident of trying to carry the powder into battery, and the story of the burning magazine, of which he had heard from Captain Peel, and said pleasant things about me, after which, to my great relief, I was allowed to talk to one of his Staff, who was told to provide me with food.

I spent Christmas Day in the battery, and while speaking to a sergeant in charge of a working party, was nearly killed by what we thought was a shot, for it lodged in the parapet close to us without interrupting our conversation. A few seconds later it burst, and a fragment cut my cap off my head without raising the skin. I dined that night with Captain Peel, the other three guests being Commodore Lushington, our Commander, and Captain Moorsom, the Commander of the Left Attack. I felt much honoured by the company in which I was placed. Mr. Daniels, Captain Peel's Aide-de-Camp, had been invalided, and so I was acting for him. The dinner was a culinary triumph, considering the

---
[1] Later, Admiral Sir W. M. W. Hewett, V.C.
[2] Captain Hugh Burgoyne, V.C., lost in H.M.S. *Captain*, 1871.

circumstances, and included all the dishes to be seen on a Mess table in England. We certainly did not realise at the moment the intensity of the suffering of our soldier-comrades close to us. We could not have done anything by individual effort of the sailors, for if such had been acceptable it would have been useless; but we certainly should not have enjoyed our dinner had we understood what the proud reticence of the Long-service soldier concealed.

One of the senior Regimental officers wrote at 4 p.m. that day: "At this hour the Division to which I belong has not had an ounce of meat for dinner; in fact, dinner there is none." This was the worst time of the winter, and to the middle of January was the climax of the misery of our men. Since Inkerman we had only had 14,000 effectives, and on the 1st January there were only 11,300 "at duty,"—it cannot be said they were fit for duty,—and there were 23,000 in hospital. From this time on, however, our men's state was ameliorated. On the 28th December the sailors obtained the first instalment of the Crimean Army Fund. A small sheep was selling at £5 that day, but by the liberality of the British Public we bought from the Fund very good tea at 6d. instead of 3s. 6d. a pound, and other articles in proportion. This Fund was due to the plain writing of Mr. W. H. Russell,[1] of the *Times*. It is remarkable that Lord Raglan and Sir Colin Campbell were the only senior Officers who did not in the first instance resent Mr. Russell's outspoken comments on the incapacity of our Government, and the inefficiency of the Departments. As I showed in *The Crimea in 1854-'94*, officers came round later to Russell's views: Lord Clyde (Colin Campbell) left him by will a keepsake, and the survivors of the Crimean War feel grateful to him, and the *Times*, for his outspoken statements.

In January snow fell, and lay three feet on the ground and twelve feet in drifts; but the Naval Brigade never ceased to send carrying parties to Balaklava. I should not like my readers to infer that the Army did nothing, for the troops at Balaklava in December and in January carried on their heads 7000 loads of siege materials from the harbour to the Engineer Parks, and 145 tons of biscuits to the Army Head-quarters; if they had not done so, not a man in the Front

[1] Sir W. Howard Russell, K.C.B.

could have existed. The half-starved, insufficiently clad, overworked, but uncomplaining Old soldier, serving at the Front, was generally in the trenches four or five nights, and in one recorded instance for six nights, in a week; those on sentry duty, 300 yards in advance of our works, having to stand motionless for two hours at a time. When they got back to camp they had but the shelter of a worn-out tent, through which the rain beating, collected in puddles; the feeblest fell asleep, completely exhausted, to awake shivering, and carried to a hospital tent but little better than the company tent, and two or three days later to a grave. The stronger men went out with picks when available, and dug up roots of stunted oak and vines for fuel, and then roasting the green coffee berry in the lid of the canteen, pounded it in a shell fragment, and boiled it. The greater number, however, unequal to so much effort for so little result, consuming their biscuit and rum, slept, generally in a wet greatcoat or blanket, until required to carry a load of ammunition or biscuit. These loads were limited to 40 lbs.; but the exertion was great, for the men on the Balaklava track waded through mud.

When going down that track on the 31st January, I had my boots sucked off my feet in the tenacious soil, and I saw eighteen horses trying in vain to move a gun-carriage similar to that which we had dragged up by hand on the same ground in the previous October.

However, the ground was now drying up, and we mounted some new guns in both Attacks during the first week of February. There was still great misery amongst the soldiers, but it was lessening, and there were a few days of fine weather early in the month.

On the night of the 3rd a party of 150 Bluejackets were dragging guns down to the Left Attack. For some reason to me unknown, they, it was said owing to injudicious treatment of the officers, turned sulky, and at a further unpalatable order given just as they got the guns on the rising ground overlooking the Left Attack trenches, the men dropped the drag ropes, and in spite of the expostulations and orders of their officers, returned to camp. Next day all these men were handed over to me for punishment on the principle of "Watch and watch," but the watch in their case consisted of manual labour. They were employed in carrying duties, and were not to be allowed more rest in camp than four hours. The unusual experiment of giving a young Midshipman the command of 150 men who had behaved badly ended satisfactorily, the men being forgiven after undergoing a week's punishment.

Towards the end of February we re-armed the 21-gun battery throughout, mounting some 8-inch 65 cwt. guns, and long 32-pounders, 56 cwt., besides two more 68-pounders, and another Lancaster, 95 cwt. gun. We had now more soldiers to guard our Position. The Right Attack trenches, which extended over a mile, had been often held by 350, and one night by 300 men; but reinforcements were now arriving. Admiral Boxer, who came to Balaklava and took charge of the Port at the end of January, effected vast improvements: he built landing-stages, and evolved order out of Chaos, and thus, when carrying parties went down to the harbour, they were no longer kept waiting for their loads.

The last week of February, the 2nd Division was annoyed by the shells thrown up from two Russian men of war, moored in the outer harbour. Their guns were slung on deck at an angle of 45°. Captain Peel worked out a scheme for the capture of the vessel, on which he did me the honour of asking my opinion. He proposed to take six boats after dark down the face of the Inkerman cliff, almost opposite the steamers, which were lying 300 yards from the shore. We were to launch the boats, board the ships, and kill or drive below the few men only who would be on deck, as we believed, after the crew had retired to rest. If we succeeded, we were to tow the ships ashore, or if necessary, higher up the harbour, immediately under the hill on the crest of which the critical struggle of Inkerman took place. I was silent, but when pressed for an opinion as to the probable result I frankly said that I thought its successs was more than doubtful; I argued, however, that our loss of men would not be in vain, for the Russians would probably withdraw their steamers, while our men would be encouraged by the adventurous nature of the undertaking. I gathered later that Lord Raglan was in favour of the attempt, but the Naval Commander-in-Chief vetoed it.

Captain Peel's scheme having become known, it encouraged other seamen, and later John Shephard, Boatswain's Mate of H.M.S. *St. Jeanne d'Arc*, invented, and constructed a small boat for one man carrying a powerful explosive. He got amongst the Russian ships without being noticed; but the ferry-boats, which plied to the north side, and back, prevented the execution of his plan. To my grief, Captain Peel now being sick, re-embarked, and the *Diamond's* men were recalled to their ship, Peel himself passing later to the command of H.M.S. *Leander*, a larger frigate.

On the 22nd March the Russians attacked the French near the Mamelon early in the evening, and were repulsed, after inflicting considerable loss on our Allies. Later, another strong column, passing up by the left or western end of the French works, moved on our No. 8 battery, just below the 21-gun battery, led by a handsome Circassian chief, who was attended by a small bugler about sixteen years of age. The lad stood on our parapet, sounding the advance, until he fell, pierced by seven bullets. There was much hand-to-hand fighting, but the end of it was that the Russians were driven back, mainly by parties of the 7th, 34th, and 90th Regiments.

Next day a flag of Truce was arranged for 12.30, and I was sent down to the trenches with a large piece of calico, which I handed over to the Senior officer in the battery, and then hurried on to our most advanced trench, hoping to reach the Mamelon before the sentries on either side were pushed out. When the flag was hoisted, I ran as fast as I could to the Front, and picking up a wounded Russian, on the north side of the ravine, sent him back by soldiers who were following me. The man must have been told we were cruel, for he made signs begging for his life. Near to him I picked up a haversack, and the Russian, when he saw that he was not to be killed, begged me to give him the black bread inside it. For two hours the combatants on either side engaged in friendly conversation.

There were some few Russian officers who spoke English, and many could converse in French. Some of them remarked on the excellent practice we made with the 68-pounder gun in the 21-gun battery, and said they hoped to open upon us with one of a similar calibre next morning, with which they intended to silence our gun. We accepted the challenge eagerly, and arranged that other guns should not take part in the duel. Soon after daylight the Russian gun opened fire, and we answered it shot by shot, no other guns taking part in the cannonade. Our practice was, however, better than that of our opponents, and the seventeenth shot caused the Russians to cease firing, and drop a mantlet over the embrasure, thus admitting that they were out of action.

On the 2nd April Captain Peel rejoined, bringing with him 200 men from his new command, H.M.S. *Leander*, and took me for his Aide-de-Camp, for Mr. Daniels had not then returned. Captain Peel's opinion was valued more and more from this time, and with Lord Raglan he daily gained influence. Before he rejoined the Brigade, he proposed a scheme for breaking the floating boom which enclosed the entrance to the harbour. His plan was to lash on either side of H.M.S. *Leander* a laden collier, and then, sending everyone below, to steer the ship himself at full speed against the obstacle. He calculated that the combined weight of the vessels would break the boom, and once inside the harbour Peel intended to engage the forts, being supported by the whole of the Fleet, which he urged should follow him. Though his plan was not adopted, his enterprise and carefully-thought-out scheme gained him increased consideration at Army Headquarters.

I nearly lost my appointment as Aide-de-Camp on the 6th April, when going up the " Covered way " on the right of our 68-pounders. Just as I reached the gun a man called out to me, " Look out! " I stood still, but had not time to move before a 13-inch mortar shell fell within six feet of me. It was fitted, however, with a long fuse, and by using my legs freely I got out of reach before it burst. Besides the great privilege of being associated with Captain Peel, I gained another advantage in that I was now entitled to draw forage for my pony. During the following week I profited by the animal's sagacity. I had been sent with a message to a party constructing a battery in front of our Left Attack, the ground of which I did not know in the same way as that of the Right, where I could almost find my way blindfolded. It was just dark, when, having delivered my message, I turned my face as I thought homewards, but inadvertently rode out to the left of the Left

Attack, just where it joined hands with the right of the French. My pony was going unwillingly, and seeing that I had lost my way I halted. I could not identify my position, so threw the reins on the pony's neck; it turned sharply round, and cantered direct to my camp.

CHAPTER VII

1855—SIEGE OF SEVASTOPOL

Narrow escape of Lord Raglan—Michael Hardy's dauntless courage—Death of Lieutenant Douglas—Selections for the Victoria Cross—Stephen Welch's Divine-like act of self-sacrifice—Sardinian outposts at Tchorgoum—Assault of the Mamelon—An intrepid Zouave—Terrible losses of the Russians.

DURING the first week in April, Lord Raglan, accompanied by General Sir Harry Jones, walked round our battery, and on reaching the guns under my command asked where he could sit down, and Sir Harry told me to place some empty shell-boxes near the 68-pounder, so that his Lordship could sit on them. There was only desultory firing at the time, but probably Sir Harry did not know that the 68-pounders received more attention from our foes than all the rest of the battery. He went away, and was scarcely out of sight when a shot cut through the parapet, six inches only above Lord Raglan's head, smothering him with stones and earth. He stood up to shake some of the dirt off his neck and head, observing in an unmoved tone, "Quite close enough."

It rained for twenty-four hours on the 8th April, and when we went to our guns on the 9th, the water was up to the level of the platforms, which stood ten inches above the ground. The Russians had apparently not anticipated a renewal of the bombardment, for they scarcely answered our fire; but we did not know at the time that they had run out of gun cartridges, and were obliged to use infantry cartridges, to make up charges for their guns. We got the range immediately with the 8-inch gun, which stood in the obtuse angle of the battery, the right face of which looked to the Malakoff, and the left face to the

Redan. The gun was served by *Queen's*, who had been in battery since October, but the *Leander's*, who had the two 32-pounders, 56 cwt. guns, were new to the work, and the shooting was wild. While I was myself getting the range with the centre gun, the captain of the right-hand gun made such erratic shots that I ordered him to "cease firing," when No. 3, the "Loader," Able-seaman Michael Hardy, asked me if the gun's crew might "change rounds," and that he might be No. 1; I assented, and after two trial shots Hardy got on the target, and made excellent practice.

During the first hour the embrasure of the 8-inch gun, which drew the greater portion of the enemy's fire, was cut down and rebuilt three times. A sergeant and two Sappers, detailed for repairing that part of the battery, were wounded, and I had personally to repair the embrasure after the first occasion of its being demolished. After three hours' firing, the 8-inch gun where I was standing became so hot from incessant use that we were obliged to "cease fire," and the men released from their work crowded up on the platform to be out of the water, which in the trench was half-way up to their knees. My other two guns continued in action; I had a telescope laid in my left hand along the gun, and was steadying my right hand on the shoulder of Charles Green, First Class boy, of H.M.S. *Queen*, who was sitting on the right rear truck of the gun.

While I was calling out the results of the targets made, a man handed round the rum for the gun's crew, and Green asked me to move my elbow, so that he might not shake me while drinking his grog. We both stood up, and he was holding the pannikin to his mouth, when a shot from the Redan, coming obliquely from our left, took off his head, the body falling on me. At this moment Michael Hardy, having just fired his gun, was "serving the vent."[1] Hardy had turned up his sleeves and trousers, and his shirt being open low on the neck and chest, his face and body were covered with the contents of the boy's head. Now, if he had lifted his thumb from the vent the result might have been fatal to Nos. 3 and 4, who were then ramming home the next charge; but Hardy never flinched.

[1] This consists in stopping with the thumb all currents of air in the gun, which if allowed to pass up the vent would cause sparks remaining in the chamber to ignite the fresh cartridge.

Without moving his right hand, he wiped with his left the boy's brains from his face. Those sitting at my feet were speechless, being startled, as indeed I was, for I had felt the wind from the Russian shot which had passed within an inch of my face. We were brought back to a sense of duty by Hardy's somewhat contemptuous "You —— fools, what the hell are you looking at? Is he dead? Take his carcase away. Ain't he dead? Take him to the doctor." "Jim, are you home?" he asked of No. 3, the Loader, who was in the act of giving the final tap, after having rammed home the charge, and seeing him nod, without bestowing another look on us, or possibly even thinking of me, he gave the order, "Run out. Ready."

From this time to his death I saw a great deal of Hardy, as we generally went to battery together, for although I had become an Aide-de-Camp I remained at battery duty, when Captain Peel did not require me.

Hardy carried down my blanket and tea-bottle, receiving my allowance of rum for his services. He was in many ways a remarkable man, for when stationed at Eupatoria in the autumn of 1854, he amassed by questionable means a number of ponies, and started a livery stable, hiring them out to officers of the Fleet. I cannot say any more of his courage than that he was as brave as Captain Peel, but in quite a different way, for I doubt whether Hardy ever felt danger.

Whenever I was in battery during this and the following bombardments, Captain Peel gave me the same charge as that held by Lieutenants, and although I never went near him unless I was sent for, he somehow managed to see or learn anything I was doing well. About 1 p.m. on the 9th I was taken ill; I had been working since daylight on a cup of coffee, in a thin jacket, and chilled by the incessant rain, shivered continuously. Captain Peel noticing my state, sent me back to camp, and in doing so expressed his satisfaction at my conduct. Later, I learnt he had told Lord Raglan of my mending the embrasure twice under heavy fire, after the sappers had been wounded, which I was not previously aware he had seen.

Before night fell on the 9th, one face of the Redan was in ruins, the guns being silenced. All that night, and throughout the 10th, a steady fire was kept up on all the Russian batteries by mortars. On the 11th I was sent early by Captain

Peel with a note for Commodore Lushington, and by him was ordered to take it on to Lord Raglan. The paper was inscribed with these words: "If the Allies intend to assault, a better opportunity than this will not offer; the fire of the Russian batteries round the Malakoff is completely crushed." When close to Headquarters and galloping fast, my pony put his foot into a hole, and turning right over covered my face and clothes with mud, and I thus appeared before the Commander-in-Chief, who was in the farmyard at Headquarters casting troop horses, apparently belonging to his escort. He astonished his Staff by warmly shaking hands with the very dirty Midshipman, as he offered him breakfast. He then read the note, but merely remarked, "Impossible, I fear."

As I rode into the battery on my return, I met four men carrying away the body of Douglas, my most intimate friend. The top of his head had been knocked off by a round-shot. On his handsome face there was still the pleasant smile which endeared him to all of us. He was singularly unselfish, and by his undaunted courage had attracted the notice of Captain Peel, who had paid him the compliment of asking him to show his indifference to danger. On the evening of the 10th, Douglas observed to me at dinner, "You have lost a good many men to-day, perhaps it will be my turn to-morrow." I answered laughingly, "Yes, and mine next day." After dinner he went over to H.M.S. *London* officers' tent, and returning said, "Our friends are in considerable trouble, for their Mess caterer, Twyford, was killed to-day. I shall now close my accounts, and you shall all pay up to-night." This we did, and in spite of my earnest remonstrance he insisted on giving back some money he had been keeping for me.

During this second bombardment, although the Russians were short of powder, yet their practice was much better than it was in October. One of their shells dropping into the magazine of the 8-gun battery immediately in our front, exploded it, one man being killed and nine wounded; and although the guns in the battery were uninjured, yet the earth from the crater formed by the explosion of the shell, twenty feet in diameter, embedded some of the guns so deeply that they were unworkable until they were cleared next day.

A shell which burst on striking the parapet near me killed

two men and literally buried three others, so that we had to dig them out; they were insensible, but all recovered. Ten days later the 21-gun battery had a fortunate escape, for the Russians dropped a 13-inch mortar shell through the roof into a magazine; it crushed the magazine-man to death, but did not explode.

I forbear to enumerate the many narrow escapes most of us had, but there were two peculiar ones which merit notice. Alongside the magazine which supplied the gun I was working we had some tools for fitting fuses; a man was actually sawing a fuse which was clamped in a vice on a little table, when a shell bursting on the parapet sent fragments all around us; one fragment struck and ignited the fuse, but the man escaped with merely a scorched wrist, burnt by the composition. We were not always so fortunate, for a shell bursting over one of our 68-pounder guns killed or wounded 13 men. I saw a remarkable escape of Lieutenant Graves, Royal Engineers, who was killed when speaking to me at the Redan three months later. On the 10th of April he was standing in an embrasure the faces of which required repair, when a round-shot struck the sole—that is, the ground surface—immediately under his feet. He was considerably shaken and bruised by his fall, but was on duty again in a few days.

It was calculated that during the bombardment the Allies threw 130,000 projectiles into Sevastopol, the Russians answering with about three to our four shots. Their losses, however, were in proportion greater, as will be understood on reference to the map at end of Chapter IX. The Russian projectiles, unless they actually struck the targets, *i.e.* our parapet, guns, or bodies, exploded behind the battery without doing damage. Many of their works were to some extent enfiladed by our guns, and thus a shot or shell missing its object often killed someone farther off. The Malakoff presented to us a target of about 200 yards wide from east to west, but it was more than double that depth—that is, from south to north—and thus few of our shells failed to explode inside the works. Their losses were terrible; and later, during a flag of truce, when one of our officers observed we had suffered heavy losses, a Russian officer replied, "You talk of your losses—why, you don't know what loss is, in comparison with what we are suffering." Sir Edward

Hamley describing the Russian hospital, states that the floor of the operating-room was often half an inch deep in coagulated blood.

By the 18th of April the Allies had beaten down the fire of the Russian batteries, and General Todleben daily expected that the French would carry the Bastion du Mat.[1]

The ammunition supply of the Naval guns was much better arranged than in October, and it was brought in without casualties through the " Covered way "; but as there were as yet no animals for such purposes, our men were employed both night and day in carrying up powder, shot, and shell from Balaklava.

Our losses were heavy. The Bluejackets were somewhat more exposed than were the Artillery, for their guns, mounted on large wheels, "ran up" in half the time that it took us to haul out our guns mounted on trucks, or little wooden wheels. After the April bombardment, and from that time on, however, the casualties in the two Services were reversed, for the Artillery manned nearly all the advanced batteries, and suffered accordingly.

One night early in May, we were replacing some guns which had been disabled during the April bombardment, and I had occasion to rebuke Michael Hardy, whose stoical courage had impressed me so greatly on the 9th of April. A party of about 60 men was in charge of a Lieutenant who had recently joined the Brigade. He was not a good officer, and had an unpleasant, querulous manner, which accounted for the trouble. Our 32-pounder guns were put in position by the guns being placed upside down on the ground, and the carriage fastened on top of it, with its trucks (wheels) in the air. A long rope was fastened to the carriage, and a turn of it taken round a handspike, which was placed in the bore of the gun; 50 men were then put on the rope, and with a sharp pull they turned the gun over into its proper position. Unless the men holding on the rope were kept in an absolutely straight line, which was difficult at night and on broken ground, the gun instead of "coming up" properly would fall on its side, and this happened several times, mainly through the fault of the officer. The Russians heard the noise, and sent several shells close over our

[1] We learned later they were awaiting the arrival of the Emperor, who was then expected.

heads. While the men were laying hold of the rope for the fifth or sixth time, the Lieutenant irritated them by some unpleasant observation, and a voice from the end of the rope was heard to say, "Will nobody send that —— fool away, and put a man there as knows how to do it?" The Lieutenant immediately ran off to report to the Senior officer in the battery the insubordinate state of the men. I waited until he was out of earshot, and then called out, for I had recognised the voice, "Michael Hardy, drop that, or you will be a prisoner." I replaced the men, just as a couple of shells fell close to us, and giving the words, "One, two, three, haul," the gun came up "righted" on its carriage. When the Lieutenant returned with the Senior officer, they found the men standing at attention, and the gun in position.

Young officers who may read this book will probably think I was wrong; officers who have served long, and know the difficulties of getting a conviction by Court Martial in such a case, will probably think mine was the better course.

In the second week of May, Commodore Lushington, at a parade, ordered his Secretary to read out his recommendations for the Victoria Cross Order, which was not, however, formally instituted till 1856. He had submitted seven names, and told us he hoped all would be approved; but in any case he meant to maintain the sequence of names. The first three were: Captain W. Peel; Midshipman —— Daniels; Midshipman E. Wood. I was naturally very pleased, but no one in the Sailors' camp then realised the value of the proposed Order, and the opposition to it amongst the senior officers in the Army raised doubts as to its being instituted. When Commanding officers professed inability to select recipients, the Government ordered the selection should be made by the Rank and File, and in one distinguished battalion a soldier was chosen who was never long under fire. He lived a comparatively safe and easy life, for on account of his honesty and steadiness he was entrusted with the rum keg, which he brought down to the trenches, and having issued to every man his tot, returned to camp.

During the second week in May, the Sardinian Army, of 15,000 men, landed at Balaklava, and occupied the left bank of the Tchernaya, from the aqueduct opposite Tchorgoum village to Tractir Bridge. Two days later, Lieutenant Dalyell of the *Leander*, my usual companion (after the death of Lieutenant Douglas), and I, leaving camp at 4 a.m., rode down the Balaklava Valley, anxious to enjoy a ride in fresh country after being confined for six months to the limited space of the Upland. The French sentries on Tractir Bridge declined, and rightly, to allow us to pass; but we went higher up the river, and the Sardinians mistaking us for Staff officers, from the gold lace on our caps, raised no objection to our going to Tchorgoum, on the opposite side, telling us, however, that it was occupied by a Russian picket. We saw no one except two vedettes on the hill overlooking the village, 150 feet above us. One of them dismounted, and fixing his lance in the ground used it for a rest for his gun, and had several shots at me, at about 300 yards' range, as I was holding Dalyell's pony, while he was foraging in a house. Some of the bullets fell near to me, and three Cossacks hearing the fire came into the road 400 yards up the village. I shouted to my comrade to mount, and as he emerged six more Cossacks joined the three men. They formed up in two ranks facing us, as Dalyell handed me a cat, which I put into my haversack, while he carried an article of domestic crockery greatly prized in camp. We hastily consulted as to what we should do, for if we had turned the Cossacks might have overtaken us before we got back to the aqueduct, so decided on an aggressive movement. I fired one barrel of my revolver at the more troublesome vedette of the two, who was, however, a long way out of pistolshot, and we then cantered at the group in front of us. They probably imagined that we had others behind us, for they turned and fled. As we rode back a company of Sardinians advanced to our assistance.

Cholera broke out in the Army during the second week in May, and the Naval Brigade moved out of the sheltered valley where it had encamped since November, to the top of the hill, near the 3rd Division. We did not escape altogether, but suffered little in comparison with the soldiers. On the evening of the 21st May I counted twenty-one bodies outside the Divisional Hospital tents, sewn up in blankets ready for burial.

During the forenoooon of the 3rd June several men of the Relief for the gun detachments were going into battery from the Woronzow road; there was little fire at the time, and the men, disregarding the order which prescribed that they should enter by the "Covered way," were walking over the open ground. As the last of the party approached the 21-gun battery, there was a shout, "Look out, Whistling Dick!" This induced the men to run, for the appalling size of "Whistling Dick" struck terror into the bravest heart amongst us. It is illogical, no doubt, to fear an enormous shell more than a bullet, for either can send us into the next world, but most of us have a greater fear of the larger destructive object.[1] All the men except John Blewitt, of H.M.S. *Queen*, safely reached the trench, and were crouching in it, waiting for the explosion. Blewitt, as he bent forward to run, was struck immediately at the back of the knees by the mass of iron, 13 inches in diameter, and fell to the ground crushed under its weight, in sight of his horror-stricken messmates. He called out to his chum, Stephen Welch, "Oh, Stephen, Stephen, don't leave me to die!" The fuse was hissing, but Welch jumping up from under cover of the edge of the trench, which must, humanly speaking, have ensured his safety, called out, "Come on, lads; let's try," and running out, he had got his arms round Blewitt, and was trying to roll the shell from off his legs when it exploded, and not a particle of the bodies or of the clothes of the two men could be found. I did not witness Welch's Divine-like act of self-sacrifice, but passing immediately afterwards helped the men, though in vain, to look for his remains. Captain Michell of the *Queen*, out of his own small income, pensioned Welch's mother.

During the night of the 3rd June, the Artillery alongside of us were firing some "carcases," but it became necessary to stop firing, as nearly every round burst at the muzzle, wounding

---

[1] For the sake of civilian readers, I explain. A mortar-shell is fired from a short, squat piece, at an angle of 45°, and having attained its greatest altitude over the spot where it is intended to fall, it descends vertically to the ground, the range being regulated by the charge of powder which throws the shell into the air. The Russians used a wooden fuse to explode the bursting charge; it was roughly made, and protruded a couple of inches outside the shell, and thus when the shell, having attained its greatest height, commenced to descend, the projecting fuse end, caught by the wind with each revolution, produced a peculiar sound, which gave rise to its name. If a mortar-shell does not explode until it reaches the ground, as is intended, the whole force of concussion is upwards, owing to the resistance of the surface of the earth, and thus men may be close to the shell and yet incur little danger from its lateral spread if they are lying at a lower level, when the only danger is from falling fragments.

some soldiers, and frightening more. I looked at some of these missiles next morning, and found that they had been made at the end of the previous century.

On the 6th June I accompanied Captain Peel round the Sailors' Battery on the Right Attack, to ensure everyone being ready for what we hoped might be the last bombardment. At 2 p.m. we fired our first gun at the Malakoff, and immediately afterwards, from the Inkerman ridge overlooking the harbour, round to Kamiesh Bay, on a frontage of five miles, shells were thrown from 550 guns with a force which shook the ground. The Russians had still about double that number of pieces in position, but they were slow in answering our fire, which we continued till dusk. Then the bombardment was taken up by mortars, which lit up the Russian works throughout the night, so constantly were shells bursting amongst our enemy. I left the trenches at 10.30 p.m., but went back again at 1 a.m. with fresh gun detachments; for my duties as Aide-de-Camp never interfered with my regular employment with the *Queen's* men, unless when actually required by Captain Peel. At daylight we re-opened horizontal fire, and early in the forenoon had silenced the Mamelon and Malakoff batteries. Nevertheless, although we slowed down our fire, we kept the guns in action to prevent any repairs being undertaken; and at five o'clock Captain Peel gave me charge of two 8-inch 65 cwt. guns, with instructions that I was to fire during the assault as long as possible, without endangering our Allies.

At six o'clock, while we were anxiously waiting the signal for attack, the setting sun had cast a broad red light over the sky, and a soft mist rising from the ground obscured now and then from our vision the troops assembling for the assault, about a mile on our right front. I have described at length the taking of the Mamelon in *The Crimea in 1854–'94*, and I now confine my story to the help the two guns I superintended were able to afford our Allies. The remainder of the guns' crews in the 21-gun battery had orders to cease firing as soon as the French started, but I was allowed greater latitude from my having been over the ground on which the Russians and French were about to fight. Soon after six o'clock a group of rockets sent up from the Victoria ridge gave the signal. At that moment there was only one Russian battalion in the Mamelon, nine being held some way back under cover. Admiral Nakimoff was visiting the Mamelon at the time, and having left his horse at the gorge,[1] was walking round the battery, when the almost total cessation of fire from our batteries, followed by the shouts of the French, made him look round.

As the signal went up, 25 men jumped out abreast of the trench, and ran up the slope of the hill towards the Mamelon, from which came but one cannon-shot. Some Russian sharpshooters were lying in a trench half-way up, and firing, killed three or four men, and then ran, they and the leading Frenchman crossing the ditch of the Mamelon simultaneously.

A Frenchman mounting the parapet waved a Tricolour, and in four minutes the Russians were driven from their work. My two 8-inch guns were ready, with fuses accurately set, and we sent several shells into the retreating Russians before I ceased firing, for fear of hitting the French following in pursuit. The leading group of Zouaves was led by one man, who, 60 yards in front of his comrades, chased the Russians as they ran. I kept my field-glass on that Zouave until he crossed the abatis of the Mamelon, where he fired his rifle and disappeared into the ditch. When his comrades fell back, he did not accompany them.

While this was occurring two columns of Russians assembled on the east of the Malakoff, on the northern slope of the ridge which connects the Mamelon and the Malakoff. I had looked carefully over this ground during the Truce in March, and knowing the lie of it, could when standing on the parapet locate the Russians, seeing as low down as their waist-belts. I was thus enabled to pour on them a destructive fire from the 8-inch guns, the shells of which, bursting just short enough for effect, literally cut lanes through the masses; but their comrades closed up as fast, and in a few mintues the Russian columns advanced, and entering the Mamelon pushed the French out. The man with the Tricolour was struck down, and replaced four times by others, and then the flag went up and down, in rapid succession. Eventually the Russians came down like a rolling wave from

[1] Opening at the rear of the work.

the Mamelon, and penetrated the trenches of our Allies. Just as night closed in, however, the work was retaken by the French as bravely as the Russians had recaptured it.

When Lord Raglan saw the French assault he gave the order for our troops to advance on the Quarries, which were easily taken; but to hold them and reverse the work was a task involving much labour and loss of life. The enemy's works looked right down into the entrenchments, and the Russians made repeated attacks on the working parties who were striving to obtain cover before day broke, but our men held on. The French took 93 guns, and had 5500 casualties; the British, including 47 officers, had 700 casualties; while the Russians lost nearly 5000 in killed, wounded, and prisoners.

Next morning I went to battery at 4 a.m., as it was intended to continue the bombardment. About eight o'clock, missing Captain Peel, I traced him as going towards the Mamelon, where I met him as he was coming out. He ordered me back, but eventually said I might go and look for a few minutes. Men spoke in whispers: it was not a place to linger in; for in the short time I was there, say five minutes, I saw a dozen Frenchmen killed and wounded. Inside, dead men were lying heaped in every attitude imaginable, some of the bodies being literally cut into two parts, while numbers were crushed under overturned cannon. That afternoon there was a truce for collecting the dead and wounded, and again going down, I looked carefully over the work, which was a marvel of labour in constructing cover from fire, enormous baulks of timber being used to support masses of earth.

During the truce Captain Peel and I strolled up to the Russian sentries, about 200 yards outside the Malakoff. We recognised a Circassian chief to whom I had spoken on the 23rd of March, and we exchanged felicitations on our being alive. Captain Peel's shirt collars excited the envy of the Russian officers, who asked how we managed it, and he replied, " We brought our laundry-women with us."

Two days later, when Captain Peel, Lieutenant Dalyell, and I were discussing the chances of the impending assault, Peel asked, " If you had to lose a limb, which one could you best spare?" I replied without hesitation, " Left arm." Dalyell agreed with me, but our Chief argued that arms are more useful for sailors than legs; eventually, however, on my suggesting that a one-legged man would probably become very stout, he came round to our view. It is remarkable that a week later we were employed in the Assault, and all three of us were wounded in the left arm.

CHAPTER VIII

1855—ASSAULT OF THE REDAN

Long months of danger blunt sensibility—Preparations—Description of the work to be attacked—The Naval ladder party is destroyed.

THROUGHOUT the week of the 10th–17th of June, in common with many of my comrades in the Naval Brigade, I suffered from low fever and severe intestinal complaints, and although I managed to evade our doctor, I was much reduced in strength, nor did I shake off the fever until I had been some time on board ship, where I was sent after being severely wounded. I was at battery again at 2.30 a.m. on the 13th June, and we re-opened fire on the Malakoff as soon as we could see. The Russians in it, however, had now not only lost the support of their guns in the Mamelon, but were being battered by the French from it, and they could only hold the Malakoff under heavy loss. Unskilled Infantry were employed to replace the trained Seamen Gunners, most of whom had been killed. The Russian batteries were crippled also by having to keep some gunners in the sea-front forts, for our steamers stood in, and bombarded them. Our gallant foe, however, managed to fire some 19,000 projectiles in twenty-four hours of the 13th–14th.

On the 16th I was lying in blankets, feeling very ill, when my friends of H.M.S. *Leander* came to see me. I was groaning with pain in my bones, but they insisted that a ride and a bathe would be more likely to do me good than medicine, and somewhat unwillingly I accompanied them to the cliffs under the Monastery of St. George, where the deep water enabled us to take headers from a rock. Strange as it may appear, I did feel rather better afterwards.

During the forenoon of the 17th, General Pélissier arranged with Lord Raglan to re-open fire on the 18th, and to assault two hours later. Late in the evening, Pélissier sent to say he had changed his mind, and wished to assault at dawn. Lord Raglan did not get the message until very late in the evening, for he was riding round the camps, and thought it was better to assent rather than to create ill-feeling by refusing, and so our troops parading at midnight got into their assigned positions before dawn on the 18th.

On the 17th I was asleep in battery, suffering from fever, and towards the middle of the day awaking, I missed Captain Peel, and found he had gone back to camp; there I again missed him, and so returned to the battery. I was cantering my pony up the "Covered way," and had got within 50 yards of the Lancaster gun, when the pony swerved to the right out of the trench, and stood still, trembling. There were many shells bursting near the battery, but none very near to the pony, which was generally steady under fire, so I applied both spurs; but planting his fore feet on to the ground, he refused to move, and just as I was shortening my reins to urge him on, I heard the noise of something falling through the air, and in less time than it takes to describe a large piece of mortar-shell fell in the trench close to the pony's forehand. He evidently had heard it when he swerved.

When I saw my Chief in camp that evening, I found with him one of our senior officers, and from what I heard when entering his tent, gathered that he was arranging for an assault. He turned to me and said, "Oh, Wood, you are not well to-day." I replied, "Not well, sir, but not very ill." "You had better go to bed; I shall not want you to-morrow morning." "I suppose, sir, that we are going to assault?" "Yes, and as you are not well enough to go up with us, you will please stop in camp." "Are you going to take your other Aide-de-Camp, sir?" "Yes; I promised him a long time ago."

I left the tent no doubt showing the disappointment I felt, so Captain Peel called me back and said, "Well, well, you may go on with me as far as the battery, but no farther." To which I immediately replied, "Is the other Aide-de-Camp to go on with you?" And he said, "Yes, I intend to take him to the Redan."

That evening in our camp I had to submit to a good deal of chaff, for it was known immediately that Captain Peel did not intend to take me out with him. On entering one of the Messes of which I was an honorary member, the conversation turned on the impending Assault, and one of the officers laughed at me, but in a friendly way, for having been forbidden to go beyond the battery. I said, " Barring accidents, I'll bet you I go as far as my Chief." Another officer observed, " I'll lay five sovereigns to one, young Wood is killed to-morrow." Dalyell replied, " Done; but bet's off if I am killed."

My friend was more irritated by the remark than I was; but the man had however, no intention of being unkind, for nine months' constant warfare with the daily losses in the trenches had no doubt blunted our senses. The question of Life and Death was discussed at meals with the utmost freedom, and there were indeed some grounds for supposing that the immunity I had hitherto enjoyed could not continue. Fifty Naval officers landed on the 2nd October, and there were only two of us present who had been on duty throughout the winter. Some of our comrades had been killed, more wounded, and the remainder invalided home, or sent to England for various reasons, the more common being that of their promotion.

At ten o'clock that night, having instructed a Bluejacket standing sentry near my tent to rouse me when the Ladder parties paraded, I fell asleep. The sentry, however, did not awake me, having been cautioned personally by Captain Peel that I was not to be aroused. The men " falling in " awoke me at midnight however, and my brother Aide-de-Camp coming to see if I was awake, we agreed that if, as was probable, our Chief was killed in the assault, one of us should stand by him, or bring in his body.

I had been taking heavy and repeated doses of laudanum for three days, and when Daniels left me, feeling thoroughly worn out, I turned over and slept again, until Michael Hardy came into the tent and shook me. I told him to go away, as I was too ill to move, to which he replied, " Shure, you'll never forgive yourself if you miss this morning's fun;" and against my will he proceeded to dress me. It did not take long, for my attire consisted of cap, jacket, trousers, and low shoes. Hardy having propped me up against the tent-pole, brought my pony, on which he put me, being obliged however, to hold me in the saddle, for I was too weak to grip with my legs. We hurried after the men for two miles down to the trenches as fast as darkness permitted, and soon after 1 a.m. reached the 21-gun battery, where I tied the pony up to a Lancaster gun.

When I reported myself to Captain Peel, he was seeing the men told off into parties, six men to each ladder, and a Petty officer to every two ladders. I asked if he had thought to bring down a Union Jack, that we might have it up in the Redan before the Regimental Colours, which, as I found later, were not taken out. He regretted that he had not thought of it, but agreed that it was then too late to obtain the flag. Somewhat later he sent me with a message to the other end of the battery, and having delivered it I was obliged to sit down for a quarter of an hour to rest, for my legs appeared to be incapable of carrying my body.

The battery was a scene of apparently inextricable confusion. The night was still dark; excited Commanding officers were looking for the Engineers who were to guide the assaulting columns, and the number of men passing into the battery, meeting and crossing each other, together with the attempts to enforce silence, which were not altogether successful, made me fear the parties would never get into their assigned positions before daylight.

When, after resting, I returned to the right of the battery where I had left Peel, the Ladder parties had moved off to pick up their loads, placed by the Engineers in a hollow to the north of the 3rd parallel. I went a short distance towards the place, and then realising that the parties must come back again towards the Quarries, waited; presently coming on my Chief, who was having the sections renumbered, to ensure every man being in his proper place on either side of the ladders. When this was done, we lay down under the breastwork, about three feet high, waiting for the signal, which was to be a flag hoisted in the 8-gun battery. While we were lying there, Captain Peel sent me on five different errands, none being of any importance.[1] On the last occasion, just at the false dawn, disregarding many bullets from the Redan, I walked straight across the open towards the Rear, instead of going round by the zigzags. Captain Peel then called me back, giving up the attempt to get rid of me.

The Russians foresaw that the impending Assault must be delivered soon, and at two o'clock that morning their bugles sounded the "Assembly," the troops getting into position about the time the Allies were moving into the trenches. General Mayran, who fell in leading his Division with great courage, mistaking the blazing fuse of an ordinary mortar-shell for the signal rocket, launched the Attack before dawn broke.

Pélissier had intended that the advance of all three of the assaulting columns should be simultaneous, but owing to some mistake in Orders, the Divisions were late in getting into the positions of "concentration," and eventually the French, after suffering great losses for about forty minutes, retired. On the extreme left of the British Attack, General Eyre pushed into some houses at the foot of the enemy's main line of works, and held them till sunset, but lost in casualties 560, including 93 officers, out of a total strength of 2000.

The Redan, as its name technically implies, was formed of two faces, each of which was 70 yards in length, meeting in a salient, the lines of parapet being continued to works on either flank. It stood on a hill 30 feet lower than the 21-gun battery, but as the ground fell between them, held a commanding position—indeed, looking down into the Quarries, some half-way between it and our 21-gun battery. The parapet at the salient itself was 17 feet high, and on the left face, where I approached it, stood 15 feet above the surface of the ground. The ditch was 11 feet deep, and varied in width from 20 at the salient to 15 feet at the faces. As the work was open in the rear, we could not have held it if we had got in, as long as the enemy was still in the Bastion du Mat and Malakoff. The glacis of the Redan was the natural surface of the ground, which met in a ridge on the line of the capital:[2] part of this ridge

---

[1] He was anxious that I should be saved from the fire we were about to encounter. This I only knew afterwards, from a letter written to his brother the following day, and at the time I was greatly irritated.

[2] An imaginary straight line, bisecting the salient angle.

ASSAULT OF THE REDAN

was seen in some degree from the adjoining flanks, though they were on a lower level than the salient, and the ridge itself was exposed to fire from both flanks. The slope up which the Stormers passed was covered by long rank grass, seamed by disused gravel-pits and holes made by explosions of mortar-shells, by innumerable rifle trenches, and craters formed by small portable mines.

Each column was composed as follows :—10 Sappers, 100 Skirmishers, 120 men carrying ladders, 60 being Blue-jackets, and 50 men carrying bags of hay or wool. Storming party:—400 bayonets; Reserve 800; working party 400.

The arrangements for the Assault contemplated that 800 men, covered by the fire of about 200 skirmishers, were to advance a distance of 400 to 500 yards over open ground, accompanied by men carrying ladders 18 feet in length. The Orders issued after dark detailed the 34th Regiment as Storming party, and detachments were ordered to form the Supports, which were lying down before daylight immediately outside the 8-gun battery, about 300 yards in the rear of the Ladder party. All had orders to move out when the flag was hoisted in the 8-gun battery, where Lord Raglan stood.

In my *Crimea 1854–'94*, I gave a full account of the operations on the 18th June, showing the arrangements for the Assault were faulty; here I limit myself to stating what happened to the column which I accompanied. The sad story of the failure, although not perhaps interesting to civilian readers, can be studied with advantage by soldiers who may have to conduct a similar operation.

When the French went out from their trenches, 7 officers, 60 Petty officers, and Bluejackets, of the Right Naval Brigade Ladder party, were all crouching close together, as much under cover as possible, behind a bank two feet high. I was lying next to Mr. Parsons, a Mate, when suddenly he knocked against me violently, and as I thought in rough play. I was asking him to leave off skylarking, when I noticed he was insensible; he had been thrown over by a round-shot, which had killed another man and covered me with dust.

Next to Captain Peel's detachment of 60 men was a party of soldiers of similar strength, and 50 men carrying wool bags. These were either volunteers or picked men of the Rifle Brigade, and in the words of their gallant leader, Captain (afterwards Sir William) Blackett, "among the best in the battalion." While we were waiting for the signal, a mortar-shell fell amidst the storming party, and blew a soldier and his accoutrements into the air. When taking my eyes off the body as it fell, I saw the signal flag as it was being run up, before it was "Broken,"[1] and shouting "Flag's up," jumped on the little bank which had sheltered us, thus inducing a shower of grape and musketry, which knocked down several men.

The Russians now manned their parapets, and thence poured on us a succession of steadily aimed volleys. Captain Wolseley,[2] who was standing near Lord Raglan,[3] said when he saw the masses of Russians facing our little body of men, "There is no hope for them."

It is difficult to describe adequately the intensity of the fire. Various kinds of projectiles cut up the ground all around us, but not continuously in their fullest force, for while there was no cessation of the shower of missiles, which pattered on the ground like tropical rain when the monsoon breaks, at times there were death-dealing gusts of increased density, which swept down the hill, felling our men as a reaping-machine levels standing crops.

Captain Peel, standing on the parapet waving his sword in the dim light, cheered on our men, shouting, "Come on, sailors; don't let the soldiers beat you." At this appeal the whole of the ladder party, some of whom had taken cover at the first outburst of the Russian fire, ran forward at a steady double, simultaneously with the skirmishers and wool-bag carriers. The skirmishers had started 50 yards in front of us, and went straight up to the abatis, where I was speaking to one of the leaders when he was mortally wounded. Although Daniels and I had previously determined to remain with Captain Peel, from the moment we started I lost sight of both my friends.

When I was riding down to the battery, I felt so weak as

---

[1] *i.e.* unfurled, by a jerk of the other lanyard.

[2] Field Marshal Lord Wolseley, K.P., G.C.B., etc. etc.

[3] Lord Raglan, who witnessed the storming of Ciudad Rodrigo and Badajos, forty years earlier, described in Napier's *History of the Peninsular War*, wrote: "I never before witnessed such a continued and heavy fire of grape and musketry," and in a private letter observed, "I never had a conception before of such a shower of grape."

to be incapable of fighting hand to hand even a boy of my own size, for I had been living on tinned milk and rice for over a week, and I instinctively realised the value of Michael Hardy, who was holding me on my pony, as a fighting man. Thinking I would secure at all events the support of one strong arm, I said, "Hardy, when we go out I shall stick to the Captain, and you must stick to me." Hardy replied, somewhat evasively, "Yes, I will stick to him if he goes well to the front;" and this indomitable Irishman carried out his resolve, and permitted no one to surpass him in the Assault.

Now invigorated by excitement, I ran forward in front of the ladder parties. Before we had gone 100 yards, several sailors were struck down, and I was hit by a bullet while cheering on the Bluejackets and waving my sword, which was knocked five yards away from me. My arm was paralysed by the jar, and I thought it was off, as I instinctively dropped on one knee. On looking down, I saw it was only a flesh wound of the hand, and jumped up hastily, fearing that anyone passing might think I was skulking. Picking up my sword, I found it was twisted like a corkscrew, so threw it down, and with it the scabbard, which had got between my legs. I had no pistol, and thus was without any weapon, but that did not occur to my mind as I ran on to overtake the leading ladder. Before I had rejoined it, my comrades had suffered considerably; the senior Lieutenant had been slightly wounded, and Dalyell had lost his left arm, shattered by grape-shot.

Captain Peel was hit, when half-way up the glacis, by a bullet which passed through his left arm. He became faint, and was accompanied back by Mr. Daniels, who was the only unwounded officer out of the seven who went out with the Right ladder party. He escaped injury, but his pistol-case was shot through in two places, and his clothes were cut by several bullets. Thus, within about 250 yards, or about half the distance to be passed over, I was the only Naval officer remaining effective. It was possible that I unconsciously brought up my left shoulder to avoid the fire from the Redan; but anyhow, having no weight to carry, I again outstripped the leading ladder men, and then retraced my steps for 100 yards, although unwillingly, for I was intensely anxious to reach the Redan, although with no clear idea what to do when I got there.

We started with ten ladders, but there were only four being carried forward when I rejoined my party; and I could see none of those entrusted to the soldiers,[1] although there were some few men still struggling forward with wool bags.

If any of my younger comrades in either Service have to undertake a similar task, I recommend them to put an officer with every ladder.

With the four ladders carried by sailors the Petty officers had replaced as carriers, men who had been killed. We instinctively inclined to our right hand to avoid the storm of missiles from two guns on the (proper) left face of the Redan, but after advancing another 60 yards came under fire of guns placed in the curtain connecting the left of the Redan with the middle ravine near the dockyard, and these caused us to bring up our right shoulders.

In the Siege-work plans made by our Royal Engineers the abatis is shown as standing 100 yards from the counter scarp, or outside edge of the ditch. Doubtless it was so after the 8th September, but on the 18th June it was certainly 20 yards nearer, and in places—for it did not run in a straight line—even closer. When I reached it, 50 yards on the Malakoff side of the Salient, I had with me only two ladders; these were carried by four and three men respectively, and I was in front of the leading ladder. Its carriers were reduced to three, and then the right-hand rear man falling, I took his place. The second ladder now fell to the ground, the men being killed or wounded by a blast of case-shot, and when we were 25 yards from the abatis my ladder carriers were reduced to two. The man in front was only a few years older than myself, an Ordinary seaman, but he had shown no other feeling than the desire to be first up. I had not carried it far when the man alongside of me was killed, and then the Ordinary seaman in front, feeling no doubt he was bearing an

---

[1] As we learned afterwards, all the soldier carriers of the first ladder were shot down by one volley, and the remaining ladders had not been taken far before all three officers with them fell, the Captain dangerously, and the two Subalterns severely wounded. Blackett (later Sir William) remained on the ground until a sergeant lifted him into the shelter of a trench.

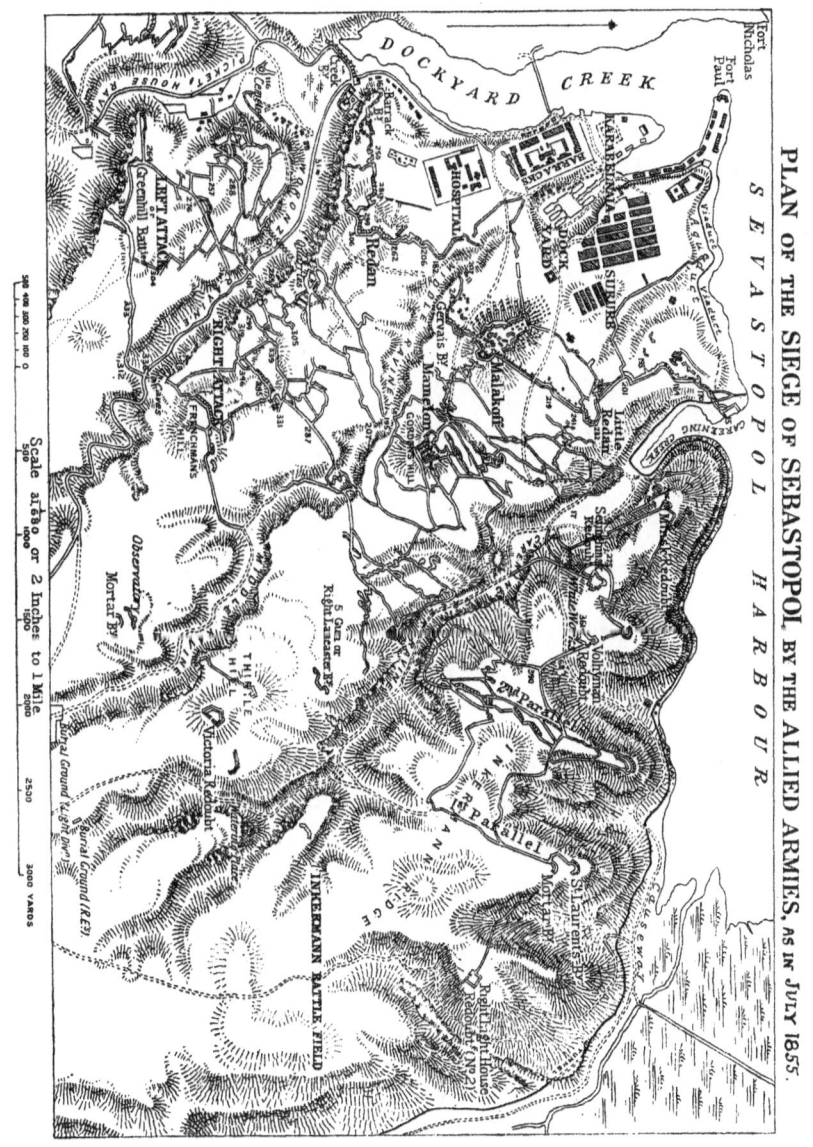

undue share of the weight, not knowing I was under the ladder, turning his head as far as he could, addressed me as his messmate. "Come along, Bill; let's get our beggar up first." Before he recognised me, while his face was still turned backwards, he was killed, and with him tumbled the ladder.

CHAPTER IX

1855—ASSAULT OF THE REDAN—*continued*

The abatis and its defenders—Hit for the second time, I collapse, but am revived by a well-drilled Corporal—Lord Raglan's remarkable kindness—I regain my pony at Constantinople—I join the Army—An impatient Cornet—Mr. Farquharson, M.F.H.

IN my heart I experienced a sense of relief, from the feeling that my responsibility was over, as even my most gallant Chief, William Peel, would not expect me to carry a ladder 18 feet in length by myself. It was now lying within 30 yards of the abatis, under the slight shelter of which a few scattered soldiers were crouching: some were firing, a great many shouting, while on the parapet 15 feet above us stood Russians four and in places six deep, firing at, and calling on us sarcastically to walk in. I looked round, and at once saw there was no chance of our accepting the invitation. The abatis where I was standing, between 60 and 70 yards from the salient, was a strong fence 4 feet thick, and 5 feet high in places, made up of stout trees, and beams from 6 to 8 inches in diameter, closed with brushwood. There were places where a man could have squeezed through the holes made by our shells, but only one at a time, and even then, assuming that he crossed unscathed the open space intervening between the abatis and the ditch, there was still a more formidable obstacle. From the bottom of the ditch the top of the parapet on which the Russians were standing was 26 feet high.

The Storming party had dwindled down to 100, and I perceived at once that unless heavy reinforcements came up there was no chance of carrying the work. While looking round to count heads, Lieutenant Graves of the Royal Engineers (see p. 73) asked me if I had seen Captain

ASSAULT OF THE REDAN

Peel. I said "No, not since we crossed the parapet," and as he passed on, he was killed. He spoke as calmly as when, repairing the embrasure on the 10th April, a round-shot cut the ground from under his feet. Now an officer detaching a bough from the abatis waved it over his head, and cheerily called on the men to follow him, but while shouting he was pierced by several bullets, and fell lifeless.

I was greatly impressed by the courage of a young Sergeant, who was trying to collect men to accompany him through or over the abatis. After calling in vain on those immediately to follow him, he lost his temper, and shouted, "I'll tell my right-hand man to follow me, and if he fails I'll shoot him." He brought his rifle down to the "Ready," and said, "Private ———, will you follow me?" I was almost touching them, and seeing by the Sergeant's eye that he was in earnest, stood for a few seconds studying the determined look on the man's face. The Private looked deliberately on the hundreds of Russians above us, and then ran his eye right and left of where we were standing, as if estimating the number of his comrades, who certainly did not exceed 100, and with as much determination as the Sergeant said, "No, I won't." The non-commissioned officer threw his rifle to his shoulder with the intention of carrying out his threat, but in doing so, struck by a grape-shot, he fell dead.

I now dropped on one knee to talk to an officer sitting under the abatis as to our chances of getting in, when he was hit just above the waist-belt by a bullet. He tossed about in great pain, calling on the Almighty. I was somewhat perturbed, but had seen too many men killed to be seriously affected, until he apostrophised his mother; this allusion distressed me so much that I rose, and walked slowly in the direction of the Malakoff, looking to see if there were any weaker spots in the abatis. I had only gone a few yards, when glancing upwards I saw a section of Russians "following" me with their muskets. Instinctively throwing up my left arm to shield my face, I was walking on, when a gun was fired with case-shot close to me. The missiles came crashing through the abatis, and one weighing $5\frac{1}{2}$ oz. struck my arm just below the funny-bone. This sent me screaming to the ground, and I rolled some yards down the slope of the hill, where I lay insensible.

I do not know how long I was unconscious, but it cannot have been many minutes; for the whole affair did not last more than half an hour. I was aroused by an Irish corporal, who shook my arm, saying, " Matey,[1] if you are going in, you had better go at once, or you'll get bagoneted."[2] I presume it was the pain in my arm which brought me back to consciousness, but I answered the man with an outburst of bad language. He drew himself up erect, and bringing his hand across his body to the rifle said, " I beg your pardon, sir, I did not know you were an officer. Can I help you ? " " Yes, help me up, but by the other hand." He then told me the " Retire " had been sounded some minutes earlier, and that all our people were going back. In spite of the number of men firing at us at less than 100 yards' distance, he helped me up carefully, taking care not to hurt my arm, and then bending down his head, ran as hard as he could towards our trenches. I followed him towards the 8-gun battery, but very slowly; for although I had not previously felt my weakness since the moment we crossed the trenches to assault, I had now become faint, and could walk only slowly, although grape and case shot fell thickly around me.

When I had gone 300 yards, I saw several men running with their heads bent down along a ditch, made direct towards the Redan for about 100 yards beyond the Quarries, during the last few nights. It was only two feet deep, but with the rank grass three feet high on the slope, gave slight shelter from view. I had walked only a few yards in the ditch, however, when the screams of wounded men, who had crawled in for shelter, and were now hurt by the soldiers running over them, caused me to get out and walk away. I had scarcely left the ditch when it was swept by case-shot from three guns in succession, and most of the men who had been running over their comrades fell killed or wounded on top of them. As I approached the trenches in front of our 3rd parallel, from which we had started, the last of the Covering party which had remained out to

---

[1] As I rolled down the slope my wounded arm, probably from instinct, remained uppermost. There was nothing to indicate I was an officer, for I had thrown away my scabbard when my sword was destroyed; my gold-band cap was underneath me, and my blue serge jacket was threadbare and dirty.

[2] Bayoneted.

fire on the Russians, were returning inside the trenches. I made for a place where the slight bank was worn down, in order to avoid the increased exertion of mounting up four feet, when a young soldier passed me on my left side, and doubtless not noticing I was wounded knocked me heavily on the arm, saying, "Move on, please." As he crossed the parapet, I caught the butt of the rifle to pull myself up, and he turned his face, saying, "What are you doing?" A round-shot passing over my right shoulder struck him between the shoulders, and I stepped over the remains of his body so exhausted as to be indifferent to his death and to my preservation, due to his rudeness in jostling me out of my turn at the gap.

On the safe side of this little parapet, there sat a sailor who made me feel ashamed of my own powers of endurance. He had been severly wounded in the right hand, and had lost two of his fingers, and thinking how helpless I had become, I stood still to admire the man's coolness and self-possession. With his left hand he had pulled out of his trousers the tail of his shirt, and holding it in his teeth, had torn off nearly three strips when I approached. With these he was bandaging up his hand in a manner which would have done credit to a class who had gone through "First Aid to the Wounded," and he answered my question as to his wound quite cheerily.

When I reached the foot of the parapet of the 8-gun battery I was unable to walk up it, and fell to the ground at the first attempt. When I did surmount it, I hesitated to step down to the banquette, fearing to jar my arm, and paused so long that a sergeant, probably not wanting to see more fire drawn on to the spot, called out, "Jump, jump, you little devil, or you will get killed." I consigned him to a hot place, and sank down where I was, when two officers seeing my state came out and carried me inside the work.

I was taken to a doctor (an Irishman) whom I had known for some time, and was greeted warmly with the exclamation, "Sit down, my dear boy, an' I'll have your arm off before you know where you are." I steadily but with some difficulty evaded his kind intention, and was eventually put into a stretcher and carried to camp by four Bluejackets. As we left the battery the stretcher-bearers and I had an escape, for a shell burst just in front of us, cutting up the ground between the fore and rear carriers, who, however, did not flinch; but as we passed through the camp of the 4th Division, as they changed arms, the iron hook which kept the stretcher apart unshipped, and I fell heavily to the ground on my wounded arm.

Whilst waiting in the operating-tent for my turn for the table, I was interested by the extraordinary fortitude of a Bluejacket, who discussed the morning's failure without a break in his voice while the doctors were removing two of his fingers at the third joint. When my turn came, I had a heated argument with the surgeons, who wished to amputate the arm above the elbow. The Navy had then an officer dangerously ill from a wound received a few days earlier, in which case amputation had been delayed too long, and all but the senior Doctor wished to take off my arm. To him I appealed to be allowed the chance, and to persuade him I underwent considerable pain. The eight who were for removing the limb declared that it was impossible that any use could be obtained from the arm, the elbow-joint of which had been shattered. To prove that it was not, I doubling my fist raised the arm as high as I could, until the case-shot met the fore and upper arm, on which the senior Medical officer decided that he would at all events try to save the limb.

As soon as I recovered consciousness after the anæsthetic, Captain Peel came to see me,[1] and telling me that he had got half-way, asked me how far the remainder of the party had advanced. Having told him, I inquired anxiously for my friend Michael Hardy, of whom I could learn nothing. At the time of the Truce next day, his body was found in an embrasure of the Redan, the only man as far as I know who crossed the abatis and ditch that day.

There were two Ladder Naval parties, but the Left, from causes beyond their control, went only a few yards, and was then ordered back, suffering but little loss. According to my Journal written at the time, 48 casualties occurred amongst our 60 men, of whom 19 were killed and 29 wounded. All 7 officers of the party, except Mr. Daniels, were hit.

[1] Extract from a letter from Captain W. Peel to Frederick Peel, M.P., 20.6.55: "Would you let Sir Page Wood know his gallant son behaved with extreme intrepidity?"

I slept for some hours, until awakened by Colonel Steele[1] coming into my tent. He brought me a letter from Lord Raglan, placing his carriage at my disposal to carry me down to Kazatch, where H.M.S. *Queen* was lying, whenever I could be moved.

When the last of our Effectives retired the batteries re-opened fire, and within an hour the Russian guns were reduced to silence; this shows clearly the error made in assaulting before we had crushed their batteries. Lord Raglan rode over to General Pélissier, who was on Victoria Hill, with whom he arranged to renew the Attack. Later on, however, Pélissier sent over to say General d'Autemarre, who was in command in the extreme Front, thought the troops were not in a condition to undertake another assault, and so the columns were brought back to camp soon after 7 a.m. Our casualties were 100 officers and 1444 of other Ranks. The French and Russian statistics are recorded together for the 17th and 18th, the former losing 3500 and the Russians 5500.

The initial error was in assaulting before the enemy's guns were silenced. Lord Raglan himself has recorded that owing to smoke he was unable to ascertain the progress of the columns of our Allies, and when it was apparent to him that they were not succeeding he determined to send his troops to the Redan to help them. Although indirectly, it is now certain that we could have helped the French more if we had bombarded, instead of sending Infantry forward, yet it is not at all certain that our Allies would have accepted this view. Whenever the assault was to be delivered, however, all soldiers will agree with Todleben's opinion that the number of British troops sent to the Redan was entirely inadequate for the task.

The Commodore had written to the Captain of H.M.S. *Queen* asking him to send a boat for me.[2]

---

[1] Later, General Sir Thomas Steele, K.C.B.
[2] Letter from Sir S. Lushington to Captain Michell, R.N. :—

"CAMP BEFORE SEVASTOPOL,
"18*th June*, 10.30 a.m.

"MY DEAR MICHELL,—You will be sorry to hear your young nephew, Wood, has been wounded by a grape-shot in the arm. The shot struck the bone obliquely, and was cut out when he got into camp. I saw him in the trenches, and he bore it like a hero. He was Peel's A.D.C., and Peel endeavoured to keep the boy from the murderous fire into which they plunged with the scaling ladders, but he would

I went down on the 20th, and though my friend and messmate, Edward Hunter, held my wounded arm up as long as he could, yet he himself being ill with fever, was unable to support it in a drive of eight miles, and the jolting of the carriage caused excruciating pain in the wounded limb, which rested on my ribs. When we reached the beach at Kazatch it was late, the ship's boat had returned, the Midshipman in charge thinking I could not be coming, and it was only after an unpleasant experience with two Greeks and being taken first of all to a French man-of-war, that I got on board H.M.S. *Queen*. I reached my uncle's ship at 11 p.m. There, however, I had every attention and kindness which it was possible for a patient to receive. The Captain gave me one of his cabins, for H.M.S. *Queen* had been fitted as a Flagship in 1852, and the accommodation had never been reduced.

I had a succession of distinguished visitors, mainly I imagine on account of my uncle's popularity, for I was only a Midshipman, and the callers commanded battleships, and included the French Naval Commander-in-Chief, who came on board on the 30th June. My uncle's courteous, polished manners were appreciated by well-bred French Naval officers. I enjoyed much more the conversation of my brother-Midshipmen, who sat with me by turn all day.

My uncle wrote on the 21st a grateful letter in my name to Lord Raglan for his kindness in having lent me his carriage, and received a reply,[1] a copy of which got me a Commission in the Army. Five days later he was taken ill, dying on the 28th June. He was one of the most uncomplaining, loyal servants the British nation ever had; ordered by the Government to carry out a difficult task with inadequate means, he died from care and overwhelming anxiety, a victim to England's unreadiness for war.

take no refusal, and went out with the rest. Wood will be at Kazatch to-day in Lord Raglan's carriage. Will you have a boat ?—Yours, in haste,

"STEPHEN LUSHINGTON,
" *Commanding Naval Brigade.*"

[1] "*June 21st*, 1855. MY DEAR CAPTAIN MICHELL,— I am very glad to have had an opportunity of being even in the smallest degree useful to your nephew, whose distinguished career cannot fail to enlist everybody in his favour. I am rejoiced to hear that he is going on well.—Believe me, very faithfully yours, RAGLAN."

My uncle, though kindness personified, was anxious to send me back at once to the Naval Brigade, not realising that the bone in my arm had been splintered, and showed some impatience when the wound failed to heal. On the 10th July I was sent down to the hospital at Therapia, on the Bosphorus, where I was nursed by two resident ladies, the Misses Baltazzi. I should have been very happy there but that the doctor in charge, every other day, used to put a probe, something like a bodkin, for a inch and a half out of sight in the wound, and when the Irish orderly seeing me wince under this examination, later found I was troublesome, treating me as a child, would say, "Be quiet, or I'll call the doctor to progue you." As the result of further probing, however, on the 19th I was taken down to Stamboul and put on board the *Great Britain* for passage to England. She sprang a leak next day, and I was transferred to H.M.S. *Perseverance*; she was actually under way when she was ordered to anchor, and wait for two officers and two horses. Our language at this repeated delay cannot be here quoted, but I had reason to be thankful, as with the two officers there came a charger and my pony, which neighed with delight at seeing me. I had tied it up to the Lancaster gun in the 21-gun battery at 2 a.m. on the 18th June, and had never seen it again till it was hoisted on board H.M.S. *Perseverance* on the 22nd July. It had been transhipped as often as I had been, so the coincidence of its eventually reaching the vessel in which I went home was remarkable. My uncle, Mr. Western Wood, M.P. for the City, owned some ships chartered by the Government, and one of them was in Balaklava Harbour on the 18th of June. The Captain had been instructed to offer me any assistance I might require, and when he visited the camp the day after I had gone to Kazatch, my comrades told him that he could not please me better than by taking my pony home. He was not going himself for some time, so shipped the pony on another vessel, which also was detained in the Bosphorus, but its Captain managed to get the pony on board the man-of-war—how I never heard.

I got back to my father's house in Essex early in August, and immediately began to worry my mother about returning to the Crimea. Neither of us foresaw the initial expense of entering the Army, and I urged that I could live on £250 per annum, and as I had cost my parents £100 in the Navy, they would only have to find £150 more. There appeared to be no chance of my seeing more service in the Naval Brigade, for there were already questions of its being re-embarked, as had been the wish of the Admiralty for some months. It was known in London the French were not anxious to carry on the war, but that our Government thought a permanent peace could not be obtained until Russia had been further humbled, even after Sevastopol was in our hands. It was generally believed that when the fortress was taken, the British troops would go to Simferopol, and that this was not merely a fancy of my own is shown by the words of a letter written by Captain Sir William Peel from Whitehall Gardens to me the day I re-embarked for the East, *i.e.* 2nd January 1856, in which, after wishing me good luck, he says, " You will have a grand campaign this year."

My parents consented to my joining the Army,[1] and during the last week in August I wrote to the Commander-in-Chief asking for a Commission in any Light Cavalry regiment at the seat of war, forwarding a copy of the letter Lord Raglan had written to my uncle on the 21st June. My letter was posted on a Friday, and I was much disappointed when I did not receive an answer on the following Monday, and for a week made the house unbearable by my impatience. My father on the Friday promised if no answer had been received by the following Monday he would go to town and ask for an interview with Lord Hardinge; but next day, when we got the *Times* at ten o'clock, I found I had been gazetted the previous evening to the 13th Light Dragoons, then in the Crimea. As it may seem strange that the Commander-in-Chief should accept the services of a person who had never been seen by

---

[1] My father wrote to the Admiralty for permission for me to resign my appointment, and received a courteous reply :—

"ADMIRALTY, 7*th September* 1855.

" SIR,—In accepting the resignation of your son, Mr. E. Wood, I am to express their Lordships' regret that so gallant an officer is lost to the Naval Service.

" *To the* Rev. Sir JOHN PAGE WOOD, Bart."

CORNET WOOD, 13TH LIGHT DRAGOONS
1855

any soldier in England, I mention Lord Raglan's Despatch[1] on the Assault had then been received.

After I had been at home three weeks, I suffered pain in my arm. The inner wound, where a case-shot $5\frac{1}{2}$ oz. in weight had been cut out, had healed up; but the outer wound, $2\frac{1}{2}$ inches long, where the shot struck close to the joint, was painful, and I could feel something moving in it.

I have always been a nervous patient under a surgeon, and personally removed eight pieces of bone. My difficulty was to see the wound, as being outside, I could not turn the arm round sufficiently. I had a firm cushion made, on which I rested the arm, opposite a mirror, and then by working with care and patience I got out eight pieces, the first $1\frac{1}{4}$ inches long, in September. They were all edged with points like needles, but it was the first only which seriously hurt me. The last bit I let our Doctor remove, at Scutari, in February 1856, for it was small, and came away easily on his opening an abscess, which had formed over the wound.

In the middle of the month I spent a short but most enjoyable visit with Captain Peel at Sandy. The morning after I arrived a deputation from Potton asked my host to link their village by tramway with the Great Northern Station at Sandy, a distance of about three miles. Having inquired the terms, he sat down and made his calculations, while they waited, and in less than an hour he dismissed them with a favourable answer. He constructed the tramway, which was taken over by the Bedford & Cambridge Railway Company, when that line was made, five years later.

Captain Peel was as good at playing host as he was at fighting, and I left the place with an increased admiration of my late Chief's character. Three months later he came to see me at Dorchester, being anxious that I should study my new profession, and not content myself with sauntering through life in the Army.

---

[1] Extract from the Despatch of Lord Raglan to Lord Panmure :—

"BEFORE SEVASTOPOL, 23rd June 1855.

"MY LORD,—I must not omit to mention the following officers of the Royal Navy who particularly distinguished themselves on the 18th June :—Messrs. Wood (severely wounded) and Daniels, who have been through the whole siege.—I have, etc., RAGLAN."

When I joined the Depot at Dorchester there were but two Duty officers, both recently appointed. There was no Mess, and one of the Cornets, the son of a Riding Master, having no private income, lived entirely in his room. The other, Reynold Clements, a University graduate, and I dined at the King's Arms Hotel, where we were soon joined by Stanley Clarke, now General Sir S. de A. Clarke, G.C.V.O., Aide-de-Camp to the King, who was recovering from recent illness. Before the end of the month more Cornets joined, and a Mess was formed in Barracks. This added materially to my daily expenses, for although I was a water drinker, all wine was shared by dining members. The Riding Master was in command, and being married did not dine at Mess. There was only one senior Lieutenant, who exercised no control, and champagne was drunk daily.

My father could only find ready money sufficient to pay for my chargers, £220; so my mother sent me to Messrs. W. E. Seagrove, the Portsea Naval Outfitters, who having supplied my kit in 1852, were willing to allow credit. They gave excellent value for the money, but had some difficulty in the unaccustomed job of fitting overalls.[1] The fit of the riding trousers was then important for an officer's reputation. That the foot of the trousers should always rest on the spur when the knee was bent, was essential for the enjoyment of a peaceful life in Mess, and the avoiding of sarcastic remarks by the senior officers on parade.

My young comrades, ignorant of the reason, at first made merry at my choice of an outfitter, as they did at my not drinking alcohol or playing cards; but they were gentlemen by birth and manners, and though I saw much practical joking, I did not suffer in any way from it. I had, however, passed my novitiate in the rough school of a gunroom Mess. The only time I ever played cards was one evening when I was reproached for not taking a hand at whist, there being only three other Subalterns present. Eventually I assented, but putting down a five-pound note, said, "Now, when I have lost this, or in any case at eleven o'clock, no one will object to my going to bed." They said, "Why, Sailor, that will last you for a week." Before bedtime I had got rid of it, and was never

---

[1] Riding trousers.

asked to play again in the few months I spent at the Depot. While we were in Ireland in 1857, loo was often played, and generally for high stakes. One of my messmates who had lost heavily gave me a bond for £50, to be forfeited if he played again for a year.

In addition to authorised deductions, for instruction of self and horses, amounting to £11, there were many bad old customs which pressed heavily on those who joined in ignorance of the initial regulated impositions, and others, such as a drink first time on Parade with troops, from £7 to £10, first time on guard 30s. I went into the Riding School on the 19th, and was sent over the bar on the 25th October, nine months' daily practice in the Crimea having settled my seat in the saddle.

Because I desired to be on Service again, and foresaw financial embarrassment, I wrote on the 24th October direct to the Commander-in-Chief, gratefully acknowledging the appointment I had received, stating I had passed my drills, and begging I might be sent to join the Service troops in the Crimea. I did not mention my Equitation efficiency, not I imagine from any desire to deceive, but because I did not feel any difficulty on the point.

I duly received an answer, signed " G. Wetherall, Adjutant-General," which showed such a keen sense of humour as to induce me, forty years later, when I was Adjutant-General, to try to obtain a copy; and search was made, but in vain, at Somerset House, where War Office records are stored, but I can recall it nearly verbatim. Sir George Wetherall, addressing the Officer commanding the Depot, ordered him to instruct Cornet Wood that he should write through his Commanding Officer, and not direct to the Commander-in-Chief. " Lord Hardinge has always understood it takes more than twenty-four days to make a perfect Cavalry officer, which time it appears Mr. Wood has been at the Depot." The letter ended however, in stating that a note had been made of my wishes.

Captain and Brevet-Major Tremayne joined early in November from leave of absence from the Crimea, and soon to our advantage, tightened the reins of discipline. Meeting a young Dragoon at the Barrack gate, who was going out for a walk some days later, the man failed to salute, and when checked, alluding to the Major's plain clothes, said with some assurance, "Oh, I don't know you, sir, in that coat." The Major said, without raising his voice, "Well, go back and stay in Barracks till you know me in all my coats—I have not got many." This at once stopped the practice, which was prevalent, of young soldiers ignoring their officers unless in uniform.

In November I had my first day's hunting, with Mr. Farquharson's hounds. We had not much sport, but I enjoyed the sensations of being on a big, smooth-jumping, 16.2 horse moving over fences without effort. The second day, however, I was a trial to the Master. Hounds had run fifteen minutes fast in a vale near Blandford. My horse followed them like a dog follows its master, and until a check I saw no one, and doubtless overrode the hounds. They "threw up" in a meadow, close to a spinney, and before I could stop, my horse careered through the middle of the pack, knocking three apparently lifeless.

On he rushed, I tugging in vain with my one hand, for my left arm was in a sling, as bone was still exfoliating. Alongside the spinney there ran a chace-way closed at either end by gates. The horse touched neither, but I shot forward on to his neck as he landed over the first, and had only just recovered stirrups and seat as he cleared the second gate. Then out of sight and sound of other horses he stopped, and I rode sorrowfully back. When I rejoined, the Master was on foot, with the Hunt servants examining casualties, and he reproved me in strong language. Major Arthur Tremayne riding up, pointed to my arm, saying, "The boy has been severely wounded in the Crimea." Mr. Farquharson dropped the limp hound he was examining, and coming forward, uncovered with a deep bow, saying, "As many times, sir, as ever you like." It is strange that while my arm escaped injury out hunting, I twice knocked it so severely as to re-open the wound, once by falling on shingle at Maldon, another time by falling downstairs in Barracks.

Mr. Southwell, whose sister I married twelve years later, joined in November. Educated at Stonyhurst and Oscott, he had been well brought up, but was delicate, and although to me he became a pleasant companion, possibly the more so from the dissimilarity of our characters and education, was constitutionally unsuited for the life in a Cavalry Regiment. To his cultivated, refined, artistic temperament the daily work and relaxation were alike uncongenial, and when I left the Regiment he retired, though his father [1] was an enthusiastic Light Dragoon. I took Southwell's part when rough practical jokes were played at his expense, and we became intimate friends.

[1] "Colonel Vivian, who commanded, immediately ordered Major Brotherton to charge with the 14th Dragoons across the bridge, but it was an ill-judged order, and the impossibility of succeeding so manifest that when Brotherton, noted throughout the Army for his daring, galloped forward, only two men and one Subaltern, Lieutenant Southwell, passed the narrow bridge with him, and they were all taken."—Napier's *Peninsular War*, vol. vi. p. 391.

CHAPTER X

1856-7—13TH LIGHT DRAGOONS

The Regiment at Scutari—Typhoid and inflammation of the lungs—Scutari Hospital—Tender and brutal attendants—My mother nurses me—Garrison life in Ireland—The Regimental Doctor—Lord Seaton—Gazetted to 17th Lancers—Join on board ship.

AT the end of the year an order was received for two Cornets to proceed to the Crimea, and I was one of those nominated. When we left the Barracks on the 1st January, we were accompanied to the station by all the soldiers and half the townspeople, for the war fever had not even then died out.

It was blowing freshly when the steamship left on the 3rd with some Infantry recruits, young officers, about 50 lads of the Royal Engineeer Train, and their horses. In my Diary letters, written up daily, there is a description of all my companions, but I cannot trace that there was any Senior officer appointed to command, and if he were appointed he certainly never asserted his authority. The breeze became a gale when we got out into the Channel, and all the men and officers except myself were very sick. No officers came to table for three days, and the horses got no attention beyond what I endeavoured to procure at the hands of some sea-sick recruits. There was an Engineer officer on board, and he sometimes visited the horses, but I do not think he had official charge of them. Before we got to Gibraltar we had thrown overboard fifteen out of fifty horses, and there a Veterinary surgeon came on board and had some of the worst cases disembarked, and to my great relief put a farrier on board. I appreciated his help, for I was never in bed during the seven days at sea till midnight, and three nights not at all, when I was trying to keep the horses alive.

It was very cold on deck, and the sea-sick recruits posted as sentries on the horse deck would always, unless watched, tie up the wind-sails, and go to sleep. I landed my own horses fit for gentle work at Scutari on the 22nd January, but the surviving Royal Engineer Train horses could not have been effective for many months.

The Cavalry officers, when they heard that they were going to Turkey from the Crimea, sent home for hounds, and so a few days after my reaching Scutari I had some hunting, jackals giving better runs than foxes in Turkey. I had on the 17th of February an unusual experience. We were running a jackal when I saw an eagle swoop some distance off; on galloping up to it, I found it had struck and killed a hare, which it held until dismounting I ran up, when it left me in possession. Four days later I was sent to Hospital.[1] I had been ailing for three days, and it was thought desirable to remove me from my brother-Subalterns, for we were crowded as regards accommodation. I became very ill, and had it not been for the Captain of my Troop, Percy Smith, who had brought the Regiment out of action at Balaklava, after showing distinguished courage, I should have added one to the many who rest under the cypress trees in the Scutari cemetery, where the doctors believed I had contracted the fever when going round guards at night. When I had been some little time in Hospital, Captain Smith brought a namesake, Doctor Smith, President of a Pathological Committee, who had been sent out by the Government, to visit me. Doctor Smith asked the young Medical officer who had charge of the case how he was treating me, and on receiving a reply said, "Oh yes, for typhoid; he'll die later from that, but now he is in imminent danger from pneumonia." Heroic measures by the application of leeches and blisters were adopted; indeed, where I had not one or the other, I was covered with mustard poultices.

Captain Smith wrote by every mail to my parents, but before the worst account reached them, the Medical officers telegraphed that while my recovery was very doubtful, I should

---

[1] My uncle, Vice-Chancellor Sir William Page Wood, bought my Lieutenancy on the 1st February.

probably live sufficiently long for my parents to see me. This telegram was received at the same time as a few lines I had scrawled on the 21st February, and on the 9th March my parents left Marseilles in the *Borysthene*, reaching Constantinople on the 19th March. In the meantime I had been at the point of death, acute inflammation of the lungs and typhoid having brought me to the verge of the next world. I heard the Senior officer desire the doctor in charge not to worry me by giving me any more medicine, saying as he left the ward, "The boy must die—let him die in peace." I was attended by Private Stanley, my soldier-servant, and two female nurses, one, Susan Cator, who had been sent out from St. Thomas's Hospital, and another whose name I suppress, for I detested her, and with reason. The bones of both my hips had come through the skin, and this woman, instead of wetting the lint before she changed it, used to tear it off roughly, bringing away flesh and drawing blood. I shuddered every time she approached me, and generally wept when Susan Cator left the ward. She always put in thirty-six hours out of forty-eight, because she knew I disliked her companion. I was relieved, however, of the woman's presence soon after my mother arrived.

My mother came to see me on the 20th March, the Lady Superintendent of the Hospital receiving her as a guest until I left Scutari. My father's life was heavily insured, and as he had to ask permission of the Companies before he passed out of Europe, he could not come to see me until a fortnight later. When my mother arrived I was too ill to recognise her, or rather to realise we were in Asia; but when she came again next morning—for I generally had lucid intervals from delirium every forenoon—I expressed my joy at seeing her, but could not believe she had been to see me the previous day.

When my mother had been three days in the hospital, she opened the ward door quietly while the brutal nurse was with me, and saw her, clenching her fist, strike me in the face. My head had been shaved for the fever, and I used to rub it continually while delirious, singing the refrain of a negro melody, which was then on every barrel organ, concerning "An old nigger, whose name was Uncle Ned." When I came to the line, " He had no wool on the top of his head," I rubbed my head until it bled. The nurse had been rebuked for allowing me to do this, and it was when I, all unconscious, continued to rub my head, that she struck me. It did not matter to me, for I felt nothing, although I knew previously that she had held my arm to prevent my doing it. My mother flew at her, and I never saw her again.

After my mother's arrival my state improved, but, as often happens in such cases, I had more than one relapse, and I asked whether I might be taken to the Naval hospital at Therapia; but, not unnaturally, the Medical authorities declined to receive me. In the second week in April it appeared to the doctors that I was not progressing towards recovery, and standing behind a screen they discussed with my mother the best course to be adopted. They pointed out that my state was so precarious that they did not care to accept the responsibility of moving me, although they believed that my recovery, if I remained in hospital, was impossible. My mother said, "Better give him the chance of going to England," and the Senior doctor replied, "We are afraid he will die between this room and the beach." When they had left the ward—for this conversation took place in the doorway—my mother came to my bedside, asking, "Did you hear? What is your decision?" I replied, "Start to-morrow." And on the 15th April we went on board the *Great Western*, arriving four days later at Malta.

We had intended to stop there a week or so, to rest me, but the fine grit off the houses restarted hemorrhage in my lungs, and so we left, travelling by short stages, and reaching Folkestone on the 1st May. It is curious that my feet were so enormous from dropsy, although I had no flesh on my bones, that there was not a pair of shoes or slippers in Paris into which my feet would go, so when we embarked at Boulogne I had to walk down the pier in my stockings.

I went to Fontainebleau the following August, and lived in a French family for two months to learn the language. I lodged over a grocer's shop opposite the Barracks, occupying apartments adjoining those of a Squadron commander of a Cavalry regiment. He was a man of some years' service, and realised that as I could not talk French, and he could not talk English, I should appreciate being left alone; but his brother-officers were not satisfied until they had entertained me. Though I could not converse with my kind would-be hosts, I could make myself understood in French, which is easier than carrying on conversation.

We had some amusing games of hide-and-seek several mornings in succession. When I was leaving my tutor's house, the officers tried to overtake me, but I evaded them; eventually, however, six of them turned out, and seeing two in front, I retreated, but there were two behind me. At the first cross street there were two more coming up both streets, and so I then gave in, and went to their entertainment. My fellow-lodger put his charger at my disposition every day when he did not require it for parade, and there was a general desire to be courteous to the young Englishman.

In spite of the remonstrances of my Troop Captain, Percy Smith, who deprecated my joining until my health was thoroughly established, I reported for duty at Cahir in Ireland on the last day of the year, being most warmly received by my brother-officers, who insisted on my hunting next day with the Regimental pack. Captain Jervis mounted me on his Crimea baggage-horse, and I was equipped with spurs, whip, and boots, contributed by different Subalterns. We had excellent sport, the baggage-horse developing brilliant and hitherto unsuspected jumping powers. He had a past history: stolen in the early days of the campaign, he was seen, recognised, claimed, and recovered by his owner from a French cart, late in the siege of Sevastopol.

I enjoyed my life, except for the want of sufficient money, which pressed on me daily. Several of my companions had about £400 or £500 a year, and it was not only that I experienced the difference of having only £250 per annum, but in our ignorance my mother and I had not calculated the numerous initial expenses of a Cavalry regiment, and thus I was always behind the world in my income.

When I rejoined at the end of 1856, I had been suffering ever since I had left Scutari from an in-growing toe-nail. I should have gone into the Hospital at Cahir at once but that three of the Subalterns, who had been for fifteen months at the Riding School, were about to be dismissed, and I did not wish to lose the chance of passing out with them; but on being "dismissed," I went to Hospital and had the nail extracted. Our Assistant Surgeon was one of the most charming of men; he kept the accounts of our Mess, Hounds, and Coach, but could not have enjoyed much practice of surgery in the Army. The Hospital Sergeant, a Light Dragoon, was not well trained, and after I was insensible left the room to look for something, with the result that the handkerchief sprinkled with chloroform dropped from my nose, and I felt the doctor slit the nail down the centre and then extract one half, the pain being sufficient to make me run round the room. Having obtained the bottle of chloroform and pocket-handkerchief, I administered the anæsthetic myself, and felt no more pain.

Soon after I joined at Cahir my brother-officers went to some races at Bansha, Tipperary, and I was left in Barracks as Orderly Officer. Besides the usual duties, I had to superintend the sale of cast troop horses, and the Orderly Officer was in those days forbidden to leave Barracks except on duty. These difficulties, however, only enhanced my desire for sport, and obtaining the Adjutant's permission, and promise to answer for me, I sent word to the kennel huntsman to take the hounds on, and to ask a "looker" to mark down a hare. This he did, and having sold the troop horses, I laid the hounds on, and for ten minutes had a delightful run by myself; Irish hares are stronger than those in England, and I had chanced on a good one. Presently, however, I crossed a high bank, dropping into a grass field, bounded on all sides by high perpendicular banks affording no foothold, while three countrymen were sitting on a gate, which was the only exit. The hounds had streamed out of sight, and after making three attempts to cross the bank I turned back from the threatening attitude of the men with shillalahs on the gate, and tried to jump the bank over which I had descended into the field; there I equally failed, and one of the Pats, with perhaps some feeling for the horse, said, "You may as well come to the gate; no horse ever got out of this field." I went up and asked them to open it, and they said tranquilly, "Half a crown each, or the best hiding you ever had." I paid, but the day cost me more, as the hounds came home in dribblets, for I never caught them again, and I had to silence the kennel huntsman.

In the spring of the year the Regiment was broken up

into small parties, and employed in keeping the peace at elections, occasionally making very long marches. The only serious trouble we ever had, however, was at Tipperary, and there some of my brother-officers had their uniforms spoiled by the unsavoury missiles aimed at the electors they were escorting.

Some of my young comrades will sympathise with my troubles in paying soldiers. The Paymaster brought me over £100 at a time, and before my Captain rejoined I disbursed in small amounts £284, without having even a lock-up desk with me.

Previous to my rejoining the Regiment it had been reported as below the standard of efficiency of Regiments at home, which was, indeed, and is the case with every corps when it has been for some time on service. The General (Infantry) in command of the District announced his intention of inspecting the corps every fortnight, and after I rejoined he came up frequently from Cork. He was, I understand, an indifferent horseman, but be that as it may, he inspected us only on foot parades and in Barrack-room arrangements.

We had three Subalterns who were unusually ignorant of their duty, and who always prepared for the day of inspection by copious notes on the wrist-bands of their shirts, on which they noted down all the information which the General ordinarily demanded, such as the price of button-sticks, braces, men's socks. I heard him ask the officer who had been so long in the Riding School, what the men had for dinner. He looked very puzzled, and replied, " Beer, sir, beer, I suppose." Another Subaltern, old in years, for he had left the Army previous to, and rejoined during the Crimean campaign, shortly afterwards, when examined by the Colonel for the rank of Captain, on being asked the hour of watch-setting, gravely answered, " Seven o'clock, sir." The standard of knowledge was not high, but these two gentlemen knew less, I think, than the others; for they were superseded on parade, others being given command of Troops, or Squadrons, from which they were sent away. I first commanded a Squadron on parade, to my great pride, on the 27th June 1857. The Commanding officer was a good-natured man, but neither constitutionally nor physically fitted for a Light Cavalry officer.

He was heavy in body, weighing 15 stone 8 lbs., as I know from having carried him across the Barrack square for a small bet.

The Major was a charming person, but he neither was, nor did he pretend to be, a soldier, although later in the year he offered the Colonel £13,000 to retire: the offer was not accepted, £14,000 being asked. In the summer, when Lord Cardigan was coming to inspect us, we had three parades in succession, that the Major might practise the words of command for the "Carbine Exercises." He was ordered to do some Field movements before his Lordship on the Curragh of Kildare. Calling the Regiment to attention, he gave the order, "Threes about," and trotted away for more than half a mile, where, by the help of the Sergeant-Major, he "changed Front" twice, and then advanced at a gallop. I looked at Lord Cardigan's face, but observed no expression in his eye as he said, "Good, Major; but you were rather too far off for me to see much."

Brevet-Major Arthur Tremayne was the next Senior, and the guiding star of the Regiment. He had taken a degree at a University, and had kept up his classical attainments, reading Greek and Latin with facility and pleasure. He was comfortably off for a bachelor, and I owe much to his thoughtful kindness. He not only lent me all his books, but bought many which he persuaded himself he wanted, because he thought that it would improve my knowledge of our profession. I occupied all my spare time, when not soldiering or engaged in sports, in reading early in the morning, and late at night, so as to make up for the five years I had been away from school; for while I was on board the *Queen* I spent most of my time aloft at sea, and in the boats when the ship was at anchor. I read a considerable amount of English Military History, and with Tremayne's help went through Virgil. I had done the Twelve Books before I left Marlborough, but on recommencing in 1857 I find I looked out absolutely every word in the first page, for I have still got the interleaved edition I used. Clement helped me in Arithmetic, in which I was deplorably ignorant. These two men and Stanley Clarke, who was often away on leave, being very popular in society, made my spare hours pass pleasantly.

When the Victoria Cross Gazette of the 24th February reached Ireland, my messmates were very sympathetic with my disappointment; they had read Lord Lyons' speech[1] of the 13th February in the previous year, when at Scutari, where I was then lying in Hospital. I had always hoped that this warm praise from the Naval Commander-in-Chief, coupled with the speech[2] of the Commodore in May 1855, would ensure my receiving the Decoration. Under the advice of the Adjutant, who reflected the view of my messmates, I wrote to the Adjutant-General, reporting what the Commodore, Sir Stephen Lushington, had read out on Parade in the Crimea, and learnt from the Equerry of the Commander-in-Chief that the letter had been duly forwarded to the Admiralty. I cannot remember to have received an official reply, but knew at the time that one of the Lords of the Admiralty was strongly in favour of the Navy following, in granting it to men who had left the Service, the procedure of the Army, but the First Lord held the Cross was not only a reward, but an incentive to valour. In spite of the remonstrances of Captain Peel, Sir Stephen Lushington, and later of Lord Lyons, who when he returned from the Mediterranean went to the Admiralty to endeavour to get the decision reversed, it was maintained.

All through the Spring of the year I was troubled by the want of money, and found it difficult to live within my income, not so much because of the ordinary expenses, for my brother-officers had generously declined to allow me to continue to pay for wine except on guest-nights, but on account of the number of small compulsory charges. The Horse Guards was issuing sumptuary Regulations for the reduction of expenditure, as is being done at the present time, and on the 18th July we had our first half-crown dinner; but a new pattern frock-coat and other expenditure was impending, and although officially the Regiments were told the cost of the Stable jacket was to be cut

---

[1] Extract from the speech of Lord Lyons, delivered at the Mansion House on the 13th February 1856: "All behaved well, but I doubt whether there is anything in the annals of Chivalry that surpasses the conduct of Captain Peel's Aides-de-Camp, Messrs. Daniels and Wood, one of whom (Mr. Wood), when wounded, placed a scaling ladder against the Redan."

[2] "I hope all seven recommended will get it, but in any case the names will stand in sequence." (Mr. Wood's name was third.) Eleven Crosses were given in the Naval Brigade.

down, being replaced by a cheaper form, yet eleven Commanding officers protesting, were told in the month of June, in the War Office, that they need not trouble themselves, as the jacket would not be altered.

I made up my mind to leave the Cavalry for the Infantry, or to take service abroad, for choice in the Foreign Legion in Algeria; but before I took any steps in the matter news from India turned my thoughts to the East. We got to Newbridge on the 4th May, being quartered with the 3rd Light Dragoons and a battery of Horse Artillery. My life would have been very pleasant there, but for the long hours spent at the Mess table, the General, a "two-bottle" man, frequently dining with us. My letters often record having sat at table from 7 till 10.40 in his honour, which to a water drinker was trying. I was not the only sufferer, for many of my messmates wanted to smoke, which was rigidly forbidden in the Mess-room, and cigars only were allowed in the anteroom; cigarettes were unknown; the cheapest cigars in the Mess were sixpence, and although I have never smoked I proposed at a Mess meeting that pipes should be allowed after dinner in the anteroom, but no one was bold enough to second it.

The Assistant Adjutant-General, Major and Brevet-Lieutenant Colonel Morris, 17th Lancers, at the Curragh had studied at the Senior Department, Sandhurst, and added greatly to the interest of our Military exercises by the schemes he gave us to work out. We re-fought many actions of Frederick the Great, and some of Wellington's Peninsula battles, which induced reading, and served to weaken, if not to break down the Mess rule of "No shop" at table.

Colonel Morris was, however, ahead of the Generals, and after he had pointed out that the Horse Artillery should have advanced previous to a charge and come into action against the troops to be attacked, we were startled by the Generals' decision, that the Horse Artillery should have *charged* with the Cavalry.

Lord Seaton, the Commander of the 52nd at Waterloo, was often down at the Curragh, and overtaking me on the 5th July, when riding back to Newbridge, he called me to him to discuss the merits of the new carbine which was then being issued to Cavalry. I was unfortunate with him ten days afterwards.

One of my horses had a hard mouth; it mattered little when I was acting as Galloper, as I generally did, but on the 15th of the month I was commanding a troop, and we were ordered to charge up to the Commander-in-Chief and then halt. My Colonel calling me, said he did not like an officer to ride without his sword being drawn when Lord Seaton was present; I was always excused drawing it when on my second charger, for I never could hold him, nor did I on this occasion. My fate brought the troop immediately opposite where his Lordship, surrounded by a numerous Staff, sat, and with my sword pointing over the horse's ears, for I had crossed my hands in my vain efforts to stop him, I careered through the officers, scattering them right and left.

When the bad news came about the outbreak at Mírath, I urged my parents to get me out to India, and suggested a transfer to the 7th Hussars. When the battery of Horse Artillery was sent out from Newbridge Barracks, my impatience became greater, and I wrote on the 7th August to an agent in London to endeavour to negotiate an exchange.

I got three months' leave on private affairs, to join a Military College at Richmond, which had just been started, to prepare officers for the Senior Department, and went to my parents' home in Essex to arrange matters. While I was there worse news was received from India, and my mother lent me money to try to effect an exchange. I had not succeeded, however, when I was recalled, and was back at Newbridge sitting on a Court Martial, on the 14th September, when I received a telegram asking if I wished to go to the 17th Lancers after the augmentation, which was always made when a Regiment was put under orders for India. This would put me under officers who had not joined when I became a Lieutenant, but I answered joyfully that I should be grateful. Early in October the transfer was approved, and that afternoon Tremayne accompanied me to Dublin, and introduced me to the Officer commanding the 17th Lancers.

That evening I crossed the Channel, and after spending four hours with my father and mother, went back to Dublin, and on the morning of the 7th, calling on Colonel Pack, Assistant Quartermaster-General, Embarking officer, asked him if it was necessary for me to embark that day, or if I should be safe for another twenty-four hours. I had not packed any kit, but I was afraid that if I did not get off with the Regiment I should be sent to the Depôt. Colonel Pack was most kind, and giving me the assurance I was safe, reminded me of the morning of the 11th April 1855, two years previously, when he heard Captain Peel send me with the message urging the immediate Assault on Sevastopol.

I spent the afternoon in packing my baggage, and saying good-bye to my comrades, and by dinner-time was nearly ready. I had arranged with the stationmaster to travel in a luggage train, which was due at Cork early next morning, a Sunday; but when my servant at ten o'clock went down for the car, he returned saying that the driver was so hopelessly drunk that he could not arouse him. I went down to the guard, consisting of twelve men, and leaving one sentry in Barracks, took the sergeant and the corporal and all the privates to the station, carrying my baggage, one box being very heavy, a Midshipman's chest in which I had packed saddlery. Tremayne and another brother-officer, who had gone down to see me off, went out with me at nine o'clock to the *Great Britain*, an auxiliary screw steamship, in which I had previously sailed; but the sea was running so high that the captain of the tug refused to go alongside. I got on board however, safely in the evening, as the ship was weighing anchor.

CHAPTER XI

1858—CENTRAL INDIA

Cape Town—Bombay—Sir William Gordon—March to Máu—Hugh Rose and Robert Napier—Tantia Topi—Meer Umjeid Ali—A loyal Sowar —The fate of a spy.

WE made a fair passage of forty-two days to Cape Town, where our spirits fell on hearing Dihlí had fallen, and the confident predictions that the Mutiny would be suppressed before the ships reached Bombay, where we disembarked on the 21st December. I was left on board to hand over the equipment used by the Regiment. The men worked well, and we got the hammocks, blankets, etc., handed in before the last train left for the foot of the Ghaut, under Khandala, which was then the terminus. There I was again detailed to stay behind, to re-sort baggage; but I caught the Regiment up in its next day's march, and with it arrived at Kirki.

The house accommodation of the Station, built for a battery of Horse Artillery and a Cavalry regiment, was insufficient, as there was already two-thirds of a Cavalry regiment in possession. The two Majors, Learmouth and Lieutenant-Colonel Morris, were kind enough to take me into a bungalow which they hired, where I had a bed and bath room for a nominal sum, my brother-Subalterns having for a time to live in tents.

I had been studying Hindustani since we had left the Island of St. Vincent, copying the alphabet[1] twenty-four times the first day, and on landing could speak a few words. Now established at Kirki with no horses, I was able to read for twelve hours daily, employing two Moonshees, or instructors, one in the forenoon, and the other in the afternoon.

[1] Each letter has three forms—initial, medial, final.

Sir Hugh Rose was just leaving Sehore to relieve Ságar, the then only remaining besieged garrison in Central India, and we were all depressed at the peaceful aspect of Kirki, and startled to find that customs of which we had read, but had not believed, were still common. A Senior officer who had been some time in India, and often dined at Mess, excused his not accepting one invitation because his dressing-boy was ill, and he could not dine out without his assistance.

I went back to Bombay on the 7th February to buy a horse, the Government having imported a number which were offered to officers. Eventually I selected a short-backed, well-bred, chestnut Arab, for which I paid £110.[1] This was certainly the cheapest horse I ever possessed, for in the eleven months from May 1858 to April 1859 he carried me, marching, for over 5000 miles. He was aptly named "The Pig," for he would take any food within reach, from milk out of a saucer to raspberry jam. I trained him myself in the "Double ride," and nobody else rode him while he was in my possession. I could have sold him for more money when I left India three years later, but that as a favour to a friend I passed him on at £90.

I had an opportunity at Bombay of meeting my sister, then on her way home with her husband, Colonel J. Chambers, who had had a narrow escape at Sialkot, when the Sepoys rose, and mortally wounded his Brigadier. My brother-in-law's[2] health had given way; he did not return to India, having served long enough for his pension.

During the month of February-March we got sufficient horses to mount two Squadrons, and the Colonel acceded at the end of May to my request to be allowed to join Sir William Gordon's troop. I saw much of him in the following year, and learned to admire him more daily. He was the most finished horseman I have known in the Army, and within three months of his joining as a Cornet from Earlston, Kirkcudbright, he won the Subalterns' Cup on his hunter, which

---

[1] Most of our officers gave much higher prices, the two Majors paying about £200 for a charger.

[2] A noted athlete and swimmer; he had distinguished himself by jumping into the Hooghly River and saving a woman. He was, for many years before his death, Professor of Sanskrit and Oriental languages, at the University of Oxford.

he had ridden in Ayrshire. He taught me more about horses than any other man has done, and how to ride them with a light hand.

We heard in March there was to be a Preliminary Examination in Hindustani, to be held at Poona in April, and officers who satisfied the Local Board would be allowed to go to Bombay to sit for an examination for Interpreter; this made me work with renewed application. I found it was difficult after morning parade, at 5 a.m., to keep awake as the weather became warmer. I always read at a stand-up desk, resting on an office stool, but I found that on a hot afternoon I went to sleep, balancing my body even when no longer awake. I then had the four legs cut down and brought into one, about two feet from the ground, and thus the stool supported my weight only while I kept my balance. My work was thrown back early in March by a severe attack of low fever, with neuralgia in the face, which swelled up to an enormous size.

At the end of March, when the mail came in, I heard that the efforts which Admiral Lord Lyons had been making in my behalf to obtain reconsideration of Sir Stephen Lushington's recommendation for the Victoria Cross were fruitless. Colonel Morris, of whom I had seen a great deal from living in the same house, and from the fact that I read to him for an hour daily, translating as I went, a book by Colonel de Brack on Light Cavalry, noticed that I was depressed, and asked me the reason. After condoling with me, he invited me to come out into the garden, as he had just received a sword, made by Messrs. Wilkinson of Pall Mall, designed on the model of a sword used effectively by Colonel Clarke of the Scots Greys at Waterloo; but Colonel Morris, who was the Champion swordsman in the Army, believing in the advantage of a light weapon, had ordered his sword to be made lighter, which Messrs. Wilkinson did, but declined responsibility, fearing that if struck by another sword it might break. Morris was a very powerful man although short, being 43 inches round the chest, and was known in the Cavalry as the " Pocket Hercules."[1] He struck the trunk of a mimosa tree with the sword three

---

[1] During the Pánjáb campaign a Sikh careering in front of the 16th Lancers challenged the Regiment. Cornet Morris, a Serre-file, galloped out, and after an exciting encounter killed his opponent.

times with as much force as he was capable of exerting, and then having examined it, handed it to me, saying, "You may trust your life to it," and utterly refused to allow me to decline the present.

On the 15th of April I went over to Poona for the Preliminary examination for Interpreter, and although one member of the Board criticised my translation of an article out of the *Dihli Gazette* in a manner which showed that he knew far less than any of the candidates, yet I was satisfied I was insufficiently prepared, realising at once that a Court Martial given to me to translate was beyond me. After two days' holiday I resumed work, and became much interested in the language, in which I was already beginning to make myself understood.

I had a severe sunstroke early in May. I had been on Adjutant's early parade, and had cantered home to tell the Captain of my troop, Sir William Gordon, of an incident which had occurred. I can only remember sitting at the foot of his bed and seeing him suddenly jump up to catch me as I fell to the floor. It was some time before I regained consciousness, finding leeches on my head, and that I had been severely bled. I suppose I must have been really ill, as the fact of the death of my former friend and Chief, Sir William Peel, from whom I had recently heard, was withheld from me until I was convalescent, and our doctor limited my studying Hindustani to eight hours daily. I was not the only sufferer, for some non-commissioned officers died from the heat, which in May was greater than is usually the case at Kirki.

The Field officers and Sir William Gordon, when going away as they occasionally did to the hill station of Mahableshwar, always left me in charge of their horses, and on the 23rd May I was offered mounts for two days' pig-sticking with Sir William Gordon, who had already gone out some twenty miles from Kirki. I was told I might "ride out" the horses as if they were my own. Having sent on ponies, for I had to go thirty miles next morning to the meet, I went to Mess, sitting opposite the Colonel. Dinner was over when an official letter was brought to him, and I noticed his face was much perturbed when at ten o'clock he left the table, so I followed him cautiously up to the orderly-room, and waited until he came out. I asked him if I could do anything for him, and he told me he had just received an order to send a Squadron immediately to Máu, and it was not known in the orderly-room where Sir William Gordon, the Senior officer of the Squadron, had gone. Gordon had told me that he would not leave his address because he had been recalled unnecessarily on a previous occasion. I asked the Colonel if I found Gordon if I might reckon on going, and on his saying "Yes," undertook to produce Sir William before daylight. The Colonel told me to jump on his horse, which was at the orderly-room door, and do my utmost. I knew the name of the house where Gordon was to sleep, and started at a gallop to find him, which I did at 2 a.m. After numberless questions from different Ramusis, or night-watchmen, I compelled one of them to accompany me to the house. Gordon had had a good day's sport, and was sleeping so heavily that I failed at first to convey to him the purport of the Colonel's message. He repeated again and again, "I dinna believe you," and at last seizing him by the legs I pulled him out of bed, when he realised the truth of my good news, and at daylight we were in the Horse Lines at Kirki. We marched on the 25th, "A" Squadron 100 strong, two Companies of Native Infantry, and 50 of the Haidarábád Contingent. We heard the people of Ahmednagar were excited about news of the march southward of Tantia Topi, but we did not know then that our Resident at Indore had telegraphed that the feeling of the Native troops at Máu made the presence of British troops essential.

Our last day at Kirki was fully occupied. My head servant informed me at daylight I should want five more servants for the march, and at noon they appeared. They demanded 50 per cent. higher wages than the current rates, to which I assented; they then asked for three months' pay in advance, which I paid, though somewhat unwillingly; and having got the money, they asked leave till an hour before I had to prepare for Parade. I thought my chances of seeing them again were small, but having no other resource, assented, and at 10 p.m. they were present; most of them remained with me until I left Central India for Calcutta, thirty months later, on my way home on sick furlough. At the Mess table that evening my companions told me they had refused the three months' advance of pay, and ridiculed my over-confidence in the Natives; but many of their servants deserted within the first week of our march.

We started at 1 a.m. on the 25th May, "the oldest inhabitants" predicting our return, as they said no troops could move over the black soil between Kirki and Indore in the wet weather, which was ordinarily due on the 12th June. When I got to the parade at midnight, I saw Lieutenant Nolan, a brother-Subaltern, standing before his horse, for which he had given £150 a month earlier, in an unhappy frame of mind; the horse had fallen close to the lines, and had cut both knees severely, and the Colonel, who was on parade to see us off, told him that he could not go, as he would not spare him a troop horse. I had bought a Persian horse two days previously, and feeling for Nolan's disappointment, told him he could have my second horse, which was perhaps more generous than wise. The horse suited Nolan, and at Ahmednagar Gordon bought me another, Nolan taking over the one I had lent him.

When we were three days out, the rain came down in torrents before it was due in the District. I got fever and swelled face again, and was miserable at the idea that I might be invalided. However, two days' rest put me right, and on the 3rd June I spent fifteen hours in the saddle. So many camels had slipped up, that much of the baggage remained behind, and after I reached the next camping-place I was sent back by Sir William Gordon to collect bullocks for transport. My companion got a sunstroke, and I narrowly escaped one, reaching the camp again with the last of the baggage at sundown. Our difficulties in moving over this roadless country, most of it cotton-growing soil, were great; we picked up three guns at Ahmednagar, but the two companies of Native Infantry dropped behind. I was kept busily employed, for there was nobody who spoke Hindustani except myself, and when we left Asseerghur our Native Commissariat contractor, being detected by the Troop Quartermaster-Sergeant in some petty fraud, deserted, and so up to Máu I had to purchase for the Squadron everything required, and as I was catering also for the Mess I had little time for myself. We did not leave Árangábád until the 19th June, being occasionally stopped for three days in succession by heavy rain, and one of the marches was practically under water for fourteen miles. That morning I saw a curious accident. We had three guns with Native drivers and European gunners; when a few miles out of Árangábád we crossed a chasm fifteen feet deep; the roadway was on a curve, and the Native drivers not being expert, the off rear wheel of a gun was driven against a parapet a foot high, which crumbled away, and the gun tumbled down to the bottom of the chasm with its three drivers and horses. The Lead and the Centre drivers were easily extricated, but the Wheel driver was at the bottom, and when the horses were eventually pulled away all the colouring matter was pressed out of his skin, for he was yellow; Natives' bones, however, are soft, and he recovered. One of the horses in his struggles seized the coronet of a horse close to him, and held on with such tenacity that we were obliged to strike the animal hard over the head with a rammer-head, to induce him to relax his hold.

I, being the only Interpreter, had many opportunities when riding on to obtain guides from village to village of talking with the Half troop of the Haidarábád Contingent, as I did indeed to every man with whom I was alone, from Kirki up to Máu. I was anxious to know why the Sepoy Army had risen against us, but never succeeded in obtaining an answer, although none of those expressed any disapproval of the Mutiny.

The difficulties of the march had not been exaggerated by the old hands at Kirki, when they predicted our return. It generally rained, but on other days we were scorched by the burning sun, and on one occasion the recorded heat in a Medical officer's double-roofed tent was 115° Fahrenheit. When therefore it seemed that Sir Hugh Rose (who was advancing from Sehore to relieve Ságar, the then last remaining besieged garrison) had stamped out the rebellion in Central India, orders were received for the Squadron to remain at Jalna till after the Monsoon. While furniture was being put into bungalows for our accommodation, the news of the outbreak at Gwáliár was received, and with it an order for the Squadron to march rapidly to Máu.

That Station, which had been sacked by Mutineers in 1857, standing on an elevated plateau, is comparatively cool even in the summer season, but the day before we ascended the Ghaut and the night we camped at its foot were really hot; metal cups, after lying in the sun, burnt the hand on being touched, the backs came off our hair-brushes, and hair-combs assumed serpentine forms. Between Poona and Máu, where we arrived on the 20th July, we forded thirty-five rivers and streams, and swam our horses across two large rivers. The Narbadá was the easiest of the rivers to cross, because boats and trained boatmen were ready, as were Native swimmers for the horses. The men of the Haidarábád Contingent thought it beneath their dignity to work, and after crossing one of the rivers wished to wait until coolies were collected to carry their saddles and equipment from the edge of the water to the top of the bank; when, however, they saw me pull off my coat and carry my own saddle, they followed my example.

When I arrived at Máu I was sent for by, and made the acquaintance of Major-General Michel[1] under the following circumstances:—After we left Asseerghur, making a comparatively short march, we arrived early at a village, and found everything we required except forage. The chief man of the village declared that he had sent for grass, and vowed that there was no dry forage in the neighbourhood; but something in his manner induced me to doubt the accuracy of his statement. At four o'clock, on again sending for him, he made men pull the thatch off some of the poorest houses in the village to give it to the horses. Meanwhile I took two Lancers with me, and found in the enclosure of his own house enough forage for a Cavalry regiment, and marched him, a Brahman, to Sir William Gordon, who ordered me to have him flogged. This was the cause of my being sent for by the General, for the Political authorities had expended much energy in trying to trace the names of the officers who had so acted. Gordon wanted to take all responsibility, but I told the General that having been ordered to reach Máu as

---

[1] He afterwards obtained for me my Brevet Majority, and did his utmost to get me the Victoria Cross.

soon as possible, the horses required something beyond dana (grain), and it was my action which induced the punishment.

I had a stormy interview with the Commissariat officer the day after I arrived. Before I dismounted, I went to his office, and reported that I had fed the Squadron from Asseerghur, and gave in a statement of the money expended. I mentioned I had two or three sacks of sweet potatoes, and a small quantity of rice, sugar, etc., surplus, and I asked him to send someone to take it over. Next day an English-speaking Native came to me, and pointing to the supplies which was in our Squadron lines, said, "I no take, you go sell," my reply to which caused him to run. His superior, the Commissariat officer, complained, and I retaliated by telling him what the Native had said, and that I thought he was to blame for not coming himself, or sending a European to relieve me of the stores.

The Officer commanding the wing of a Native Cavalry Regiment kindly offered me a room in his house, which I accepted the more willingly as the offer carried with it the use of a rough shed for my favourite horse. My host, although a clever man, had been for many years away, working under a Political agent. He had charming manners, but he neither knew his drill nor had he aptitude for the work of a Cavalry leader. He was short-sighted, suffering from inflammation in his eyes, and prematurely aged in constitution. After I had been a week in his house, he went to Sir William Gordon and borrowed my services as a Squadron commander, there being only one available for two and a half Squadrons. The Adjutant, twenty-two years of age, weighing over 20 stone, was a brave man, but unsuited for his appointment.

While Gordon's squadron was marching northwards, Sir Hugh Rose had beaten the rebels at Gwáliár, reinstating the Maharaja, and Sir Robert Napier, taking up the pursuit after a forced march of 25 miles, in which 5 officers and 85 soldiers in one battalion fell from sunstroke, overtook and defeated Tantia Topi, 30 miles north-west of Scindia's capital.

Tantia had left Gwáliár the day before its recapture, and by similar promptitude evaded Sir Robert Napier, carrying off Scindia's Treasury, and a vast number of horses and camels. Tantia was neither well-born, rich, nor brave, but clever and unscrupulous. While he had Scindia's treasure-chest, and the Rao Sahib as a figure-head, he enjoyed the sympathy and respect of the ten millions of Central India, who are mostly Hindoos. To Tantia, acting under Nana Sahib, had been attributed the arrangements of the treacherous slaughter of Sir Hugh Wheeler's force when it surrendered at Kánhpúr. This he denied when about to be hanged in 1859, but he was one of our most persistent and elusive foes.

Central India, composed of six kingdoms, was subdivided into 69 Feudal States, the stability of which is guaranteed by the British Government, and there are in addition 79 petty Chiefships, making 148 in all. Bhopál and Jaora are Muhammadan, but Scindia was the only Hindoo ruler who exerted himself actively on the British side, and thus even in States whose rulers were outwardly loyal, Tantia was able to recruit Bundelas [1] and Wilayatis,[2] and to arrange for food and horses to be in readiness for him as he passed through the Districts. He usually got all he wanted, and when no longer encumbered with guns travelled great distances, circling round between Jhánsi and Ajmír in the north, Betul and Asseerghur in the south.[3]

The northern, eastern, and western sides of this parallelogram are from 350 to 400 miles in length, and the southern side about half that distance, so in spite of the fact that a dozen columns pursued the flying horsemen from various places, he eluded capture for many months.

We had been six weeks in Máu when Tantia Topi was reported to be approaching Jalra Patan, and on the 21st August a small column, consisting of two squadrons and two battalions Native Infantry, moved out to Indore. I was sent with the Native Cavalry, as Sir William Gordon had five officers, and this wing of 200 sabres had only one Duty officer

---

[1] Bundelas, a tribe of Rájpúts, inhabitants of Bundelcund.

[2] Wilayati, literally a foreigner; those with Tantia came from the North-west Frontiers of India.

[3] These towns are situated:

Jhánsi	.	. latitude, 25° 20′ N.;	longitude,	77° 55′ E.
Ajmír	.	. ,, 26° 30′ ,,	,,	74° 20′ ,,
Betul	.	. ,, 21° 40′ ,,	,,	78° 20′ ,,
Asseerghur	.	. ,, 21° 15′ ,,	,,	75° 50′ ,,

besides the Commanding officer. Some days later, as we reached Soosneer, and I thought were marching with sure confidence to attack, the column was halted, and in the evening I was sent for by the Officer commanding it, and told to go the following morning as near as possible to the enemy's camp, estimated to be twenty miles distant. I was cautioned not to run unnecessary risks, but at all hazards to keep the Officer commanding the column aware of any advance of the enemy. When I left at daylight next morning the Infantry were entrenching the position, and the Gunners making gun-pits. This puzzled me considerably at the time, but I afterwards learned that all my Superiors did not feel the same confidence in the Native troops which their Regimental officers professed.

About eleven o'clock I was riding in a shallow valley in front of my party of twenty men, and probably the hot sun had made me drowsy, for although a few minutes previously I had seen a large hyena which crossed our path, I was startled by hearing the clang of horses' hoofs, and looking round, saw my escort retreating. I thought they might be flying from a tiger, but looking up saw 300 yards ahead two men in red coats, who as I afterwards learned belonged to Umjeid Ali's [1] party of the Gwáliár Contingent. While I was looking at the two warriors in front, I noticed that they had their backs turned to me, and they seemed undisturbed by our approach, so I continued to ride towards them, and was rejoined by my escort. Our Staff arrangements in the column were not good, for although the Officer had sent out these men, he had not thought it necessary to inform me they were on the same business, which might easily have given rise to accidents, as they wore identically the same uniform as their former comrades the rebels. Nothing occurred during the day to indicate the enemy would move farther south. They were probably distributing the spoils of Jalra Patan. Meanwhile a column of Europeans, with Gordon's Squadron of the

---

[1] Meer Umjeid Ali, a well-born Muhammadan, was a Silidar (non-commissioned officer) in the Contingent. Although the King of Dihlí wrote personally to him, Umjeid Ali refused to be untrue to his salt, and in spite of all opposition joined the British troops. He served later as an officer in the Central India Horse, dying an honoured pensioner.

17th Lancers, was hurrying up to reinforce us, which they did three days later, but the European Infantry marched with great difficulty in the oppressive heat.

We moved on the 10th September towards Tantia, who had 30 guns and many warriors obtained in Jalra Patan, and for three days marched in order of battle. The Infantry felt the intense heat, though they were spared unnecessary fatigue by the Native Cavalry, which passed through all high-standing grain crops and swamps. In fording the Kala Sind River we lost a good deal of baggage, many mules being washed away. On the 12th the rain came down so heavily that it was impossible to move our camp, nor did our enemy attempt to march. On the 14th the Advance Guard, a Squadron of the 17th, 98 all Ranks, Native Cavalry 190 sabres, and 3 guns, arrived at Rajghur. As we halted in sight of the enemy's camp they began to strike tents. The European Infantry were much exhausted by the previous march, on which several men had died from sunstroke. We waited impatiently for them to come up, as a strong Cavalry picket crossing the river halted for two hours within half a mile of us. Then the General rode up, and said the Infantry could not advance, and must encamp where they were.

Two battalions of Native Infantry now came up, and volunteered to attack; but the General naturally wished to wait till the Europeans could take part in the action. He left me with one Squadron of Native Cavalry, with orders to hold my ground at all costs till the Europeans had rested.

Two Squadrons of the enemy advanced as I was placing vedettes, and conformed to my dispositions, on a ridge about 400 yards distant. As the Native officer opposite to me placed a pair of vedettes exactly opposite to mine, I got off my horse after I had gone about 500 yards, and sitting down, waited to see if he had sufficient self-confidence to choose a spot on his own initiative; this he did not do, however, and he remained sitting on his horse waiting for me.

I had been in position two hours, and the sun was setting, when looking through my field-glasses I observed a Native woman approaching from the river, walking with a long swinging stride. The Native endeavoured to pass through our line of vedettes at about 200 yards from where I was sitting on my horse, and having noticed that the stride had perceptibly shortened, I called to the nearest vedette to bring the person to me. Stripping off the clothing round the Native's body, we found it was a man, and after a few questions he admitted he was a spy. I sent him into camp, and he was shot next day.

When I got back into camp at night I realised the General's anxiety, for one-third of the European Infantry had fallen out exhausted, and several had died from the heat. I had not a particle of skin on my nose, which was swollen to an enormous size, and my eyelids were blistered by the sun.

CHAPTER XII

1858—SINDWAHA

Rajghur — Tantia Topi makes a running fight — Loses 26 guns — Intense heat—Many soldiers die—A loquacious Native fights me—Dhokul Singh—Death of Adjutant, 8th Hussars—E. R. C. Bradford's gallant charge.

WE mounted at 3.30 a.m., and moving slowly forward, reached the river at dawn. The ford was difficult, and if we had attacked the previous day not more than one horseman could have passed there at a time, though there was an easier crossing higher up.

When we got across the river we found the enemy had moved to the eastward, and Captain Sir William Gordon was ordered to pursue with the Cavalry, while our Infantry followed. We soon came up with their Rear Guard, and then the Squadron of the 17th Lancers halted while a troop of Native Cavalry under a Subaltern advanced in skirmishing order, firing while mounted, as was the custom. After a quarter of an hour in which very little progress was made, the General called me and said he wanted to get forward and reconnoitre, and did not like being stopped by a few men. I took on a line of skirmishers at a brisk trot, and soon came on a Horse Artillery gun, abandoned by the enemy; but 100 yards farther on three men stood by their gun with a match ready to fire. I could have wished to have opened out, but there was just the chance that the gun might not go off, or that its charge would go over our heads, which indeed happened as we closed on it and cut down the three rebel gunners, who stood bravely up to die. The Native Cavalry skirmishers now got out of hand, and pursued at speed faster than I approved; but I consoled myself with the reflection that they would stop when confronted by any considerable body of the enemy, and this indeed soon happened.

A quarter of an hour later I was cantering on in pursuit by the track on which we had taken the two guns, followed by a Dragoon named Dhokul Singh; one of our men shouted to me, "Look to your left, or you will be shot." Turning my head, I saw a Rebel who had planted his spear in the ground, and with his gun resting on the spear was aiming at me. I called to my orderly, "Go and kill him," and without checking my horse looked round to see what would happen. Dhokul Singh rode at him with uplifted sword, prepared for cut 2;[1] the man held his fire till his adversary got within three yards and then fired, missing his aim; Dhokul Singh's sword cutting his face into two bits, knocked him to the ground. As my orderly galloped up to rejoin me, the man jumped up again, and continued to fight others, until he was speared by the on-coming Squadron of the 17th Lancers.

The track I was following passed through a belt of jungle, with trees and bushes standing three or four yards apart, and I slackened my pace to a slow trot. Glancing down, I saw a Rebel under a bush close to me, but as he did not raise his gun I took no notice of him, but looked ahead, as I came on an open patch in the jungle, where a hundred yards from me 500 Infantry were standing in column, with 100 of the Gwáliár Cavalry, rather nearer on the flanks. The dozen Cavalry soldiers following me immediately turned; the front Rank of the Infantry fired, and the horsemen raising a shout, galloped at us. I had not much fear for myself, for my horse "The Pig" was fast, but when we had fled 300 yards through the jungle, we came on prickly growth two feet high, and all turned outwards to avoid it. The Gwáliár horsemen were too close for me to venture to turn, so, taking my horse hard by the head, I drove him at it, and he went over, or through, in a succession of bounds. This put me on the safe side of some of my own men, one of whom galloping up behind, and travelling faster than I was then going, caught the back of my knee on the point of his, and lifted me out of the saddle on to my horse's neck. By the help of its mane I got back, and in doing so chanced to look to my left, where I saw the Subaltern

[1] A cut at the head.

who had come with me riding at a "collected gallop," all unconscious that at his heels followed a fine bearded Sowar, who was poising a spear within two feet of his back. I shouted, "Look behind you!" and he did. Now, I have often read of the "Chifney Rush," and have seen George Fordham rouse a horse in winning a race, but I do not suppose that either of these celebrated jockeys made so great an effort as did that Subaltern, whose horse soon put him into safety, for the Squadron of the 17th Lancers was now approaching.

I reported to Sir William Gordon that there was a well-posted enemy in his front, but was not explicit, and we were neither of us perhaps sufficiently careful; at all events, he "lost direction" in passing through the patch of jungle, and thus did not follow me, and come fairly on the enemy, passing 100 yards on their flank; in the result they effected their retreat without our closing on them. We took, however, during the day, 26 guns, a large mortar, and 10 guns were picked up, abandoned by the enemy, in the course of the week.

At 4 p.m. the same body of Infantry stood in the plain, as if to invite us to attack, although their horsemen had retreated. The senior Subaltern of the 17th Lancers wished to charge, and Sir William Gordon sending for me, asked my opinion. I pointed out that our Infantry had halted 8 miles and the Artillery 6 miles behind us, the horses had been moving since 3 a.m. without anything to eat or drink, and I thought it was not worth the probable amount of casualties we should suffer. I urged, however, that if we were to charge, I should be allowed to go forward with a few men to make certain there was no intervening nulla[1] between us and the enemy; Sir William decided against the attack, as I thought then wisely, but my opinion was much stronger an hour later, when, after the enemy had retired, I found there was an impassable nulla between us and where the Infantry stood.

At 1 p.m. the Adjutant of the Native Cavalry with which I was serving complained to me that he was suffering from the sun, and I begged him to get off his horse and lie under a tree. He demurred to doing so, as he thought his action might be misinterpreted. I endeavoured to laugh him out of his apprehension, urging him to rest. I left him, and con-

[1] Ravine.

tinued the pursuit, and about an hour later he fell in a dying condition off his horse. When Sir William decided not to attack, he moved back towards our own Infantry's encamping-ground at Biora, and I remained out with a few men to bring in my comrade's body. There was but very little risk; although we were still close to the unbroken Infantry, they naturally did not wish to fight, and moved off to continue their retreat, as our Squadrons moved towards Biora. I followed the enemy for 1½ miles, going into a village to look for water as they went out of it, catching Tantia Topi's umbrella peon[1] with the Chief's big sunshade. I had some difficulty in transporting the body, for the officer weighed 20 stone, and I had to impress a number of villagers, who carried the body on a door, by reliefs.

Some innocent inhabitants were killed by the Native Cavalry, and I saw a villager cut down by one of the party of the faithful Gwáliár Contingent, who rode at a man apparently unarmed, and although I galloped as hard as I could, shouting to the horseman not to strike, before I could get up he had cleft the villager's shoulder through. I reached the spot before blood came, but turned my head away, because it seemed the man was cut in two.[2]

The heat was great, and though our human casualties, except from sunstroke, were but trifling, the day's operations were costly to us as regards horses. We started at 3 a.m. with 200 in the wing of the Native Cavalry Regiment with which I was serving, and next day 135 only were effective. In the teams of the four guns, six horses died while in draught, although they did not accompany the Cavalry, and got but two miles farther than the Infantry.

Tantia Topi led the flight in an easterly direction, and we moved in a south-easterly direction for the next five days,

---

[1] Footman.

[2] In the following April I camped at Biora for one night on my way from Gwáliár to Máu, and rode over to the village. Calling the Head man, I narrated what I had seen on the 15th September of the previous year, and asked whether my surmise that the sufferer was a villager was correct. The Head man said, "Yes, he is still alive, but a cripple." I had the man brought to me, and although a ghastly sight, being paralysed, and unable to work, with the patient resignation of the Asiatic, he was thankful to be alive, and was profuse in gratitude for a small present I gave him.

making short marches, for the heat during the last few days had had a prejudicial effect on men and horses, and now rain fell in torrents, making all movements over the black cotton soil difficult. Tantia's objective was Bhopál, ruled over by an able woman, the Begum, who had always been loyal to the British cause, and General Michel's duty was to save her capital. When we crossed the Parbati River, we turned northwards; the Native Cavalry, preceding the Europeans, at Bersia came under the command of Major H. O. Mayne, who had recently raised some Irregular Horse, fine riders and skilled men-at-arms, but of a motley appearance as regards dress and equipment.

General Michel joined us at Bersia, and foreseeing that the Europeans could not reach that place for several days, permitted the Native horsemen to go forward in a northerly direction. We camped 40 miles to the south-east of Sironj, and endeavoured to locate the enemy and ascertain how best to close on him. I was sent out to reconnoitre roads, and felt my ignorance, my only knowledge of the duty being derived from Lefroy's *Handbook on Artillery*. Returning from one of these reconnaissances, I marched on a track continuously under water for six miles. A column approaching Sironj from Sipri, almost due north of that place, caused Tantia to move; but as we numbered only 8 officers and 350 Natives it was impossible for us to make any serious attack on his Force, numbering just then 10,000 men, with six guns.

Tantia having captured Esaughur, the chief of which, loyal to Scindia, had refused to surrender, while we were 12 miles to the westward, adopted such drastic measures with his countrymen as effectually prevented any Native in that district from giving us assistance or information. He killed the male adults, and collecting the women's clothing in heaps, had it burnt. Major Mayne begged the General to allow him to return to General Michel, but this was refused until Michel sent a third peremptory order, and we then turned back. Mayne proposed to march 30 miles, but unfortunately was ordered not to go more than 10 miles. In the result, having marched 140 miles farther than the Europeans, we arrived at Mongroulee one day after a successful little fight which had come about unexpectedly.

General Michel, to catch Tantia, who was between him and the Sipri column, with the impassable Betwa River to the east, having moved northwards, was encamping near the village, when Tantia Topi approached on the other side of it, neither Force being aware of the proximity of its enemy. Michel, on sighting the Rebels, at once extending his Infantry, advanced to attack, and Tantia giving way disappeared; but a part of his Force moving through the jungle chanced on the rear of Michel's Column as it was coming into camp, and killed some soldiers, and the dooly-bearers carrying them. Gordon was sent to the Rear with his troop, 43 Lancers all told, and arriving just as this slaughter was being perpetrated, gave the order, " Open out and pursue at the gallop," and his men followed into the jungle. The Rebel horsemen fled, but the 43 Lancers killed rather over 90 Infantry, Gordon himself slaying three. Tantia crossed the Betwa, and for some days eluded our scouts.

We now marched in a south-easterly direction to cut the rebels off from Ságar, but they had turned northwards, in which direction we followed them. On the 17th October, the General promised us a fight next day, and to my disappointment I was detailed to command the Rear guard. As the Advance and Rear guards were invariably performed by Natives, I was nearly always on one or the other, the horses of the 17th Lancers being saved as much as possible. I suffered considerably from indigestion and face-ache, but persuaded our doctor not to put me on the Sick report. Nothing, however, occurred on the 18th, and that evening, when we encamped at Nurot, we had given up all hope of another fight for some days. Orders were given to march at sunrise in a north-westerly direction to Lalitpúr, where Tantia was supposed to have gone. After nightfall news was received that Tantia was moving eastwards, and at 3 a.m. we started in a north-easterly direction.

We had marched 16 miles, when at 7.30 a.m. I came with the Advanced guard on a small picket of the enemy's Cavalry to the south of Sindwaha. Not anticipating a fight, I was riding the horse I had bought at Ahmednagar, which I could not hold with my maimed arm, so the moment I had satisfied myself the enemy was in force, ordering the Native officer to stand fast, I galloped to the Rear, passing the Mounted column as it came on. My friends all shouted to me, " There is firing, where are you going?" But I answered not a word, going towards the Rear until I came to the groom, who was leading "The Pig," which had a sore back. Disregarding the man's entreaties, I changed horses, and within one minute was again passing at speed to the Front.

Our Force consisted of two half battalions of Infantry, which were still 3 miles behind, 4 guns, on the waggons of which a few European Infantry were carried, the Squadron 17th Lancers, 2 Native Squadrons, and the Cavalry of the Sipri column, which had come temporarily under our General's command. It included 1½ Squadrons 8th Hussars, and 2 Squadrons of a Native Cavalry Regiment. Our Infantry was not in sight, and Tantia Topi imagining he had only Cavalry in his front, for once determining to stand, took up a strong position on a low range of hills, the gentle slopes of which were studded with conifers and patches of jungle. His Force consisted of 10,000 men and 4 guns, which were well served, although they fired only round-shot. At the foot of the enemy's position was a marshy stream 30 feet wide 2 feet deep in water, and more than that in mud in parts, running generally east and west, bordered by fields of jowarry, or Indian corn, from 8 to 10 feet high.

Tantia advanced a body of Infantry on our left to seize the village, while his Cavalry came down on our right, and some Rebel Infantry got into a large field of jowarry, covering the centre of the position. Our battery came into action near the fields, and the two Squadrons with which I served moved to its right as escort. My Commanding officer's eyes were painful, and he directed me to take over the executive command, and sending me to the General to ask what he wished us to do, I was told to draw as much fire on ourselves as possible, to divert the enemy's attention from our Artillery, so we halted on the edge of the nulla,[1] which was impassable in front of us, under the fire of the enemy's footmen, who were in the jowarry fields.

Several cannon shots were dropped in succession in front of the Squadrons, one killing the Left Troop leader's horse, and two horses in the Rear Rank. The Trumpeter sitting exactly behind me was now struck by a bullet in the mouth, and this

[1] Ravine.

followed by the well-aimed cannon shots made the men uneasy, and to ensure their remaining steady I turned about, and ordered them to " Tell off," feeling then much more uncomfortable from the sound of the bullets and cannon shots at my back than while I was facing the direction from which they were coming.

The Officer commanding the Native Cavalry on our right, under whose orders the 8th Hussars and the 17th Lancers were acting, was to the east of the jowarry fields, which covered a considerable track of ground. The Colonel had received orders from his Senior officer he was to avoid an engagement until further orders, and when some of Tantia's Cavalry crossed the nulla, he went off to the Right Rear at a trot. Sir William Gordon protested, but the Colonel said that his orders were imperative. The enemy's Cavalry followed up, coming on boldly, and had nearly ridden into the Rear of Gordon's Squadron, when he reversed his front, uttering the usual expressions of an angry Briton against the giver of such an order, and led his men forward at the charge. The boldest of the enemy's horsemen who had come across the nulla where it was passable were all killed, for the collision occurred close to the stream, where though its banks were easy the bottom was tenacious mud. In tumbled Europeans and Rebels in one confused mass, and four of our men falling in amongst a crowd of the enemy were killed. The charge cost our small Force 24 horses, most of which scrambling out riderless, went off with Tantia's horsemen.

The effect of this counter stroke, with the sight of the European Infantry doubling up towards the village, was a general retirement of the enemy, some 300 footmen only covering the retreat. The charge was not visible from where we were standing, but we heard the cheering, and could see some of the enemy's Infantry beginning to retire from the hill 600 yards in our front.

I moved off to the right, and crossing the nulla at the place used by the enemy's Cavalry when advancing, was going forward, as a dozen rebels ran out of the jowarry field, and stood up in a group, the leader, a fine broad-shouldered Wilayati, over six feet in height, armed with musket, sword, and shield; a smaller Wilayati, wearing a doublet of flexible mail and iron skull-piece with flexible curtains, and ten or eleven Sepoys, Bengal Infantry,

RISALDAR MAJOR DHOKUL SINGH
AIDE-DE-CAMP TO THE COMMANDER-IN-CHEIF, BOMBAY ARMY

in coatees, cummerbunds, and langotis.[1] Their numbers were so small, twelve or thirteen, that I went on at first, ordering a half troop on my left to ride over them. This they did not do, and with another officer I attacked them, but without breaking their ranks. A hundred yards to the right of where this occurred stood a half troop of my Right Squadron, and going up to the Native officer I called on him to charge, but without any effect.

The Wilayati gave me a personal challenge, coupled with opprobrious language, in much the same terms as those in which the Philistine vituperated David, calling to our men, "Come on, you dogs of the Government!" The Native officer spurred his horse, but held him hard by the head. I shouted, "Dhokul Singh, Dhokul Singh," the name of my orderly at Rajghur, who was out of sight behind the high jowarry, when one of the half troop said, "I will go with you, Sahib," and cantered towards the group of men, who knowing their time to die had come, were resolved to sell their lives dearly. I did not notice that my man had his carbine on his thigh; he cantered to within a few yards of the rebels, and as he passed, fired a shot without effect. I had started my horse at the same moment, and reached the five men standing in the corner of the group. They came to the motions of "Ready—Present" in the methodical manner in which our soldiers were trained, and as I lunged at the nearest man, five fired: I ducked my head to the horse's crest, and the bullets passing over me wounded two horses of the half troop, still 100 yards off. The Wilayati throwing down his empty gun, drew a long two-handed sword, which he carried on his back, and I noticed while I was fighting with two of the Sepoys who were trying to bayonet me that the leader had to shift his left hand down and hold the blade in order to draw it out of the scabbard. "Your body will be food for the dogs," he cried; to which I replied, "Cease talking, come on," and drawing away from the group as he ran at me, with sword uplifted over his head, waited for him with the point of my sword low. The Wilayati cutting too soon missed my leg, and overbalancing fell on his face. I backed my horse, and got the point of my sword within a couple of inches of his back, when two of the Sepoys running out of the group, thrusted at

[1] Body coverings which nearly reach the knees.

me with their bayonets, and I was obliged to bring the point of my sword back to keep them off.

The Wilayati jumped up and came behind me, but as he did so I saw over the heads of two Sepoys, with whom I was personally engaged, Dhokul Singh approaching at speed from the west, or far side of the group, through which he charged like a skittle ball amongst the pins. He knocked down two without seriously hurting them, riding straight at the Wilayati, who was now close behind me, with his sword again in the air. Dhokul Singh cut 5 (body cut), but missed his stroke, and I exclaimed sarcastically, " Bravo ! " The soldier was furious at my remark, and as he circled his horse and " collected " it to a slow canter, shouting " The Sahib says 'bravo'!" rode directly on the Wilayati, who stood with his long sword in the air. Neither man condescended to guard; each cut with all his strength, Dhokul Singh using cut 2, as he had at Rajghur, when he fought the dismounted Rebel. The Wilayati's sword falling on the cap lines of my orderly's chaco, severed them, cut through the cantle (rear peak) of the saddle, dividing the crupper, and slightly wounding the horse's spine. Dhokul Singh's sword cleft the Wilayati's face in twain, felling him to the ground.

Lieutenant Bainbridge of the 17th Lancers, who passing when the rebels ran out of the jowarry saw the scene, had galloped off 300 yards to the Right to ask for assistance for me, and while I was fighting with two men of the group, for the others would not quit their formation, for fear of being attacked by the Half troop of Native Cavalry, I felt the thud of horses galloping behind me, and although I could not turn my head the effect was at once apparent in the eyes of my opponents. Putting both spurs into my horse's flanks, I drove him into the middle of the group, the men of which put their muskets down, and some of them clamouring for painless death at my hands, cried, " Shoot us, Sahib, shoot us, please " (Goli-se marna). Without attempting to hurt, they mobbed me, until, passing my sword into my left hand, I struck two men with my fist in the face. Then with a revulsion of feeling they separated, just as some of the Native Right Troop and a troop of the 8th Hussars, led by Lieutenant Harding, Adjutant, came up. He and the men, who having been my fellow-passengers on board ship for two months knew me, were

SINDWAHA, 19TH OCTOBER, 1858

GENERAL ORDERS BY H.E. THE VICEROY AND GOVERNOR-GENERAL LIEUTENANT-COLONEL.—BRINGS SPECIALLY TO NOTICE THE GALLANTRY OF LIEUTENANT WOOD, 17TH LANCERS, WHO ON THIS OCCASION (ACTION AT SINDWAHA) ALMOST SINGLE HANDED, CAME UP TO AND ATTACKED A BODY OF THE ENEMY

cheering, and Harding calling me by my nickname "Sailor," shouted, "You take that one, and I'll take this fellow," pointing to two rebels, who having run for about 50 yards, were then standing at bay.

Harding rode down at the man he had selected, who waited to fire until they were so close that Harding in raising his sword for cut 2 at the man, had his jacket set on fire by the rebel's cartridge, and fell mortally wounded. My man stood 50 yards from where the group had dispersed when I rode amongst them, and with his right foot placed on an antbear heap, awaited me with fixed bayonet. I approached him at a smart canter, with elbows close to my sides to protect the lungs, and the point of my sword low down under the horse's forearm. I guided the horse so as to take the point of the bayonet on its chest, but the Sepoy when he saw that I was "riding home" wavered, and attempted to club his musket. As he swung it, butt uppermost, over his head, the point of his bayonet caught in the cummerbund which he wore over his coatee. This delayed him for a second, and my sword entering under the left armpit went through him up to the hilt, the butt of his musket falling over my shoulder, but without hurting me seriously, as my horse stopped. As the Sepoy dropped off the point of my sword, I galloped after the others. Four stood 60 yards farther on, with their backs to conifers. The nearest awaited the attack till the colour of my sword blade unnerved him, and he withdrew out of reach, under the spreading branches of a cedar, where he was speared by a Native Lancer, his comrades falling at the same time. This takes much longer to tell than it did in action, but I was so exhausted by the fight as to be obliged to dismount and sit down for a few minutes to recover my breath.

The brigade having come up, we followed the enemy's horsemen, but the Brigadier insisted on our proceeding in a dressed line at the walk, and consequently the rebels got farther away from us every minute. General Michel riding up to me, reproached us. I said, "Sir, do you not hear the Brigade-Major shouting to me to keep in line?" The General, though apparently unwilling to interfere with the Executive Cavalry leader of another Division, used a strong expression, and I replied, "Well, there are some fir trees 200 yards in front of us, and when we reaching them pass out of sight, I will gallop." This we did, he accompanying us to the Sujnaur River, across which the Rebels escaped. There were very few killed, except by the Native Cavalry, and a troop of the 8th Hussars, which being next in the line of advance, broke away with us, and came on in the pursuit.

As we rode into our camp, which had been pitched near the scene of the fight, one of the Natives approached me: "Sahib, what must I do with this animal?" When we were going forward in pursuit, he had run to me, crying, "My horse has been killed, save me." I caught a riderless horse, and held it while the soldier mounted; now, after riding it all day, he wanted to be rid of it, to cook his food. I stood over him till I had seen the horse watered and fed, and then having had it tied up to a tree near the Guard Tent, went to get some tea. Returning in an hour's time, I had the khójir (Native saddle) removed, and noticing it was heavy, cut open the layers of silk and linen of which the seat was formed, finding gold mohurs to the value of £90; this I distributed in the Squadrons, stipulating that the lazy soldier should not share in my find.

Lieutenant E. R. C. Bradford,[1] a fellow-Marlborough boy, talked over our adventure that evening. He is singularly modest, but I had heard of his determined conduct in the charge initiated by Captain Sir William Gordon which decided the fight. Mayne's Horse, about 200, came on a gol (literally circle) of the enemy's Infantry, covering the retreat. Their formation represented our square, but was in effect wedge-shaped. As the horsemen approached, they struck the thin edge of the formation where the rebels stood 5 or 6 deep. Bradford energetically pointing out this would occur, turned his horse, and broke through the thickest of the enemy, 18 or 20 deep. He was followed by 20 Sikhs, and though there were some men and many horses slightly wounded, Bradford was untouched. Said I, "Edward, when you went through the gol, did you cut or thrust?" Most men would have swaggered a little, but he replied simply, "I shut my eyes and galloped."

[1] Later, Colonel Sir Edward Bradford—Chief Commissioner, Metropolitan Police, 1890-1903.

SINDWAHA

I bought the coat of mail worn by the smaller Wilayati for 10 rupees, of a camp follower; but it was not received by my mother, to whom I sent it. I fell asleep that night depressed by a feeling that I might be blamed for the hesitation of my men, but by next day the 8th Hussars men had told the story, and the Officer commanding the Cavalry informed me I had been mentioned in his Despatch,[1] and Dhokul Singh was promoted to be Corporal.[2]

[1] Extract from General Orders by H.E. the Viceroy and Governor-General:—

"*January* 16*th*, 1859.

"16. L—— in separate command during a portion of the day, brings specially to notice, etc. etc., as does ——, the gallantry of Lieutenant Wood of the 17th Lancers, who having, from paucity of officers, volunteered, during the campaign, to serve with Native Cavalry, on this occasion (action at Sindwaha), almost single-handed, came up to and attacked a body of the enemy."

[2] As Risaldar Major Dhokul Singh Bahadur, he was Aide-de-Camp to the Commander-in-Chief, Bombay, for many years in the eighties.

CHAPTER XIII

1858-9—A PURSUIT

A pursuit—Highlanders march in three days 73 miles and attack—Varied duties—Ride on a giraffe—A well-dressed rebel mistaken for a loyal Sepoy.

WE halted on the 20th October, uncertain in which direction the main body of the rebels had gone after we had driven them across the Jamni River. We afterwards learned that the Infantry had separated; some going northwards, joined Maun Singh, and others travelled with Tantia Topi for another fortnight.

We marched on the 21st to Lalitpúr, and having encamped, nearly all of us were asleep in the afternoon, when fifty rebel horsemen came into the village in ignorance of our presence. Sir William Gordon mounted, but did not overtake the fighting men, bringing in only some of the camp followers. Tantia doubled back between us and the Betwa River, passing within four miles of our camp; we followed, and our European Infantry, consisting of a wing of the 71st and 92nd Highlanders, for the next three days covered long distances. We generally started in the middle of the night; our first march, on the 23rd October, was 27 miles; next day, 29 miles; and on the 25th October, 17 miles. The General had promised the Infantry a halt, but as we came on the spot selected for our camping-ground near Kurai, the rebels arrived there at the same moment.

I quickly shifted the saddle on to "The Pig," and accompanied the Native Cavalry out to the flank, while our Infantry advanced in an extended line. Organised resistance soon ceased, and during the pursuit the mounted troops spread out on an extended frontage, the Cavalry separating into three bodies. I had led a Squadron against a collected body of the

Rebels, and then, to avoid seeing them killed, I followed, with a dozen soldiers, a formed group of men; leaving my followers engaged in exterminating them, I rode at a Sepoy who escaped into a jowarry field. I pursued him, but when I got into the middle of the field regretted having done so, for the stalks were stiff and strong, and I had to spur my horse sharply to induce him to move. If the Sepoy had realised my difficulty, and awaited my coming, I must have fought at a disadvantage; he went through the grain however, and halted on a clear spot. As I approached he threw down his musket, which was empty, and drawing a sword, cried, " Sahib, I know I must die, but it is not an officer's duty to kill individuals; send a private to fight me. I shall either wound or kill you." I replied, " It is more likely I shall kill you," as I cantered at him. He was an active man, and threw himself down on his back so suddenly as to escape the point of my sword, irritating me by cutting at my horse's hocks. Now I had given £110 for the horse, and having no money to replace it, I lost my temper, calling to the Sepoy that I had taken him for a warrior, and not a horse-slaughterer. Before I could turn the horse, my men, who had come up, by getting round the Rebel in a circle effectually prevented my fighting him by approaching at speed, as all Cavalry soldiers should do. He kept five or six at bay for some minutes by snicking their horses' faces, until he fell to a pistol shot.

We killed in the pursuit about 150 of the rebels, and the General estimated their total losses at 350. Tantia fled towards Ratghur, and then turning south-west moved by Garaispur towards Bhopál, where, forestalled by another small column, he crossed the Narbadá.

After the pursuit I fell ill with a severe attack of fever and ague, complicated by acute toothache, and was carried into Bhilsa, where fortunately for me the Force halted for three days. I persuaded the doctor to let me go back to duty a day too soon, and thus got another touch of fever, but succeeded in concealing the fact, and recovered by the 6th November.

When we reached Hosingabad three days later, troops at that town and others coming up were formed into a Cavalry column of 7 Squadrons, and D Troop Royal Horse Artillery, under command of Colonel Benson, 17th Lancers, who had just arrived from Jalna. I was nominated as his Staff officer, doing also the duties of Interpreter and Bazaar Master; and I should soon have got ill again, had not the Colonel let me have an intelligent Corporal of the Regiment to assist me with the office-work.

I was indeed so hard worked that my English letters remained unopened in my pocket for five hours on the 14th November, when we halted at Betul to collect grain for the horses, before following the rebels to Multai. We had saved the Treasury from Tantia, which he had hoped to seize, but were now obliged to wait, or the horses must have starved.

Besides the ordinary routine work of a Staff officer in the Field, the duties of Bazaar Master were varied and numerous. On the 14th November I was engaged nearly all the forenoon, while sitting in Sir William Gordon's leaky tent with my face tied up in a pepper poultice, in dispensing justice like a Kadi in the *Arabian Nights*. There appears a Native, who after prostrating whines, " I was buying sugar in the Bazaar, and had a rupee tied in the fall of my puggaree, when this child "—producing an urchin six years old—" calls out, ' Look behind you, a man steals the rupee.' I looked behind me, and the rupee was gone." The culprit gives up the rupee, receives twenty-four lashes on the spot, and disappears. A Native Corporal reports that the Squadron which marched at daylight to join another column has left baggage on the camping-ground, would the Sahib provide transport? This I order from the town, and he goes. A doctor writes: "Dear Sir, I learn that you have flogged one of my dooly-bearers, will you state for what cause and on what evidence?" I reply, "Dear Sir, I flogged your dooly-bearer on what I considered to be sufficient evidence.—Your faithful servant." Colonel Benson's servant appears and says, "My master's cart is broken, please mend it." I send a Native messenger with him into the town to the wheelwright's shop. Dhokul Singh, my orderly at Rajghur, and who came to my assistance at Sindwaha, says, "Oh, father and mother, why have you left us? There is nothing for me but Death." I reply, "I obey orders, but say at once what you want." "Oh, master, four of us gave our boots to the cobbler yesterday, who disappeared, and the Commanding officer said I might stay behind the Regiment to search for him. I have found the cobbler, but he is helplessly drunk: what is to be done?" I reply, "Wait;" and sending to the cobbler's house, in a short time his friends bring the boots, and Dhokul Singh rides off, saying he "will try to live for the happiness of seeing me again."

Tantia Topi had hoped to enter the Dekhan, but confronted by hostile forces in every direction, he dismissed the footmen who had followed him south of the Narbadá, and they dispersed in the Pachmarhi Hills, while his horsemen turned down the valley of the Tapti. Colonel Benson followed him, and for ten days we rode through jungle, the wretchedly poor villages being unable to furnish adequate supplies for our horses, which for two days had no grain. We went close to Ellichpoor, making a round of 40 miles in order to obtain food for our animals, while another column in command of Colonel Parke, which was close to the Narbadá, took up the chase, and Tantia, fleeing westward, made for Khandeish, vigorously pressed by Colonel Parke, whose men and horses were fresh. Tantia doubling northwards, eluded his pursuers, but ran across five companies of Infantry before he was aware of their presence, losing 150 men, but succeeded in crossing the Narbadá at Burwanee.

We had struck the Asseerghur-Máu road to the north of the former place and were moving northwards, when Colonel Benson, at 3 a.m. on the 30th November, received an urgent message to reach Máu as quickly as possible, as Tantia once across the Narbadá had headed for Indore, ten miles to the north of the Máu Cantonments, which were denuded of British troops, and we made a record march.

We arrived at the bank of the river at noon, got the last load across by 6 p.m., and starting two hours later rode into Máu at 8 a.m. on the 1st December, a journey of 50 miles in twenty-six hours, of which six had been occupied in crossing a big river. Greater distances have been accomplished in recent years in less time, but Cavalry soldiers in those days generally made even the longest marches at a walk.

We halted twenty-four hours at Máu for information, but left on the morning of the 3rd for Rutlam, hearing Tantia had ridden in a north-westerly direction. It is possible he learnt we were between him and Indore, or perhaps Colonel Parke was too close at his heels to allow the wily Mahratta time to turn.

Colonel Parke overtook him near Udaipúr, 40 miles north of the Narbadá, chasing him to Dewud, whence Tantia turned in a south-westerly direction towards Baroda. He ran against another column sent out from that place, suffered more loss, and then headed north-east to Banswara.

On the 9th December, Colonel (Brigadier - General) Somerset took over the command from Colonel Benson, and halted for three days, uncertain of Tantia's movements, and the military situation being complicated by the fact that Firoz Shah was crossing the Ganges to join Tantia. It was necessary for us to keep within reach of Jaora, for the Nawab's brother was with Tantia, and had vowed he would plunder the city, into which we marched on the 14th.

The Nawab came to meet us, and in the evening sent elephants, on which we proceeded in procession round his somewhat squalid capital, and later to his palace. While waiting for dinner some horrid exhibitions were given, amongst others a sheep being killed by a lynx, and we were shown the Nawab's menagerie, which was varied, though not extensive. A giraffe was brought round, led by a string in its nose. Eventually it was halted under the balcony on which we were sitting, when an officer observed, " I'll lay a rupee that Wood doesn't dare ride that beast." " Done with you," said I, and pulling the spurs from the heels of my boots, I opened my legs and dropped on to the creature's back. The motion was not unpleasant while it walked, but when it began to trot I became uncomfortable. It carried no saddle, but round its neck was a circlet of ornamental worsted, by which I held. While the creature trotted in a circle I maintained my seat, but presently jumping high from the ground he pulled over the attendant, who held on manfully for 50 yards while being dragged, but then let go, and the giraffe broke into a canter. I was not much inconvenienced at first, but soon the ungainly motions gave me all the sensations experienced by a landsman crossing the Channel between Dover and Calais in a choppy sea, and I was wondering how I could get off, when the giraffe turned a corner, and I saw in front his stable. Fearing for my head, I let myself down, and should have escaped with only a shaking but that the creature's knee struck me in the chest, and sent me backwards to the ground.

His hind foot came down on my face, and knocked me insensible, cutting a hole in either cheek and in my lip, and making a mash of my nose. For the next three days I was carried in a dooly.

In Christmas week our destination was changed four times. On the 23rd we were marching towards Purtabghar, when General Somerset was ordered to "hand over his Command to Colonel Benson, and move with all speed towards Sehore, bringing as many Highlanders as he could mount on camels, 8 guns, and Lieutenant Wood." We marched day and night to Ujjain, where we were ordered to turn back and march to Agar, and from thence to Mehidpur. On the 27th we left Mehidpur at 3 a.m., and marched continuously till 7 p.m. on the 31st, having one halt of four hours, one of two hours, and others of only an hour. The men carried only cloak and haversack.

At Zirapur we overtook Colonel Benson with two Squadrons and two guns, who having chased Tantia from near Maundsar for over 80 miles, had had a fight the previous day, and taken six elephants. Both he and Sir William Gordon, who was the hardest of the hard, looked very thin and ill. General Somerset asked them to come on with us, but they declared that neither men nor horses, which had been without grain during the four days of forced marches, could move.

We moved on 16 miles to Khilchipur, and with rests of twenty minutes to feed the horses, marched 40 miles continuously till the evening of the 31st, closing on the rebels, now only 10 miles in front of us. I sent two spies from Sarthal to stay with them until they halted, for we knew that we were close on them, every now and then coming on foundered horses. My two spies were captured, but telling plausible stories escaped with their lives.

When I had shown the troops where to bivouac—for we had dropped tents and all baggage on the 26th—I induced a horsekeeper to go out to the enemy. The man was stupid, for when I inspected him before he started he had a tin pannikin marked "17th Lancers" tied to his cummerbund. I stripped him and a torch-bearer whom I had obtained from a village, and made them exchange every particle of clothing, and my horsekeeper was thus fairly disguised, having nothing appertaining to a European about him; and I accompanied him three or four miles, till we got near a Piquet of the Rebels.

While I was away the Commanding officers had been to see the Brigadier, and pointing out that such incessant marching was having a prejudicial effect on the men's health, begged that he would go on as soon as the troops had eaten. This decision was announced to me when I came back later to have some food, and I asked my General what he proposed to do when we came on the enemy's Piquet; but he determined to go forward, and so at midnight we moved off. When we were 3 miles south of Barode we were fired on, and turning back to the General, who rode 100 yards behind me, I asked him what he would do. He was then sorry he had not accepted my suggestion, and asked what I advised, and I said, " Lie down until daylight : " and so we did. I brought twelve men of the Highlanders up to the head of the column in place of the few Lancers who had been there, enjoining the Sergeant that the sentry should awake me when he saw the first streak of the false dawn.[1] I awoke about half an hour before it appeared, witnessing a strange sight. There was not one single man in the little Force awake. The Sergeant and the twelve Highlanders were sleeping soundly; every Lancer had his arm through his horse's rein, which was standing with drooping head; and the drivers were stretched alongside the gun teams. Kicking the Sergeant and the Piquet up, I bade them run down the column and awake the men, and we advanced. Three-quarters of a mile distant, in a large group of trees, we saw camp fires, and I rode with an orderly of the 17th Lancers into the grove, which was occupied by camp followers, whose only anxiety was to escape. Disregarding them, the column pressed on, following a cloud of dust which marked Tantia's retreat. He had camels and elephants, and the latter certainly must have moved earlier or we should have overtaken them.

When we had gone about 6 miles and I was ahead guiding the column, the horse of one of the rebels putting his feet inside the standing martingale, came down in front of

---

[1] The light on the horizon about one hour before dawn.

me, and I told Trumpeter Brown[1] to shoot him. Presumably the Trumpeter had not much confidence in his skill, for he would not fire until he had placed the pistol close to the rebel's head. Eventually Brown fired, and the man ducking his head the bullet missed him, and I peremptorily forbidding another shot, let the man run off into a field of jowarry, his horse still remaining cast on the road. He must have escaped, for when we returned in the afternoon the horse was gone.

Two miles farther on we were hurrying through a village with high mud walls, and a roadway so narrow as only just to take the guns. The leading gun detachment was in front, and the Squadron 17th Lancers half a mile out on either flank, and had dropped somewhat behind, as the guns followed a track, and the Lancers were moving through poppies, which being in full bloom and high, were tiring to the horses. The 150 Highlanders were as near behind the battery as they could keep.

I did not know at the time how ill the Brigadier was, suffering from a disease from which he died a few months afterwards; but on this occasion, when in actual presence of the enemy, he came out grandly as a leader of men. As he, Captain Paget, and I rode out of the village, there were 2000 horsemen drawn up 700 yards from us in one long line, and on seeing the gun they cheered, and advanced at a slow trot. I turned to General Somerset and said, as I put my hand over my sword, " We have only to die like gentlemen ; " to which he replied, " Die ? Not at all. Paget, gallop." Captain Paget always talked in a drawling voice, and on this occasion he did not quicken his intonation, as he ordered, " Leading gun—gallop." And gallop it did for 100 yards, and came into action, thus enabling the remaining three guns to emerge from the village. The Rebel horsemen were within 400 yards of us as the first gun was fired ; the projectile, a round-shot, hit the horse of the leader, killing it, the rider and horse turning a somersault. This caused a delay. Three or four men jumping off their horses, picked up their leader, who was a man of note. The second round was high, but the third and fourth shot found the target,

---

[1] It is said he saved Sir William Gordon's life at Balaklava by shooting a Russian officer who attacked Gordon when he was helpless from wounds.

causing the line to halt, and now to my intense relief I saw coming through the village the leading camels.

Riding up to the first man, I said, "Jump off." The kilted Highlander had come 150 miles on a baggage-camel with rough paces, and had lost skin; his feelings caused him to border on the insubordinate, as he replied, "Na, na; I winna brak ma neck." It was no time to argue, and jumping off my horse I pulled at the nose string of the camel and brought him down, and the Highlander then slid off, quickly followed by others, and in much less time than it takes to tell the story, a dozen men were standing on each side of the guns. While I was forming them up, we heard a cheer, and saw the Squadron 17th Lancers, divided into two troops, with about half a mile interval, bring their lances down, as they galloped at the enemy, who, demoralised by our Artillery fire, turned and fled. So far as I recollect, we had only one man speared.

We moved on after the Rebels, for we had seen nothing of their treasure, which we wanted less for our pockets than to break up their Force, realising that when Tantia could no longer pay his men handsomely they would disperse. We had gone 10 miles from Barode when on approaching a low range of hills we came on hard soil and lost the trail (pag). I asked the General if he would follow the track while I rode to a village in a gap in the hills half a mile to our left for information, and I trotted off, followed by an orderly of the 17th Lancers, while the column proceeded at a walk. Just before I reached the village I came to some sandy soil, and tracing without difficulty camels and elephants, sent the orderly back to ask the General to turn the column.

I saw the chief man of the village and asked him for chupattis (bread), as I had had nothing to eat since a scanty meal on the previous evening. I did not at first realise I had shut my eyes, but when I looked at my watch I found I had been asleep for half an hour, sitting alongside my horse. Most of the people were on a high hill which overlooked the village, and shouting to them, I asked which way the English Force had gone. They replied it had followed the main track, outside the range of hills which formed a basin, at one entrance of which their village stood. I asked if I could save distance by riding across the valley to another pass which I could see a mile on, and they answered in the affirmative. Mounting, I rode on, followed by a horsekeeper of the Artillery, who was riding bareback on a horse which was too exhausted for draught.

We had gone a few hundred yards, when a man came from behind a hut, so neatly dressed as to make me think he was one of the Bombay Native Infantry, some of whom were following us, but 60 miles in the Rear. I approached him to ask how he got up, when he came to "the charge," and I then saw he was one of the rebels. I was about to attack him, as the horsekeeper shouted to me, "Enemy's Cavalry in front," and looking ahead I saw a Squadron of the Gwáliár Contingent coming through the pass for which I was making. I reflected that if the man fired, and missed me, the Squadron would catch me, unless indeed our column was close behind it, and so saying to the Rebel, "Not just now," as he went into a hut, I rode on, with much anxiety as to whether the Squadron I saw, which was crossing my front without regarding me, was the first or last of the Rebel Cavalry in the pass, where, however, I met the Advance guard of the 17th Lancers. The General after some discussion decided he would return to Barode, where we arrived at five o'clock on the evening of the 1st January, having marched—if direct distances from village to village only are counted—171 miles since the morning of the 27th.

When I had obtained a guide to lead the column by the nearest track to Barode, taking an orderly I went off to look for the Sepoy whom I had not ventured to fight half an hour earlier. I found the hut without difficulty in which he had disappeared, and having dismounted, approached, feeling sorry I had come, when I saw that I had to go down on my knees to get through the door, and was considerably relieved when I found the place empty.

CHAPTER XIV

1859—THE END OF THE MUTINY

Passive disloyalty of many Central India chiefs—A record in pig-sticking—Eighty hours' work without sleep—The rebels exhausted by fatigue give in—Field Forces are broken up.

WE halted till the 4th January at Barode, and then moved in a north-westerly direction to Chuppra, where our baggage column rejoined us on the 9th, to our great comfort; for we had not changed our underclothing since the 25th December, bivouacing with what we carried on our saddles. A great number of camels had broken down, and some had died, being unable to support the fatigue of the forced marches we were making. Commanding officers were vexed with me because I always had a small string of camels following us without loads, which they regarded as a waste of power, not realising that when they were once distributed to Corps I had no means of bringing along ammunition should any of the camels carrying it become non-effective.

As we were passing through Sarthal, two Lancers who were employed by me for Intelligence purposes caught a man hiding behind a hut, and took off him an order written by an agent of the Jalra Patan Rajah, commanding certain villages to have ammunition and stores collected for Tantia's forces. The bearer of the letter was sentenced to be shot, but I obtained a reprieve for him, being anxious to punish the writer of the order. On arriving at Chuppra, I arrested and placed him in charge of the chief of the town, who undertook to be responsible for him. That evening I had a visit from another Jalra Patan official, who offered me a thousand rupees to give up the letter. He left the tent quicker than he entered it; but the Brigadier, to whom I reported the circumstance, would not sanction my request to have it made known that the letter-writer was in a waggon, under a Horse Artillery sentry, and I suffered in consequence of my General's decision; for that night, in spite of my precaution in having a servant to sleep in the doorway of the tent, it was rifled of all its valuable contents, including my medals, uniform, etc. The two tin clothes-boxes in which they were packed were found 200 yards from the tent, as were some articles of uniform, but the medals I never recovered. When the official was tried at Ajmír, he escaped punishment, the Political officer averring that nearly all the Minor States in Central India assisted the rebels as far as they could without getting into trouble with the Paramount Power.

General Michel rejoined us on the 12th, and I was appointed Brigade-Major. This did not give me any more work, but the day on which he arrived I had particularly heavy cases as Bazaar Master, and I should have become ill had not the General, noticing my face, and with many kind words, relieved me of those duties, which indeed were sufficient for a man who had nothing else to do. The General never tired of doing me a kindness, and years after it was the subject of a joke between us, that a mixture of croton oil, red pepper, and something else, he had prescribed for toothache, had burnt a hole in my cheek. We found the alternations of cold and heat trying, generally marching at 2 a.m. The thermometer was low at night and the sun scorching at midday, and my baggage-camels dying after a long march in September, I had lived since that time in a small single roof tent intended for Natives.

In the third week in January we moved to Kotá, on the Chambal River. The city stands on a sandy plain of bare sandstone slabs, with intervening rain holes, and some scrub jungle of camel thorn; but close to it there are magnificent gardens with trees of many varieties, ranging from bamboos to the leafy mangos. Near a large lake there was a beautiful residence, but I was more interested in the citadel, going there as soon as I had encamped the troops, to look at the place where the commander of the rebels met his dramatic death after the capture of the city in 1858. He with a few desperate men had retreated to the upper walls of the citadel, and the chief sat quietly on his horse till the leading files of the Seaforth Highlanders ran at him with levelled bayonets, when, putting his horse at the low parapet wall, it jumped, and man and horse fell a lifeless mass on the rocks 56 feet below.

While at Kotá I had my first day's pig-sticking, which is undoubtedly the most exciting of all sport, both from its danger of falls, omitting that of the tusks of the boar, and because, as in a steeplechase, only one man can win, he who first strikes the pig. Kotá was celebrated for the amount of game close in to the city, and on the 24th January, having procured beaters, half a dozen of us rode out before daylight to the nearest covert, $2\frac{1}{2}$ miles from the city walls. The beaters were scarcely in when up jumped a sow and eight or nine small pigs, and we had some difficulty in preventing the more excitable sportsmen from pursuing them. I was on the left of the horsemen when I saw, 400 yards away, a dozen black objects which in the dim light I took for buffalo, and was afraid to speak; but the sun was just rising at the moment, and I then saw that they were pigs, and shouting rode for the biggest boar of the sounder.[1] The pig ran from the left to the right of the line, and Sir William Gordon, riding as he only could, cut in, and would have got the first spear but that the pig escaped into a nulla covered with small trees, and we failed to find him again. I knew I could find the others, however, and guided the party back. We had three short runs, but the pigs all got back into the jungle, and we then adjourned to breakfast in a garden of the Rajah's close at hand, sitting under orange trees bearing ripe fruit. After breakfast we remounted. I had sent my horse back to camp, and was on a big Native pony. The beaters put out three pigs, but the sportsman "rode them" too soon, and all three turned back into the thick jungle. After another similar mistake, Sir William Gordon made the party promise to be more patient. When the beaters went in again, in a few minutes about thirty pigs broke covert and separated, as did our party. Sir William Gordon got first spear of those who rode with him, while Major Lewis Knight had alone followed a pig, and killed it.

[1] Herd.

This success made him very keen for another hunt, and he came into my tent late at night, for when I got back to camp I had to make up the day's work, and offered to mount me next day if I would arrange another beat. I replied I had no horse available, and I did not care to ride another man's horse on such rough ground; but on Knight's explaining that the offer of a mount was not for my pleasure but for his own, since he could not work the beaters without my help, I accepted the mount on his £200 horse, being told "to ride it out" as if it were my own.

I got very little sleep that night, as the Artillery and heavy baggage were moving off at 3 a.m. to cross the Chambal River, and I had to hand over the guide, and to see them off. I came back after doing so, and had an hour's sleep till 5.30 a.m., when I got up to do some brigade work before we went out at nine o'clock.

From what I had seen the previous day, I put the men in so as to get the pigs out on the soundest ground. We waited with breathless anticipation, I especially, since it was only my third day of pig-sticking, and I had never before managed a hunt. In a few minutes the beaters began to shout, and out came a big black buck, followed by a number of hares, two jackals, and then amidst a herd of deer there came a pig. I called to my companions, and drove the pig clear of a nulla, sending him towards Knight, who galloping fast was unable to turn when the pig did, and he escaped in some broken ground. He was apparently lost, and when I sent the beaters over the line they saw no signs of him. Looking round at the moment, I viewed the pig rather more than a quarter of a mile off, only just showing as a black speck, and calling to my friend we rode. Knight coming up to me, told me he would like to see his horse extended, so I gratified him, and we pushed the pig for about three-quarters of a mile, when the other two sportsmen cut in, and one of them got first spear, although Knight and I had done all the galloping.

The pig having sat down, I rode slowly up, thinking he was mortally wounded; but as I approached he rose and charged exactly at my horse's chest. I lowered my spear, which caught the pig on the nose, sending him over backwards and cracking the spear. As we were despatching the animal, the beaters brought on by the horsekeepers crossed the plain in line, and drove before them a large sounder, nearly as many as came out the first time. I mounted, straightened my spear as well as I could, and followed a boar beyond the covert from which he had originally come. I passed the other three sportsmen who were following a pig, and my own horsekeeper, but my tongue was so dry I could not ask for help, and though close behind the boar, from exhaustion could not kill it. The boar was equally exhausted, and disregarded men working in a field who threw stones at him. Eventually he stopped in a dry ravine, whence he charged me. I was obliged to turn and gallop to save the horse, for my spear was no longer reliable. The boar then made for a watercourse, with overhanging steep banks, down which he slid, and swam across. I dismounted, and ascending the far bank, saw the pig lie down in a run covered with bushes. My companions had now followed me, and getting one of them to stand in the watercourse, and holding the spear by the shaft-head, I struck the boar. He turned and charged my companion, and Lewis Knight killed it. This must be a record: five pigs in an hour and a half, amongst four sportsmen.

From Kotá, making short marches, we followed our General, who had ridden on to Nasírábád, being uncertain where Tantia Topi had gone, the last reports locating him as 150 miles north-west of Ajmír. While we were encamped at Shaporah I saw in a Political officer's tent an essay on "How to Watch the Passes of the Aravalli Range," and copied it, without anticipating, however, how useful it would become. We were encamped at Musooda, a small town 25 miles south-west of Nasírábád, on the night of the 12th–13th February, when we received a letter from the General, stating that Tantia being unable to subsist his followers in the Bikaneer District was moving southwards on the western side of the Aravalli Range, and that General Somerset was to make a forced march of 40 miles at least, and endeavour to block the passes. Our only information of the passes was the paper I had fortuitously copied. It was impossible for us to march 40 miles carrying the kit we had with us, and as we could not rearrange it at night, in order to save time we marched immediately for Ramghur. There we spent several hours in selecting the best camels, and having loaded up two days' grain and fifteen days' groceries, we started again, and marched not only 40 miles, but day and night, for nine days. The Force consisted of 4 Squadrons 17th Lancers, 2 weak Squadrons of the Bombay Cavalry, D Battery Royal Horse Artillery, 130 men of the 92nd Highlanders, and 140 of the 4th Bombay Rifles on camels. I have now before me the hours of our marching off and coming into camp, and after an experience of forty-six years I think that no one in South Africa or elsewhere ever sat longer hours in the saddle than did our men. We knew, however, less of mounted soldiers' work, and performed even the longest marches at a walk, covering only 4 miles in the hour.

I never underwent such continuous fatigue, and lost the holding power of my legs after being for 80 hours without sleep. On the 15th February we marched from 6.30 a.m. to 11.30 a.m., and I was occupied till we marched again at 4 p.m. sending out spies, of whom I had a continuous succession coming and going. The price paid to each man averaged 6 rupees, and while we were riding down on the east side of the range of mountains I spent 113, which involved a great deal of conversation, and effectually prevented my lying down to rest. When we got on to our ground at 10.30 p.m. on the 16th, I had to interview men who arrived with information, and just as I was about to lie down, a post rider arrived with the English mail. I could, no doubt, have got a non-commissioned officer from the 17th Lancers to assist me; but every man, including those who were supposed to be sentries, was asleep by the bivouac fires, and so I went on sorting until 2 a.m., when I had the "Rouse" sounded, and at 3 a.m. we were again travelling. The order of march was slightly varied daily, but was simple. One hour after the "Rouse," the column passed by the Brigade-Major's torch-bearer; there the Advance Guard picked up the guide, and so nobody but the General and I knew where we were going, and treachery was impossible, even if the camp followers had not been too tired to think of it. We marched till 1.30 p.m. that day, and then, having travelled 30 miles, halted to let the men cook, and also because I was uncertain in which direction the enemy had gone.

We got this information about 6 p.m., and at 8 p.m. were making for a village 32 miles distant. I had seen the Column off without mounting, my bivouac being on the track, and as I was tired told the horsekeeper to put me up in the saddle. He put me over, on to the ground the far side, and grumbling at him I told him to come round the off side, and put me up; he did, with a similar result, and then I discovered I had no power in my legs. Calling to an elephant-keeper, I bade him make the elephant sit down, and hand me a rope, up which I was hauled, and stretching out on its load, a hospital tent, I followed the Column, awaking only when the elephant passing under trees brushed my face against the boughs. My horsekeeper had walked close behind the elephant, and at 4 a.m., mounting my horse, I cantered up to the head of the Column, receiving very grumpy answers to my cheery " Good-morning," uttered as I cantered past the Squadrons. When we halted for breakfast, I asked a friend why they were all so cross at 4 a.m., and received the naïve answer, " Because your voice was so cheerful."

We had nearly arrived at the limit of human endurance. Many officers had straps sewn on to the front of the saddle, by fixing their wrists in which they were able to sleep when on the march; but I counted three Lancers on the ground at one time, who had tumbled off while asleep. The horses became so leg-weary that they would lie down before they were picketed on the lines, and many refused to eat. The Australian Squadron horses showed least endurance; then the Cape Squadron; the Arab Squadron outlasted all others. I saw " The Pig " lie down one day as I dismounted, but he ate his food greedily, without offering to rise.

The rebels got through the range of mountains, and we missed them by an unfortunate circumstance. We had actually marched off for Kankroli, when a horseman arrived from an officer who was at Amet, with two companies of a local battalion, stating that the Rebels were close to him, and that the town people were openly hostile. We made a detour of 10 miles, and found the enemy had never been within 6 miles of the place, and later we learnt if we had gone to Kankroli we should have arrived there at the same time as the Rao Sahib, for Tantia at that time was not with his troops.

On the 23rd, when we were within 10 miles of the Banswara jungle, some Rebels whose horses' feet were worn to the quick, and others who were so exhausted as to be unable to sit in the saddle, submitted. Ordinarily, we shot everyone, but I begged the General to try the experiment of not shooting them, and two or three days later Jaroor Ali, the Chief of the fighting men escorting Firoz Shah, asked to surrender. We should have got all of them in, but that columns were brought in to surround them, and the Prince, fearing treachery, moved on. We marched up to the north of Bundi, and then turned southwards again, still chasing the men, who would have come in if we had been more patient, till on the 4th February we were again on the Chambal, near Chenwassa. Here I got another sharp touch of fever. I had marched for 3000 miles in Central India since the end of August, and my blood was in so bad a state that the slightest cut on my hands festered. We moved to Biora, and encamped on a spot where we had halted on the 15th September in the previous year, and then after some fruitless marches between Pachor and Biora, looking for reported rebels, we finally received an order to break up the Force;[1] the 17th Lancers being ordered to Gwáliár.

The General had gone back to Máu, whence he wrote asking for my Record previous to coming under his command. Later I heard that he was trying to obtain for me the Victoria Cross for the episode at Sindwaha, but had some difficulty, however, on account of his having irritated the officer who made the favourable report on me; for the day after the action a Divisional Order was issued, pointing out that "Cavalry is not justified in pursuing a beaten enemy in dressed lines at the walk." The officer now declined to move in the matter.

[1] Extracts from a Report by General Somerset, to Assistant Adjutant-General :—

"CAMP, PUCHORE, 15*th April* 1859.

". . . my Brigade-Major, Lieutenant Wood, 17th Lancers, with whose previous services and conspicuous gallantry in action, the Major-General is already acquainted, . . . as my only Staff officer he has shown the most unvaried zeal, particularly on occasions of rapid pursuit of the enemy, when his position did not admit of his taking advantage of the few short hours others had for rest."

I only heard of this long afterwards, for Sir John Michel[1] never told me when I stayed with him; also that he had applied for my name to be noted for a Brevet as soon as I became a Captain; but the application was returned, noted, that "His Royal Highness the Commander-in-Chief always declined to promise promotion in advance."

After we started for our Station we were twice recalled, when rebels crossed the main road from Máu to the north. They were no longer organised bodies, but bands varying in numbers from time to time infested the jungle country of Narsinghar and Sironj till 1860. When at last allowed to proceed towards Gwáliár, we marched by the regular stages, till an order was received to hasten as much as possible. A battalion of the East India Company Army at Morar had become so insubordinate as to cause apprehension of mutiny, and there was grave misconduct in Bengal. The men had not been asked, but were transferred with the Native Army to the Crown, by Act of Parliament, and many European soldiers flatly refused to serve on, demanding re-engagement, and bounties. Eventually they gained the first point, and those who stood out for the bounty were discharged. More consideration would have prevented any difficulty arising, but the idea of the Rank and File that the Queen's Regiments would refuse to act against them was, I believe, unfounded; and certainly it was so in the 17th Lancers, as anyone could learn from the language of the men when making forced marches in May. The trouble at Morar happily subsided when the Government admitted its mistake, and we eventually got into Barracks on the 15th May.

Three weeks later I was warned for duty at Kirki, 690 miles to the south, where I was to receive, mount, equip and train a large draft of Recruits from England, who were to march up to Gwáliár after the Monsoon. I was unwilling to go, for my horses had marched continuously for 342 days; moreover, I was happy in the Regiment, although my pay had dropped from £80 to £36, 10s. per mensem, and I enjoyed the friendship of Sir William Gordon, from whom a horse-lover could learn something daily. Both he and Major White being in advance of their time in liberality of mind, wished

[1] He had got the K.C.B. for his services in Central India.

to prevent my paying for wine I did not drink at Mess, but I declined to lend myself to any request for an alteration of the system, as the Colonel had refused a similar suggestion made by Major White without my knowledge when we were at Kirki. The Colonel himself was acting on principle, and was personally kind to me, and, influenced I think by Captain Duncan the Adjutant, sent for me before I left Morar and asked me if I would like to be Adjutant on my return. I replied, " I thought you were going to give it to the Sergeant-Major," and he said, " No, I shall give it to the man I think will do the Regiment best, and I advise you to work up for it, if you wish to have the appointment."

CHAPTER XV

1859—BEATSON'S HORSE

Tantia Topi executed — I rejoin 17th Lancers and am sent to Poona to train recruits—Sir John Michel at Máu—Am sent to Beatson's Horse at Árangábád—Novel cure for scorpion bite—General Beatson—I qualify as Interpreter—Ordered to Bersia—Tiger-hunt on foot—Irregular Cavalry.

WHILE we were halted at Biora, another Squadron of the Regiment farther north made two forced marches, being ordered to attend the execution of Tantia Topi, who had been given into the hands of our Political agent at Sipri, Major Meade, under the following circumstances. Maun Singh, a vassal of Scindia, quarrelled with his overlord some time previous to the Mutiny and was outlawed by him, but being too powerful on account of his fighting retinue, and the difficult country over which he ruled, to be suppressed, had never been seriously molested.

Tantia Topi in passing through Maun Singh's country invited him to join him, and on his refusal imprisoned the Rajah. Maun Singh escaped, and in April of the following year, when Tantia sought an asylum in the Rajah's territory, Maun Singh, after some deliberation, sent to Major Meade at Sipri and offered to give up the fugitive. Tantia became suspicious of Maun Singh's intentions, and left the Rajah, who, however, decoyed him back, and when he was asleep had him surrounded by Native soldiers sent by Major Meade. When Tantia awoke, perceiving the trap into which he had fallen, he said, "What sort of friendship is this?" The Rajah answered, "I have never considered you as a friend." Tantia was hanged under painful circumstances, his executioners being without experience.

My servants engaged at Kirki the night before we left, at the end of May 1858, had gone home just before I received the order to proceed there, and I had been obliged to obtain a fresh set in Gwáliár. I had no difficulty in obtaining good men, because, although my servants were "Strangers in the land," yet such is the freemasonry in the class in all countries, no sooner had I told them they could leave me and go home on their finding substitutes, than such were produced. Nevertheless, I must admit that I had some misgivings when I handed over my horses to men I had only known for a fortnight. They were to lead them about 700 miles to Poona, where I, starting a few days later in the Bullock train, hoped to arrive in twenty days.

I left Morar on the evening of the 29th May, and early next morning breakfasted 40 miles south of Scindia's capital. I found Maun Singh, who had given Tantia into our hands, living for a few days in a temple immediately opposite to where I halted. He came over to see me, and after the usual compliments, showing me his rifles, of which he was proud, invited me to try a shot with a Westly Richards. Now I had not used a rifle since I left the Crimea, and being unwilling to discredit the shooting powers of the British officer, I hesitated, until Maun Singh said to me bluntly, "Do not be afraid. I am not an ordinary Native; it is not overloaded." I was then in the dilemma of either appearing afraid or of showing myself a bad shot, and accepted the latter alternative. Taking the rifle from the Rajah, I looked around for some object which I might miss without discredit. The head of a squirrel was showing over a stone 50 yards distant, and throwing the rifle to my shoulder, I immediately pulled the trigger. The Natives shouted, and one of them running up, held in the air the body of the squirrel, the head of which had been decapitated by the bullet, as if cut with a knife. I declined the Rajah's suggestion to have another shot.

I stayed in a temple next night at Goona. The Commanding officer and acting Political agent, Major Mayne, offering me hospitality, gave me an escort as far as Biora for myself and horses, which I had just overtaken. This was the more acceptable as two Eurasians had been killed by rebels three days earlier. We reached Pachor without further incident, but 8 miles south of it encountered a deluge of rain with a strong wind from the south, which our oxen declined to face, and the bullock cart carrying a sergeant, 17th Lancers, detailed as a Drill Instructor to help me, going off the track, upset in a nulla. Pulling off all my clothes except my shirt, I walked back, and after considerable manual labour succeeded in extricating the sergeant and his conveyance. I overheard the Natives talking in the night, and the observation made by one throws a curious light on our rule in India at the time. The speaker mentioning with approbation my efforts in extricating the non-commissioned officer's cart, added, " and the Sahib never beat one of us."

I reached Máu late on the 11th June, and calling soon after daylight on the General, Sir John Michel, learnt I had been appointed Brigade-Major of Beatson's Horse, the Headquarters of which were moving to Árangábád, where I was to join my new Chief; so I waited until the 18th for my horses, staying with Sir John until they arrived. He was kindness personified. A man of mental and bodily vigour, having been at the Senior Department, Sandhurst, he was educated to a higher degree than were most officers in the Army. When I was at Máu I found him engaged one afternoon after luncheon trying to teach Mathematics to two of his Staff, and it was pathetic to see his eager face fall with disappointment when he saw their drowsy heads sink on the table.

I had been unwell ever since I had left Gwáliár, troubled with intestinal complaints and indigestion, which I did not shake off till the end of July. Nevertheless, I travelled at the rate of 25 miles a day, and arrived at Árangábád without further incident. I witnessed, however, a curious instance of " One pain is lessened by another's anguish." When settling down in a village for the night, one of the grooms uttered a piercing shriek, having been bitten by a big scorpion. I was perturbed by the man's agony, and inquired if there was any doctor within reach. The Head man said, " No; but there is an old woman who can treat the groom." I summoned her, and she said she could without doubt alleviate the man's sufferings, if I gave her a piece of tobacco. This was simple, for I had only to buy it of the other grooms; and my aged visitor sitting down, proceeded to chew an enormous lump of the strongest tobacco of the country. Under her direction the man was held down, and then the practitioner sat astride on his chest, and with considerable force opened one of the patient's eyes, into which she ejected a volume of tobacco saliva. The sufferer gave a yell, then jumped up, and avowing he was quite well, proceeded to cook his supper.

I arrived at Árangábád after some long stages, and reported myself to Colonel Beatson, the Commander of Beatson's Irregular Horse, which was for all purposes, except serious cases of discipline, under the Viceroy. He was fifty-five years of age, and had entered the Service in 1820, when sixteen. He had a handsome face, was 5 feet 7 inches in height, weighing 14 stone. He was a man of remarkable energy, always riding an hour before daylight. He was not particular about uniform, but insisted on a sword being always worn, and went so far in being ready for service as to ride daily with a supply of groceries in his wallets. He worked all the forenoon, and dined at two o'clock, riding again between four and five, had some tea at seven, and went to bed at nine o'clock.

I had marched over 30 miles when I reported my arrival, but he desired me to accompany him for a ride in the afternoon. Accepting the order cheerfully, I asked him to lend me a horse; this he did for two days, but on the morning of the second day I rode one of his horses so eagerly in chasing a deer, that he was not so willing later to mount me. The General was busily engaged in preparing for a civil action he had brought against Mr. Skene, a Consul, to prosecute which he proceeded to London three months later.

The General ordered me—for though put as an invitation it was practically an order—to come and live with him, stating he lived "Camp fashion,"[1] and our fare would be plain. Plain it was, but this did not disturb me so much as the want of refinement. He had lived in great discomfort, with iron cups and metal plates, which were seldom washed. I nevertheless soon got to like my Chief, admiring his boundless energy, and my butler improved the serving of our meals.

I rode down to Poona from Árangábád in September.

---

[1] "Camp fashion Mess" implies that each member brings his own stool, plates, cutlery, and drinking mug.

The Colonel followed me about a week later on his way to Europe, and I spent the next two months at Poona and Bombay preparing for my examination. I overtaxed my strength in endeavouring to read seven hours daily with Moonshees, and five to seven hours by myself. A Doctor insisted on my doing less, but I was young and foolish, and as a result, on the 3rd October, when at Bombay, I awoke with severe pain in my ears, which continued for a week, leaving me so deaf that I had difficulty in hearing the Examiner dictating Hindustani.

I was better on the 15th, when the colloquial examination was held, and therein I reaped the advantage of the continuous practice I had had in the twelve months since leaving Kirki. I was naturally fluent, and as I took up for the examination 2000 words, had an unusual vocabulary at my command, and passed the examination for Interpreter without difficulty, at a cost of from £180 to £200. I rode back to my Station with renewed health, the deafness passing away when I ceased to overtax my strength.

I remained at Árangábád three days, employed in packing the Brigade office papers, and then started to join the Officer commanding the 1st Regiment, who was now in command of the Brigade. From Árangábád to Bersia, where I arrived on the 10th November, I averaged just over 20 miles for eighteen days; but my servants were very footsore, and my horses' legs gave evidence of the constant work they had done for fifteen months. On the 13th the Commandant and I went out to Sindhara, where, dividing our troops, consisting of 200 Cavalry and 150 Infantry,[1] into three parties, we made a circuit simultaneously in hopes of catching Adil Muhamad Khan.

Firoz Shah and the Rao Sahib, although in the neighbourhood, were no longer accounted fighting men. The small bands of rebels were acting as did Robin Hood, plundering the well-to-do and sparing poor people, and thus had friends in every village. We concentrated on the 20th November at Shamsabad, where on the previous evening a tiger had carried off a boy from the village. The Commandant and I went out next morning after breakfast. He was well equipped

[1] Baréli Police.

with two rifles and a gun; I had only a shot-gun, Major Tremayne's present, which I loaded with bullets.

Two of the villagers conducting us to a ravine, said, "Now there are two places where this tiger always comes out— here, and another farther on, near some water." The Commandant stood at the first place, where there was a clear field of fire, while the villager, with a confidence I could not share, placed me in dense jungle on a narrow path, two feet wide, bordered by grass as high as our heads, observing, "We will stand here, for it is almost certain the tiger will come along the path." I climbed a tree, and insisted on the villager doing the same; but the covert was drawn blank.

In the second drive, the Commandant stood 5 yards from the head of the ravine, and I felt obliged to stand alongside of him. When he tried for a tiger in the same place some months earlier, he missed his first shot, and in turning to the Native who had his second rifle, he saw him running with his companions. The Commandant stood firm, and looked at the tiger, which, bounding past him, seized one of the flying Natives and literally bit off his head.

I personally was not disappointed that no tiger came out of the ravine; but one of the Natives, with a misplaced confidence in my skill, attracted I believe by my fluency in the language, was anxious for my success, and for the third drive took me on my hands and knees for 100 yards into the jungle, close to a shallow pond, but to my intense relief of mind the tiger broke back.

While we were hunting for rebels and tigers, I received an offer to raise a Regiment of Irregular Cavalry, under the orders of Major H. O. Mayne, and by the same post a note from Sir John Michel directing me not to leave Bersia until further orders. Some days later, on our return to Bersia, the post brought the Army Order dissolving the Brigade, and the Commandant a confidential letter reverting him to his Regiment, and directing him to hand over the command temporarily to me. I never heard the details of the case, culminating in a Court of Inquiry held while I was at Bombay, in which he had incurred the displeasure of the Commander-in-Chief and the Viceroy, but I gathered that his intentions were laudable, and that he had done the right thing, but in the wrong way, in preferring charges against officers which he could not substantiate.

He left on the 1st December, handing me over the command of 535 men and 542 horses, with a Government debt of £25,000, and a large approved debt to the Regimental banker, it being the custom for the Commanding officer to initial the promissory notes of the men who borrowed money, as an indication that they would, while the soldier was serving, assist the banker in recovering the sums due.

The banker financed the Chunda, or Horse Regimental Insurance Fund, which being £500 in debt, and with an increasing liability, paid him 5 per cent. interest. The banker was an important personage in the Regiment, and until the Commandant left on the 1st December, the portly Brahman when riding out of an afternoon was escorted by a guard of honour. He sent monthly for the Regimental pay to Sehore, a distance of 35 miles, charging a percentage of 1.32 on all Ranks, *i.e.* taking 6d. out of the Privates' 16s. monthly stipend. Ten days after assuming command, I abolished his escort, and announced my intention of sending the Government camels to Sehore, under a guard, for the money. The Adjutant, who was older than myself, warned me that I should be held personally responsible for any loss; but I did not agree, if the proper precaution of having a sufficient guard was taken, and from that time forthwith the soldier got all to which he was entitled.

The theory of the Irregular Horse system before the Mutiny was simple. The Government paid 50s. monthly for a trained, armed, mounted soldier, without incurring any further liability for the man, horse, their equipment, or food. There were two plans: one in which the soldier owned and rode his own horse, which was obviously effective only in peace-time, unless the soldier had ample private means. The usual plan was for the Native officers to own a certain number of horses, generally varying with their Rank; but in Beatson's Horse there were Lieutenants with more horses than had certain Captains. The most incompetent officer owned forty-five, and some sergeants had four, which was in many ways convenient, as affording sufficient margin of profit in ordinary circumstances, and enabling the non-commissioned officer with his section to be detached on duty. Such detachments might enrich or ruin the owner of the horses, for, owing to the difficulties of transport in the roadless country in which we were stationed, the price of gram, a horse's ordinary food, varied at the outposts from 40 to 160 lbs. to the rupee.[1]

In nearly all Regiments, except where the riders were relatives of the horse-owners, the former got 16s., and the latter 34s., for each horse. Under this arrangement, in most parts of the country during peace the sum paid by Government (£2, 10s.) enabled the owner and rider to live, and maintain his equipment in fair order, and support a wife. It also enabled the horse-owner to keep a man acting as groom and grass-cutter for two horses, and yet to make a profit, after paying all charges, including 24s. per annum towards a Horse Insurance Fund, from which in case of loss not attributable to negligence, he received compensation varying from one-half to three-quarters of the average cost price of horses in the Regiment.

When Colonel W. F. Beatson received permission in 1857 to raise 1000 Irregular Horse, he undertook, with an imprest on account, to put them into the Field within six months. This was approved, but it was not anticipated to what the advance would amount. The Colonel allowed £40 for many of the horses, and £10 outfit for each rider, to be repaid by monthly instalments of 4 rupees and 1 rupee respectively, thus encumbering the Regiment with a crushing debt from which it could never recover. This, however, was not the full extent of the evil; for though the advances were given generally to men of position, later the proprietary, or right of owning a horse, was in some cases transferred to men of straw, and thus the Government lost security for their money.

The Regiment had been raised in a hurry, and showed all the imperfections due to haste. Many of the Native officers had served as non-commissioned officers; some of the non-commissioned officers had served as Privates in the Haidarábád Contingent. Others had been recruited from the Irregular Levies of the numerous minor potentates of Central India.

---

[1] The calculations are given in sterling, but at that period the rupee was worth a penny more than its face value.

The Native officers were generally illiterate,[1] and even the better educated were under the impression that in the mixing of Hindustani and English words in command, the latter were Persian.

In each troop there was a sergeant who could read and write, and he kept such accounts as there were, showing how much had been repaid to Government; for the monthly instalments had been suspended while the Regiment was on Field Service. These men, however, like many uneducated men, had marvellous memories, and it was from them I adjusted and made out the accounts of the Regiment, of which there were none previously in existence, showing to whom the £25,000 advanced to the Regiment in two years had been paid. The greater number of all Ranks were Mussulmen, but there was one troop of Hindoos, in which a sergeant named Burmadeen Singh was the ruling spirit, having much more influence than the Native officers. He was a fine athletic man, but like most of his race, not a horseman; he was twenty-five years of age, and had lived according to the strictest letter of the Brahminical law, a life of absolute purity, without tasting meat. The majority of the men were poor riders, and the Regiment as such was undrilled. I never wished to see Irregular Cavalry drilled with the precision of British or Continental Cavalry, but these men were unable to advance 20 yards in a line, or wheel to the right or left without jostling each other. I adopted Rank Entire or Single Rank, as advocated by the Duke of Wellington after Waterloo for all Cavalry.

Although there was little Military knowledge in the Corps, some of the men came from warlike races, and from 1 to 1½ Squadrons might have been selected out of the 535 who, as Irregulars, would have been fairly efficient. Nevertheless, my difficulties were great, chiefly owing to the want of education, and the consequent want of intelligence, of those whom I had to instruct. My new command was intensely interesting: for fifteen days I spent all my time from daylight to dusk in the

---

[1] Some weeks after assuming command, when presiding at a Native Court Martial, my colleagues gravely sentenced a forger to be imprisoned for a long period, and to have his nose slit. I had much difficulty in persuading them to omit the sentence of mutilation.

Horse Lines, where out of a total of 542 horses 80 were sick. There were 20 sore backs, many severe cases of mange, 4 of farcy and 9 of glanders, none of which were separated from the effective horses. Indeed, so ignorant were all in the Regiment, that the Adjutant thought it his duty to tell me that the owners of the infected horses objected to having them separated. This was done, however, and within forty-eight hours I found the officer [1] who owned 45 horses was deliberately starving 4 of the glandered horses. Their market value if sound was something under £15 a horse, and he would have got from the Insurance Fund £20 for each, if it should die. I checked this inhuman practice by striking them off the Insurance Fund.

The premium to the Fund was based on the assumption that 40 to 50 horses would become non-effective annually, and that the owners were to be allowed £15 on each. A short calculation will show that even this sum was not financially sound, but when I assumed charge the horse-owners received £20 for each non-effective horse, and 4 died in the first week of my command. Every owner of 2 horses was supposed to have a groom who was also a grass-cutter, and whose duties cutting grass occupied him at least six hours a day; but some of the more careless owners had not replaced the grooms, who for various reasons had become non-effective, and in consequence but few horses were properly cleaned. At (durbar) or orderly-room, I pointed out the impossibility of the horses remaining healthy unless they were properly groomed, and on being met by the objection that it would be derogatory to a warrior to clean his horse, I replied that I would take off my coat in the Horse Lines and thoroughly groom a horse, that I insisted on every horse being cleaned either by a groom or by the soldier who rode him; and that evening, having done an hour's hard work, when I replaced my turban and coat, I said plainly that dismissal would be the fate of any soldier who declined to follow my example. After this I had no more trouble on that point.

I daily regretted my want of knowledge of the Veterinary art, but by dint of hard work and diligent study of *Youat on*

[1] He commanded a troop, but could not ride without holding on, having spent his life manufacturing puggarees.

the Horse, and *Miles on the Horse's Feet*, aided by the Doctor, who compounded medicines, the non-effective list was reduced to 48 in the course of three weeks.

The Second in command was away on sick leave, so the only European officers were the Adjutant, who came from an Infantry Regiment, and the Doctor. The Adjutant, three or four years older than myself, was short-sighted, a fair rider, without any love for horses, but an excellent office man. He was a born accountant, never tired of figures, and preferred being at such work to spending his time in the saddle or amongst the men.

John Henry Sylvester, the Doctor, was a man of unusual ability, and had carried off all the prizes in all subjects at the end of his school career. He had made a considerable sum of money when at Bombay by practice amongst wealthy Natives, but disliked his profession, and would have made a good Cavalry officer.

During the Court of Inquiry, he and the Adjutant, having taken opposite sides, were not when I took command on speaking terms, and consequently I had trouble in inducing them to exchange even a word at meals, which was the only time at which they met. I succeeded gradually, mainly by so placing bread on the table as to oblige them to ask each other and not me for it. Bread was a luxury for which we sent to Sehore, a distance of 35 miles, at the cost of a shilling for each journey.

When my brother-officers were on better terms, I persuaded them to accompany me to look for a hare, in some broken ground close to our lines. Unfortunately, the Adjutant being on low ground, and without his spectacles, saw above him what he took to be a hare, but was the fawn-coloured puggaree of the Doctor's helmet; I was at some little distance, but realising when he raised his gun what was about to happen, I shouted, though too late, and Sylvester's helmet was struck heavily, one or two pellets lodging in his neck. This accident retarded the reconciliation.

Two days later, getting news of rebels, I rode to Sindhara, and starting at 1 a.m. with 20 men from that outpost, searched but unsuccessfully for the band, and was back for dinner next day, having covered 62 miles in 26 hours. Fifteen days' hard work followed, during which time, fond as I was of riding, I only once got into the saddle. I effected some improvement in the Horse Lines, as the men were happy and willing to learn; the reforms instituted did not affect them financially, as they did the horse-owners.

I suspected that the horses detached on outpost duty were not adequately fed, grain being always dearer in the jungle than in the cultivated country, where camel, and in some cases wheeled transport was available, and I now paid a series of surprise visits to the outposts, riding out 20 miles, and returning to eight-o'clock breakfast.

CHAPTER XVI

1859-60—THE SIRONJ JUNGLES

The Rescue of Chemmun Singh—Justice in Native States—A Regimental banker—Insubordinate Native Officers—Burmadeen Singh.

AT the end of December I was sitting at dinner with the Adjutant and the Doctor, when a letter was brought from Sindhara stating that a band of Rebels was in the neighbourhood, and having translated it, I invited the Adjutant to go out to the outposts. He demurred, saying he had been out often with no result. Though he was evidently disinclined to go, I pointed out there was always the hope of taking the enemy by surprise, and that as I had been fortunate in seeing service, I should like him to have a chance; then he said plainly that he would only go on complusion, and I dropped the conversation, telling my servant to bring my horse round with sword and pistol in an hour's time. When the boy returned to say the horse was at the door, my messmates endeavoured to dissuade me, saying it was impossible to find a small band in such a vast track of jungle,[1] but bidding them "Good-night," I stated for Bilko. The night was dark, and the bullock track, between two and three feet wide, led through trees so dense that I was restricted generally to a walk, and often could only guide the horse by looking upwards towards the sky. I obtained no news at Bilko, and inspecting the detachment I proceeded to Shamsabad without obtaining news, neither post having any further information of the enemy.

I reached Sindhara at nightfall the 28th, meeting the detachments which marched into the clearing on which the village stood, on the north side, as I went in at the south. They had been out since early morning on an unsuccessful

[1] Eighty miles by one hundred.

search for the Rebels, who on the evening of the 27th had carried off an influential Landowner named Chemmun Singh. This man had always been loyal to the British Government; he had accompanied my predecessor in several expeditions after Rebels, and on one occasion led a Native officer in command of a Squadron to the band's bivouac. There was, however, no fight, though the outlaws derided the Squadron, calling out, "Where is the Sahib? Come on and fight us now without him." The Native officer did not accept the invitation.

The Rebels burning down Chemmun Singh's village, which was 5 miles to the north of Sindhara, tried to kill him, and from that time until the 27th he lived in Sindhara under the protection of the Outpost. He was enticed out, however, and with a nephew carried off by a robber chief named Madhoo Singh, who hesitating to hang him without instructions, sent to the "Tontea," a rebel of higher rank, in hiding west of the Parbati River, who undertook to attend on the 29th and decide Chemmun Singh's fate, of which there was practically no doubt, and also the amount of ransom of a goldsmith who had been captured.

We knew nearly all the villagers assisted the robber bands; we had good reasons for suspecting that the Rajahs and minor Chiefs helped them as far as they could without being found out; it was therefore very important to save the life of the only landowner in the District who had openly sided with the Government.

It was nearly dark as I reached the village, on the outskirts of which sat all the women in a circle, uttering their lamentations, which took the curious form of blubbering while slapping the mouth. Sitting down amongst them, I made the acquaintance of Chemmun Singh's wife, and taking her aside, asked if she was really anxious her husband should be rescued; and when she satisfied me she was, I explained to her she had better stop crying and help me. When I got her to talk sensibly, I elicited that there was a man in the village who had been in the band, and I offered him £5 to guide me to their haunts. He was not covetous of the £5, but very anxious to have in writing a pardon, which I gave him with the reservation that it was not to condone the murder of white men.

With this he was content, as his infractions of the law had only reference to people of his own colour, and he consented to guide me.

The Outpost consisted of a weak company, some 60 strong, of the Barélí Levy (Police), which had been raised in the previous year, and 35 all Ranks Beatson's Horse. When I was ready the men were still cooking, and as nearly everyone in camp except a small guard had been marching for eight hours, the Native officer told me he did not think I should get any good out of them, so I elected to take a Corporal and 9 men, and 4 Cavalry soldiers, who having been on guard had remained in camp, and Burmadeen Singh, a sergeant, Beatson's Horse, who volunteered to come although he had but just returned to camp.

Our latest information of the band we were seeking put their numbers, varying slightly from day to day, at from 20 to 25 men, and assuming that we should surprise them, the Party that marched with me was, I considered, sufficient. Starting at 9 p.m., we marched steadily northwards. The night was very dark, so it was necessary to go slowly, and my horse ("The Pig"), cautious as he was, slid down a nulla, which he had not seen. At twelve o'clock, the guide, who had been taking bhang[1] every time we halted, trembling violently, pointed to a light, which he said was burning in one of the Rebels' hiding-places.

The ground being rough we dismounted, and leaving our 6 horses with 3 soldiers, proceeded on foot. In spite of constant cautions, I could not make the men careful enough to avoid breaking sticks and branches, and as we learned later the Rebel sentry reported to the Chief, Madhoo Singh, that he had heard footsteps. The Chief and another man getting up listened, but thought that it was only the sound of passing deer, and having shifted bivouac three times since the 27th, decided to lie down. When we got to within a mile the guide absolutely refused to lead any longer, but walked after me, I holding his hand to prevent his taking bhang, as I feared he would fall insensible.

Between one and two o'clock on the morning of the 29th, I crawled up to within ten yards of the hollow in and around

[1] Prepared opium.

which the band was sleeping. I was then perturbed to find that the numbers were greatly in excess of what I had anticipated, and the thought came into my mind to retreat; for I reflected that failure might discredit the action of Sir John Michel, who had been so kind in giving me the command, and I pictured in my mind newspaper articles on "The folly of appointing young English officers to command Natives, who overtax their powers." Fortunately my men could not see my face,—indeed, if I had not been in front of them the night was too dark,—and after a moment's hesitation I thought of Chemmun Singh's impending fate, and moreover realised that my only safety lay in attacking; for although we had succeeded in approaching the band unheard, once we attempted to retire we must have been discovered and overwhelmed, so beckoning to the men, they came up silently, and this time so noiselessly as not to attract the attention of the sentry, who with the prisoners and another man were the only persons awake, Chemmun Singh being tied up to a tree.

I stepped forward a little, and looked on the crowd of men, who to be out of the wind were lying asleep in the dry pond. In the depression forming the pond, the jungle was less thick than outside it, but there were trees in it with branches 3 feet from the ground, against one of which the sentry was leaning, when the click of the men's hammers as they cocked made him look up, and the firelight fell on my white Bedford cords. He asked without raising his voice, "Who is that?" I replied, "We are the Government," and turning to my men, shouted "Fire, charge." Having given the word, I ran at the sentry, without perceiving there were two men sleeping immediately under my feet, in the cummerbund of one of whom my foot caught, and I went headlong into the hollow. The ground was so rough that the Cavalry sergeant and private also fell as they ran forward. The Rebels jumped up, scuttling away unarmed, the sentry and four or five brave men covering their flight.

I rose as quickly as I could, with my left hand over my neck to save it from the sentry's sword, and attacked the nearest Rebel, a Brahman wearing a Sepoy's coat. We cut at each other three times in succession, the boughs intercepting our swords, and as he drew his hand back the fourth time, I going close to him with the point of my sword behind my right foot, cut upwards, wounding him in the fleshy part of the thigh. He staggered to my left, which brought him before Burmadeen Singh, who twice cut in vain at him, his sword catching in the trees, when I shouted, " Point, give the point." Burmadeen Singh now disappeared, and I ran after him, tumbling into a natural drain from the pond, on top of my Sergeant and the rebel Brahman, whom he was killing, using vituperation like that with which John Balfour of Burleigh addressed Sergeant Bothwell;[1] scrambling up, I ran after the last fluttering white clothing I could see, for I was apprehensive that if once they stood, I might yet be beaten. Failing to overtake them, I turned back, and found the prisoners had escaped, the Corporal and men of the Baréli Levy were still on the edge of the pond, where they had stopped to reload, and four or five rebels whom they had wounded when they fired into the sleeping mass, had crawled away out of the firelight. The Police compensated for their want of activity in charging, by the noise they made, which was perhaps more effective, shouting " Bring up the Horse Artillery, bring up the Cavalry," until I commanded silence. The private Cavalry soldier behaved well, until having wounded a rebel, he saw blood flow, when he became idiotic at the sight, falling on the guide, whom he mistook for one of the enemy. Eventually, to save the guide, I had to knock the soldier down with my fist, by a blow under the jaw.

I made every man of the party bring away one gun, and having broken the remaining firelocks and swords, we started homewards. The Cavalry soldier was half unconscious, and the Sergeant dragged him for two miles by his waist-belt, while I took charge of the guide, who was speechless and dreamy from opium. When we rejoined the horse-holders, I left the Non-effectives to find their way back to Sindhara, which I reached at daylight, the three prisoners, including the goldsmith held for ransom, having got back a quarter of an hour sooner, of which fact I was apprized by Chemmun Singh's wife kissing my boots as I re-entered the village. I rode into Bersia rapidly, suffering from face-ache. I had ridden 86 miles since I had left the dinner-table on the 27th, and Nature declined

[1] Scott's *Old Mortality*.

to answer any longer to the demands made on my constitution.

When I met my messmates at breakfast, they observed, " I suppose you have not done anything ? " and I replied, " Yes, a good deal, but I am too tired to talk, and you will have to copy the report presently." I did not realise I had earned the Victoria Cross, for in my official narrative, apprehensive of being considered rash, I minimised the affair, giving the enemy's numbers as about 60 men. I do not think that I should have received the Decoration, but for the report of Lieutenant Bradford from Sironj with the actual number 83, which corresponded nearly with Chemmun Singh's statement of 80, made later.

On the 31st December we received a telegram calling for volunteers for China. I went on parade and asked the men, and all the Regiment except 29 expressed their willingness to go. I telegraphed the fact to the Adjutant-General of the Army, sending at the same time to the Staff officer of my General a copy of my telegram, and apologising for having sent it direct. He answered my official letter with the unconventional remark written in the margin, " My dear Wood, no gammon," but wrote at the same time a sympathetic letter, saying he had not seen any Native Cavalry he was anxious to take to China. In thanking him for his letter I asked if he would get me sent to China, on any unpaid work; for although I saw it was possible to choose a Squadron, or perhaps two, of men with whom it would be a pleasure to serve, yet not anticipating I should be allowed later a free hand in disposing of the 1st Regiment of Beatson's Horse, I was unwilling to remain in a Corps which I thought, all danger of a rising in the south of India being over, was no longer worth the Government money expended on it in monthly pay. The two Regiments had cost about 5 lakhs to raise, or £50 per sabre; they had, however, exercised some moral influence, and had been usefully employed in checking Tantia Topi's attempted raid in the Dekhan, but now the rebellion was over I felt their state of efficiency did not justify their cost.

It required perseverance to discipline the men, of which they had acquired little in their eighteen months' service. Guards habitually undressed, the sentry only being clothed and armed. I cautioned three sergeants in Orders, and dismissed the next three I caught undressed while on guard in the first fortnight of December. The Native officers gravely represented that no one could remain dressed for twenty-four hours, so I referred them to Outpost reports, which showed that I had just passed from post to post in a continuous ride of thirty-six hours, covering 110 miles,[1] which was, however, less than Europeans had done twelve months earlier, when chasing Tantia Topi.

I spent my days when not inspecting outposts as follows:— Getting up before daylight, I exercised the Regiment by troops till 8.30 a.m.; saw the Native officers at orderly-room at 10; and then tried to disentangle and arrange the Regimental accounts till 5 p.m., when I went to the Horse Lines, and there remained till 7 p.m. This probably had an exhausting effect on my nervous system, and made me anxious to get away from what I feared must under the existing conditions remain an unsatisfactory Corps, inasmuch as it was financially unsound. When not engaged in trying to unravel the Regimental accounts, disciplining or drilling the men, I spent my time in patrolling the jungles to the north of Bersia. On the 9th January I went to Sindhara in the afternoon, and searched all night for a leader named Mulloob Khan, the Tontea (one-armed). This man was very troublesome from his courage and determination, and it was to him that the doom of Chemmun Singh (see p. 179) was remitted.

I perceived there were some men in the Regiment who might become good soldiers, and having issued an Order that no one would be promoted unless he could ride fairly, read and write his own language, it became necessary to establish a school. I provided a hut at a cost of about £5; the furniture consisted of the piece of praying-carpet which good Mussulmen carried on the saddle, and a payment of 6d. monthly from the voluntary pupils remunerated the master, who soon had bearded men of forty years of age under instruction.

Early in February an incident occurred indicating clearly

---

[1] I got cold in my face during the ride, and suffered considerably, Sylvester warning me on my return to Bersia, that if I shook my head all the teeth in the left side of my jaw would tumble out. Forty-eight hours of rest, however, brought me round.

the difficulties of keeping order in the numerous States and petty Chiefships of Central India. A Lieutenant, fifty years of age, appearing at orderly-room one morning, said, "The rebels are gone, there remain only robbers: may I have leave?" "For how long?" "I cannot say—my business may take six months, but I will return the moment it is done." "Six months is a long time, Lieutenant." "Yes, but I have always done my duty, and I must have leave, or resign." "Why so urgent?" Becoming excited, he doffed his turban, saying, "Look at my head, unshaven for months, and which I have sworn shall not be touched till I have satisfaction for my nephew's death." "But what happened to him?" "He was the Head of our family, and travelling, at nightfall was near a village owned by an hereditary enemy. My nephew sent to ask if he would be received as a friend. Being assured of hospitality, he went in, was well entertained, and in the morning seen out of the village with due ceremony, but three miles out was attacked in a pass and killed, with all his servants but two who escaped." "Take your leave, Lieutenant; come back when you can." Five weeks later he reappeared with a cheerful face. "I am glad to see you back, Lieutenant. Have you done your business satisfactorily?" "Quite so, my master, and my head is shaved." I asked him no more questions, but one of his friends told me he had fully avenged his nephew's death.

I had some trouble with the banker, for instead of being grateful for £400 I had assisted him to recover, he continued, in order to gain a few shillings, to lend, on terms of usury, money to the Rank and File. Three times I detected him, warned him in Orders, but without effect, and a week later, proving he had lent two rupees to a trumpeter, I turned him out of the Regiment. This did not do away entirely with the evil, for the Senior Troop non-commissioned officers who kept the pay accounts also lent on usury, but against them it was difficult to prove a case. Many petitions sent direct to Lord Canning were referred to me for report, but as from the day I assumed command every decision affecting pay was published in Regimental Orders, I had no difficulty, the Military Secretary to the Government accepting as satisfactory replies a copy of the Order on the subject.

There were two officers[1] whose domestic life shocked even their Mussulmen comrades' indulgent opinions, and who, moreover, could not ride at all, and of these I induced the resignation by ordering a weekly Officers' Ride without stirrups. A sergeant in the Regiment had been employed in the Riding establishment of the Haidarábád Contingent, and putting him in command as Drill Instructor, I led the ride, with the result that those whom I wished to leave the Corps, after a succession of falls, departed without giving me further trouble.

Some few officers and non-commissioned officers took great pleasure in riding feats such as are now familiar to Londoners from the Military Tournaments, and these I made a weekly institution. The Natives were disappointed to find their horses bitted with spikes were invariably beaten by my horses ridden in English bits with low ports, in all feats which required the horses to gallop true and boldly, as in tent-pegging, for on the spear striking an embedded peg the hand of the rider, however firm his seat may be, involuntarily interferes to some extent with the horse's mouth. On the other hand, Burmadeen Singh generally beat me at quarter-staff play, and in wrestling never failed to throw me.

On the 18th March I visited the Bhilsa outpost, and met Bradford, the Adjutant of Mayne's Horse, with whom I conferred on a troublesome subject. Having ascertained the practice in that Regiment, on my return I issued an Order framed on it. All the riders in the 1st Regiment of Beatson's Horse had been enlisted on the personal security of the horse-owners. When I took over the command there had been a succession of robberies, the perpetrators of which were undoubtedly men in the Regiment. It did not affect the European officers, who lived a quarter of a mile away, but the succession of petty thefts in the Lines was the more annoying that many of the Native officers did not assist in the detection of the culprits. My order was based on the principle of placing an actual though limited responsibility on the horse-owners for their riders' conduct. The Native officers and non-commissioned officers in the Regiment did not so much resent this order as another change I had been making in the Regiment, which affected the riders but little, but touched

[1] One was the former puggaree manufacturer who owned forty-five horses.

their pockets, such as enforcing strictly payment of the monthly instalments of their debt.

The Horse Insurance Fund, which was £500 in debt on the 1st December, with a constantly increasing liability, had been put on a better footing. Horse-owners who neglected their horses were penalised by the removal of the horse from benefits of the Insurance, the subscription ceasing at the same time, and the sum payable for the replacing of a horse was reduced from £20 to £15. All these alterations, although carried out with the concurrence of the Native officers assembled at orderly-room, were undoubtedly distasteful to many; and, moreover, in the course of three months I had reduced the debt to the Regimental banker[1] from £550 to £150, by putting pressure on wealthy men who, able to pay, yet, like most Natives, were unwilling to do so until compelled.

The order was issued on the 22nd of March, and in the ordinary routine the Native officers would have spoken to me on the following day if they thought the order pressed unduly on them. They knew, however, that I should be alone the day after, as the Medical officer was away on leave, and the Adjutant had arranged to visit an Outpost on the 24th, and hoped, being alone, I should give way. On the 23rd the two senior Native officers assembled all the officers unknown to me, and wrote a "Round robin." Next morning, instead of the Squadron Commanders coming at ten o'clock, all 19 officers of the Regiment appeared. Seeing them walking up, I called for my sword and pistol, which I placed on the table, feeling that something unusual was intended. The Native Adjutant, an inoffensive opium-eater, said he had a Petition to read, but that as he had been a soldier for many years in the Haidarábád Contingent he wished to dissociate himself from the Petition, which he had not signed. When it was read, I ordered the Regimental clerk to get a Persian Dictionary, saying that I thought three of the words employed were actually mutinous. This proved to be so, and I spent half an hour endeavouring to persuade the malcontents, some of whom I liked, to rewrite the Petition in more respectful and guarded language.

[1] Before I turned him out of the Lines.

I explained I realised how distasteful much of that which I had been doing must be to many of them, and I understood their object was to induce my removal from the temporary command of the Regiment, but I pointed out that if the Governor-General wished to remove me he would be more inclined to do so if the Native officers did not put themselves in a false position.

I showed how the Petition might be worded so as to express exactly the same meaning in soldier-like language; but after a prolonged discussion, though feeling uncertain how the order would be accepted, looking steadily at the Senior officer, who was the best fighting value of the nineteen, I rose and ordered them all back to their quarters, suspending them from duty, and ordering them to leave their swords at the Native Adjutant's quarters.

They filed out of the room and retired. I sent camel orderlies for the Adjutant, the Doctor, and Sergeant Burmadeen Singh, who was still at the Sindhara outpost, but it was obvious many hours must elapse before they could arrive.

I worked all day in the orderly-room, and at five o'clock, with some misgivings, went down to the Lines, where I remained till seven o'clock. Nothing occurred except the unusual circumstance of there being no officers present, and some of the men looked at me with an expression I had not before noticed. After nightfall Burmadeen Singh came to my hut, and I told him to find out the feeling of the Regiment and return at ten o'clock. He did so, and reported that two of the Senior officers were inciting the men to kill me, but many Muhammadans were unwilling, and Burmadeen did not think there would be any concerted attack on me. He never told me, but I learned later, that he personally had taken care there should be no such attack.

As before stated,[1] he had great influence in the Hindoo troop, and it happened that the guard on the magazine was furnished by it. Burmadeen, forcing the guard, issued ammunition to the troop, which remained under arms all night between the Lines and my hut, disappearing before daylight. This decided indication of the feeling of the Hindoos effectually damped any desire of an overt attack on me, and at daylight

[1] *Vide* chap. xv. p. 172.

Bradford and 20 of his men galloped in from Bhilsa, a distance of 50 miles.

His first words were, "Now, won't it be fun if they rise?" "There are 500 here, have you more coming on?" "No, I've only these twenty, but they are real good men." Though the odds were great, Bradford's presence changed the situation. I had passed an unhappy night: putting out my candles at eleven o'clock, I endeavoured to go to sleep, but unsuccessfully, and after an hour, finding the strain on my nerves too great, got up and worked till 3 a.m., when I fell asleep. The little Poona groom, who had been with me since May 1858, remained up all night with my favourite horse saddled. Next day the Political agent at Bhopál offered to send a company of the 95th (now the 2nd Derbyshire) to support me, but I declined, and next day released all the Native officers except the two Seniors, who had been the ringleaders, whom I placed in close arrest, sending the others back to their duty.

The excitement now quieted down, and Bradford left me three days afterwards, when we were satisfied the trouble was over. I reported fully to the Adjutant-General, for although the Regiment was serving under the direct orders of the Viceroy, matters of discipline went to the Commander-in-Chief, and eventually when the case was settled, four months later, the two Native officers' conduct was declared to be "insolent, seditious, tending to mutiny." They were "dismissed, with the confiscation of their horses, arms, and equipment to Government, losing the right of owning horses."

At the end of March I rode up to Goona, 120 miles, to see Major H. O. Mayne, under whose command I was to come somewhat later, as he wished to talk to me as to his future plans. Leaving Bersia in the evening, I got to Shamsabad at dark, and rested till two o'clock, when I rode by Sironj to Goona, arriving at tea-time. Before dinner I saw twelve men tested who wished to join Mayne's Horse. They were provided with stout strong single-sticks, with which they fought mounted, in single combat, by pairs. One of them, who called out to his antagonist not to hit hard, was rejected on the spot, on the ground that if he feared a single-stick he would still more fear a sword. The others were sent in succession at the gallop over a wide ditch, and a mud wall 3 feet high, and although there were many falls, they all succeeded eventually in crossing it.

At four o'clock next morning Major Mayne had the Regiment out, and I was astonished at the silence and discipline maintained, so very different from the men to whom I was accustomed.

After breakfast we had a long and fruitless hunt for tigers, but on our way home found a bear, which fell riddled with seven bullets. I was much impressed with the excitement of the hitherto placid elephant, which trumpeting loudly knelt violently on the bear, crushing it flat, and then tossed it between fore and hind feet, as if playing catch-ball.

SINDHARA

CHAPTER XVII

1860—CENTRAL INDIA HORSE

A long ride with insufficient sleep induces sunstroke—Disguised as Rebels we are well received—The death of Lieutenant Jennings—The Rajah of Narsinghgarh has a pain—I resign my appointment—and return to England, seeing Irregular Cavalry on my way to Calcutta.

WE rested on Sunday the 22nd, doing some business after Divine service; going next morning for a long but fruitless beat for a tiger, and then decided to have another drive for bear. Blair, one of Mayne's officers, accompanied me to a ridge along which the bear was expected to pass. My companion got into a tree, and I remained on the ground, until Blair urged me to climb at all events on to a low bough. After half an hour's waiting, I saw my companion's eyes sparkle, for he was in a tree within touch of my arm, and he fired into a bush 40 yards off, when out sprang a large tigress straight for our trees, making me feel glad I was off the ground. Blair fired again, but missed, and the tigress paused immediately under the bough on which I was standing, but without noticing me. Holding on by one hand, I dropped the muzzle of my gun close to her back; but a twig catching the hammer, the first barrel missed fire, the second bullet as I thought hitting the tiger in the foot. She went on lashing her tail, a magnificent sight, till Blair turning round got another shot, and she rolled over apparently dead. I being eager to see whether I had hit her, jumped down, and got within 30 yards, when Bradford, who was then approaching on an elephant, shouted to me to keep clear as the tigress was moving. As he spoke she leaped on to his elephant, getting close to him before he fired, when she fell dead, turning a complete somersault, and as she did so her tail hit the elephant, which up to this moment had behaved perfectly; when touched by the tigress's tail, she rushed on the carcase, and tossed it as she had tossed the bear.

After dinner, Bradford and I started at 11.30 p.m., having lingered too long over our coffee to make it worth while to lie down, and rode back the 100 miles, he accompanying me as far as Sironj. I was short of sleep, having had only three or four hours' rest each night since leaving Bersia, and was thus unable to stand the heat, which was intense. In the evening my track ran through a narrow valley bare of trees, and the rocky formation emitted a burning glow which scorched my skin. I felt I was gradually losing consciousness, but could see three miles off the trees at Shamsabad where my servants were waiting, so, thrusting my right hand in the cloak straps, I galloped on. Just before I reached the village I rolled off my horse unconscious, and when half an hour later I recovered my senses, my servants were pouring water over my head and neck. They were still thus occupied when a Native came up with my favourite sword, given to me by Colonel Morris, which had jumped out of the scabbard without my missing it.

I made several unsuccessful attempts to catch the Tontea (Mulloob Khan) and Madhoo Singh, my friend Bradford driving these men and their few adherents from Sironj on to my outposts, and I returning the compliment. The first week in May, a man who had given information to Bradford was killed near Sindhara, so taking 25 horsemen I made a long night march in search of the band, but without success. When I got back to the outpost on the 8th, I found an order for the Regiment to proceed to Goona, and riding into Bersia, I was occupied all day in obtaining waggons for my magazine, the officers and men having sufficient private transport kept in a state of constant readiness to move their own effects.

We all knew that the villagers were assisting the band of robbers who lived in the jungles, but there was difficulty in proving the complicity of the Head men, who asserted their loyalty to the Government. On the 9th May, having given orders for the Regiment to march next day, I selected 25 strong men; and after dark, having disguised them and myself as Rebels, we started on foot in the direction of Sindhara, reaching a village 2 miles to the west of it soon after daylight, a distance of 23 miles. We came on a patrol from our outpost, which fled, not unnaturally, as it consisted of only four men.

We remained concealed all that day, being well entertained by the villagers, and at nightfall went nearly to Bilkheri. The actual distance was only 15 miles, but the men were all footsore, and I had large blisters on my feet, on which I wore Native sandals. Lying up during the day, after much difficulty we found a man to guide us, but either intentionally or from nervousness, he guided us so that when we got close up to the robbers there was a shallow river intervening, and the noise we made getting down the bank enabled them to escape, although we got to within a few yards of them. The villagers were generally completely deceived as to our identity, for I always remained out of sight, though my skin was nearly as dark as a Native's. The villagers duly informed us of the march of the Regiment from Bersia northwards, and proposed we should go a few miles westwards and seize a rich trader, in the Narsinghgarh District, who was able to afford a large ransom.

That night we made another long march towards a light many miles north, which I hoped indicated the bivouac of a band of robbers, but were again unsuccessful; and the following morning, finding my men were exhausted, I collected all the ponies I could to mount the more footsore. In the course of the forenoon we met a wedding party on ponies, the arrangements of which I was obliged to upset, telling the bridegroom that if he came on with us to Dehri or to Katra, where there was a post of Mayne's Horse, I would return the ponies.

I had sent to warn the non-commissioned officer in command we were in disguise, but unfortunately not knowing exactly where the post was, I remained in the Rear, trying to bring along some of the footsore men for whom I had not got ponies. Mayne's men had heard that I had passed on, and thus when my leading man approached they stood to their arms and challenged. The soldiers halted, except one unlucky Hindoo who was mounted on a mare, and she being ridden without saddle or bridle, cantered up towards the horses of the post. The sentry fired at my man, putting nine pebbles into him, and the Sergeant in charge, as he lay on the ground, was about to spear him, when he gasped out, "I am Wood Sahib's servant," which averted further misfortune. When I came on the scene the Hindoo was apparently dying, blood spirting out of his lungs; but he eventually recovered.

I arrived at Goona with the Regiment on the 17th, but was no sooner in camp than I was sent back to my old hunting-ground, Sir Richard Shakespeare, the Governor-General's Agent, having telegraphed that "either Bradford or Wood" was to stop out till Madhoo Singh was caught. I made one or two very long marches, in incessant rain, with no change of clothing, but was back in Goona again at the end of the month, and on the 6th June was ordered out after a somewhat larger band. Bradford represented to Major Mayne that his men were jealous at my having gone out twice in succession, so was given the work; and Mayne, as I now think wisely, refused to allow me to go with him, which I was anxious to do, as it was said that the band I surprised in December had been reinforced. I handed over to Bradford, Lieutenant Jennings, who had been attached to me when I was ordered out. This officer had lost his parents, brothers and sisters, murdered at Dihlí, and was anxious to encounter the Rebels. Bradford at my request took him, and they marched throughout the night, but failed to find any trace of the party.

After an hour's rest at daylight, Bradford keeping 20 men, sent 40 under a Native officer, to scout, and meet him on the far side of a belt of jungle. At 8 a.m., when passing under a high hill covered with rocks and jungle, Bradford looking up saw the men of whom he had been in search. They so little anticipated being disturbed that they continued their cooking. Bradford giving the order, "Charge," led up the hill, being the only one who escaped falls, Jennings having two ere he reached the top. Bradford, followed by three Sikhs, got among the Rebels as they fled, and killed several without serious resistance. He was returning from the pursuit when he heard of his Subaltern's fate. He had ridden with uplifted sword at an undaunted rebel, who had held his fire till the last moment, and as Jennings, shot through the body, fell out of the saddle, the Sepoy, seizing the young officer's sword, killed him with it. The Rebel must have been a man of determination, for he resisted bravely, until he fell under the swords of four Sikhs.

Bradford took a few prisoners, one supposed to be Madhoo Singh, whom I had often chased. The man stoutly denied his identity, till I sent Burmadeen Singh to Sindhara for one of my spies; he identified him, and Madhoo Singh admitting the fact, agreed to help us to catch the Rao Sahib and Firoz Shah, for whom a reward had been offered.

I lost my Adjutant soon after reaching Goona, and his successor was not a good accountant, which added to my work. The India system of holding up the men's pay not only added to my daily work, but impaired my efforts to get rid of money-lenders, who were always usurers. I managed to pay my men for the month of May by utilising Government money which accrued from various sources, such as the confiscation of "Assamees," or right of possessing a horse, the Regimental market value of which stood at the end of May, in spite of the uncertainty of the fate of the Regiment, at £35, or £15 beyond the value of the horse. I was discharging men, sending away over 200 of the least efficient between the 20th and 30th of May, and as I drew 34s. from Government for each horse, paying the men only up to the day of discharge, since the horse belonged to Government, I had about 11s. in hand for each horse; but these transfers of moneys from one account to another caused me much labour, as my only accountant was a man who did not speak a word of English. At the end of one week the balance I had in hand which had accrued as mentioned above, amounted to £7000.

I took the Native officers into my confidence as regards all money transactions, and often had the Senior officer at work with me from 7 a.m. till 5 p.m. In reorganising the Regiment I should have liked to have promoted Burmadeen Singh, who in force of character and skill at arms on foot was one of the best; but he was not clever, and I was confronted by the order I had issued in December that all future promotions should be given to those only who could read and write in one language. Burmadeen worked steadily at the Nagari character, which was his mother tongue, but did not make much progress, and could not be said to come up to the required standard. I lent him £35, by which he became the possessor of his own horse, and thereby ceased to be the servant of a Native officer.

All financial transactions, including a detailed account of

the expenditure on four horses which I had personally purchased from Government, and kept for the benefit of the Horse Insurance Fund, were published in Regimental Orders. This arrangement had the advantage of showing exactly what profit could be made out of the Assamees, after providing the feeding of the horse, and the upkeep of saddlery.

I retained about 100 out of the 535 men whom I had taken over on the 1st of December of the previous year, filling up the Regiment to its original strength by enlisting high-class men, who were the more ready to enlist as many of the Regiments, including two raised by Hodson in the Pánjáb, had recently been disbanded.

On the 2nd July, hearing of robbers moving in the District to the south of Barsad, I rode 36 miles at speed to Jamner, where I had a troop. I did not dare go nearer than 15 miles or so of the band, until my spies located it, for the Tontea always moved when he realised I was within two hours' ride of him; but on the 14th I had a fast gallop to a hill in the jungles, when he only just escaped us. I was arranging another surprise, when on the 16th, at 2 a.m., I received the following order from the Brigade-Major at Goona: "I send you a copy of a statement made yesterday by Madhoo Singh, agreeably to the Commanding officer's desire. He wishes you to go down to Narsinghgarh at once, and apprehend Baba Bhut, Kamdar to the Rao Sahib, Risaldars Rustum Ali Khan, and Eman Khan. The first is in the house of the Rajah's chief agent, Bishund Dhutt. Apprehend them by means of the Rajah himself; take him with you, and do not let them have a moment's notice. If you want more men, let us know sharp, and how many."

Having read the depositions of Madhoo Singh, I started at 3 a.m., and by trotting where the track was possible, reached the outskirts of Narsinghgarh, 40 miles distant, at 3 p.m. Placing the troop in the jungle so as to surround the fort, which stood above the town, I rode up, accompanied by Fyz Ali Khan, the troop Native officer, and a Trumpeter. The men were uneasy at our going alone, and begged to be allowed to accompany us. This I forbade, for although Madhoo Singh's depositions showed what we had suspected for some time, that the Rajah was disloyal to the Government, yet I hoped to arrest the two

Native officers who had been turned out of the Regiment, and were now supplying the Rebels with information, without outwardly coercing the Rajah. I left the Trumpeter on the drawbridge of the fort, ordering him if he saw a struggle to sound the "Gallop," and asked to see the Rajah alone, and he somewhat unwillingly dismissed his armed retinue, when telling him the purport of my orders, I requested his assistance in arresting the three men. He denied their presence in the first instance, alleging he had never heard of Baba Bhut, adding that Rustum Ali Khan had gone to a village some way off, and that Bishund Dhutt was on duty at Pachor, 20 miles away, but that he would send for him. I then informed him I had seen Rustum Ali Khan as I ascended the hill, on which he admitted the two officers were in his palace, and went with me to their quarters, where I made them prisoners. He would not, however, order a horse for a considerable time, to ride to the house where Baba Bhut was staying. It was so long in coming that I placed mine at his disposal, but this he declined; and when eventually the horse was brought, he sent it back again, and then delayed for different articles for over an hour, sending in succession for a sword, cummerbund, pistol and dagger. At last he said, "If you go out of the courtyard, I will follow you," but looking back I saw him hurrying into the palace, whence he sent a soldier to say he had a bowel complaint and could not come.

I then went to Bishund Dhutt's house, but warning had been given to Baba Bhut, and it was empty. At six o'clock, as I was starting for Pachor, Bishund Dhutt, who had been in the town all the afternoon, appeared, and I arrested him. I stayed that evening at Lakanwas, a village of mixed races, 7 miles from Narsinghgarh, the head man of which was loyal,[1] and after nightfall, taking 15 men, rode back, and searched the house of Baba Bhut for the Tontea and Firoz Shah, but unsuccessfully; for, as we learnt later, the latter escaped in woman's clothes from the palace, while the Rajah parleyed with me.

I wrote a full Report that night, stating that I had addressed the Rajah in respectful language, and the only harsh expression used was in pressing him either to come with me or to refuse,

[1] He told Lieutenant, now Sir E. Bradford, a month later, my visit to the Rajah cleared Narsinghgarh of rebels for a time, and saved Lakanwas from being looted.

saying, "If your Highness will be kind enough to refuse to accompany us, I shall arrest you, as I have been ordered to take you with me, as I have already told you." In a subsequent report I regretted this expression, explaining it was not drawn from me until the Rajah, whom I knew to be disloyal, had deliberately lied, and had delayed me for over an hour, as I believed to give time for a proscribed Rebel to escape.

The Agent had been previously very kind to me, and in January had written to the Viceroy, who proposed sending British troops into the Narsinghghar District, "I assure you I believe the services of these two officers, Lieutenants Bradford and Wood, will be of more avail in restoring order than any number of English soldiers." He had, moreover, unknown to me, recommended me for the Victoria Cross for the attack on the band by which I released Chemmun Singh. Nevertheless, he was now much displeased with my conduct. He had recently reported the District had settled down, the Native Princes as being generally loyal, and on hearing that I had threatened the Rajah with arrest, wrote that he was "certain I had acted without orders." When he received a copy of my instructions, he censured all concerned, pointing out Narsinghar was outside the Goona District, observing, "If Lieutenant Wood had arrested the Rajah, he would probably have lost his life, and have involved us in a petty but most inconvenient warfare." I resented the censure as unjust, and resigning my appointment, asked to be allowed to leave Goona, when my successor could take over the Regiment. Soldiers, including the Commander-in-Chief, Bombay, and Sir Hugh Rose, Commander-in-Chief in India, supported me. The latter having represented "Lieutenant Wood only did his duty in carrying out the orders he received," Lord Canning, the Viceroy, before I left India in November, replied, "He would approve of Lieutenant Wood being again employed under the Supreme Government."

My former schoolfellow Bradford and I continued in turn the pursuit of the brigands, but under considerable difficulties, as, except on the hilltops, most of the country was under water. We marched in torrents of rain for forty-eight hours, and my men and I were five and a half hours in travelling

10 miles, the camels carrying my baggage falling heavily. On the 25th I returned to Goona, which at that time abounded with game, but unfortunately I had little or no leisure for sport: pigs were plentiful around us. A wolf was killed in our Horse Lines at early morning stables; I saw five tigers shot one day within 10 miles of the Station, and had a herd of nilghai [1] within my skirmishers when exercising the Regiment in extending order on our drill-ground.

We lost some men from cholera during the month of August, nearly all of which I spent at Goona, Bradford going out to the jungles. This enabled me to clear up the accounts of the Regiment, but my friend was no more proof against the incessant work in jungles, which gave even our Native servants repeated attacks of fever, than I had been, and the doctors now proposed to send him to England for a change of air.

On the 15th I was galloping on a cart track to the Brigade-Major's office, when my pony, making suddenly for a short cut in high grass, was unable to turn quick enough, and collided with a tree. I felt a blow, and on recovering my senses saw my pony stretched on the ground near me with his head the reverse way to which we were travelling. On the tree there were three deep grooves cut, marking where my shoulder, knee, and foot struck, but the pony must have been stunned by falling on his head. My friend the Doctor was summoned, but though personally fond of me, he disliked his profession; the first remark made, "I suppose you are not hurt," effectually closed my lips, and I went on parade that evening and for a week with my arm in a sling, only discovering two months later, when bathing with a Doctor in the North-west Provinces, that my collar-bone had been broken, and the bones had reunited one on top of the other.

Towards the end of September, Bradford being too unwell to remain in the jungles, I went out after the bandits, and was caught for two days in succession in heavy rain, which gave me fever, and impaired my hearing still more than it had been. Early in October a Medical Board ordered me to Calcutta to appear before a Presidency Board, with a view to my going to England for a change of air. Shortly before I left the

[1] Blue cattle.

Station a new Commandant[1] came to inspect the Regiment, and with his permission, after I had exercised it, I handed over the command to Fyz Ali Khan, who had less than four years' service, but was one of the best Native officers I had met. He worked the Regiment at the trot and gallop without making any mistake, and was warmly commended. My friend Burmadeen Singh was still a sergeant, for I was unwilling to infringe my order requiring elementary education of all officers. He brought me one evening a bag containing 350 rupees (£35). "What is this?" "Oh, the money you lent me to purchase my Assamee, and as you are going away you would doubtless like to take your money, and so my friends have lent it to me." "Please hold it until you can repay me by instalments, after you have saved the money." About twelve months later I received a draft from a Bombay banker with a note from Burmadeen enclosing the first instalment of £10. In returning it, I answered by asking him to accept the price of the Assamee and horse as a present. My successor, Captain Martin, who took over the command on the 4th October, endorsed my views on education, and followed the system I had inaugurated; but at my request he promoted Burmadeen Singh to be an officer, and he received the 2nd Class Order of Merit for his gallantry on the 29th December 1859.

The Regiment owed the Government nearly £25,000 when I assumed command on the 1st December 1859, and when my final account was passed a year after I left Goona, my recommendation that £13,300 should be written off was approved. The Government had given me a free hand as to recovering or writing off the Public debt, and was satisfied with my action in having got £12,200 back out of the £25,000 which had been advanced when the Corps was raised.

I made a Record ride to Gwáliár, my messmates and the

---

[1] He wrote about my resuming command of a Regiment later :—

"Your untiring zeal, great patience and tact are well known to me. I am not acquainted with any man who has stronger or better claims, or, with your professional abilities, would do it greater justice. I consider that you have great qualifications for such a command, and that you carry with you the respect and goodwill of all, having maintained strict discipline at the same time.—With best wishes, believe me, sincerely yours, JAMES TRAVERS, *Col.*,
"*Commanding Central India Horse*.

"*To* EVELYN WOOD, Esq., 17th Lancers."

Native officers of the Regiment having posted their horses for me on the road at 8-mile stages. Leaving Gwáliár in a mail cart, I was due at Dholpúr at daylight; but owing to two accidents in the road we did not get in until nearly noon, and although I had felt the sun, I imprudently started again at four o'clock, getting a sunstroke when the sun was going down. I came to my senses finding water being poured over my head and neck; this revived me, but I was still so giddy that I could not see the door of the bungalow, and my orderly who accompanied me to Ágra had to lead me to bed.

I left Dihlí, after a visit of two days, on the 3rd October, by Palki Dak, passing through Mírath at night, and reached the foot of the Himalayas at daylight on the 21st. As this mode of travelling must be unknown to the present generation, I describe the vehicle, which may be likened to a wooden bedstead having the outward appearance of a coffin. The bottom of the couch was made of ropes, with four uprights and connecting rods from which cloth or canvas walls were suspended. The structure being slung on poles was carried by four men, ordinarily relieved by four who ran alongside, and usually covered 5 miles an hour. I paid for eight bearers, but the contractor sent me six, keeping the payment for the other two in his own pocket, and moreover the first stage, instead of being 14 miles, the usual distance, was 24 miles. The fare from the foot of the Himalayas under Nynee Thal to Sítápúr, 190 miles, was £7, 10s. 10d., with the usual present of 1s. for each stage, say £8 sterling.

I spent four pleasant days with the Lieutenant-Governor of the North-west Provinces, Mr. George Edmonstone,[1] meeting Mr. Couper, who was the cleverest man I saw in India. In talking of the Narsinghgarh affair, Mr. Edmonstone observed, "Yes, you were censured; but if it had occurred five years ago, Lord Dalhousie would have given you an Army Order to yourself."

On my journey from Gwáliár to the Himalayas, and Calcutta, I saw several Irregular Cavalry Regiments, to the Commanding officers of which letters had been written on my behalf. The systems varied in all. In some, as Hodson's Horse, the Horse Insurance Fund was 4000 rupees in credit, in others it was in debt, and in others again it did not exist.

[1] Later, Sir George Edmonstone, K.C.B.

Some Regiments were extraordinarily dressed with gaudy, unsuitable clothes, and accoutrements made in London, in many cases bad copies of the follies of the designers of our European uniform; in others, and particularly the Jat Horse at Banáras, commanded by Major Murray, which considered in all aspects was the most satisfactory I saw, everything was provided on an economical yet satisfactory basis. Káhnpúr saddles cost complete 34s., and the one uniform coat 16s. 6d.

I made the acquaintance of the Adjutant, Lieutenant Hennessy, under somewhat unusual circumstances. I arrived at the Station an hour before daylight, and knowing that Major Murray was married, asked for the Adjutant's bungalow, and was shown by the night-watchman into his room. Henessy was lying asleep, and his room being in darkness my hand rested on his arm, the feel of which made me draw back in alarm, for it was like a 7-inch hawser. While the servants were getting me coffee, I induced him to tell me the story of the strange state of his arm. He was covering a retreat in Oude, and being pressed heavily, the Regiment charged, driving back the Rebels. Hennessy was returning from the pursuit, his horse exhausted, when he passed a Rebel Captain, who fired at him, and Hennessy drawing his pistol fired back. Neither shot took effect, and the Captain ran at him so determinedly that Hennessy had not time to draw his sword, but threw himself off, just escaping the sword of his opponent. They then stood up, and fought in styles characteristic of the East and West. Hennessy cut the Rebel three times over the head and forehead, and had his arm snicked again and again, until he was obliged to wield his sword with his left hand, while his opponent had to keep his left hand up to his forehead to prevent the blood running into his eyes. Eventually both were so exhausted that they sat down to rest before renewing the fight, when some of Hennessy's men passing, in spite of his entreaties, speared his brave foe.

I liked the Commanding officer much. If he had lived in these days, he would not have troubled himself about the parade which was to come off for Sir Hugh Rose, who was then on his way up country; but in 1860 there were many old-fashioned Generals, and the one in command had had a rehearsal of every movement each Corps was to perform on the following day.

I sat up till past 2 a.m. hearing Murray say his lessons, the explanations of nearly all the Cavalry Drill book, and as I went to bed told him, "Well, I have heard you your lesson, but it is labour thrown away; for you will see that Sir Hugh will upset this arranged program before you have been five minutes on Parade." And so he did.

I called on the Commander-in-Chief next morning, and was received with great kindness. In repeating what Lord Canning had replied to his letter, that " he would approve of my being employed again under the Supreme Government," added, that he, Sir Hugh, would give me the command of the first Cavalry Regiment that became vacant. He desired me to attend him as Galloper next day, which I did, when everything fell out as I had predicted to Major Murray; and the Chief animadverted severely on much of what he saw. The Jat Horse, however, were praised by him.

Leaving Calcutta on the 24th November, I got back to my father's house in Essex three days after Christmas, after an absence of rather more than three years.

CHAPTER XVIII

1861-2-3—THE STAFF COLLEGE

I meet my future wife—Reading for Staff College—Death of the Prince Consort—The Military Secretary—The Canada war scare—Life at Camberley—Charles Kingsley—Viscount Southwell—A heavy fall over a gate—A Muhammadan missionary on the Elbe—A dream shows question in Examination papers.

EARLY in January I attended before a Medical Board in London, and by it was advised to place myself under the care of Mr. Toynbee, a celebrated aurist. He promised there would be considerable improvement in my hearing, but said in one ear it would never fully recover, as inflammation had caused the tympanum to adhere to the bone, and added it would be unwise for me to return to India for at least two years. I became a Captain in April, paying £1000 to Government, and £1,500 over Regulation to the officer who retired in my favour. My country still retains the Regulation sums for my Commissions, except the Cornetcy, which was given to me. Sir John Michel, on learning of my promotion, at once, and unknown to me, renewed his application for a Brevet Majority for my services in Central India, which after repeated requests was granted in August 1862.

While I was in India I had not sufficient leisure to attend to my left arm, which from the loss of bone and from being for months in a sling, had shrunk considerably, and so after a month's rest at home, I took lessons with the gloves, foils, and sabre, using both hands equally, by which means I greatly increased the strength and use of the left arm.

Early in the spring I went to Mortlake to stay with my former comrade, now Viscount Southwell, and met the lady who seven years later became my wife. Southwell had never tired in the three years I had been away of expatiating on my merits, real and imaginary, to his four sisters, and thus they were all disposed to receive me kindly as their brother's friend. The second had recently married Mr. Justice, afterwards Lord, FitzGerald;[1] the other three resided with Southwell.

When I had rested for a few months, I took up my books again, and early in September went to reside with Captain Lendy, who prepared young men for Woolwich, and officers for the Staff College. He was a handsome man from near Perpignon, in the south of France. All his family had been Royalists, and on returning from Algeria at the time of the proclamation of the Republic, out of which grew the Third Empire, Lendy left the Army, and settled in England. He was assisted by Herr Zöbel and a Swiss, Monsieur Delissert, both of whom were clever in imparting knowledge. My first interview with Captain Lendy was decidedly depressing, for after stating my object I was questioned with immense rapidity as to my knowledge, which was limited, being confined to a good knowledge of Hindustani and a slight acquaintance with French. His remark, " Ah, then it is difficult," made me all the more anxious to succeed, and for many months I worked hard.

In spite of the fact that on going to India I had given up £150 of my allowance, and on my getting command of Beatson's Horse the other £100, I was in funds for once in my life, and should have liked to hunt; but until I had been up for the Examination in July in the following year I took no pleasure except that of rowing, working as many hours a day as my head would allow, and getting exercise by sculling up and down the Thames, summer and winter, in an outrigger which I purchased on going to Sunbury. Delissert was such a pleasant and enthusiastic teacher that I regretted I was forbidden to do any French after the first few weeks, Captain Lendy explaining that I knew enough to secure two-thirds marks, and must turn to German, which I did, being instructed by Herr Zöbel. Both these men were more successful in teaching me than was Captain Lendy, whose mind was so quick that it was difficult for him to exercise sufficient

[1] He not only showed me unbounded hospitality, but in my absence on Foreign Service watched over the interests of my wife and children.

patience with any one who was entirely ignorant of a subject. He himself, besides knowing the answer to any possible question which could be asked in any Examination paper, had also a marvellous memory for dates. One morning when sitting at early study with him, the post was brought in, with it a parcel for me containing Haydn's *Dictionary of Dates*. My tutor, with the vivacity of his race, looking up, asked me the name of the book, and on my answering observed, " Yes, it is a good book, but you should have it all here," pointing to his forehead. " Oh, that is impossible; no man could have all in his head." On which he replied confidently, " I have it all." I then said, " Well, Captain Lendy, I will open the book with the paper-cutter, and if you answer three questions which I shall take at random, successfully, I will admit you know the book." My first was the date of Hampden's death ; " 1643 " came without a moment's hesitation. The next was the date of the Catholic Emancipation Act, to which he replied immediately, " 1829." I then asked, " Will you tell me the dates of the Numantine Wars ? " " Ah," he said, " that is a little difficult," and he counted on his fingers for less than a minute, and replied, " 143–133 B.C."

Early in 1862 I went to Heidelberg, and lived in the family of a German Professor for two months, when I returned to Sunbury, working steadily until the examination, which was held in July. I had never done any Euclid or Algebra at Marlborough, and I found both of them troublesome ; it appeared to me to be easier to learn by heart the first four books of Euclid than to attempt to understand them. My fellow-pupils at Sunbury, three of whom rose to be General officers, used chaffingly to ask me if I could remember the problems if they changed the letters; but such changes did not affect me, as I remembered the relative positions of the letters. Like most men who have spent on Active Service the years generally given to study, I was slow in acquiring knowledge of Military Drawing, and indeed had made so little progress that just before the Examination Captain Lendy advised me not to waste the time by attending at the Hall. Herr Zöbel, however, told me, as indeed he told his employer, that he was mistaken : " Major Wood cannot draw, but he understands." And this was the case, for I was amongst the few in the Examination who got the section of that ugly-looking plan entitled "Kirkcudbright" correct. As I passed out of the Hall at Chelsea, seeing beads of perspiration starting from a friend's forehead who was clever at hachuring, I asked him later what was the matter, and he said that he had just discovered that in his section he had made the highest hill the deepest valley on the plan.

On the third day of the Examination, a brother-officer in the 17th Lancers called on me to ask my advice. Said he, "Is it any use for me to have a try at the German paper?" "What do you know?" "Nothing, until last night, when I bought Dr. Emil Otto's Grammar, and have not been to bed; at this moment I believe I can say the first five Declensions backwards or forwards. Naturally, I cannot speak a word, and know nothing more of it." I replied, "You might try, for Dr. Max Müller marks highly for Grammar; and at all events you will only lose an hour, after which you can come out."

This proved to be good advice for him, for he got the minimum, 50 marks, but unfortunate for me, for when the marks were totalled he had made 1904, I scoring only 1903.

On the evening of the last day of Examination I went to Oxford with Southwell, and started at daylight next morning to pull down the Thames. I had been pulling daily for a year, and so was in hard condition. My friend had been leading a London life, and his arms and face caught by the sun were painfully swollen, and he became so exhausted that he drove into Reading, the lock-keeper's son replacing him in the boat; and as Southwell was still indisposed next day, I took the lad as far as Maidenhead, where I was anxious to arrive, as Southwell's sisters were coming to dine and spend the evening. Southwell did not know that I loved his sister, and indeed resented it as soon as he became aware of the fact, some months later.

Before the result of the examination became known, I heard from a friend that I could not hope to join the Staff College while in the 17th Lancers,[1] and arranged to exchange into the 73rd Perthshire Regiment. The difference of one mark in the Examination entailed a considerable pecuniary loss to me, as if I had been able to wait until the 17th Lancers returned from India, due before my course at

[1] By the Regulations only one officer from a Regiment could be at the College.

the Staff College would expire, I should have received much more for the exchange.

I now made another financial arrangement with my parents, who always wanted to give me more than they could afford. At my request, they reduced my allowance when I went to India, and stopped it at the end of 1859. I had saved enough money in the East for all my expenses up to date, and had still some in hand; but we now arranged that I should draw £80 per annum, and I did so until my father's death, four years later, gave me a small income.

I joined the 73rd at Plymouth at the end of November, and with one exception was fortunate, for a more pleasant, agreeable set of officers it would have been difficult to find, and the people round the "Three Towns" being far off London, were very hospitable; indeed, it may be assumed that hospitality in country houses exercised in favour of officers varies in inverse ratio to the distance from London.

The difference in the behaviour of the men and of those with whom I had served in the 13th Light Dragoons was remarkable, the 73rd having more prisoners one morning than the 13th showed in a week; yet the battalion was really a good one, as is shown by the Adjutant-General, later Lord Airey, putting his only son in it.

The Colonel of the Regiment, Hugh M. Jones, who was universally liked, observed to me the day after my arrival, "I suppose as you have come from Cavalry you do not know much about Infantry drill, but I could not think of ordering an officer of your service to attend drill parades. I may, however, mention there is afternoon drill for the Subalterns four days in the week, at which you can, if you desire, attend, and look on." I naturally, after this, drilled as a Subaltern, until I was satisfied I could command a company fairly in the intricate movements in which Senior officers of that period delighted. Our Cavalry drill, complicated and useless as much of it was, has always in my period of service, until the last few years, been much in advance of the Infantry book.

I arrived in London on leave on the morning of Monday, the 16th December, when the news of the death of the Prince Consort, on Saturday–Sunday night, was announced. The sorrow was universally deep, and Dean Milman expressed correctly the feeling of the Nation in a sermon delivered a week later in St. Paul's Cathedral, when he observed, "From the Highest to the Lowest it is felt that a great example has been removed from amongst us."

In December I made the acquaintance of the Military Secretary, an aristocratic-looking, clever, well-informed, but hot-tempered gentleman, with a delicate constitution, which accounted for his not having been allowed to serve in the Crimea. This disappointment had soured a naturally generous man so far as regarded his treatment of applicants for War Service. Nevertheless, he was inflexibly just, and under a stiff and sometimes repellent demeanour concealed a kindly nature mingled with a keen sense of humour. He dominated the Army through the Horse Guards for eleven years.

The progress of the war in America indicated there might be trouble in Canada,[1] and it became known that half a dozen officers were to be sent out to that country on Special Service; so, asking for an interview, I was ushered into the General's room. "Well, what do you want?" "To go to Canada." "We are sending only Cavalry officers out." "I left Cavalry, sir, six months ago, but I will exchange back again, if I may go." "No; the selection will be limited to half-pay officers." "I will retire on half-pay, sir." "You would lose the place you have obtained at the Staff College, and I do not believe you would succeed in another competitive entrance Examination." "I'll chance it, sir, if I may go out." "Look here, young man, you want to go on Service, but it does not go down here." "That is evident, sir." "Get out of my room."

I hope, if any of the young officers who applied to me as Adjutant-General to aid them in getting out to South Africa, forty years later, read this book, they will recall that my reception of them was more sympathetic. There was no intrinsic difference in our aims, however; we both desired to get the best men for the work to be done for our country. The innate generosity of the Military Secretary's mind may be seen by the following story. He sent for a young officer, who was playing billiards at a Club, relative to an application he had made for some post, and the young man hastening

[1] On the 8th November, Captain Wilkes of the *San Jacinto* seized the Confederate Commissioners Slidell and Mason on board the British Mail steamer *Trent*.

to obey the summons, placed in his pocket a piece of chalk which he was handling at the time. He was badly received, and his application refused. As he left the General's office he chalked up on the door, "Cave Canem." The messenger-in-waiting being short-sighted, the legend remained unnoticed until the General saw it when he was leaving in the evening, and as he had not received anyone else that afternoon there was no doubt as to who had thus expressed his opinion of the Military Secretary, and so the following morning the young officer was sent for again, and taxed with having written the notice. He at once admitted it, and expressing regret, had his application granted! My next interview with the Military Secretary was of a more pleasant nature than when my application to be sent to Canada was refused. He accompanied the Commander-in-Chief and many other General officers to inspect the work done at the Staff College, and was pleased to make some complimentary remark on my drawing of "The Polygonal System," on which I had spent many weary hours; but the effect of the praise I received from the Staff was lessened by the fact that many of them regarded the drawing upside down!

At the end of January I took my horses to the Staff College—a thoroughbred which had run third for the Goodwood Cup, an ordinary hunter, and the pony which I had brought from the Crimea. In 1863 the officers passed into the Staff College by competition, being allowed to take up a great number of subjects, which had helped me materially, as though ignorant I was quick at learning; but the system had the great disadvantage of never allowing a student time to master any one subject. When I had been for a month at Sunbury, Captain Lendy made me drop French and take to German, observing, "You know quite enough French to get two-thirds marks, and you must give your time now to other subjects." Once in the College, the competition to get out of it was on a different system, the number of subjects being limited, and there was also a minimum aggregate number of marks essential to ensure a pass being awarded. This minimum was based on the assumption that everyone would score 565 in every subject. Now, Mathematics counted 1200, and although scarcely anyone got more than 800 or 900, yet as the average man got over 600, he had a great advantage over the mere linguist in obtaining the aggregate minimum, since full marks for a language was only 300.

A few days after my arrival, the Professor of Mathematics, in his opening lecture, turned over the first seventy pages of Todhunter's *Algebra*, saying, " It is no use talking to you about this ; all of you will understand that," most of what he said being incomprehensible to me, who had never got farther than the simplest of Simple Equations. When the lecture was over, I explained to him my ignorance, and that it would be practically impossible for me to keep up with the class. He was kind and sympathetic, offering to give me private instruction ; but I wrote to the Council of Military Education as to my position, and stating that while I had no desire to compete, I asked permission to take up either Russian or Chinese, not for marks but only to show I was not idle, and to obtain the minimum aggregate, in order to pass out. The answer was to the effect that mine was not the first case, and although the Regulation as it stood did not oblige officers to take up Mathematics, yet in the opinion of the Council it was desirable that every officer should do so, and that if I wished to obtain the certificate of having passed through the Staff College, I must score so high in all the other subjects as to get the minimum number of marks. In any case, I should have to do a certain amount of Trigonometry, for which I should not receive any credit. The letter ended with strongly worded advice to give up the idea I had formed, stating that two of my predecessors after making a somewhat similar request, had been obliged later to revert to Mathematics. This advice, however, I did not accept, and two years later did sufficiently well in French, German, Hindustani, and other subjects, to gain three places on passing out, on the position I held in the Entrance Examination.

Many of my companions of the College were no longer young, and some found it difficult to alter their habits to the College life. A clever Artillery officer was much vexed because after the first week, during which his messmates consented to play whist with him after dinner as an act of politeness refused to do so any longer ; thus he was left without amusement in the evening, being unwilling to follow the custom of most of the officers, who studied till bedtime. For a week or ten days I played chess with him, at the end of which time he returned to Regimental duty, although there was no doubt he could have passed well, had he been willing to alter his mode of life.

I soon made the acquaintance of the Reverend Charles Kingsley, whose Rectory, Eversley, was about 6 miles from the College, and spent many happy Sundays in the family circle. Thousands of his readers may have often pictured in their minds what kind of man wrote *Westward Ho*, but few can have realised his delightful simplicity and charm of manner, which made him a most eloquent preacher in spite of an occasional stammer. This did not affect him in the pulpit, where his great command of language enabled him to bridge over a word he found difficult, by substituting a synonym, and I never heard more perfect word-pictures than those he preached of David's life on four successive Sundays in 1864. He loved not only his fellow-men but all Nature, and his children "learnt without tears" the names of every tree, plant, wildflower, and weed. I asked him once if he would not shorten the service by omitting the Litany when he read the Communion service, and he replied he had started by doing so, but the labourers, possibly feeling they were being defrauded, complained, saying, " Unless we get the whole, we shan't come."

Throughout the two years' course I hunted as a rule five days a fortnight. For the first year I went home every Saturday night, thus giving the Professors the impression that I was not studying; but I was never in bed after six on a hunting morning, and always did three hours' study on my return, and so lost less time than my instructors imagined.

In the spring of 1863, when my affection for Miss Paulina Southwell became evident, I was given to understand that, irrespective of monetary considerations, neither Lord Southwell nor any of his family would consent to receive me into it, unless I became a Catholic. I had loved the lady from the first day I met her, on my return from India. I had many Catholic friends and sincere admiration for their religion, an admiration which deepened year by year after my marriage, as I saw it so perfectly exemplified in my wife's Christian life. I could not, however, accept the suggestion that I should abandon the Church in which I had been brought up, and possibly resented the conditions on which only the prize was obtainable. I read many Catholic books, and Newman's *Apologia pro Vita Sua* two or three times over when it was published a year later, but seldom met Paulina Southwell during the next four years, nor did we exchange a single letter, till I asked her, in August 1867, to marry me. My friendship for Southwell, dating from 1855, deepened yearly, and we remained on affectionate terms until his death, in 1878; nevertheless, while guardian of his orphan sisters, he never lost sight of the possibilities of unhappiness incidental to mixed marriages, and therefore, in spite of our friendship, he was unwilling to receive a Protestant into his family. His fears, however, were unfounded, for though a difference of religion of man and wife is not generally conducive to domestic happiness, yet it never raised a discordant note between Paulina Southwell and me in the twenty-three years of our union.

On the 29th December 1863, while staying with Sir Thomas Barrett Lennard, I had a heavy fall, nearly breaking my neck. I got away with hounds from one of the Belhus coverts, close on a fox. I was riding a thoroughbred mare on a snaffle, and she swerved from a small fence on to a high gate, jumping as she breasted it. We turned right over in the next field, my body remaining on the saddle while my head was twisted back between her feet, with one of which, in struggling to rise, she hit my head. I was taken to Belhus, and next morning, when my mother returned to see me, her look of horror made me crawl to the looking-glass after she had left the room. I had fallen on the crown of my head, and my neck had swollen till it protruded beyond the cheek-bones, giving the appearance of large double goitre. I hunted again three weeks later, at Dewlish, in Dorsetshire, when on a visit to General Sir John Michel, to whom I owed much in my career. I strolled into the King's Arms, Dorchester, to look at the room where Clement, Stanley Clarke, and I messed in 1855, and hearing the hounds met at Dewlish next day, hired a cob. I had no riding-clothes, and in my skull-cap[1] presented an unusual figure on the lawn. We found in the home covert,

---
[1] The wound in my head prevented my wearing a hat.

and the hounds crossed a flight of rails, not high, but being strong, nearly all the field rode off at an angle to avoid them. I welcomed the chance of seeing if my fall had unnerved me, but when the pony went so close as to touch the rails with his knees as he rose, I felt my heart flutter; but he knew his work, and carried me well.

I spent the summer vacation of 1864 visiting the battlefields of Frederick the Great and Napoleon. I had advertised, in the spring of the year, in leading German papers asking to be received into a German family for six weeks, stating that I was a student of the Staff College. I selected one of the more expensive offers, and went to Dresden. On my arrival, I received a letter from Monsieur Delissert, who was my tutor at Sunbury in 1861. He had become proprietor of a school at Ouchy, in Switzerland, the pupils being nearly all Germans, and invited me to join him on a holiday walking tour. My acceptance of the offer precluded the possibility of my staying at Dresden, and my prospective host courteously offered me the assistance of his son, a young man who spoke no English, for a short walking tour, which I carried out in the Saxon Switzerland. At Heidelberg in 1862, and at Dresden in 1864, I paid or was asked to pay only half the sum I expended for my sons a quarter of a century later, but it is right to state they were better accommodated and boarded.

The day after the young man left me to return to Dresden I was going down the Elbe, and when near the Bastei[1] my attention was attracted by a noise in the fore part of the steamer. Strolling forward, I found an Indian dressed in the Irregular Cavalry uniform, a long dark green coat, red puggaree, cummerbund, and knee-boots. He had the look of the "Derby Dog" in his face, and the excitement of the Germans was sufficient to startle anyone, for they were shouting at him at the top of their voices single English words. Going up behind him, I said gently in Hindustani, "Can I be of any assistance to you?" Jumping round, he replied, "All praise to the Almighty, I once more hear a civilised tongue."

His story, which I translated sentence by sentence to the Germans standing around, was peculiar. After leaving our

[1] In the Saxon Switzerland.

Service, he had lived in Jerusalem for twenty years as a Muhammadan missionary, with what success he did not say, and was travelling to England as a mendicant. He had papers on him from Consuls and other persons in authority, and a letter signed by the Governor of Agram, Croatia. The interest that the Germans took in the strangely dressed man now increased, and they collected £8, 14s. in gulden, which they asked me to give him. One gentleman was so impressed by the story that he asked me to bid him welcome to his house in Berlin, if he passed that way on going to England. When I conveyed this polite offer, the mendicant said with some indignation, "God is our provider; we should take no thought for the morrow." While thinking how to render pleasantly the somewhat curt reply, the German proverb came into my head, which I used, softening the Indian's remark into a polite expression of gratitude, and ending with the explanation, "He holds, 'Jeder Tag hat seine Sorge.'" I found that the numberless questions which the excited Germans launched at me was tiring, and taking up my small handbag I endeavoured to get ashore unperceived when the steamer stopped under the Bastei; but the Indian was too quick, and catching me on the gangboard by the skirt of my frock coat, with the apposite Eastern expression, "I clutch the hem of your garment," followed me up to the hotel where I intended to remain. I explained the situation to the manager, adding that the man had £8, 14s. in silver, but that I would be answerable for his bed and board that night, and then I left him.

A quarter of an hour later, while I was having tea, the waiter ran to me, saying, "Your black friend has taken off most of his clothes on the river bank : will you please speak to him ?" Going outside, I saw the Indian kneeling on a prayer-carpet on the sand, divested of all his clothing except a loin-cloth. I said, "What are you doing ? Put your clothes on ; you must not kneel here naked." He looked reproachfully at me, and said, "Kneel down too ; it is the hour of evening prayer ;" and then it dawned on me that he thought I was a Mussulman. After dinner, I paid my bill and the missionary's, and walked away at daybreak, fearing I might be saddled with his company for an indefinite period.

Two days later, I went from Dresden to see the battlefield of Bautzen, and having noticed there was apparently a station 8 or 9 miles from the town close to the scene of action, I asked for a ticket to the place, Förstchen. The booking clerk said, repeating the name two or three times, " Do you really want to go there?" And on my replying in the affirmative, he went out on to the platform, and said to the guard, "This gentleman wants to go to Förstchen;" and the guard looked me over as if I were demented. Before the train started, he repeated the question, "You really want to go to Förstchen?" And at the next station before arriving at my destination, he came to the carriage door and said, "Give me your ticket; there is no one there to take it." The station consisted of a long platform, and when the train passed on I felt as if I were on a desert island. Walking southward towards the battlefield, I came on a group of children, who screaming fled. One of them was lame, and him I caught, and with chocolates and coppers soon made him sufficiently at home to talk; and the other children, who had stopped to see what became of their companion, now came back. I sent one of them to call his father, who was at work; and the man, about five-and-forty years of age, proved to be an excellent guide. He had lived with his father, who was present at the battle as a spectator, and had practically worked on the battlefield all his life, and told me the name of every natural feature.

From Dresden I went to Munich, Prague, and thence into Switzerland to see my friend Delissert. I joined his party, and have never had so good accommodation at such moderate terms. One of the elder boys generally walked ahead, and made a bargain. In order to ascend the Righi, we started from an unfrequented village—indeed, we were never on beaten tracks. Every room I slept in was scrupulously clean, and the cheapness may be understood from my bill at one place, which for a supper, with two meat courses and second course, half a bottle of wine, bed, with a roll and coffee next morning, was five francs. I acquired some colloquial proficiency in German, and then returned to Camberley.

The instruction at the College was unsatisfactory in many respects; for example, the French teacher's one idea of imparting knowledge of his language was to read the letters of the great Emperor to his brothers and subordinate Generals, and thus the words, "Napoleon à Joseph, Mon frère," had the effect of clearing the study of all who could get out without being rude to this courteous Professor. The Fortification and Drawing Instructors knew their subjects, but were not good teachers. I had the advantage of sitting under two distinguished lecturers: Colonel, afterwards Sir Edward Hamley, whose *Operations of War* is a Military text-book, and who so bravely led his Division at Tel-el-Kebir; and the other, Colonel Charles Chesney, celebrated for his *Waterloo Lectures*, which were republished in all Continental capitals, who was one of a clever family, his brother being the author of *The Battle of Dorking*. Colonel Hamley expected his pupils to accept his deductions as well as his facts, and did not encourage original research.

After his lecture on the battle of Blenheim, there being no books which treated of the battle in the then meagre Staff College library, I obtained in London Cox's *Life of Marlborough*, which I offered to the two men whose society I most enjoyed. They were about my own age, but took College life more seriously than I did. One gratefully accepted the loan of the volumes, but the other answered gaily, "No, I shall serve up Hamley, Hamley, nothing but Hamley; that always gets me full marks." When Colonel Hamley was succeeded by Colonel Chesney on the conclusion of the first lecture, I went to my friend, who was a wonderful précis writer, and said, "After this lecture, you will have to think for yourself." Charles Chesney's ideas of teaching were diametrically opposed to those of his predecessor. He mentioned the salient points in the standard authorities who had written on the campaign or battle, and then said, "And now, gentlemen, no doubt you will be good enough to read all these authors and give me the advantage of your studies." The result showed my forecast was correct, for my friend, the précis writer, who had hitherto got one or two marks out of a hundred more than anyone else, now came down to our level.

At the end of 1864, many of my instructors having foretold I should fail in the Final Examination, I settled down to work harder, and to enjoy less hunting. The confinement, however, immediately affected my nervous system, and the aurist under whose care I had placed myself when I returned from India, wrote to the Commandant, unknown to me, deprecating my undertaking any additional work. Colonel William Napier, a son of one of the three distinguished Peninsular Napiers, had married the daughter of Sir Charles Napier, the conqueror of Scinde; he had been kind to me during my terms, and was a man of unusually broad generous mind, for within three months of my joining, when acting as President of a ball committee, I struck out the names of many of his friends whom he had asked as public guests to the ball. Sending for me to his office, he demanded an explanation, and I told him that none of the people whose names I had omitted had ever invited anyone from the College into their houses except himself, when he observed, "Please send out the invitations in my name:" and it was done.

I had ridden successfully one of his horses which he found uncontrollable, entirely from his habit of catching hold of the horse's mouth when approaching a fence. The horse was naturally a slow, nervous fencer, but in the Commandant's hands became so excitable that I have seen him run backwards when checked on approaching a fence. I rode the horse for a month, and then handing him back to the Commandant, he enjoyed two days' hunting, the horse jumping perfectly; but the third day out he resumed his habit of rushing, with the result that the rider got a broken leg. Later the horse came into my possession, and carried me or one of my sisters for many years.

The Commandant sending for me, read my Medical attendant's letter, and telling me that the Professors thought I should probably fail to get the aggregate number of marks, observed that he was himself leaving the College to assume command of a brigade in Dublin, and as he knew all about me from my two years' residence at the College, he would be glad to take me as his Aide-de-Camp, whether I passed or not, and suggested I might avoid the worry, and possible annoyance of failure by not going up for the Final Examination. I thanked the Commandant warmly, asking for a fortnight to consider the question of the appointment, but said at once that having looked at a fence for two years, I could not refuse to go at it and cross it, and would sooner fail than not try.

I had a curious premonitory dream in the last week I

spent at the College. I thought I knew fairly well the usual questions on Bridging, and had given but little time to it. I dreamt the night before I was to be examined I could not describe General Eblé's bridges made over the Beresina for Napoleon's retreat, and getting up studied it carefully, from 1 to 3 a.m. It was the first question in our paper set at 10 a.m.! The Professors were mistaken, and having done better than anyone anticipated in the Final Examination, I went over to Dublin at the end of the year, and joined General William Napier.

The night after I arrived in Dublin I dined at the Mansion House, when discussion was carried on across the table with a gentleman sitting next to me about the Clones agency. It was impossible for me to avoid hearing the conversation, and as a result of what I learnt that evening I supervised for twenty-one years the management of my brother-in-law's estate, about 9000 Irish acres. Six months later, Sir Thomas Lennard, who had married my second sister, went down with me to Clones, the third time it had been visited by the owner for upwards of eighty years, he having succeeded his grandfather, who lived to be nearly a hundred years old.

CHAPTER XIX

1865–7—" ON THE STAFF "

Recognition of an opponent—A good Veterinary Surgeon—"Vagabond" —Fenian scares—I supervise the management of an Irish estate— Difficulties of marriage settlements—Sir Thomas Lennard—His offer of £5000.

ON the 22nd May, when accompanying General Napier, who was inspecting a battalion at Mullingar, my eye rested on an officer whose face I recognised, and when the parade was over I asked him, " Are you the man who fought me in the public-house in Air Street, Regent Street, and gave me such a hammering ? " He replied, " I am the man ; but I do not admit that I gave you a hammering, for you left me speechless."

In taking lessons from various pugilists in London, I had gone in 1862 to an ex-" Lightweight Champion," and after a few lessons I was foolish enough to accept his proposition that instead of paying 7s. 6d. for each lesson, I should pay him £5, and then have as many lessons as I desired. The result was that after I had had two or three lessons, instead of taking the trouble to stand up himself, he invariably set me to box with the first pupil who happened to come in, and thus it was I met the gentleman, not knowing he was in the Army. Though neither of us lost our tempers, we had what was virtually, and is now called, a glove fight, except that our gloves were heavier and better covered.

I suffered so continuously in the summer of 1865 each time I got seriously wet from recurring attacks of fever, which affected my ears, accompanied with neuralgia and swollen face, that I went over to London in July, when my dentist informed me that I should always suffer when ill from other causes unless I had eight stumps of teeth at the back of my mouth removed. I then made a round of doctors' houses, asking if they would give me chloroform, but they one and all declined, so I went back to Dublin, and asked a physician who had been most successful in treating a gnawing pain from which I had suffered in the stomach, but he, while declining to allow there was any disease of the heart, was not willing to administer to me an anæsthetic, so returning to England I sought out Dr. Nicholas Parker, who had attended one of my sisters. He was himself ill, and had given up practice, but consented to give me chloroform, and, having arranged with the dentist, I went up to London, accompanied by my mother and four grieving brothers and sisters. After a careful examination, Dr. Parker postponed the operation, telling me to come back again in a fortnight. When I returned, the attendant family had dropped to three, after another fortnight to one, and eventually there was nobody with me, when the doctor said cheerfully, "Yes, you are fit to-day; go away and have a good luncheon, for you won't want to eat much for a day or two." Since that period, although I cannot say I have been free from neuralgia in the head, I have suffered much less from face ache.

I accompanied my General to the Curragh in the summer, and there became so ill I was obliged to go away. Doctor Hudson, the Physician of the Meath Hospital, did more for me than anyone else at the time, chiefly by keeping me on a milk diet.

In the autumn of the year, my battalion, the 73rd, was ordered to Hong Kong, and I expected orders to embark with it. This I should have done, but that the pleasant Colonel who commanded it when I joined, retired, and was succeeded by a man I disliked, so I paid £500 for an exchange to the 17th Regiment.

At the end of the year I bought "Vagabond," the best horse I ever possessed, from a farmer at Finglas, just outside Dublin. It had been sold within three weeks at varying prices, from £85 to £15. I saw the animal cross some apparently impossible fences, his rider wielding a heavy bludgeon with which he struck the horse violently over the head. Eventually I begged him to desist, for I was afraid he would either stun the horse or that it would break its legs, and I became its owner for £45, the farmer betting a friend £10 he would get it back in a week for £15. The certificate of the Veterinary surgeon, Mr. Ferguson, is worth quoting for young horse-owners: " I have examined the chestnut ——. I regard it as unsound, and advise you to buy it." Next day I called on Mr. Ferguson, and said, " Oh, I bought that horse, and here is your fee; and now will you tell me where he is unsound?" Said he, " Are you a busy man?" " Yes, I am, but I can listen to you for five minutes." " But it will take me the forenoon to tell you all the places in which that horse is unsound."

The horse objecting to jump, gave me five severe falls the first day I rode him after the Ward Union Hounds. I cannot write *with*, for after the first fall, on which the farmers shouted, " Take that brute away, or he will kill you or some of us," I never saw the hounds, but rode the line for 8 miles, crossing every fence. The same farmers came to me a fortnight later, wanting to know what drug I put up the horse's nose to tame him, and it was some time before I could induce them to believe that I had improved the horse's temper by consistent kindness. During thirteen seasons, while carrying my wife, my brother who rode it while I was in South Africa, or me to hounds, the horse never made a mistake. He was, however, a trial to one's patience, for the first time I rode him from Stephen's Green to my General's house, about 4 miles, it took me over two hours, the horse walking about on his fore and hind legs alternately.

I should have had a pleasant life in 1865–6 but that I suffered from continuous ill-health. I went to a famous physician in London, afterwards created a baronet for his devoted care of the Heir to the throne, and to many doctors of lesser note. The disease from which I was suffering was neuralgia of the nerves of the stomach, treatment for which presents but comparatively little difficulty now, but forty-five years ago it was not so. I managed to hunt, but occasionally suffered such acute pain as to be unable to sit in the saddle.

On the 9th of February 1866 I received a telegram to the effect that my father was very dangerously ill at Belhus, and leaving Ireland that night I remained with him until he died, a fortnight later.

VAGABOND

Shortly after I returned to Dublin I lost my appointment, my Chief being made Director-General of Military Education, and I was ordered to join my Regiment, then at Aldershot. My mother went to Brighton, and keeping my horses at Redhill, I lived with her two months, hunting with the Surrey Stag Hounds and adjoining packs. I was still suffering severely from neuralgia in the face and stomach. Early in March, when hunting near Cranleigh, we had had a slow run for two hours, and being close to the station, and wet to the skin, I went into a shop and bought every article of clothing, from a suit and shoes to undergarments. Shortly before the train started, a London citizen who might have been Mr. Jorrocks himself, bustled into the train, reeking with spirits, and upbraided me for leaving the hounds until the deer had been taken. I told him I had delicate lungs, but he derided the idea of changing clothes, adding, " Look at me ; I have had three glasses of hot gin and water, and I shall be all right." And so he was. I being in bed for the next fortnight with double pneumonia, became so ill that a Medical Board declined to allow me to join at Aldershot until I regained my health.

On the 30th June, having ceased to cough, I joined at Aldershot the battalion to which I had been recently appointed, in which my eldest brother, Sir Francis, had previously served and was a guest at the time. I did not do duty with it, for after a few days I was appointed Deputy Assistant Quartermaster-General in charge of the Instructional Kitchen of Cookery.[1] I knew little of cooking, but thought with study I might acquire sufficient knowledge, but was startled to find that the kitchen was only to occupy a part of my time, the more important duty being to instruct officers in Military Drawing and Field Sketching. This was an unpleasant surprise, for except Mathematics, Drawing was my weakest subject at the College, and going to London I asked to see the Military Secretary. I explained my difficulty in undertaking such a task, but my explanations were not well received, the General observing, " A Staff College officer ought to be able to do anything." I said meekly, " But perhaps you do not know I was

---

[1] I received at the same time an offer to go abroad with a General officer whom I had known in India as his Military Secretary, but declined the offer, feeling sure that we should not find each other's society congenial.

the duffer of my class. I am not thinking of myself, but of those whom I have to instruct." He replied, " Well, you have got to do it." And I left the room.

Going back to Aldershot, I heard accidentally that the Brigade-Major in the North Camp had been ordered to rejoin his battalion, and applied officially to be transferred to the post. Meantime I prepared for my first class of students, and feeling incapable of teaching what I did not thoroughly understand, I got my friend Herr Zöbel to come from Sunbury for forty-eight hours, in which time much that had been vague and undefined in my mind, even after two years at the Staff College, became clear, and when Zöbel went back on the third day I reported to the Assistant Quartermaster-General that I was ready to begin.

Before the class assembled, however, I had become Brigade-Major in the North Camp, under General Sir Alfred Horsford, by whom I was treated with the greatest kindness. He was handsome, clever, with great knowledge of the world, and had done well in the Indian Mutiny; although he did not know details of the Drill book, he handled troops well, but was not fond of soldiering in peace times. When in the spring of 1867 I asked whether we ought not to exercise the Brigade, prior to Divisional parades, my General replied calmly, " Yes, certainly ; a good idea—I quite approve. Carry on, but do not ask me to attend." He supported me, however, so my work was very pleasant.

He was popular in society, having many friends, being especially intimate with Sir John Cope of Bramshill, 10 miles from Aldershot, where he spent a great deal of his time. This of course became known, and gave rise to an amusing incident, of which Sir Alfred, who had a keen sense of humour, himself told me. Approaching the Lieutenant-General, Sir James Yorke Scarlett, Sir Alfred said with much warmth before other General officers, " The Duke told me, Sir James, that you said I was seldom here." The Lieutenant-General said very calmly, " You have been misinformed, Horsford: what I said was, you were never here."

Sir Alfred believed in a celibate Army, and told numberless stories in support of his views. When in command of a battalion, Rifle Brigade, a soldier came up for permission to marry. " No, certainly not. Why does a young man like you want a wife ? " " Oh, please, sir, I have two rings (Good Conduct badges) and £5 in the Savings Bank, so I am eligible, and I want to marry very much." " Well, go away, and if you come back this day year in the same mind, you shall marry ; I'll keep the vacancy." On the anniversary the soldier repeated his request. " But do you really after a year want to marry ? " " Yes, sir, very much." " Sergeant-Major, take his name down. Yes, you may marry. I never believed there was so much constancy in man or woman. Right face. Quick march." As the man left the room, turning his head, he said, " Thank you, sir ; it isn't the same woman."

I invented a knapsack a month or two after I joined, and was told to consult with Dr. Parkes,[1] one of the most advanced Medical officers in the Service. I went down to Southampton where he lived, and he satisfied me that one on which he was then working, arranged to spread the weight over the body, a modification of which was eventually adopted, was better than mine ; my principle of the alteration of the pouches, however, was accepted. Previously the pouches were made rectangular, and as no man's body is exactly flat there was obviously inconvenience in this arrangement, especially as one of the tests of soldiering in those days was to bring the rifle across the body as closely as possible without hitting it, with the result that the edges of the pouches were found to be inconvenient.

In December, there being rumours of a Fenian outbreak, my General was sent over to Ireland, and a fortnight later I was ordered to join him. On the last day of the month he was offered command of a Division. Now his tact and knowledge of the Army was profound. He asked Lord Strathnairn (Sir Hugh Rose) to leave the question in abeyance until an outbreak occurred, saying that any supersession of a General officer in peace-time would be unpopular in the Army, and thus it was arranged, the General in question not being informed of what was hanging over him. After I had been three weeks in Dublin, I got leave to go to England until wanted. In the middle of February I received an urgent telegram from the General to rejoin. He had gone to

[1] Author of Parkes' *Hygiene*.

Killarney, where we remained for six weeks, with a large body of troops, but learned most of the Fenian movements from the London morning papers. I satisfied myself that some of the reports of the assembling of Fenians were untrue, for on receiving a report of a large body of men having been seen drilling in a field near Tralee I went there immediately; but though the field was wet, there was not a footprint on it. We went in April to Mallow, as a Police barrack had been attacked and burned at Blarney, one station on the Cork side of Mallow Junction. As we travelled up, a bridge near Mill Street had been set on fire, but without being sufficiently damaged to interrupt the traffic, and although there was doubtless much disaffection, the arrangements for a rising were despicable.

We returned to Aldershot at the end of March, and going up to London I bought five couples of hounds. Getting up at 3 a.m., I trailed an anise-seeded rabbit over the Long Valley, coming back an hour later to hunt it. I never had more than three companions, but I persevered until the weather became so hot that the scent would not lie in the Long Valley.

I have often been asked whether I am nervous out hunting, and my answer in the affirmative has been frequently discredited. I cannot recall the time when I have not been for the first few fences, but so far as I know my mind, my nervousness does not affect my riding, as is shown by the following story of the early sixties. I was riding frequently with the Essex Stag Hounds horses hired from the farmer horse-dealer who acted as huntsman to the pack. He was driving me from Ingatestone to the meet one Tuesday morning, when I observed, "What sort of a mount have I got to-day?" "Well, Major, I cannot say I know very much about him, but I believe he is a very good one." It was a low, strong, cob-like horse, with great power and breeding. The deer having been uncarted, as we rode down at the first fence my teeth were chattering so as to be painful, and I crossed the first two holding my jaw with my left hand. We had a brilliant thirty-five minutes, in which the horse performed well, making only one mistake, in which although we got down we did not part company, and when we had secured the deer the owner of the horse said, " Major, will you get off, and ride this gentleman's horse? for he may be a customer."

When we were driving home from the public-house where we regained the cart, the huntsman said to me, "I owe you a good turn, Major, to-day." "Why?" "Oh, you have sold that horse for me." "Done well?" "Oh, I haven't made a heap of money, but I like quick returns." "Then you have not had the horse long?" "No, I only bought him yesterday afternoon at Tattersall's."

I stayed at Reading for the Ascot week with a cousin, and on the Thursday accidentally met the Southwells. My former General, William Napier, accosted me in the enclosure, asking whether I could get him some lunch, and I replied, "Oh yes, come across the drag enclosure, and you can have what you like; I am sure to know many men there." Threading our way through the coaches, I looked up, and saw Miss Paulina Southwell. The General, to whose wife I had confided my feelings, said, "Oh, don't mind my lunch; stop here, and talk to your friends." I said, "No, sir," and went on until we got to the Guards' tent, where a friend made us welcome. I am not a lunch-eater, but the General had a hearty appetite, and asked me if I could get him a chair. That lunch appeared to be about the longest I ever attended, but I waited patiently, and insisted on piloting my former General across the course before I left him, when I returned to Lord Southwell's coach, and saw the lady whom I had not met for a long time, and with whom I never corresponded until, two months later, I wrote and asked her to marry me.

I was very foolish at that time, for I tried to reduce my weight, which has not varied four pounds in forty years, in order to ride in some races. I had ridden a good hunter in the Tweezledown[1] steeplechases soon after I returned from Ireland, but the horse was hopelessly outclassed, and in July I rode four races in succession one day, on a diet of a limited number of biscuits, for which folly I suffered considerably; for a fortnight later, after being very wet on parade, I got fever, and early in August fainted three times one morning in my office. I went to London and saw doctors, who prescribed perfect rest, and as my brother-in-law had decided to appoint another Agent, I went over to his estate in Ireland, hoping that the change of air might improve my health. I was

[1] Aldershot.

still weak when I got to Clones, where I wished to see a tenant who had not paid his rent for eleven years. The annual sum was trifling, under two pounds, but the example set by the man was bad on an estate which had arrears of over £11,000 on a rental of £8000. My brother-in-law's London solicitor was coming over to go through the estate accounts with me, and the day before he arrived, taking a car, I went out to see the recalcitrant tenant. I was uncertain of my reception, so, although the day was fine, I wore an overcoat, in the pocket of which I carried a big revolver. The driver pulled up alongside a punt, in which I was ferried over to the island on which McElnea lived, in a little cabin, and on entering I saw a fine tall man, nearly seventy years of age. He did not offer me a seat, but there were three stools, and I sat down on one, remarking, "You do not offer me a seat, but I am not well, and so sit down." "Who the divil are ye? Are ye the landlord?" "No, but I am his brother-in-law, and very like him." "Well, is it about the rint that ye have come?" "It is." "Sorra a penny will I pay! Divil a man is there in Oirland to make me." And as he spoke in came two fine specimens of humanity, over six feet in height. I looked at them, and putting my hand into my pocket, said to McElnea, "Well, I am going back into Clones, and you can pack up." "Pack, is it? and why would I pack?" "Because when I get into Clones I shall issue a process against you, and you will be out in a week." Changing from his defiant to a cringing tone, he said, "Why, yer honour will not be turning me out of the ould place; I am a very ould man, and I have always lived here." I replied, "We do not want you here, and I will give you your crop and £5 to go away." "I would much sooner stop, may I?" "If you pay a year and a half's rent to-morrow, and a year and a half every year until you are clear, you can remain." He paid, and on the next gale [1] day, saying he could not be bothered with accounts, paid up all arrears, and gave no further trouble.

I had discussed daily with my mother and sisters, since the Ascot meeting, the question of my marrying Paulina Southwell. I did not apprehend any difficulty with her about religion, but realised that my financial position did not justify

[1] Rent.

my asking her to marry me, and that moreover I was too fond of my profession to abate in the slightest degree my desire for War Service on any possible occasion. Eventually, on my way to Clones, I wrote to her explaining my unsatisfactory financial position and my feelings as a soldier, and asking her whether she would consider the question of marrying me, on the distinct understanding that she would never by a word, or even a look, check my volunteering for War Service.

After I had settled my brother-in-law's business, I went to Turkeenagh, a mountain 12 miles from Scarriff, where I had a share in a moor. I was too ill to walk, but enjoyed the air and the society of my companions. We had had a successful day with the grouse on the hills looking down on Lough Derg, when, getting the *Irish Times*, I saw an expedition was going to Abyssinia, under General Napier. I packed my bag, and, sending a boy to the nearest public-house for a car, drove 38 miles to Nenagh station, *en route* for London. I telegraphed to Miss Southwell that I had received no reply to my letter written ten days earlier, and asking her not to answer until she heard again from me. Writing in the train, I explained the object of my journey to London was to try to get to Abyssinia, and although I could not advise her to marry me before I embarked, I should be glad to do so if she wished; adding I was unlikely to see anyone in Abyssinia whom I should prefer to her, as I had not done so during the six or seven years I had spent in England and Ireland since our first meeting. When I got to London, I received her answer saying that fully understanding my feelings about War Service, she accepted me, but that she would await my return from Abyssinia. I found it was not William, but Robert Napier, afterwards Lord Napier of Magdala, who would command; moreover, the Staff of the Expedition would be chosen almost exclusively from those serving in India, and I was married a fortnight later.

There were monetary difficulties, as I was poor; indeed, an old friend in common, Canon Doyle, had teased Miss Southwell, when she sought his advice, by saying he knew only one great objection besides that of religion, which he explained later, was "Major Wood's dreadful impecuniosity." This lack of means gave an opportunity to my brother-in-law of showing me his character. My mother's brother-in-law when dying had left a large property to his childless wife, with verbal instructions to "take care of Emma's children." She had given without demur £5000 to each of my brothers and sisters when they had married, but although she had not been to church for fifty years, she objected to my marrying a Catholic, and refused to settle anything on me. Sir Thomas Barrett Lennard heard that the marriage might not take place, and wrote to the following effect: "There are many disadvantages in being as casual about money as I am, but this time there is an advantage in it; please accept the cheque I send for £5000. I am content to take my chance of your surviving your aunt, and of my eventually getting the money back." I naturally thanked him warmly, but other arrangements were made. Six weeks after my marriage I arranged with his London solicitor to make certain alterations at Clones, and for twenty-one years had the satisfaction of remitting a large annual income to my brother-in-law, without his being troubled with work which he disliked.

Sir Thomas, who married my second surviving sister, is a fine classical scholar, and has ever been a capable and indefatigable worker in County business, going as thoroughly into every matter of self-imposed duty as he does in the pursuit of his principal recreation, the breaking in of horses and making them hunters. I have never known a man with better hands, nor one who can encourage more successfully a wayward four-year-old to execute his rider's wishes. He never cared for shooting, but in order to recompense me for supervising his Irish estate, he preserved pheasants in the coverts at Belhus for my pleasure,—foxes, however, being the first consideration; indeed, at the end of one season there were to my knowledge thirteen left on the estate of 4000 acres.

He has repaid me many times over in the last forty-five years, by unvarying kindness. While he lived at Belhus, his house, before and after my marriage, was my home; and in 1874, on hearing I was wounded, he offered to go out to the West Coast of Africa, disregarding the climate, which had carried Insurance premiums up to 45 per centum, and the fact that he had at the time a large family.

I had been away ten days on my honeymoon when I was recalled by my General, who had the command of a large gathering of Volunteers at Liverpool. He took with him two senior Colonels who commanded battalions at Aldershot; but they appreciated the pleasures of the table, and falling victims to turtle soup at the Adelphi Hotel the evening we arrived, remained in bed until the Review was over, and we were back at Aldershot.

CHAPTER XX

1867-71—ALDERSHOT

Sporting Essex farmers — An eccentric groom — Drunk and incapable in the street—Ill-health induces me to think of joining the Bar—A fine example on parade—Sir James Yorke Scarlett—A student of the Middle Temple—School feasts—A Low Church Colonel—An audacious order—Sir Hope Grant, his lovable nature.

THE winter of 1867-68 was for many years the best season's hunting I enjoyed, although I was occasionally suffering from ill-health. General Napier had lent me a hunter, and besides "Vagabond," already described, I bought a bay mare named "Fractious." When I was sent over to Dublin at Christmas 1866, my friend Mr. Leonard Morrogh wrote me a note, saying that, owing to a week's frost a horse bought by a Colonel in the Indian Army had been kept in its stable at Sewell's Yard, and having refused to leave the yard, had given stablemen heavy falls. The mare was known to be very clever over a banking country, and Morrogh, hearing its owner who gave £70 before the frost would accept £20, advised me to go and look at her. The frost was breaking up when I drove down and had the mare out. She was nearly as broad as she was long, with straight shoulders, but with great power over the loins, and with good hocks, although they were much disfigured, having been fired with something like a fire-shovel. I liked the appearance of the mare, and seeing that she "used" her shoulders well, asked the foreman to put a saddle on her and trot her up and down. He saddled her, but absolutely declined to mount, as did everyone else in the yard. I said to a lad, "It will be worth 5s. for you to trot her up and down on the straw;" but he said, "No, my life is worth more than 5s." This compelled me to mount the mare. She stood still until I *asked* her to move, when she went straight up on her hind legs, narrowly missing falling back. This she repeated twice, the third time walking on her hind legs so as to bring my knee against the wall as her fore feet came to the ground. I realised the mare's intention, and instead of pulling her away from the wall, pulled the inside rein sharply, which brought her down with her jaw on the wall, the jar being so great as to almost stun her. Taking advantage of the horse's bewildered state, I applied both spurs, and she trotted quietly out of the yard. Although her shoulder was short and badly put on, she never fell until I shot her, six years afterwards, except twice—once in a rabbit hole, and once when a bank broke under her.

I had a small pack of drag hounds, the farmers living round Rivenhall, where my mother lived, allowing me to take the Drag anywhere I liked, out of love of my father's memory. One farmer in reply to my request to cross his fields, sent me a message, "Tell Muster Evelyn if there be any one field where he can do most damage, I hope he will go there." Some of the younger ones assisted me by taking on the drag occasionally, so I hunted under favourable conditions, "Vagabond" and "Fractious" carrying me, or my sister, fifteen times in twenty-three successive days. I generally rode "Vagabond" with the Drag the day before I hunted him with the Stag Hounds, and saved him all I could by putting the horse in the train whenever it was possible; but as the kennels were five-and-twenty miles off, I could seldom get a short day. One day I rode him 19 miles to the meet, had a good run of two hours, and then 29 miles home, after taking the deer north of Bishop's Stortford, and without putting him off his feed.

I had a groom, excellent when he was sober; he came into my service in December 1865, and up to the end of 1866, when I was at Aldershot, had not given way to his besetting vice; but there the attractions of the canteens were too great, and he became troublesome. He should have arrived at my mother's house with the horses some hours before I did on the 14th of February 1868, but did not appear till nightfall. When I went to the stable just before dinner, I found that the horses had apparently been fed and watered, but the man was drunk. Seeing his condition, I endeavoured to avoid him, especially as my mother's coachman was also under the influence of liquor although not intoxicated; but the groom approached me rapidly, and as I thought with the intention of hitting me over the head with a lantern, so, knocking him down, I held him by the throat while I called the coachman to bring a halter and lash his legs. The groom had a keen sense of humour, and after the trembling coachman had tied his feet he pulled one out, observing, " Oh, you're a blessed fool, to tie up a man!" and in drunken tones he apostrophised me and all my family, finishing up with the expression, "And you're about the best of a d——d bad lot." I was nervous of leaving the man over the stable for fear he might set fire to it, so putting him into a dog-cart my brother and I drove over to the Petty Sessions House at Witham, where we saw the Inspector of Police, who declined to take charge of him because he was not "drunk and incapable in the street." I asked, "If you saw him drunk and incapable in the street would you then take charge of him for the night?" "Yes, certainly, but not while he is in your carriage." I cast off the undergirth, and having tilted up the shafts, shot the groom into the roadway, calling to the Inspector, "Now you can properly take him up." He reappeared next day, contrite, and remained with me two or three years, until he became so troublesome I was obliged to part with him. He was engaged by the Adjutant-General of the Army, without any references to me, and eventually having challenged him to fight, was knocked down, and dismissed.

My eldest child, born at Brighton in the summer, was for some time delicate, the nurse and I watching her at night by turns for two months. I had never been really well since I left the Staff College, and this night-watching rendered me altogether incapable of work. I was endeavouring to carry out my official duties while spending two or three hours every evening at Brighton; this necessitated my spending the night in a luggage train between Brighton, Redhill, and Aldershot, with the result that at the end of August I broke down, and was obliged to go away for a change of air. Towards the middle of the next month I fainted five times one afternoon from the intensity of the pain in the nerves of the stomach.

All through 1868 I was suffering from it, and it was not until a year later that Doctor Porter, attached to the 97th Regiment, in the North Camp, cured me. When he had done so, he asked to see me alone, and said, "Now I have cured you of neuralgia, but I fear I have made you an opium-eater for life." I laughed, saying, "I think not." "But you must feel a craving for it, don't you?" "Only when the pain is on." "But haven't you got to like it?" "No; I have never got rid of the feeling that it is exactly like soapsuds." I remained ill so long, however, that I had to face the contingency of being obliged to leave the Service, and having some taste for Military law elected to qualify for the Bar. During my service at Aldershot I had made an epitome of every important decision given by Judges Advocate-General relative to Courts Martial in the United Kingdom, and some years later Colonel Colley [1] asked permission of the War Office to have my notes printed, for the guidance of his class at the Staff College. The application was refused, with the quaint answer: "Permission cannot be given on account of the many conflicting decisions." It is only right I should add the office being then Political, the holders changed with the Government.

The Heads of the Army inculcate uniformity of punishment, but they do not always succeed. In the spring of the year, Frank Markham, Sir Alfred Horsford's Aide-de-Camp, Cricket Club Secretary, asked me for a fatigue party to roll the officers' ground in anticipation of the match. I said, "No, you can have a working party." "Oh, but I have got no funds." "Then go over to the —— and get some defaulters to roll your ground." "I have been there already, and the Adjutant says if I go after Monday I can have as many as I want; but that is too late, for we play on Monday, and so I cannot wait." "What does he mean by saying he has got no defaulters now?" "I asked him that, and he explained that the Colonel being away there were no defaulters, but he is coming back on Monday, and then there will be as many as I can want."

There came to Aldershot in the early summer a battalion distinguished for the best Barrack-room discipline in the Army. At that time it was commanded by a courteous gentleman,

[1] Later, Major-General Sir George Colley.

typical of the old school. A delightful host in his Mess, on matters of duty he was accurate to the verge of pedantry. Captain ——, a pillar of the Regiment, being not only a good Company commander, but having business attributes which enabled him to manage successfully all the Regimental institutions, was courting his cousin, whom he afterwards married. He had obtained leave from noon to go to London on "urgent private affairs," which were to meet the young lady in the Botanical Gardens, and just as he was starting for the one o'clock train at Farnborough,[1] an orderly came to him, saying, "The Colonel wants you in the orderly-room, sir."

Captain —— got back into uniform, and, putting on his sword, for in the "Wait-a-Bits"[2] officers attending orderly-room always wore swords, knocked at the door, and entered. The Commanding officer was writing, and nodding pleasantly, said, "Yes, wait a bit, please," and proceeded to finish what was apparently a carefully worded official document; at all events, it so seemed to the Captain, who stood fidgeting with his watch and calculating whether he could catch his train. At last, his patience being exhausted, he said, "I beg your pardon, sir, but you wished to see me. May I know for what purpose, as I want to catch a train?" "I wish, Captain ——," replied the Colonel, "to impress on you the necessity of being accurate in any documents you send in to this office for my approval." "I am not aware," the Captain said, "that I have sent any in, sir, for I have had no prisoners for some time." The Colonel then handed to him two passes, which the Captain scanned carefully, without finding out what was wrong. It was indeed difficult to make a mistake, as everything except the dates and the signature was printed. After close perusal, he handed them back, saying, "I am sorry, sir, but I cannot see anything wrong." The Chief replied slowly, "You have applied for leave for two privates in your Company to be absent from the 25 to the 27 of July, and if you look, you will see, in each case, there is a 'th' and two dots wanting." This was too much for the Captain's temper, and he said with much heat, "Have you sent for me, sir, and caused me to lose my train, and thus fail to keep a most important engagement in

[1] The Aldershot Railway was not then projected.
[2] A local nickname, from an expression often used by the Colonel.

London, to tell me to put a 'th' and two dots?" "Yes, Captain ——, I have. And I hope when you have the honour of commanding this Regiment, like me you will appreciate and teach the advantages of accuracy. Good-morning." During the operations then practised in and about the Long Valley he was a trial to excited Aides-de-Camp, who galloping up would exclaim, " The General wants you to advance immediately and attack." To which the Colonel would reply, " Kindly say that again—I am rather deaf." And after still more excited repetition would say calmly, " Let us wait a bit, and see exactly what is required." This peculiarity had no doubt become known, and was partly the result of an explosion of anger, and subsequent regret, on the part of the Commander-in-Chief, who one day with his Staff was sitting on Eelmoor Hill South, practising eleven battalions in a new formation imported from Germany, as many movements have been since that time. The idea was to advance in a line of columns, and by filling up the interval from the Rear of each column to lull the enemy into the belief that there was only a line advancing towards him. Five times in succession the battalions advanced and retired, each column being formed of double companies—that is, two companies in the front line. The Chief now said, " I am going to try the same thing, but forming the battalions in double columns of subdivisions."[1] When the Chief gave the order to half a dozen Gallopers, he said, " Advance in a double column of companies, filling up the intervals from the Rear companies." Five of us took the order as we knew the Chief intended, but not as he said, for we had all heard he intended to change the formation; but the sixth Galloper gave the " Wait-a-Bit " battalion the literal order, and thus, after the Colonel had begun the formation, looking to his right and left he saw that the others were forming double columns of subdivisions, and he proceeded to conform. This involved delay, and the Chief galloping down shouted at him with an oath, " You are the slowest man, Colonel, in the British Army." He had been wounded in the Crimea, and did not therefore carry a sword. Sitting erect on his horse, with his eyes straight to the front, he threw up his maimed hand and saluted, and the Chief rode

[1] That is, each battalion would have a frontage of one company composed of two halves of different companies.

back, vexed with himself and all the world, at having lost his temper. Before we got to Eelmoor Hill again, I told the officer who had taken the message that he ought to explain what had happened; but as he absolutely declined, I told the Chief, who turning his horse cantered back to the battalion, and made in a loud voice a generous apology. I do not know that I admired the Colonel particularly for his self-restraint in the first instance, but he gave me a lasting lesson on hearing the apology, for his face did not relax in the slightest degree nor did his eyes move. When the Chief had ceased speaking, up again went the maimed hand with a grave, punctilious salute— a grand example to his battalion of young soldiers. When the troops were going home, the apology was repeated; and then the Colonel, holding out his hand, said pleasantly, "Pray, sir, say no more about it; I am fully satisfied."

A few months later a Cavalry Colonel was called during a manœuvre a "d——d fool," for which at the Conference a full apology was made. The Colonel, a most lovable character, although a high-class gentleman in essentials, habitually used words as did our soldiers in Flanders two hundred years ago. He was an excellent Cavalry leader, although not by any means a finished horseman, and had a habit of heaving his body up and down in the saddle when excited. When the Chief had finished his apology, the Colonel blurted out, " I do not mind, sir, being called a 'd——d fool,' but I do mind being called a 'd——d fool' before all these 'd——d fools' of your Staff."[1]

Bad language was then used constantly on every parade, until Sir Hope Grant assumed command two years later. He resolutely setting his face against the practice, did much to stamp it out.

In the sixties our Generals delighted in practising complicated movements in lines of columns, especially one which was the terror of many Commanding officers, and which consisted in turning one or more battalions about, and then having moved to a flank, in fours, to wheel the column while in fours. The result was often ludicrous; indeed, I have seen five Captains standing in the leading company of a battalion, which had

[1] The custom was so widely spread, that the "Wait-a-Bits," an old-fashioned but one of the steadiest battalions I ever knew at Aldershot, asked me when I was Brigade-Major to be allowed to give up their place in line of columns in order to avoid standing next to a very vituperative though brave Commanding officer.

been ordered suddenly to " Halt," " Front." A line of thirteen battalions changing front forwards and backwards, on a named company, of a named battalion, was often practised three times a week, when I went to Aldershot in 1866, and the Lieutenant-General nearly always placed the Base points for the new alignment, to the mathematical accuracy of which both time and energy were devoted, and which induced much bad language.

Those at Aldershot now, who may see this book, will be interested to read that I met Captain Tufnell of the 34th coming in one evening in October with eleven and a half couple of snipe, shot between the Queen's Hotel and the bathing pond on Cove Common.

I was more intimate with that Regiment than any other, my brother having served in it for some years. I admired greatly the Colonel, of whose gallantry I had been a witness on the 18th June 1855, and thus it came about that, although I dined once a week with each battalion in the North Camp, I generally spent any other free evening in the 34th Mess. In May 1869 two French officers came to the camp bringing an introduction from Lord Southwell, and asked to see an officers' Mess. I sent an orderly over to the 34th to say we were coming, and just as we approached the hut one of the officers came out, saying, " Will you delay them a moment till we throw a rug over our drums ? " I could not stop the officers without giving an explanation, and so walked on, thinking it best to chance their noticing the drums. It was difficult to avoid seeing them, however, as there were five on each side of the very narrow entrance to the anteroom, and the senior French officer asked me their history. I told him frankly, expressing regret that I had inadvertently shown them something of an unpleasant nature, and he replied politely, " Pray do not let it disturb you ; it is only the fortune of war." [1]

In July we sent a flying column from Aldershot to Wimbledon, and officers who know the present state of the Mobilisation Stores which are sufficient for an Army Corps, may be interested to read that in 1869 we had not enough " line gear "

---

[1] At Arroyo dos Molinos, in the Peninsular, 1811, the French 34th was captured by the English Regiment of the same number. The representative bands rushed at each other, with the result that the baton of the Tambour Major and ten of the French Regiment drums remained in the hands of our 34th.

at Aldershot for one Squadron of Cavalry. An officer of the Control Department went to Woolwich on the Saturday, and bringing it across London in cabs, had it sent out in waggons at the trot to overtake the column at Chobham, which had marched two hours earlier.

I moved over to the South Camp at the end of the year, becoming Deputy Assistant Adjutant-General, and although I was sorry to leave Sir Alfred Horsford, I learned more in the Divisional office, especially as my Senior officer being in delicate health, I was often left in charge. To serve directly under Sir James Yorke Scarlett was a great privilege. He was a gentleman in the highest sense of the word, and although not an educated soldier, yet the tone he imparted to all under his command was to elevate the sense of duty and discipline.

When I had been under his command for some time, I thought it my duty to point out the result of one of his many charities, for both he and Lady Yorke Scarlett, who had fortunes, were never tired of doing good to others around them. Sir James used to pay for a cab for every woman leaving the Maternity hospital, and I told him that the moment his cab put the woman down at her hut on the eighth day after her baby was born, she took up her basket and walked into the town to make good the week's marketing. Said he, "What a capital thing to save her one journey!" During his absence in London I arranged a visit of the Inns of Court Volunteers, many of the Rank and File in those days being Queen's Counsel, or Barristers of high standing, and provided lunch at the conclusion of the operations. When the General returned, I told him what I had done, and that I had taken what was in those days the unusual step of debiting the Staff with the expenses according to our pay. He asked, " Well, and how does it work out ? " " Oh, sir, the result is that you will pay four or five times more than what I do." " Quite right," he said aloud ; and then dropping his voice, in a low tone, to me, " And mind you, Wood, if there is any shortage, let me pay it."

In the following year Sir James was as usual leading a line of skirmishers of one Force against another many yards in front,[1] as he had led the Heavy Brigade at Balaklava against

[1] *The Crimea in 1854-'94.*

three times its numbers. This was the habit of our Generals,[1] as I have shown in another book. Sir James was leading an attack up the Fox Hills, near Mitchet Lake, and with cocked hat in hand was cheering on the troops. Three times I respectfully pointed out that he was very far forward, to be rebuffed only with a curt expression beginning with an oath. On the third occasion he turned round and said, " Young man, have I not ordered you twice to hold your tongue? If I like to lead my skirmishers, what the —— is that to you?" Said I most respectfully, " Ten thousand pardons, sir, but it is the enemy's line in retreat you have been leading for the last ten minutes." He was short-sighted, and did not wear glasses, so was unable to see the distinguishing mark, a sprig of heather worn in the shakos of the troops he was attacking.

At the end of April, having passed my examination, paying £140 for the fees, I entered as a Law student in the Middle Temple, my Examiner being kind enough to say that my papers were very satisfactory. The questions in History, although requiring an effort of memory, were not beyond me, except in one instance. I was fully equal to the first question, which was: " Give a list of the Sovereigns of England from William the Conqueror to Queen Victoria, showing how, when, and in what particular there was any departure from strict hereditary succession." Girls, no doubt, are generally taught History better than our schoolboys, for my wife laughed at me when I returned in the evening stating I had failed entirely to answer the question—" State what you know of the Pilgrimage of Grace." A charming Queen's Counsel examined me, and being in the room a few minutes before the hour stated, I had picked up a Virgil, and was reading it, when passing up the room, he looked over my shoulder. He said pleasantly, " Is that your favourite author?" To which I replied, " Yes, it is the only one I know." Taking the book out of my hand, and seeing I was in the Eleventh Book of the *Æneid*, he opened it at random at the passage in the Second Book—

"Et Jam Argiva Phalanx instructis navibus ibat
A Tenedo tacitæ per amica silentia lunæ."

---

[1] General Pennyfather led many charges at Inkerman, where Sir George Cathcart was killed at the head of two companies, and as Generals did in war, so did they then in peace.

Showing me the passage, he said, "Write out that page." This I found easy, and when he had looked it over he said, "Well, it is a very good translation; but your rendering, 'tacitæ per amica silentia lunæ,' 'in the favouring obscurity of a moon in its first quarter,' is somewhat free." I said, "Yes, but I am a soldier, and over thirty years of age, and Virgil, who knew a good deal about campaigns, must have meant what I have written." "Can you quote me any authority for ' Lunæ tacitæ ' being a moon in its first quarter?" "Yes, Ainsworth's Dictionary, which if everyone will not admit, is good enough for me, and I looked it out only three weeks ago." He laughingly said, "Well, if you will tell me that you looked it out only three weeks ago, I also shall accept it." Then he observed, "After your very frank remark about your limited knowledge, I must put you on in something else;" and to my relief he took up a "Cæsar," which although I have not read always appears to me to be the easiest of all Latin authors, and I had no difficulty in satisfying him.

I took the opportunity of being in the Headquarters Office of striking out a new line of management in the Divisional School Feast. I had mooted the question when I was a Brigade-Major that the feast as arranged, assembling the children in the largest riding school for tea and cake, was not making most of the holiday, and I suggested that the children should be taken out to one of the parks around Aldershot. I was met by the usual objections: it had never been done before, the owners of the neighbouring parks would be unwilling to receive 1500 children, and moreover it would be impossible to transport them, besides the risk of accidents. I found no difficulty, the Bishop of Winchester gladly placing his park at my disposal. T. White & Co., the Outfitters, and all the Brewers employed, lent me waggons, with the result that some 1500 children spent a most enjoyable afternoon, the ride backwards and forwards being perhaps the greatest pleasure, and for many years my plan was followed.

At the end of 1869 the Agent on my brother-in-law's estate died of scarlatina, and it became necessary to appoint a successor. Sir Thomas Lennard desired me to make the appointment, and after advertising I selected three names representing what appeared to be the most desirable candidates, and to these I wrote, asking them to come and stay with me for at least forty-eight hours, my object being to find out which was most likely to suit an agency where the agent must fully represent the landlord, who very seldom visited the estate. My second child was but a few weeks old, and as the accommodation in our hut was limited, and a person with normal hearing must know nearly everything said in the hut, the opportunities of finding out the guests' nature were favourable.

My choice fell on Frederick Wrench,[1] who had not long left the University. He had never been an agent, but had worked for six months in the office of Mr. John Vernon, an agent of high standing in Ireland, who strongly recommended the young man, and undertook to give him, or me, any advice as long as we required it. Wrench and I worked together for twenty-one years, during which time we never had a difference of opinion. Five years after he had taken over the Clones agency, he telegraphed to me to come to Dublin, and meeting me, said, " If you will tell the Trustees of an estate that you think well of me, I shall get another agency worth £800 a year; but they want a personal interview, not a written opinion." He held it until he took over the management of the Colebrooke estate for his brother-in-law, Sir Victor Brooke, and was eventually selected by the Secretary for Ireland[2] for the Irish Land Commission, where I believe he has given as much satisfaction to those who know what his work has been, as he did to my brother-in-law and to me.

In the summer I obtained a half-pay Majority by purchase. This was convenient, because the battalion to which I had been transferred against my will in 1866 (after paying £500 to exchange to the battalion which was due to remain in England) was ordered for Foreign Service, and I must have paid another £500, or embarked with it. Shortly afterwards, a Colonel of Cavalry I had known since 1856, when we were quartered for a short time together at Scutari, before I was sent to Hospital, tried to persuade me to exchange with a Major of his Regiment, offering to lend me £3000 on my personal security at 3½ per cent. He was

---

[1] The Right Hon. F. Wrench, Irish Land Commissioner.
[2] The Right Hon. Arthur Balfour, M.P.

very fond of his Regiment, and foreseeing that he must soon retire, was anxious that I should succeed him. I explained, however, that my private income was not sufficient to enable me to do justice to a Cavalry regiment, and so, although very grateful, I declined his offer.

My friend the Colonel was very Low Church, and one day, as we came out of All Saints', at the conclusion of the Cavalry Brigade Divine service, he said, "Are you Churchwarden?" "Yes, sir." "Very well, I am going to report you for the way you go on in church." "What do I do?" "Why, you say 'A-a-a-men' in three motions. Why the devil don't you say 'Amen,' and have done with it?" "Does it hurt you, sir?" "Yes." "Stop your saying prayers?" "Yes." "Do you try?" "Well, as well as a wicked old man can; but I ask you plainly—will you stop it?" "No, I will make no change."

Within a week I received a rebuke from the Secretary of State for War, addressed to me personally as Churchwarden, for having permitted intoning at a Parade service, which (quoting an Army circular, dated before I was born) was against Regulations. Two Sundays later, I turned the tables on my friend, when at the conclusion of the service I asked, "I beg your pardon, sir, but are you in command of the Cavalry Brigade?" "Yes—why?" "Because I am going to report you for allowing the opening sentences, 'I will arise and go to my Father' to be sung." "Well, why can't it be sung?" "Because by the canons of the Church we are forbidden to sing or chant until we have confessed our sins to Almighty God." "Is that really the case?" "Yes." "Well, I say, old fellow, you like it, don't you?" and I admitted I did.

I believe I gave the most audacious order ever issued in peace-time on the 9th July. Her Majesty the Queen had reviewed the troops between Long Hill and the Steeple Chase brook. The arrangements were thoughtlessly made; for the Cavalry, which had the shortest distance afterwards to get into position, came past before the Infantry, which had to go nearly a mile farther. The scheme arranged was that the Division should concentrate behind Miles Hill and Eelmore Hill close to the Canal, and should then advance past Her Majesty's carriage, placed on Eelmore Hill South, and attack Cæsar's Camp. I was detailed as guide to Her

Majesty. I went as slowly as possible, but it was impossible to take longer than ten minutes to drive from Long Hill to Eelmore Hill South, and thus the Queen's carriage was in position before even the head of the column of Infantry had reached the spot where it was to wheel about. Her Majesty sat with evident impatience for over half an hour, when General Sir Henry Ponsonby beckoned me to come on one side, and warned me as follows: " Unless something is done immediately, the Queen will go back to the Pavilion." Picking up my writing-tablet, I wrote as follows: " Lieutenant-General Sir James Yorke Scarlett. The Cavalry will attack immediately up the Long Valley, and reversing the front attack back again, by which time it is hoped that the Infantry will be ready to advance. By Command.—Evelyn Wood, Major." I sent an orderly at speed to the Lieutenant-General, who was then under Miles Hill, and within a few minutes, he himself leading, the Cavalry galloped up the valley and down again, to Her Majesty's evident gratification. The moving and exciting scene occupied her attention for the best part of a quarter of an hour, and then the Infantry came on. At the conclusion of the Review, after the Queen had thanked the Lieutenant-General, I told him, as we rode home together, of my action, of which he quite approved.

Next month, to my regret, I vexed him a little by declining to tell him where I was going with a Squadron of the 12th Lancers, being determined that nobody should know whence we intended to start. I had made a scheme that we should bivouac out over night, and march from westward into Aldershot next day, somewhere between the Canal and the Aldershot and Farnham Road, the Cavalry Brigade watching for us in any position that the General might select. I rode round the previous day and looked at various spots, and as I was leaving Dogmersfield Park, which I had given up as unsuitable, I called at the house, saw Sir Henry Mildmay, and told him that although I did not intend to request his permission to use his park, I wished to tell him what I had intended to ask, if satisfied with the water supply.

Next morning I got a note from him saying he considered it his duty to help the Army in every way, and he would supply as many barrels of fresh water as the men of the Squadron required, and hoped that all the officers and I would dine with him, when he would give us something better than water. We dined with him, and early next morning went away towards Woolmer, lying up in Alice Holt wood. The Cavalry Brigade came out to the valley of the Wey, but instead of leaving a standing patrol to watch the avenues of approach from the south, sent small parties patrolling up and down the Farnham-Bentley Road. We watched until a patrol had passed westwards, and then proceeded at a slow trot,[1] crossed the road, which was the only danger point, got inside the line of outposts, and had no difficulty in reaching the men's Barracks at twelve o'clock. The Cavalry Brigade did not hear till the afternoon that their line had been pierced, and returned between four and five o'clock in an unhappy frame of mind.

Early in August I got a lesson from a Major in an Infantry regiment who had asked leave " on private affairs." I returned the letter to the General commanding the Brigade, calling attention to the Divisional Order requiring a special reason to be given in an application for leave in the Drill Season, and the answer was " Sea bathing at Margate," to which I sent back the usual formula, " The Lieutenant-General regrets he cannot sanction leave during the Drill season for the purpose alleged." This evoked a humorous protest. The Major, who was in temporary command, replied that he had only three days previously received the Lieutenant-General's approval to an application he put forward for three of his Subalterns to shoot grouse in Scotland ; that he himself, when young and unmarried, used to shoot grouse ; now that he was elderly and poor, his solitary surviving pleasure was to see his children playing on the sands at a bathing-place, but he could not see why that should make a difference in obtaining a privilege. I knew that my General would, if told, refuse the leave, but felt so strongly the absurdity of our official position that I wrote " Leave granted. By Order," and never since have I asked an officer his reasons for desiring leave of absence.

[1] Which pace I was bound not to exceed, neither could we trot farther than a mile at one time.

My General was going away, and although I was not the officer of his choice, he having recommended one of my most intimate friends, Major William Goodenough, for the post, yet I had been most kindly treated by him, and every day I worked with him I got to like him better. We knew he was to be succeeded by General Sir Hope Grant, who had the reputation of being very Low Church, and I seriously contemplated resigning my appointment, but was deterred by the wiser counsels of my wife, who urged me to wait and see whether her religion would in any way interfere with the smoothness of my relations with the General. She was right, for both he and his wife became two of our most intimate friends, as kind as any we ever had, and we enjoyed their friendship till they died.

In the spring of 1871 I negotiated with three different Majors, arranging to pay various sums, from £1500 to £2000, for an exchange. I had settled with one Highland Regiment, but a Captain who had been a Colour-Sergeant at the Alma wrote me a manly letter, appealing to my feelings as a soldier not to stop his advancement by coming into the Regiment. Ultimately, in the autumn of 1871, shortly before purchase was abolished, I paid £2000 to exchange into the 90th Light Infantry.

All through the spring and summer months I was employed by Sir Hope Grant in prospecting ground for camps for the manœuvres, which were eventually held the following year. I saw a great deal of my General, and of his Aide-de-Camp, Robert Barton, Coldstream Guards. They were well matched in nobility of soul and in their high sense of duty. I have heard of many noble traits of Hope Grant, and of his indomitable courage, moral and physical. My General, with all his lovable qualities, had not much sense of humour, and one day when we were riding from his office back to Farnborough Grange, where he resided, we passed the 3rd Bedfords, a smart Militia battalion, commanded by Sir John Burgoyne.[1] When Sir Hope came opposite the Guard tent, the Guard turned out, and it was obvious that the sentry was not quite certain how to " Present Arms." A man lying down

---

[1] Who a few weeks later conveyed Her Majesty the Empress Eugénie from the French coast to England in his yacht.

in a Company tent in his shirt sleeves, ran out, disarmed the sentry, and presented arms very smartly, and then looked up in the General's face with a grin, for approval of his smartness. My General, however, saw only the enormity of a sentry being disarmed.

In September H.R.H. the Duke of Cambridge came down to handle the Army Corps, the larger proposed manœuvres having been countermanded. He left the Adjutant-General and Quartermaster-General in the War Office, bringing down only the Deputy Adjutant-General, who was very ill, and indeed never once went on parade.

My General, Sir Hope Grant, had taken over temporarily with the Staff the command of an Infantry Division, and I was left as the Duke's Staff officer, and was thus brought into daily relations with him. Although he had not been educated in the higher sense of a General's duties, his natural ability made it pleasant to serve under him. I had difficulty, however, in getting him to understand that when he gave me instructions at six o'clock in the evening and invited me to dine at eight, it was utterly impossible for me to obey both commands, for to get the Orders out I was obliged to remain in my office till a very late hour of the night. Indeed, for one week I was not in bed till three in the morning. The Aldershot printing-press establishment was then in its infancy, and I generally had to check three revises of Orders.

At the end of October, Sir Hope Grant's application for an extension of my appointment having been refused, I left Aldershot, and shortly afterwards visited the battlefields to the east of and around Paris with General Arthur Herbert, Majors Home and Leahy of the Royal Engineers. We had an enjoyable trip, slightly marred by the necessity of saving money; for after spending seven or eight hours in studying a battlefield it is unpleasant to travel all night in a second-class railway carriage, in order to save the price of a bed.

MAJOR WOOD'S QUARTERS, ALDERSHOT, 1869-70-71

CHAPTER XXI

1871-2-3—90TH LIGHT INFANTRY

Stirling Castle defended—Arthur Eyre—Colonel Eyre—Route marching—Dunkeld—A survivor of Albuera—Back to Aldershot—On Staff for Cannock Chase Manœuvres—Ordered to the Gold Coast.

AT Christmas 1871 I joined my new battalion, the 90th Light Infantry, as Junior Major, assuming command of three companies at Stirling Castle. I had seen the Germans man the walls of Thionville instead of having a march out a fortnight earlier, so I put the detachment through the same exercise in the Castle, having the drawbridge raised for the purpose. The Officer in charge of Barracks protested against the drawbridge being touched, saying it had not been moved in the memory of man, and would probably break. I persisted, however, and nothing untoward occurred. My new comrades saw parts of the Castle that they had never before visited, their attention having been confined to the way out of it into the town, over which it stands.

Some few days after I joined, I went over early to Glasgow to pay my respects to the Colonel, who was there with three companies, two being stationed at Ayr. The Colonel was away on leave, and when I entered at half-past nine the dingy little anteroom, there sat four or five officers who had just breakfasted; rising, they bowed, with awkward shyness, which was the more marked in contrast with the self-possession and polished manners of a young officer with an eyeglass, who came forward and talked to me as if he were receiving me in his mother's drawing-room. After a few minutes' conversation, he said, "If you will excuse me, sir, I will go into the next room and have my breakfast;" and when he closed the door I asked his name, and was told it was Arthur Eyre. " Is he a son of the late Sir William ? " " Yes." " He was not only brave in action, but very determined in the maintenance of discipline, as you will understand from my story. In June 1852 (mid-winter), during a Kafir war, his battalion, 73rd Perthshire, made a forced march from King William's Town to the Döhne, Kabousie Nek, to endeavour to surprise Sandilli. The men carried their packs: two blankets and greatcoats, seven days' biscuits and groceries, and 70 rounds. There was much grumbling in the Ranks, and 60 men straggled out of their companies, though fear of the Kafirs kept them between the battalion and its Rear guard. When the murmurs of the laggards could no longer be ignored, Eyre asked them what they meant. ' We cannot march farther, sir, carrying all this load.' The Colonel halted, ordered the 60 men to ' pile ' their blankets and ' Stand clear.' Then moving the battalion 50 yards away, he made the Pioneers burn the blankets, and resumed the march. I have no doubt the facts were as I narrate." As I finished speaking a deep voice came from an elderly Captain on the sofa, who had not previously spoken: " It's tr-r-rue, every wur-r-rd, for I was there as a Pr-r-ivate in the Regiment." The officer who corroborated my story was Captain Rennie, who, promoted into the 90th from the 73rd, gained his V.C. at Lucknow.

I had some little trouble when I first took over the command of the detachment at Stirling. On checking the distances entered by the Acting Orderly Room Clerk of the Route marching, I found to the Bridge of Allan and back entered as about 10 miles, which was nearly twice the actual distance. The first day I marched with the men we went for a walk of about 12 or 13 miles, and many of the Rank and File were certainly tired, and when going out at the end of the week (for the exercise was carried out twice weekly) nearly half the detachment was absent. I took no notice, but on our return had the names of all the men who had reported Sick that morning " put on the gate." Next morning the men asked to see me, and urging that they had not committed any crime, protested against their being confined to Barracks, which they felt the more that under the easy-going system of the place at least half the detachment slept out nightly in the town. I agreed that they had not committed any crime, but as it was obvious that sleeping out was not conducive to good marching, their names would remain "on the gate" until they had done another march. After this, we had no trouble in doing any distances up to 15 miles.

At the end of January I informed the men that there would be a voluntary Parade the next day for Divine service, to be held as a Thanksgiving for the recovery of the Prince of Wales from enteric fever. I explained that attendance was absolutely voluntary, that I intended to go myself, but that I wished the men to do exactly as they pleased. Those who did not attend Divine service would carry out their usual duties. Before we marched off next day, the Senior non-commissioned officer reported that all the men except the guard and one other man were present on parade. I inquired with some little curiosity who the one man was, but the name told me nothing except that he was Irish. When the men broke off after the service and were entering their Barrack-rooms, I heard derisive cheering as I was going down the hill, and turning back, I found the one soldier who had not attended the Parade being drilled in Marching order. On inquiring the reason, I learnt that the morning was ordinarily that for Route marching, so the Acting Orderly Sergeant, resenting the man's declining to go to parade, had determined to carry out the letter of my order that those who were not attending Divine service should perform their usual duties. This one man was a shoemaker, and had anticipated being allowed to work in the shop, but to the delight of his comrades had to carry his pack while we were in church.

While quartered at Stirling I several times visited Dunkeld, the scene of the heroic defence of the Cameronians, now the Scottish Rifles, against the Highlanders, being greatly impressed by the courage and determination of Cleland, who, when his Lowlanders, all Glasgow Covenanters, upbraided him for having brought them into the Highlands to be massacred by their foes, saying, "It is all very well for you; when they come down, you can mount your horse and ride off," replied, "Bring out the horses;" and when they were led forth, said,

"Now cut their throats." With a revulsion of feeling the Cameronians refused, and on the 21st August 1689 withstood the determined and repeated attacks of 5000 Highlanders till 11 p.m., when they raised a Psalm of triumph and thanksgiving, as their foes drew off and dispersed. On my third visit, I asked the caretaker to show me Cleland's grave. She said, with much astonishment, "Wha's that? If ye come here, I'll show ye a real Christian's grave," and she took me over to the opposite side of the graveyard and showed me the tomb of a Bishop. I said, "I am not interested at all; I wanted to see where Cleland's body lies, who, with his officers, gave up his life in defence of this building." "Ah, man," she said, "but this was a Christian." "Well, and why should not Cleland have been a Christian?" "Nae, man; ye said he was a sodger."

When I joined the 90th Light Infantry, it came to my knowledge that although it had been in possession of its new Colours for two years, the tattered remnants of those that had been previously carried were still in the Quartermaster's Store at Glasgow, and after some correspondence the Regiment accepted my suggestion, and I was asked to arrange with the Provost and Council of Perth to hang the Colours in the Cathedral of the City in which the Regiment was raised. The arrangements necessitated two or three visits to Perth, and on the first occasion, as the Councillors accompanied me back to the station, which was close to the Council Chamber, I asked one of them, pointing to a distinguished-looking old man, with a long white beard, who he was, and received the somewhat contemptuous reply, "Oh, he is of no importance—only an old Peninsula soldier." I repeated my question to the stationmaster, who was more sympathetic, and at my request obtained his initials from the Goods Office. When I got back to Stirling, I went up to the Mess-room, where we had Army Lists for eighty years past, and was rewarded by finding the name of the distinguished-looking old man, who had been present in a Fusilier Regiment at the battle of Albuera in 1811. William Napier wrote marvellously graphic English, but of all his work one piece stands out pre-eminent, "The Attack of the Fusilier Brigade at Albuera," and I committed to memory rather more than a page of his account of the climax of the battle. On the 27th June we went up to Perth—16 officers and 14 non-commissioned officers, and the Commanding officer asked me to return thanks for our reception at the luncheon given to us by the Provost and Council. On rising, I said, " I should have been glad to do so, but that I stand in the presence of one who has taken part in a more stubborn struggle than it has ever been my fate to see," and I recited Napier's stirring description. As I finished the last sentence, " The rain flowed after in streams discoloured with blood, and 1500 unwounded men, the remnant of 6000 unconquerable British soldiers, stood triumphant on the fatal hill ! " I said, " I call on Lieutenant —— of the Fusiliers to answer for the Army."

He was at the end of the Council Chamber, having taken, literally and metaphorically, a back seat, and rising slowly and with difficulty, for he was more than eighty years of age, he doddered over to the table, and leaning heavily upon it, said simply, " Let me greit ! " And " greit " he did; but presently brushing away his tears, and drawing his body up to its full height—and he was 6 foot 2 inches—he made an admirable speech, the gist of which was that he had lived in the City of Perth since 1814, and no one had ever asked him anything about the Peninsula; no one had ever spoken to him about the battle of Albuera; "but now," he concluded, "when I have one foot in the grave, I see before me officers in the same coloured coats, and with the same sort of faces, and instead of talking about what they did in the Crimea or the Indian Mutiny, they recount in wonderful language the crowning scene of my Military life." Then sinking back into a chair, he added, " I shall die happy."

Two Colour-Sergeants out of the three at Stirling were intelligent men, and I had a considerable amount of success in imparting the method of Road Sketching to them, for they were both highly commended when they reached the Camp as among the four best in Aldershot, which seems to indicate that what one has often heard is true—that it is not always the most proficient artist who makes the best teacher; for they were certainly much more successful draughtsmen than was I, their master. I got the Captains of the three companies to teach their men the art of making straw mats to cover the ground of their tents; to exercise the men regularly in pitching and striking camp; and in drilling at one-pace interval, which was introduced the following year at Aldershot. The battalion went to the Camp at the end of July, and a fortnight afterwards I was put on the Staff of the Second Army Corps, and sent down to Blandford to select and prepare camps for the Force under the command of General Sir John Michel.

I had taken down three horses, but the distances to be covered were so great, and the hours so long, that on the 10th I was riding a hack hired at the King's Arms. I had been upon the Racecourse Down, and was returning by appointment to meet a Cavalry regiment reaching Blandford that afternoon. When I got close to the meadows I had selected for the Camp, I saw the Camp Colour men waiting for me, but between us was a high hedge. I rode to a gate, and getting off tried to open it, but it was chained up so strongly that I found it would take me a long time to unfasten it. The meadow was just at the foot of a Down, so that I could not approach the gate straight, as the fall in the ground was too steep, and I was obliged to ride in a slanting direction, and at the gate post. The horse failed to clear it, and falling, got up with my leg under its shoulder. I at first thought that the ankle was broken, as I had lost all sensation in it. I was carried into the King's Arms, where I was attended by many doctors.

It was known that I had been an advocate for some time of the "Hospital" as against the "Regimental" system, and I had to undergo a considerable amount of chaff when it was known that nine different doctors attended me in one week! The treatment was changed nearly as often as were the Medical attendants: one gentleman prescribed hot fomentations; another ice, with perfect rest. I did not make much progress for the first week, when a young Doctor came in, and after looking at the ankle, which was then very big (and even after thirty-three years is still so), asked, "Do you wish to have a stiff ankle all your life?" "Not by any means." "Then get up and walk round the room." "But I can't move it." "Try, and when you have walked round once, rest." This was advice after my own heart, and I followed it.

On the day of my fall, my wife was coming down to spend the Sunday, and she arrived to find me in a small lodging, to which I had been carried in order to avoid the noise of the hotel, which was crowded with officers of the Staff of the Army Corps. Mr. Glyn,[1] the Liberal Whip, was then living at Ranston, and hearing of my accident, came to see me, and eventually sent his wife with instructions to stop outside my lodging until I came away in the carriage. I have never had kinder hosts, and they put a wing of the house at our disposal, overwhelming us with their attentions. I did not get into Camp till the end of the month, when I was able to ride with my foot in a slipper.

When we got back to Aldershot from Manœuvres, Captain Blake, of the Royal Marines, a barrister of the Middle Temple, came to see what progress I had made; for he had been sending me a series of Examination papers for the previous two years. Throughout 1870-1 I studied from 4 to 7.30 a.m. and never missed being in my office at 9 a.m., and it was thus I acquired any slight knowledge I possess of legal books.

I drew up, and circulated, in October 1872, proposals for Mounted Infantry. General Sir John Fox Burgoyne had predicted that in all wars of the future Mounted Infantry would play an important part. My attention had been turned to the subject by his correspondence, and the scheme which I drew up then has been closely followed, except that I always advocated, and still recommend, a certain number of men being carried on light waggons. In the spring of the following year I urged this point in a lecture on Mounted Infantry that I gave at the United Service Institute.

When I went to Aldershot from Stirling in the Spring of 1872, I asked Mr. Thomas White, who was not only my outfitter, but whom I regarded as a friend, to hire for me a house in the best sanitary position. He replied that he had taken two houses himself, in the highest part of the town, for his wife and relations, and proposed that I should take a house in the same block. This I did. Here I nearly lost my two children from Diphtheria, and as my wife was not allowed to go near them, I had an anxious three weeks, sending my

---

[1] Later, Lord Wolverton. I knew him in the sixties, as he rode brilliantly with the Essex Stag Hounds.

wife out of the house at short notice, and sitting up half of every night. Eventually, when the children were convalescent, I placed them at an hotel near Hungry Hill, and thus had four houses on my hands at one time. Except for two days, I carried out my Military duties as Commandant of the School of Instruction for Auxiliary Forces, as it was difficult to delegate the work to anyone else, the School being always full, and the officers, my pupils, being enthusiastically eager to learn. Eventually, from having been up so many nights, when the tension was over I was unable to sleep, and on the 1st April the Medical officer in charge of the Regiment expressing some concern about my appearance, I told him of the insomnia, which he ascribed to a want of will power, and said he would send me to sleep then and there. Pulling a syringe out of his pocket, he injected into my arm what proved to be an overdose of morphia. Half an hour later, I was sitting at the dinner-table, when calling to my servant, " Catch me," I subsided on the floor, and as I opened my eyes at eight o'clock the next morning learnt that my second son had been born at 4 a.m. My wife was soon convalescent, and the summer passed pleasantly, for I frequently had command of the battalion. We invariably moved off " Right in Front," and were so wedded to this custom that the battalion always faced on its return from a Field day in the opposite direction to which it stood on assembling for exercise, and these idiosyncrasies of the Commanding officer I endeavoured, and successfully, to overcome by always moving " Left in Front."

At that time the two senior Majors in the Army were promoted on New Year's Day, and I, as one, became in January a Brevet-Lieutenant-Colonel, after $10\frac{1}{2}$ years' service as Brevet-Major.

In the month of August I was sent to Rugeley, in Staffordshire, as the Staff officer of General Sir Daniel Lysons, who taught me more of the details of Camp life than anyone else under whom I have served. In the month of May I had chanced to go into Sir Garnet Wolseley's office in London, and found him poring over a Dutch map of Ashanti, and he told me, in reply to my question, that there was a King there who required a lesson to bring him to a sense of the power of

England. I said laughingly, "There is a river half-way—the Prah—I will steer your boat up;" and he turned round sharply, saying, "So you shall, if we go." It was while going up that river many months later that Sir John Commerell was wounded.

I had been only a few days at Cannock Chase when I received a letter from Arthur Eyre saying it was known at Aldershot that an Expedition was about to start for the West Coast, and asking me to interest myself in his behalf. I did so readily, from the following circumstance. When riding one afternoon with my wife in the previous autumn, I noticed Eyre trying five hunters in succession over the practice-jumps under Tweezledown Hill. The horses had been bought by brother-officers at Tattersall's two days before, and their owners preferred that their capabilities as hunters should be tested by some person other than the purchasers. Marking the look of determination with which Eyre rode, fixing his eyeglass by contracting the muscles of his brow, I observed to my wife, "If I go on Service again, that boy shall come with me." So, on receiving Eyre's note, I endorsed it with the curt remark, "The son of a good soldier, his mother is a lady;" and he was selected.

It was the end of the month when I received a telegram from Sir Garnet Wolseley: "We go out on the 12th September. You go with me on Special Service." Sir Garnet's original intention had been to take two battalions, each about 1300 strong, made up of picked men from the most efficient battalions in the Army at home, each of which was to furnish a company under its officers, and I was to have commanded one of these battalions. The Commander-in-Chief, however, vetoed this principle, which has, nevertheless, since been accepted in the organisation of Mounted Infantry Regiments, and Sir Garnet was told he was to try and do the work with what natives he could enlist, and that if he failed he might have the three battalions first on the roster for Service. This sound principle where large numbers are concerned was very unsatisfactory when every man, whether an officer or in the Ranks, was of value.

My soldier-servant, Private Rawson, begged leave to be allowed to go with me, but the Secretary of State refused his permission in a letter the wording of which, considering that 25 officers were embarking, is peculiar: "Mr. Secretary Cardwell considers that the climate is particularly fatal to the constitutions of Europeans." On receipt of this quaintly worded refusal, I wrote to the Army Purchase Commissioners—I having been a Purchase officer up to the rank of Major—to ask what I was worth that day, in other words, how much the country would give me if I retired, and received for answer the sum of £4500.

I had declined to join in the petition to Mr. Cardwell, which was originated and put forward by two of my friends who are still happily alive. One of them, however, having been an Artilleryman, had paid nothing for his steps. The claim in the petition to have the purchase-money returned at once was not only illogical, but if granted would have been grossly unfair; for if A had purchased over B, B would undoubtedly have resented A getting his money back and retaining the seniority that he had purchased with the money.

It was stated, and I believe with accuracy, that if the petitioners had confined their request to the Secretary of State that the money should be payable to their heirs on their decease, Mr. Cardwell would have supported the application. But as the matter stood, on accepting promotion to the rank of General, I, like my brother Purchase officers, helped the Consolidated Fund of the Nation.

CHAPTER XXII

1873—ASHANTI

Elmina—Ex-Governors' wives—Essaman, the first successful Bush fight—The head of the road—Kossoos' cruelty—A Fanti order of battle.

THE steamer in which Sir Garnet and his Staff left Liverpool on the 12th had been newly painted, which added to our discomfort. She rolled so heavily as to throw a watch out of the waistcoat pocket of one of the Staff overboard as he leant over the ship's side, and on more than one occasion we thought she had turned turtle as we were all tossed out of our berths. We reached Cape Coast Castle on the morning of the 2nd October. I was sent to Elmina, a Dutch fort, about 12 miles off, to the west of the chief village[1] of the settlement.

There were six officers in the Fort, of whom three had fever, and the other two startled us by the offer of "Square-face"[2] instead of five-o'clock tea, and one of them still more so by drinking the glass poured out for but declined by Arthur Eyre, after he had drunk his own. It was, perhaps, more remarkable that they were alive than that they were not well, but the climate at that season was, it must be admitted, intensely depressing.

Amongst my instructions was an order impressing upon me the necessity of exercising great care over the scanty supply of rain water, there being no springs. All the potable water was collected from off the roof of the Castle into iron

---

[1] The fort, St. George della Mina, named from the gold mines in the vicinity, is said to have been built by French merchants in 1383, though the Portuguese allege that they built the first fort. The Dutch held it from 1637 to 1872, when England took it over. St. George stands on a rock close to the sea, just above high water, and St. Iago, a fort inland, 100 feet higher, commands both St. George and the town built on either side of the Beyah backwater.

[2] Trade gin.

tanks, so before daylight the next morning I went to the issue place, and after a few West India soldiers had been supplied, I was astonished by the approach of a long line of elderly black women, each with a large earthen jar on her shoulder. "Who are these people?" I asked the interpreter, "and why should they consume our water?" To which he replied glibly, "Please, sir, all ex-Governors [1] wives have liberty take water." I allowed it for the morning, but had the women informed that I could not recognise their claim for the future.

The state of Elmina was peculiar. The Ashantis had attacked the loyal part of the town, which was separated from that inhabited by Ashantis and their friends by the Beyah backwater from the sea, and had been repulsed by Colonel Festing, Royal Marines. The main body of the Ashantis remained at villages about 15 miles from the Coast undisturbed by us until after Sir Garnet Wolseley's arrival.

I was instructed to summon the Chiefs of the villages who were supplying the Ashantis. Those in the hamlets so close to us as to feel insecure, obeyed my summons; but the Chief of Essaman wrote back, "Come and fetch me if you dare;" the Chief of Ampeene, a village on the Coast, sent no answer, but cut off the head of a loyal Native, and exposed it to our view. The strangest answer came from another Head man, who was evidently of a vacillating mind; for he wrote, "I have got small-pox to-day, but will come to-morrow."

I was ordered to punish these men, and without telling any of my officers what I was about to do, collected sufficient Natives in the loyal part of Elmina to carry our ammunition, and hammocks for wounded men, into the Castle at sunset, and having had the gates locked, spent the night in telling them off as carriers for their respective duties. When Sir Garnet Wolseley and the Headquarter Staff, with some White and Black troops, landed at daylight just under the Castle, we were able to start within an hour—180 White men and 330 Black soldiers.

A small party of Haussas under Lieutenant Richmond led the Advance, and then came a section of the West India Regiment under Lieutenant Eyre, followed by Sailors and Marine Artillery, and two companies of Marines. For an hour we marched across a marshy plain, often through water, and in

[1] The English Government took over the Fort in 1872.

one place up to our knees for 100 yards. On each side, as we passed away from the marsh, were wooded undulations, with shrubs bordering the path, which was about a foot wide. Beautiful creepers, purple, red, mauve-coloured sweet-peas, and bright yellow convolvuli met the eye at every moment. Farther on, the Bush, which was in patches only close to the plain, became denser, and occasionally we passed through defiles which, if held by an enemy, must have cost us many lives. We were near the village of Essaman at 7 a.m., when the Advance guard received a volley fired at 100 yards distance; occasionally some brave men awaited our approach until we were so close up that the slugs did not spread in the body of the first of our men killed. The enemy stood around the clearing on a hill upon which we formed up, and the 2nd West India Regiment, with the hammocks, became enfolded in dense smoke.

The Special Service officers were serving under the eye of Sir Garnet Wolseley, and apparently wishing to justify his choice in selecting them, adventured their lives freely. Colonel M'Neill, Chief of the Staff, led the advance. The command of the Column was entrusted to me, and Sir Garnet, who was carried in a chair, had no definite duties, which was also the case with his Staff, so that they were free to enjoy themselves, which they did by leading the advance with a lively audacity which, whilst it excited my admiration, caused me some uneasiness when I reflected on what might happen if they fell. Led by these Staff officers, the Column pressed on, and we never again during the campaign advanced so rapidly on our foes.

The enemy left the village of Essaman as Captain Brackenbury[1] and Lieutenant Charteris[2] reached it. The surprise of our foes was complete, and we found the place stored with provisions and powder. Having rested for an hour, we marched on to Ampeene, about 5 miles off, situated on the beach. Its Chief fled with most of his people, after firing a few shots. It was 12 noon, and the heat was intense as we started, as it had been for the last four hours whenever the Bush was clear enough for us to see the sun. All the Europeans had suffered considerably, and Sir Garnet proposed that

---

[1] Now General Sir Henry Brackenbury, G.C.B.
[2] Son of Lord Elcho—died of fever.

we should rest content with what we had done; but I had undertaken to visit the Chief of Ampeene, who had beheaded the loyal Native, and expressed my desire to fulfil my promise. Sir Garnet, in the first instance, said I might go on with the Native troops only, but the Sailors, with whom my relations were always happy, wished to accompany me with their 7-pounder guns; then the Marines were unwilling to be outdone by the Bluejackets, and thus at two o'clock the whole party went on to the village, a toilsome march of $5\frac{1}{2}$ miles along the edge of the sea, through deep sand. We had no casualties at Ampeene, where Sir Garnet and his Staff embarked in a launch for the Commodore's ship, returning to Cape Coast Castle, while after destroying the village I turned back towards Elmina, which was reached at 10 p.m. Some of the officers never recovered their health during the campaign after this march. We covered 22 miles, most of the time under a burning sun.[1]

This action, though not of much importance in itself, was the first successful Bush fight in West Africa, and therefore not only the experience but its result was valuable. All previous attempts had ended disastrously from 1823 downwards. A few white men under the Governor then sold their lives so dearly that the Ashantis quarrelled for his heart, hoping they might assimilate with it his undaunted courage. The details of this fifty-years-old story were remembered, and thus the effect of the fight on the Ashantis, who had hitherto been the attacking party, was great; but the effect on the Coast tribes was even greater.

We had left them, although they were supposed to be under our protection, to defend themselves, until they had ceased to believe in our power or courage to oppose the foe. The orders issued before Sir Garnet Wolseley's arrival were in themselves demoralising; for instance, an officer sent to Dunquah was directed to give "every moral aid" to the Fantis, but he was "on no account to endanger the safe concentration of the

---

[1] Sir Garnet Wolseley wrote:—

"CAPE COAST CASTLE, 5.38 a.m., *October* 15*th*.

"What hour did you get back last night? I watched you through a glass till you got close to the Marines we left on the beach. . . . I have to congratulate you on the very able manner in which you did everything yesterday. I am very much obliged to you. The operations were well carried out, and all your previous arrangements were admirable."

Haussas under his command." The Chiefs of the Fantis gave the same sort of order, for we learnt after the campaign that a King who furnished a contingent of fighting men for our service strictly enjoined his brother, who commanded them, not to venture under fire on any account, whatever the white officers might say.

Sir Garnet Wolseley in his Despatch dwelt on the moral effect of the Expedition into the Bush, and two months later received the approval of Her Majesty.[1]

On the 26th October, leaving Elmina in charge of Captain Blake, and Bluejackets of H.M.S. *Druid*, I marched at daybreak to Simio, which I reached about eleven o'clock. I had with me half a company of the 2nd West India Regiment, and 35 Elminas of No. 2 Company, and was joined by a large party of Fantis from the neighbourhood of Abbaye. The latter showed great disinclination to move farther north, and absolutely refused to stop at Simio for the evening. They returned, therefore, to Abbaye, but their Chiefs remained with me. I proposed to attack the Ashantis at Mampon next morning, and sent to Captain Blake to ask him to come up and help me; but I was not able to carry out my intention, for I was ordered back to Elmina by the General, which, considering what we learnt later of our Black Allies, was fortunate.

It was some weeks before I raised my (Wood's) Regiment of four companies, to something over 500 strong. The 1st Company was composed of Fantis, enlisted near Cape Coast Castle, and it would be difficult to imagine a more cowardly, useless lot of men. The 2nd Company, which was the only one of fighting value, and which did practically all the scouting work, started on a modest footing of 17 men, enlisted generally in the disloyal part of Elmina, or that part sympathising with the Ashantis, and some few Ashanti Haussa slaves that we took in one of our first reconnaissance expeditions. The 3rd Company, Haussas, had been brought from Lagos, and were described as the sweepings of that Settlement, all the best men available having been previously enlisted. They were first put

---

[1] "I have Her Majesty's commands to convey to you and Lieutenant-Colonel Wood, who under your general direction was in immediate command, Her Majesty's approbation. . . . I observe with great satisfaction the terms in which you speak of the services rendered by Lieutenant-Colonel Wood, V.C."

under the command of Lieutenant Gordon, who had been the moving spirit at Elmina before we landed, but he being sent to the Hospital ship, they were commanded by Lieutenant Richmond, until he in turn succumbed to the effects of the climate.

I was then in some difficulty, but Martial Law having been proclaimed, the Civil prison was under my jurisdiction, in which there was a fine stalwart Black, whom I asked for what he had been imprisoned. He said for attempted murder. "What made you do it?" "I was drunk." "Well, if I let you out, and enlist you, will you undertake not to murder me, drunk or sober?" He promised cheerfully, and I got the advantage of that promise on Christmas Day, which we spent at Prahsu. The Sergeant had been of great use, and maintained an iron discipline, in a way of which I could not approve; for he kicked and cuffed every Black whom he could reach, and who was not as brave and active as himself. The men therefore hated him. He had remained quite sober until Christmas Day, when I was sent for by one of the officers, who said the Sergeant had got a loaded rifle, and had cleared the camp of No. 2 Company. When I reached the spot he was dancing, and mad drunk, defying all and sundry. I told off a dozen men to stalk him, and then approached him unarmed. He recognised me, and did not offer to resist. I walked straight up to the man, saying, "Stop this nonsense, and give me that gun;" and he handed it over. It was no sooner out of his hands than three or four of his men, who had doubtless suffered at his hands, jumped on him from behind, and knocking him down, tied him. This was apparently a sufficient lesson, for he gave no further trouble for the next three months we spent in the country. The Haussa company was later withdrawn, being replaced by 160 men from the Bonny and Opobo rivers, under command of Prince Charles of Bonny, who had been educated in Liverpool. The men were small, beautifully made, very clever at all basket-work, but with no special aptitude for war.

The 4th Company enlisted in the Interior, east of Sierra Leone, were Kossoos.[1] They came with a great reputation for courage, saying they preferred to fight with swords, and we gave them Naval cutlasses; but their only marked characteristic

[1] Wild pigs.

was intense cruelty. It is said that they did charge on the 31st December under Lieutenant Clowes, who was an excellent leader, after I had been wounded; but although I credit them with the intention, the fighting could not have been serious, as they had few or no casualties. Later on in the campaign, I personally took an Ashanti prisoner, while scouting at the head of the road, and knowing that he would not be safe away from me, had him put outside my living hut, where he was fed for three days. I was out of camp for half an hour, superintending the bridging of a stream, when Arthur Eyre ran to me, crying, "Pray bring your pistol; I want you to shoot one or two of these brutes of Kossoos. They have got the Ashanti prisoner away, and are practising cutting him in two at one blow." I hastened to the spot, but the man was beyond human aid, his body having been cut three parts through. I had the Haussa sentry who stood over him brought before me as a prisoner, and called upon him to recognise the Kossoos who had taken him away; but the man said he could not tell one Kossoo from another, adding he took no notice, as several men having come with a non-commissioned officer, he understood I wanted the man killed. The Kossoos realised that Englishmen would disapprove of their conduct, for when they were paraded within a few minutes of my arrival, they had anticipated that I should inspect their swords, and every cutlass was bright, and without a sign of the bloody use to which it had been put. I learnt afterwards that they had told the Ashanti to stand up, as they wanted to practise cutting him in two at a stroke, and, with the stoicism of his race, the man made no difficulty.

A peculiarity of the battalion was that while the 1st or Cape Coast Castle company could talk to those raised at Elmina, but never would do so, as they were deadly foes, neither company could talk to the Kossoos, or the Haussas, or indeed understand them. . There was, however, one advantage in this diversity of language and interests; for whereas corporal punishment was our only deterring power, except execution, and neither company would flog its own men, I made the Kossoos flog the Haussas, and the Haussas flog the Kossoos, and so on all round.

During the month of December, Chiefs Quamina Essevie and Quacoe Andoo came to offer me assistance. I had had a great deal to do with Essevie when I first landed. Andoo was such a fluent orator that we nicknamed him "Demosthenes"; and Essevie, though he said but little, was evidently a man of determination. They both accompanied me on our first expedition to Essaman and Ampeene, twelve days after we landed, with the carriers. Andoo had brought carriers in for me, and when I told him I was going out, he begged to be allowed to go home and do fetish. I was somewhat inclined to refuse, but reflecting that the man had come in on the understanding that he was a free agent, I assented, and he returned at 1 a.m., four hours before we started, and we are still on friendly terms. Essevie joined me early in December with twenty-two sons of his own body begotten, all between the ages of twenty and twenty-three, he himself being a man of about forty years of age, and the finest of the family. He brought also about twenty of his relations, but all his men were engaged on the following terms, which were approved by Sir Garnet, "that we be discharged on the day upon which Lieutenant-Colonel Wood, from any cause whatsoever, ceases to command the Regiment."

On the 6th November, in obedience to an urgent order from the General, I made a long march, which lasted from 8 a.m. till 10 o'clock at night, to join him at Abrakampa, which village, held by Major Baker Russell, had been invested by the Ashantis, but whose attack was, however, limited to a heavy expenditure of ammunition.

The morning after I arrived, 1000 Cape Coast Castle men, who had been sent by Sir Garnet to fight under my command, joined me at Abrakampa, and were paraded in the clearing facing the Bush. The order of battle was extraordinary. In the British Army, officers and their men quarrel for the post of honour, but here each company struggled, and edged away to the west, where it was supposed there were fewer Ashantis than in the front (north). The Fantis were fine men in stature, bigger than the Ashantis, and all armed with Enfield rifles. Behind them stood their Chiefs, handling whips, and yet again behind the Chiefs were Kossoos with drawn swords. My warriors being ordered to advance, moved forward a dozen paces, while their Chiefs belaboured all within reach, and in time drove all the men into the Bush, remaining themselves, however, in the clearing until some of Sir Garnet's Staff assisted me by using "more than verbal persuasion." One gifted Officer used so much persuasion to a Chief as to break a strong umbrella! With much shouting and firing the warriors slowly advanced, followed closely by the menacing Kossoos; but once in the Bush the Fantis got beyond control, for 100 Kossoos could not drive on 1000 Fantis, and nothing more was done, the Ashantis falling back until a party of Haussas and Cape Coast Castle men cut off their retreat at the village of Ainsa, when a few of them, taking the offensive, put the Cape Coast Castle men into such a panic that they fired into each other, killing 20 of their own men, and coming on the Haussas, who were in the act of crossing a stream, ran over them so hastily as to drown one of the company. They ran on till they reached Cape Coast Castle, 20 miles away, and there dispersed. The General, writing of them, said: "Their duplicity and cowardice surpasses all description."

While the King of Akim told us frankly that their hearts were not big enough to fight in the way the white men desired, yet individuals behaved well enough to satisfy even exacting Englishmen. The personal servants of the Staff Officers as a rule showed courage in action when accompanying their masters, and the two Elmina Chiefs while with me never showed signs of fear,—Essevie, the father of many children, being remarkably courageous.

It should be recorded also that the Fantis, when deserting, never stole their loads. Although they dropped them under the influence of fear when fighting was going on, they took the opportunity as a rule of leaving them close to a guard before they ran home.

The women had most of the qualities which are lacking in the men. They were bright, cheerful, and hard-working, and even under a hot fire never offered to leave the spot in which we placed them, and are very strong. As I paid over £130 to women for carrying loads up to Prahsu, I had many opportunities of observing their strength and trustworthy character; for to my knowledge no load was ever broken open or lost. They carried 50 or 60 lbs. from Cape Coast Castle to Prahsu, a distance of 74 miles, for 10s.; and the greater number of them carried a baby astride of what London milliners used to call a "dress improver."

When I moved into the Bush with the few men I had enlisted, although I was immune from fever I suffered considerably from exhaustion. In my Diary for the 12th November is written: "When I got into the clearing where we halted, I could only lie down and gasp." My head, eyes, and forehead ached, and I remained speechless until I was conscious of being severely bitten, when I struggled up, and obtaining a lantern, found my stretcher was placed on an ant-heap. All the officers, in carrying out work which would only be that of an ordinary day in Europe, were affected by the exhausting nature of the climate. Our men behaved badly; but then, as I have explained, we could not talk to them, and the command of the companies constantly changed hands, from officers falling sick. The Haussa company commanded by Lieutenant Gordon, after ten days was put under Lieutenant Richmond, who in his turn became sick, and although he tried determinedly to remain at duty, he never really recovered the exhausting march of the 14th October, except for one week at the end of November, in which he rendered us great assistance by his stoical demeanour under fire. Another Lieutenant spent nearly all the campaign on board the *Simoom*, a Hospital ship lying off Cape Coast Castle. He landed for duty eight times, but only did one march, when he was obliged to return. The climate affected our tempers, too, and most of the officers preceded their words with blows. Eventually, after issuing several Orders forbidding the practice of striking or kicking our soldiers, I wrote a Memorandum, which I passed round to the officers, to the effect that I would send back to Cape Coast Castle for passage to England the next officer who struck a soldier in Wood's Regiment.

Three days later a man came with a bleeding shin, and babbled out a complaint of which I understood nothing but the words "Massa ———." Calling for the doctor, whose courage in action was only equalled by his more than human kindness to all under his charge, for he never took food or lay down to rest till he had seen all the officers, I said, "Surgeon-Major, examine No.[1] ——— and report on his injury, and how he came by it." I did not venture to ask the company

---

[1] As every Black man was apparently called Quashi or Quamina, we knew them only by the numbers suspended from their necks.

Commander, for being as straightforward as he was brave, he would at once have answered, "I kicked him," and indeed there could be no doubt that he had done so, for the man's shin was marred with hobnails and mud. The doctor reported in writing: "I have examined No. ——, and, his statement to the contrary notwithstanding, am of opinion he injured his shin by tumbling over a fallen tree." I called the officer concerned and read the two memoranda to him, observing, "If another man in your company injures his shins in that way, you will go back to England." He saluted, and went back to his bivouac, when I said to my friend the doctor, "How could you write such an untruth?" "To save you from a great folly. I knew if I told the truth you would have sent him home. You have not got a braver officer here, nor one more devoted to you, and you will never be killed in this Expedition if he can save your life; that is the reason I told a lie." I was really very glad, for the occurrence had the desired effect; although I do not pretend to say that no officer struck another Black, yet they all realised that I was in earnest in endeavouring to suppress the practice. I sympathised fully with those who lost their temper! Our officers were brimming over with energy, and had to deal with Races naturally indolent, and the climate was, as I have said, very trying.

Ten days before I left Elmina, Captain Redvers Buller[1] came over from Cape Coast Castle, carried in a hammock, and the moment he reached the Castle, taking out his note-book, said, "Please order me a cup of tea, and give me some information as quickly as you can." I asked, "Why this hurry?" "Because I feel I have got fever coming on, and I am not certain how long my head will last." He wrote down carefully all I had to tell, and then, having drunk a cup of tea, started back. He soon became delirious, and imagined that the Fanti carriers were Ashantis surrounding him. Seizing his revolver, he fired three shots, but fortunately in the air.

The General also suffered considerably, and when I went on board the *Simoom* to see him, I felt doubtful if he would ever get to Coomassie.

We lost touch with the Ashantis for three weeks in November. They were moving back towards the Prah, and

[1] General the Right Honourable Sir Redvers Buller, V.C., G.C.B.

avoiding the main track running from south to north until they got clear of our advanced post, which was then near Sutah. I was now ordered to take charge here, the General writing to me, "There has been a terrible want of energy lately at the Head of the road, so I want you to go up there, for I expect very different from you. I will send you some more officers when the next mail comes in. Have the enemy's position constantly under your scout's supervision, so that I may hear when he begins to cross the Prah, as I may possibly come up with 500 Sailors and Marines, and attack him."

CHAPTER XXIII

1873-4—AT THE HEAD OF THE ROAD IN ASHANTI

A gloomy forest—Two brave Company leaders—Major Home—Wood's Regiment become carriers—Major Butler invades Ashanti with 20 Native Police—Amoaful—I am wounded—A forced march—Ordasu—Arthur Eyre killed—Sent down with wounded—The disobedient Bonnys—Chiefs Essevie and Andoo.

THE day after we occupied Sutah, which the Ashantis had quitted the previous morning, I went out with 6 European officers and 300 men to advance to Faisowah, and left No. 1 Company (the Fantis) at Sutah, to bring up our baggage as soon as some carriers were obtained from the Fanti camps in the neighbourhood. The enemy's Rear guard of 4000 men under Amanquatsia had been reinforced two days earlier by 5000 (slaves) fresh troops from Coomassie, and the Commander had orders to retake the offensive.

The country in which we were operating was a dense forest of gigantic trees, many 150 feet high, laced together with creepers supporting foliage so thick as to shut out the sun, which we never saw except in the villages; indeed, the light was so dim that I could not read my English letters until we came to a clearing, and the dreary monotony of endless green was oppressive beyond description. There were scarcely any birds or animal life except small deer the size of a terrier, and rats and venomous insects; few flowers, except round the villages, where the undergrowth was not so thick as near the Coast. On the other hand, it was close to the villages that most of the fighting, such as it was, occurred, where the system of African cultivation offered good cover to our enemies. They clear the ground by fire, then sow, in the ashes of the trees, and when the soil is exhausted abandon the spot, and build another village. This is easy, as four men can make a hut, the walls formed of palm leaves, within an hour. On the sites of these deserted villages there rose lofty vegetation, impenetrable except to naked savages crawling on their hands and knees.

Our track ran almost due north, passing occasionally through swampy ground, there being water up to our knees in one place for over 900 yards.

At 2 p.m. the Advanced guard under Captain Furse, 42nd Highlanders, who was acting as Second in Command of Wood's Regiment, was fired on half a mile south of Faisoo, but drove the Ashanti Rear guard back across the river, and from the open ground of Faisowah. He took a prisoner, who, seeing our numbers, advised us not to go on, stating that as it was Adai—that is, the Ashanti Sunday—they would not retire. Furze under these circumstances asked for orders. Now, I had been ordered to "harass the enemy, hang on his rear, and attack him without ceasing," so I gave the order "Advance." When we came under heavy fire in the clearing of Faisowah, I extended Richmond's Kossoos to the east of the track, and Woodgate on the west side with the Elmina company, in which there were 25 Haussa Ashanti slaves, whom we had taken in previous reconnaissances. The Haussas I extended in line behind, intending to pass through them if I were obliged to retire. Sergeant Silver and two white Marine Artillerymen were with me, using a rocket tube, and their cool, courageous bearing was an object lesson to the Blacks who could see them.

There was a heavy expenditure of ammunition for half an hour, when, as I had no reserve of it, and the Ashantis were extending round both flanks, I said to Arthur Eyre, the Adjutant, "Now, neither of the men in front of us will come away as soon as they are told, but Woodgate will be the slower, so go to him first, and order him to retire at once; and then come back to me, and you shall go to Richmond." This he did; and my forecast was correct, for after I had got Richmond and his Kossoos safely back through the extended Haussa line, I had to wait for Woodgate. For a mile our retreat was carried out in perfect order, but just south of Faisoo some carriers came up with my Fanti company, which I had left to bring up the baggage, and who, though not actually under fire, fled panic-stricken. They threw their loads down on the ground, unsteadying the greater part of the Kossoo company, and all the Haussas, who rushed along the narrow path on a frontage of 11 men—a path which only accommodated two men abreast in the Advance. The Elmina company only kept its ranks; the officers of other companies, Gordon, Richmond, Woodgate, and Lieutenant Pollard, R.N., by holding a few men together, kept back the Ashantis, who followed us up 4 miles.

Our casualties were slight—one killed and eight wounded, while four men who fled into the Bush, reappeared, one a month later. The bush on either side was so thick that the Ashantis could only crawl slowly through it, and did not dare come down the path, as they were shot by the European officers. I feared at one time that Sergeant Silver, Marine Artillery, would be trampled upon till he was insensible, and drew my revolver to keep back the crowd from him. I was just about to fire, when a black man seeing my face knocked down the nearest Haussa who was pressing on Silver, and kept back the fugitives until the Sergeant recovered his breath. I halted at nightfall, when we had retreated 7 miles, intending to stand; but the Ashantis, imagining I had been reinforced, became panic-stricken, and fled northwards — recrossing the Prah three days later.

Sir Garnet reported: " This attack caused the whole of the Ashanti Army to retreat in the utmost haste and confusion, leaving their dead and dying everywhere along the path."

The effect on the European officers of their exertions on the 27th was marked. Next morning I was the only effective officer, and spent the day in instructing three companies in aiming Drill. I had been on my back on the 16th, after two very long marches extending over twelve hours, although the progress made was comparatively small; but possibly on this occasion the excitement of the fight kept me up, and I did not suffer at all. Lieutenant Richmond was never again effective during the Expedition, and the health of his predecessor Gordon was seriously broken; but he had been for months on the Coast prior to Sir Garnet's arrival. Lieutenant Woodgate struggled on, but some days afterwards I found him lying insensible on the track; and some conception of our duties may be formed when I state he had £132 on him, mostly in silver, for we were all paying carriers as they put down their loads. Arthur Eyre, also, whose irrepressible energy always led him to overtax his strength, had to go on board ship sick, and came back to me only when we reached Prahsu.

The energy of the Commanding Royal Engineer of the Expedition, Major Home, was inexhaustible. I was warned by our Surgeon-Major that my friend, who was living with me, must break down unless he tried his system less. At the doctor's suggestion, I issued a circular Memorandum that "officers under medical treatment were not to go out in the sun without the doctor's sanction." Home resented this order, and told me that he did not intend to obey it. A few hours after, on returning from visiting parties cutting a path towards the Ashantis, he intimated his intention of going southwards, and, instigated by the doctor, I begged him to lie down instead. He absolutely refused to do so, and told his hammock-bearers—for he was being carried—to proceed. I shouted to the Rear guard, composed of men from the Bonny River, to stand to their Arms, and then explained to Home that he would suffer the indignity of being stopped and brought back by the little black men, unless he obeyed my order. He did so, and lying down on my bed, desired me to get a messenger to go back to Cape Coast Castle with a letter, reporting me to Sir Garnet. This I did; and he, being too weak to write the letter, dictated it to me, and I steadied his hand while he signed it, for he was in a high state of fever. I wrote on the outside, "The poor fellow is off his head," and agreeably to my promise sent the messenger off at once. We duly received an official answer to his question whether he was to be considered as under the orders of anyone but Sir Garnet Wolseley. It was to the effect that as Commanding Royal Engineer he received his orders from the Leader of the Expedition, but as an officer he was under the Senior in whose camp he might be on duty.

The Ashantis having recrossed the Prah, I asked that I should have a fortnight in which to teach my men to shoot. They, under Major Home's directions, had built Barracks for Europeans at every halting-place up to Prahsu, and I suggested that the work at the Head of the road should be taken by Major Baker Russell, whose Regiment had been at Abrakampa, or some other clearing, for six weeks; but on the day the order was issued the whole of the carriers deserted, and the General was obliged to order Russell's and Wood's Regiments, as well as the men of the 2nd West India Regiment, to carry loads for a fortnight, for without this help the rations for the Europeans could not have been got up to the Front.

I spent Christmas Day at Prahsu, helping Major Home to build a trestle bridge across the river. The King of Coomassie sent down ambassadors to arrange terms of peace. They were somewhat alarmed on first crossing the river, but became reassured when in the camp of Wood's Regiment, where they were kindly treated. Unfortunately, in the afternoon they were shown the action of a Gatling gun, and the sight of the bullets playing on the water in a reach of the river (which is broad at Prahsu) so alarmed one of them, that, by a complicated arrangement of a creeper fastened to his toe and to the trigger of a long blunderbuss, he blew off his head that night. We duly held an inquiry, much to the astonishment of the most important ambassador, who, after listening to the evidence, showed some impatience at our endeavouring to record the facts accurately, and observed, " The man being a coward was afraid to live, that's all."

I was ordered to take the body over the river, that the man might be buried in Ashanti, and the Bonnys being clever at all basket-work, in a very short time made a perfect Hayden's coffin.[1] When we were standing round the grave, I was astonished by two of the Ashantis throwing earth on the coffin, in precisely the same reverential way we see at our Burial services, and on our return to camp asked the ambassador what was the meaning of it. He said briefly, " For luck," adding a widow always did it at her husband's funeral, hoping that she would thus get another spouse by whom she would have children. Imagining that the custom must have been adopted from seeing our missionaries bury their dead, I asked if the practice had originated since white men came to the country, but he replied that it had been in use hundreds of years earlier.

---

[1] So called from the gentleman who proposed in the early seventies openwork coffins for burial in England.

Before we advanced from the Prah, I received the following original letter from Major W. Butler:[1]—

"AKIM SWAIDROO, *January 2nd*, 1874.

" MY DEAR COLONEL,—The King of Accassi's Queen has been carried off by the Haussas, and her chastity is in danger. Express messengers have arrived to announce her detention at Prahsu when tending plantains. Please do what you can to save Her Majesty's honour—or the plantains—for I cannot make out which is rated at the highest figure by the King. I am *en route* to Iribee.—Yours in haste,
"W. BUTLER."

The messenger brought a slip of paper also, with the significant words, " Please send me some quinine." I had to send Her Majesty back under escort, as she preferred the society of a Haussa to that of the King. Major Butler had expended much energy, and all the ready eloquence for which he is distinguished, in endeavouring to induce the Kings to the east of the Cape Coast Castle–Prahsu road, to march with him across the Prah. His reports were a series of buoyant hopes due to the man's indomitable nature, alternating with despair at the successive disappointments which he had to undergo. We heard that he finally crossed the Prah with 3 Fanti policemen, but he was followed a few days later by 400 Akims, who could not be persuaded even by my courageous and persuasive friend to incur any risk from the enemy's bullets.

On the morning of the 30th January, a few minutes after we reached the clearing south of Egginassie, where Wood's Regiment was to bivouac as Advanced guard, Home asked me for a Covering party for the Fanti road-cutters. I walked round and looked at the faces of my seven officers, who were asleep; all had fever. I thought Woodgate looked the brightest, so I awoke him, though he had been on Piquet all night. " Covering party ? Yes, sir ; I'll start at once." " Have some breakfast first." " Oh no ; I've got some biscuit, and there's plenty of water about the track." That evening Russell's and Wood's Regiments had cut a pathway that would take three

[1] Now General Sir William Butler, G.C.B.

men abreast, up to the outpost of the Ashanti Army, which was holding the clearing, and village of Egginassie, the southern end of Amoaful, which gave the name to the fight of the next day.

The General's plan was to advance, with one European battalion, by the pathway which ran from south to north, while a column under Colonel McLeod, 42nd Highlanders, consisting of 100 Sailors and Marines, and Russell's Regiment, with two guns and rockets, cut a path in a north-westerly direction. A similar column under my command was to cut a path to the north-east.

The brunt of the fighting was borne by the 42nd under Major Cluny Macpherson, which advanced with great determination, pressing back and breaking through the front line of the Ashantis. As the Bush was very dense, this fact was not known to the Ashantis on the east and west, and they continued to work round our flanks, penetrating between them and the 42nd Highlanders on both flanks.

The right column before I was wounded had cut 200 yards of track, the procedure being as follows: two workmen, each wielding two cutlasses, slashed at the Bush, being protected on either side by Sailors or Marines. We had been working an hour or two, when besides slugs which rattled round us, fired generally by Ashantis lying prone on the ground, there came several bullets over our heads, fired rather behind us, where I was superintending the advance. I called to the men behind me to go into the Bush and see who was firing, and shouted, "42nd, don't fire this way." At first nobody moved, and with an angry exclamation I ran back, and was parting the thick bush with my hands, when Arthur Eyre, pulling me by the skirt of my Norfolk jacket, protested, "It is really not your place," and pushed in before me. There was immediately an explosion of a heavy Dane gun, and when the smoke had cleared away, I saw Eyre was unhurt, and he exclaimed, "There are no 42nd men there; the fellow who fired at us is black, and quite naked." Two or three volleys cleared that part of the Bush, but between nine and ten o'clock, as I turned round to speak to a Staff officer who was bringing me a message from the General, an Ashanti lying close to me shot the head of a nail into my chest immediately over the region of the heart. Sticks were flying freely all the morning, and when I recovered from the stunning effect of the blow, I asked Arthur Eyre, who was bending over me, "Who hit me on the head?" "No one hit you, sir." "Yes, somebody did, and knocked me down." "No, I'm afraid you are wounded." "Nonsense! It is only my head is buzzing, I think from a blow." He pointed to my shirt, through which trickled some blood, and said, "No, you have been wounded there." He helped me up, and said, "Let me carry you back," but asserting I was perfectly able to walk alone, I asked him to stop and ensure the advance was continued. I walked unconsciously in a circle round and round the clearing we had made, and so had to submit to being supported back to Egginassie, where the ammunition-carriers and hospital stretcher-bearers had been placed. As most of the enemy were firing slugs, my body could only have been seriously hurt in the spot in which the slug struck; for Woodgate had stuffed my pockets with the War Office note-books, which he asked me to carry, and when I protested, said, "Well, as you are sure to be in front, I should like to save your chest."

My friend the Surgeon-Major, who had been taken away from Wood's Regiment a fortnight previously, to serve on Headquarters Staff, came to see me, and put a probe into the hole through which the head of the nail had passed. The first doctor who examined me had expressed an unfavourable opinion, based on his diagnosis of the very weak action of the heart. Noticing my friend's face was unusually grave, I said, "I believe you know I am not afraid to die, so tell me frankly what my chances are." He replied, "There is some foreign substance just over your heart; I cannot feel it with the probe, and do not like to try any farther, but as you are alive now, I can see no reason why you shouldn't live;" and this satisfied me I was not to die that day. It, however, was not the opinion of the other Medical officers, and the Principal Medical officer of the Expedition, afterwards Sir William Mackinnon, Director-General of the Army Medical Department, a friend of mine, went to Sir Garnet, who was on the west side of the clearing, to ask him to say good-bye to me before I was carried back to a clearing at Quarman, three-quarters of a mile farther south, where it was intended to establish a hospital. Sir Garnet Wolseley has an optimistic temperament, which has carried him onward through his remarkable career, and he absolutely declined to say "good-bye" to me, alleging that he would see me again at the Head of the road within a week, as indeed he did; but Mackinnon said, "No, sir, you never yet saw a man live with a shot in his pericardium."[1] The stretcher-bearers put me down in the clearing, and a man of the Army Hospital Corps dosed me with Brand's Essence of Beef, and brandy, until I somewhat petulantly asked him to leave me alone, and attend to somebody who required assistance more. "But you are very bad, sir," he said. Ten minutes later the Ashantis attacked the clearing. My Sierra Leone servant, putting my rifle between my feet, and revolver on the stretcher, sat down tranquilly alongside with his Snider. However, the measures for defence taken first by Captain C. Burnett,[2] and somewhat later by Colonel Colley,[3] who managed to be present at every fight or skirmish from the time of his landing, repulsed the attack, which was never serious. Next day there was a skirmish, after which the Sailors paid me the compliment of asking Commodore W. N. W. Hewett,[4] my friend of the Crimea, to get them placed under my command, as they were not happy under a Military officer who did not understand them.

The Force moved slowly on, and on the evening of the 3rd of February was only 16 miles north of Amoaful. That morning I received a note from Arthur Eyre, lamenting my absence, both for my sake and for that of his comrades, who had worked so hard since early in October. Eyre wrote that Sir Garnet and his Staff had forgotten the promise made after our very hard work, that, come what might, Wood's Regiment should be represented when the troops entered Coomassie. Eyre ended his letter, "Our last company has now been left to garrison a post, and we shall never see Coomassie till it

---

[1] From Sir Garnet Wolseley to Secretary of State for War:—

"AMOAFUL, 1st *February* 1871.

"The Officers commanding the columns performed their difficult task most excellently. . . . Lieutenant-Colonel Evelyn Wood, V.C., was wounded, while at the head of his troops."

[2] Now Lieutenant-General C. Burnett, C.B.   [3] Later, Sir George Colley.
[4] Died as Admiral Sir W. N. W. Hewett, K.C.B.

falls." After reading the pathetic appeal twice over, I sent for the doctor, and in order not to give him any chance, assured him that I was perfectly well. This was not absolutely accurate, for I had been lying on my back since noon on the 31st; but I showed him Eyre's letter, and in accordance with my assurances he sympathetically replied that I might try and overtake the General.

I started half an hour afterwards, and sent a runner to the Chief Staff officer, Colonel W. G. Greaves,[1] with a message that I was coming up, and intended to carry forward the most advanced company in accordance with the General's promise. I was detained for 5 hours by the Commandant of a post, who declined to allow me to take on the company until a strong patrol he had sent out returned; but eventually moving at a quarter to six, we marched all night, Furze, Woodgate, and Arthur Eyre. Rain fell in torrents, and it seemed that every step we took forward on the greasy path brought us at least half a pace backwards, but finally at four o'clock we came up with the Headquarters. Colonel T. D. Baker[2] warmly congratulated me on my arrival, saying, "The Chief is asleep, but he told me to give you his love, and say he is delighted you have come up, and wishes you to take the advanced section of the Advanced guard, when we move at daylight." I took over the duty from my friend Major Baker Russell, who grumbled good-humouredly at my luck in getting up in time to replace him in the forefront of the fight. He had enough, however, for we were together all the morning. He observed, "As you are here, I must tell you that there is an Ashanti about 60 yards in front of us with a heavy blunderbuss; I hope you won't let him put its contents into you." We had been ordered to do everything we could to save the lives of the Ashantis, and I took over from Baker Russell a wretched interpreter, himself an Ashanti, whose duty it was to advance with me, calling out in the vernacular, "It is peace, it is peace. Don't fire." This man knew his countryman's position behind the tree, and showed the greatest disinclination to accompany me when, about six o'clock, we advanced; but the ambushed Ashanti fired over our heads.

[1] Now General Sir George Greaves, K.C.B.
[2] Later, General Sir Thomas Durand Baker.

AT THE HEAD OF THE ROAD IN ASHANTI

We were three-quarters of a mile from Ordasu, a village on the river Ordah, which the Ashantis had anticipated holding; for when eventually we drove them out of it, their food was still boiling in the cooking vessels. I spent four hours trying to get the Bonny men to advance. They had never been taught to fire, and their idea was to lie prone on the ground, and, elevating the muzzle of the Snider in the air, fire it as quickly as possible. My friend Essevie, who was there, with a few of the Elmina company, showed the courage which he had always displayed, and kicked and buffeted all black men, including his sons, with the greatest impartiality, to drive them on; but we made little progress. I think it was a mistake to allow the Blacks to head the advance. They had built barracks, they had made bedsteads, they had taken every outpost, no European soldier being disturbed at night, and we should have got on faster if Europeans had been placed at once at the Head of the track. There were few casualties—in fact, nearly all were confined to the weak company of Wood's Regiment, which lost 1 officer and 3 men killed and 10 wounded, while the European Regiment supporting us with a strength of 450 men had only 17 men wounded, most of them slightly.

The density of the Bush may be realised by this fact: while I was teaching a Bonny man to fire, an Ashanti in the Bush discharged his gun so close to the Bonny man's head that the slugs did not spread, and the force of the charge threw the man's body from west to east across the path. While Baker Russell and I were talking, he standing up with the complete indifference to danger he always apparently felt, I ordered Arthur Eyre to kneel down, like the other Europeans, but he had scarcely done so when he was shot through the body, and from the look in his face I saw that his last hours had come. He held up his hand for me to remove his rings, saying, "Good-bye; please give them to my mother." The bullet had pierced the bladder, and he suffered so terribly, in spite of the doctor giving him all the morphia that his system would accept, that I felt relieved when he[1] died two hours afterwards. He had accompanied me, except when in Hospital, in every patrol and skirmish I undertook, and whenever he foresaw danger invented some excuse to get

[1] The only surviving child of a widow.

between me and the enemy. He had inherited his father's impulsive temperament and all his determined courage, and was moreover a delightful companion.

When we got into the clearing at Ordasu we halted for an hour, and the 42nd Highlanders coming up with heads erect and shoulders back, moved on into the Bush on either side of the track. Colonel McLeod was old-fashioned in his ideas. I never saw him willingly deploy to the right, or outwards. When at Aldershot he was accustomed to deploy to the left, and would move his battalion from the left up to the right to deploy back again; but there was certainly no more stoical man in the Army when bullets were flying. When he had extended a company, half on each side of the track, he called for the Pipe-Major, and saying, "Follow me," walked down the path, followed by another company. The resistance soon died away, and the Column moved on in single file towards Coomassie.

Just before it started, Major T. D. Baker [1] came to me and said, "The Chief says you are to take over the Rear guard." A wounded Marine had just been decapitated by Ashantis, who had crossed the path immediately behind the Headquarters Staff. I protested that I had been walking since 10 a.m. on the 3rd, and to put me on Rear guard would result in my not reaching Coomassie till after dark. I mentioned the name of an officer senior to me for the duty, but Baker said, "No, I suggested that, but Sir Garnet wishes you to do it." Shortly after we left the clearing we came on the body of a Chief, who had been shot by the 42nd Highlanders, while near him were three slaves who had been decapitated by one of the Chief's relations, for the Ashantis have a theory that when a great man dies he should be accompanied into the next world by slaves as body-servants.

At the southern entrance of Coomassie Lieutenant Maurice,[2] Sir Garnet's secretary, met me at 9 p.m., and said, "The Chief says you are to take up a line of outposts covering the town." As the night was pitchy dark, I observed, "Where is the Chief, and where is the enemy supposed to be, and where am I to

[1] Later, General Sir Thomas Durand Baker, K.C.B.
[2] Now General Sir Frederick Maurice, K.C.B.

COMASSIE, 4TH FEBRUARY, 1874

GENERAL SIR GARNET WOLSELEY, TO SECRETARY OF STATE FOR WAR. "IT IS WITH THE GREATEST REGRET I HAVE TO REPORT THE DEATH OF LIEUTENANT EYRE, 90TH LIGHT INFANTRY, WHO WAS MORTALLY WOUNDED IN ACTION. I CANNOT REFRAIN FROM STATING WHAT A GREAT LOSS THE ARMY HAS EXPERIENCED IN THE DEATH OF THIS GALLANT OFFICER."

go?" Maurice replied, "I asked him that, and he observed, 'Evelyn Wood is sure to know, leave it to him.'" I went away a few hundred yards from where I understood the Headquarters Staff was lying, and, halting close to some huts, sent an Ashanti for clean water; for the stream we had just crossed had been polluted by the bodies of human sacrifices. I had barely fallen asleep when a Staff officer came to me and told me to fall in my men, and proceed to the Palace, which was on fire. I went at once, but the fire was nearly out when we arrived, and I slept till daylight, when I was again summoned, and ordered down to the Coast, with a convoy of sick and wounded.

I left Coomassie on the morning of the 5th February, with the remnants of Russell's and Wood's Regiments, and a company of the Rifle Brigade, escorting some 70 wounded and sick Europeans, nearly all the former belonging to the 42nd Highlanders.

Although no serious attack was probable, my charge occasioned me some anxiety. All the wounded who were unable to march were in cots slung on long bamboo poles, carried by eight men, and so in single file, which was the only arrangement of which the path admitted, our line of march extended over nearly two miles.

When Sir Garnet went forward to the Ordah River, the troops accepted cheerfully four days' rations for six, and thus it came about that on the evening we arrived at Ordasu, where Arthur Eyre was buried, except a small bit of biscuit, the wounded had no rations of any kind. Just as we had lifted the cots of the wounded off the ground and placed them on tripods of bamboos, an impending storm broke, the heavens opening, rain fell as it does only in the tropics, and within ten minutes there were 10 inches of water on the ground.

I had ½ lb. of tea and some sugar, which my servant carried in a haversack, and, assisted by Furse of the 42nd, after infinite trouble, I made a fire over a projecting root of a big Banyan tree. In turn we held an umbrella to shelter our fire from the rain, and finally had the satisfaction of raising the water to boiling-point, and into it I put all my tea and sugar. When we had handed round the last pannikin, I said I would have given a sovereign for a tin of tea, and Furze remarked, " I would have gladly given two." Next day we moved onwards, and met a convoy of Supplies, so there was no further scarcity. I received orders to halt, send the convoy on with the Rifle Brigade, and remain behind, following the Europeans as Rear guard.

The strength of the white soldiers was husbanded, and wisely so, in every respect. They were never put on outposts. Up to the Prah — 74 miles, just half-way to Coomassie—they slept in large bamboo huts which accommodated 50 men, provided with comfortable beds, filtered water, washing-places, latrines, cooking-places, sentry boxes, commissariat stores. A Hospital and Surgical ward was erected every 8 or 10 miles. Everything, in fact, was so arranged that the Europeans had nothing to do except cook their food and lie down on their arrival in camp. All these arrangements were carried out by Major Home, to whom Sir Garnet expressed his warmest thanks. They were deserved. During the Expedition, Home and his officers had cut a fairly smooth track, about 8 feet wide. He bridged 237 streams, laid down corduroy over innumerable swamps, some of which required three layers of fascines, and in one place alone, between Sutah and Faisowah, stretched over 800 yards. When the Ashantis in their retirement approached the main path, near Mansu, Home was there with 43 Natives, and had just built a fort. His men—Fantis—were untrained, and he had only 40 rounds of ammunition. The General ordered him to fall back towards the Coast, but Home held his fort, and the enemy, not being able to pass him, moved farther northwards in the Bush before they regained the track.

When we were coming down country, some of the worst traits of the Bonny men became evident. They absolutely refused to carry their own sick and wounded, and after I personally coerced 8 men into carrying a Bonny who was very ill, when I had gone back to look for another sick man on the line of march, they deliberately carried their comrade into the Bush 50 yards off the track, and there left him to die. The exertion of walking from front to rear of the Column was great, and thus it was that, when coming along slowly—for I was suffering from intestinal complaints, and could walk only by resorting frequently to laudanum and chlorodyne—I heard a noise in the Bush which attracted my attention. My servant told me he thought it was nothing, but I persisted in looking, and there found the Bonny man whom I had put into a hammock an hour earlier. I had him carried to the next encampment by some of Baker Russell's men, and upbraided Prince Charles, the Captain of the company, who spoke and wrote perfect English, for the conduct of his men. They, however, received my reproaches with apparent unconcern. Next morning I arranged that the Bonny company should march behind the sick; but when moving off, Prince Charles informed me that his men absolutely refused to carry, saying that they never regarded a sick and wounded man in their own country, and always left him to die. I halted the Kossoo company, and directing them to cut some stout bamboos, told the Bonnys that I should begin with the right-hand man, and unless they picked up their sick comrade they would suffer severely until they obeyed orders. They refused, so I had the right-hand man thrown down and flogged until I was nearly sick from the sight. Then I had the next man treated in a similar manner, but he received only 25 lashes when, turning his head, he said, "I will carry." The company then gave in, and undertook to carry their comrade down to the Coast.

Two marches farther on, from the carelessness of an interpreter, and the peculiar reticence of the Native character, I nearly had a man flogged unjustly, the remembrance of which would have been very painful to me. The Native soldiers for choice carried everything on their heads, blanket, ammunition, rifles and cooking-pots, and thus when a shot was fired in the Bush, or a man moved unexpectedly, everything came down with a crash, and as we had several false alarms, I was obliged to provide against this trouble. This I did by issuing two cross belts for each black soldier. For two successive mornings I noticed that one man in the Elmina company was still carrying loads on his head. I fined him a day's pay, and when I saw him disobeying orders the third morning I had him made a prisoner. He still refused to carry his kit except on his head, so I sent for the doctor, and said to the Elmina, "When the men have eaten, I shall flog you."

While I was having a cup of cocoa, a deputation came to the tree under which I was sitting, to beg their comrade off, saying, " You have put us in front on every occasion; when you, or your white officers went out, whether they belonged to our company or not, we have always escorted them, and we beg you will not flog this man." I explained that he must obey orders. They still gave me no indication of why the man had refused to obey orders, but when I saw him and asked for a reason, he replied simply, " The belts hurt me ; " and on my further questioning him, he opened the front of his shirt, and showed a deep hole in his body, which he had received from a slug in action at Ordasu, and into which, without troubling a doctor, he had stuffed a lump of grass! I rejoiced in my persistence in questioning the man, which was the means of saving me from doing a great injustice.

I spent some anxious days at Elmina on my return, for Arthur Eyre had kept all such Public accounts as we had, as well as my private accounts, and I provided the food and liquor for all the officers of Wood's Regiment, charging them the actual cost, and although my friend had kept accurate accounts up till his death, it was difficult for me to arrange satisfactorily with the officers, who seldom messed with me four or five days at a time. Finally, I embarked on board the *Manitoban,* and came home with our General, to whom the success of the Expedition was due. When he went out there was a cloud of evil auguries ; advisers differed, and the causes of anticipated disasters varied, but nearly all predicted failure. The successful result was due primarily to Sir Garnet Wolseley. His mind it was that animated all, for to his other great qualities he added that fire, that spirit, that courage, which gave vigour and direction to his subordinates, bearing down all resistance. Every one acknowledged his superior Military genius, and when, on coming home, I was asked by the Adjutant-General and the Military Secretary what my brother-officers and I thought of Sir Garnet, I replied, " If he had gone down, I doubt whether there was any man big enough to have entered Coomassie with only one day's rations."

As I was leaving Elmina, I said to my friend Essevie, " You have done very well throughout the four months you have served with me, and I should like to send you a present from England. Have you any preference?" After a moment's reflection,[1] he replied, "Well, I should like a tall black hat." Before the ship sailed, however, he wrote me a letter, asking if I would sell him one of my umbrellas. I sent him both as a present; but the request put another idea into my head, and on reaching London, having ordered him a 23s. Lincoln & Bennett black hat of the largest size ever made, I called on Mr. Lawson, Secretary of the Army and Navy Co-operative Society, and said I wanted him to make the biggest umbrella ever seen—the sort of thing which would take two men to carry—and with a different and startling colour between every rib. "Do you know that will cost you over twenty guineas?" "Possibly; but I should like to send a black man something of which he may be proud." And he booked the order. A few days later he wrote to me that, as I probably knew, my idea was not original, and he had found in the City an umbrella such as I desired, which had been ordered by the Colonial Office for a Chief on the Gambia River three years previously; but the sable Potentate having misbehaved, the umbrella was still on sale, for, as Mr. Lawson quaintly wrote, "There is no demand." He bought it for me for £12, and also made for me a ten-guinea walking-stick, ornamented with gold bosses, and the hat, umbrella, and stick, on receipt at Cape Coast Castle, were handed over to Essevie and Andoo, on a Full-dress parade of the garrison, which marched past these somewhat unusual emblems of honour.

Twenty-two years afterwards, my eldest son took part in the next expedition to Ashanti, and was sitting one day in the market-place of Coomassie, when he saw a Native carrying a handsome gold stick. He, like most Englishmen, thinking that money would buy anything that a black man possessed, called to him, "Hey, sell me that stick." The man replied, "I cannot; it belongs to my Chief." "Oh, he will take £5 for it." "No," said the man, "he would not take any money for it;" and somewhat unwillingly he handed it over for closer inspection. My son read on it, "Presented to Chief Andoo by Colonel Evelyn Wood, 1874." Essevie was dead

[1] He wore only a small loin-cloth on his gigantic body.

but Andoo still lives, and was in Coomassie with the Expedition of 1895–96.

My mother was staying at Belhus, the seat of Sir Thomas Barrett Lennard, when I arrived home, and the tenantry and local friends gave me a great reception, as did, a week later, the 90th Light Infantry; for when I went down to stay with the officers at Dover, the Regiment turned out and carried me up the heights to the Barracks in which the Regiment was quartered.

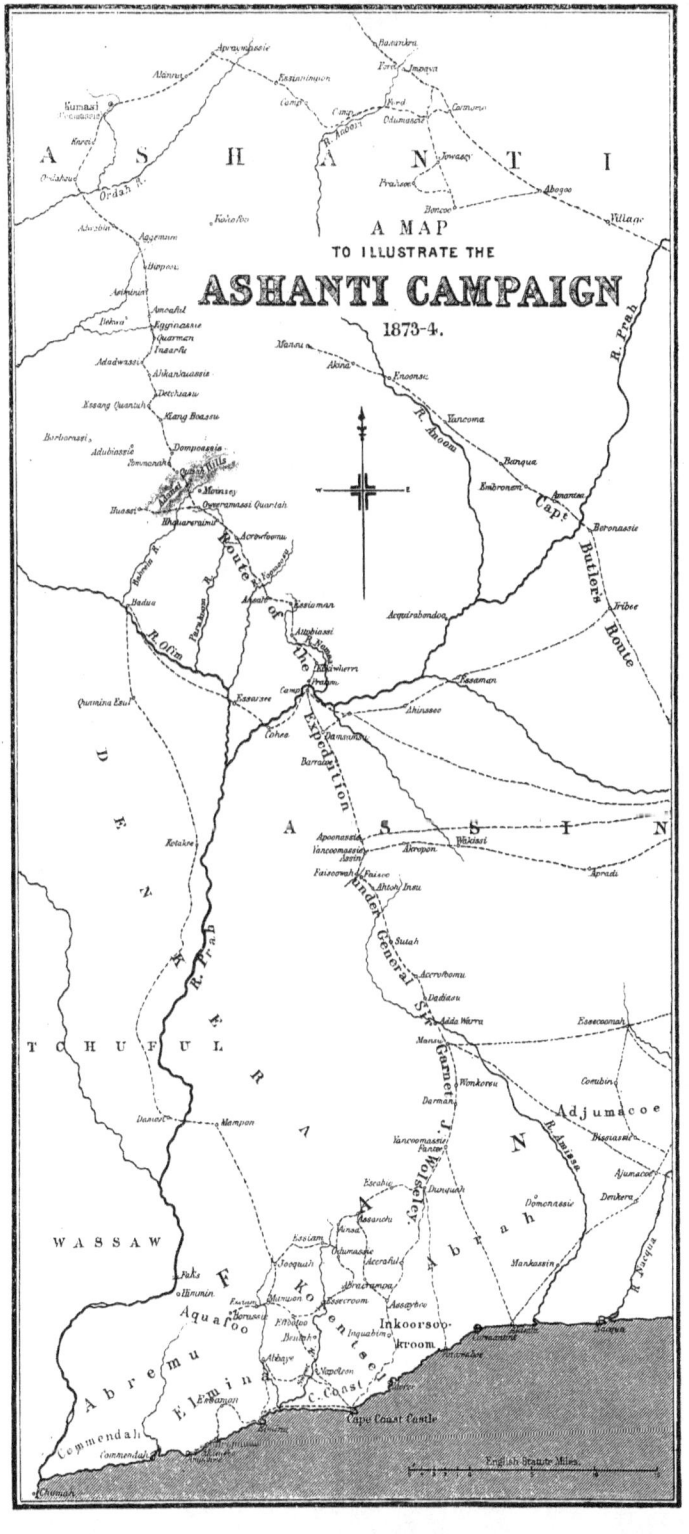

CHAPTER XXIV

1874-8—ALDERSHOT: SOUTH AFRICA

Civic hospitality—Garrison instruction—E. R. P. Woodgate—I decline to be permanent Examiner for Promotion — Thomas White invites me to join him in business—Am offered the Commandantship of Staff College—A Glassite—" War-Game "—Sandilli—The Gaikas—The Fingoes—The Perie Bush—Rupert Lonsdale.

SOON after our return from the West Coast we were honoured by a command to Windsor, officers of the rank of Lieutenant-Colonel and upwards only being invited to dine at the Royal table and to remain the night at the Castle.

I had intended to postpone being called to the Bar, but my friend and tutor Captain Blake, Royal Marines, thinking I might be too busy later to read further, advised me to apply at once, and I was called during the Easter term.

At a Dinner given by the Lord Mayor to Sir Garnet and the Ashanti warriors, I sat near the Prime Warden of the Fishmongers' Company, and in the course of conversation he learnt I was a grandson of Sir Matthew Wood, which resulted in my being invited to join the Livery of that Company, which I did a few weeks later.

At another Civic Feast I sat next to a retired Rear Admiral, who was annoyed at Sir John Glover's name being noted to return thanks for the Navy. This was a mistake; for Glover, one of the most indomitable of men, had left the Navy as a Lieutenant, with the honorary rank of Captain, and the Admiral had reason, therefore, for his vexation, which he showed throughout the dinner. He presumably must have seen my name on the plan of the table, which he studied from time to time. In an interval between two speeches he ex-

pressed to me an opinion shown by the following conversation :—
"A great deal of unnecessary fuss is being made over these men who have been to Ashanti." "Yes, sir." "They have done just nothing at all to what I did when I was there." "Pray, when was that, sir?" "In 1823." "Oh, that was when Sir Charles Macarthy was killed?" "Why, were you there?" "No, sir, I wasn't there." "Oh, but you must have been—you know about it." "No, I wasn't there, but it has been my business to read about what took place before we went there." "Well, I will tell you a remarkable story of what happened to me that year. We were going up the Niger to attack a village at daybreak, and although the days were hot, the nights were cold, and I was wearing two pairs of trousers. We were fired on before we reached the village, and a ball from a jingal nearly as big as my fist went in at my hip, wrapping round it bits of both pairs of trousers." "Really, sir, I am thankful you are alive here to-night to tell the tale." "Yes, but more wonderful still, that ball went through my body and came out the other side." I had been sipping wine for three hours, and perhaps being nettled by the Admiral's disparaging remarks on my friends, observed quickly, "What, sir, and both pairs of trousers wrapped round it?" The moment I had spoken I reflected that he had distinguished himself in trying to reach the North Pole, that he was old, and I had been disrespectful; but I was immediately relieved by his cheerful answer, "Yes, and that's the most extraordinary part of my story—the bits of both pairs of trousers came out with the ball"!

I received three months' leave for the recovery of my health, at the end of which I had hoped to join the Headquarters of my battalion at Dover, but the Lieutenant-Colonel then in command did not wish to have a full Colonel with him, who would often, in Field operations, have command of the brigade, and persuaded my brother-officer and junior, Major Rogers, to come from the Depot to Headquarters.

I joined at Hamilton on the 1st July, and the Officer in command of the Depot, when I called on him, said to me politely, "Now, Colonel, there is only enough work for one of us here, and I am fond of work." I said, "May I assume, then, that it is a matter of indifference to you where I live, or how often I come into barracks?" "Quite so," he assured me. "Come when it suits your convenience, no oftener." So I lived pleasantly for two months in the Manse at Dalserf, immediately over Mauldslie Castle, at which my wife and I spent half of each week.

The miners, who lived all around, were then earning high wages, and I had great difficulty in obtaining milk for my family, until I called on a farmer and asked him as a favour to let me have some, I sending for it. He assented, though not graciously, observing, " Every man should keep his ain coo."

Early in September I was ordered to Aldershot as Superintending officer of Garrison Instruction, with my office at that camp. Some years previously there had been a serious outbreak of scarlatina at Sandhurst, and the cadets had necessarily been removed, the College not being re-opened for a considerable time. To educate the cadets, whose studies had been interrupted, as well as with the average intake of candidates through Sandhurst — about 300 per annum — classes were formed in the principal garrisons of the United Kingdom, as far east as Colchester, south as Shorncliffe and Cork, and in the north at Edinburgh. The young gentlemen were gazetted to Regiments on probation, and taught the Sandhurst course as far as possible by Staff College graduates, in classes of from 15 to 25. My duty was to visit them as often as I thought necessary, and see the Syllabus was duly followed, and that Instructors and pupils were doing their best for the Service. I learnt a good deal about schools in England, for as a rule I talked to all the young men in the class, and they, with the feeling that they were in the Army, gave me valuable information as to our Public schools, the general tone of which was, according to the information I received, undoubtedly very high.

The difficulties at some Stations in the way of regular teaching and progress were serious, where the temptations for asking leave of absence were unceasing. One Instructor complained bitterly to me. "Although I have got," he said, "as gentlemanlike a set of young men under Instruction as it is possible to find in the whole world, it has been heartbreaking to try and keep them together for concerted work. First of all, their mammas and their sisters wanted them to dance all night, while by day they were constantly away at Epsom, Ascot, and Goodwood. Then I hoped, the Season being over, I should get them to work, but with the middle of August came requests for leave for grouse-shooting, followed in September by applications for a few days' partridge-shooting, and early in October out-lying pheasants demanded attention. Now one of the best young fellows in my class wants leave for cub-hunting." "Oh," I said, "you should put your foot down; tell him to cub-hunt at daylight, and get here at ten o'clock." "He would do that cheerfully," was the answer, "but he is Master of the Hounds, and his kennels are 200 miles from London"! I enjoyed my life, doing most of the travelling in the summer and early autumn, and enjoying a considerable amount of hunting. I took a house near the Staff College, and after doing a day's work in the office at Aldershot often got a ride in the afternoon with the College drag hounds.

After riding with the drag, about tea-time one evening, my friend Lieutenant E. R. P. Woodgate[1] walked up from Blackwater Station, carrying his bag, and in his abrupt, decided way said, "Can you put me up for the night? I want to talk to you." "Yes, certainly." After dinner, he observed, "I want to go to the Staff College." "Well, what do you know?" "I was well taught at Sandhurst, but I have not read much since." Next morning, I gave him after breakfast a complete set of examination papers, and observed, "Do as much of these as you can, and I will look over them to-night after dinner." As the result, I said, "With two months' instruction you would probably succeed in the competition for entrance to the College, but it may take you three." "What will it cost me?" "About 20 guineas a month." "Then I must abandon the idea, for I have only got £14 available." I thought of my friend's case in the night, and next day wrote to a tutor who had been successful in teaching me, and whom I had obliged with a small loan of money some years before. I made no allusion to the loan, but asked him if he would, as a personal favour to me, teach my friend as much as he could for £14. This he did, and so successfully that Woodgate had no difficulty in getting into the College. He reappears farther on in my story. The Council of Military Education

[1] Later, General Woodgate, mortally wounded at Spion Kop, in the Boer War.

were troubled by the irregularities of Boards of Examination on officers for promotion, for neither candidates nor Boards realised the discredit of "obtaining aid from books or other sources," and I was invited to become Examiner for all Boards in Great Britain. Although the suggested salary was tempting, I declined, explaining officers would, if trusted, come in time to see their duty in its true light, while their hands would always be against an individual, whose questions would moreover become stereotyped.

In order to have a little money for my favourite sport of hunting, I accepted the office of Examiner in Tactics, but it was monotonous work reading 100 answers to the same questions.

My friend Major-General Arthur Herbert got me appointed to his Division for the Autumn Manœuvres in the following year, and on the 23rd April 1876 I was appointed Assistant Quartermaster-General at Aldershot, where I served with a pleasant, but one of the most determined men I ever met in my career, Colonel George Harman, later Military Secretary. He was a fine horseman, slight in build, but with a handsome, aristocratic face, and never afraid of saying the most unpleasant truths to his superior officers if he thought it was his duty to do so. Not having been to the Staff College, he liked me to arrange the tactical schemes, and to the best of my recollection I framed, and got permission for, the first example of Minor Tactics, in June 1877, to be carried out by Field officers. The idea was so popular that the system took root, and has been continued to this day. Previously to this Drill Season no officer under the rank of a General had had, as a rule, the opportunity of handling the three Arms of the Service in tactical operations.

In the spring of that year, towards the close of the hunting season, I was at my brother-in-law's, going through the accounts of his Irish property, when I received a telegram saying that my eldest son, a child of six years old, was ill, and Surgeon Alcock telegraphed to me to buy some salicylate of soda, which was not then a drug supplied in Army hospitals. When my wife and I reached the North Camp, I was warned by my friend Alcock that the child was very ill, with a temperature of 104°, and that unless the salicylate of soda brought his temperature down, he could not live. Alcock explained that the drug, although often given in America, was not in common use in England, and its effect was uncertain, so I watched with intense anxiety the effects of three doses, given in close succession. We found the boy wrapped in cotton-wool, with his knees drawn up to his chin, and he screamed with the apprehension of being touched before I got to the bedside. Within an hour the painful look in his face relaxed, and after the third dose had been swallowed his knees gradually resumed a natural position, and the child slept, being able the same evening to look at the picture-books we had purchased for him as we passed through London. He recovered, but eight years later had a second, though less severe attack, which obliged me to remove him from Wellington College, and I was compelled to have him watched with great care for two years, allowing him to do but very little work. I was advised by three of the leading physicians in London, who examined him, that it was hopeless to expect he would be able to do anything but sedentary work.

Six years later, when the lad wished to enter the Army, I took him to one of the Doctors who had given the unfavourable opinion and asked him to re-examine him, as I should not feel justified as a General in allowing him to go up, unless I were satisfied he was sound, whatever the Medical Board might decide. After a severe test the opinion was favourable, and four years later he hunted successfully the Regimental pack of Foot beagles.

I had what I always consider was a flattering offer about this time from Mr. T. White the Outfitter (a miniature Whiteley), who supplied most of the officers and non-commissioned officers of the Aldershot Division. When he was a young man, working in his father's small shop at Hartley Row, on the Bagshot-Basingstoke Road, His Royal Highness the Prince Consort, having induced the Treasury to purchase 10,000 acres, initiated the Aldershot Camp. Mr. White came to Aldershot, which was then only a hamlet, and prospered with the rising town. He was not only my provider, but a friend for many years; indeed, our business relations commencing in 1866 have continued without intermission with the Firm until this date, and every time I have gone on

COLONEL WOOD'S QUARTERS, ALDERSHOT, 1876-77

Service my telegraphic requisition has been, "Send me what you think is necessary." This confidence has always been justified. When Sir Daniel Lysons commanded the 1st Brigade, he and I worked a good deal with Mr. White, inventing and improving camp equipment for officers, whose amount of baggage was then closely limited; and later the General and I went through Mr. White's books on a proposition being made to start a Local ready-money establishment, similar to the Army and Navy Stores.

Mr. White coming to me one day, asked for a private interview, in which the following dialogue occurred :—" Colonel, you have been of great use to me about Camp Equipment and with your advice generally, and I have been thinking for some time that I should like to make you a proposition, but I hope if it displeases you you will forgive me." I said, "What is it?" "Can I induce you to leave the Service, and join me in business?" "Yes, the subject would require thought as to terms, but if they were sufficiently good I would consider it for the sake of my children." "Well, may I ask what terms you would require?"

After ten minutes' calculation, I replied, "£3000 a year taken out of your business, and invested in any security approved by me, payable to me as long as I wish to retain it, irrespective of the time and attention I give to the business, or to our agreeing or disagreeing on any points." Mr. White jumped, nearly falling off his chair, and observed, "£3000 a year is a large sum: pray may I ask what your pay is now, sir?" "£664, including allowances." "The difference, you will allow me to say, is very great." "It is, yet not so great as the difference in serving Her Majesty Queen Victoria and Thomas White." "Oh, sir, I am afraid I have vexed you." "No; on the contrary, you have paid me a greater compliment as to my capacity for business than I am likely to receive from anyone else."

In August, my friend General W. Napier, the Governor of the Military College, Sandhurst, offered me the post of Commandant there, under him. All my relations with him and with his family had been of the happiest description, but I did not like the idea of settling down at Sandhurst before I commanded a battalion; this feeling influenced me again when I was informed I might be considered for the Staff College. Moreover, I thought Colonel Colley,[1] then Military Secretary to Lord Lytton, Viceroy of India, would make a far better Commandant of the Staff College in every respect (except in personally encouraging the drag hounds), and I asked a common friend to write and urge him to become a candidate. Colley replied that he was engaged in too important work, and I hesitated for some time as to whether I should ask for the post. My Regiment was amongst the first upon the Roster for the Colonies, and the prospect of serving as a Major on 16s. a day was not attractive when balanced against the advantages of the Staff College—£1000 a year, a good house, and the immediate proximity of Wellington College, where I intended to send my sons.

When the offer was definitely made, I consulted Sir Alfred Horsford, who had been one of my kindest friends ever since I served with him in the North Camp at Aldershot. I pointed out the pecuniary and other advantages, and when I had ceased speaking, he said, "Do you want my frank opinion?" "Certainly, sir, please." "Well," he answered, "accept it; and if your Regiment goes on Service you will be a miserable man for the rest of your days." This settled the question in my mind.

Early in November, when coming from Belhus, where Sir Garnet Wolseley[2] and Colonel W. Butler[3] had been shooting, Butler mentioned in the course of conversation that if worse news came from the Cape, the 90th would be put under orders. Sir Garnet condoled with me, for although he was in the War Office at the time he was not aware of the state of the Roster for Foreign Service. He told me in confidence then, what I had suspected for some time, that we were on the brink of a war with Russia. Indeed, at Aldershot, not long before, I had given a lecture on "The Passages of the Danube and the Passes of the Balkans."

The Ministry had intended to employ another General officer in Command, but he having stipulated for a larger number of men than the Government was willing to employ, at all events in the first instance, Lord Beaconsfield's choice

---

[1] Major-General Sir George Colley, killed in action 1881.
[2] Field-Marshal Lord Wolseley.   [3] General Sir William Butler, G.C.B.

fell on Sir Garnet, and he told me how much he regretted that I should not be with him. I said, "Perhaps Cetewayo will give us a fight," but he replied, "No, Shepstone will keep him quiet until we are ready." Colonel Butler said, "When we fight Zulus, we shall want 10,000 men, and I shall go out on the second wave of Special Service officers." And so he did.

The Officer commanding my Regiment was then, and may possibly have been all his life, a "Glassite," but had latterly accepted the idea that it was immoral to fight. All the time I was at Aldershot I performed his duties on Courts Martial, as he was unwilling to take an oath. At the end of December, at his request, I accompanied him to London, when he asked that he might be allowed to remain in England, on leave, till the 1st April 1878,[1] when his command would expire, and that I should take out the battalion. He endeavoured to convey his wishes to the Adjutant-General and Military Secretary, but entirely failed to make them understand his position; indeed, I believe they imagined he was suffering under some physical ailment, for the words he frequently used were, that he "had the strongest reasons for not wishing to go into Camp."

He embarked on the 11th January, and on the 27th I followed the battalion, having indeed been very unhappy since I saw them off at Southampton with the band playing "Far away."

The battalion had its complement of Lieutenant-Colonel and two Majors, I (the Senior), being on the Staff, was supernumerary, so when a month later I was sent out, it was "On Special Service," with the promise given to me verbally by the Commander-in-Chief, the Adjutant-General, and the Military Secretary, confirmed in a Memorandum which was handed to General Thesiger, that I should succeed to the command on the 1st April. But this understanding was not fulfilled.

The battalion on arriving at Cape Town was divided; five companies were sent to Fort Beaufort, where the Gaikas were restless, and three companies to Utrecht, in the Transvaal.

When I got to the Amatola Mountains, six weeks later, the five companies were gradually withdrawn from the Colonel

---

[1] Later he asked to remain on till November 1878, in order to complete thirty years' service, and thus get the full pension of 20s. per diem.

commanding, and he remained in charge of some Hottentots at Fort Beaufort until June, when he returned home, being retained in nominal command of the Regiment till November, when he completed his thirty years' service.

My fellow-passengers on board ship were General the Honourable F. Thesiger, who was going out to Command at the Cape, Major Redvers Buller, and other Staff officers. We arrived at East London, British Kaffraria, on the 4th March, and a more uninviting spot than it was then, it would be difficult to imagine. It consisted of corrugated iron huts, surrounded by broken glass bottles and empty jam tins, dotted about on bleak, bare sand-hills, through which the muddy Buffalo River cut an opening 250 yards wide to the sea, depositing a barrier of sand, which up to that time had presented insuperable difficulties to forming a satisfactory harbour, although the problem had engaged the attention of the most eminent of our British Marine Engineers. There were no roads; the so-called hotel provided shelter and food, but while there were bath towels there were no baths, and the one closet was common to Whites of both sexes and Kafir servants.

A few days before our arrival, two boatmen had been washed off a lighter in crossing the bar and drowned, as capsizing in a heavy roller it remained upside down. This fact, and the prospect of being battened down in a chamber with my horses, and tossed about in the rolling waves, added considerably to the interest of the arrangements for passing through the breakers, which all of my companions preferred to undertake in a lifeboat. This alternative was not open to me, as I felt bound to accompany the groom and my horses; but nothing occurred, except that in two successive heavy waves as we crossed the bar the horses were knocked off their feet.

The General and his Staff were going to King William's Town, 50 miles distant, to which place there was a railway. I had no difficulty about a horse I bought from a Dutchman at Cape Town, but a well-bred, weight-carrying hunter named "War-Game," standing 16.2, could not be fitted in any horse box or truck available, and I handed it over to a Kafir with orders to lead it up to "King," the familiar local abbreviation of the chief town of the eastern provinces. Later, hearing of a larger truck up the line, I succeeded in getting the horse safely to the Settlement, and it falsified all the predictions of those who advised me that an English horse would be useless for service in South Africa. "War-Game" was knee-haltered and turned loose with the horses of my companions, although in the Transvaal, on account of horse-sickness, I stabled him in wet weather wherever shelter was available. The animal kept his condition, and was brought home at the end of the Zulu War, carrying me well to hounds for many seasons. He was very troublesome on board ship, for in the rough weather we experienced near Madeira he got his foot over the front of the box, which was on deck, and at another time had both hind feet over the side of the ship at one moment.

The General relieved by Lieutenant-General the Honourable F. Thesiger had reported that the war was over. This was accurate as regards the outbreak in the Transkei. In that open country the Galekas in attacking our fortified posts had been easily defeated, without inflicting any loss on our people; but coincident with the General's arrival at King William's Town, the Gaikas under Sandilli broke out in rebellion, and moved westward towards the Buffalo Range, a lower feature of the Amatola Mountains.

Sandilli, born in 1822, had fought against us in the wars of 1846, 1848, and in 1850–53, and commanded a devotion from his followers which he did not deserve. He had, so far as I know, no redeeming trait in his character. When he was twenty years of age, he assented to his mother[1] being put to death by torture, by the advice of witch doctors, a profession which might easily, and should have been suppressed in 1857, when one of these pests persuaded the Kafirs on the Kei River to destroy everything edible, with the result that 67,000 died of starvation. Sandilli was born with a withered foot, so could not lead his men in action, who nevertheless, such is the tribal spirit, would accept death to save him. In all the previous wars from 1835, in the time of General Sir Harry Smith, to that of General the Honourable Sir George Cathcart, 1851–52, Sandilli had always managed to evade capture.

One of his sons, Edmund, had been in a Government

[1] She was rescued by a missionary.

office, and his apparent object in joining his father's rash attempt to regain Kafirland for the Natives was the fear of his younger brother, Guonyama, a real Savage, being elected to the Headship of the Gaikas. All through 1877 the witch doctors were urging the important chiefs to rise; Sandilli hesitated until the Galekas under Kreli had been defeated, and then it was an accidental beer-drinking quarrel between Galekas and Fingoes which precipitated the outbreak.

The Fingoes, a remnant of eight tribes originally in the south-east of Africa, flying from the Zulus, became slaves to the Galekas, and their first cousins the Gaikas, to whom they acted as hewers of wood and drawers of water, the Kafirs despising every sort of work, except that of herding cattle, their fields being cultivated by the women. In 1835 the Fingoes were taken under British protection. They accepted missionaries, and many were in 1877 more prosperous than their former masters, having more wives and more cattle, and thus an antagonistic feeling arose between the Gaikas and their former slaves.

When General Thesiger and his Staff reached King William's Town on the 4th March, the farmers alarmed by Sandilli's rebellion had crowded into the towns, abandoning their farms even within one mile of the Settlement. There were near Fort Beaufort, 45 miles to the west of King William's Town, two or three hundred Gaikas under Tini Macomo, who however were not anxious to fight; but on the 9th March news was brought in of Sandilli's being near Grey Town, and of his men having murdered three Europeans at Stutterheim, on the eastern edge of the Buffalo Range. The position was curious; for while Sandilli's men were attacking a village, they sent their women to sit down near it, so as to be out of danger.

When the news was received, I was dining at the Mess of the 24th Regiment, and had asked to sit next to a man whose name was already well known in the Colony, Captain Brabant, a Member of the Legislative Council. He had served as Adjutant of the Cape Mounted Rifles, and when the Corps was disbanded took to farming near King William's Town, and had been successful. He was a man of middle age, somewhat impetuous, with great personal courage, an iron constitution, and for his age very active habits; these qualities, combined with some Military knowledge, marked him out as a Colonial leader of men. I found him socially as a soldier an agreeable comrade.

The General told me next day he intended me to proceed to Keiskamma Hoek, 25 miles to the north of King William's Town, where I was to endeavour to command harmoniously some Colonial farmers. There had been considerable friction between Colonists and Imperial officers in the Transkei Campaign. That afternoon Captain Brabant had a warning letter written by a friend in Keiskamma Hoek, stating that Mr. Lonsdale, the Magistrate, had been repulsed by Sandilli's men, and that an attack on the village was expected at daylight. Brabant urged me to start at once, and I agreed to go after dinner, which would in any case bring us in before daylight; but the General would not sanction it, as I was to take out two companies of the 24th Regiment next day, leaving one about half-way, at Bailie's Grave.[1]

The Buffalo Range and its adjoining hills, over and above which our operations were carried out for the next three months, is about 12 miles north of King William's Town, which Settlement lies in a hollow of a plateau bounded on either side by parallel ranges of mountains. The track from King William's Town to Keiskamma Hoek runs generally for 12 miles in a north-westerly direction, passing over an undulating country nearly bare of trees, when the traveller sees in front of and above him a wall-like mountain, covered for miles with lofty trees and dense underwood. The southern side is precipitous, and, under the term "Perie Bush," extends for 6 miles from the Buffalo River on the east to the King William's Town–Bailie's Grave–Keiskamma Hoek road, on the west. Bailie's Grave post is a small square earthwork, 12 inches high, a relic of the war of 1851, on a neck,

---

[1] The name given to a little post from the fact that in 1836 a Colonist of that name with 24 Hottentots had been surprised there by Gaikas, and after a brave resistance killed without one man escaping. It was not known for many months what had become of the party, in spite of a protracted search ordered by Sir Harry Smith. Eventually a belt worn by Macomo was recognised as having belonged to the deceased Hottentot leader, and later his Bible was repurchased from the Gaikas, with a pathetic note on the fly-leaf that the detachment was surrounded, their ammunition nearly exhausted, and they must soon be killed.

which runs generally from east to west, and connects this wall-like side of the Buffalo Range with a mountain 2 miles south-west of Bailie's Grave, called the Intaba Indoda, to the west of which there is also a precipitous fall to the southward, bounded by the Debe Flats. The track north of Bailie's Grave post, bending northwards, passes under, in succession, Goza Heights and the Gwili-Gwili Mountains, which tower 2000 feet above Keiskamma Hoek, the original "great place" of Sandilli's father, well known in the war of 1851–52. The scenery in the valley is beautiful beyond description. The Basin, in which Germans had formed the most fertile farms I saw in the Colony, is surrounded by fantastic hills. It possessed seven churches,—each, it is true, only the size of an Aldershot hut,—six being Lutheran, and one Church of England.[1]

The main feature in the Range is the so-called Buffalo Poort, at the head of which the river rises in a ravine (locally called a kloof), which extends 5 miles in a southerly direction, being at its mouth $2\frac{1}{2}$ miles wide from east to west. At its head, where the spring rises, the slopes are comparatively gentle, the gorge being about 50 feet deep; but it falls away rapidly, and at the mouth of the valley a man standing on the rocks above may throw a stone which, according to where it alights, will travel 600 or 800 feet below him. All this valley is clothed with magnificent forest trees, and most of it with thick undergrowth, and is so rugged that within one pace there is often a drop of 20 or 30 feet; and in one of our skirmishes two Gaikas being pressed by us fell nearly 100 feet, and were killed.

To the eastward of the Poort, or valley, there is another hollow, the stream of which joins the Buffalo River under a bold granite precipice, called Sandilli's Krantz, and again farther east a valley called the Cwengwe forms the boundary of the tangled mass of forest-clad rocks in which the Gaikas hid for three months. Sandilli's Krantz covers 30 acres of rocks, formed by

---

[1] When the German legion, enlisted towards the conclusion of the Crimean War, was about to be disbanded, all who cared to go to South Africa were sent out, to the great advantage of the Colony. They were industrious, hard-working, and successful gardeners, giving their old country names to prosperous villages, such as Wiesbaden, Hanover.

a portion of the cliff having broken away, and unless one has lived in the cave it is nearly impossible to find an individual in it, and throughout the war of 1851–52 it was undiscovered by Europeans.

The whole Buffalo Range extends 12 miles from north to south, and 8 miles from east to west, the highest points being on the northern and eastern sides. These are in themselves considerably above the edge of the valley called the Buffalo Poort, and from the western side of the Poort the ground slopes gradually, covered with bush, but interspersed with open glades. In these glades the Gaikas fed their cattle and basked, for the warm sun is as necessary to the red Kafir as is his food.

When my party, one company of the 24th, Lieutenant Rawlings, and 10 mounted men of the 90th Light Infantry, reached Keiskamma Hoek, we found the Magistrate, Mr. Rupert Lonsdale, preparing for another reconnaissance. He was reticent as to the previous day's proceedings, in which he had lost two men, but I learned later that he had led in the advance, and had covered the retreat. He had reconnoitred up on the mountain, and was passing under one of its highest points, Mount Kempt, with 60 White residents of Keiskamma Hoek, and about the same number of Fingoes, when they were fired on by Kafirs in ambush, and had to retire.

For the next three months Lonsdale dined with me at least twice every week, and had many other meals with me, and thus I got to know him very well. He had served in the 74th Regiment, until a marriage on insufficient means forced him out of the Army, and he chanced to go to the Cape to nurse a sick brother. He told me many amusing stories of his short Army life; one instance, which occurred at Colchester Camp, I repeat.

Lonsdale was fond of playing cards, and one summer morning, when his party broke up about 3 a.m., he saw, to his astonishment, an officer of his acquaintance walking up and down between the huts, carrying a lighted candle, and humming Handel's " Dead March." Startled, Lonsdale said, " What are you doing here in your nightshirt?" " Don't you know," the man replied, " I am dead, and they're burying me? Just listen to the band;" and he again started his mournful dirge. Lonsdale,[1] seeing his state, humoured him for a few minutes, and taking his arm, they walked up and down to this dismal music. Finally, when passing the door of the man's hut, which stood open, my friend said, "Here we are at the cemetery," and leading him into the hut, put him into bed. Then, blowing out the candle, he said, "There you are, 'dust to dust, ashes to ashes,'" and covering him over with the bed-clothes, added, "We will fire the three volleys in the morning." Next day the man was ill, and did not remain long in the Service.

Lonsdale was about thirty years of age, of slight but strong build, and he strode along at the head of his Fingoes, setting a pace which even they, who when paid will run 6 or 7 miles for hours in succession, found severe. The Fingoes themselves were nearly always led by certain men of character, not necessarily Heads of Locations who controlled them in camp, but other men, who became self-constituted leaders in action. These were Gaikas married into Fingoe families, and though this fact was not in itself sufficient to render such men loyal, yet if, as in some cases, their fathers were not "Out" in the 1851–52 war, they had come to consider themselves Government men. Four were to my knowledge shot leading their Fingoe fellow-villagers against the Gaikas.

About six months previously, Lonsdale had raised 250 Fingoes, and sent them to the Transkei to serve under Mr. Frank Streatfield, a Kentish gentleman, who at the time of Kreli's rebellion had broken up an ostrich farm in Albany, preparatory to his return to England. Offered the command of Native levies, he cheerfully accepted the duty, and did excellent work, living with me generally when we were on the Buffalo Mountain. He was unknown to his men prior to the last six months, and so had not the great advantage of Lonsdale, who had known for two years all the 900 Fingoes he raised in his District. The Magistrate is in the mind of the Fingoe, or of the Kafir, of far more importance than the Governor, or any General, inasmuch as the Magistrate not only

---

[1] I wrote to the Military Secretary of Rupert Lonsdale, in the following December: "Brave as a lion, agile as a deer, and inflexible as iron, he is the best leader of Natives I have seen."

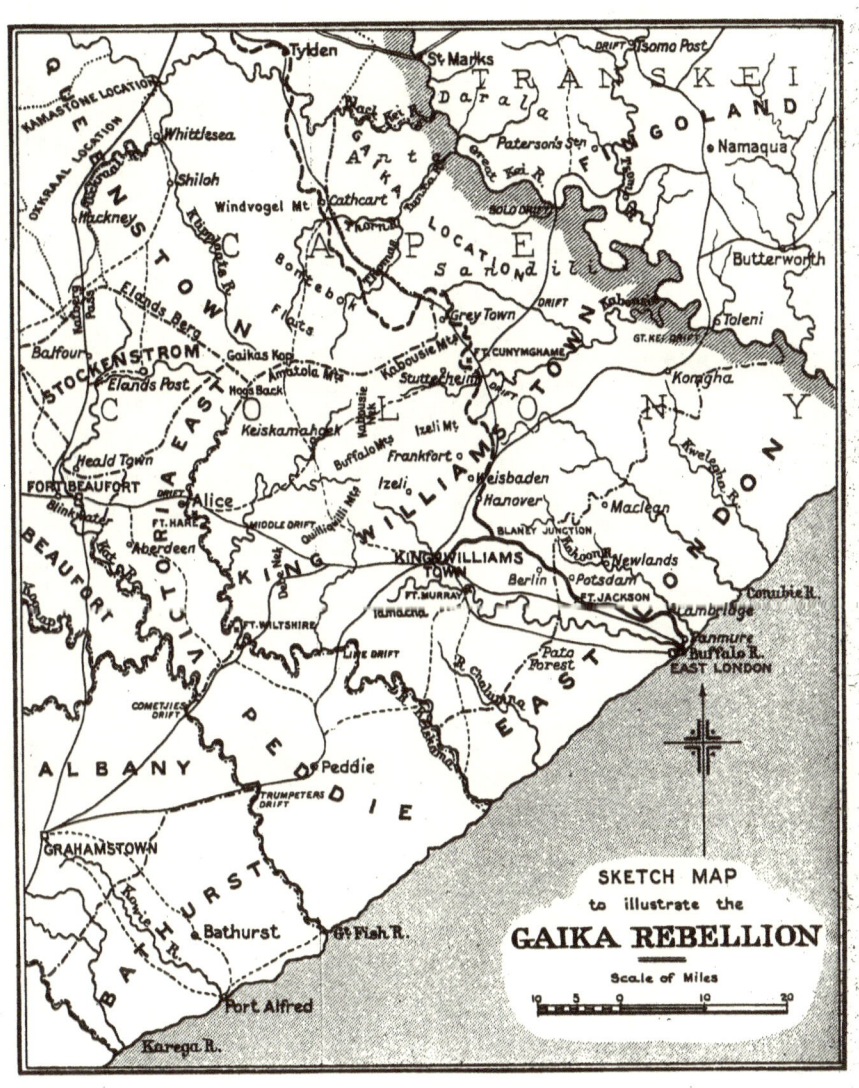

rewards, but he punishes. Thus Lonsdale had the unstinted devotion of his men, actuated not only by respect, but by self-interest. They were absurdly overpaid, receiving 2s. per diem and free rations, being able to live on 2d. a day, and at a time when the British soldier got 1s.

CHAPTER XXV

1878—THE GAIKAS AND PERIE BUSH

British and Dutch Volunteers—Brabant—Bowker, a Colonial Staff Officer —Gaika woman sells her child for a shin bone of beef—Volunteers return home—The Tutu Bush—Saltmarshe killed—Stevens wounded —A brave Colour-Sergeant — Redvers Buller slides down a cliff — Death of Sandilli.

THE General's intention was to drive the Gaikas from the Gwili-Gwili Mountain, the north-west end of the range, where most of them were, towards the south of the Buffalo Poort, where a line of our people awaited them. The Keiskamma Hoek column, composed of 300 Whites (85 being soldiers) and 300 Fingoes, was to climb the rugged western face of the mountain, begin and direct the attack, while Commandant Frost with 500 mounted men was to ascend from the direction of St. Matthew's, north-east of the Hoek, and join hands with me. Streatfield with 250 Fingoes was to ascend the Rabula Height, and Captain Brabant with about 200 Whites was to go up from Bailie's Grave and follow in support of the right of Wood's column. Troops were placed east of the mountain to prevent the Gaikas going towards the Kei.

On the afternoon of the 16th, when riding towards Kabousie Nek to concert measures with Commandant Frost, I met him riding with Major Buller to call on me. He lived near Queenstown, whence he had brought 500 Burghers, many Dutchmen. He was for a South African farmer wealthy, and in addition to great moral courage his personal cool bravery was remarkable even amongst daring spirits. I saw him watch unmoved his eldest boy, serving as a Burgher, fired on at close quarters by a Kafir. The lad escaped, though the stock of the carbine he was aiming was cut in twain by the Kafir's bullet. Frost later, from his place in the Legislative Assembly, criticised in strongly worded adverse terms the Burgher system of using untrained Levies without discipline.

Having arranged our concentration for daylight on the 18th, I rode southward to Bailie's Grave to impress on Captain Brabant the part he was to play in the drive, as to ensure success he must wait until we passed him. At sunset on the 17th, Mr. Bowker and his troop of Grahamstown farmers had not arrived. Mr. Barber with 50 Cradock men, many being Dutchmen, had been for some days at the Hoek. Their leader was over six feet high, strongly built, with a fine handsome face, and such frank manners as to render all duties with him a pleasure.

At 9 p.m. I paraded my little Force, Mr. Bowker having arrived. Above the Hoek our Fingoe scouts had counted over 1000 Gaikas on the Gwili-Gwili Mountain, and I had seen enough of the climb, 2000 feet above us, to have made me uneasy, but that our Fingoes were within 300 feet of the crest, which I hoped to reach at daylight, while the Gaikas were still chilled by cold. Although the entire distance was only 8 miles from the Hoek, the actual ascent was severe, and would in daylight, if opposed, have been costly in lives. Leaving at 10 p.m., we marched in single file through thick bush up a path so steep and rugged as to oblige us to dismount at 1 a.m. Messrs. Lonsdale, Barber, and I led, and without having halted we reached the crest only at daylight, climbing the last 300 yards through boulders of rock which a dozen determined men might have held for hours.

Fourteen days of very hard work combined with little sleep had brought a return of my neuralgic pains, which, although not severe, obliged me to take doses of chloral and bismuth, and foreseeing that I might be on the mountain for three days, I took the precaution of getting a large bottle from a doctor in King William's Town, who enjoined me on no account to finish it until the third day. When we started my pain was worse, and it increased as I climbed, with the result that when we reached the top of the mountain and I sat down on a stone to rest, I had finished the bottle, and was tormented with acute thirst. I asked each Burgher as he came up for a drink, but there was not one of them who had put any water in his bottle of "Cape Smoke," and so I had to endure the thirst until, the day having broken, we moved on, and came to a stream.

The Gaikas retired from the clear plateau of the Gwili-Gwili Mountain, and after breakfast Barber's and Bowker's Colonials and Streatfield's Fingoes descended into a deep ravine which intervenes between Gwili-Gwili and Rabula Heights, whence the Burghers emerged late in the afternoon, exhausted by their climb.

Captain Brabant had an easier ascent, up which, indeed, we took waggons two months later. When he gained the crest at daylight, he saw two miles below him, to the eastward, some Kafirs and cattle in an open glade, and advanced till he had dense bush on either hand.[1] The Kafirs opened fire, and Brabant fell back with some slight loss, Streatfield, who went to help Brabant out, having an officer killed. This impatient disregard of orders spoilt the General's plan. Late that evening a path across the intervening ravine was found, which Frost's men and the Hoek columns crossed next day. The night was cold; most of the men had a blanket, but as we were carrying three days' food, the officers had left their blankets below. I personally did not suffer, for Mr. Lonsdale emerged from the Bush at sundown, near Brabant's bivouac, too tired to attempt to return, so Captain Nixon, Royal Engineers, and I sheltered under the Magistrate's waterproof sheet.

When we were having our coffee before advancing next morning, Captain Nixon, who had given me much aid as a Staff officer, warned me that he had overheard the Burghers say that they intended to refuse to enter the Bush. I took no notice until the men were falling in at daylight, when the two Leaders came to me, saying that the men declined to go into the Bush, as it was not a fit place for Europeans, and they suggested that the driving of the main valley should be done by Fingoes. I replied, "I do not agree with you; we

[1] The Colonial papers attributed Brabant's reverse to Colonel Wood having for some reason failed to support him. Our Burghers only laughed at the local papers, but it was republished in the *Times*.

have got our orders, and you are to take your men through the Bush." "But the men will not go, they are all determined." "Well, gentlemen, I shall write to the General that you refuse to obey orders, and having sent off my letter I shall go in with this company of the 24th Regiment. We shall probably not do the work as well as you can, but if I become a casualty I do not envy your position." I said no more, and in a quarter of an hour the Burghers entered the Bush, from which they did not emerge till late in the afternoon, when some of them, hearing I was going through the ravine to the south end of the range, where Captain Brabant had been repulsed, formed a guard round me so that I could not be hit except through the bodies of my escort. Until they went home, we never had another difference, and they endeavoured to anticipate my wishes.[1]

Next morning Commandant Frost and his men followed the Hoek column across the ravine, and bivouaced in the glade whence Captain Brabant was driven on the 18th of March; Brabant moving a mile farther south on the mountain range. As we advanced the Kafirs disappeared in the Bush, followed by Mr. Lonsdale and his Fingoes. Neither Kafirs nor Zulus fight on two successive days, unless compelled to do so.

When Lonsdale's Fingoes went down the Buffalo Poort, 500 women and children came out of the Bush as the Fingoes advancing came near them. The poor creatures had nothing on except a blanket, and this we were obliged to remove to search for powder and lead, which many of them carried. When the operations ceased for the day, I was willing to let them return to their husbands, as I could not feed them; but they refused to go back, not knowing where they would find their men, and moreover fearing ill-treatment at the hands of

---

[1] The High Commissioner, writing on the 15th August 1879, after pointing out the important bearing which the position of the Flying Column in Zululand had on the safety of Natal and the Transvaal from January to July, said: "I would beg to call attention to the excellent Political effects of the dealings of these two officers with the Colonial forces, and with the Colonists in general. Up to 1878 there had always been amongst the Colonists something of a dread of the strict discipline which was, as they thought, likely to be enforced by a Military officer were they to serve under him, and a great distrust of Her Majesty's officers generally to conduct operations against the Kafirs. This feeling has now, I believe, disappeared amongst all who served under General Wood and Colonel Buller."

the Fingoes. The starving women sat on a hill which rose from the plateau on the mountain for twenty-six hours, and suffered severely from cold and want of food. I was called to them, as one wished to complain to me of a Dutchman who she said had taken away her child. The Dutchman, who was in Commandant Frost's Contingent, admitted he had the boy, but added that he had given its mother a shin bone of beef for the child; this the mother acknowledged, but she was unwilling to give back the beef even to obtain her boy. I compromised the matter to the satisfaction of both parties, by giving the man five shillings for his beef and restoring the child to its mother.

There was another woman with a baby apparently on the point of death, and I gave its mother a small bag of biscuits. When we carried out the same operation on the 8th May, about half the number of women came out of the Bush, and on seeing them I said to the interpreter, "Why, Paliso, here are some of the same women." " Oh no, master; these are Seyolo's, and the others were Sandilli's women." " I can see identically the same women," I replied, and accosting a young woman with fine eyes, I talked to her through the interpreter for a few minutes, and then asked her if she was up in the same place last moon. "Yes," she replied. "Is the woman here who had the sick baby?" "Yes, she is eight or ten farther down." "Well, I recognise you—do you recognise me?" She looked steadily at me, and replied, "No; all White men's faces are exactly alike." Which is the reproach we level at the Kafirs.

On the 20th a thick fog prevented our seeing more than 40 yards, so movements of troops became impossible, and many of the Gaikas passed out of the Perie Bush unseen by us on the mountain or by the troops who were guarding the roads 2000 feet below us. Frost and I went to Brabant's bivouac, and arranged a drive for the 21st March. The Hoek column was to line the path which led to Haynes' Mill; Frost was to remain on the crest near Brabant's bivouac, to prevent Kafirs breaking back towards Gwili-Gwili; while Brabant, who knew more of the Perie Bush than any other Colonial present, was to descend the other precipitous side and work eastwards towards the path lined by the Hoek column.

THE GAIKAS AND PERIE BUSH

Brabant had greatly underrated the difficulties of his task. He entered the Bush at 8 a.m., and almost immediately came on a precipice, down which his men swung themselves on monkey ropes.[1] He failed to move eastwards, and after a determined effort emerged at 5 p.m. on the plain almost due south of where he entered the Bush, consequently neither Frost's men nor the Hoek column saw a Kafir, and at sunset I sent the troops down the mountain, having there no food for men or horses.

The apparent result of our three days' operations, and four days' residence on the mountain, was not commensurate with the discomfort we underwent. We killed an unknown number of Gaikas, took several horses and some cattle, with 17 casualties, Whites and Blacks, but on the other hand the Gaikas had never before been harassed in the Buffalo Poort.

When the troops descended, I rode down the mountain and round by Bailie's Grave to General Thesiger's camp at Haynes' Mill. About 6 miles from the camp I came on a small Draft recently landed, consisting of a young officer and a dozen men, on their way to join the Headquarters of the battalion. Their waggon had broken down, and they were in a state of excitement, having just killed a Kafir. After a few minutes' conversation, I went on to the General's camp, but missed him, he having gone round by the eastern side of the mountain to see me. I dined with the General's Staff officer, and at half-past nine, with a bright full moon, started back on a well-worn waggon track. When we got about 80 yards from the waggon, four shots rang out sharply, striking the ground at my horse's feet. The two orderlies Frontier Light Horse unslung their rifles to fire back, but I stopped them, and on riding up found the small Draft, which apparently had not yet recovered from their excitement, had mistaken us for a party of Kafirs coming to attack them. The Musketry Instructor of the battalion was living with me as a guest, and had told us the day before we went up the mountain of the great improvement he had effected in the shooting of the men. He was consequently much chaffed when it became known that the Regimental Armourer and three first-class shots had missed four horsemen at 80 yards distance.

---

[1] The growers which hang from and interlace the forest trees.

I had been in the saddle several days from 4 a.m. till 7 p.m., and rode throughout the night of the 21st–22nd March, when my horse died of exhaustion. The work told on me, and I had to go to bed for three days, having a high temperature. I was at duty again, however, on the 27th, when we received orders for another drive. The General went up the Cwengwe Valley to Mount Kempt, leaving the direction of the operations in my hands, regarding which the Staff officer, Captain F. Grenfell,[1] wrote, "The Lieutenant-General gives Colonel Evelyn Wood the greatest latitude for these operations."

Commandant Frost having joined the General's column, which consisted of two companies of the 24th Regiment, with two guns, at Mount Kempt, was sent round from the northeast to ascend the Gwili-Gwili Mountain. Captain Brabant, placed under my orders, was to ascend the Rabula Heights. On this occasion the orders were executed, but the result of the operations was meagre, for the Gaikas evaded us; we now pitched our camp on the mountain plateau, and our presence annoying the Gaikas even more than the drives, as they could not emerge from the Bush to bask in the sun and graze their cattle.

The next week we saw but little of the Kafirs, for all the White men were employed in cutting broad paths in the Bush, while the Fingoes were carrying our tents and baggage up the mountain. When we had got enough food up, we tried another drive, but the result was unsatisfactory; the paths, however, annoyed the Gaikas, as they could not drive their cattle across the glades without being seen, and thus some fell into our hands immediately.

Nearly all the Burghers had now gone home: they disliked being on the mountain, where their horses suffered from cold. They had enlisted for three months, a month of which was to be allowed for the return journey, and although in deference to the General's wish they had stayed on for another drive, their patience had now become exhausted. Like all amateur soldiers, they varied greatly in quality. Many were landowners, well off, and serving for the love of their country; others were men attracted by the pay of 5s. per diem, which was more than they could earn in the towns and villages or

[1] Now Lieutenant-General Lord Grenfell, G.C.B.

on farms. To the reproach that they were leaving before the fighting was over, they replied, "We got leave from our employers for three months; if we stay on, will the Government guarantee us work, if our employers refuse it?" And to this reasonable question no answer was obtainable.

On the 5th April, 700 Fingoes having arrived from the Transkei District, the General arranged another drive, to start from Mount Kempt, where he took up his position, straight down the Buffalo Poort to Haynes' Mill. The Fingoes were, however, undisciplined, and fired away twenty rounds a man, without any adequate results. It is only fair to state that they had no such leader as had the Hoek Fingoes in Mr. Lonsdale, whose men were not given more than five rounds for a day's operations. We moved that morning at 4 a.m., and were in our assigned positions at six, and after eleven hours, in which 1500 Fingoes searched the Bush while the soldiers lined the paths, the result was indeed incommensurate: 3 Gaikas killed.

When I returned to the Hoek late at night, I heard that Captain Warren,[1] Royal Engineers, with a troop of the Diamond Field Horse, had been surrounded by 1500 Kafirs, and arranged to start at 3.30 next morning to his relief. Sleep was impossible, for Mr. Streatfield arrived at midnight, and Mr. Lonsdale at 2 a.m., and it was necessary to concert with these gentlemen the movements of the Fingoes westwards.

I heard at daylight, when at Bailie's Grave Post, the correct story of Captain Warren's skirmish the previous day; he had skilfully ambushed Seyolo,[2] whose men fled. On the 4th April, Seyolo induced the tribe to rise, and with 500 men was seen crossing the Debe Flats early on the 5th April, making for the Tutu Bush. Captain Warren concealed about 50 men in a hollow, from which they fired with effect. Seyolo charged bravely, but 20 of his men fell, and the tribe scattered in the Bush, leaving many of their wives behind.

I anticipated the General would come down from Mount Kempt, and so waited for a couple of hours, when he appeared, and approved of my suggestion that I should go westward, and

[1] Now Lieutenant-General Sir Charles Warren, K.C.B.
[2] The Gaika was the legitimate Head of his section of the tribe, but was deposed by General Sir George Cathcart in 1852, and imprisoned for a time, his younger brother, Siwani, being made Chief.

prevent the Kafirs breaking out north-west to the Amatola Basin. At Burns Hill I found a company of the 90th Light Infantry, and two miles farther off I heard of another. Ordering the men of both companies to eat, and parade as soon as possible in shirt sleeves, they marched off within an hour, going up the Makabalekile Ridge. I preceded them with 8 men, my personal Escort, and picked up near Burns Hill 80 Fingoes and 80 Hottentots. I carried them on with me, leaving orders for two Squadrons of the Frontier Light Horse, coming from Bailie's Grave, to follow me. The Bush on the Makabalekile Ridge extends for about 1500 yards, then there is an undulating plateau, named Tutu, extending a mile from east to west, and a mile and a half from north to south, the plateau being bounded on its east side by a deep ravine running practically north and south, called the Zanyorkwe. Just as my 8 men arrived, riding in extended order, a body of Kafirs ran out of the ravine, but were driven back by my escort, and the Fingoes coming up, I extended them at intervals along the edge of the Bush. When two hours later the Frontier Light Horse and a company of 90th Light Infantry arrived, I sent them down into the Bush, and was superintending these movements when I saw the Fingoes, whom I had left fairly steady, running rapidly. Cantering up to them, I soon perceived the reason: bullets were striking all around them, the line battalion on the high ground to the east of the Intaba Indoda Ravine having mistaken the Fingoes for Kafirs. As I led the former back to the edge of the Bush, hoping that the Regiment, which was only 1400 yards off, would recognise I was a European officer, the Artillery dropped a shell 40 yards from us; I noticed the Fingoes, like myself, had not the same fear of shells that they had of the bullets, and after three or four minutes the firing ceased, except for an occasional over-shot fired at Seyolo's men, who were in the Bush close underneath us. We learned next day that the Transkei Fingoes had disappointed the General, for they were driven back three times, and for several hours left the body of two of their White officers in the hands of Seyolo's men.

I lost four horses, which was provoking, but in a manner which made me admire the audacity of the Kafirs. After I had re-established my line of Fingoes, some 20 Gaikas ran out in the open, from a spot where the Fingoe line was weak. The position was awkward, because I had nobody with me except my personal escort of 8 men and the horse-holders of the Frontier Light Horse, the other men being all below in the Bush. When we fired, the horses broke away from the horse-holders and careered over the plateau, four of them running northwards in a narrow glade where the Bush closes in on either hand. The horses chased by my orderly ran close to the trees, from which Gaikas darting out pulled them into bush so dense that our men who were in the ravine, and later emerged close to the place, saw neither Kafirs nor horses.

At nightfall we marched back to Burns Hill, where I had to provide food and shelter for the hungry, coatless companies, 90th Light Infantry. They sheltered in the Mission Church, and as there were sheep close at hand, lumps of mutton were soon broiled on the fires. Next day Lonsdale's and Streatfield's Fingoes moving from the Rabula Valley through the Tutu Bush, killed 20 of Seyolo's men with but few casualties, while with the 90th companies and Frontier Light Horse I held the plateau. On the following day the Fingoes advancing from the Rabula, with two companies of the 90th and Frontier Light Horse, again went through the Tutu Bush and drove out some of Seyolo's men, who, after a skirmish with the General's small Force, then encamped at Bailie's Grave, succeeded in getting across to the Buffalo Range. Next day I heard that another small tribe had broken out and were making for the Tutu, and I followed them with a few mounted men, but only overtook their women, the men escaping into the Zanyorkwe Ravine.

Now for about three weeks the Rebels remained unmolested, and Seyolo appreciating the situation, coming down from the Intaba Indoda Bush, destroyed all the Fingoe huts within two miles, carrying off large supplies of food and cattle. On the 23rd April he attacked Streatfield's Fingoes, but was beaten back, although they were obliged to shift their camp, as it was too close into the Bush.

Captain Bowker,[1] whose men had all gone home, came to

[1] Bowker was one of eleven children not one of whom was under 6 feet, and three of his brothers were 6 feet 3 inches. Like many others of those serving with us, he had seen his cattle driven off, and had known his relations and friends murdered by

me as a Staff officer, and was very useful in many ways, as I was new to the country. He told me a great deal that was interesting, and was one of those who agreed with me as to our obligations in sparing Kafirs who no longer resisted. Many of the Colonists with whom I had talked had disagreed with me on this subject, alleging that as the Kafirs never spared us we should treat them in a similar manner. Several said to me on the Buffalo Mountains, "You don't understand; the women you want to feed would gladly inflict nameless tortures on you if you were their prisoner."

The Volunteers having gone home, the General was now left with only one battalion and two guns, for the Transkei Fingoes being untrustworthy had been disarmed. We could not satisfactorily clear the Intaba Indoda Range with Lonsdale's men, and so for three weeks the Gaikas were unmolested. The broken country in the valley of the Zanyorkwe River, about 6 miles from north to south, and 10 miles from east to west of the ravine, is clothed with thick bush, the densest part of which gives its name, Tutu, to all the adjoining woods. The neck of land connecting the Kafirs' stronghold with the Buffalo Range, 4 miles farther east, is generally speaking covered with bush, with an opening of a mile near Bailie's Grave; thus our difficulties were greatly increased by the vicinity of these two natural strongholds of the Gaikas.

The General had urged the Colonial Government to collect more Volunteers, and I was instructed to raise all the Fingoes I could in the District to the north-west of King William's Town, Tini Macomo, son of Sandilli, and Chief of the Fort Beaufort District Gaikas, being then in the Tutu Bush. General Thesiger took me to Fort Beaufort, and being satisfied there

Kafirs; but he had a high type of mind, as is indicated by the following story. In a petty skirmish in 1864 he was fired on by a Basuto, who missed him but killed his horse. Bowker fired on the Basuto as he ran, and broke his arm. The man fell, but when Bowker approached stood up stoically to meet the death he anticipated. Bowker bound up his arm and let him go, thinking no more of the matter. Many years after, when Bowker was travelling with his wife in a waggon in Basutoland, buying cattle, he halted at a kraal at sundown, and as usual the Basutos crowded round him. He noticed one man who stared at him closely and then disappeared, but came back within an hour, with all his family, bearing on his head a bundle of firewood, a sheep, and some milk and vegetables, saying, "I offer these gifts to the man who broke and mended my arm." The firewood could not have been worth less than half a crown, as the country is treeless, and the only fuel is the manure of cattle.

were no armed rebels in the District, ordered the 90th Light Infantry to Burns Hill, to work under my command, the Lieutenant-Colonel remaining at Fort Beaufort, in command of some Hottentots.

I was glad to see the Water Kloof, of which I had read a good deal. It appeared to our forefathers very difficult, but they never penetrated the Perie Bush, with which it cannot compare as a natural stronghold for the Black man. The Water Kloof ravines are not nearly so deep or rugged as are those in the Perie, and the Bush is broken up by intervening patches of cultivation.

At the end of April the General's preparations for driving the Tutu Bush were complete. He was to direct the operations on the eastern, and I on the western side; he kept under his own command the 2nd 24th Regiment, some Fingoes, 4 guns and White Volunteers under Von Linsingen, who had raised also 600 loyal Kafirs. Generally speaking, Bowker's Rovers were to hold the mouth of the Zanyorkwe Ravine, Lonsdale and Streatfield were to move from it, with the two companies of the 90th Light Infantry under Major Hackett up through the Bush, while Von Linsingen was to advance from Debe Flats, and join me on the Tutu Plateau, which I was to gain by passing up Makabalekile Ridge, with three companies of my Regiment, and about 100 men of the Diamond Field Light Horse, and a company of Hottentots.

On the evening of the 29th April, Seyolo, who was aware of our operations, undertook to hold the ridge himself against me, and boasted that he would capture the guns if they were taken up the Bush path. He commanded on the Tutu Plateau, while Tini Macomo was to hold the Tutu Bush itself.

At daylight on the 30th, the General having got into position on the eastern crest of the Zanyorkwe Ravine, shelled the rebel bivouac. Tini Macomo at once dispersed into the Tutu Ravine, while all Seyolo's men hastened westwards to support their piquets, who were already ambushed on the Makabalekile Ridge. It was covered with bush from 150 to 200 yards wide, from north to south, and extended for 1500 yards, through which the attacking Force had to pass before it reached the open plateau.

The General had written to me on the 29th, saying he

expected to see me on the plateau half an hour after daylight, to which I replied, "I will start in good time, but I shall not be there so early if Seyolo knows what to do."

One of the best companies in the battalion was commanded by Captain Stevens, who was fortunate in having an excellent Colour-Sergeant. It was the last company to come in from Fort Beaufort, and I invited Stevens and his Subaltern, Lieutenant Saltmarshe, to mess with me. I gave them a good dinner at seven o'clock on the 29th, and awoke them soon after midnight, when they, being young, consumed a 2 lb. tin of Cambridge sausages and a couple of chops. Saltmarshe seeing that I took nothing but a cup of cocoa, said to me chaffingly, "You don't eat, sir; are you nervous?" I said, "Yes; but even at your age I could not breakfast heartily at 1.15 a.m., having dined at 7 p.m. the previous evening." At dinner-time, Stevens, who had been intimate with me at Aldershot, had asked whether he might lead the Attack, and I replied that such was my intention. I was somewhat later in getting into position than I had intended, for after extending a company on either side of the timber-waggon track, which was about 6 feet in breadth, I was obliged to post personally a company and two guns which I intended to fire along the southern crest of the Tutu Plateau, on which I knew that any Kafirs reinforcing those already on the Makabalekile Ridge would pass. The Officer commanding the company was short-sighted, and so unfortunately was the Lieutenant in command of the two guns, and although later several bodies of Kafirs passed within short range not a round was fired at them. When I cantered up, after placing the guns, Stevens said, "You promised we should lead, and you have left us behind." "Yes," I said, "but now come on." Riding in front of the company, I led it on the track into the Bush. We had scarcely got 100 yards when a fine stalwart Kafir advanced as if to shake hands; he had apparently heard the guns moving on the flank, and did not see us until I told one of the men to shoot him. Fire was now opened on either side of the path, on which the company was advancing in file, and I told Stevens, who was in front, to press on. As he did so, Mr. Saltmarshe ran after him, but catching him by the collar as he passed, for I was still mounted, I said, "Go back to the rear." "Why?" he asked, somewhat impatiently. "Because I order you;" then seeing from the lad's face he felt the rebuke, I added, "I do not want, my boy, all my eggs in one basket." Ten minutes later, when we had advanced 400 or 500 yards, or one-third of the distance to the plateau, the firing increased in intensity, especially on the northern side, although nearly all the bullets cut the trees, and at one time my pony's back was covered with leaves, which fell like snow in a winter scene at a theatre. The Gaikas approached closer and closer, till a Kafir, almost touching Stevens, fired, and knocked a big hole in his face. I was sitting in the centre of the company, and beckoning to Saltmarshe, as his Captain was carried away, said, " Now it is your turn." I noticed that, although his face was set, and he was still eager to fight, yet the fall of his friend had sobered him, for he asked in a quiet voice, " What am I to do, sir ? " " Go to the head of the company, fire two or three rounds, then advance 50 yards and drop again." He had made one advance only, when a Gaika fired so close to him that his chest was knocked away by the charge. The Rebels now made a rush, and the Hottentots, who were on the southern side of the path, whence there came but little fire, ran down the path, carrying with them half a dozen of my men, who had been near Saltmarshe. Colour-Sergeant Smith, a little man, so short that I often wondered who could have enlisted him, had a heart entirely out of proportion to the size of his body, using most opprobrious language to the men, led them forward again.

I sent back for Major Cherry, who was in command of the detachment, as the company was now without officers. At that moment Captain Stuart Smith, Royal Artillery, asked if he might bring up a gun, and on my saying I was afraid we should not get the horses clear of the muzzles, he observed cheerfully, " Oh, it does not matter if we shoot them ; " and in a couple of minutes he had two guns unlimbered, and firing case into the Bush close on the ground from whence most of the fatal shots had come. Major Cherry now led on the company, and in a few minutes the Gaikas drew off, and we got on to the plateau with but little further loss. I then reaped the advantage of my ride the previous day to Alice (Fort Hare), where I had bought several yards of calico, for with a strange want of forethought the signalling equipment had been left at Cape Town.

I was now able to report to General Thesiger across the ravine, for we were standing only 1600 yards apart, and the Gaikas had been driven below the plateau into the ravine. This fight ended disastrously for Seyolo's men; our columns converging at the common centre, met them as they tried each avenue of escape, and after nightfall, crossing the King William's Town–Keiskamma Hoek road, they took refuge in the Perie Bush.

When we were on the mountain plateau in March, we felt the want of guns, to prevent the Kafirs coming out to bask in the sun without taking the trouble to attack them, so I was anxious, now we had to follow Seyolo's men, to take the 7-pounders up, although I had been told it was utterly impossible to get anything on wheels up the face of the Rabula Mountain, which looks at a distance precipitous. Captain Stuart Smith, under the orders of Major Harness, Royal Artillery, accomplished the feat. He hooked in 48 oxen, and then, putting a pair of staunch wheelers in front, attached them to the horns of the leading pair of oxen. The horses, although often on their knees, kept the oxen in a straight line, and the whole team, urged by some twenty Africanders with long whips, eventually got both guns up to within 100 feet of the crest, whence they were hauled up by a company 90th Light Infantry. We began work after nightfall on the 7th, and by daylight on the 8th were on the mountain: with 4 companies 90th Light Infantry, 2 guns, the Frontier Light Horse, and 1500 Fingoes. Sandilli and Seyolo had been warned of our attack by the so-called loyal Kafirs, and the actual number of Gaikas killed was less than in other drives; but a determined attack led by Major Redvers Buller so demoralised the Rebels that they never again attempted to resist white men. Buller, with a Squadron Frontier Light Horse, following some straggling Kafirs on the wooded precipice overlooking Haynes' Mill, was fired on, and though he drove the enemy from the edge of the Bush, they held some rocks 50 feet down, and a few men sat in high trees, which enabled them to fire on the plateau.

Just as I arrived from another part of the elevated plateau, which consisted of a series of terraces, Captain McNaghten, Frontier Light Horse, fell mortally wounded. Major Buller reported that there were only 30 Kafirs immediately below him, the man who shot McNaghten being in a tree farther westward along the precipice. He explained that most of the enemy were behind a big rock, 40 feet down, a place so steep that you could not go down without holding on, or sliding, so it was difficult to turn them out as I wished, and he demurred to the inevitable loss of men in the operation. I suggested that it was only the first man down who was likely to be shot, and signalling to Captain Laye,[1] who was on a terrace 200 feet below me, he brought up his company. While he was climbing up, I told Commandant Lonsdale to take his men into the Bush and extend them higher up the valley, and Commandant Maclean to do the same farther westwards, with orders to work round the spot where the Kafirs were lying concealed. I explained the operation and its dangers to Captain Laye, telling him he was to sit and slide down the rock, ordering one of his most trustworthy men to keep close to him. Just as the company, which had extended while in "dead" ground, approached the edge of the precipice, Buller jumping up, shouted, "Frontier Light Horse, you will never let those redcoats beat you," and forming himself into a toboggan, he slid down, under fire, which fortunately passed over his head, and most of the Kafirs disappeared before he regained his footing.

Coincident with Buller's slide, some of Lonsdale's Fingoes arrived at the rocks, and getting below the Gaikas, they were caught as in a trap, but selling their lives dearly, killed two of our men. The Fingoes lost a few men, and an old woman came to me with a large hole in her face, a bit of the jaw-bone having been shot away. She was unconcerned, however, and when I proposed to hand her over for Medical aid, declared she would much sooner have a plug of tobacco to chew. A young Fingoe had an altercation with our doctor, a Colonial, and I was appealed to to settle the dispute. Two of the Fingoe's fingers had been shot off by slugs from a Gaika's gun, and the hand was in such a mash that the doctor wished to amputate the fingers at the second joint. My coloured soldier objected strenuously, and said that if he might have six weeks' leave he would come back again. And so he did.

[1] Now Major-General Laye, C.B.

His cure, which was that ordinarily adopted by the Natives in such cases, was peculiar. Returning to his village, he was pegged down on the ground, the maimed hand being buried in the earth, without any bandage or dressing upon it, and the man was not allowed up until it had healed over. It was, however, an unpleasant sight, for all the ragged bits of skin remained, and the man would have had a more useful hand if he had submitted to the doctor's operation.

From this time till the end of May, the object of the Gaikas was to evade our men. Forty or fifty Fingoes worked through Bush which required 500 men on the 18th March, and daily the small parties killed a score of Rebels.

In the third week of May, Major Buller nearly caught Sandilli in his cave, where he lived unmolested throughout the war of 1851–52; there was, however, a back exit, to us then unknown, by which the old man escaped. Major Buller, with two companies 24th Regiment, the Frontier Light Horse, and Lonsdale's Fingoes, remained near the cave for forty hours, which prolonged visit caused Sandilli to move northwards.

From the 12th March, when I left King William's Town, I scarcely ever slept for two nights in succession on the same spot. Constant work, shortness of sleep, and the great alternations of temperature, often over 40° between midnight and noon, and the want of nourishing food, told on me. I was unwell on the 10th May, but the General being 80 miles away, visiting the Transkei, the 3000 White and Black soldiers on and around the Buffalo Range were under my command, so I stayed on the mountains until a high temperature and pulse 104° obliged me to go down. For a fortnight the glands in my groin, armpits, and neck had swollen; my skin peeled off like a mummy, and chilblain-like openings appeared on my hands. I gave four Hottentots, who are more intelligent than Kafirs, £2 to carry me down to the Rabula Valley, where Dr. Alcock, my Aldershot Doctor, thus diagnosed my case: "Overwork, want of sleep and of nutritious food." Milk and eggs every four hours, with "All night in," soon restored me, and on the 27th I accomplished a long ride, involving many hours in the saddle.

The Gaika Rebellion was now over: Tini Macomo in the

THE GAIKAS AND PERIE BUSH

Water Kloof, Seyolo in the Fish River Bush, and Sandilli in the Perie, were hiding in caves. On the 29th May a patrol of Lonsdale's men skirmished with a few Kafirs near Mount Kempt, and were startled at the resistance, until they recognised amongst the slain Dukwana, an elder of the Emgwali Mission, who had shot several of our officers, and was now killed in protecting the flight of Sandilli. He fell mortally wounded, and with his death the rebellion ended. He had fought in 1835, '46, '48, '51–'52, and had always previously escaped. A fortnight after his death ladies were riding about unescorted where no small armed party could have ventured since March, and in three months what we may hope was the last Gaika revolt had been suppressed.

The number of Regular troops employed by General Thesiger in suppressing this outbreak was far less than those engaged in 1851–52, but we never had the same number of Gaikas under arms against us, and the area was smaller; moreover, tactics had undergone a change. When the 90th Light Infantry came under my command, the battalion had received an order, emanating from Headquarters, Cape Town, that it was never to be employed in the Bush. In 1851–52, Colonel Eyre, with the 73rd Regiment, broke this established rule, to the immense disgust of Kreli, who in the quaint words of the interpreter excused a defeat by saying, " No two men stop one Bush; one man come, other man go." To enter the Bush boldly in the face of Kafirs is not only the most efficacious, but the safest method. I can only recall one out of the many White leaders shot in 1878 who was killed in the dense Bush. In nearly every case our loss occurred just outside the Bush, or in paths from unseen foes.

By the middle of June the Regular Troops were concentrated, and the Volunteers recently collected were sent home. I was ordered to prepare the 90th Light Infantry for a march to Maritzburg, in Natal. I was offered at this time the command of the Colonial Forces, to be organised into three battalions, with a salary of £1200 and £300 travelling expenses; I considered the offer until I learnt the Colonial Government did not intend to let the Commandant nominate the battalion Commanders. I had been tempted by the pay, but on the other hand wished to command the 90th Light

Infantry, and not being allowed to suggest my own choice of subordinates settled the question.

General Thesiger was generous in his praise. In his Despatch, dated King William's Town, 26th June 1878, he wrote:—

"From the 9th to the 29th May the troops under Colonel Evelyn Wood gave the Rebels no rest.

"Para. 62. Colonel Evelyn Wood, V.C., C.B., 90th Light Infantry, on Special Service in South Africa, has had command of a separate column of Imperial and Colonial troops, from the time that I assumed the direction of Military operations in the Field. I cannot speak too highly of the good service rendered by this Officer. He has exercised his command with marked ability and great tact. I am of opinion that his indefatigable exertions and personal influence have been mainly instrumental in bringing the war to a speedy close.

"I would beg to draw attention to those officers who are especially brought to notice by Colonel E. Wood.

"(Signed) F. THESIGER."

He wrote to me on the 21st June, "I have written to His Royal Highness I could never have succeeded if it had not been for your active and energetic aid."

END OF VOL. I.

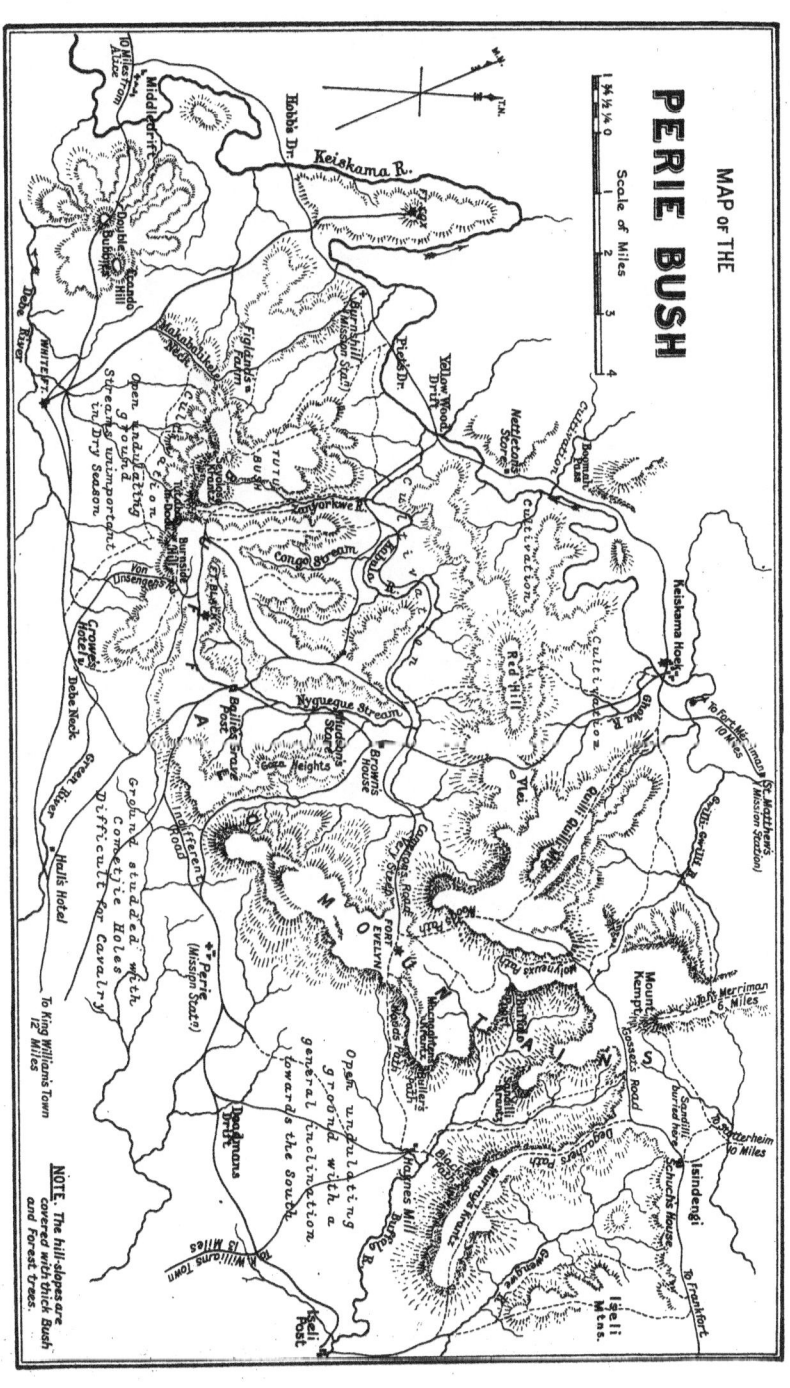

FROM MIDSHIPMAN TO
FIELD MARSHAL

FROM MIDSHIPMAN TO FIELD MARSHAL

BY

EVELYN WOOD, F.M,
V.C., G.C.B., G.C.M.G.

IN TWO VOLUMES

WITH TWENTY-FOUR ILLUSTRATIONS AND MAPS

VOLUME II

METHUEN & CO.
36 ESSEX STREET W.C.
LONDON

First Published in 1906

Printed and bound in Great Britain by
ANTONY ROWE LTD
Eastbourne

CONTENTS

CHAP.		PAGE
XXVI.	1878—FROM KING WILLIAM'S TOWN TO UTRECHT	1
XXVII.	1878—PREPARATIONS FOR WAR	14
XXVIII.	CHRISTMAS 1878—THE INVASION OF ZULULAND	24
XXIX.	1879—IN ZULULAND	37
XXX.	1879—THE INHLOBANE, 28TH MARCH	48
XXXI.	1879—KAMBULA, 29TH MARCH	57
XXXII.	1879—THE PRINCE IMPERIAL	70
XXXIII.	1879—ULUNDI	79
XXXIV.	1879—COMPLIMENTARY HONOURS	88
XXXV.	1880—H.I.M. THE EMPRESS EUGÉNIE	97
XXXVI.	1881—THE LAND OF MISUNDERSTANDINGS	105
XXXVII.	1881—AFTER MAJUBA	114
XXXVIII.	1881—A ROYAL COMMISSION	126
XXXIX.	1881—MARITZBURG	138
XL.	1882—CHATHAM AND ALEXANDRIA	146
XLI.	1883—SIRDAR	155
XLII.	1884-5—THE SUDAN	169
XLIII.	1885-6-7-8—COLCHESTER DISTRICT	182
XLIV.	1889—ALDERSHOT	193
XLV.	1889-90—REFORMS AT ALDERSHOT	205

CONTENTS

CHAP.		PAGE
XLVI.	1891-2-3—TRAINING OF TROOPS ON PRIVATE LANDS	217
XLVII.	1893-6—QUARTERMASTER-GENERAL	227
XLVIII.	1897-90—ADJUTANT-GENERAL	239
XLIX.	ADJUTANT-GENERAL—*continued*	251
L.	1901-2-3—SECOND ARMY CORPS DISTRICT	262

LIST OF ILLUSTRATIONS AND MAPS

	PAGE
EVELYN WOOD, F.M. . . . . . *Frontispiece*	
Painted for the Fishmongers' Company by W. OULESS, R.A., 1906	

BURIAL OF RONALD CAMPBELL AND LLEWELYN LLOYD UNDER FIRE 51

INHLOBANE MOUNTAIN 56

KAMBULA HILL 68

NATAL AND PART OF ZULULAND 144
This illustrates Campaigns in 1879, 1880, 1881

THE SUDAN 180

FROM MIDSHIPMAN TO FIELD MARSHAL

CHAPTER XXVI

1878—FROM KING WILLIAM'S TOWN TO UTRECHT

The unreadiness for war of a Regimental system—A Baca hairdresser, Pondoland—Its white Queen, Mrs. Jenkins—General Thesiger—Purchase of Regimental Transport—Faku—Cetewayo's Military kraal, Luneberg, its Military occupation—Manyoba.

ON the 26th June, my new Command, the Natal Column, consisting of 4 guns, 5 companies 90th Light Infantry (in which I was still a supernumerary Major), and a company Mounted Infantry, left Kei Road, Major Buller with 200 Frontier Light staying behind for a week to enlist men, was to overtake us. Up to Kokstadt we marched over treeless rolling plains, and in spite of the fact that we crossed 122 (unbridged) rivers, it frequently happened there was not sufficient water for the Column. I rode, therefore, every march three times. Leaving my excellent Staff officer, Captain F. Grenfell,[1] K.R.R. Corps, to encamp the Column, I went on to the next camping ground, as local information was unreliable. It was generally offered by Storekeepers, whose estimate of the quantity required was often based on the assumption that all Europeans would consume bottled beer. This, indeed, many of our men did, at 2s. a bottle. Our canteen President bought at Mount Frere £40 worth of stores from Mr. McGregor,[2] who had become a prosperous colonist. He interested me by extolling Colonel Eyre, though he was present

[1] Now General Lord Grenfell, G.C.B.   [2] Ex-private soldier, 73rd Regiment.

in the march from the Perie to the Döhne, when Eyre burned the blankets and food of the stragglers—*vide* p. 248, vol. i. Two other former 73rd men rode 40 miles to see "A friend of Master Arthur Eyre, their own Colonel's boy."[1]

The arrangements for equipping the battalion which now came more closely under my command left much to be desired, and I doubt whether the officers realised more clearly than those in authority at Home the necessity of good boots and flannel shirts in order to maintain soldiers efficient. I was obliged to buy flannel shirts for the Rank and File which cost the men 12s. each, as they had been allowed to go on service wearing cotton, and some with only one of that nature. This accounted for many having fever on the Amatolas, as the temperature varied from 75° at noon to 30° at night.

Nor was the administration more creditable to our Military rulers. In order to economise passage money, no non-commissioned officer or soldier with less than eighteen months to complete twenty-one years, was allowed to embark, while all the recruits were sent out. Thus the Sergeants and old soldiers left at Home had nothing to do, while the officers had insufficient non-commissioned officers to help in training the recruits. Incomplete and unsatisfactory, however, as were the Regimental arrangements, they were virtually all that existed in South Africa, the Departments being represented by very few officers; and thus no sooner was I ordered to march, than I received a requisition for 5 non-commissioned officers, and selected men to form a Hospital, and 5 to form a Commissariat department. In the result this left but 7 duty Sergeants with the 5 companies of rather more than 500 men.

The difficulties of crossing the numerous rivers in the journey of 500 miles exercised our patience. When the team of 16 or 18 oxen failed to pull the waggon and its load out of a river, another team of similar strength was hooked in, often with the result that one of the wheels was wrenched off by a boulder of rock which stopped the progress of the vehicle. This procedure was suitable, moreover, only when the "pull out" was fairly straight; if, as frequently happened, the gravel forming the ford was deposited on a curved line, every waggon had to be hauled out by one team assisted by manual labour,

[1] Killed in Ashanti. *Vide* p. 279, vol. i.

and to lift or extricate a waggon with its load equal to 6000 lbs. dead weight involved much labour. Even with comparatively easy fords the crossing of a river—for example, the Kei, between 80 and 90 yards wide, only 4 feet 6 inches deep —took five hours; the first waggon entering the water at 7.30, and the last pulling out at 3.30, the waggons taking on an average forty-five minutes to cross; and although I had arranged for a short march, we did not encamp till nearly 11 p.m. the day we crossed the river.

At Colossa, a village which Captain Grenfell and I visited in advance of the Column, I asked him to go into a kraal to ask where was the nearest drinking-water. He observed that there was not much chance of ascertaining, as he had no interpreter; but I replied that I thought he would find the mother of some children whom we saw playing could speak English, as I noticed they were playing like English children a "dolls' dinner party," with white berries to represent food, on little bits of tin representing plates, and none but the children of a Fingoe, or one who had been about white people, would be so advanced in their amusements. The result proved that my surmise was correct.

When we were travelling through Bacaland to the north of Pondoland, I was riding with an interpreter and 2 white soldiers two hours' march in advance of the Column, and near Tchungwassa, a valley under Mount Frere, came on a native who had the head of another between his knees, and was engaged in curling every separate bit of wool on the man's thickly covered skull. The Bacas and neighbouring tribes spend hours in order to produce results which seem to us funny. I have seen the wool on a man's head twisted up to represent the head of a castle in a set of chess men, and a bird's nest is a favourite device. Sitting down, I asked the hairdresser why he was taking such pains, and he explained because there was a wedding feast in the next village. "How much are you going to charge him for the job?" "Oh, nothing; he is a friend of mine." "Well, how much would you charge him for what you are doing if it was a matter of business?" "I always charge a shilling when I am doing it as I am now." "Do you know who I am?" "Yes, you are the General of the Army coming here to-day." "Well, what will you charge to dress my head?" I fully expected the man would say 5s., but looking at my scanty hair, with a merry twinkle in his eye he exclaimed, "Oh, I will do you for three pence!"

I had a visit from Macaula, Chief of the Bacas, when I entered his territory, a fine big savage, 6 feet 3 inches in height, and broad in proportion. He was the happy owner of 22 wives, and informed me that he had 59 children. I said laughingly, "Why not make it 60?" He observed, with great gravity, "I had forgotten one; I heard this morning as I was coming here that I had another, and so it is 60." He was very anxious to buy my weight-carrying hunter "War-Game," as, weighing 15 stone, it was difficult to find a pony to carry him, and asked if I would sell the horse. He was startled by my statement that he cost 24 oxen as a four-year-old, a trek ox there being reckoned at £10.

The object of our long march was to impress the Pondos with a sense of British power, and I had been warned on leaving King William's Town that I might have to coerce Umquikela, one of the Chiefs of Pondoland. He and his relative Umquiliso had given the Colonial authorities much trouble, for there was continual warfare between the tribes, with the result that those who got beaten invariably fled into the land set aside for tribes under our protection, and, moreover, Umquikela had recently misbehaved. The Governor, Sir Bartle Frere, informed General Thesiger that while he was confident I should not fight if it was possible to attain our end without bloodshed, yet it had been determined that Umquikela should be deposed from the position of Chief unless he behaved better. This black Potentate was under the influence of traders, to whose advantage it was that he should retain his independence. He received much good advice from a widow, Mrs. Jenkins, who lived at Umfundisweeni,[1] about 40 miles to the south of Kokstadt. Mr. Jenkins had lived amongst the Pondos for many years, and was deservedly held in high esteem by them, so much so that his widow stayed on, being known by the name of the "Pondo Queen." She was embittered against the High Commissioner, and the Colonial Government, and, like

[1] The place of teaching.

other advocates for the rights of the "Black man," was under the impression that the Government could do nothing right, and her favourites could do nothing wrong. Prolonged correspondence by telegraph, and indecision on the part of the Colonial Government, caused the Column to be halted for over a month at Kokstadt, an uninviting, treeless, barren waste, to the great vexation of all Ranks. To me it was less irksome, as I had the interest of the Political situation, the two Resident magistrates being ordered to work with me, and, moreover, I had a delightful companion not only in Captain Grenfell, whom I have mentioned, but in Lieutenant Arthur Bigge,[1] Royal Artillery. He came to me with a good reputation, and I saw a great deal of him in Camp, although on the lines of march but little, having chosen him to make a road sketch from King William's Town to Maritzburg, which he did very well. He and Grenfell accompanied me to Umfundisweeni, where I was sent by the High Commissioner to interview Umquikela.

I went down on the 17th of August with an escort of 20 Mounted Infantry, and Mrs. Jenkins, outside whose garden I pitched my tent, did her best to induce Umquikela to meet me. She was an interesting old lady, but had lived so long amongst the Pondos as to lose the sense of justice where they were concerned. She was very angry with Macaula, Chief of the Bacas, because he had just killed a number of Pondos, and she inveighed against his conceit in having 22 wives, as he was too small a chief to have that number. I asked whether that was her only objection? She said, Yes; she thought it was presumptuous of him. She told me in the course of conversation it was difficult to explain, how earnestly she prayed for the Pondos when they invaded Bacaland. I asked, was not that rather hard on the Bacas, because they had done nothing wrong? I got no reply to this, and politeness as a guest prevented my saying that her prayers did not seem to have influenced the result, for although at first the Pondos, owing to their great numerical superiority, carried all before them, yet for some unaccountable reason they became panic-stricken, fled, and were slaughtered in great numbers by the pursuing Bacas.

[1] Colonel Sir Arthur Bigge, K.C.B., K.C.S.I.

Umquikela at first agreed to meet me on the 17th, but I had assented to it being altered to 8 a.m. on the 18th, explaining that I could not wait longer, as I was due at the Ixopo, 50 miles to the north-east of Kokstadt, on the 19th. At nine o'clock on the 18th I received a message asking me to wait till 2 p.m., and shortly after that hour Mrs. Jenkins, who was playing the part of " Sister Anne " in *Blue Beard*, triumphantly pointed out to me a crowd of natives coming over the hill about three-quarters of a mile distant. There, however, Umquikela remained, and nothing would induce him to come nearer. Mrs. Jenkins, his adopted mother, sent him many messages, and at five o'clock in the evening told me she fully admitted I had given him every chance, and said she thought it was of no use for me to remain; so I started on my 40-mile ride back to Kokstadt, which I reached before daylight, and at three o'clock that day was on the Ixopo, where General Thesiger came to dine and sleep, in the little inn. With the kind thought which he always had for others, he, although a teetotaler, brought down a couple of bottles of Perrier Jouet champagne. We stayed up most of the night talking of the Pondos, about whom, and also the Magistrates in the neighbourhood, the General wished to report to the High Commissioner. Before we parted it was nearly morning, and to my great pleasure he told me the Column might move on by easy marches towards Maritzburg, leaving behind two Companies of the Buffs, which were in the neighbourhood.

I brought to the attention of the General the fact that the Imperial Government was paying 30s. per diem for every waggon throughout the month we remained at Kokstadt, and urged that sufficient waggons and oxen should be purchased to complete with Regimental transport any force which might be sent into Zululand. This the General undertook to consider, and when on the 31st of August I rode into Maritzburg a few hours in advance of the Column, he told me the principle was approved, and I was to report to him the cost.

I left Maritzburg on the 7th September, having spent a week in formulating a scheme for Regimental transport, and on my way up country with my Staff officer, Captain E. R. P. Woodgate,[1] received authority to purchase sufficient to equip the

---

[1] General Woodgate was mortally wounded at Spion Kop, Natal, January 1900.

FROM KING WILLIAM'S TOWN TO UTRECHT

90th Light Infantry, at a cost of £60,000. On reaching Utrecht on the 17th, I inspected the Left Wing of the battalion, and found that the men were as badly provided with kit as were their comrades with whom I had been serving in the Amatola Mountains. Insufficient Regimental Necessaries had been brought out with the battalion—as previously stated. I had hoped that the Left Wing, which had been stationary, would be better equipped, but the Regimental reserve store of Necessaries landed with the companies consisted of four flannel shirts, and four mess tins, and no steps had been taken prior to my arrival to complete the men with equipment. The District Commandant, writing from Pieter-Maritzburg, at first resented my strong representations on the subject, but it was time that somebody spoke out, because 5 soldiers had just been sent up from the Base, not only unarmed, but unclothed. I was supported, however, by General Thesiger, and from that date until the end of the Zulu Campaign, my suggestion that no soldier should leave the Base without being properly equipped was carried out.

When I returned to Natal in 1881, I found the battalions had slipped back to the old state of unreadiness, for when I inspected two at Lang's Neck I found many of the men had only one, partly worn, pair of boots. There can be no doubt that the Regimental system of that time, which practically left all Supplies in the hands of the Quartermaster, and induced the Company officers to regard him as a Store holder who might be expected to produce anywhere, and at the shortest notice, anything required, was faulty.

The War Office arrangements left much to be desired. When the battalion was ordered out in consequence of the Gaikas having revolted, it might have been reasonably expected that the men would have to encamp, and possibly to fight. They were generally very young, for all recruits were embarked, and although there was an excellent system amongst the non-commissioned officers, yet many of the older ones were not allowed to go out. Thus the battalion was deprived of some of its most experienced old soldiers in order to save their passage money, which at the time might be taken as £12. Such maladministration was comparatively of little importance when fighting Gaikas, but it would have been serious if the battalion had to meet the Zulu Army in the field soon after it disembarked. This our young soldiers did successfully twelve months later, but it was after marching 1000 miles, and living in what was, after we left the Perie Bush, a healthy climate, for, with proper sanitary arrangements and the absence of public-houses, the young soldiers improved out of recognition.

When I had looked round the little village of Utrecht, which possessed a Laager, or square walled enclosure, 10 feet high,—without loop-holes or platform from which men could fire over its walls; a magazine standing on an ironstone soil, with no lightning conductor,—and had taken the necessary and obvious steps to improve the situation, I rode on the 19th to Luneberg, a German Lutheran Mission Station 36 miles to the north-east. The pastor, the Reverend Mr. Filter, spoke English, but neither his family nor his flock spoke aught but German, so I had considerable colloquial practice for the next four days, during which I bought oxen, waggons, and Indian corn, at a cost of £2500. The average price of new waggons, with all their equipment, and a team of 18 oxen, varied from £260 to £300. I liked the straightforward ways of the German settlers, for, three days after I gave one of them a cheque for £270, he returned it to me, saying one of his cows had "lung sickness" and he feared that his oxen might be contaminated already, so he did not venture to send my purchase to Utrecht.

After some conversation with Mr. Filter and his family, I went to see Faku, the Chief sent by Cetewayo to frighten the Dutch settlers away from the border, which he had done effectually. I was curious to see the so-called military Kraal about which I had read while still in England. It was made of wattles, 6 feet in height, and 22 yards in diameter. He asked me, "Are you going to invade our country?" "No, not without orders; and so far as I know such orders are not contemplated." He was impressed by my being unarmed, carrying only a riding-whip, while he sat surrounded by twenty of his warriors. The result of my visit was that he sent to Cetewayo, saying he was satisfied that no immediate invasion of the country would be made from the Luneberg-Utrecht side, and the Maqulusi tribe, which had been assembled in the Inhlobane Mountains, was sent home.

1878] FROM KING WILLIAM'S TOWN TO UTRECHT

Next day I started with my interpreter, Paliso, who had accompanied me from the Amatola district, Kaffraria, to ride southwards, and then along the Yagpad (hunting road). I intended to stop the night at Potter's store, 35 miles distant, on the Pemvane River, which, as I was told at Luneberg, the owner, from his friendship with the Maqulusi, had been able to keep open, although the district had been abandoned by the Dutchmen. When I reached it, however, I found it was practically empty, and its owner had left.

The Zulus were in a state of excitement: four regiments had recently gone to Ulundi on the King's summons, and four more were then moving down. The men to whom we spoke were so truculent in their behaviour, asking when the Germans were going to obey Cetewayo's orders and leave Luneberg, and showing, moreover, so strong a desire to take my kit, that I decided to go on another 35 miles until I got out of the disputed territory. In my 70-mile ride that day the result of Cetewayo's message was apparent, for there was only one farmhouse with a roof on it, and most of the gardens and fields were being cultivated by Zulus. The mules pulling the Cape cart with my luggage were quite fresh at nightfall when I crossed the Blood River, but my three horses all showed signs of fatigue, and after I halted, the horse I bought at Cape Town, which had gone gaily up to that time, died after ten minutes' pain.

I spent the next ten days purchasing and organising transport, in obtaining which and some mealies I expended £10,000, which rose to over £50,000 by the 1st June 1879. I was obliged to employ my one Staff officer in examining roads, and thus I had to do more than I was really able to carry out to my satisfaction.

On the 1st October, General Thesiger wrote to me that the High Commissioner wished to encourage the Luneberg settlers to remain on their farms, in spite of Cetewayo's notice to quit, and asking me if I could raise a Volunteer force. I replied that this was impossible; and on the 16th, the General being away, his chief Staff officer, reiterating Sir Bartle Frere's wishes, directed me to be prepared to take the Utrecht garrison to Luneberg, and suggested that I should tell the Germans I was coming. Next day the High Commissioner writing to me in the same strain, as had the General on the 1st October, explained his anxiety to prevent the Germans moving, and his hope that I would do all I could to help them, adding that, of course, he did not intend me to take any Military steps without the General's approval. He ended his letter by expressing his gratitude for the work I had done in Pondoland, and for my successful dealings with the Chiefs there. To the chief Staff officer I wrote that the main risk of the movement would lie in its being known in advance, and that if the troops arrived at Luneberg before the Zulus got warning, in my opinion nothing would happen; and in this view I was supported by the Landdrost of Utrecht, Mr. Rudolph, who knew the Zulus well.

During the first week in October, Witch doctors went round the kraals on the border, "doctoring" with charms the males who did not belong to the regiments summoned to Ulundi; and on the 14th, Mr. Rudolph warned me that unless I supported the Luneberg settlers at once they would leave, as the friendly Zulus in the neighbourhood, apprehensive of being massacred, had slept out of their kraals for several nights. On the 15th I forwarded the Landdrost's official letter to the chief Staff officer, explaining that, owing to the importance of keeping the Germans at Luneberg, which was our line of communication with Derby, and because of the number of friendly Zulus around the settlement whose service I wished to engage, I had decided to take two Companies there to support the Germans. I was urged to do so by a Dutchman named Piet Uys, whose acquaintance I made at this time, and whose father had been killed by Zulus at Weenen in 1838.

I wrote privately to the General the same day, saying I had considered the responsibility I incurred in leaving Utrecht for a day or two with only one Company (until the Company I had called up from Newcastle could arrive), and had come to the conclusion that if he were present he would approve of my action. I continued, "I believe many people will consider two Companies too few for Luneberg. I think we ought to have more; but if the Zulus come there, I hope our men will not fight less well than their predecessors did at Lucknow. It is possible you may not approve at Maritzburg of my action, but believing you would do so if you could see and hear all I see and hear, I feel I should be unworthy of the

FROM KING WILLIAM'S TOWN TO UTRECHT

confidence you put in me if I hesitated to do what I thought was right." My General, with the generosity with which he always treated me, replied, "You have taken a serious responsibility upon yourself, and I doubt very much if you have acted wisely. However, you may depend upon my backing you up, as of course, in your position, you are bound to act in whatever way you consider necessary under what, I presume, are very pressing circumstances." The High Commissioner, regarding my action in the Political point of view, wrote, "I think Colonel Evelyn Wood deserves our gratitude and acknowledgments for taking the responsibility and saving us from the disgrace of leaving the Germans without protection." Later, the Governor of Natal, who did not generally agree with Sir Bartle Frere's views, wrote to the same effect, saying that my action had effectually stopped any further raid.

I wrote to the General on the 22nd October: "I am sorry I have not your full approval of the course I have adopted, though with your usual kindness you support me. I thought it over for twenty-four hours. On the one hand, I incurred certain Military risks incidental to all warfare, and especially when engaged with such small forces as are usually employed against savages; on the other hand, I risked the almost certain abandonment of the Pongola Valley, involving the loss of the assistance of the farm Kafirs and separation from the Swazies. . . . Though I fully appreciate your generous kindness in endorsing my action, I am anxious, if ill results come from what I think was my duty, it should be known I acted after receiving a copy of your letter to Sir Bartle Frere.[1] I suppose you hardly realise how anxious your unvaried support makes me to act in accordance with your wishes. A 'safe man' would not have run the risk, but I did what I believe you would have told me to do if you had been here."

When Parliament met in February 1879, the Secretary of State for the Colonies, in answering a question put by a Member of the Opposition, explained Luneberg was outside the district on which there had been an arbitration, adding, "Colonel Wood could not have taken any other course consistently with his duty."

[1] This letter refuses the assistance on account of Military risks.

I started two Companies on the 16th October for Luneberg, but the next morning they had only got 7 miles on their journey, being stopped by the difficulties of a mountain-track over the Elandsberg—and it became necessary for me to join them, in order to ensure their progress, as I was anxious to get the Companies intrenched at Luneberg before the Border Zulus knew of the movement. By dint of considerable exertion they reached the Mission Station on the afternoon of the 18th. I had ridden into Luneberg on the 17th, when I had to undertake a distasteful task. I had purchased from Mr. Filter an ox, for the men's rations; but on my asking him to be good enough to have it killed, he said that was impossible, and that I must kill it myself. I asked, "Surely some of your farm Zulus will kill it?" "Yes, certainly," he assented; "but they will kill it as slowly as possible, inflicting as much pain as they can before the animal dies, transfixing it with assegais in non-vital places." I then tried to make my Fingoe interpreter, Paliso, slaughter the ox, but he absolutely declined, saying that he had never done such a thing; so, finally, I had to go in the kraal, and shoot it.

When I had settled the Companies in their camp, I sent to tell Manyoba (whose kraal was 5 miles from Luneberg, and who, in the absence of Faku, was Cetewayo's representative) that I wished to see him, but received no answer; and after waiting two hours I rode out to his kraal, accompanied by Paliso.

In the kraal there were women only, and they informed me that the Chief was away on a hill. About 2 miles off I saw a crowd of men, and suspecting it was Manyoba and his kindred, I went on. On riding up I found about 100 men sitting down, most of them with guns, and the remainder with assegais. I asked for Manyoba, but was assured that he was away. I knew that he had been seized by the Boers some years before, and imprisoned for a considerable time on account of cattle thefts, and believed he feared the same sort of treatment. One or two men came out of the crowd, and said they wanted to know why I wished to see their Chief. I explained that I had brought soldiers to Luneberg, not to attack the Zulus, or, indeed, to cross the border, but because Faku and, indeed, Manyoba had threatened to kill the

Germans unless they left the settlement. The Zulus wished to argue as to our rights, but this I declined, saying that as the Chief was not there, they could give him my message, and I should go back. I was riding away, when there came a shout of "Stop!" and Manyoba, surrounded by a guard of a dozen men, came forward. Two of the younger men caught up their guns, which were on the ground, but the Chief told them to put them down, saying, "They are only two." I stayed twenty minutes, and I think reassured Manyoba; but he must have had a strange idea of our power, to be nervous of one White and one Black man, when he was surrounded by 100 of his tribe.

CHAPTER XXVII

1878—PREPARATIONS FOR WAR

Purchasing Transport—Canvassing Boer leaders—Maude's accident—He is carried 45 miles—Lysons crows like a cock—Pretorius, a Boer leader—Benighted on the Veldt.

THE General having desired me to go to Wesselstroom, and ascertain whether it was possible to get any Dutchmen to come out in that district, in the event of a Zulu War, I went up on the 8th November, and was told by the Landdrost that the feeling was so hostile to the Imperial Government that he doubted any Dutchman coming out. He said if I could persuade Swart Dirks Uys and Andries Pretorius to join us, they would bring over many others. Piet Uys told me that the feeling of his countrymen was so intensely bitter that he doubted whether any of them would come out, but he would do his best to help, not because he loved us, but because he realised the importance of the Border question.

I left Captain Maude with Mr. Swart Dirks Uys to buy ponies, while I returned to Wesselstroom to purchase waggons. Mr. Henderson, the Field Cornet, accompanied me. He was riding a mare whose foal, only twelve days old, cantered along in front of us. I should have preferred to have travelled faster than the baby colt was able to go, but as Mr. Henderson had remained sixteen hours in Wesselstroom to show me his farm, I could not easily shake him off, though I foresaw that he would cost me the loss of valuable time, which indeed was the case. He had a beautiful farm, utilising the sources of the Pongolo River, and he detained us till a herd of 100 horses could be driven past for me to admire. Eventually, after losing three hours of valuable daylight, we left, and mounting a steep hill to the south of his farm we had a glorious view, overlooking 40 miles towards Ulundi. There Mr. Henderson said "Good evening" to us, after pointing out the direction of his brother's house. We quickened our pace, for a storm threatened to break every minute. Coming to a very bad place on the side of a steep hill, I made Paliso and two 90th orderlies, Walkinshaw and Stringer, dismount and walk, holding back the mule cart, while I led the horses, and at 5.30 we reached a plateau where a streamlet crossed the track. Here I decided to halt, instead of making for Mr. Henderson's house, for rain was falling heavily, and lightning played vividly around us, attracted by the iron-stone which cropped out on the surface of the ground. We soon had a tent up, off-saddled, and unharnessed the mules, when we saw that the mule waggon was stuck on the spot where I had had the cart handled down. Maude walked up to see what was wrong, as a boy came in, saying, "Please, Sare, him waggon turn over." I sent up my servant Fox and two men, keeping one mule driver to catch the horses and mules, which we tied in a circle.

It was now quite dark, and rain was falling in torrents. I sent a Zulu for water, and put the men's rifles inside the tent. Taking one of T. White's[1] lanterns, I started soon after seven o'clock, with matches in my pocket, and one hand held carefully over a cracked pane of the lantern, but I found that not even a whole pane would keep the candle alight in the furious gusts that swept over me. I trudged on, but got off the track, and was even grateful to the lightning, which helped me to regain it. I found the men breathless from exertion. The waggon driver had lost his nerve, and fearing to drive against the scarped side of the hill, went over the edge of the road, and when Maude got up, the waggon was 30 feet down the slope, all four wheels in the air, and the mules entangled in a heap. When I reached the spot, they had got the limber on to the track, and the waggon body within 7 feet of it, having lifted it up by inches. I got down underneath, and in half an hour we raised it up, and then scotching the wheels, placed it on to the limber. The hill was so steep that the men could not carry up the loads, so they formed line, and passed up the articles. There were two sacks of "mealies" (Indian corn) which were too heavy for the men to carry, so I made Fox and Walkinshaw

---

[1] Messrs. T. White & Co., Outfitters, Aldershot.

take either end of the sacks, while I lay with my face against the side of the hill lower down, and with chest and elbows forced up the centre of the sacks, rolling them upwards. When we got the load (a very small one) up, I found that the driver and the mules were demoralised, and so decided to run the waggon down by hand. Two men went to the pole, but I said laughingly, "If anyone is to be killed over this job, it had better be an officer; you go behind," and as I tied the lantern, which belonged to my friend Woodgate, in front of the waggon, I added, "If the waggon fetches away, he will never see his lantern again." I took the pole, and at Maude's request let him help me. At the end of it there was a ring, through this we passed a reim,[1] and knotted it, each taking an end round our wrists. Although I did not anticipate the serious accident which ensued, I thought it would be safer if we "reimed" up the wheel, for which there was no drag chain, but our united strength failed to move the waggon, and so I was obliged to take off the reim, and with a strong pull we started it. For 30 or 40 yards we did well; then the waggon came faster, and presently, to my horror, I found we had lost control over it. It flashed across my mind that my jest might come true, as, though holding back all I could, I had to increase my pace. I realised in the darkness that Maude had stumbled by the increased weight on my arm. Running on my heels, I made a heavy tug at the pole, and hanging back drew the waggon so close to me that I felt the fore rack on my shoulder, and feared I should soon be like a pancake![2] As the waggon pressed more heavily on me, putting my left hand on the ledge of the hill, which was about the height of my waist, I vaulted better than I had ever done before, or have done since, rolling over above the waggon. As I scrambled on to the track I saw to my horror what seemed in the darkness to be a bundle, while the waggon, released from the guidance of my hand on the pole, turned to the right, and careered down the slope out of sight. Hastening to the bundle, I found it was Maude on his face, doubled up, senseless. When after some minutes he said, "Oh! my chest is knocked in!" I was so miserable that

[1] Rope made of ox hide.
[2] I measured the track next morning, and found I had taken the wheel to within 5 inches of the scarped outside of the hill.

I could not answer him. He murmured, "Lay me on my back." I sent a man down the hill after the waggon, to fetch a table. He brought back a broken half of it, on to which we lifted my friend. As we carried him down the hill, the front men being so much lower than those behind, Maude's body began to slip off, so I had to walk backwards, holding his feet, until I noticed Private Stringer was much exhausted, when I changed places with him. Now Paliso was $2\frac{1}{2}$ inches taller than I, so I got an undue weight, and before I reached the tent had no breath left in my body. We placed Maude on the bed in the tent, cutting off his clothes, he groaning all the time. I poured some brandy and water down his throat, and put a hot-water bottle to his feet, which were icy.

I then wrote a hasty note to Major Clery at Luneberg, and sent Private Stringer and Paliso off with it. It was 25 miles away, on a track neither of them had ever seen, and although the rain had ceased, the mist was so thick it was difficult to see 50 yards off. They had, however, the guiding line of a mountain range, and a river along which they rode. I said to Stringer as they started, "You must ride till you and your horse drop from fatigue to get a doctor, and his quiet "Yes, sir," assured me that if he failed it would only be from one of these causes. As they disappeared in the mist, I shouted, "Borrow some of the officers' horses, and come back at once." They reached Luneberg about 3 a.m., and Stringer announced that he was then ready to start back, while the Kafir lay down and could with difficulty be aroused. He was a Fingoe, and had, moreover, ridden 16 miles with me in the morning, while Stringer had been in camp.

When I got back to Maude, I found he was able to speak, and ask for tea or soup, which I gave him through the tube of my syphon eye-douche; and about one o'clock I lay down and tried to sleep, but every time Maude moved, or groaned, he awoke me. About five in the morning he asked for cocoa, and I wrote a note to Mr. Henderson, whose house was close to us, for some Kafirs to pull out the waggon. I collected some articles from the wreck—the men's tent, and horse food, and washed more dirt off my friend's face. When the doctor arrived he declared that, as far as he could see, there was no serious damage; the wheels had passed over Maude's chest, and he was very sore all over. When the Kafirs were ready we lifted him on to the stretcher, but he groaned so much from his weight pressing against the sides, that I stopped at Mr. Henderson's and got the loan of a rough bedstead, placing that on the stretcher. We were very tired, and the Zulus occasionally kept step, which gave poor Maude the movement of being tossed in a blanket. As night fell, and with it rain, I decided to make my way into an empty house we found on the way. We got into Utrecht—45 miles—on the following evening, and at the end of ten days my friend was at work again.

I was up early on the 21st November, and arranged for my Cape cart to start with our baggage at 1.30; but about eleven o'clock Captain Woodgate came in, and said that both the drivers were drunk, and nobody else could catch the mules. I observed philosophically, "Perhaps one may be sober by 1.30, which will be plenty of time, and one driver can get the cart to Newcastle, so send the more sober of the two."

I was harried all the forenoon by pressing business, but, to my delight, Major Moysey, Royal Engineers, came to join, and thus I was relieved of one part of my manifold duties. A succession of people,—the Principal Medical Officer, the Landdrost, and various Settlers, and Captain McLeod, my assistant, the Agent [1] accredited to the King of the Swazis,—occupied the time until 3 p.m., when, just as I was starting, Faku, Cetewayo's representative near Luneberg, and another Induna, arrived with an important message. The message was amusing: the Zulu Monarch declared that, when he sent orders for the Germans to leave Luneberg, he did not know it was Transvaal territory; but that now he was aware of it, he would make Umbeline keep his people in order, and so perhaps I would be good enough to withdraw the soldiers. I declined this request, but consoled the Ambassador with a present of tobacco. At the close of the interview the post arrived with important letters from the General, one putting the 13th Light Infantry under my orders.

At 4.30 p.m. I started, with my Orderly officer, Lieutenant Harry Lysons.[2] The Cape cart had 27 miles to go, but Lysons knew a short cut, and a ford across the

---

[1] I had been appointed Political Agent for North Zululand and Swaziland in October.
[2] Son of my friend, General Sir Daniel Lysons.

Buffalo River, just south of where it is joined by the Incandu and Ingagane Rivers. We cantered to the Buffalo, 12 miles, without drawing rein, well under two hours, including a stop at a Fingoe's kraal, from whom I hoped to buy mealies. He was a prosperous settler from the Cape Colony, speaking English well. The day was now closing in, and after we were across the river, Lysons hesitated. He had guided me as straight as a line drawn on the map hitherto, but the ground on the right bank of the Buffalo is difficult to understand, and there is no doubt that, having crossed the main stream once, we kept too far to our right, and came back to it. We now realised we were wrong; but after turning northwards, darkness came over us, and "our rest" became, not "stones," but puddles. Vainly attempting to read my compass, for it was now quite dark, we plodded on at a walk. Light rain fell incessantly, and a black cloud, the precursor of heavy storms, blotted out every star, and compelled us to dismount and feel for footpaths, which crossed and recrossed each other in the most bewildering manner.

About eight o'clock we came to a river, the whirling waters of which we could just distinguish lying below us, with steep banks on either side. After wandering up and down for twenty minutes, our horses jumping round every few minutes, when the flashes of lightning were more than usually vivid, I found a place where oxen had descended, and holding the horses I sent Lysons down to explore, as on the far bank we thought we saw a light. He slipped twice going down, and when he reached the water, being nervous he might be drowned, I called to him to take off his waterproof coat, adding that, as I should probably not hear him, I would sing loudly until his return. I waited an hour, the horses turning round and sliding about, endeavouring to get their faces away from the rain, and after the first quarter of an hour I sang "Far Away" till I was tired of the tone of my voice, but could not hear a sound. I began to calculate the chances of my ever getting "War-Game" and Lysons' pony down the bank, and came to the conclusion that I should either lose my Orderly officer or my horse, who constantly rested his nose on my shoulder. When the heavy rain came on about five o'clock, I had shifted my un-read English letters from my pocket to my wallets; but now, thinking I ought to try and find Lysons, even though I lost my horse, I put the letters back in my pockets, fearing, however, to find them in a shapeless pulp in the morning. Just then Lysons greeted me so cheerily from the opposite bank, I thought he must have a Kafir with him, but when, having again waded across the river, he rejoined me, he said he could not find the lights, and he believed he had wandered in a circle. As he reported very badly of the descent, we led the horses up stream for 300 yards, but the banks being more unfavourable we returned. So far as I could make out from my watch, it was about eleven p.m. A heavy storm, obscuring everything, obliged us to stand still, and I sat down and slept for ten minutes, but a loud peal of thunder frightening "War-Game," made him jump so violently as to hurt my arm, which I had passed through the reins. I then decided to try and descend step by step, utilising the lightning for a light. I went down the bank, "War-Game" following me like a dog. It was nervous work walking exactly in front of him, but unless I did so he would not advance a foot! When he reached the water I rewarded him with a piece of sugar, which I generally carried for my horses.

We got across the river about midnight, and after wandering for about an hour in and out of small ravines, another storm compelled us to halt. We lay down as close to each other as we could for warmth; but as "War-Game" jumped at every vivid flash of lightning, and pulled at my arms, I could not sleep. Lysons slept, not soundly, but still he did sleep. I stood up from about 12.30 a.m. till 4 a.m. wondering occasionally which of the two shivered most, master or horse. I felt nervously at my letters every five minutes to see whether they were still dry. About 4 a.m. the water was so deep under Lysons I made him get up, and he presently heard a cock crow, towards which we led our horses. After walking for ten minutes I asked, "Do you hear him now?" "No, not at all. Shall I challenge?" He then screamed such a cock-a-doodle-do that my horse jumped into the air, and nearly knocked Lysons over; but his challenge was immediately answered, and ten minutes' walk brought us to a Kraal. After much shouting we got a Kafir out, and I let off my only Zulu sentence, asking the way to Newcastle. I could not say "Come and show us," but a half-crown in my left hand, and a grip of his neck with my right, indicated what I wanted, and the Kafir trotted off, bringing us to the bank of a river, through which we waded with some difficulty. The water came in over the top of my boots, Lysons on his pony going in up to his waist. When we got to the far side, being now sure of the track, I threw the half-crown to the astonished Kafir, who probably never earned one so easily before, and we cantered into Newcastle.

After an hour's sleep, and having had some breakfast, we drove northwards, but the jolting of the Cape cart was intolerable. Presently, looking back, I observed a farmer following us in a "Spider."[1] I knew him as a man who had ox-waggons for sale, and suggested he should take me into his carriage. This he did, and in a four hours' drive I learnt a good deal about Colonial life. While we sheltered in one of his farms, occupied by a Dutchman, who could not speak a word of English, but who made some tea for us, frying beef and eggs together in one pan, we escaped one of the heaviest storms I ever saw. I have often read with incredulity travellers' stories of hail-stones being as large as walnuts, and can scarcely, therefore, hope my readers will believe my statements when I say that I have seen many such under the Drakensberg range of mountains. I bought a span of oxen during the storm, and then started again at three o'clock. The farmer was to have taken us a short cut, but what was generally a little rivulet was now a whirling river, and we had to go round by the ordinary track.

We stopped that night at Meek's farm, 30 miles north of Newcastle, and next morning, rising at daybreak, got the loan of the Spider and two of Mr. Meek's ponies. The ground was heavy, and neither animal would pull, so we started in a somewhat undignified fashion, my Orderly officer pushed the cart behind, while Paliso, the interpreter, and I hauled on the shafts until we got up the hill, and could start with the advantage of the downward incline.

When we reached the farm of Andries Pretorius, there were twenty of his kindred awaiting my arrival. They were all surly, and although it is customary in that part of the

---

[1] A light four-wheeled American carriage.

country for the host and his family to come out and assist in unharnessing a guest's horse, nobody offered to help, except Pretorius. He apologised for his kindred, explaining they detested the sight of an Englishman. He was careful to impress on me, however, that were I not his guest he would be equally discourteous. He had a remarkable face, hard, resolute, and unyielding. When we went in—Mr. Meek interpreting—I explained the object of my visit. "I know," I said, "there is a strong feeling against the Imperial Government, but you have many relatives on the border, and their farms, now valueless, will be very valuable when we settle the question." Pretorius replied: "We have sworn an oath to be true to Messrs. Kruger and Joubert, who went to England to see your Government, and we will not move till we hear the answer to the deputation, and we will not help you till the Transvaal is given back to us." "I shall not, then, have the pleasure of your assistance."

We talked for two hours as "friends." Pretorius argued on the Annexation question, and, as I thought, got the worst of it. He said, "You came into my house, saying 'How dirty it is; turn out.' And now you cannot clean one little room named Sekukuni! And what a small broom you have got, to try and sweep up Cetewayo! He will destroy that broom." I observed, "Well, your house was very dirty, and tumbling down; moreover, it had just then taken fire. My house was next yours, and as you could not put out your fire, I was obliged to try to do it. It is true that the broom was not large enough to sweep up Sekukuni, and it may be destroyed in sweeping up Cetewayo, but my Queen can send out 45 Regiments instead of the 5 stationed here, and if the little broom is destroyed you will soon see more brooms." "But why do you light a big fire before you put out a little one?" "We hope when we put out the big fire, that the little one will go out of itself." "Then," said he, "tell me honestly—do you prefer to have with you your own soldiers, or Dutchmen, when fighting Natives?" "For shooting Natives and taking cattle, I prefer Dutchmen. In the Perie Bush, in Kaffraria, I had 300 Dutchmen in my command, but when I had a position to carry, and the Kafirs were standing up to us, I took soldiers. In four months I never had a Dutchman killed in action." Although this honest opinion was not appreciated by Pretorius or by his family, we had much conversation, and finally, when I left the farm, all the Dutchmen came out and expressed the hope that personally I might come safely out of the Zulu War.

I did not abandon the General's scheme, on account of this failure, and when at the end of November the Staff at Maritzburg wrote that the Cabinet had finally decided not to accede to the General's request for reinforcements, expressing the hope that war would be avoided, I made an effort to win over the Dutchmen living in the Wakkerstroom and Utrecht districts. On the 4th December, after a conference which lasted from 9 a.m. to 5 p.m., I induced some of them to say that in the event of war they would accompany me. The man of most influence won over was Piet Uys,[1] who, for himself and his sons and nephews, declined to receive pay.

I spent the next three weeks in purchasing transport, and having sketches made of all tracks leading over the Transvaal frontier towards Ulundi.

[1] Extract from a letter from Lord Chelmsford to Colonel Evelyn Wood:—

"MARITZBURG, 10th December 1878.

"You have done wonders with the Dutchmen, and I am quite sure the High Commissioner will be as much obliged to you from a Political point of view as I am from a Military one.—CHELMSFORD."

Sir B. Frere to the Secretary of State for the Colonies:—

"MARITZBURG, 23rd December 1878.

"I have but little doubt but that the firm, conciliatory, and judicious treatment of these gentlemen by Colonel Evelyn Wood will have an excellent effect, not only locally, but generally throughout the South-eastern Transvaal districts.—B. FRERE."

CHAPTER XXVIII

CHRISTMAS 1878.—THE INVASION OF ZULULAND

A woman the ultimate cause of the Zulu War—Preparations for a campaign —Christmas Day — Forming an advanced base — A disappointing Honours gazette—Conference with Lord Chelmsford—I decline to be Resident in Zululand—Seketwayo's vacillation—Captain Woodgate's indifference to danger—We defeat the Makulusi, Nodwengu, and Udloko Regiments, and hear of Isandwhlana—Boers as waggoners— They pull over a champion team in a Tug-of-war.

SIR THEOPHILUS SHEPSTONE came to stay with me, Christmas Eve 1878, for three days, and gave me much valuable information about the Zulus. He was particularly kind, and I appreciated it the more because the High Commissioner having made me a Political Agent for North Zululand and Swaziland, had virtually taken the control of our policy in those countries, as regards the natives, out of his hands. This, however, increased my work, and I had more than I could do. My diary shows that at 6.30 a.m. I was inspecting Mounted infantry, and a more ragged crew perhaps was never got together, except the professional beggars on a stage. I was much dissatisfied, for the first horse I looked at was about to get a sore back, his saddle cloth being twisted up under the saddle. Many of the men had only 10 rounds of ammunition, instead of 75. I got back to breakfast at 8 a.m, when Captain Barton[1] rode in from Major Buller's camp, where he was doing good work, which justified my recommendation of him for Special service. During breakfast time, a hurried meal, I gave him instructions, as he was going to Wesselstroom to buy horses, grain, and vegetables. At nine o'clook I had a second inspection of the 90th Light Infantry, looking at

---

[1] Coldstream Guards, serving in Frontier Light Horse; he was Aide-de-Camp to Sir Hope Grant at Aldershot in 1870-1871.

every man's boots, which were unsatisfactory; this took till 11.30. My excellent Major was much vexed by my telling him that the kits of no two companies were laid out in the same manner, for this, though perhaps not of great importance in itself, takes the inspecting officer more time. Nor were his men's "small books" signed for the previous month. Then I passed on, telling the Royal Engineer officer what was required in the Laager to make it defensible.

The Landdrost now appeared, with the Townspeople, and asked how many soldiers were to be left to protect them. "I am not going to leave any, except the halt and the maimed." "The Townspeople can defend the Laager, and the halt and maimed my stores, and if I lose them it won't much matter to me." One of the local leaders said, "If you lose your stores you will starve!" I replied, "I shall have two months' supplies at Balte Spruit, 20 miles in advance; and all I promise the Utrecht Townspeople is a decent burial on my return." Then the Senior doctor came and asked me our plan of campaign. Surgeon-Major Cuffe, however, was a good organiser, and took all trouble in that respect off my hands. Then a Captain came and told me he could not work with his Senior officer, and must leave him. I suspected that the complainant had a hot temper, but sent him to work on Transport duty. Next, Major Clery appeared,[1] and said that Captain Barton had annexed a waggon. The dispute turned on a point of grammar. Clery wrote, "Send them back." Barton read this to mean "oxen." Clery meant "waggon and oxen." They both quoted Lindley Murray at length. Captain Woodgate then wanted me to look at, and buy, two horses which were outside. I told him to ask Clery to buy, or reject, the horses. At this moment I was reminded that I was to give an address on the Zulu nation and its army on the following Friday night, to which I had not yet given a thought! When I could obtain ten minutes without interruption, I was considering how to equip 1000 natives without any means at hand. To this number I later added another 1000, and as officers speaking Zulu had to be found, as well as blankets, guns, and something to carry powder and bullets, or ammunition, it will be understood the work was of an engrossing nature.

[1] Now Major-General Sir C. Clery, K.C.B.

I began work at daylight on Christmas Day 1878, and went to a Church parade at 7 a.m., and then did some odd jobs till 8.30, when we had a Sacrament service, for which Major Buller and Captain Barton rode in ten miles. It was pleasant to see our boldest polo players, who had hustled me the previous evening, Bright, Hotham, and Lysons, at the service. All three were fine bold boys; Bright had been the stroke oar of the Eton Eight. They came in to breakfast, which caused some little difficulty about knives and forks, as Sir Theophilus Shepstone was still with me. He worked with me for a couple of hours after breakfast, and then I did business with the doctors and commissariat.

I saw my guest off about midday, but when I returned from a ride to Major Buller's camp, I found that Sir Theophilus had come back, for his mule driver was drunk, and all the mules were lost. This was, however, my gain, as I could not see too much of my guest, and it cleared up our relations. He wrote to me later from Newcastle, he had previously imagined Sir Bartle Frere was under the impression that he was not supporting me; the idea was, however, erroneous. Sir Theophilus and I had disagreed as to putting in force the Transvaal Commando law. He thought it would be better to make it applicable to Whites and Blacks, and I wanted it enforced only for Natives, in order to obtain drivers and fore-loupers for my waggons, and the black men who formed Wood's regiment, many of whom, however, came voluntarily, as indeed they well might, at 1s. a day. I always received the warmest support from Sir Theophilus, and the misunderstanding was caused, I think, by my diffidence in expressing, after so short a residence in the country, any opinion which did not coincide with that of one who had spent his life in South Africa.

On the 26th December I started a Company, 13th, and one of the 90th Light Infantry with a convoy of waggons to fill up Balte Spruit, a position I had selected 20 miles to the southward of Utrecht. About midday I received a message from Captain Woodgate that all the waggons were stuck in a ravine 10 miles distant, and later it became necessary to encamp a company at three different places to assist the oxen when they were unable to "pull out" by themselves.

At the end of the month I got a very kind letter from the

General—now Lord Chelmsford—relative to the Gazette of Honours and Rewards for the Operations in the Amatola Mountains, which had just been received.[1]

The confidence which the General gave me enabled me to urge a more concentrated advance than he had at first intended, and this was eventually adopted, as was another suggestion I made, that we should purchase all the Transport we might require, as being not only a cheaper arrangement, but the only feasible plan to ensure success. Any disappointment I felt about the Gazette was mitigated by the fact that several officers whom I had recommended received promotion, including two in the 90th Light Infantry. Some other selections, although made, no doubt, on what appeared to those in Pall Mall adequate grounds, caused much amusement in the Colony, for of two of the Seniors who became Companions of the Bath, one had been relegated to the command of 30 privates and the Regimental band, 500 miles from the scene of action, and the other assumed charge of a few loyal natives in a peaceful district.

The Military Secretary treated me with great kindness, and allowed me to write to him freely, so I urged on his attention the omission of Brevet Major Hackett's name; and took the opportunity of telling Sir Alfred Horsford that the delay in gazetting me to the command of the Regiment had caused me to serve ten months in South Africa at 2s. a day less pay than Captain Woodgate, or indeed any of the captains employed on Special service, received.

When my last company joined at Utrecht, the officer in command informed me he had heard all his way up that Colonel Wood was a wonderful judge of oxen. This was an unfounded reputation, for I knew very little about cattle. I had no Veterinary Surgeon, and was therefore obliged to look closely at every beast myself; but the average price and quality was undoubtedly satisfactory.

The incessant work, however, now began to tell on me, and my glands swelled as they had done when I was over-

---

[1] He wrote: "I was sorry not to see your name in Orders for some reward, for all your good service, and for the help you have given me, but it is only deferred. Your loyal and excellent work will not, and shall not, go unrewarded, if I have anything to say to it."

worked in the Amatola Mountains, although for pleasure and on principle I played either lawn-tennis or polo for an hour or two every evening, the subalterns of the 90th being always available for a game.

On the 1st January one of my spies informed me that Cetewayo had assured Sirayo that he should not be given up to the British Government. Sirayo was not himself in fault, but the action of his sons, and especially of the elder, Melokazulu,[1] was the ultimate cause of Cetewayo's downfall.

Sirayo, whose district was on the borders of Zululand, adjoining the Buffalo River, had, like all important chiefs, many wives, and two of the younger ones absconded with young Zulus resident in Natal. Melokazulu followed with an armed party, and surrounding the kraal, took the women back into Zululand, where he shot them. In the following year I asked him in the course of conversation why he did not shoot the men, and he answered simply, "Oh, my father did not pay for them as he did for the women, for whom he gave cattle, and besides, the men were subjects of the British Government." "Did your father know that you had gone after the wives?" "No." "Did he approve of your having shot them?" "I don't know. I told him they were dead, and he made no remark."

I moved what was now called No. 4 column, consisting of the 13th and 90th Light Infantry, 4 guns, a varying number of horsemen, on the 3rd January to Balte Spruit, near the Blood River, which we crossed on the 6th, after hearing that Cetewayo had not accepted the terms offered by the High Commissioner.

I received a letter on the 9th January from the General, requesting me to move down and demonstrate to the southward, to take pressure off him as he crossed the Buffalo, and also, if he was unopposed, to meet him personally about halfway from our respective positions.

I told the Zulus in our neighbourhood, and as far east as the White Umvolosi, that they must decide before daylight on the 11th January whether they intended to be friends, or foes. When, after the 11th, Colonel Buller seized a large number of cattle, I asked some of the Zulus why they had not driven

[1] Reported as killed in Bambaata's rebellion, June 1906.

them off, and they answered, "Oh, we never thought you would begin on the day you mentioned."

On the evening of the 10th, I moved with about two-thirds of the column, having laagered and entrenched one-third, towards Rorke's Drift. It rained incessantly, and the Blood River behind us, usually only 3 feet deep, became 11 feet in the course of a few hours, while it was impossible to move a waggon over slight watercourses, without putting on 50 men to help the oxen. I started at 2.30 a.m. for the Itilezi, and soon after nine o'clock met Lord Chelmsford on the Nkonjane Hill, 9 miles from Rorke's Drift. No. 3 column had started the previous day, but the difficulties of crossing the Buffalo were considerable.

I had an interesting talk with Lord Chelmsford for three hours, while Colonel Buller was sweeping up cattle to the south of the General's line of advance. After we had discussed the many affairs in which we had been interested since we met three months earlier, he pressed me, in the name of the High Commissioner, to accept the office of Resident of Zululand. I urged that the Resident ought to speak the language, and that, moreover, I was too fond of soldiering to leave the 90th Light Infantry for Political employment. He was greatly pleased to learn that I had got forty-two days' supplies for man and beast at Balte Spruit, besides a week's rations I had with me, as No. 3 column had only collected fifteen days'. Mr. Hughes, my Commissariat officer, had been indefatigable in adding to my stores, for which purpose he had been sent three weeks earlier from the Transvaal.

Before I left Lord Chelmsford, I warned him that, according to the information given by my spies, the first serious Zulu attack would fall on the column which he was accompanying. Three days later, on the 14th, I informed His Lordship that no forward movement had been made from Ulundi, but on the 17th I wrote, " My spies say that the Zulu Army," or, as they expressed it, " Cetewayo, is moving westward."

On the 14th January I sent to tell Seketwayo, a Chief of considerable importance, who had been negotiating with me since the 2nd, that I could no longer herd the 2000 head of cattle we held taken from his territory, but if he would come in, he should have them. The matter was complicated, as a considerable number of the cattle belonged to Cetewayo, or rather to the Royal House. The Chief could not make up his mind, and having waited five days I sent the cattle away to the Free State, where they were sold.

Being uneasy concerning Zulus to the north of our left flank, I directed Colonel Buller to send there the Frontier Light Horse under Captain Barton, who took between 500 and 600 head of cattle, clearing the Pemvane and lower Bevane Rivers, while the column was moving forward slowly, much impeded by heavy rain, to the Umvolosi.

I had obtained the General's approval to my going in a north-easterly direction to clear the Ityenteka Range, including the Inhlobane mountain, of Zulus under Umsebe and Umbeline, hoping to be back before the General was ready to advance with No. 3 column. Having reached the Umvolosi River on the 19th, we built a fort at Tinta's Kraal, which, humanly speaking, should have been impregnable if held by two companies, and off-loading seventy waggons I sent them in the afternoon back towards Balte Spruit, escorted by Captain Wilson's company of the 90th, with orders to fill up the waggons and return to Tinta's Kraal, where I intended to leave him, and a company of the 13th.

About 7 o'clock in the evening I got a note from Colonel Buller, saying that he had been engaged for some hours on the Zunguin mountain with several hundred of the Makulusi tribe, who were pressing him back, and, as he was writing at sunset, had crossed in small numbers to the right bank of the Umvolosi. This disturbed me considerably, for they were now within a few miles of our empty waggons, and it was not only the chance of the loss of the company and £21,000 worth of property, but it would have been difficult to replace the waggons. I knew that the Convoy was not more than 3 or 4 miles off, for there was a muddy ravine which could only be passed with difficulty, and that Captain Wilson intended to begin to cross it at daylight.

Captain Woodgate, seeing I was perturbed, asked me the reason, and on reading to him Colonel Buller's note, at once went to the Company, although we were just going to have something to eat. He had the oxen inspanned at once, the drivers and foreloupers on learning the news being anxious to get away to a place of safety. His unconsciousness of danger was shown by handing his horse to a Zulu when he dismounted to help the waggons across the ravine, with the result that he never saw it again for three days. Nothing of importance, however, occurred, for Colonel Buller, by showing a bold front to the Makulusi, held them on the river, and they retired after dark to their stronghold on the highest part of the mountain.

On the night of the 20–21st we made a long night march with the 90th Light Infantry, two guns and the mounted men starting at 11 p.m., and at daylight climbed the western end of the Zunguin mountain, along which we advanced during the day, taking some cattle and driving 1000 Zulus off it, they retiring to the Nek connecting it with the Inhlobane. Looking down from the eastern extremity, we saw about 4000 Zulus drilling under the Ityenteka Nek; they formed in succession a circle, triangle, and square, with a partition about eight men thick in the centre.

We descended at night for water, and rejoined the 13th, the 90th Light Infantry having been nineteen hours out of the twenty-four under arms, and having covered a considerable distance. In mileage, however, it was not so great as the distance covered by Wilson's company escorting the waggons, which filled up at once and returned to the Umvolosi, marching 34 miles in twenty-six hours.

We heard the guns[1] fired at Isandwhlana, 50 miles off, that evening as we sat round a camp fire.

There was a thick mist on the morning of the 24th which delayed our advance, but when it cleared we moved forward and came under fire from Zulus hidden in the rocks under the south-western point of the Inhlobane. Leaving the 90th and two guns to follow the waggon track with the baggage, I went to the right with the 13th Light Infantry, Piet Uys and his troop of 40 Burghers, with whom I was disappointed, as it was necessary for Piet and myself to ride in front to

---

[1] These were fired by Lord Chelmsford's troops returning from Sirayo's district to the wrecked camp. Our Senior officers asked my opinion, what was the probable cause, and I said guns fired after dark indicated, I apprehended, an unfavourable situation.

induce his men to go on to cover the advance of the guns. When we reached the rocks from whence the fire had come, it was clear we could not hope to get the guns down, so, after driving back a few Zulus who were in broken ground, I turned northwards, and went to a hill under which I had ordered the 90th to halt with the waggons and outspan. When I got there the oxen had just been loosened from the Trek-tow, but to my great vexation they were without any guard, and the 90th, which ought to have been with them, was three-quarters of a mile in front, advancing rapidly in line, without any supports, against some 4000 Zulus.[1] I looked up the ravine, which farther to the southward had stopped my onward progress with the 13th Light Infantry and guns, and was concerned to see about 200 Zulus coming down it towards the 90th's Ammunition carts, which had been left with some bugler boys, who had no firearms. I had just told an orderly to call Colonel Buller, when I was accosted by a Kafir who had ridden 48 miles from Utrecht bringing a note from Captain Gardner, recounting the disaster of Isandwhlana, of which he had been an eye-witness. Buller came to me at once, and telling him in one sentence of the misfortune which had befallen No. 3 column, I sent him up the ravine to drive back the Zulus, while I galloped to the 90th and expressed a strong opinion to the Senior officer— not belonging to the Regiment—who had contravened my orders. The Zulus in front of them made no stand. The young soldiers were very steady, and expended less than two rounds of ammunition per man; but the Zulus fled from the sight of the advancing line, and went ten paces to one covered by our men. The Frontier Light Horse and the Dutchmen pursued them until they climbed the Inhlobane mountain, and then after a halt of two hours I ordered the column to fall in, and, against the advice of some of the senior officers, read to the men the note I had received.

[1] It appeared later I had greatly under-estimated the Zulu force, imagining it was the Makulusi regiment only, but the High Commissioner learnt from his agent, and reported to the Secretary of State, not only was the Makulusi routed and dispersed, but that the Nodwengu and Udloko regiments shared in their fate. Later, Sir Bartle Frere wrote: "The Zulus are greatly impressed with the skill with which this force (Colonel Wood's) has been handled, and are afraid it may push on to the Inhlazatze, and threaten the Royal Kraal."

We moved back as far as our camp of the previous day, and next morning returned to our fort on the Umvolosi River. I was now in some difficulty. I did not want to abandon Supplies, and I had 70 loads for which I had no waggons. The Dutchmen, who were well provided with waggons, and were themselves wonderful drivers of oxen, came to my aid. Piet Uys and his men, who had only about 1000 lbs. weight on each waggon, loaded up to 8000 lbs., and then we moved slowly westwards, halting on the 28th at Venter's Drift, where I was within reach of firewood, our greatest want in that part of the country. There were trees growing in the ravines south of the Ngaba Ka Hawane Mountain.

Here I received a considerate note from Lord Chelmsford, giving me a brief account of the disaster at Isandwhlana, and telling me I had a free hand to go anywhere or adopt any measures I might think best, ending: "You must now be prepared to have the whole of the Zulu Army on your hands any day. ... No. 3 Column, when re-equipped, is to subordinate its movements to your column. Let me know how it can assist you." I replied to Lord Chelmsford on the 31st January that I was in a position on Kambula Hill which I anticipated being able to hold even against the whole of the Zulu Army. I understood he did not wish me to incur risk by advancing, and I would not move unless it became necessary to do so in order to save Natal.

In spite of the carriage for stores lent to us by the Dutchmen, we had some trouble before we succeeded in finding a good military and sanitary Position, and even to men who did not feel much compassion for oxen, to make them pull 8000 lbs. through swamps is trying to their feelings as well as to the oxen's hides. It has often been a wonder to soldiers in South Africa how the Dutch, under Pretorius and other leaders forty years earlier, took waggons up and down mountains which appear to us impracticable for wheel traffic, but the maximum weight in a waggon on Commando was 1500 lbs., five adults being allowed a waggon between them, which of course made a great difference on a bad track. The difficulties of transport caused me to halt every second or third day, as I was obliged to make two journeys with my loads, and I soon had warning that I could not remain in the valley of the Umvolosi, by the loss of horses and oxen, followed by that of a man of the 90th, who died of very rapid enteric fever. The Military situation, although I tried to conceal the fact, affected my health. I never slept more than two or three hours at a time, going round the sentries for the next three months at least twice every night. We shifted camp five times before we finally took up the position in which the greater part of the Zulu Army attacked us on the 29th March, and as we constructed slight entrenchments in every camp, and improved the formation of the encampment so as to obtain the greatest amount of fire from all sides, the men were kept employed, and gained valuable experience. We worked on Sundays, saying our prayers in a practical manner, for I had Divine Service parade on ground immediately adjoining the spot where two companies were at work throwing up redoubts, and let the men put down their picks and shovels and join in the Service, which, during the sixteen months in which I either read it myself or caused one of the Staff officers to do so, never kept the men standing more than ten minutes, and I have never seen soldiers so attentive.

From December 1878 I had Native scouts 20 miles in front of our Force, and patrols 6 miles out an hour before daylight, but in the afternoon we amused ourselves, although the early morning was a period of anxiety. My spies informed me of impending attacks, which were predicted for each new and full moon, which periods are held by the Zulus to be auspicious. Mounted men were stationed 6 miles in front by day, and two companies beyond our cattle at grass. The arrangements for security during night were peculiar. It rained regularly when the sun went down, throughout the months of February and March, which added to our difficulty of ensuring security without impairing the health of the soldiers. To save them, the outlying pickets were allowed tents pitched in a circle, 200 yards outside the Laager. Groups of 8 men were placed 100 yards farther out, 6 lying down under blanket shelters, while 2 watched and listened. Beyond on the paths most convenient for the enemy's approach, under a British officer, were small parties of Zulus,[1] whose marvellous hearing by night, and sight

---

[1] They were drawn from the Border Zulus I enlisted at Luneberg in November, and attached to battalions, 6 to each company; their powers of hearing were extra-

by day, enhanced the value of our precautions. After the disaster on the Intombe these men asked to speak to me, and said: "We want to go home to our families, for you are going to be attacked by the whole of the Zulu Army." "Well, that is just the reason why you should stop with me; I have been paying you all these months, and you have never yet been in danger." "Oh, we are not nervous about ourselves, you are sure to repulse the attack, but some of the Cetewayo's men will sweep round in Raiding parties on both flanks, and kill our women and children, who are near Luneberg." "I promise you I will insure your wives and your cattle if any harm comes to them while you are with me," on which they saluted and went back to the kitchen fires quite content.

It is interesting that at some Athletic sports on the 19th February, in the country pastime of throwing the assegai, the Zulus, who since Chaka's time had been taught not to throw long distances, but to rush on their foe and stab him with the short assegai, were easily beaten, the first prize being won by a Hottentot about 5 foot in height, who propelled an assegai 70 yards, the second man being a Colonial born Englishman, while no Zulu threw an assegai farther than 50 yards.

Our team in the Tug-of-war, which had only been once defeated, was thoroughly beaten by Piet Uys and his Dutchmen. In 1872, when we were at Aldershot, I wished the battalion to enter a team for Divisional Athletic sports. I could get no volunteers, the battalion had never pulled in a Tug-of-war, and showed no inclination to begin; eventually I had to appeal to the Sergeant-Major, who practically coerced the Colour Sergeants into producing one man a company. When I looked at them, selecting a man who seemed to be about my own size, I said: "I do not think you will be much good for this job,—I doubt whether you can pull me over."

ordinary; they could see farther than we could with field glasses,—their vision was surpassed only by the telescope. They lived near the battalion cooking fires, and were the cause of considerable difficulty with respect to their clothing. I could not buy soldiers' greatcoats in Africa, but it was the dumping ground of cast-off full dress uniforms of the British Army, and I obtained from Maritzburg old Cavalry tunics, those of the Heavy Dragoon Guards being the only ones into which the Zulus could squeeze their bodies, and in these it was only the top buttons that would meet.

"I can do that, sir, and without much trouble." Taking up a rope, I told him to try. He gave one look at me, and then pulled me off my feet; and although I sacrificed my spurs by digging them into the ground, he took me across the parade ground without any apparent effort. My judgment was decidedly faulty; although he was not more than a stone heavier than I was, his arms and back were abnormally powerful. I was much interested in training the team, which beat in succession every battalion at Aldershot, the Garrison Artillery at Portsmouth, every regiment of the Guards, a Brigade team of the Guards, a team from H.M.S. *Excellent* at Portsmouth, and a team of the Royal Marines. We sent it about to different garrisons, and it was never beaten until it met the 96th Regiment, which had an equally well trained team, each man being about half a stone heavier in weight, the effect of which was decisive.

When we were marching up from King William's Town to Natal, our men vanquished the Frontier Light Horse, composed of fine men, as they did when at Utrecht, and again at Kambula Hill, but they could not make the Dutchmen take their pipes out of their mouths. I said to Piet Uys, "I do not think your pipe will be alight in a quarter of an hour." He laughed, and at the end of the quarter of an hour the laugh was against me, for the Dutchmen, averaging 14 or 15 stone, with enormous knotted arms, and hands like iron, waited until the 90th were exhausted, and then without an effort pulled them over.

In each camp we occupied I made a lawn-tennis ground, playing it, and polo on alternate afternoons, when I was not out on reconnoitring expeditions.

CHAPTER XXIX

1879—IN ZULULAND

A bibulous officer—The disaster on the Intombe River—Uhamu joins me—We go to his district and bring in his 300 wives and families, 1100 in all—Piet Uys and his sons—Redvers Buller's kindness of heart—Zulu woman's rapid parturition—Officers sent to Free State to purchase Transport—The Mounted Troops bivouac under the Inhlobane—Piet Uys charges me to protect his children if orphaned.

AT some athletic sports held in February, I was strolling amongst the competitors when I received a vigorous slap on the back, and, turning round, was greeted effusively by an Officer with the exclamation: " How are you, old boy?" He was not able to stand steady, and I sent him away under arrest, in charge of Captain Ronald Campbell. Next day, when he was brought before me, I asked: " What have you got to say?" Now, I have had to deal with many similar offenders, but never before had such an honest answer; most men attribute their inebriety to an incongruous mixture with salad, or to the effects of a very small amount of alcohol on an empty stomach under a hot sun, but my officer replied: " Drunk, sir, drunk; nothing but drunk." " This is very serious, and I should like some hours to think over your case." " Quite simple, sir; you must either let me off, or try me by Court Martial." When I saw him again I said: " It is not the question of our safety only, but also of our honour as soldiers; if you are in charge of the Piquets when this happens again, you might cause a great disaster." " In the language of the soldiers, sir," he replied, " if you give me a chance I shall never be drunk again while under your command." He kept his promise, showed great courage in action some weeks later (for which, indeed, he had been noted when tiger shooting on foot in India), and his reformation was complete. A year later, when in Cape Town, I came across him one day when I had arranged a dinner to many of my former comrades, the Club being placed at my disposal for the purpose. Although the dinner was convivial, and I invited my bibulous comrade, I should have been doubtful of his reformation if he had abstained altogether, but he took an ordinary amount of wine, and left about midnight perfectly sober.

Before he joined me in 1878 he was drinking heavily, while attached to another regiment at Maritzburg. One day the Mess Sergeant said to the officer managing the Mess: " Unless I get some relief, sir, I must go back to duty." "Why, what is wrong?" " So-and-so goes to sleep every night on the sofa in the ante-room, and as he never wakes up till between one and two o'clock, I cannot close the Mess." " Sergeant, don't mind him,—lock it up, and go to bed," the officer replied; and so he did. Next morning about 2 a.m. the honorary member awoke, and, rolling off the sofa, collided with the coal scuttle, and then fell over a high fender guard. This alarmed him considerably, and crawling away he clutched the legs of a centre table, which he overturned. The crash aroused the Sergeant, who hurried in undressed, grasping a lighted candle, when the officer exclaimed in a piteous tone: "Where am I—in Hell?" The Sergeant, standing erect in his night-shirt, said: "No, sir, Officers' mess." The Officer sat up, and at once asserted his authority, saying decidedly: "Then, bring me a brandy and soda."

During the night of the 12th-13th March I was awakened by a messenger with the news of the disaster to a company of the 80th Regiment, which was marching from Derby to Luneberg. Four companies crossing the Intombe River, 5 miles from Luneberg, had camped at the station when the water rose, and the 5th Company was unable to cross. A raft was employed, and one-third of the company had reached the west side of the stream of the river at nightfall. Half an hour before daylight next day an attack was made by Umbeline, assisted by Manyoba's[1] tribe. Nearly every one on the east bank of the river was assegaied, many in their tents, and the Zulus, taking to the water like otter hounds, crossed and endeavoured

[1] The nervous Chief who feared I was going to arrest him in September.

to overwhelm the 34 men on the Western bank. Some 10 of these, however, were not only skilfully but courageously handled by Sergeant Booth, who successfully brought the party back. In all 40 of our men were killed.

I went over at daylight to the scene—40 miles distant—to inquire into the disaster, and to ensure our system for security being adopted for the future, returning in the afternoon to camp, as I had arranged a long ride for next day.

Uhamu, a brother of Cetewayo's, came into our camp[1] in the Cape cart which I sent for him, he being so enormously bulky that it was difficult to find a horse to carry him. He had made many appointments, but in the procrastinating Zulu fashion had failed for various reasons to keep them, until Colonel Buller had ceased to believe in his being willing to come over to us. Finally he went to my Assistant Political Agent, Norman Macleod, in Swaziland. He was no sooner in our camp than he asked me if I would be good enough to go after his wives. "How many are there, Uhamu?" "I don't know but about 300," he replied vaguely. "But you have got two now with you," I urged. "These are only slaves,—I should like to have the others." "I am not willing to take the responsibility of escorting all your wives unless you will come with me." "Oh, in such a case, Great Commander, I would sooner do without them."

Uhamu's head Place was in a rugged country, 45 miles from our camp, between the Black Umvolosi and Mkusi Rivers, and Ulundi being within 40 miles of the kraal, there was the possibility of our return being cut off if either of Uhamu's men let it be known, by Cetewayo's adherents, they were collecting the women in anticipation of our arrival.

Looking, however, to the Political effect of getting out the tribe, I decided to go down, and on the 14th March started with 360 mounted men under Buller, and 200 of Uhamu's men, many of whom had fought against No. 3 Column at Isandwhlana. Some of my officers objected to my leaving Buller and the White men and accompaning Uhamu's people, by a short cut

---

[1] Sir Bartle Frere eulogised my agent, Captain Macleod, and me for our "temper, judgment, and patience" in getting Uhamu over from his brother; and a Zulu agent told Bishop Colenso, and Sir Bartle later, that Cetewayo's altered tone was due to the defection of Uhamu.

over the Zunguin Mountain, which would save three hours' travelling. I argued that there was absolutely no danger while their Chief was located in my camp, especially as the men looked forward to bringing their wives and children back with them.

I took with me Captain Woodgate,[1] Mr. Llewellyn Lloyd,[2] my interpreter, Lieutenants Bigge,[3] Bright,[2] and Lysons.[4] We joined Colonel Buller under the Inhlobane, down the slopes of which some aggressive Zulus came, and fired at us at long ranges. I allowed two or three men to return the fire, and then had two shots myself, and the bullets falling amongst the Makulusi—for they occupied the mountain, silenced their fire.

About 2 p.m. we saw a few cattle to the south of us, and Piet Uys despatched his two boys, aged fifteen and thirteen, with half a dozen men to drive them to us. Master Dirks Uys shot a Zulu. When the father heard the firing he tried to look unconcerned, and was too proud to ask me (for his eyes were not as good as mine) if I could see what the lad was doing. Lysons told me later that he kept on repeating, "Are they coming back yet?" The men brought back about 100 head of cattle, and I said to my friend Piet, "I am glad the lad has come back. I saw that you were nervous." "Yes," he said, "I am always nervous if I am not there myself," a feeling which I understood. Nevertheless he risked them in every skirmish, though the warmth of his affection for his youngest born—Piet was a widower—was evident. In an argument he said something which I thought unworthy of the bigness of his character, and I remarked, "Why, you risk Dirks for us, you should not talk of farms and property"; and he replied, his eyes filling, "You are quite right, I would not give Dirks for all Zululand!" An hour or two later Piet called out that he saw Zulus, and galloped off with his two boys, but on this occasion nothing happened, for the Zulus he had sighted were some of Uhamu's men, who, taking advantage of our presence, were coming to join us.

---

[1] General Woodgate, mortally wounded at Spion Kop.
[2] Both killed in action a fortnight later.   [3] Now Colonel Sir Arthur Bigge.
[4] Lately Colonel Commanding a battalion of the Bedfordshire Regiment; now on Staff in India.

We marched steadily till sunset, when we off-saddled for an hour, to let the horses graze, and, moving off again at dusk, at 9.30 p.m. reached the spot I had arranged with Uhamu, having taken three hours to pass over the last seven miles. We descended a mountain by a goat path, and all the Europeans dismounted; but I, being tired from having been touched by the sun in the forenoon, threw the reins on my pony's neck and let him choose, or rather feel, the path,—it was too dark to see, and we got down without accident.

At sunset Uhamu's 200 men who accompanied me had asked me to stop, declaring they were tired. This I refused, and when we got down they had nearly cooked their food, having passed down by a still steeper but shorter path. Before I went to sleep I had some of the women, for whom I came, brought out of a cave three miles off, as I foresaw there would be delay next morning, and every hour added to the chance of our being caught by some of Cetewayo's regiments. During the night I sent 6 miles away to some caves where I heard there were more women, being unable to sleep soundly, although greatly fatigued, for one troop of the Frontier Light Horse, linked [1] in line, nearly walked over me, after they had eaten all the grass within reach. Buller came and pulled them away; indeed, every time I awoke in the night I saw him walking up and down, for he felt we were in a precarious position.

At daylight we shook ourselves, and began to start—a long stream of humanity. The Refugees numbered between 900 and 1000, men, women, and children. Many of the latter, although only five years old, walked from 6.30 a.m. till 9.30 p.m., when they had covered 30 miles. I sent Captain Barton on in front, while Colonel Buller and I remained behind. At 8.30 we were assured by Messrs. Calverley and Rorke—two traders who had often been in the district—that we had got the whole of the women and children. My engagement was that I would remain till daylight,—that is, six o'clock. At 8.30 Colonel Buller marched, a small Rear guard, remaining with me till 10.30, as even then stragglers were coming in, the last few being shot at, and two assegaied in our sight but too far off for us to save them. My friend Buller had stoutly

---

[1] Horses are linked by a headrope being passed through the head collar, and then through that of the next horse.

declared that he would have nothing to do with the verminous children, nevertheless during the march I more than once saw him with six little black bodies in front of and behind his saddle, children under five years of age.

As we passed under the Inhlobane, the Makulusi tribe, which had been reinforced by one of Cetewayo's regiments from Ulundi, fired a few shots at us without any effect, and we bivouaced at nightfall on a small effluent of the White Umvolosi, where Vryheid now stands.

Next morning I started the procession at daylight, remaining myself on the top of the Zungu in range to see the Rear guard into camp. I had sent in for all mule waggons available, to save the children a farther walk of 10 miles, and was waiting at the top of the pass, up which we had climbed on the 22nd January, for a dozen women who were loitering half up the mountain. It was past noon when I desired Piet Uys to descend and hurry them up, holding his horse for him, for it was too steep to ride down. When he returned he said, in his curious mixture of Dutch, German, and English, "Kurnall, die vrow sie sagt now too sick, presently have baby, then come quick." "Piet," I exclaimed, "oughtn't we to send some of these women back to see after her?" "Not necessary, Kurnall, she come." Calling Mr. Llewellyn Lloyd, my interpreter, I apprised him of the situation, and said, "You are not to go into camp until that woman gets there." Finally, waiting for the waggons longer than I expected, I did not reach camp till 5 p.m., and, having had nothing to eat or drink since our morning cocoa at daylight, I was annoyed to see Lloyd sitting in his tent with a cup of tea, and observed in a somewhat irritable tone, "I thought I told you not to come into camp until the woman who was about to bring a baby into the world had arrived. "Yes, quite so," he replied, "but she has been in camp a long time. Half an hour after you told me, she passed me like one of Waukenphast's pictures, doing five miles an hour easily, and I, suspecting that she had left her baby in the rocks, made her angry by insisting on seeing it, but she had it right enough under her arm."

Throughout the weeks of waiting for reinforcements I had frequent letters of encouragement from the High Commissioner and Lord Chelmsford; the latter writing to me frankly, said I had caused irritation amongst the local Civil authorities by the insistent tone of my communications. I have no doubt that this was accurate, but on the other hand many were supine, some actually obstructive. I was unable to induce the Field Cornet of Wesselstroom to take any effectual steps to send back 400 men who had deserted, out of the 600 enlisted when we crossed the border.

The Transvaal Boers rejoiced in our misfortune, and openly stated that they intended to rise; some of the Natal authorities objected to my sending any Refugees into the Colony, advancing the most absurd reasons. The Political Agent, sent from Pretoria to Utrecht to assist me, instead of doing so wrote at length that he was advised that the action of the Administrator of the Transvaal, in putting the Commando law in force for the Kafirs, was illegal. The Civil authorities on the Natal and Transvaal border clamoured for protection, and urged me, but in vain, to fall back to ensure the protection of certain villages.

The Utrecht Landdrost begged me to encamp close to that village, while the Landdrost of Wesselstroom, the chief village of the Wakkerstroom district, spent much time in endeavouring to persuade me to encamp in front of his village. When I intimated that I was not interested in Utrecht, as I had ample supplies at Balte Spruit, they expressed anxiety for the safety of that depot, and importuned Lord Chelmsford on the subject, who referred the correspondence to me, and to whom on the 3rd March I wrote in reply: " I have often considered your proposition about the Zulus masking this position, and going on to attack Balte Spruit and Utrecht. I do not believe they are equal to such a manœuvre, and are incapable of remaining in presence of a Force without attacking it or running away. If all our mounted men were absent I should feel anxious, but so long as they are here I could always make the Zulus attack us by sending the mounted men to follow them if they marched to Balte Spruit. I doubt Cetewayo turning out more than 30,000 men; if he does, he would do better to send 20,000 here and 10,000 against you. Moreover, the moral effect of our being in Zululand is considerable, both on the Swazis and the Boers." I discussed fully in this letter a scheme I had long considered about attacking the Inhlobane, but when Colonel

Buller burnt the Makulusi Kraals, bringing away 500 of their cattle, the necessity was less apparent, and I did not recur to the plan until asked to take pressure off the Force relieving Ekowe.

The Civil authorities were not, however, the only demoralised people. The General, in deference to the apprehensions of the inhabitants, sent a garrison to hold a village 30 miles behind our camp, and the Commanding officer marched round by Newcastle, adding 12 miles to his journey to avoid crossing a bit of Zululand 10 miles on the safe side of Kambula, and on arrival pitched his men's tents inside the cattle laager, which was several feet deep in manure; he became sick in a few days and went away. The next senior officer, on hearing of the disaster to the Company of the 80th, on the Intombe 45 miles distant, recalled a Company which was 10 miles behind our camp, at Kambula, for fear of its being surprised, although there were still four companies 80th Regiment at Luneberg, and another company from our camp, coal digging, all between him and the enemy. Indeed, the overweening confidence felt by many before the war had now changed into unreasoning apprehension.

The one great heroic figure throughout the time when men's minds were depressed was undoubtedly the High Commissioner, Sir Bartle Frere. He spent many days and nights in supporting all my demands, and in coercing unwilling and timorous Civil subordinates. With great address and moral courage he prevented an outbreak of the Boers, projected after the destruction of No. 3 Column.

On the 12th March I took the opportunity, when acknowledging the thanks by the High Commissioner and the General, to point out how much I owed to the Staff officers, Mr. Llewellyn Lloyd, my interpreter and Assistant Political Agent, Captain Ronald Campbell of the Coldstream Guards, Captain Vaughan, R.A., Director of Transport, and Mr. Hughes, Assistant Commissary-General, who worked literally day and night to carry out my wishes.

The difficulties of transport for the increased force, which was coming out to reinforce Lord Chelmsford's command, being always before me, I wrote urging that we should purchase sufficient at once, as hiring was not only extravagant but impracticable. The Chief replied on the 14th March that he had handed my offer to provide waggons to the Commissary-General, and was surprised that he did not jump at the offer, but added, "I do not like to interfere with his arrangements; please do as you like best yourself. I congratulate you on the surrender of Uhamu, the entire credit of which belongs to you. You can do anything you like with your column; if you like to attack the Inhlobane, pray do so."

I had previously asked permission to send officers to the Free State to purchase mule transport, foreseeing that the final advance on Ulundi might be delayed until the grass on the veldt would no longer suffice for oxen, and thus render the movement impossible without mule transport. After writing in vain repeated reminders for five weeks, I decided to act on the qualified sanction of my Chief in his letter of the 14th, "Please do as you like best yourself"; and on the 23rd sent two officers to the Free State, giving the senior, Captain Bradshaw, 13th Light Infantry, a cheque for £56,000, drawn on the Standard Bank of South Africa. They did very well indeed, enabling me to supply the 2nd Division, without which, as Lord Chelmsford wrote later, the advance would have been impossible.

The only comment made by the War Office on my action was to the effect that, as the money could not be all expended at once, I ought to have drawn two cheques, each for £28,000 at different dates, as I should thus have saved the amount of interest unnecessarily paid to the Bank. In my reply, while admitting my mistake, I remarked I had already spent for the Government over £50,000 without the assistance of a Paymaster, and it was therefore reasonable to debit the salary of such an officer against the amount of interest I had unnecessarily incurred.

The day Captain Bradshaw left was one of some anxiety. I had arranged a raid, by all the mounted men, in a North-Easterly direction to the Southward of Luneberg, to destroy the crops of one of our most troublesome foes. A convoy of 40 waggons was going in the opposite direction, South-South West to Balte Spruit, escorted by Infantry, and there was a working party, with an Infantry escort, employed in removing Potter's Store, which I had purchased and was moving from the Pemvane River to Balte Spruit. When we stood to our arms an hour before daylight the fog was so thick that we could not see 40 yards, and it did not clear off till the forenoon. I decided, however, to let the movement proceed as ordered, preferring the risk of surprise while I was present, to any which might occur in my absence.

Next morning, when I saw the convoys safe back in camp, I started and, overtaking Colonel Buller's 300 men, and 500 of Wood's Irregulars, reached Luneberg at sunset on the 24th. Next day we spread out over the basin of the Intombe River, cultivated by Umbiline's tribe, who were Zulus, although he was a renegade Swazi. We destroyed all the crops we could, and after two long days' work returned, on the evening of the 26th, to Kambula Hill.

In a letter dated the 19th, Lord Chelmsford called my attention to a paragraph in a Maritzburg newspaper, from a Correspondent with No. 4 Column, alleging that I was fretting at the inaction imposed on me by the General, and wrote, "You can undertake any operations you like, and I shall hear of it with pleasure. I hear all Cetewayo's army will be concentrated about Ekowe in a few days, so we shall have a hottish encounter." I replied on the 27th, "I do not often see the letters of the Correspondent, and hold no communication with him. If I did I should certainly tell him I am perfectly unfettered, your only action being to support me in every way. Buller has started, and at 3 p.m. I follow, to try to get up the Inhlobane at daylight to-morrow. I am not very sanguine of success. We do not know how steep the Eastern end may be, but I think we ought to make a stir here, to divert attention from you, although, as you see by our last reports, it is asserted that you have only Coast tribes against you, and that all Cetewayo's people are coming here."

In the forenoon of the 27th March, the two columns which were to attack the Inhlobane at daylight next morning marched; I followed in the evening, intending to lie down 5 miles under the Western edge of the Inhlobane. The more important part of the operation was intrusted to Colonel Buller, under whose orders I placed the two battalions of Wood's regiment. The 1st battalion, under Major Leet, bivouacing near the White Umvolosi, where Vryheid now stands, was intended to ascend the Western end of the mountain; both columns were to get as high up as they could before daylight on the 28th. In the orders I stated that, as Cetewayo was said to be advancing with his whole army, scouts were to be sent to the South and South-West, to watch the avenues of approach from Ulundi.

I took with me Mr. Lloyd, Assistant Political Agent and Interpreter, Captain the Honourable Ronald Campbell, Coldstream Guards, and Lieutenant Lysons, 90th Light Infantry, Orderly officer, my personal escort, eight mounted men of the battalion, and seven mounted Zulus under Umtonga, a half-brother of Cetewayo's, whom the father, Umpande, had originally designated to succeed him. Before I went to sleep I had a long talk with Piet Uys, who was to accompany Colonel Buller, and had stayed behind to see me, while the Colonel had bivouaced 5 miles farther to the east. Mr. Potter, a Captain in the 1st Battalion, Wood's Irregulars, also came to me. Both men knew the Inhlobane, and Potter had often been up on it. I asked whether, if we should have the bad luck after taking the mountain to see Cetewayo's army advancing, we could get down on the North side, and Mr. Potter assured me that we could,—by leading our horses. Piet Uys was confident that Colonel Buller would get up, without serious loss, and we agreed that, except in the probable contingency of the Zulu main army coming in sight, our operation ought to be a success; then Piet turning to me, said, "Kurnall, if you are killed I will take care of your children, and if I am killed you do the same for mine." We had heard, indeed, for several days that Kambula was to be attacked, but were informed that the Zulu Army could not leave till the 27th, as there had been a delay in "doctoring" one of the largest regiments. This was inaccurate. It had started on the 25th March.

CHAPTER XXX

1879—THE INHLOBANE, 28TH MARCH

The ride to Death—Buller surmounts the mountain—Fate of two heroic Coldstream Officers — Campbell and Barton — Major Leet, V.C.— Chicheeli's description of Barton's death—Buller's heroism—Ronald Campbell as tender hearted as he was brave.

AT 3 a.m. on the 28th I rode Eastward, with the Staff officers and escort. Captain Campbell and I were silent, but the two younger men chattered till I wondered whether their voices could reach the Zulus on the Inhlobane. When Ronald Campbell spoke on Lloyd's challenge for his thoughts, he replied, "I am hoping my wife is well and happy." Lloyd and Lysons, jubilant at the prospect of a fight, remarking on my silence, asked, "Are you doubtful, sir, of our getting up to the top of the mountain?" "Oh no, we shall get up." "Then, of what are you thinking?" "Well, which of you will be writing to my wife to-night, or about which of you young men I shall be writing to parents or wife?"

Colonel Buller, to avoid risk of being surprised, had shifted bivouac twice during the night, but at daylight we struck his track and followed it. We met a Squadron of his Force coming Westwards, the Commandant having lost his way the previous night, and I directed him to move to the sound of the firing, which was now audible on the North - East face of the mountain, where we could just discern the rear of Colonel Buller's column mounting the summit. I followed the Squadron, but when it came under fire, as it did not advance rapidly, I passed to the front, the track at first being easy to follow, from worn grass and dead horses of Colonel Buller's command lying on it. Hard rock now replaced the beaten down grass, and as we came under fire I unconsciously, by leading directly towards the rocks whence the bullets came, missed the easier gradient, up which Buller's men had ridden, losing only one officer. The ground was now steep and very rugged, so we dismounted and put the horses of my White and Black escort in a cattle kraal, the walls of which were 2½ feet high. Campbell invited me to leave my horse. I said, "No; I am a bad walker," and pulled it after me, Mr. Lloyd being close on my left hand. Half a dozen of the foremost of the Irregulars had dismounted sooner, and followed me until Lloyd and I were within 100 feet of the crest of the mountain, and we came under well-directed fire in our front, and from both flanks, the enemy being concealed behind huge boulders of rock.

The men of the Squadron 200 yards behind us now opened fire, and Mr. Lloyd said, " I am glad of that, for it will make the Zulus shoot badly." He had scarcely spoken these words when a Zulu rose up from behind a rock 50 yards above us, and, touching Lloyd with my elbow, I observed, " He won't hit us in the face," for he laid his gun directly at my waistbelt. He fired, and Lloyd fell back, exclaiming, " I am hit!" "Badly?" "Yes, very badly; my back's broken!" I tried to lift him on my shoulders, but he was taller than I, and the ground being steep I stumbled, when Captain Campbell climbing up said, " Let me lift him," and carried him on his shoulder 50 yards down to where the horses were standing in the cattle kraal, under the walls of which the escort were sheltering. I climbed a few yards higher, when a Zulu fired at me from underneath a rock, 20 yards distant. The charge struck my horse immediately in front of the girth, killing it instantaneously, and as it fell, striking my shoulder with its head, knocked me down. I heard an exclamation from my comrades, and scrambling up called, " No, I am not hit!" and as they began climbing the hill, added, " Please stop where you are. I am coming down, for it's too steep to get on any farther, in this place." When I got down to the kraal, I saw Mr. Lloyd was dying. He could no longer speak; obtaining some brandy from Lysons, I tried to pour a little down his throat, but his teeth were already set.

I told Captain Campbell to order the Irregular horsemen,

II.—4

who were taking cover under rocks below us, to clear the caves from whence the firing had come which killed my horse. He found much difficulty in inducing the men to advance, as they alleged the position was unassailable; and eventually, leading four of my personal escort, with Lieutenant Lysons, he climbed up, Bugler Walkinshaw going with him. I called Walkinshaw back before he was out of sight, for I wanted help for Mr. Lloyd; and thus he, one of the bravest men in the Army, missed the chance of gaining the Victoria Cross. In a few moments one of the men told me that the cave was cleared, but that Ronald Campbell was dead. He had led the small party of three or four men, passing up a narrow passage only 2 feet wide between rocks 12 feet high for several yards, and was looking down into the cave, when a Zulu fired, almost touching him, and he fell dead. Lieutenant Lysons and Private Fowler,[1] 90th Light Infantry, undauntedly passing over the body, fired into the cave, and the few Zulus in it disappeared through another opening.

By the time the men brought Ronald Campbell's body down, Mr. Lloyd was dead. Telling Walkinshaw to put his ear down to his heart, he made sure, and then I tried to put the bodies up on my baggage animal. The fire from the rocks on all sides was fairly accurate, killing many out of the 21 ponies we had with us. As bullets were striking all round me on the stones, my pony moved every time I got Campbell's body on my shoulder. Walkinshaw, who was entirely unconcerned at the bullets, said, "If you will hold it, sir, I will put the bodies up"; and this he did.

It then occurred to me that in the wallets of the saddle under my horse, which was lying with all four feet in the air, was Campbell's wife's Prayer book, a small one I had borrowed before starting from Kambula, as my own was a large Church Service, and I said to Walkinshaw, "Climb up the hill, and get the prayer book in my wallets; while I do not want you to get shot for the saddle, you are to take all risks for the sake of the prayer book." He climbed up in a leisurely fashion, and, pulling the saddle from underneath the horse, brought it safely down on his head. We then moved down the mountain 300 yards, to find a spot on soil clear of rocks.

[1] They both received the Victoria Cross.

INHLOBANE, 28TH MARCH, 1879

COLONEL EVELYN WOOD TO LORD CHELMSFORD. "MR. LLOYD FELL MORTALLY WOUNDED AT MY SIDE—CAPTAIN CAMPBELL LEADING IN THE MOST GALLANT AND DETERMINED MANNER WAS SHOT DEAD. WE BROUGHT THEIR BODIES HALF-WAY DOWN THE HILL, WHERE WE BURIED THEM, STILL UNDER FIRE."

The operation of digging a grave was laborious, as our only implements were the assegais of the native escort, and when it had been completed to about 4 feet in depth, the men got flurried by the approach of some 300 Zulus from the Ityenteka Nek, and, lifting the bodies, placed them in the grave. It was not long enough, and although I realised the possibility of our having trouble with the approaching Zulus, yet as they were still 600 yards off and were most of them bad shots at that range, I had the bodies lifted out, and the grave made a proper length to receive them without the lower limbs being doubled up. When I was satisfied, I read an abridged form of the Burial Service from Mrs. Campbell's prayer book. We were now assisted by the fire of some of Colonel Buller's men, who, seeing our difficulty, opened on the advancing Zulus, and, being above them, checked their approach. The officer commanding the Irregulars asked permission to move down the hill to regain Colonel Buller's track, and by it he finally reached the summit without further casualties. He had lost only 6 men dead, and 7 wounded, up to this hour.

As all firing on top of the mountain had now ceased, I decided to move back, and see how the other column had fared. Passing one of the Irregulars who had been shot in the thigh, I put him up on one of the dead men's horses, and as there was no apparent hurry, Umtonga's men drove with us a flock of sheep and goats. We stopped occasionally to give the wounded man stimulants, being unconscious that the main Zulu Army was moving on our left, across, and towards our path. When we were under the centre of the mountain, Umtonga, whom I had sent out to a ridge on our danger flank, gesticulated excitedly, explaining by signs that there was a large army near us. Cantering up, I had a good view of the Force, which was marching in 5 columns, with the flanks advanced, and a dense Centre—the normal Zulu attack formation.

I sent Lieutenant Lysons to the officer commanding the western party with the following order :—

"BELOW THE INHLOBANE. 10.30 a.m. 28/3/79.

"There is a large army coming this way from the South. Get into position on the Zunguin Nek. E. W."

The plateau which Colonel Buller's force had cleared was 150 feet higher than the Lower Plateau on which the western column stood, but both parties saw the Zulu Army a considerable time before I did, as I was 1000 feet below them. Buller had seen it at 9 a.m., and the western force had seen it rather earlier, Buller being engaged in covering a party of 25 of the Frontier Light Horse under Captain Barton, Coldstream Guards, who were descending the eastern slope to bury one or two men killed in the assault. Sending word to Captain Barton to retire, Buller fell back to the western end of the mountain, and forming some selected men into a rear guard, he took them down the almost precipitous edge of the Upper Plateau. The path was down the apex of a salient angle, with long sides, and the head of the descent was well suited for defence. Buller's men had previously collected a great number of cattle, which had been driven down towards the Zunguin Nek at 7 a.m. Colonel Buller and all his party would have got safely away had not the Makulusi, and the men of the Regular regiment with it, taking courage at the advance of the Zulu Army, emerged from their caves and harassed the retreat, during which some valuable lives were lost. Colonel Buller came down, practically the last man, and was at the foot of the descent from the Upper Plateau, when, seeing men nearly surrounded by Zulus, he went back on two occasions, and brought out in succession two on his horse. Piet Uys came down with him, until he was one of his sons having difficulty with his horse, and, going back, was assegaied by a Zulu crouching behind him.[1]

---

[1] The death of Piet Uys was a great loss to us, and Lord Chelmsford supported the earnest representations I made in his favour, as did also Sir Bartle Frere, who knew a great deal about him. He was intensely Patriotic, and had done not only good service to No. 4 column, but to South Africa, for although he had opposed the Annexation, the justice of which he denied as regards his countrymen, he admitted its necessity in the interests of the country at large, and he lent all his great influence, in opposition to many of his oldest and dearest friends, in pressing on the attention of his countrymen their duty in combatting our savage foes. He had armed, equipped, mounted, and provisioned his numerous family at his own expense, bringing all his sons into the field. He had persistently refused to accept pay for himself, or for any of his relatives, who, after his death, declined to accept the arrears of pay which I offered. He constantly acted as Arbitrator in compensation cases for damage done in the operations to the property of Dutchmen, and no decision was ever questioned by the sufferers, or by myself, who had to decide on

THE INHLOBANE, 28TH MARCH

About 80 of the First Battalion of Wood's Irregulars were overtaken and killed, and with them, to my great regret, Captain Potter, and Lieutenant Williams[1] of the 58th regiment. The main Zulu Army being exhausted by their march, halted near where Vryheid now stands, but some of their mounted men came on, and a few of the more active and younger footmen. Before leaving camp I had given orders for a barricade of planks, 5 feet high, to be erected, and securely bolted into the ground with supporting struts, to run between the redoubt and the south end of the cattle laager, to stop a rush from the ravine on to the fort. To those who objected that the Zulus would charge and knock it down by the weight of their bodies, I replied it would cause a delay of several minutes, during which 300 or 400 rifles, at 250 yards range, ought to make an additional barricade of human bodies, and I now sent an order to the Senior officer in camp, to chain up the waggons, and to continue the strengthening of the barricade. I wrote I had seen between 20,000 and 25,000 Zulus, and remained on the Zunguin Mountain till 7 p.m., hoping to cover the retreat of any more of our men who might come up, being particularly anxious about Captain Barton,[2] of whom we had

---

the claim. When one of his own farms was accidentally damaged, he would not allow it to be reported. I asked for 36,000 acres of Government land to be set apart for his nine children, and was supported in my request by the High Commissioner, whose last official letter before leaving Natal some months later was to urge on the Colonial Office the importance of giving effect to my recommendation; but I doubt if it would ever have been carried into effect had I not been afforded the opportunity of stating the case personally to Her Gracious Majesty the Queen, who ensured the provision being made.

[1] When the latter joined me, not very long before, I had a very favourable report of him from the Assistant Military Secretary, Colonel North Crealock, and my experience during the few days in which he worked under my command fully justified it.

[2] I tell now the manner of Robert Barton's noble end, although it was fourteen months later that I obtained the details. He had shown not only distinguished courage, but in actions great humanity, and in the previous January nearly lost his life in trying to take a Zulu prisoner, the man firing his gun so close to Barton as to burn the skin off his face.

When, on receipt of Colonel Buller's warning, he descended the mountain, he trotted on westward, followed by the men of the Irregular Squadron who had been with me at the eastern end, and who, before I returned, had gained the summit without further loss. As they reached the western base of the mountain, some of the Ngobamakosi regiment headed them, and they tried to cut their way through, but, after losing some

had no news since he descended the eastern end of the mountain.

I never knew until that day the depth of regard which Buller felt for me. I was sitting on the summit of the Zunguin range when he climbed up it, and, seeing me suddenly, uttered so fervent a "Thank God!" that I asked for what he was thankful, and he explained that he thought I had been cut off at the eastern end of the mountain. It rained heavily on the evening of the 28th. All the mounted men had been on the move day and night since the 23rd, when we went to Luneberg; but at 9 p.m., when a straggler came in to say that there were some Europeans coming back by Potter's Store, Redvers Buller immediately saddled up, and, taking out led horses, brought in 7 men, who were, as we believed, the sole survivors of the parties at the east end of the mountain.

So far as I know, the only officer who got down the western end of the Inhlobane on horseback was Major Leet, who commanded the 1st battalion Wood's Irregulars. Six men, retraced their steps eastwards, and, though many fell, Barton got safely down over the Ityenteka Nek.

When I was with Her Imperial Majesty the Empress Eugénie, in May 1880, on the Ityatosi River, I asked Sirayo's son, Melokazulo,[1] who was a mounted officer of the Ngobomakosi tribe, if he could tell me whether any of his men had killed my friend, whose body had never been found. He said, "No; for I followed you, although you were not aware of it, and, when failing to overtake you, I turned back, I was too late to overtake those who were going eastward, and the pursuit was taken up by mounted men of the Umcityu regiment. I know a man named Chicheeli, who was a mounted officer of the Umcityu, and I believe saw what took place." I said, "Send for him," to which he replied, "He won't come unless you send for him. He will believe Lakuni."[2] Chicheeli came, and talked quite frankly, giving me a still higher opinion of the powers of observation of the savage than I already had. After describing the coat and other clothes that Barton wore, he said, "The White man was slightly pitted by smallpox." Now I had lived at Aldershot for two years in daily intercourse with Robert Barton, and at once said, "Then it is not the man I mean." Chicheeli, however, declined to be shaken from his statement, and repeated that the marks on his face were slight, but that there was no doubt that he had had smallpox. Opening my portmanteau, I took out a cabinet-sized photograph and a magnifier, and, examining the face closely, I then perceived that what I had for two years taken to be roughness of skin was really the marks of smallpox, which Chicheeli had noticed as he stood over the dead body.

Chicheeli told me that on the Ityenteka Nek he followed several White men and

---

[1] Reported as having been killed in Bambaata's rebellion, 1906.
[2] This was my name among the Zulus. The word describes the hard wood of which Zulus make their knobkerries, or bludgeons.

weeks earlier, at the Athletic Sports, we had a Tug-of-war between the officers of the 13th and 90th Light Infantry, captained by Leet and myself, and as the 90th pulled over the 13th Leet wrenched his knee out of joint, and I had told him to remain in camp on the 27th. This, however, he did not do, and as he could only hobble, he tried, and successfully, to ride down the mountain. I believe he got down before the counter attack; but while on the Lower Plateau, and being followed up closely by the enemy, he showed distinguished courage in going back to help a dismounted officer, for which he received the Victoria Cross.

On the night of the 28th March, as I sat at dinner, I could not keep my mind off Ronald Campbell, who had sat opposite me for three months, and had anticipated every want with the utmost devotion, and I cannot write now, even after the lapse of a quarter of a century, without pain of the loss the army sustained when my friend fell. As I visited the outposts at least twice every night from the date of Isandwhana till after Ulandi, 4th July, my clothes were nearly always damp from walking through the long grass, which, when not wet from the

killed them, one man, as he approached, turning his carbine and shooting himself. When he, with several others, got down on the plain, 7 miles from the mountain, he overtook Captain Barton, who had taken Lieutenant Poole up on his horse. He fired at them, and when the horse, being exhausted, could no longer struggle under the double weight, the riders dismounted and separated. Chicheeli first shot Lieutenant Poole, and was going up towards Barton, when the latter pulled the trigger of his revolver, which did not go off. Chicheeli then put down his gun and assegai, and made signs to Barton to surrender. I asked, " Did you really want to spare him ? " " Yes," he replied ; " Cetewayo had ordered us to bring one or two Indunas down to Ulandi, and I had already killed seven men." Barton lifted his hat, and the men were close together when a Zulu fired at him, and he fell mortally wounded; and then, said Chicheeli, "I could not let anyone else kill him, so I ran up and assegaied him." I said, "Do you think you can find the body?" "Yes, certainly," he said; "but you must lend me a horse, for it is a day and a half."[1] I sent Trooper Brown, V.C., with him next day, and, with the marvellous instinct of a savage, he rode to within 300 yards of the spot where fourteen months previously he had killed my friend, and then said, " Now we can off-saddle, for we are close to the spot," and, casting round like a harrier, came in less than five minutes upon Barton's body, which had apparently never been disturbed by any beast or bird of prey. The clothes and boots were rotten and ant-eaten, and tumbled to pieces on being touched. Brown cut off some buttons from the breeches, and took a Squadron Pay book from the pocket filled with Barton's writing, and then buried the remains, placing over them a small wooden cross painted black, on which is cut "Robert Barton, killed in action, 28th March 1879," and then he and Chicheeli buried the body of Lieutenant Poole.

---

[1] Equal to 60 miles.

heavy rain which fell constantly through the months of February and March, was soaked with dew, and I had forbidden either of the Staff accompanying me, because, as we slept in our boots and clothes, anyone who walked round the sentries got saturated up to the waistbelt. I had, however, once or twice suspected that I was being followed, and one night, turning suddenly in the darkness, I knocked against a man, and then recognised Campbell's voice, as he answered my challenge. I said sharply, "Why are you disobeying orders? What are you doing here?" "I have always the fear, sir," he replied, "that one night you won't hear the challenge of one of the sentries, and you will be shot." On two occasions on which I was in bed with fever for three days, he nursed me as tenderly as could a woman, and I never saw anyone play a more heroic part than he did on the morning of the 28th March 1879.

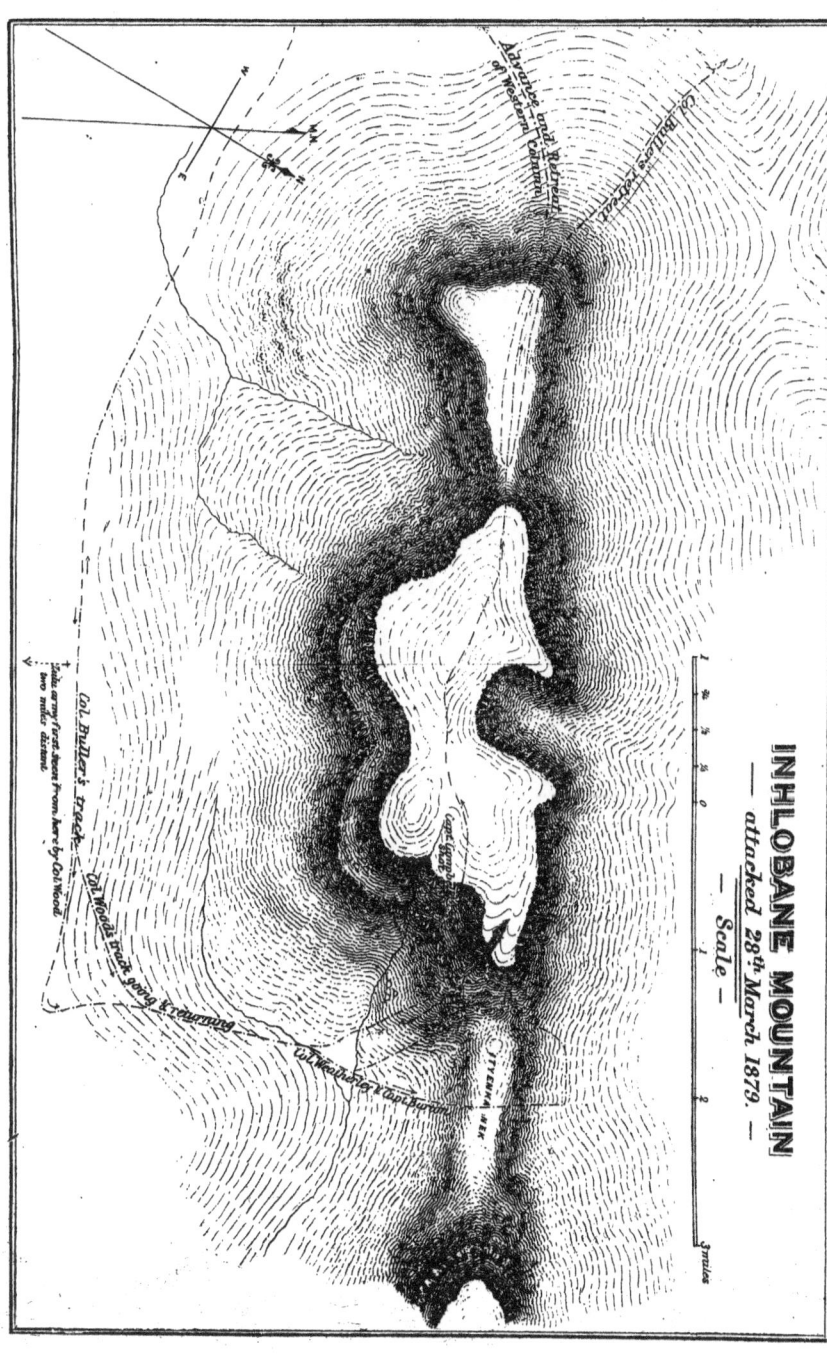

CHAPTER XXXI

1879—KAMBULA, 29TH MARCH

Mist delays the advance of 23,000 Zulus—Piet Uys having fallen, Burghers leave us — The position under the Ngaba-ka-Hawane — Bigge — Nicholson—Slade—Buller teases Zulu Right Wing into a premature attack—I shoot three Zulu leaders in five successive shots—Hackett's Counter attack—His wound—His character—Death of Arthur Bright —I recommend Buller for the Victoria Cross.

I WENT round the sentries twice during the night, although I did not anticipate an attack until daylight, feeling sure the large masses of Zulus I had seen could not make a combined movement in the dark. When the night was past, the mist was so thick that we could not see more than a hundred yards. Captain Maude, who had temporarily replaced Ronald Campbell, asked me if the wood-cutting party of two companies was to go out as usual. Our practice was that they should not start till the front was reported clear for 10 miles, but until the sun came out there was no chance of the mist clearing off, and after thinking over the matter I decided the party should go, because we had never been able to get up reserve of fuel, and it was possible the Zulus might not attack that day. Our men would certainly fight better in two or three days' time if they had cooked food, and so I accepted the risk, but ordered two subalterns to keep ponies saddled to recall the companies in good time. Fortunately, though 5 miles away, the place was behind the camp.

All the mounted men had been continuously in the saddle since daylight on the 23rd, and it was difficult to get a trot out of the horses;[1] but Commandant Raaf went out with 20 men to the edge of the Zunguin plateau, and when the mist

---

[1] One of my ponies had carried me 94 miles in fifty-four hours, without corn, getting only the grass he could find when knee-haltered.

lifted, about 10 a.m., reported the Zulu Army was cooking on the Umvolosi and a tributary stream.[1] He remained out himself to warn me when they advanced.

All our arrangments in camp were perfected, with the exception of the barricade, to which we had added some strengthening pieces.

The Dutchmen came to see me early in the day, to say that, as Piet Uys was dead they wished to go home, and, except half a dozen who had hired waggons to us, they departed. Great pressure had been brought on my gallant friend Piet to induce him to withdraw from the column. His friends told him he was a traitor to their cause, but Uys always replied that although he disliked our policy, he thought it was the duty of a White man to stand up with those who were fighting the Zulus.[2]

Between 80 and 100 of Uhamu's men, who held on to the cattle they had driven from the Inhlobane, were overtaken and killed near the Zunguin Mountain on the 28th, but in the battalion which had gone out with Colonel Buller there were very few casualties. Nevertheless, Zulu-like after a reverse, the two battalions of Wood's Irregulars, about 2000 strong, dispersed.

I spent the forenoon, after saying good-bye to the Uys detachment, in writing a report on the previous day's reconnaissance, and letters to the bereaved relatives of those who had fallen.

At 11 o'clock Raaf reported that the Zulu Army was advancing, and I sent the officers to recall the wood-cutting parties, and had all the Trek oxen driven in, except about 200 which had strayed away from the drivers, whose duty it was to herd them. We got the two companies back in time for the men to have a hasty dinner before the attack actually began. The commanding officers asked if the battalions might not be told to hurry their dinners, but I said, "No; there is plenty of time," for by the system enforced in the column during daylight, as Lord Chelmsford saw five weeks later, our

[1] Where Vryheid now stands.
[2] When in December 1878 I was endeavouring to get Dutchmen to join, some queried my impartiality as Arbitrator in deciding claims for captured cattle—the South African form of prize money,—and I rejoined, "I'll not take any for my personal use." I gave my share towards erecting a memorial to Piet Uys in Utrecht, and all the soldiers of the column contributed.

tents could be struck, and the men be in position in the laager, within seventy seconds from the last sound of the "Alert."

At 1.30 p.m. Colonel Buller suggested he should go out and harry the Zulus into a premature attack, and this he did admirably.

We had shifted camp several times for sanitary reasons. My friends the Dutchmen could never be persuaded to use the latrines, although I had one dug specially for them; moreover, Wood's Irregulars and the oxen had so fouled the ground as to induce fever, unless the camp was often shifted. The position in which we received the attack was on a ridge running in a south-westerly direction, an under feature of the Ngaba-ka-Hwane Mountain.

The waggons of the 13th Light Infantry formed the right front and flank, 4 guns were in front of the centre, and the 90th Light Infantry on the left. The Horse Lines were in the middle, and the rear face of the Laager was held by the Irregular Horse; 280 yards in front, on ground 20 feet higher than the Laager, was a redoubt, its main lines of fire being in a northerly and southerly direction, while 150 yards to the right front of the main Laager was a cattle Laager, into which we crammed upwards of 2000 oxen. The outer side of it stood on the edge of a deep ravine, into which the Laager drained. The wheels of the waggons were securely chained together, and the space between the forepart of one and the rear of the other was rendered difficult of ingress by the poles (or dyssel-booms), being lashed across the intervals.

Two guns under Lieutenant Nicholson were placed *en barbette*,[1] at the front end of the Redoubt. The other four guns came into action under Lieutenant A. Bigge[2] and Lieutenant Slade,[3] by sections on the ridge, connecting the Redoubt with the main Laager. The men belonged to Garrison Companies, but I have never known a battery so exceptionally fortunate in its Subalterns. Lieutenant Nicholson, standing on the gun platform, fought his guns with the unmoved stoical courage habitual to his nature.

Major Tremlett was renowned as a fearless sportsman, and both Bigge and Slade were unsurpassable; they with their

---

[1] Gun placed on raised ground, thus firing over the parapet.
[2] Now Colonel Sir Arthur Bigge, K.C.B.
[3] General F. Slade, C.B., lately Inspector-General, Royal Artillery.

gunners stood up in the open from 1.30 p.m. till the Zulus retreated at 5.30 p.m., and by utilising the ridge were enabled to find excellent targets with cover during the first attack on the southern slope, and later on the northern slope, and suffered but little loss.

The direction of the Zulu advance was, speaking generally, from south-east, but when they came in sight they stretched over the horizon from north-east to south-west, covering all approaches from the Inhlobane to Bemba's Kop. When still 3 miles distant, 5000 men moved round to our Left and attacked the side held by the 90th Light Infantry, prior to the remainder of the Zulu Army coming into action. This fortunate circumstance was due to Colonel Buller's skilful tactical handling of the mounted men, whom he took out and dismounted half a mile from the Zulus. The Umbonambi regiment suffered a galling fire for some time, and then, losing patience, rushed forward to attack, when the horsemen, remounting, retired 400 yards, and, repeating their tactics, eventually brought on a determined attack from the Zulu right flank. The Umbonambi followed up the horsemen until they were within 300 yards of the Laager, when their further advance was checked by the accurate firing of the 90th Light Infantry, greatly assisted by the enfilading fire poured in from the northern face of the Redoubt. I saw a fine tall Chief running on well in front of his men, until, hit in the leg, he fell to the ground. Two men endeavoured to help him back as he limped on one foot. One was immediately shot, but was replaced by another, and eventually all three were killed.

We now sent the Artillery horses back into the Laager, keeping the guns in the open, on the ridge between the Redoubt and the main Laager. I had instructed the officer commanding to serve his guns till the last moment, and then, if necessary, leaving them in the open, take his men back to the Laager, which was within 188 yards.

The attack on our Left had so slackened as to give me no further anxiety, when at 2.15 p.m. heavy masses attacked our Right Front and Right Rear, having passed under cover up the deep ravine, on the edge of which the cattle Laager stood.

Some 40 Zulus, using Martini-Henry rifles which they had taken at Isandwhlana, occupied ground between the edge

KAMBULA, 29TH MARCH

of the ravine and the rear of the Laager, from the fire of which they were partly covered by the refuse from the Horse Lines which had been there deposited, for, with the extraordinary fertility of South Africa, induced by copious rains and burning midday sun, a patch of mealies 4 feet high afforded cover to men lying down, and it was from thence that our serious losses occurred somewhat later. The Zulu fire induced me to withdraw a company of the 13th, posted at the right rear of the cattle Laager, although the front was held by another half company for some time longer.

I could see from where I stood on the ridge of land just outside the fort, leaning against the barricade, which reached down to the cattle Laager, that there were large bodies in the ravine, the Ngobamakosi in front, and 30 men (leaders) showed over the edge, endeavouring to encourage the Regiment to leave the shelter, and charge. I, in consequence, sent Captain Maude to order out two companies of the 90th, under Major Hackett, with instructions to double over the slope down to the ravine with fixed bayonets, and to fall back at once when they had driven the Zulus below the crest.

A 13th man coming away late from the cattle Laager, not having heard the order to retire, was shot by the Zulus lying in the refuse heap, and followed by four from the cattle Laager. I was running out to pick him up, when Captain Maude exclaimed, "Really it isn't your place to pick up single men," and went out himself, followed by Lieutenants Lysons and Smith, 90th Light Infantry; they were bringing the man in, who was shot in the leg, when, as they were raising the stretcher, Smith was shot through the arm. I was firing at the time at a leader of the Ngobamakosi, who, with a red flag, was urging his comrades to come up out of the ravine, and assault the Laager. Private Fowler, one of my personal escort, who was lying in the ditch of the fort, had asked me, "Would you kindly take a shot at that Chief, sir? it's a quarter of an hour I am shooting him, and cannot hit him at all." He handed me his Swinburne-Henry carbine, and looking at the sight, which was at 250 yards, I threw the rifle into my shoulder, and as I pressed it into the hollow, the barrel being very hot, I pulled the trigger before I was ready,—indeed, as I was bringing up the muzzle from the Zulu's feet. Hit in the pit of the stomach, he fell over backwards: another leader at once took his place, cheering his comrades on. At him I was obliged to fire, unpleasantly close to the line of our officers leading the counter attack. I saw the bullet strike some few yards over the man's shoulder, and, laying the carbine next time at the Zulu's feet, the bullet struck him on the breastbone. As he reeled lifeless backward, another leader seized and waved the flag, but he knelt only, though he continued to cheer. The fourth shot struck the ground just over his shoulder, and then, thinking the carbine was over-sighted,[1] I aimed on the ground 2 yards short, and the fifth bullet struck him on the chest in the same place as his predecessor had been hit. This and the counter attack so damped the ardour of the leaders that no further attempt was made in that direction, although several brave charges were made to the south of the cattle Laager, against the right flank of the Redoubt. While I was firing at the leaders of the Ngobamakosi Regiment, who, from the ground falling away towards the ravine, were out of sight of the main Laager, the two companies 90th Light Infantry came out at a steady "Double," Major Hackett leading, guided by Captain Woodgate, who knew exactly where I wished the companies to go, and how far the offensive movement was to be carried out. Lieutenant Strong, who had recently joined us, ran well in front of his company, sword in hand, and the Zulus retired into the ravine. The companies, however, were fired on heavily from the refuse heaps, at 350 yards range, and Major Hackett was shot through the head; Arthur Bright fell mortally wounded, and the Colour-Sergeant of Bright's company, Allen, a clever young man, not twenty-three years of age, who had been wounded in the first attack, and, having had his arm dressed, rejoined his company as it charged, was killed.

    The Umcityu and Unkandampenvu had charged so determinedly over the open on our Left front, as had part of the Ngobamakosi up the slope to the Redoubt, from the south side of the cattle Laager, that I did not at first realise the full effect of Hackett's counter attack, and apprehended the mass still crouching below the crest would rush the Right face of the Laager. They would have had some 200 yards to pass over

[1] We paced it afterwards—195 yards.

from the edge of the ravine to the waggons, but, owing to the ground falling rapidly, would have been under fire from the Laager for 100 yards only. I therefore went into the main Laager, being met by Colonel Buller, who asked me cheerily for what I had come, and I replied, "Because I think you are just going to have a rough and tumble"; but Hackett's charge had done even more than I had hoped, and having looked round I went back to my position just outside the fort.

At 5.30 p.m., when the vigour of the attack was lessening, I sent Captain Thurlow and Waddy's companies of the 13th Light Infantry to the right rear of the cattle Laager, to turn out some Zulus who were amongst the oxen, which they had, however, been unable to remove; and I took Captain Laye's[1] company to the edge of the krantz on the right front of the Laager, where they did great execution with the bayonet amongst the Undi Regiment, who were now falling back. I then sent a note to Buller, asking him to take out the mounted men, which he did, pursuing from 5.30 p.m. till dark, and killing, as it happened, chiefly the Makulusi tribe, who had been his foes on the previous day.

When the enemy fell back in the direction in which they had come, they were so thick as to blot out all signs of grass on the hillside, which was covered by their black bodies, and for perhaps the only time in anyone's experience it was sound to say, "Don't wait to aim, fire into the black of them."

At 3 a.m. on the 30th, one or two shots from the Outpost line roused the camp, and the Colonial corps opened a rapid fire to the Front, immediately over the heads of the two line battalions and artillery, who stood perfectly steady. Rain was falling, so, while Maude was ascertaining the cause of the firing, which was a Zulu who, having concealed himself till then, jumped up close to one of our sentries, I sat in an ambulance near the battery until the Colonials having put three bullets into the top of it, I thought it would be better to get wet than be shot by our own men. After five minutes the firing was stopped. The scare was excusable, for the nerves of the mounted men had been highly strung for some hours, a fourth of those who had ridden up the Inhlobane having been killed.

In the next few days we buried 785 men within 300

[1] Now General Laye, C.B.

yards of our Laager, which we were afterwards obliged to shift on account of the number of bodies which lay unseen in the hollows. We learnt after the battle that when the Zulus saw our tents go down they thought it was in preparation for flight, and that unsteadied their Right Wing.[1] They never fought again with the same vigour and determination.

The Line battalions were very steady, expending in four hours on an average 33 rounds a man; though that evening I heard that some of them had thought the possibility of resisting such overwhelming numbers of brave savages, 13 or 14 to one man, was more than doubtful. I had no doubt, and lost all sense of personal danger, except momentarily, when, as on five occasions, a plank of the hoarding on which I leant was struck. This jarred my head, and reminded me that the Zulus firing from the refuse heap in the right rear of the Laager were fair shots. A few had been employed as hunters, and understood the use of the Martini rifles taken at Isandwhana.

Besides the men killed, we had 70 wounded, and amongst them my friend Robert Hackett. Born in King's County, Ireland, he was one of several soldier brothers. He was decidedly old-fashioned, and I have now before me an indignant letter, written four years before his terrible wound, urging me to use my influence to stop what he regarded as the craze for examining officers like himself, nearly forty years of age. He pointed out the injustice of expecting old dogs to learn these new tricks, and argued that as he had bought his commission without any liability to be examined for promotion, it was unjust to exact any such test from him now; and added that, as no Staff appointment would tempt him to leave the battalion, and it was generally admitted that he was efficient in all Regimental duties, all he wanted was to be left alone, and not troubled with books.

He was, indeed, a good Regimental officer; he managed the Mess, the Canteen, and the Sports club, and, indeed, was a pillar of the regiment. He kept a horse, but seldom, or never, rode, putting it generally at the disposal of the subaltern of his

---

[1] Zulu Chiefs told me in 1880, when they saw our tents struck at 1.15 p.m., they made certain of victory, believing we were about to retreat, and they were greatly depressed by our stubborn resistance.

company. He played no games, and lived for nothing but the welfare of the men of his Company, and the reputation of the Regiment.

At Aldershot, in 1873, he gave me a lesson which I have never forgotten. I was senior Major, being in temporary command of the Regiment, and spoke to him about three young officers who did not pay their mess bills when due, and when the delay recurred the third time, I said, "Unless these bills are paid to-morrow morning, you will put the three officers under arrest." The Commanding Officer being away, I was in the Orderly-room when he reported, "The bills you spoke of have been paid, sir." "You see," I remarked, "it only required a little firmness on our part to get the Queen's Regulations obeyed." He saluted, but said nothing, and when I saw him in the afternoon I said, "Hackett, I do not quite understand your reticence. Why don't you help me in making these young officers pay their bills by the proper time? Why do they delay?" "Oh, it's not wilful, sir," he replied—"only impecuniosity." "Oh, that can't be the case," I argued, "because when they had to pay, they paid." He only answered "Yes"; but something in his tone made me say, "If you are right, can you explain how they got the money at such short notice?" "That's quite simple, sir," he answered; "I paid the bills myself." After this I thought less of the effect of my firmness!

When I visited him in the Hospital the morning after the action, he was a piteous sight, for a bullet had passed from one temple to another, and, without actually hitting the eyes, had protruded the eyeballs, injuring the brain. He was unconscious of the terrible nature of his wounds, possibly from pressure on the brain, and observed to me, "Your Commissariat officers are very stingy in not lighting up this Hospital tent; the place is in absolute darkness." We were all so fond of him that nobody ventured to tell him the truth, and it was not until he was in Maritzburg that the doctors begged a lady, who was a constant visitor at the Hospital, to break the news to him.

When we received, on the 4th January 1879, the Gazette of the Promotions and Honours for the suppression of the Gaika outbreak, I addressed the Military Secretary as follows: "Lord Chelmsford writes to me a kind letter about the omission of my name when honours were being served out, but I am not likely to trouble you on my own account, especially as one Commanding Officer rewarded has never been within 500 miles of bloodshed, but I confess Brevet Major Hackett might have attracted your, or His Royal Highness', favourable eye. A man of long service, old enough to be father of the junior Captains, he has, I believe, been for many years the bed-rock of the 90th Light Infantry. An excellent Regimental officer, ever ready to counsel or aid those of his brothers whose follies, or scanty purses, brought them into trouble. He has successfully neutralised the bad points of two Commanding Officers."

When in the Hospital at the close of the action, I did not speak to Arthur Bright, who was dozing, but after we had had something to eat I sent Maude over to see how he was going on. Maude came back saying that he was sensible, but very depressed, although the doctors said a bullet which had passed through his thigh had not touched any artery or bone. The two doctors had more than they could do, and may therefore be readily excused for not having noticed that the other thigh bone had been shattered; and Bright died, happily without pain, before morning. Over six feet in height, and very handsome, he exercised, through his high moral tone, great influence amongst the subalterns. He had been captain of a boat at Eton, was our boldest and best Polo player, and was a gifted draughtsman, possessing also a beautiful tenor voice. He had only fifteen months' service when he took command of the company of which Maude was the Captain. This company had been unfortunate, for Stevens, its Captain, was dangerously wounded on the 30th April 1878, when Saltmarshe was killed; and now, in one day it had lost its only duty officer, Bright, and the gallant Colour-Sergeant Allen.

For two or three days after our victory I had some anxiety on account of our convoy of wounded men, which Buller escorted to the Blood River. My battalion was unfortunate, for, in addition to the two officers of the 90th whom we buried, we sent away three wounded in the convoy. I was obliged to keep Maude to help me, in spite of his company being without an officer.

Lieutenant Smith, whose arm was badly hit, was invalided

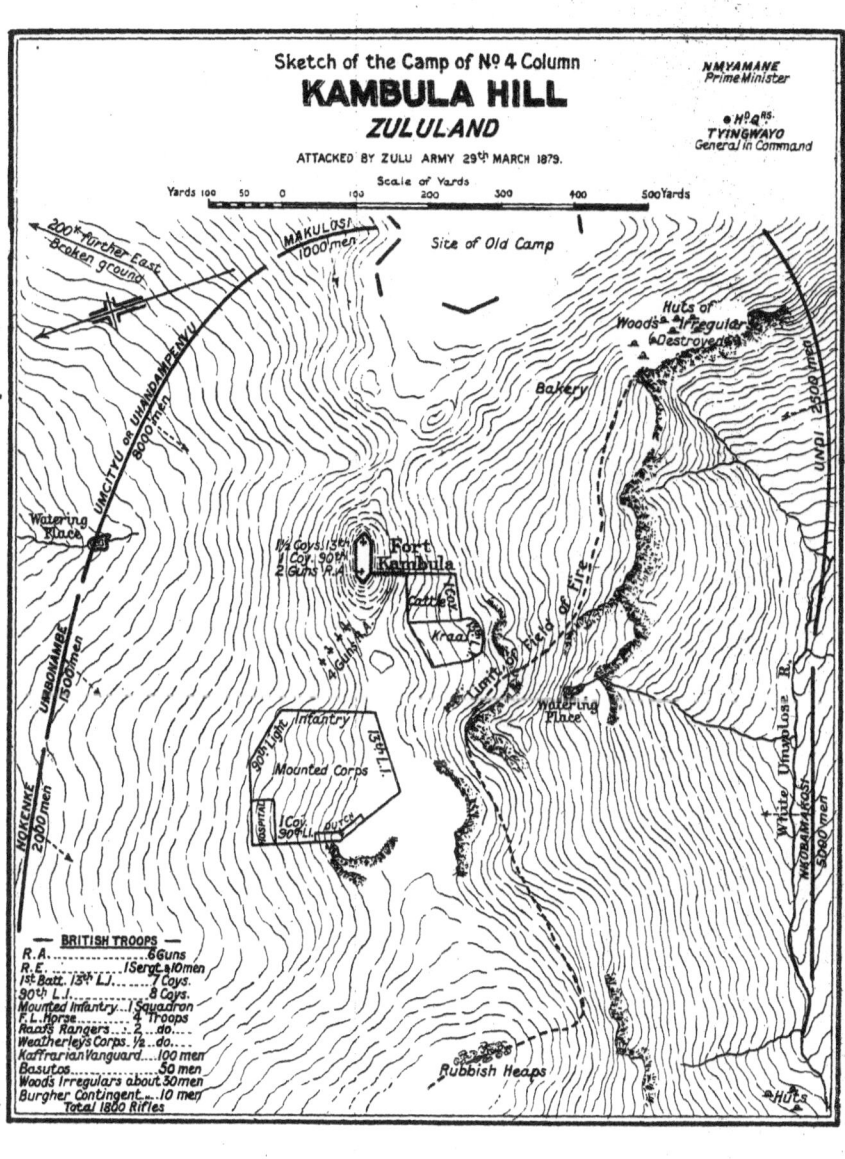

to England. After seeing his family, he went to stay with Lady Wood, and, while he was giving his account of the fight in the drawing-room, his soldier servant was telling my wife's servants about it in the kitchen; and, alluding to the time when I walked across the open to the Laager, he said, " We saw three Zulus following him, and we knew he couldn't hear 'em, so we turned our faces away that we might not see him assegaied!" " Ah," the cook said, with deep emotion, " that would have been a sad day for his wife and children!" when the soldier observed cheerfully, " Oh, we weren't thinking of them, or of him either, for the matter of that, but what would have become of *us* if 'e'd been killed?"

I heard from Lord Chelmsford, who said he observed in my official report of my attack on the Inhlobane that I had made no reference to his having induced it; and, while thanking him for his generosity, I replied that I considered I was bound to help him, and that the operation I undertook was, moreover, feasible, and would have been carried out without any serious loss except for the coincidence of the approach of the Zulu main army.

30*th March.*—Although nearly all of Wood's Irregulars had deserted the previous evening, we still had the Zulus attached to the companies, as well as the drivers and fore-loupers of the waggons, and, knowing it was hopeless to expect them to bring in, without reward, any Zulus as prisoners, I made it known I would give a " stick " of tobacco for any wounded or unwounded Zulu who was brought into camp. During the fight it was difficult to spare wounded Zulus who could sit up, for, when I took out a company from the Redoubt for a counter attack at 5.30, an officer shouted, " Look out for that wounded Zulu behind you." He fired immediately, killing a soldier who followed me. When all resistance was over, I was anxious, not only for the sake of humanity, but in order to make an accurate report, to ascertain what regiments had attacked us. So I instructed our men to bring me, if possible, a representative of every Zulu regiment engaged.

Next morning, 15 or 20 grand specimens of savage humanity stood in front of me, while the interpreter took down their names and the names of the officers commanding the regiment to which they belonged, and we learnt that the Zulu army had numbered over 23,000 men. When I had obtained all the information I required, I said, " Before Isandwhlana, we treated all your wounded men in our Hospital, but when you attacked our camp, your brethren, our black patients, rose and helped to kill those who had been attending on them. Can any of you advance any reason why I should not kill you ? " One of the younger men, with an intelligent face, asked, " May I speak ? " " Yes." " There is a very good reason why you should not kill us. We kill you because it is the custom of the Black men, but it isn't the White men's custom ! " So, putting them in charge of an officer and a couple of Colonel Buller's men, I had them sent safely past our Outposts, as far as the Zunguin mountain.

We got in a considerable number of wounded Zulus, and as our Hospital establishment was not capable of dealing with our own cases, I was obliged to hand them over to their countrymen attached to the companies of infantry ; and to ensure the wounded men being well treated, I promised our Zulus an ox to eat at the end of the week. There was, however, but little animosity when once the fight was over, because all the border Zulus were so intermarried that we had cases of men fighting in Cetewayo's regiments against brothers in Wood's Irregulars.

It is not often that the narratives of victors and vanquished agree, so it is interesting to note that the Governor of Natal, in reporting to the High Commissioner on the 21st April, wrote :

" The whole of the Zulu border population have returned to their homes. In conversation with our Natives, they give accounts of the two days' fighting with Colonel Wood, which agree with the published accounts in every respect. The Zulu losses on the first day are stated to have been severe. The Europeans who fell selling their lives dearly."

I had heard many stories of the gallantry shown by Colonel Buller in the retreat from the western end of the Inhlobane, but I had some difficulty in arriving at anything definite, because he guarded closely all the mounted men from receiving orders except through him, and I knew from his character that he would repudiate the notion of having done anything more than his duty.

A few days after the fight he went out with a troop of the Frontier Light Horse to endeavour to find Captain Barton's body, but could not reach the spot, as he was opposed by Zulus in force, making a raid in the direction of Luneberg, carrying off cattle, and killing men, women, and children. While he was out I received written statements from Lieutenants D'Arcy and Everitt and trooper Rundall, whom he had rescued at the risk of his life, and their reports were verified by those of other officers who were present. This enabled me to put forward a strong recommendation that his name should be considered for the Victoria Cross. A day or two later, on his return from another raid, in which he had been unsuccessful, I said, as he was leaving the tent after making his report, "I think you may be interested in something I have written," and I handed him the letter-book. He was very tired, and observed somewhat ungraciously, "Some nonsense, I suppose!" to which I replied, "Yes, I think I have been rather eulogistic." When he handed me back the book his face was a study.

CHAPTER XXXII

1879—THE PRINCE IMPERIAL

Collecting Supplies and Transport—Summary justice on a dishonest trader—Mistaken identity—Fresh bread—Our system for baking—A practical lesson to a young officer—The Flying Column returns to Natal—An overworked Leader.

FIVE companies of the 80th Regiment now joined my column from Luneberg; and, the evening before they marched in, Buller came to me and asked if a protecting certificate might be given to his Regimental Sergeant-Major. " What do you mean ? " I asked. " Well, he is about the best man in the Frontier Light Horse," he replied, " but he has just been to me to say that he is a deserter from the 80th, and as he is sure to be recognised to-morrow, he intends to be off to-night, unless you will condone his offence, and give him a protecting certificate." This I did, and the man served with credit until the end of the war.

I spent the next two months in collecting provisions, not only for my own column, now numbering 2500 Europeans, but in anticipation of the wants of others, as I knew insufficient steps were being taken at Helpmakaar; and by the 15th May I had succeeded in collecting at Balte Spruit 100 days' food for 4000 Europeans, and a fortnight's food for the horses and animals of No. 4 Column.

In February, when the Column was encamped at Kambula, a trader, who had a brother-in-law in the Volksraad at Pretoria, came into camp with waggons, asking to be allowed to sell groceries to the troops. I saw the man, and he assured me that he had no alcohol of any description; but I would not allow him to unpack his waggons until he had given me a certificate in writing that his verbal statement was accurate.

In the evening I received a report that a small raiding party of Zulus was murdering natives to the north of Rorke's Drift, and I ordered Captain Maude to go with a few mounted men and two companies of Wood's Irregulars to the spot. At nine o'clock the party was still in camp, waiting for some of the natives who had not finished cooking, and I sent Ronald Campbell down to try and start them. He came on the trader, who was selling trade gin at 1s. a glass to the soldiers, some of whom were already drunk. Campbell had the man seized, and sent for me. There was a full moon, and I executed summary justice by its light: ordering the man to be tied up to the wheel of his own waggon, I sent for two buglers, and gave him two dozen lashes on the spot, upset the whole of his liquor (which must have been a considerable loss, for he had a large quantity under the groceries), and informed him that unless he trekked at daylight, I would impound his waggons and oxen for the rest of the campaign.

I received, a few weeks later, various legal letters concerning an action with Damages laid at £5000, to which I paid no attention, as I was in an enemy's country. The Administrator and I had interfered with the sale of liquor at Utrecht, and the trader, who got summary justice, also wished to " take the Law of me."

In the month of May I was riding one morning into Utrecht, attended by bugler Walkinshaw, when, a few miles to the north of Balte Spruit, we met a horseman, who, stopping me, asked if he " was on the right track to Colonel Wood's Camp, and also whether the road was safe ? " I told him he was quite safe until he got to Balte Spruit, as there was a Company there, but that after he turned out of the valley to the eastward, there was a certain amount of risk, unarmed people travelling only with an escort. " What sort of a man is this Colonel Wood ? " he asked. " Well," I replied, " some people like him, and some dislike him." " I have been told that he is very rough." " Yes, that is so, when he is vexed." " I am an officer of the High Court of the Transvaal, and I am going to him with a writ. Do you think he will be violent with me ? " " Oh no, I'm certain he won't." " Then you think there is no risk as far as he is concerned ? " " None whatever; but you had better not mention your business in the camp, as his own battalion is at

Kambula Hill, and it might be bad for you if the men got to know your errand." "Why? What do you think they would do to me—kill me?" "Oh no; the worst that would happen to you would be to be tarred and feathered." "I don't like this job that I am on. I think, if you'll allow me, I'd like to turn back and ride with you into Utrecht, and send the document by post." Accordingly we rode along together, and I showed him the post office in the little town before I went about my business.

Lord Chelmsford came to visit me early in May, and stopped for several days, bringing with him the Prince Imperial, who returned to me as a guest a fortnight later. The young Prince impressed me much by his soldier-like ideas and habits, and was unwearied in endeavouring to acquire knowledge and Military experience. The Prince accompanied Colonel Redvers Buller on some patrols, and on his return from one on the 21st May I observed at dinner, "Well, you have not been assegaied, as yet?" "No; but while I have no wish to be killed, if it were to be I would rather fall by assegai than bullets, as that would show we were at close quarters."

I went out to the north side of the Inhlobane and buried Charles Potter and Mr. Williams. Uhamus' men had stood bravely by the white men. Many dead Makulusi lay around, and Captain Potter's body was alongside that of a Chief of Uhamus' tribe. I was obliged to postpone till later the burial of Piet Uys, whose body lay on the lower plateau of the mountain, 1000 feet above us, as Makulusi held the ground.

Though my relations with the Commissariat Departments were friendly, it was, I thought, essential to write forcibly, and on the 25th April Lord Chelmsford supported my views in a letter. "It is of no use, however, thinking of Ulundi, until Commissariat and Transport are in better order."

I irritated the Heads of Departments—for there were "Heads" although there were no bodies—by my plain speaking. I represented frequently that an Ordnance Department scarcely existed, and that the Hospital arrangements were totally inadequate. I pointed out that No. 4 Column had been for a fortnight without castor-oil, in spite of the fact that there was a daily post from Newcastle to the Column, and that from Maritzburg up to Newcastle there were two mail carts weekly.

I was taken to task for having used the word "disgraceful," but maintained it, asserting that there was no other word which adequately expressed the want of system.

Eventually, after much expenditure of time occupied in angry correspondence with Civil authorities, showing that the natives sent to me from the Wakkerstroom district who had deserted, carrying away Government horses, guns, and blankets, had never been sent back, my friend Mr. Rudolph, the Landdrost, was placed over the two districts of Utrecht and Wakkerstroom, and then attention was paid to my requisitions.

Lord Chelmsford consulted me at this time with reference to an Expedition proposed against Sekukuni, although we were less prepared to undertake such than we were when the previous attack was abandoned in September. I wrote to his Lordship, " In my opinion we are not strong enough, either in Generals, Troops, or Departmental officers, to attempt more than we have on hand," and he decided that the matter must stand over until we had settled with Cetewayo.

No. 4 was now renamed "The Flying Column," and I was told during the month that I was to help General Newdigate by offering him the results of my experiences, and also by supplying him with waggons. This I did to the extent of 37, about the number I had then bought in the Free State, Lord Chelmsford writing to me that the 2nd Division would be unable to advance until I provided the waggons.

I had been cutting firewood and digging coal for General Newdigate, and from the 19th of the month sent to the Second Division 40,000 lbs. daily. By Rudolph's exertions I got Zulus to act as drivers, and was enabled to use the waggons which had been lying idle, and had already cost us in a short time £4000. As the nominal strength of the 2nd Division was only about 2500, we soon handed over as much coal as they could carry; its great economy consisted in that 1 lb. was of better value for cooking purposes than 3 lbs. of wood. I should have been ready to advance by the middle of May had not I been obliged to lend waggons, for I had collected sufficient to carry twenty-five days' food for men and ten days' mealies for horses.

A draft of 80 men for the 13th Light Infantry landed early in May, but only 45 came into the field, the others being invalided between Durban and Utrecht, a march of about 250 miles.

On the 1st of June we encamped on the Umvunyana River within a short distance of the 2nd Division, and I describe here the system by which I kept the Flying Column supplied with fresh bread throughout our advance, which was necessarily slow, to enable the cattle to graze.

I generally accompanied the Advance guard, and when satisfied there were no considerable force of the enemy within striking distance, the bakers with the ovens followed me in mule waggons. Having chosen the site for the camp, I personally selected the site for the bakery, which was at once dug out, and fires lighted. Although the weather was no longer as wet as it had been, yet we seldom got the first batch of bread out under eight hours, for if the "sponge" was put in before the ground was thoroughly dry, the bread was not fit for consumption. The bakers worked all night, and stopping behind the next day until the Rear guard moved off, baked up to the last moment; sleeping that day and the following night, they started again on the third day with the Advance guard, and thus worked throughout alternate nights. The boon to the Column was great. I sent a daily present to the Head Quarters Staff, and to General Newdigate, under whom I had served at Aldershot.

I attribute the health of the Flying Column to some extent to the fresh bread, but also to the fact that the men invariably had a meat breakfast. Early in June the Commissariat wrote to me complaining that I had overdrawn thousands of rations. This did not perturb me. Sending for Colonel Buller, I told him my difficulty; and, going out himself with a squadron, he returned in a few hours with enough cattle to repay our overdraw, and to leave a handsome surplus in the hands of the Commissariat.

Our difficulties may to some extent be realised by the statement that on the 1st June it took us two hours and a half to start our ox waggons, owing to the inexperience of the drivers; but in the evening we encamped near the 2nd Division, from which the Prince Imperial, with an escort of six Colonials, had gone out that morning on duty.

At sunset the British officer and four survivors of the party rode into the 2nd Division camp, reporting that the Prince, who had been sketching sites for camps, had been killed. Next morning we sent forward a party of Basutos, who picked up the Prince's body, shortly before a squadron of the 17th Lancers, sent out from the 2nd Division, arrived. I defer the story of his death, as I learned it from the mouths of the attacking party, 17 of whom told me the facts on the spot in the following year; but I may here state the body was unmutilated except for wounds, for he had fought until the end, and was pierced by eighteen assegais. Two White men were lying 50 yards from him.

The officer, arraigned before a Court-Martial for misbehaviour, alleged the Prince was in command of the party, but I have had a strange and convincing piece of evidence before me for many years, in the Prince's own hand-writing, that he was serving under the British officer, and was therefore in no sense responsible for the disaster. Light rain was falling early on the 1st June, and when the party started the Prince was wearing a Pocket Siphonia.[1] He had been unusually well taught; his plans submitted for redoubts to defend depôts showing not only great natural talent, but that he had thoroughly assimilated the sound instruction imparted at the Royal Military Academy at Woolwich. On previous patrols he had taken full notes, and on the 1st June had filled the sheet of a writing pad thus: "1st June.—Started from Itilezi to find camping-ground for 2nd Division; party under Captain ———"; and then follows an itinerary with a panoramic sketch, the last entry being dated 1.30 p.m. The Prince, tearing these notes off the pad, had put the paper into the ticket pocket of the waterproof; and when, after the war, various articles belonging to His Imperial Highness were recovered, the coat, having been sent to Chislehurst, was being sponged and straightened out, for the waterproofing had caused it to stick together, a lump in the ticket pocket was noticed, which was found to be the sheet of the writing pad. I was kept up very late that night, many correspondents coming to me to furnish Natives to ride to the nearest telegraph office with an account of the misfortune.

[1] A very light waterproof of the day, advertised: "To be carried in the pocket."

A young Transport officer appeared from the Base, and reported he had lost three of his waggons; disregarding the remonstrances of his superior officers, who wished me to send a conductor, I insisted on the young man going back himself. Although he did not find the waggons, which arrived safely next morning, yet the Transport officers realised that it was useless to come into the Flying Column camp until they had brought in all their party.

On the 5th June, when the two columns were encampéd 20 miles from Ibabanango, the Head Quarters Staff were having tea with me when my orderly officer Lysons arrived with a message from Redvers Buller. He was skirmishing with a large Zulu force, which was following him up. As the Staff departed, they shook me warmly by the hand, wishing me good luck. Taking out my watch, I laughed, saying " I am obliged to you, but you are much mistaken if you think we are going to have a fight. It is half-past three, and there are less than two hours of daylight; and, with the Zulus 5 miles off us, there is no chance of our being engaged to-night." My forecast was correct.

On the 7th of June the Flying Column was sent back to Natal to bring up more provisions, off-loading our food, and taking back the empty waggons of both forces. Oxen make no difficulty in crossing any place with an empty waggon, but as the rivers can only be entered and traversed at certain places, especially the Nondweni,[1] the crossing of such was a question of many hours, and gave rise to some anxiety. Although we now knew that Umbiline was dead, and that renegade Swazi had been our most active foe on the sources of the White Umvolosi, I nevertheless kept two squadrons out 10 miles on the north, or danger flank; and to ensure them being on the alert, always visited them before daylight, which gave me little opportunity for sleep; but we arrived without incident at Landtman's Drift on the 9th of June. We started back again on the 13th, and as I had just received a report that our scouts covering the coal-cutting parties had been driven in, considering that I had 660 vehicles to convoy, my position was one of considerable anxiety. On the veldt they were able to travel fifteen abreast; but when we crossed the Nondweni on

[1] Locally called the Upoko.

the 16th there were only three practical places, and each required repairing parties of a hundred men with pick and shovel. The drivers all knew which was the danger flank, and I foresaw that they would try to cut in as the front of the Column became reduced from fifteen to three waggons, and therefore placed officers on the top of the steep bank of the river to ensure that the waggons had halted, and descended in regular rotation; for once a collision occurred on a slope, the oxen telescoped, and it took us a quarter of an hour to disentangle them.

I was in the river superintending a party digging out the egress on the south side, when, looking round, I saw five waggon drivers racing for the descent on the north side, while the officer on duty was sitting with his back to them smoking, apparently quite unconcerned. The water being up to the horse girths, and the bottom strewn with rocks, rendered rapid movement impossible, which added to the irritation I felt. I was overworked, had had no sleep while on the line of march, and, forgetting manners and propriety, I lifted up my voice and cursed him, saying, "You d——d infernal —— idiot of an officer." The words were no sooner out of my mouth than I regretted the vulgarity and want of dignity shown in losing my temper. It flashed across my mind that the lazy officer belonged to another Corps. Regimental feeling would allow me (a 90th man) great latitude in addressing one of my comrades, but the fact of my nominally commanding the 90th would add to the vexation of an officer of another Regiment on hearing such language applied to him. My contrition was increased by the echo: in the deep valley, seven times those vulgar swear words were repeated, gradually becoming fainter in the distance. Suddenly I heard the cheery voice of the lazy one's[1] Commanding officer, "Ay, ay, sir, I'll talk to him;" and then followed a string of expletives in comparison to which my language might be considered fit for a drawing-room.

My want of self-control was excusable, since I had come to the end of my physical strength. From the 2nd of January, except to wash, I had never undressed nor had my boots off, and had been sleeping like a watch-dog! and, besides

[1] Lately Commanding a district in the United Kingdom.

my military duties, I was still acting as Political Agent, which took up a certain amount of time. When I rejoined Lord Chelmsford on the Nondweni River, I was obliged to have my face tied up for a week, suffering from continuous neuralgic pains in the eyes, coupled with gastric neuralgia.

CHAPTER XXIII

1879—ULUNDI

A woman in a basket—"Wait for the waggon"—Bill Beresford earns the Victoria Cross — Zulu attacks on our square feeble, and isolated — Rundle's guns always outside square—Lord Wolseley arrives—I return to England—Tribute to the Prince Imperial.

GENERAL NEWDIGATE played a joke on me as we passed his camp. When leaving for the frontier with the empty waggons, I sent him a very old woman, virtually nothing but skin and bone. She was bright and intelligent, but so emaciated that we lifted her about in a basket no larger than a fish basket given in a London shop. I had personally carried her out of a burning kraal to save her life, and, not wanting to take her farther from her own people, I sent her over to General Newdigate on the day I marched back to Landtman's Drift, with my compliments, and expression of a hope that he would feed her. This he did; but when I returned to my camp on the evening of the 16th, for I had ridden nearly to the spot where we intended to encamp next day, I found the old woman waiting for me, the General having sent her back by an orderly, who carried her as if she were a parcel of fish, saying, " General Newdigate's compliments, and he thinks you would like to have the old woman back again."

I was ahead with the Advanced guard, when the bands of the 13th and 90th Light Infantry, as they passed the 2nd Division camp, played with fine sarcasm, "Wait for the Waggon," there having been considerable emulation in the two Columns, the 2nd Division wanting to lead, and the Flying Column wanting to keep its place. It did so, led into Ulundi, and followed in the rear of the 2nd Division when Lord Chelmsford came back to the high ground.

On the 1st of July we descended the Entonjaneni to the

White Umvolosi, 5 miles south of Ulundi. Moving off before 7 a.m., it was nearly two o'clock before the last of the 100 waggons of the Flying Column were laagered, and had the Zulus shown the initiative and audacity which characterised them early in the war, they might have inflicted severe loss upon us, if they had not indeed destroyed a portion of the force. They were, however, then discussing the terms of peace to be offered to Lord Chelmsford, and on the 2nd of July, at a meeting attended by the Prime Minister, Mnyamane, who was present at the attack at Kambula, and Sirayo, and four other Chiefs, it was resolved to send to the British General "the Royal Coronation white cattle." These had indeed started, and were within 5 miles of our camp when the Umcityu (sharp pointed) Regiment drove them back, and insisted on the Chiefs giving battle.

On the 3rd of July I sent Colonel Redvers Buller across the Umvolosi to reconnoitre the ground on which Lord Chelmsford fought on the following day, and although he lost three men killed and the same number wounded, the information obtained was worth more than the lives of a larger number of soldiers. That day at twelve o'clock I had 120 of our trek oxen, which, taken at Isandwhlana, had been sent by Cetewayo to us, driven back across the Umvolosi. These cattle had been accepted only on the condition that Cetewayo complied with the demands which the High Commissioner had made on him.

That afternoon Lord Chelmsford told me he wished the Flying Column to lead the attack. Parading the Column, I said, "Now, my men, we have done with laagering, and we are going to meet the Zulus in the open; you will remember how on the 24th of January I read out to you the news of the disaster at Isandwhlana, so I expect that you will to-day believe that anything I tell you is, to the best of my judgment, correct. I cannot promise that you will all be alive to-morrow evening, but if you remain steady, and wait for the word of the officers before delivering your fire, I promise you that at sundown there will be no Zulu within reach of our mounted men, and that you will not see any from an early hour in the day."

At 6.30 next morning we moved over the river, marching in hollow square; we stood on some rising ground selected by Colonel Buller the previous day, and on which for five-and-twenty minutes we were attacked by 12,000 or 15,000 Zulus. The Regiments came on in a hurried, disorderly manner, which contrasted strangely with the methodical, steady order in which they had advanced at Kambula on the 29th of March, for now not only battalions, but regiments, became mixed up before they came under fire. There were most Regiments represented on our left; the actual front of the square was attacked by the Udloko and Amahwenkwee, about 3000 men. Usibebu was the only Chief who came within 600 yards of us, and when he was wounded, his Regiment, the Udloko, generally lost heart, although, the moment the firing ceased and I rode out to the front of the square to where Lieutenant H. M. L. Rundle, Royal Artillery, had been working two machine guns, I counted sixty dead bodies in the long grass within seventy paces of the front of the Gatlings.

When the attack slackened and our men began to cheer, led by men who had not been at Kambula, I angrily ordered them to be silent, saying, "The fun has scarcely begun;" but their instinct was more accurate than mine, who, having seen the Zulus come on grandly for over four hours in March, could not believe they would make so half-hearted an attack.

As we marched back to our camp the men remarked that their General's forecast of the previous day was accurate.

Although I was satisfied that the war was now over, inasmuch as single men of Wood's Irregulars, of which there were about 500, were willing to go anywhere in Zululand with a message, we did not omit any precautions. Scouting parties preceded the Column, and flankers were pushed out, as we moved towards the coast to meet Sir Garnet Wolseley, and not until the 20th of July did I take my clothes off at night. The day after the action, I wrote to Lord Chelmsford's Staff officer: "His Excellency has frequently been good enough to speak with approbation of the order, regularity, and celerity of this Column. I feel that eighteen months of incessant work in the Field, which has not been without anxiety, more or less constant, makes it advisable, both in the interest of the Service, and for the sake of my own health and efficiency, that I should have a relaxation of work if only for a short time. I desire, therefore, to place on record that the good service done by this Column is due to the cheerful, untiring obedience of soldiers of all Ranks, which has rendered my executive duties a source of continued pleasure, and to the efforts of the undermentioned Staff, Regimental, and Departmental officers, many of whom have worked day and night to carry out my wishes. . . ."

Lord Chelmsford that evening published a congratulatory order to the Troops, ending thus:—

"The two Columns being about to separate, the Lieutenant-General begs to tender his best thanks to Brigadier-General E. Wood, V.C., C.B., for the assistance rendered him during the recent operations."[1]

I received a letter dated the 9th July, Port Durnford, from Sir Garnet Wolseley: "Just a line to congratulate you on all you have done for the State. You and Buller have been the bright spots in this miserable war, and all through I have felt proud that I numbered you among my friends, and companions-in-arms."

On the 15th of July, Sir Garnet Wolseley and his Staff arrived at sunset, and intimated his intention of seeing the Column next morning. In order to mark the difference between War and Peace service, I had caused a supply of pipeclay to be brought from Natal, and throughout the night of the 14th our men were employed in washing out the coffee colour with which we had stained our white belts in January, and pipeclaying them, so that next day when we marched past, although the clothing was ragged, the men's belts and rifles were as clean as if they had been parading in Hyde Park.

I entertained the General and his Staff, and at dinner Sir Garnet Wolseley asked me: "Who were the Natives I saw going westwards over the hill at the rear of the camp?" I replied: "Wood's Irregulars, who were engaged to serve

---

[1] Lord Chelmsford to the Secretary of State for War:—

"ENTONJANENI, 7th July 1879.

"I cannot refrain from bringing again to your special notice the names of Brigadier-General Evelyn Wood, V.C., C.B., . . . whose service during the advance towards Ulundi from the advanced Base, and during the recent successful operations near Ulundi, have been invaluable.

"Brigadier-General Wood, although suffering at times severely in bodily health, has never spared himself, but has laboured incessantly night and day to overcome the innumerable difficulties which have had to be encountered during the advance through a country possessing no roads."

only with me personally; I paid them up and sent them home." He said, "You were in a great hurry." I reminded him that in December 1873, when one of my Sierra Leone men had lost his eye in action, he disapproved of the Regimental Board which I had convened, and which had awarded him £5. I did not mention I had personally paid the £5, but added: "I was so afraid of your economical spirit that I have compensated Wood's Irregulars, and let them go."

Next morning Sir Garnet Wolseley spoke to me on his proposed arrangements for attacking Sekukuni. I knew what was coming, as I had seen a letter he had written to Lord Chelmsford, saying, "I mean to send Wood up, as we can trust him, to settle Sekukuni." Sir Garnet said: "Now, I know that you have had hard work, but I want you to do some more, and propose to give you an adequate Force to bring Sekukuni to terms." I replied: "I haven't had an unbroken night's rest for eight months, and am not of the same value as I was last January, and therefore do not feel justified in accepting any command for the present. If you will not let me go to England, I must go to sea for a fortnight or so, for without a rest it is impossible for me to do for you, or the Country, good service." "Well, then, how about Buller, is he fit?" "No, he has said nothing about it; but he is even more 'run down' than I am, his legs being covered with suppurating Natal sores;"—and so the Chief acquiesced in our departure, and issued the following order:—

"In notifying the Army in South Africa that Brigadier-General Wood, V.C., C.B., and Lieutenant-Colonel Buller, C.B., are about to leave Zululand for England, Sir Garnet Wolseley desires to place on record his high appreciation of the services they have rendered during the war, which their military ability and untiring energy have so largely contributed in bringing to an end. The success which has attended the operations of the Flying Column is largely due to General Wood's genius for war, to the admirable system he has established in his command, and to the zeal and energy with which his ably conceived plans have been carried out by Colonel Buller."

Sir Garnet Wolseley informed me he would urge the Commander-in-Chief to promote me to the rank of Major-an accurate and truthful man, for he put in his head and added,—"they had carts and wheelbarrows."

The Cape Town people also entertained us, and the ladies of the Colony gave me in 1880 a very handsome embossed silver shield for my services in the suppression of the Gaika outbreak, and later I received an address with a beautiful service of plate from the inhabitants of Natal.

Steaming by St. Helena and Ascension, we reached Plymouth on the 26th August, where my wife, brother, and sisters met me, and I went as soon as possible on a visit to my brother-in-law at Belhus, where my mother was staying, Sir Thomas Lennard's tenantry giving me a great reception. The village of Aveley was decorated, and the inhabitants taking out the horses pulled the carriage up to the house.

The Fishmongers' Company, of which I had become a liveryman in 1874, entertained me at dinner on the 30th September. I took the opportunity, on being asked to speak on South Africa, to try to do justice to Sir Bartle Frere, whom I termed, and after twenty-five years' experience still regard, as the greatest High Commissioner South Africa has seen; the greatest not only in his treatment of barbaric peoples, but in unflinching courage and rectitude of purpose. The trust he placed in me was the means not only of winning over some valuable allies, but of neutralising the position of many colonists of Dutch extraction, who otherwise would have swelled the number of discontented Boers who assembled at Pretoria to protest against our Government.

I spoke also of my comrades, mostly deceased, who had done so much for England, purposely making no difference between officers, non-commissioned officers, and privates who had distinguished themselves. While some newspapers unduly praised me, I was taken to task for naming anyone by a few anonymous correspondents of the daily Press. After paying this tribute of respect to the memory of those who had given up their lives while under my command in defending the interests of the country, I spoke of the Prince Imperial as follows: "In remembering those brave spirits and that gallant youth—the son of England's Ally—whose mother is our honoured guest, I am reminded of the question and answer in Shakespeare, for humanity is the same in all ages. When Rosse said to Siward—

> 'Your son, My Lord, has paid a soldier's debt:
> He only lived but till he was a man,
> The which, no sooner had his prowess confirm'd
> In the unshrinking station where he fought,
> But like a man he died,'

the bereaved parent asked, 'Had he his hurts before?' and on being told, 'Ay, on the front,' replied—

> 'Why then, God's soldier be he,
> Had I as many sons as I have hairs,
> I would not wish them to a fairer death.'

Of the gallant Prince Imperial we may say, 'Ay, all eighteen wounds on the front.'"

CHAPTER XXXIV

1879—COMPLIMENTARY HONOURS

Honours from County of Essex — Visit to Balmoral—Cawdor Castle—Hughenden Manor—Promotion by selection disapproved—Entertained by the Bar of England—Forecast of Boer Rebellion.

I ATTENDED on the 20th of September the sale of Sir Thomas Lennard's hunters at Belhus, then an annual event of much interest in the County, and it having been stated in the papers I should be there, many of the labouring classes came to see me. An elderly woman, who had walked many miles, pushing her way through the crowd round the show-ring, asked a policeman eagerly, "Which is 'im?" She had pictured in her mind an imposing heroic figure in a splendid uniform, and on my being pointed out, a middle-sized man in plain clothes, observed in a disappointed tone as she wiped her perspiring brow: "What, 'im kill all them Zulus! Why, my old man would clout un."

On the 14th of October the County of Essex entertained me at Chelmsford, presenting me with a handsome Sword of Honour and a service of plate, and in a speech at dinner, while thanking the inhabitants of Essex, I replied to the adverse anonymous critics who had objected to my naming my comrades in previous speeches by explaining the necessity of bringing the Nation into closer touch with its private soldiers. I had long thought that with a Voluntary Army it was useless to expect the best results, unless where bravery and devotion to the interests of the country is concerned, all ranks receive consideration, and I deliberately acted upon the conviction, in spite of adverse criticism.[1]

[1] Much has since been done in this direction. The parents of soldiers wounded on service are now relieved from painful anxiety by weekly telegraphic reports.

A friend, the able editor of a newspaper, while remarking on my speeches in terms personally complimentary to me, observed: "Sir Evelyn Wood does not appear capable of perceiving the seamy side of his profession." I was too fond of my friend to answer him in print, for I feel sure that if I had written to his paper he would have put in my letter, but, as I told him privately, the occasion was not one for bringing to notice the seamy side, of which there is, doubtless, in military life more than anyone could desire, but there are also many noble aspects in such a career; for, as I remarked in speaking of the death of Ronald Campbell, Coldstream Guards, "When the noise and excitement of a war is over, the soldier who has seen men die for each other, or for Duty's sake, can never again be altogether unheroic in his life."

I received in September a command to stay at Balmoral, and left town on the evening of the 8th. I was most graciously received by Her Majesty, who honoured me with her conversation throughout dinner, and again the next night, in addition to an hour's interview each forenoon and afternoon, and then on until the 11th. My original invitation was for one night only, and when I was told on Thursday that I was expected to stop till Saturday I was much concerned, as I had promised to visit Lord Cawdor, who was naturally anxious to hear about his son, Ronald Campbell; and moreover, Sunday travelling is practically impossible in Scotland. The Equerry-in-Waiting informed me that it would not be etiquette for me to express any wish in the matter, so I approached Lady Ely, who was equally determined that she would not speak to the Queen, and explain my position. I then said, "Well, Lady Ely, then I shall," believing that the Queen, who had been so gracious, would not wish to put me to inconvenience, or disappoint Lord Cawdor. This had the desired effect, and when Her Majesty sent for me in the afternoon she opened the conversation by saying, "I believe it will not be convenient to you to remain till Saturday?" and I replied, "Most inconvenient, Your Majesty." I was greatly impressed, not only by the Queen's accurate judgment, but by her profound knowledge of details of the recent operations.

I went by Elgin to Nairn, and spent an interesting twenty-four hours with the family of my late friend. On my return south I received the following courteous letter from Lord Beaconsfield, and I went to Hughenden on the 23rd.

"HUGHENDEN MANOR, *Sept.* 15*th*, 1878.

"DEAR SIR EVELYN,—The Queen wishes that I should see you, but it is not only in obedience to Her Majesty's commands, but for mine own honour and gratification, that I express a hope that your engagements may permit you to visit Hughenden on the 23rd inst., and remain there until the following Friday.—Your faithful servant,

"BEACONSFIELD."

There was a house party, those interesting me most after my host being Mr. Edward Stanhope, then known as "Young Stanhope," afterwards Secretary of State for War, and Sir Drummond Wolff. Lord Beaconsfield asked me to come and stroll with him on the terrace the morning after my arrival,— a walk which we shared with his peacocks,—and he asked me many questions about soldiers and South Africa, I endeavouring to parry his queries respecting Sir Bartle Frere. In the course of his conversation he expressed unbounded admiration for Sir Garnet Wolseley, telling me that when he embarked for South Africa he had said to him: "Now, I trust you—you trust me." Then passing on to other soldiers, he asked if I had known Colonel Home. I explained that I had lived for many weeks in a hut of leaves on the West Coast of Africa with him, and, moreover, had been associated with him at Aldershot. His Lordship said: "That man had the biggest brain of any soldier I have met." I agreed heartily, but then Lord Beaconsfield rather spoilt the value of his judgment by observing, "Why, it was Home who made me acquire Cyprus!" Home foresaw clearly that England must, for the sake of India, acquire a predominant interest in Egypt, and at one time had made a plan for building a gigantic fort in the bed of the sea, three miles outside Port Said.

The second night, after the ladies had left the dining-room, somebody remarked on the news in the evening papers that Mr. Waddington had been appointed French Ambassador at the Court of St. James, and went on to say how extraordinary it was that the French found it necessary to nominate an

Englishman to that position, appealing to Lord Beaconsfield for his opinion. His Lordship replied: "The fact is, the French have never had a native Frenchman worthy of the name of statesman." I observed gently: "My Lord, have you forgotten Colbert?" He turned to me, saying somewhat sharply: "You don't seem to be aware that Colbert was a Swiss!" I did not think it necessary to contradict my host, and a much older man, by stating the fact that, although educated in Switzerland, Colbert was born at Rheims, and submitted to the suppressing looks of my fellow guests, who chorused: "Yes, Colbert was a Swiss!" I was sitting next but one to His Lordship, and then in a low tone observed: "My Lord, how about Sully?" Sir Drummond Wolff from the end of the table called out: "What is that you are saying?" "Oh, nothing, I only made another suggestion;" but our host, drawing himself up, said in his slow, measured voice: "I now feel I made a rash and inaccurate statement. Sir Evelyn Wood challenged it, and I could not agree with him when he instanced Colbert, but he has now reminded me of Sully, who was not only a Frenchman, but a very great minister. I admit my mistake."

In the drawing-room, later in the evening, Drummond Wolff came up to me and said: "I say, how on earth did you manage to remember Sully?" "When I was small," I replied, "my parents were poor, and we had few toys, but in our nursery there was a French history book, *The Kings and Queens of France*, and I often looked at a picture of Sully standing at the door with a portfolio of papers, having surprised Henri IV., who was on his hands and knees carrying two of Gabrielle D'Estrées' children on his back."

I saw by Lord Beaconsfield's manner that if I stayed till the end of the week, as I had been invited, I should never escape a searching inquisition respecting Sir Bartle Frere's action in declaring war, so on Wednesday night I asked my host's permission to take my leave next morning. As we were going to bed, I said: "You will allow me to thank you, and say good-bye, as I am going by the earliest train." He replied: "There is no earlier train than 8.23, and as I am always up at 7 I shall have the pleasure of seeing you." As this was just what I wanted to avoid, I told the butler I would have my breakfast at 7.30 in my bedroom, and at that hour rang, and asked why it had not been brought. He answered that it was in an ante-room, close at hand, where a fire had been lighted. I had scarcely sat down before I heard the measured step of his Lordship on the stairs, and as he came in, after greeting him, I asked him whether he had read an article in a magazine which I had open on the table. He replied somewhat shortly, "No," but he had come to talk to me about other matters, and he proceeded to put many searching questions as to Sir Bartle Frere's procedure with the Zulu nation.

We all knew in December that the Government had refused General Thesiger the reinforcements he had asked, as the Cabinet wished to avoid war, but the High Commissioner and the General were of opinion that matters had then gone too far to avoid it. Lord Beaconsfield asked me: "Will you please tell me whether, in your opinion, the war could have been postponed for six months?" "No, sir." "For three months?" "I think possibly." "For one month?" "Certainly." "Well, even a fortnight would have made all the difference to me, for at that time we were negotiating with Russia at San Stefano, and the fact of our having to send out more troops stiffened the Russian terms." "But, sir," I said, "you surely do not mean to say the sending out of four or five battalions and two cavalry regiments altered our military position in Europe?" He said: "Perhaps not,—but it did in the opinion of the Russians, who imagined we were sending an Army Corps." He then went on to say: "You are young; some day you may be abroad, and let me urge you to carry out, not only the letter of the Cabinet's orders, but also the spirit of its instructions." Two years later, after Majuba, I had to ponder often on this admonition.

On the 16th October the Military Secretary informed me that the Colonial Office had brought to the notice of the Commander-in-Chief "the very valuable Political services" I had rendered when in command of a column in Zululand. Sir Bartle Frere had brought the services of my friend Colonel Pearson also to notice, and the fact that the only result in my case was an expression of His Royal Highness's gratification, which caused him to make a note in the records of the War

Office, did not detract from the pleasure I had on reading of Pearson's being made a Knight Commander of the Order of Saint Michael and St. George.

There were many discussions amongst the Heads of the Army on the question of my promotion. His Royal Highness the Commander-in-Chief was conscientiously opposed to it, and indeed to all promotion by selection, having been a consistent advocate of advancement by seniority. He held an officer should command a battalion when he was forty, but on the other hand maintained that a Colonel should become a Major-General only by seniority. He said more than once, " Men are much of a muchness; I find officers very much on a par."[1] Lord Penzance's committee pointed out, however, that if the system advocated by the Commander-in-Chief was maintained the average of Majors-General would be sixty-four. The senior Staff officers appointed by him naturally reflected his views. There was, however, a Colonel of very decided opinions then in the office, for whom the Adjutant-General sent, and asked: " Would you object to Evelyn Wood being put over your head?" He replied: "Do you consider he would make a good general?" "Yes, his reports are good." "Then, sir, I think you should promote him; and having said that, may I further add I do not think you have any right to ask my opinion."

Sir Garnet Wolseley did his utmost to get me promoted on Public grounds. In addressing the Commander-in-Chief from South Africa, on the 18th July,[2] he wrote: " I earnestly hope that Your Royal Highness will be enabled to recommend Colonel Wood to Her Majesty for the permanent rank of Major-General, not as a reward for what he has done, but in the interests of the Queen's Army, and of the State." The Chief, ignoring the Public grounds question, replied: " Evelyn Wood I know as an excellent man. . . . I have my doubts, however, whether Wood has not received his full reward with a K.C.B. and a Good Service Pension." The Commander-in-

---

[1] Lord Penzance's Royal Commission on Army Promotion. August 1876.

[2] *Military Life of H.R.H. Duke of Cambridge*, by Colonel Willoughby Verner, page 62: "I intend to send Brigadier Wood, he being the best Commander of those in South Africa. His name is in every one's mouth, from Bugler up through all Ranks, as the man of the War . . ."

Chief was misinformed as to the rewards he mentioned. He had given me the Good Service Pension in March 1879, on General Thesiger's strong remonstrance that I was the only officer unrewarded for the Gaika War, and the K.C.B. was given for my services in Northern Zululand, before the battle of Kambula.[1]

On the 1st November the Bar of England gave me a dinner in the Middle Temple Hall, the first, I believe, to a soldier, unless we consider Drake belonged to both Services, at which the Lord Chancellor paid me a gracious compliment: " The law is silent in the midst of Arms, yet, as we see to-night, the lawyer and soldier combined can, after Arms have been laid aside, speak with the eloquence which befits the one and the vigour which characterises the other."

Early in December 1879 my mother's health gave us cause for anxiety, and on the 13th of that month my sister, Lady Leonard, in whose house she was staying, said: " I am afraid that you are feeling very ill." "Yes, very ill!" " Would you like us to telegraph for Evelyn to come and see you?" "Yes, please do so." As my sister was leaving the room, mother called her back, and asked: " What time is it?" "About six." " Then please write on the telegram, 'Not to be delivered till 11.15 p.m.'" "Why?" my sister asked. "Because he is giving an important dinner party at his Club, and if the telegram goes now he will leave the table, and it will spoil the party." I was, in fact, entertaining the Attorney-General Sir John Holker, and some friends who had thrown themselves warmly into the dinner given to me by the Bar. At 11.15 the telegram was placed in my hands as I was saying good-night to my guests. My brother was with me, and we left by a luggage train at 2 a.m., reaching Belhus early on Sunday. My mother spoke to me about ten o'clock that night quite rationally, asking about the dinner party, and died at five o'clock next morning, so painlessly that I was unable to credit the fact that she had passed away.

[1] See page 85, and
Despatch from Lieutenant-General Thesiger to the Secretary of State for War :—
" KING WILLIAM'S TOWN, *June* 26*th*, 1878.
" I am of opinion that his (Colonel Evelyn Wood) indefatigable exertions and personal influence have been mainly instrumental in bringing the war to a speedy close."

Her last act of unselfishness was only similar to her conduct throughout her life. There are few men, I suppose, who remain in quite as close touch with mother and sisters when they marry as they were while bachelors; but in my case, with the mother, as with two sisters, my marriage only brought one more into the circle of devoted relations.

I assumed command of the Belfast District on the 22nd of December, and to this day am ignorant why I was sent there, as the Commander-in-Chief had given me on the 29th of October the command of the Chatham District, which I took over on the 12th of January 1880, from General (now Sir) Edward Bulwer, brother of Sir Henry Bulwer, who was Governor of Natal in 1879. My only difference of opinion with the General was as to the terms on which I purchased horses, furniture, *et cetera*, concerning which he showed much more consideration for me than for his own pecuniary interests.

When Her Imperial Majesty the Empress Eugénie read in the newspapers the account of the Fishmongers' banquet on the 30th of September, and the allusion to her noble son beautifully expressed in Shakespeare's language, she sent for me, and, after several prolonged interviews, I was commanded to Windsor, where Her Majesty was graciously pleased to honour me with the charge of the Empress on a journey she was undertaking to the spot where her gallant son perished. The Queen enjoined on me the greatest care for the safety of her Sister, and I replied I could only accept full responsibility if H.I.M. the Empress would follow my instructions as if she were a soldier in my command. This was arranged, and on the 25th of March the Empress sailed from Southampton for Cape Town and Durban.

Her Imperial Majesty had sent me a cheque for £5000, desiring me to purchase everything required, and to defray all charges. I handed back on our return to the Empress' Secretary £3600. I was allowed to take my Aide-de-Camp, Captain Arthur Bigge,[1] and Lieutenant Slade[2] as an extra Aide-de-Camp. Both these officers had distinguished themselves by the courage with which they fought their guns in

---

[1] Now Colonel Sir Arthur Bigge, K.C.B., K.C.S.I.
[2] Now General Slade, C.B., Royal Artillery.

the open at Kambula twelve months earlier. The Marquis de Bassano, Lady Wood, and the Honourable Mrs. Ronald Campbell, the widow of my Staff officer and friend who fell leading so determinedly at the Inhlobane, Dr. Scott of the Army Medical Department, two maids in the service of the Empress, Walkinshaw, my bugler, who had served with me in 1878 and 1879, and a complete establishment of servants, made up the party.

When we reached Cape Town, I had communications from well-educated acquaintances in the old Colony and Natal, loyal to our Government from conviction and personal interest. I wrote to my uncle on the 20th April, after an interview with a Dutch gentleman: "From what this gentleman told me, and from what I learn from other sources, it is clear to me that affairs in South Africa are in a very unsatisfactory state. Joubert and Kruger are now in this Colony agitating amongst the Colony Boers for the restoration of the Transvaal. There are many members of the Cape House whose seats depend on the vote, and thus pressure is brought on the Ministry here. I do not suppose we shall restore the Transvaal: if we do, we shall be obliged to re-annex it in ten years, for the sake of both Whites and Blacks. If it is not to be restored, the cause of order and progress will be greatly strengthened by the Imperial Ministers saying, 'We cannot restore the Tranvaal.'" I suggested he should tell some of his friends in the Cabinet what I had learnt. He had long before resigned his seat on the Woolsack, owing to failing vision, but was on intimate terms with his former colleagues.

CHAPTER XXXV

1880—H.I.M. THE EMPRESS EUGENIE

Cetewayo in captivity—Boers welcome me in Utrecht—Value of a Zulu wife—The Inhlobane—Ityatosi—How Cetewayo killed Masipula—How the Prince Imperial fought 18 Zulus.

WHILE we were at Cape Town I paid Cetewayo two visits, and sat with him for some time. He expressed great pleasure, and, unless he was a good actor, felt such at seeing me. He was a man of considerable tact, for he had taken the trouble to procure a photograph of myself. He discussed the merits of his chiefs in the course of conversation, and said it was quite correct that he had ordered Faku to drive the settlers away from Luneberg. As he put it humorously, " I said they were to go away lest they should be hurt." He told me many interesting stories of my proceedings in Zululand, and mentioned that he was always nervous lest I should make a raid with the mounted men and carry him off to Ulundi, thus confirming the information obtained by Sir Bartle Frere.[1] The ex-monarch asked me for a rug; and so appropriating a thick handsome one belonging to my wife, I sent it when we got back to Government House, where the Empress was staying. But Cetewayo returned it with a message that it was not nearly big enough to cover his body, and with some difficulty I found one which gave him satisfaction.

We left Maritzburg on Thursday the 29th of April, with waggons, cooks, servants, waggon drivers, and mules. The party consisting of eighty persons.

H.I.M. the Empress had proposed, in the first instance, to ride throughout her journey, but foreseeing that this might

[1] See vol. ii. p. 32.

be inconvenient I had purchased a "Spider," and after our first day's journey, finding it too heavy for a pair, in spite of the predictions of the oldest inhabitants, that it was impossible to drive four horses from such a low seat, I drove the Empress or one of the other ladies 800 miles before we re-embarked.

They greatly enjoyed the scenery in the Tugela Valley. The camp was pitched one day on a slope overlooking a ravine, 150 feet below the tents. Up to Helpmakaar, the track is carried through a beautiful though rugged country, and on the 5th May we mounted 650 feet in 5 miles, and descended 1800 feet in the next 5, travelling on an unfenced road, scarped out of the mountain-side.

When we reached Utrecht the whole of the population turned out to see me, and from the moment we crossed the Blood River I had a succession of Black visitors, including 10 men enlisted in October 1878, who had been attached to Companies of my Battalion, and who had lost wives killed in the raid made by Umbilini after the battle of Kambula. They were the men who had thrown their knobkerries in the air when they learned I was to decide, and pay the amount they claimed for their wives. In every case the claim was certified by Mr. Rudolph, the Landdrost, as correct, and I handed over cheques amounting to between eight and nine hundred pounds, which I told them would be honoured at Newcastle. They saluted according to their fashion, and walked off without the slightest doubt of their getting gold for the pieces of paper tied up in the corner of their blankets.

When the last of them had departed, one man came forward and said, "Will you do something for me?" "Oh! but you are not one of the men whose wives I insured?" "No; but I was in Wood's Regiment, and my wife was killed." "When was that?" "In August." "But then you could not have gone straight home when I dismissed you in the middle of July near Kwamagasa?" "No; it is true I stayed for some little time with relatives in Sirayo's country, and the raid took place while I was there." "That is, you contributed to your own loss?" "Yes; I have no claim, but perhaps, as my wife was killed, you will do something for me?" "How long had you had her?" "Five years." "What did you give for her?" "Ten cows."[1] "That is a good deal." "Well, it was the current price when I married her." "Wives will be cheaper now, for we have killed a good many men, and no women. Had you any children?" "Two." "Boys or girls?" "Girls." "Were they killed?" "No." "Then they are worth a calf a piece?" "That is so." "What sort of value was your wife?" "Excellent; she could hoe well." "Well, for the sake of calculation, if you have had her five years she could not be as good as she was when you got her, and eight cows was the outside value when you married her, according to the current rate at this time; so if we take off one cow for the two girls you have still got, and two cows for wear and tear, if you get the price of five cows you will be fully compensated?" "Yes; I shall be perfectly content." I satisfied myself that his loss was correctly stated, and then having prize money which was somewhat of a white elephant to me, I eventually gave him £24, with which he departed expressing deep gratitude.

While we were encamped on the Blood River the whole of the Uys family came to see me, as did also Sirayo and his two sons. They accompanied us to Kambula, and on the 16th the Empress, standing in a little redoubt on the hill, was able to see not only where Lieutenants Bigge and Slade had fought their guns in the open for four hours, but also where the Ngobamakosi Regiment, of which Melokazulu was a mounted officer, attempted to come out of the ravine, to storm the laager. We had taken up a tombstone for the graves near the camp, and on the 21st, in Mrs. Campbell's presence, I had the tombstone to Ronald Campbell carried up the Inhlobane by men who were fighting against him when he lost his life on the 28th of March.

The Empress rode and walked up the eastern end of the mountain where Colonel Buller ascended and descended by the Devil's Pass, at the foot of which he gained his Victoria Cross. The ruggedness and steepness of the descent may be gathered by the fact that I had all 14 ponies belonging to the party driven slowly, and allowed to pick their path down, and the only one which accomplished the descent

[1] A cow is equal to £3, and a calf 30s.

without a heavy, fall was my own pony, which I led, and indicated to him where he should put his feet.

While we were near the Inhlobane I rode many miles to the eastward and to the north of the mountain searching for the body of my friend Robert Barton, but was no more successful than were the 25 natives whom I employed for three weeks for the same purpose. Uhamu came to visit me at Tinta's Kraal. He naturally did not tell me, but I learned from others, that both he and Mnyamane, who were the most powerful chiefs, were oppressing their lesser brethren. Mnyamane had then taken 400 cattle from Sirayo, and 600 from his people, on the ground that it was his fault the Zulu dynasty had been destroyed.

We had arranged that the Empress should reach the Ityatosi some days before the sad anniversary, the death of her only son, June the 1st. When we arrived there we were troubled by the intrusive action of a lady correspondent of an American newspaper, who endeavoured with much persistence to obtain "copy" for her paper. I sent for the head man of the kraal,—and it is remarkable how the natives trust any Englishman whom they know,—and after an explanation of the case, he signed a witnessed deed of a lease of all his land on a radius of 2 miles from the spot where the Prince fell. We explained the law of trespass, and after giving the Zulus some blankets they formed a long line, and clasping hands danced away, showing how they would resist passively the approach of any one who endeavoured to go on the property.

I have already described, by Chicheeli's help, how he killed Robert Barton. We were able to give the remains a Christian burial. When we arrived at the Ityatosi I sent out for all the men who had been engaged in the attack on the reconnoitring party when the Prince lost his life, and while waiting for them to assemble, Lieutenant Bigge and I rode to the Inhlazatze Mountain, with the double purpose of returning Mr. Osborne's call, who had waited on the Empress when she entered Zululand by crossing the Blood River, and also because I wanted to confer with him about the lease I had taken of the land around Sobuza's kraal, the spot where the Prince was killed. Leaving at 1 a.m. we were able to spend several hours with Mr. Osborne, and got back in time for dinner, the ponies doing the 74 miles without any sign of distress.

I had long wanted to know the truth of the story of the death of Masipula. When we were marching on Ulundi the previous year I was out in advance of the column reconnoitring, and when sitting under a tree the interpreter said, " The last time I was under this tree I said good-bye to Masipula, Umpande's Prime Minister ; " and he told me this story. During the later years of Umpande's long reign the position in Zululand was somewhat analogous to that in the days of our Regency, when George the Third was no longer capable of managing the affairs of the nation. Masipula felt it his duty to check Cetewayo continually in his desire of raising more regiments, and when the king died, Cetewayo delayed until he was crowned by Shepstone, and then sent a message to Masipula, " The King is dead." The meaning of this intelligence thus formally delivered was, " As you were his minister so many years, you ought to die." Masipula not accepting the hint, sent back a message that he greatly regretted Umpande's death; and Cetewayo waited patiently for another three months, and finding that Masipula would not take the hint, sent for him. He told my informant he knew that Cetewayo would kill him, and the Englishman asked, "Then why go ? Ride over the border into Natal, and live there." The old chief drawing himself up proudly, observed, " And do you think that, after being his father's minister so long, I would refuse to obey the son's orders ? "

I asked Mr. Osborne, " Can you tell me whether Cetewayo poisoned or strangled Masipula ? for I have heard that he had his beer poisoned, and another story that, after receiving him, in the evening he sent men into the kraal assigned to him, and that when the executioners entered, Masipula placed his head in the noose which was already in the rope. Tell me if you can, was he poisoned, or strangled ? " Mr. Osborne was a cautious man, and his solitary life among the Zulus perhaps increased this habit, although within 40 miles of us not any one except Captain Bigge and our orderlies could speak English, he dropped his voice, and in a low tone answered me in a monosyllable, " Both " ; and added, the poison not having taken effect as quickly as was expected, the ex-Prime Minister was strangled.

While we were encamped on the Ityatosi, near Seobuza's kraal, I had prolonged interviews with 18 Zulus, whom I examined separately, and from them obtained a detailed account of the surprise of the reconnoitring party of the 1st June in the previous year, in which the Prince Imperial fell, the natives later putting themselves in the exact positions they held that afternoon. There were between 30 and 36 Zulus who took part in the attack.

The Patrol having rested on a hill to the north of the river, descended at three o'clock to Seobuza's kraal, and the Zulu scouts who were watching it hastily assembled all the men within reach. These crept up the bed of the river, and were close at hand concealed in a mealie field, when a friendly Zulu, who was acting as guide, and was killed a few minutes later, informed the British officer in command that he had seen Zulus near, and then it was that the party was ordered to mount. The Zulus purposely waited until this moment, realising that it would be the most favourable moment to attack, and fired a volley. The horse of one of the white escort was shot, and he was immediately assegaied. That of another soldier fell in an ant-bear hole, and the rider was stabbed before he could rise. The rest of the party, except the Prince, galloped hard to the ridge, not drawing rein until they reached some rocks 820 yards from the kraal, when one of them looked round, and they then rode away, still fast, but not at the headlong speed at which they had started. The Zulus in pursuit ran first after the two white soldiers who were on the flanks, three or four men, headed by Zabanga, following the Prince. His horse had jumped just as he was mounting, and his sword fell out of the scabbard. He was very active, and was vaulting on his horse in motion, when the wallet on the front of the saddle broke away, and he fell to the ground, being at this time only 60 yards behind the fugitives. There were seven men who actually fought the Prince. When Langalabalele, pursuing the fugitives, first saw Zabanga [1] he was running away from the Prince, who was rushing at him. Zabanga, crouching in the grass, threw an assegai at him. The

---
[1] Killed at Ulundi, 4th July 1879.

first assegai stuck in the Prince's thigh, and withdrawing it from the wound, he kept his foes at bay for some minutes. In the native's words, "He fought like a lion; he fired two shots, but without effect, and I threw an assegai at him, which struck him, as I said at the time, but I always allowed Zabanga's claim to have killed him, for his assegai hit the Prince in the left shoulder, a mortal wound. He fought with my assegai, and we did not dare to close with him until he sank down facing us, when we rushed on him."

On the 1st of July I drove the Empress and Lady Wood from Maritzburg to the foot of the Inchanga Mountain, where at the terminus of the railway a train was waiting. The road was engineered down the side of the mountain, and the Empress liking to travel fast, I let the horses canter most of the way down. I was always nervous when driving Her Majesty, and when I handed my wife into the train, I said, "Now my personal responsibility is over I shall not mind if the train goes off the line." We had indeed a narrow escape; when I had assisted the ladies out of the carriage I handed the reins to a Sergeant of the Army Service Corps, who was waiting to take the team back. He had gone only half a mile at a steady trot when the connecting rod which fastens the fore-carriage to the after part of the "Spider" snapped in two. If this had happened half an hour earlier, when we were cantering down the mountain road, the Empress and Lady Wood would have had a severe accident.

After giving a personal report of the journey to Her Majesty, for which purpose Lady Wood and I received a command to Osborne, I resumed my work at Chatham.[1]

This gave much interesting occupation, and an opportunity I had long desired of reducing the number of useless sentries who wasted their time in many places in the garrison.

The Commissary-General at the War Office corresponded with me at this period, and later, on the question of my succeeding him, which he desired. I had been successful in providing food and transport in 1878–79, and now, being anxious for the efficiency of his Department, in the absence of

[1] The War Minister, apprehensive of criticism in the House of Commons, declined to allow me to draw any, even half-pay as a Colonel, for the six months I was absent from the Command.

any specially qualified officer in it, he wished that I should succeed him. He proposed this to me on several occasions, once when writing with reference to the confidential reports I had furnished on officers who had served under me during the Zulu War, concerning which he wrote: " I take this opportunity of stating, with reference to the reports you have sent me, that no more faithful or honest descriptions of officers' characters have ever reached me."

CHAPTER XXXVI

1881—THE LAND OF MISUNDERSTANDINGS

Preliminaries to Rebellion—Modelled on Hampden's conduct—To South Africa—Dutchmen from Cape Colony deprecate resistance to Government—Death of Sir George Colley—An appreciation.

SOUTH AFRICA, sometimes named "The land of Misfortune," may be more aptly termed "The land of Misunderstandings." The problem of ensuring good government in a vast country inhabited by a few dominant white men, in the midst of warlike native races, has always been difficult.

Many Governors and Generals have been recalled by a dissatisfied Home Government, mainly because it did not understand the local conditions of the country, and twenty-five years ago the solution of the Zulu question, instead of solving the Boer-British difficulties, brought their opposing interests into sharper antagonism.

In 1880, before the gold industry had been developed, Mr. Kruger and his friends worked against Confederation, mainly, I believe, from the wish, after regaining their independence, to be left alone. The successes of 1881, and the accumulation of vast wealth from gold mines turning the farmer's head, encouraged him later to strive for the mastery in South Africa.

The proclamation annexing the Transvaal, in 1877, promised as much Self-government as the circumstances of the country permitted. Sir Bartle Frere confirmed this pledge, and the Boers hoped on for its fulfilment, though the nominated Assembly of officers, and other Britons, in November 1879, in nowise satisfied their aspirations.

The answer brought back by the Deputation to the Colonial Minister in London showed the Boers they had little to hope for by peaceful measures; but, as Kruger and Joubert told me in May 1881, the step which eventually determined their resort to arms was the perusal of a despatch from the Administrator, published in *The Times*, arguing with perfect honesty of purpose, the people must be contented, since taxes had never been so satisfactorily collected. "These English cannot understand our love of freedom," they said, and the prearranged refusal to pay taxes by Bezeidenhout, at Potchefstroom, for which he was indemnified in advance, was the first overt act of rebellion, following the precedents of Eliot, Hampden, and Pym in the early Parliaments of Charles I.

The British Authorities, determined to strengthen Pretoria, called in two-thirds of the Lydenburg garrison. The Boers waylaying it on the 20th December, demanded it should retrace its steps. The Senior officer refused to do so, and was extending for action when the Boers opened fire from cover, destroyed or captured the detachment.

Major-General Sir George Colley had succeeded Sir Garnet Wolseley as High Commissioner for East South Africa, but had been requested to regard his authority in the Transvaal as dormant, to be exercised only in case of necessity.

Unfortunately Sir Bartle Frere, the strongest Governor South Africa has ever seen, was no longer at Cape Town. First the Conservatives, later the Liberals, had retained him as the keystone of the much-desired Confederation. He had left Cape Town in September 1880, and his successor, Sir Hercules Robinson, only arrived at the end of January 1881. On the 25th December the Acting Governor in Cape Town cabled a resolution of the Cape Legislature, urging Lord Kimberley to send a special Commissioner to the Transvaal to avert hostilities. Lord Kimberley replied on the 30th December that "the moment was not opportune."

Throughout January 1881 Mr. Brand strove strenuously for concessions to the Boers, telegraphing on the 10th and 12th to Lord Kimberley, and many messages passed between Brand and some of the British Authorities in South Africa.

On the 23rd January, General and High Commissioner Sir George Colley wrote to Mr. Joubert calling on him to dismiss his followers, and undertaking to submit any representations the Boers might wish to put forward. Although the hostile camps were within 4 miles, Joubert's refusal to disperse unless

Annexation was cancelled, dated 27th January, was not received until 15th February. On the 28th January, Colley attacked Joubert in position on Lang's Nek, in Natal, and was repulsed.

On the 28th January, Lord Kimberley telegraphed to Mr. Brand, through the Free State British Consul, " Inform President, that if armed opposition ceases forthwith Her Majesty's Government will thereupon endeavour to form such scheme as they believe would satisfy all enlightened friends of the Transvaal community."

On the 3rd February, in telegrams passing between Mr. Brand and Sir George Colley, he learnt of Lord Kimberley's message to Brand of the 26th January, and, asking Sir Hercules Robinson, received a copy of it, and next day begged Mr. Brand "to give every publicity to it."

On the 5th February, Mr. Joubert wrote to Sir George Colley protesting against the attack of the 28th January, made before he had had time to reply to Sir George's letter of the 23rd; but Joubert, at the same time using the Free State Territory, sent troops round the British flank, and stopped the post on the 7th February, on the Ingogo River, 7 miles south of Colley's camp at Mount Prospect. The General tried to reopen the Newcastle road next day with 5 companies and 2 guns; was heavily attacked; retained his position until sunset, when the Boers drew off, and after dark Sir George Colley fell back on Prospect Camp. Although the Boers held the ground next morning for a short time, the engagement reopened the communication a few days later.

On the 4th January I received a note from the Military Secretary asking me in the name of the Commander-in-Chief if I would return to South Africa to serve under Sir George Colley, to whom I was one senior in the Army List, and requesting me to go to London to discuss the question. I agreed to go out on the Adjutant-General's observing, "Your Rank, Pay, and Allowances will be the same as at Chatham."

In a "Letter of Service" received on the 6th, it was stated that I was going out as a "Colonel on the Staff." This I declined by telegraph, recalling the previous day's conversation, and was again ordered to the War Office. Though the Adjutant-General predicted I should repent it, I maintained my decision. In the result a fresh "Letter of Service" was handed to me, with the rank of Brigadier-General, which I had held at Chatham, and also when I left the Colony eighteen months earlier, after having commanded in two campaigns and five fights a strong brigade of all Arms.

Lord Kimberley sent for me and explained his views of the question of the Zulu and Swazi States after the Annexation should be annulled, which he gave me to understand he already accepted in principle. I took leave of Her Majesty the Queen, who was very gracious to me, on the 7th January, and sailed on the 14th, reaching Cape Town on the 7th February.

We heard on the 8th, at Cape Town, of the action on the Ingogo; and the mail steamer being delayed, I transhipped into a transport, reaching Durban on the afternoon of the 9th. I left immediately, arriving at Government House early next morning, where I was kindly received by Lady Colley, with whom I had danced at her first ball. I found a letter from Sir George Colley, dated the 4th February, couched in graceful terms, as follows:—" I was right glad to hear you were coming out, and thought it very generous of you to be ready to serve under a junior and less experienced officer. I propose to give you half the troops, to relieve Lydenburg."

The situation had changed since he wrote, and so I left Maritzburg in the evening, sleeping a few hours at Estcourt, as the tracks were heavy and the mules had much difficulty in pulling the cart. I stopped on the 14th at Ladysmith, after travelling from daylight till 9 p.m. for two hours, to clear up some work about which the Colonial Secretary had telegraphed to me, and then drove on through the night, arriving at the Biggarsberg at daylight, where I received a letter from Sir George Colley, dated Mount Prospect, 16th February. He had heard I was coming up, and warned that a Force was on my left, estimated to be from eight to fifteen hundred men, adding he did not know the position it was supposed they intended to hold.

I found on the Biggarsberg two infantry Battalions, and two Squadrons of Cavalry, but the Senior officer had taken no military precautions. Having ascended the top of the mountain, and assured myself there was no enemy in the immediate neighbourhood, I left orders for the troops to march after an early dinner, and went out at nine o'clock with a small escort of 15th Hussars, to reconnoitre. I could see no signs of the Boers on our side of the Drakensberg Mountain,[1] and turned eastwards in the afternoon, arriving on the Biggarsberg-Newcastle track at sunset.

I approached the rise overlooking the Ingagane River, cautiously as a matter of habit, and it was well I did so, for just below me there was a party of 200 Boers pillaging a public-house on the north bank. They had cleared the building, destroying all the liquor, and were leaving. As they never looked back, I was able to ford the river and follow them until it was clear where they intended to cross the Drakensberg into the Free State. None but the leaders knew why Joubert declined to attack us.

When I returned late to the camp I sent for the Commanding officers, and told them that I had seen a Boer Patrol; and while I had no reason to suppose that a large body was close at hand, yet even a small number of mounted men might hold the Ingagane position and render our crossing difficult. They had made one march, so I asked if they would prefer to make a night march to get to the bank, and cross with the first streak of dawn, or wait and take the chance of the Boers occupying it. They unanimously preferred to march, as we did at 1 a.m.

We began to cross at daylight, but the water had risen since the previous evening, and as single men could not resist the current, we were obliged to form a chain to ensure getting them over in safety. We moved on to the Horn River, 7 miles, and the difficulties of the track may be understood from the fact that our last waggon did not get into camp until 10 p.m., the oxen being on the trek-tow[2] twenty hours.

Next morning, preceding the troops, I went early to Newcastle, and had the pleasure of meeting Sir George Colley, who had ridden through the previous night from Prospect Camp. I told him Lord Kimberley's views on the steps to be taken after the Annexation was annulled, and Sir George protested

---

[1] They had broken up their laager at Leo Kop that morning.
[2] Rope by which oxen pull a waggon.

in a telegram dated the 19th February, against any division of the country.

On the 8th February, Lord Kimberley had telegraphed to Sir George Colley, " If the Boers cease from armed opposition, Her Majesty's Government will be ready to give all reasonable guarantees as to their treatment after submission, and that scheme will be framed with a view to permanent friendly settlement of difficulties."

On the 13th February, Sir George telegraphed the purport of a letter from Mr. Kruger asking for a Royal Commission, which he was confident would give Boers their rights, adding, if Annexation were upheld they would fight to the end. On the 16th, Lord Kimberley, understanding Colley was shut up in Prospect Camp, telegraphed to me, " Inform Kruger that if Boers will desist from armed opposition, we shall be quite ready to appoint Commissioners with extensive powers, and who may develop scheme referred to in my telegram of 8th inst. And that if this proposal is accepted you are authorised to agree to suspension of hostilities on our part."

I had not answered this telegram, hoping to hand it to Sir George, which I did on the 19th February. Sir George replied that day to Lord Kimberley, " Latter part of your telegram to Wood not understood. There can be no hostilities if no resistance is made; but am I to leave Lang's Nek, in Natal territory, in Boer occupation, and our garrisons isolated, and short of provisions, or occupy former, and relieve latter ? "

Lord Kimberley replied the same day,—" It is essential that garrisons should be free to provision themselves and peaceful intercourse allowed, but we do not mean that you should march to the relief of garrison or occupy Lang's Nek, if arrangement proceeds. Fix reasonable time within which answer must be sent by Boers."

I ascertained, in the course of conversation, that Sir George had no information of the Left Flank and Rear of the Boer position, and suggested that I should go as far as was necessary to see if there were any considerable number of troops in the Wakkerstroom district.

He demurred somewhat to the risk, but eventually, after proposing to come himself, to which I objected on the principle that two valuable eggs should not go in one basket, allowed me to proceed; and at 11 p.m. on the 19th, I left Newcastle, and crossing the Buffalo with 100 Hussars, we proceeded to a hill overlooking Wakkerstroom, and ascertained there was no large Force of the enemy in that direction.

When I returned next evening, after a ride of 60 miles, Sir George told me he wished me to go back to Maritzburg and expedite the transport of provisions, of which there were at Newcastle only thirteen days' supply. I received two telegrams in succession from Dutchmen living near Fort Beaufort, who had served with me in 1878, requesting me to transmit to the Boer leaders then on the Nek, the opinion of the Fort Beaufort district Dutchmen that they ought to submit, when no doubt they would get all they wanted from the British Government. I sent the telegram to Sir George Colley with a note saying I was anxious to assist him, and not engage in any correspondence myself with the Boer leaders. He thanked me warmly, saying he fully appreciated my loyal desire to help him, and mentioned that he thought it was best to let Mr. Brand deal with all such communications. I left Newcastle at 3 a.m. on the 22nd, but was detained several hours on the Ingagane, as the change of mules had strayed and ours were too exhausted to do a double stage; but later, we were fortunate in the weather, and next day, by driving from 3 a.m. to 7 p.m., got to Maritzburg.

During the night, 26th to 27th, Sir George Colley occupied the Majuba Mountain, thinking the Boers intrenching its lower slopes were about to forestall him on the summit. I heard from him at breakfast-time; he was on the mountain; but in the afternoon we had an alarming telegram, followed by a succession of similar messages; one announcing Sir George's death, urged that unless the 15th Hussars and an Infantry Battalion moved up to Prospect at once, the camp there would be in a critical position. I recalled the troops who had already started, for the effect of their move would have been to leave the ammunition, and the twelve days' supplies at Newcastle, with 250 sick and wounded, guarded by 100 men, in order to put 700 more men into Prospect Camp, where there were already 1200 soldiers, and would also have added a march of 17 miles and one more difficult river, through which the supplies would have to be dragged.

At 8 p.m. I asked the Chief Justice to come to Government House, and was sworn in as Acting Governor of Natal and Administrator of the Transvaal. I could not rest, as telegrams were brought to me every half-hour, but managed to get away at 5.30 a.m. on the 28th. Though we started before daylight, the track was so greasy that it was dark before we reached Estcourt, only 50 miles away. There I received a fresh bundle of telegrams, which kept me up till midnight, and Walkinshaw called me again before 4 a.m. That night we slept at the Biggarsberg, and as an officer there had telegraphed to me that a Dutchman had been watching for the post cart, asking if I was on it, I took on an escort of six men. I saw no Boers, however; and as the team could not pull the cart, I rode the horses of the escort in turn, to Newcastle, where I arrived on the 3rd March. Next day I visited Prospect in a deluge of rain, which made the track so greasy that the horses could with difficulty keep on their feet at a walk; and on the 6th, when I again rode up, it took us five hours to travel about 20 miles.

I wrote to my wife, "Colley is gone: the best instructed soldier I ever met." In 1877 I wished him to take the Staff College, when I thought it was to be offered to me, solely because I thought he would make a better Commandant.[1] Except by Lord Wolseley, and one or two others, Sir George's long and valuable life is unappreciated, and forgotten in its culminating and dramatic disaster. For him success was impossible, no smaller mind would have attempted to achieve it with the totally inadequate means at hand. He did not know what it was to fear, and rated others by his own undaunted heart. He had suddenly to face a rebellion carefully prepared in a vast country, which he was to rule only in case of emergency, and until the end of November; when the Administrator of the Transvaal telegraphed for troops, all that officer's reports had been reassuring.

Colley was justified, in a military sense, in moving on the 26th. The hill he occupied is in Natal. The forty-eight hours, to which his letter of the 21st had limited his offer

[1] *Vide* vol. i. p. 294.

"to suspend hostilities," had long since elapsed; and, moreover, as he telegraphed on the 10th to Mr. Brand, he could not "allow any communication with the Boers to affect his military operations" while they were trying to starve out the British garrisons.

CHAPTER XXXVII

1881—AFTER MAJUBA

The Military situation compels inaction—Ambiguous telegrams from the Cabinet—Piet Joubert asks me to meet him—Lord Kimberley approves of my doing so—His instructions—I urge Military action—Walkinshaw's endurance—The Boers disperse—Boer flag at Heidelberg—Pretoria—A painful journey.

THE following was the Military position of the frontier when I arrived at Newcastle: at Prospect there were 1200 Infantry and a few Mounted Infantry. All the troops had been engaged once; about two-thirds, twice, and all three engagements had ended in a withdrawal of the British troops. In the camp at Prospect there were six weeks' rations for men, and at Newcastle twelve days', with six days' forage. Although we were so short of forage, no horses had been allowed to graze for two days, for fear of a raid by the Boers, still over 25 miles distant. I found of two and a half Squadrons of Cavalry, one Squadron was kept continuously on outpost duty. These I withdrew, replacing them by six scouts, only farther out than the Squadron had gone.

Rain had fallen for ten successive days, and on one occasion for twenty hours without ceasing, causing the Incandu River at Newcastle to rise 7 feet in one day.

The Colonial Secretary urged me to bring the troops back to Newcastle, and asked to have the Natal Police moved back to Colenso. The Inniskilling Dragoons, a battery and a half Royal Artillery, and the 83rd Regiment were marching up country, but did not arrive till twenty-three days later, when, although the Dragoons led their horses all the way, they had only a hundred of them fit for work, in spite of the fact that they had taken eighteen days to cover 140 miles. The tracks, called roads, in Natal were indeed almost impassable, but by leaving their waggons the troops could have arrived a week earlier.

There was no necessity for an immediate advance, except as regards Potchefstroom. Sir George Colley had been very anxious for that Garrison. He wrote on the 15th January: "Unless I can in some way relieve the pressure on Potchefstroom before the middle of next month, that Garrison and its guns must fall into the Boers' hands," and this anxiety induced his movement on the 28th January. Although he had not the power to ensure success, he kept the Boer forces occupied, and it should be remembered to his credit that none of the garrisons fell.

I received simultaneously the two following telegrams:

"SECRETARY OF STATE FOR WAR TO SIR EVELYN WOOD, BRIGADIER-GENERAL.
"*1st March* 1881.

"Although Sir F. Roberts is going out with large reinforcements, we place full confidence in you, and do not desire to fetter your military discretion."

"LORD KIMBERLEY TO SIR EVELYN WOOD.
"*1st March.*

"When did Sir George Colley communicate to Kruger the fact that the British Government would appoint Commissioners with extensive powers for the friendly settlement of all difficulties, and what answer was given?"

And on the 3rd March, Lord Kimberley ordered me to inquire whether an answer would be sent to me; and again, on the 4th March, asked for a reply.

Most of the Ministry, possibly, but certainly a majority of the Nation, would have been better satisfied if I could have consulted my own wishes, and driven the Boers from the Nek before the Transvaal was given back. With the troops then at hand, however, success against a well-posted enemy, four times as strong, was unattainable. Before the reinforcements arrived the dominant will of the Premier decided the question.[1]

---

[1] I had thought much during the weary hours spent on the post-cart between Maritzburg and Newcastle of the Military Situation, and of the Duke of Wellington's

On the 3rd March, Mr. Brand telegraphed to me, stating he had written to Kruger to urge him to suspend hostilities, and begged me, as one formerly on friendly terms with some of the Boers, to contribute to a peaceable settlement. I replied thanking Mr. Brand, and endorsing his sentiments for our Boer friends, said I would gladly abstain from a forward movement till the 10th March, if the Boers made a similar promise.

I telegraphed Brand's message and my reply to Lord Kimberley, and he next day replied approving my message. When sending a copy of my telegram I added, "Referring to the above, please consider with this my telegram to Brand. I views expressed in his letter to Viscount Castlereagh, dated the 1st of August 1808. ". . . You may depend, I shall not hurry the operations, or commence them one moment sooner than they may be commenced, in order that I may acquire the credit of success." And again, a year later, in a letter written at Badajos to Marshal Beresford, he insists "above all on a determination in the Superiors to obey the spirit of the orders they receive, let what will be the consequences."

In addressing privately the Secretary of State for War many months later, referring to this period, and the conduct of Detachments employed at Majuba, I wrote: "The depressing effect of the Majuba affair on officers and men at Camp Prospect lasted for some time, but we should undoubtedly have taken the Nek about the end of March; and I think such a victory would have been a gain to all, English, Dutch, Kafirs, and to Humanity generally, and that it would have been cheaply purchased, even had you lost your generals and a large number of troops. I confess I am disappointed at some of the criticisms on my duty in England. It is assumed by many that the generals in command of troops should disregard the orders of the responsible advisers of the Crown, if such orders are distasteful to him and the troops."

Mr. Childers, who always treated me with the greatest consideration and kindness, in replying on the 21st July, thus expressed his views: "I do not think you need be in the least way unhappy about Newspaper criticisms. Everyone knows you are guided by Instructions from home, which the telegraph makes now more detailed than ever."

In a letter to my wife, dated the 4th May, endeavouring to console her for the vexation she felt at the unsparing criticisms on my conduct, I wrote: "My life has been spent in worrying the Boer leaders about the murderers of Messrs. Elliott and Barbour. You ask me how much of the feeling in England was known to me? I reply, I always anticipated a great outcry, for I have read History, but such outcry will, I hope, never influence me in Public events. I could not go beyond the clear words of the Instructions I received. So long as I serve out here I shall loyally carry out, not only the words, but the spirit of the orders of the Ministry, if that body is led by Gladstone or Stafford Northcote. We are all astonished here at the Praise and Blame measured out to me on the subject. I should utterly despise myself if I allowed personal feelings to sway me in a matter of Life and Death. I wished to fight, not because I am willing to purchase reputation by expending our soldiers' lives, but because I believed, and believe that by fighting, the peace of this country could be assured, as it will not be now. I am as vexed at the Praise as I am at the Blame, which is so freely accorded to me. Do not distress yourself, Dearest; I value my own sense of duty much more than the opinion of anyone."

suggest I wait for a day or two, as I shall not be ready for another week, and then I must act if Potchefstroom is to be saved. When I move, I am confident, with God's blessing, of success."

I received late, on the 4th March, a communication from Mr. Piet Joubert, enclosing a telegram from Mr. Brand, and asking would I meet him? I replied, I would meet him on the 6th; and while informing Lord Kimberley, added, " My constant endeavour shall be to carry out your orders; but considering the disasters we have sustained, I think the happiest result will be that after a successful action, which I hope to fight in about fourteen days, the Boers should disperse without any guarantees, and then many now undoubtedly coerced will settle down." Later in the day I telegraphed : " Joubert is coming to meet me. Shall follow strictly the lines of your instructions."

I rode out about 17 miles to O'Neill's, an empty farm at Prospect, on the afternoon of the 5th, and was deciphering telegrams till 9 p.m., when I asked Walkinshaw for my eye-douche, the rose of which could not be found; and I desired him somewhat impatiently to call me at 4 a.m., at which hour he held a jug over my head. " What's the use; you left the rose behind?" "It's here." "Where was it?" " On the mantelpiece." It was only months later I learned he had ridden to Newcastle and back, 34 miles, swimming twice the Ingogo River, in fording which an officer and some men had been lost on the 8th February.

I met Mr. Joubert and three Boer leaders on the 6th March, and at their request, in order to allow time for Mr. Kruger, who was then near Rustenberg, to reply to Sir George Colley's communication, agreed to an armistice for eight days, *i.e.* to midnight on the 18th March. The Boers undertook to pass eight days' supplies to the invested garrisons, and inform them of the Truce, which was to count only from the arrival of the supplies. I telegraphed this arrangement to Mr. Brand, and begged him to ensure the faithful transmission of the news to Potchefstroom, which he undertook the same day to do.

I telegraphed to the Secretary of State for the Colonies, and for War: "Want of food prevents advance for about ten days. Ingagane and Incandu are impassable. I have therefore lost nothing in suspending hostilities, and gained eight days' food for the garrisons most in want." Next day the Cabinet approved my action, not only in the Political, but also in the Military point of view.

On receipt of this message I replied to Lord Kimberley, 8th March: "Do not imagine I wish to fight, I know the attending misery too well; but now you have so many troops coming, I recommend decided though lenient action, and I can, humanly speaking, promise victory. Colley never engaged more than six companies; I shall use twenty, and two Cavalry regiments, in directions known only to myself, and I undertake to enforce dispersion."

That same day Lord Kimberley, telegraphing with reference to my telegram of the 5th March, in which, while suggesting an amnesty for leaders, I urged, "The happiest results will be after a successful action, which I hope to fight in about fourteen days," replied, "There will be complete amnesty. . . . We will now appoint Commissioners for friendly communications to Boers." Later in the day he telegraphed, "Prolong Armistice as needful."

On the 11th March, in referring to my telegram of the 9th, showing the food supplies in the garrisons, I asked if the Armistice was to be prolonged, stating, "The situation on military grounds scarcely justifies prolongation, certainly not beyond the 18th March." And in reply I received orders "To prolong the Armistice, and inform the Boers, if they desisted from armed opposition, a Royal Commission, consisting of Sir Hercules Robinson, Sir Henry de Villiers, and yourself, will be appointed to consider the giving back of the Transvaal, subject to British Suzerainty, a Resident at Capital, and provisions for guarding native interests, Mr. Brand being present as representing the Friendly State."

On the 12th March, Lord Kimberley telegraphed: "In order to enable me to answer questions in Parliament, inform me whether suggestions for Armistice proceeded from you or Joubert, or from whom?" I might have replied briefly, "From you. See your telegram of 16th February."[1] Although Mr. Kruger on the 16th March, in the conference under Lang's

---

[1] Telegram from Secretary of State for the Colonies to Major-General Colley:—

"16*th February* 1881.

"Your telegram of the 13th. Inform Kruger that if Boers will desist from armed opposition we shall be quite ready to appoint Commissioners with extensive powers,

Nek, claimed the credit of the Armistice, as being the result of his letter of the 12th February to Sir George Colley. However, appreciating Lord Kimberley's difficulties in the Houses of Parliament, I replied: "Mount Prospect, 14th March. Whole history of Armistice. 3rd March, Brand appealed to me, as former friend of Boers, to stop bloodshed, by arranging temporary cessation of hostilities. 4th March, Sent my answer to you. 5th March, You approved. 3rd March, Brand appealed to Joubert to meet me to arrange armistice. 4th March, Joubert sending me Brand's message; asks how far I will co-operate so (sic) he wishes to stop his patrols. 5th March, I offered to meet him on the 6th."

During the next few days I had much discussion with some of the Boer leaders, who were, however, unable to give definite opinions on many points, as Mr. Kruger,[1] whom they all regarded as their chief, was still absent. I wrote to Lady Wood on the 15th March: "Buller, who went with me to meet Joubert yesterday, thinks the Boers will go on fighting. I think they will not, if we concede all that Lord Kimberley has telegraphed."

His Lordship had sketched roughly to me before I left London his views regarding the Government of the territories inhabited mainly by Natives after the retrocession of the Transvaal, but his views were not in accordance with the wishes of the Boers, who subsequently, in consequence of the recommendation of two of the Royal Commissioners, obtained what they wanted.

I told the Boers plainly on the 15th that the Government would not consent to the recall of our garrisons until the country was handed over by a Royal Commission, and on this point, which had been represented as one of paramount importance, they gave way. We talked for hours on the 16th, and I telegraphed that evening to Lord Kimberley as

and who may develop scheme referred to in my telegram to you of 8th inst. Add that if this proposal is accepted, you are authorised to agree to suspension of hostilities on our part."

[1] From Sir Evelyn Wood to the Secretary of State for the Colonies:—

"NEWCASTLE, 13*th March*, 9.50 a.m.

"Kruger sending Reuter's 22nd February message, with Mr. Gladstone's statement that steps to avoid bloodshed will be taken, asks how far my instructions go. I have replied I am still awaiting your orders, and shall be at Prospect to-day."

follows: "After eight hours' talk I am confirmed in the opinion expressed in my telegram of the 5th instant, namely, 'Considering the disasters we have sustained, I think the happiest result will be that after a successful action which I hope to fight, the Boers should disperse without any guarantees.' On the 19th, the Boers who were in telegraphic communication through the Free State with Parliamentary and other supporters in London, abated their tone considerably, and in writing that night to my wife I said, "Buller now thinks they will not fight; if they do, we shall beat them."

On the 20th, Lord Kimberley replied to my telegram of the 16th as follows: "I have not heard from you the result of your communication to the Boers relative to my telegram of the 17th inst. We rely upon you, unless Military Necessity requires immediate action, to give us time to consider points on which you may not be able to come to agreement with the Boers."

On the 21st March the Boers accepting Lord Kimberley's terms, including any separation of land in the interests of the natives which the Royal Commission might consider necessary, agreed to disperse; and while informing Lord Kimberley, I telegraphed to the Secretary of State for War asking him to see the telegram, and added, "If authorised, can advance 24th, but may be delayed by rivers." On the 22nd, Lord Kimberley approved of the conditions under which the Boers undertook to disperse; and on the 24th nearly all their waggons had moved off, about 1,800 remaining on the Nek to receive me as I descended from the Majuba with the Boer leaders, who had ascended to show me the respective positions of the contending forces on the 27th February.

At a breakfast given to me on the Boer position there were three young couples who were to have been married six months earlier, but the girls, like all the Boer women, declined to have anything to say to lovers or husbands until Peace was made, and it was, I believe, mainly owing to the influence of the women that the spirit of the Rebellion was maintained.

It is remarkable that none of us ever heard either Boer leader boast, or even speak in a tone of exultation, of their successes. This was not the case with the young men, but the leaders on every occasion ascribed the result of their struggles to the intervention of the Almighty. Mr. Brand asserted that another check to our arms would have brought into the field all the young Dutchmen of South Africa. As I telegraphed to Lord Kimberley, "A check, humanly speaking, was impossible;" and in spite of Brand's experience, assuming one occurred, I could endorse his opinion only as regards the Free State men, of whom there were about 300 on the Lang's Nek position on the morning of the 24th March.

I had much interesting conversation with Mr. Joubert during the intervals of the negotiations. He was by far the most far-seeing and moderate of the Boer leaders. I was told on the 24th, when the Boers were dispersing, that Joubert had had considerable trouble to obtain the assent of the different Commandoes (detachments) to Lord Kimberley's conditions, many of the leaders objecting strenuously to any interference with the power of the Boers to deal with the Natives. Joubert did not tell me, but I learnt while on the Nek, that the evening before it was decided to accept the British terms, Joubert, after a long discussion, said, with some heat, and decision, " I advise you to accept these terms, which are liberal; and if you refuse them, you had better nominate another Commandant-General, for I do not mean to fight."

When talking to him alone I said, "You dislike our reservations about Native territories. Why not stand out, and let us have another fight?" "Oh," he replied, "I do not want any more bloodshed." "Well, as you are not quite satisfied with the terms, why not fight again; you say you have won three times?" "Yes, but we shall not win again now, and I am in favour of a peaceful settlement."

On my return to Newcastle I received the following telegram: " 22nd March. Her Majesty's Government desire to convey to you their high sense of your conduct in the recent proceedings, and the skill and judgment you have shown throughout in your communications with the Boer leaders."

I had heard from Lord Kimberley on the 1st April that he thought it desirable I should go to Pretoria and explain the Situation, and replied I had already placed relays of horses, and was starting on the 3rd April.

I travelled in a "Spider" drawn by two Artillery horses, and at Paarde Kop, a few miles out of Prospect, the driver having dismounted to adjust some harness, left the horses' heads, and they started off while I was in the carriage. The man made a determined effort to stop them, and catching the rein, was dragged a hundred yards, when the horses breaking into a gallop he let go. As the Spider bounded over an ant-bear heap I was tossed out, falling on my spine on the off horse's head. Very little damage was done to the carriage, and in a short time we were again on the track.

When I reached Heidelberg at sunset on the 4th, I found the Boer flag flying over the Court House in the market square, and going up to speak to the sentry, who did not understand English, he showed such decided intention of shooting me if I interfered with the flag, that I went back to the hotel, and sending for Messrs. Pretorius and Smidt, desired them to have the flag hauled down. To this they demurred, and attempted to argue the point. Eventually bidding them good-night, I said, " You have got several hours to think about it, but if at 6 a.m. to-morrow—now, please compare your watches—that flag is flying, I shall pull it down with my own hands, and assuming the same man is on sentry he will shoot me. This will be unpleasant for my family, but honestly speaking I think it will be a gain for England. You gentlemen believe, and rightly, Mr. Gladstone has great power with the British Public, but not even he will be able to give you back your country if you are so foolish as to shoot a Governor, who dies insisting on your carrying out the terms under which you dispersed from Lang's Nek. There cannot be two Governments in the country at one moment."

At daylight next morning I looked out from my window and saw the flag was flying,[1] and exactly at six o'clock, telling Walkinshaw what I was about to do, I walked across the square to the flag-staff. As I approached it, saying a little prayer, for I thought that my last moment had come, the non-commissioned officer in charge of the guard hauled down the flag, and Smidt coming out, admitted that his argument of the previous evening had been fallacious.[2]

[1] The Boers did not haul down their flags at sunset.
[2] I thought I was the only British officer in Heidelberg, but Colonel Fortescue, K.R.R. Corps, came in that evening from Lydenburg, as he mentioned to Mr. Butcher, M.P. for York, and myself when we were riding in Hyde Park in 1900.

AFTER MAJUBA

I left Pretoria on the 8th, sleeping at Heidelberg that night, where I met the Boer leaders, who apologised for Cronje's dishonourable conduct in withholding the terms of the armistice from the Potchefstroom Garrison, and they begged to be absolved from any complicity in the act, which they desired should be undone as soon as possible by the surrender being cancelled, and the Arms and Ammunition returned. This was done, and a Garrison replaced for a short time.

I was more injured in my fall than I realised at the time, and in the next two or three days the irritation set up in the spine was so severe as to make my feet swell to an enormous size. I had necessarily to ride about at Pretoria, and thus made myself worse; and when leaving Heidelberg on the return journey was in such agony that I could travel only propped up with pillows and rugs, with my feet higher than my body. When I was lifted out of the Spider at Standerton, and the doctor asked me to turn over, I said, " That is impossible; you must turn me." I had lost all power of movement. Rolling me over, he injected some morphia close to the back-bone, and in a few minutes, saying, " Oh, this is Heaven," I slept soundly many hours in succession, for the first time since the accident.

I vexed the High Commissioner somewhat by my persistence in urging him to come up to Natal and open the Commission. He probably thought I was unreasonable in not estimating sufficiently the importance of his Constitutional position, as regards the Ministers of the Cape, who at this time, as indeed was often the case, were uncertain how long they would hold office. On the other hand, Lord Kimberley wishing me to persuade the Boer leaders to provide for our current expenditure, was asking what arrangements I proposed as to Revenue and Expenditure of the Government during the interval before they got Self-government. I pointed out that we could hope to get nothing out of the country, and for that reason I wanted the interval shortened, and had therefore been urging the High Commissioner to come up as soon as possible. I explained to him, and to Lord Kimberley, that as the entire expenditure for the purposes of governing the Transvaal was only one-twelfth of the military expenditure, which could not be reduced without the troops being sent away, we had every reason for giving over the country as soon as possible. In the meantime the young Boers who had not seen the troops assembled in the North of Natal, were somewhat impatient with their leaders, and inclined to get out of hand.[1]

I had plenty of occupation before the High Commissioner arrived, for I held daily conferences with the Boer leaders for the purpose of bringing to justice the murderers of Major Elliot, Paymaster, who was shot while crossing the Vaal River, into which the Boers forced him and his companion, Captain Lambart; and the case of Doctor Barbour, who was murdered under somewhat similar circumstanees, a few hundred yards inside the Free State boundary. There was no doubt of the identity of the murderers in either case, but to obtain a conviction was unusually difficult, as martial law had not been proclaimed. Sir Henry de Villiers, my colleague, the Chief Justice of Cape Colony, advised me that to try the men by court-martial would be to create *ex post facto* legislation, and with the prevailing feeling in the Transvaal, trial by Boers for such deeds would have been useless.

The Free State judge who tried Barbour's murderers, in spite of the evidence given by Mr. —— that he saw —— fire at Barbour, advised the jury : " If you are not certain that —— shot Mr. Barbour, you should give the prisoner the benefit of the doubt," and so they did. Similarly, Major Elliot's murderers were acquitted, in spite of Captain Lambart's evidence, who escaped only by diving like a duck in the Vaal River.

When not inquiring into such and somewhat similar cases of outrage, not, however, involving loss of life, I spent many hours, averaging 16 daily, in considering the affairs of Zululand, where the system of dividing up the country amongst a number of Chiefs had become unsatisfactory. Several Chiefs complained of acts of oppression by Usibebu, and Mnyamane complained of oppression at the hand of Uhamu. In the opinion of Lord Kimberley the terms of settlement had not

---

[1] With reference to the Boers' conduct, I suggested another appeal to arms. From Sir Evelyn Wood to the Secretary of State for the Colonies :—

"*19th April.*

"I should allow them to reoccupy Nek. We are quite ready. This will give a decisive military result, and the happiest result for the country. I guarantee we dislodge them."

contemplated any interference on the part of the British, so in telegraphing to him on the 13th April I said, " All these Chiefs have asked me to inquire into the matters in dispute, and to give a decision which they bind themselves to carry out, but I am not certain how you will regard my giving any decision. Shall I do so, or let the Chiefs fight it out?" Next day His Lordship told me to decide the matter, which I did four months later.[1]

[1] Extract from the Secretary of State for the Colonies to Sir Evelyn Wood :—

" 1st *November*.

"I am quite satisfied with the result of your visit to Umbandeen, which will no doubt have been very useful, and I think you have done all that was possible in the circumstances to settle Zulu affairs.—KIMBERLEY."

CHAPTER XXXVIII

1881—A ROYAL COMMISSION

Charles Dickens' story of the Fleet Prison paralleled—I ask permission to leave Royal Commission, but am refused—Gallop after wild ostrich—A jail delivery in Pretoria—Visit to the Inhlazatse, and Lotiti—My Dissent to the Report of the Royal Commission—Hotel at Beumbei—Delagoa Bay.

ALTHOUGH I had delegated to the Colonial Secretary much of the routine work of the Colony of Natal, I had to take action on some cases, and in writing to Lord Kimberley on the 31st May I mentioned that in 1878 I had met in the Colony a magistrate who was then, I thought, inefficient; that in 1880, when I next saw him, he had sunk still lower, and was in 1881 a drunkard; and on inquiry I found the Colonial regulations were so framed as to practically check any action on the Governor's part, and I was advised by the Colonial Secretary to leave the matter alone. Eventually, however, the magistrate's conduct became so flagrant that I assembled a Committee of inquiry, and the result indicated that Charles Dickens, in *Pickwick*, need not have drawn on his imagination for "Jemmy" or "Number 20," confined in the Fleet Prison. There was one person in the jail of the little town where the magistrate resided, who was taken out every night by a constable to the hotel that he might play billiards with the magistrate, and on several occasions the prisoner brought the constable back at night drunk. The jailer was always ordered to wait up until the game was finished; but as it was frequently protracted till past midnight, he eventually warned the prisoner that unless he came in at reasonable hours he would lock him out!

On the 7th May, Sir Henry de Villiers arrived, and assisted in endeavouring to persuade the Triumvirate, as I had been trying to do since the 29th April, to institute a searching inquiry into the murder of Major Elliott and some other Europeans. This was a work of much difficulty, as the Boers were unwilling to admit, although the victims were dead, that they had been killed under unjustifiable circumstances.

Next day the High Commissioner, Sir Hercules Robinson, arrived, and on the 8th the Royal Commission was formally opened. It was obvious that the views of Sir Hercules and myself differed on many essential points. It appeared to me also that Sir Henry Villiers wished to set up a form of Government incompatible with the paramount authority of England, whereas I appeared to him to be unwilling to repose that confidence in his fellow-countrymen which he felt. After a fortnight's close attention to the work of the Royal Commission I called on the President, for whom I had hired a farm outside Newcastle as a residence, and informed him I should like to withdraw from the work imposed on me. He laughingly explained that he had had a similar suggestion from Sir Henry that morning.

Many of the subjects under consideration were new to my colleagues, and required, therefore, more consideration from them than it was necessary for me to give who had been in that part of South Africa for nearly two years previously; and while they were thus engaged, by laying on horses I was enabled to inspect the Garrisons at Wesselstroom, Utrecht, and battalions encamped along the line of communication, going as far as the Biggarsberg, and Ladysmith.

On the 1st June the High Commissioner and Sir Henry started in a carriage, I remaining behind for a few days to do some military work which had fallen in arrears during our sittings, which extended from seven to eight hours daily. By riding up with relays of horses I was able to cover the distance much quicker than was possible in a spider.

It was my misfortune, while maintaining cordial relations with my brother Commissioners, to differ entirely with them in many matters brought before us, and I protested against my colleagues telling the Boers that we were waiting at Newcastle for Lord Kimberley's reply to the reference we had made on the question of boundaries. I pointed out to Sir Henry de

Villiers, who had told them in conversation why we were waiting, that the fact of our moving up to Pretoria must show the Boers that the British Government had accepted the advice of the majority of the Commission, against mine, which, as the Boers knew, was antagonistic to their views. My brother Commissioners had telegraphed on the 1st June to the following effect: "The Boers say [1] that they left the Boundary question with the Royal Commission for the sake of peace at the Nek, in full confidence that they would lose nothing by doing so. The leaders do not now wish to retract, but they point out that the people would not acquiesce." My brother Commissioners for these reasons recommended that we should give back the whole of the Transvaal, including the country adjoining Native States. I dissented, maintaining we had carried concessions to the utmost limit, and pointed out that the Boers admitted I had told them distinctly on the Nek that I would do my utmost to prevent their ruling any territory bordering on Native territories.

At the same time I pointed out to the Secretary of State for War the inconvenience of the Natal frontier when any question of a Military offensive is contemplated, explaining it had every possible defect, without one compensating advantage.

On receipt of this decision against my recommendations I telegraphed to Lord Kimberley: "When peace was made my views on the most important question, that of the Boundary, were well known here, and were, as I thought, the views of the Government, as expressed in your telegram of the 17th March. These opinions are so entirely opposed to those of my colleagues, which you have since approved, that I am induced to represent to you that as the Border Natives look to me for protection, and may possibly regard my future action with suspicion if I continue to serve in the Commission, I am compelled in justice to you to suggest for your decision whether your policy might not be better carried out by withdrawing me from the Commission, and allowing me to devote all my time to Natal, the Army, and the Zulu settlement. My chief colleague, with whom my relations are

---

[1] Mr. Brand told them at the Nek, unknown to me, that if they gave way he was confident the British Government would not curtail the Transvaal.

cordial, wishes me to remain, and advises me not to ask you, but I have no fear of your misunderstanding my motives."

To this telegram the Government replied on the 9th: "We appreciate your motives in suggesting retirement from Commission, but cannot accept your offer. We attach much importance to the retention of your services on Commission, your retirement from which cannot fail to have prejudicial effect on prospects of peaceful settlement. Our agreement with majority on Boundary question does not imply any diminution of our confidence in you."

On the 12th June, about 25 miles outside Pretoria, my Aide-de-camp and I enjoyed some good runs after a herd of wild ostriches, which we chased with hunting whips merely for the pleasure of a gallop, for when the birds could run no farther we left them to recover their breath. I do not know whether it is the habit of the ostrich in all places, but these were not difficult to run down, inasmuch as, after running at speed for a mile, say from East to West, they would turn and go back in a parallel line, and thus two men by judiciously nursing their horses could overtake them.

From the 13th of June to the end of July I sat six days a week discussing with the Triumvirate and their advisers the many and varied questions incidental to giving back the Government of the Transvaal.

I was anxious to agree with my colleagues on Public grounds, and one of my military advisers urged me to do so for personal reasons, but I felt bound to record my Dissent [1] to

---

[1] My Dissent was published in *Blue Book, Transvaal Royal Commission Report*, Part I., C. 3114, pages 34 and 56–66, issued in 1882, but a subsequent edition issued soon afterwards omitted my Dissent, which I therefore republish.

Sir Evelyn Wood, while concurring generally with the views of his colleagues, feels bound to record the grounds of his dissent on certain points, at the end of which Dissent he has signed the report.

DISSENT.

As regards the question treated in paragraph 16, viz. the trial of those accused of murder during the late hostilities, Sir Evelyn Wood desires to place on record, that, in a telegram of the 30th March, he gave an opinion adverse to the trial of these persons, either by Boers or by ordinary process, and recommended the creation of a Special Tribunal: eventually, however, the Commission recommended the course which was adopted.

the recommendations formulated by Sir Hercules Robinson and Sir Henry De Villiers.
The Chief of the Staff, Sir Redvers Buller, took nearly all

2. With reference to the territorial question, Sir Evelyn Wood is unable to concur with his colleagues in the arguments which led them to recommend the abandonment of the Scheme of Separation of Territory agreed to at Lang's Nek. Paragraphs 44 to 53, of this report, give the arguments of the Boer Leaders against the separation of any territory East of the 30th degree of longitude.

These objections must have been just as evident to the Leaders, when treating with Sir Evelyn Wood at Lang's Nek, as when treating with the Commission at Newcastle. At Lang's Nek, they acquiesced in the principle of separation of territory; that they did so is, Sir Evelyn Wood thinks, a proof that they preferred peace, with the proposed separation, to a continuance of war.

To contend afterwards that the Royal Commission ought not to decide contrary to the wishes of the Boers, because such decision might not be accepted, is to deny to the Commission the very power of decision that it was agreed should be left in its hands.

In paragraphs 53 and 54, the majority of the Commission hold that sentiment was the mainspring of the late outbreak, and imply that none of the peace stipulations antagonistic to this feeling can be enforced, without detriment to the permanent tranquillity of the country. Sir Evelyn Wood cannot concur with even the premisses of his colleagues, and he is convinced the approximate cause of the late outbreak was a general and rooted aversion to taxation.

His colleagues appear to have received the statements of the Leaders as expressing the feelings of their followers. In Sir Evelyn Wood's opinion, the views of the Triumvirate should have been accepted with reserve; and he could not attach the same value that the majority of the Commission did, to the Leaders' account of Boer sentiments. As it was, his colleagues arrived at their conclusions on this question in Newcastle, before the Commission had entered the Transvaal, and practically before they had any opportunity of learning the wishes of the inhabitants, except through the mouths of the Leaders.

As Sir Evelyn Wood cannot accept the conclusions of his colleagues, based on the arguments of the Boers, still less can he accept those they have arrived at in paragraphs 56 and 57, on the aspect of the Native question. It is argued that by concessions to the Boers on the Territorial question, the Commission would obtain large powers for the British Resident, and also gain the consent of the Boers to conditions not contained in the peace agreement, viz. :—

The creation of a Native Location Commission; the right of Veto on Native Legislation; and the settlement of the disputed boundary of the Keate Award territory;—all of which will, the majority of the Commission think, form the best guarantees for the protection of all Native interests.

Schedule 2 of the Agreement of the 21st March 1881 left to the Commission to define, and to the British Government to determine, what powers should be assigned to the Resident, and what provision should be made for the protection of Native interests, while Schedule 3 made complete self-government *subject to Suzerain rights*.

It is not apparent to Sir Evelyn Wood that in the Convention any powers greater than those justified by the peace agreement have been so assigned to the Resident: and the creation of a Native Location Commission: the power of veto on Native Legislation: and the settlement of the Keate Award question, appear to him to be matters so directly affecting Native interests, as to be entirely within the scope of the Agreement of the 21st March: however, be this as it may, he cannot believe

the routine work off my hands, but I continued to pay attention to questions of army training, as I foresaw they might have great importance in the future.

that any power the Government or the Resident may derive from the Convention will prove as beneficial to the Natives as would the existence of British Rule Eastward of the 30th degree of longitude.

It is admitted that all the Eastern natives would prefer the retention of British Rule in this country, and also, that it would benefit them; it is, however, argued that these are the Natives best able to protect themselves.

To a certain degree this is correct, but we have recently destroyed the military power of the Zulu nation, and have disarmed the people.

In the interests of the Transvaal, but at England's expense, we subdued Sikukuni, and we have checked the acquisition of firearms by all Natives.

Sir Evelyn Wood maintains, therefore, that the Eastern tribes are not so capable of defence as to be independent of our protection; and while admitting they are not so defenceless as are those on the Western border of the Transvaal, he submits that the arguments of his colleagues prove more conclusively the importance of protecting the Natives on the West, than the desirability of withdrawing protection from those on the East side of the Transvaal.

Sir Evelyn Wood's colleagues admit the desirability of retaining the Eastern territory under British Rule, and the substantial benefit to the Natives living therein and to the Eastward of it; but they argue that those in the West, who, by their position are unavoidably excluded from our protection, would have suffered loss by missing those favourable conditions which have been secured to them by the Convention. The value of the said conditions must be a matter of opinion until tested by time; and the necessity for making concessions to obtain them is not, Sir Evelyn Wood submits, apparent: but whichever may be the more accurate view, in summing up numerically the interests concerned, the question cannot be confined to those named, but should be considered to extend indirectly to all the natives in South-East Africa.

Sir Evelyn Wood agrees with his colleagues in thinking that the grounds for retaining the country East of the Drakensberg, are less cogent than those for retaining the whole territory East of the 30th degree, and he admits that the relatively small number of the Transvaal natives, East of the Drakensberg, does not alone justify the proposed rectification of boundaries, but he cannot follow his colleagues in the rest of their argument, and thinks that, while studying how best to balance the interests of Boers and Natives, they have overlooked, what was to him, the most important factor in the question, viz.:—the interests of the English Colonies in South Africa. The proposal for a separation of territory proceeded from Her Majesty's Government. In the month of March, when the negotiations at Lang's Nek were approaching completion, Sir Evelyn Wood submitted to the Secretary of State for the Colonies, what he considered would be (for British and Native interests) the most suitable boundaries for the Transvaal in case we left it.

The Commission being opposed to the retention of the territory lying to the Eastward of the 30th degree of longitude, Sir Evelyn Wood suggested as a compromise, the retention of the District which lies to the East of the Drakensberg: but it was far less in the interests of its native population that the smaller measure was suggested, than for the sake of tranquillity in Swaziland, Zululand, and Natal. His colleagues have balanced the Eastern and Western Native question, by a comparison of numbers, but a glance at the map will show how very much more important it is to our Colonies to have quiet on the Eastern than on the Western borders. Separated as we now

I used the privilege accorded to me by the Secretary of State of addressing him personally, in trying to provide for

shall be by the Transvaal from the Eastern Natives, it will be impossible for us to exercise over them the influence for peace due to our paramount position in the country. It is from this cause, he thinks, trouble to England may arise, and this is the consideration which has led him to dissent from his colleagues on the Territorial question.

3. As to the question of belligerency, touched on in paragraphs 107 and 108, it should be borne in mind that although, by the Agreement of the 23rd March, immunity was granted to both the Leaders and to their followers, yet this did not apply to those "who had committed, or were directly responsible for acts contrary to civilised warfare." This is apparent from Schedule 4, of the Agreement of the 21st March, in which the Leaders engaged to co-operate with the British Government in bringing such persons to justice. Sir Evelyn Wood is therefore unable to agree that there was any question of amnesty in such cases, though the attitude of the Boers, no doubt, precluded the possibility of obtaining evidence.

4. In paragraphs 121 and 122, the question of compensation for damages due to war is considered, and the liability of the Boers, under the terms of the peace agreement, is questioned by one member of the Commission.

Sir Evelyn Wood, who negotiated the agreements of the 21st and 23rd of March, holds them to mean that the Royal Commission was empowered to settle questions of compensation for acts which were in its opinion not justified by the necessities of war, and also questions of compensation for acts fairly subjects for compensation.

In support of this view he stated that, during the peace negotiations, he had quoted, as an instance, the case of a Kafir whose crops had been consumed by the Boer Forces on Lang's Nek. This act was evidently justified by the necessities of war, but nevertheless in this case, as in that of all subjects of the Queen commandeered against their will, the justice of compensation was alike evident.

5. The next point on which Sir Evelyn Wood desires to touch, is the question of Sub-residents mentioned in paragraph 139.

While concurring with his colleagues that it was desirable to interfere as little as possible with the internal affairs of the Transvaal State, he was, however, of opinion that, in a country as large as France, it could not be expected any one individual, however active, would become acquainted with the real state of feeling of the Natives, and of their treatment by the Boers ; and he considered that complaints, however just, would rarely, if ever, reach Pretoria. As regards the Natives external to the State, he held it would be impossible for a British officer resident in Pretoria to ascertain, without aid, their complaints, wishes, and intentions, or to exercise that peaceful influence over them so desirable in the interests of South Africa.

6. Lastly, on the question of remitting the expense of the successful war with Sikukuni, Sir Evelyn Wood dissented from the opinion of his colleagues. Until Sir Garnet Wolseley subdued Sikukuni, no Government was able to obtain taxes from his people, and he occasioned the Boer Government constant trouble and expense ; the last expedition, under President Burgers, having reduced the Republic to the verge of bankruptcy.

When we last collected taxes in the country, the people were well disposed and paid cheerfully. Seeing, therefore, that the Boers are about to reap the benefits, both financial and peaceful, brought about by the war, it seemed to Sir Evelyn Wood but just that the Transvaal State should give some return to England for the expense incurred.

EVELYN WOOD, Major-General.

the eventuality which occurred in 1899. I thought it would arise much sooner from the Boer State becoming bankrupt, as I had not foreseen the finding of gold mines. I wrote, 31st May: " It may be well to record in the War Office that when you send out the next Expedition to this country, all the Cavalry and Artillery should come from India. English horses require at least three months easy work after a sea voyage."

I had urged the importance of training Mounted Infantry, from 1874, and wrote to Mr. Childers on the 18th July 1881: " I desire to urge on your attention that the —— were surprised —— from having no Mounted men. I advocated, before I left this country in 1879, that in every battalion there should be some Mounted men to act as scouts." I shall shortly submit to H.R.H. a scheme for maintaining in peace time about twenty-five horses per battalion, and to instruct a succession of young soldiers in each company—say for four months, to ride sufficiently well to act as scouts."

Three Zulus came down from the interior, sent by their chief Umzila, for having been concerned in the killing of a Boer. The Chief's message was to the effect that he believed the men were guiltless, and had acted merely in self-defence, but as he trusted in the justice of the English he had sent them in to be tried. The situation was peculiar, for I personally had no confidence that they would be accorded a fair trial after we had left the country, and as they had walked 200 miles under the impression the British were to remain in the country I caused the interpreter to explain to them the actual position, coupled with the admonition that I thought in a few days' time the climate of Pretoria would be unfavourable to their health; and we saw no more of them.

During the conversation with them, while the interpreter who had spent his life in South Africa was putting their story into English for the benefit of the Royal Commission sentence by sentence, I observed: " These men live near the tribe who have the curious practice of piercing their baby girls with an assegai over the hips, and under the shoulder blades." My brother Commissioners doubted the existence of such a practice, and the interpreter stoutly averred that he had never heard of it. I explained to the President the operation of putting the assegai through the muscles, and then a round stick in the holes, which is moved every twenty-four hours until the skin is healed. The baby girl on arriving at maturity has thus four holes in her to take the arms and legs of her future baby : whom she carries on her back while at work. The President asked the Zulus if this practice was universal in the tribe near them, and they answered : " Yes, all the baby girls are treated in that way."

On the 1st August, three days before the Retrocession, a Kafir came in from Rustenberg, about 60 miles distant, complaining that his son had been killed by a Boer, under the following circumstances: the Boer had taken an unusually fine beast out of the Zulu's herd, and the lad drove it back. Twice this operation of taking and recovering was performed, and then, according to the father's story, the Boer took the lad between his knees and broke his neck, as one wrings the neck of a chicken. I sent the depositions to Mr. Kruger, who expressed great concern at the supposition even of such an atrocious deed, and assured me that he would send off his State Attorney that evening to inquire into it. This he did, and ten days later I received a letter from him to the effect that he was sure I should be glad to hear that the State Attorney had come to the conclusion the lad's neck had been broken by a fall from a rock.[1] To this I could make no reply, but the conclusion at which the President of the Transvaal had arrived was the less satisfactory to me as I was aware that the State Attorney had been driven out in a carriage, with the attorney of the accused, by a near relative of the Boer who was supposed to have killed the lad, and that, moreover, having been close to the place, I could not remember the rocks whence the lad was stated to have fallen.

We left Pretoria on the 5th August, and on the 4th I had a Jail delivery. There was, however, one man in it serving a sentence of seven years for a peculiarly atrocious sexual out-

---

[1] In justice to Mr. Jorissen, I should mention that he informed a civilian, attached to the Royal Commission, that the case was, in his opinion, one of murder. Mr. Kruger's information as supplied to me was, moreover, erroneous, for later we heard the Court sentenced the Boer to a month's imprisonment for killing the Kafir herd. On the other hand, the Transvaal High Court ordered a man who seduced a Dutch girl to pay the parents a solatium of £1000, and £7, 10s. a month for the maintenance of his child until it was twenty-one years of age. This statement gives, I think, a fair indication of the mind of the Transvaal Boer twenty-five years ago.

rage, and, thinking Mr. Kruger would prefer he were not at large, I sent over to say that I had cleared the prison of all ordinary malefactors, and while I could not leave this man locked up without food or jailers, I assumed Mr. Kruger would sooner he was in prison than at large, and asked him whether he would undertake that the man should not die of starvation. The President sent back to say that he had no jailers, no money to hire them, and begged I would do whatever I liked,—leave the man locked up, or let him out, but he hoped not to use the jail for some time, and so one villain more was let loose in the Transvaal.

When the Commission broke up I went to the Inhlazatze Mountain in Zululand to interview the Chiefs put in authority under the arrangements made at the conclusion of the Zulu War. I gathered that there had been some improvement in the working of the settlement from the previous year, although there was still much oppression by the greater Chiefs, and it was evident that we were trying to civilise the Zulus quicker than was convenient. By the orders of the Secretary of State for the Colonies I impressed on the assembled Chiefs that they should inaugurate a system of Industrial schools. This proposal when understood was received in silence by all except Usibebu, who remarked quaintly, that he had already got a Bishop and a clergyman, and he thought that was enough for any black man.

When the interview was over I sent the Cavalry, which had been taken less as an escort than a guard of honour, back to Natal, and with Major Fraser,[1] Lieutenants Slade[2] and Hamilton,[3] and Mr. Brampton Gurdon,[4] rode to Lotiti, the head kraal of Umbandeen, King of the Swazis, intending to travel from this place to Delagoa Bay, and return to Maritzburg by Man-o'-war.

On the evening of the 1st September, when riding towards Mabamba's kraal, near the Inhlobane, where we intended to sleep, I saw several Zulus, carrying firewood on their heads, running to intercept us, and we halted till the leading man

[1] Now Major-General Sir Thomas Fraser, K.C.B.
[2] Now Major-General Slade, Royal Artillery.
[3] Now Major-General Sir Bruce Hamilton, K.C.B., Aldershot.
[4] Now Sir William Brampton Gurdon, Bart., M.P.

approached. After saluting, they stood staring at me. I said: "Why were you running?" "To see you, Lakuni." "Well, are you satisfied?" "Yes, we are glad to see you,—that's what we wanted." "Where is the satisfaction?" "Oh, we wanted to see you, because you fought against us." "Yes, I killed several of you." "That is true, but you never interfered with any of our women, and they were protected by you, and after the war you took no cattle from us; and as for your killing us, you are a soldier, and have to do what you are told, as we had." He and his companions lit fires for us, and procured milk from the surrounding kraals, and there came together a great assembly of both sexes, who gave me an ovation.

We had heard in Natal that there was a hotel at a place called Beeumbei, where we sent a letter addressed to the manager asking him to provide accommodation, as our arrival might not coincide with that of the Man-o'-war's gun-boat which was coming up to take us to Durban. Just as we were starting I received a kind letter from the Zulu Chief, Mr. Dunn (ordinarily called the White Zulu Chief), urging me not to attempt to go farther than Lotiti, as the party would probably get fever, which might be fatal. That the advice was not only kind, but well founded, is shown by the fact that of seven men who preceded us somewhat earlier or followed later all contracted fever, and five of them died,—the flat and marshy land between the Lebombo Mountains and the sea being at that time peculiarly fatal to Europeans. When riding towards Lotiti we passed two Swazis, and I said to Mr. Rudolph: "Look at the far man—I know his face—ask him if he has ever met me." The Swazi, greatly pleased, replied: "Yes, I took a message to Lakuni in Newcastle six months ago." We spent eight hours at Lotiti trying to explain to the King the position between the Boers and the British Government.

His Majesty, on our taking leave, proposed to have an ox slaughtered, but I told him that my retinue would prefer to have it at our resting-place that evening, and he asked in what other way he could show his respect for me, for I had sent him in 1878 and 1879 one or two horses and other presents on behalf of the Transvaal Government. I suggested that a present of chickens would be acceptable, and the King, who was a stout young man, attended by his Prime Minister and chief warriors, proceeded to chase fowls, which they knocked down with knob-kerries, until the exertion was too much for him, and to our relief he allowed some of the Royal attendants to provide for our larder.

We had a guide from a kraal between Lotiti and the St. John River, which flows into Delagoa Bay, and he led us to the hotel at Beeumbei. We fully anticipated some kind of accommodation, and so were proportionately disappointed on seeing the so-called hotel was a straw hut arranged like a pagoda, about ten feet in diameter, on the upright support of which was pinned our letter asking for accommodation, and the guide who led us to the spot confided to us there was no human creature within 20 miles. There was a cask of Cape brandy in the hut, but nothing more.

The position was somewhat serious, for we had brought very few stores, and we had run out of every article of food except Umbendeen's fowls. We had for three days no rice, bread, vegetables, except sweet potatoes, or salt, the absence of which was perhaps the most felt after two meals of boiled fowl without anything to accompany it.

On the 8th September we had absolutely no food except these fowls, of which I was so tired I was unable to eat them, and went to sleep supperless. At 4 a.m. I was awakened by Slade shouting that the Gun-boat's cutter had arrived with a hamper of food and a dozen of champagne, to which my companions did full justice on the spot, I declining to lift my head until daylight. We had a pleasant pull down the St. John River, and getting on board the gun-boat reached Maritzburg via Durban late on the 11th September.

CHAPTER XXXIX

1881—MARITZBURG

Advice as to entertaining—Bishop Colenso—The opening of the Legislative Council—Preparations in the event of Boers declining to ratify the Convention — A long ride to the Drakensberg — Isandwhlana—My unpopularity dies out—How Colonists died around Colonel Durnford —Return to Chatham.

THE day after my arrival I received much advice as to my social duties, from official and unofficial personages, male and female, all kindly meant; but I made no distinctions in invitations, and disregarded also the suggestion I should not entertain, but save my salary and take it home.

I was under no misapprehension as to my unpopularity, for at the end of May, when I thought it was possible that the offer of the Governorship of Natal might be made to me later, I desired a friend to inquire whether the feeling in the Colony was so bitter, as to render such an appointment undesirable in the public interest.

After the Zulu War of 1879, Natal had given me a beautiful testimonial in recognition of my services in the Zulu War, and my correspondent asked the Honorary Secretary of the Committee, who not only selected the offering, but who had moreover come to Chatham in 1880 to present it to me, on behalf of the Colony, for an opinion. That gentleman answered: "Yes, the feeling is very bitter against him. Although some few still respect him, the majority regard him as the mouthpiece of Mr. Gladstone."

I therefore answered my adviser: "Yes, I am quite aware of the fact that I am unpopular, and I must be now as the instrument of the Government; but a long experience has shown me that dinner parties judiciously arranged afford satisfactory opportunities of dispelling unfavourable impressions. I do not suppose for a moment that the question of dinner influenced the Colonists, but it gave them an opportunity of seeing me, and learning my views. The Durban people had but little opportunity of meeting me, but Messrs. Escombe [1] and Robinson [2] lived there. Both were in the Legislative Council, and were therefore brought in contact with me more frequently than many others, and when I left the country the inhabitants of Durban give a dinner and a ball in my honour, at which such pleasant things were said of me that I do not venture to repeat them. A more important gain, however, was that owing to my better acquaintance with the ministers they treated me as a friend, asked me later how much they ought to give an able Governor, and on my advice raised the salary by £1500 per annum.

One entertainment I gave was of an unusual nature, but afforded me great pleasure. Thinking my guests would be happier without my company, I got Redvers Buller to ask me and my Aides-de-camp to dine, so as to enable me to invite forty-five soldiers, a Sergeant, three of the escort of the 15th Hussars, and the band of the 58th Regiment, which played at Government House at least three times a week. The escort had been with me since March, and as a soldier, regarding the band as comrades, I had objected to pay them, and indeed never gave them anything beyond refreshments. I told Slade, my Aide-de-camp, I wanted the table dressed with flowers, and that the wines and food should be exactly as if I was entertaining the Legislative Council, which was done.

I entertained within three months three bishops, a dean, and an archdeacon, a Church of England missionary who had come from India to carry out a series of Revival services, and a Church of England chaplain who was the brightest of them all. He had behaved courageously in the fight near the Ingogo River, and with a copious vocabulary, a musical voice, and a seraphic face, filled every Sunday an iron Drill Hall which he hired, in spite of his charging a shilling entrance.

The greater dignitaries of the Church agreed in one point, their dislike to Bishop Colenso. He was about sixty-eight years of age, with a noble face, an accurate reflection of his mind. Although I could not defend his retention of the

[1] Who was made a Privy Councillor. [2] Who was made a knight.

Bishopric when he ceased to accept the Mosaic authorship of the Pentateuch, I considered it to be my duty as Governor to attend the Church of the lawful Bishop of the Colony.

It was difficult for him to believe anything good of a white man, and although I became intimate with him, I never heard him admit anything against a Zulu. This mattered the less, however, as a great majority of Boers, and some Colonists acted on precisely opposite principles, and Colenso's championing of the black races was absolutely disinterested.

He was greatly distressed because he heard I had referred to Cetewayo at the meeting of Chiefs under the Inhlazatze as a scoundrel (Ishinga), which was absolutely incorrect. On the other hand, it was commonly said that two years earlier, immediately after the Zulu War, that the Bishop generally referred to me as "the man of blood."

The Bishop lived frugally, giving away a great part of his stipend in charity. As his house, Bishopstowe, was 7 miles from the church, I induced him occasionally to come in to Government House from Saturday to Monday; and though he and I disagreed on most Zulu questions, as indeed he had done with all my predecessors, yet I believe he felt that he was ever welcome by me. In a letter dated the 22nd October I wrote: "I trust whatever views you take of our respective duties, it will make no difference to our private relations."

I generally attended his church as a point of duty, though I went also to the Bishop of Maritzburg's church, and to the Army chaplain's. What the Bishop of Natal read was uncontroversial sound doctrine, but as a preacher he was singularly ineffective. Very short-sighted, he held his manuscript close to his eyes, thus his beautiful snowy white hair was the only thing visible to the small congregation.

In the house he was a delightful companion. He made my acquaintance as I passed through Maritzburg in 1878, mainly, I believe, because he supposed I had been oppressing Umquikela, chief of the Pondos, and now in 1881 I found him a delightful guest. Sitting alone together one evening, I asked: "Are you the man who wrote that terrible Arithmetic over which I shed tears at school?" "Did you really shed tears over my Arithmetic?" "Yes, often." "Well, when I was a small boy I shed tears over every Arithmetic put into my hands, and I resolved I would write one by which boys would learn without tears." I replied: "Ah, Bishop, but you could not write down to my level."

One of the other bishops, when attacking Dr. Colenso, virulently observed to me: "I do not know why you call him Bishop; he is not one." "Well, he is the Bishop of Natal." "But he is only a bishop from what the lawyers say." I answered: "They did not appoint him, the Queen did, and She is the only Head of the Church whom I recognise."

On the 6th of October I opened the Legislative Council, and the comments in the local papers were varied and amusing. The writers, despairing of finding something on which they could remark, turned to my delivery of the Speech. The Editor of the Radical paper observed the only good point in it was the perfect delivery; but he wound up by saying it was exactly like Edison's phonographic machine!

Another paper declared that I spoke exactly like a Sergeant-Major giving an order to a Squad, while the Government Gazette remarked on my foreign habit of rolling my r's. This last interested me most of all, because I still remember the tears which came into my eyes at Marlborough in 1847 as I counted the verses in the Bible which each boy had to read on Sunday afternoon, and saw that my fate would bring me to the 40th verse of the 18th Chapter of St. John, and when my turn came I popped up and said, "Now, Bawabbas was a wobber."

Early in October the British Cabinet became perturbed by reports that the Raad sitting in Pretoria would not ratify the Convention under which the Boers had assumed the Government of the Transvaal in August, and Mr. Gladstone determined that they should either ratify it, or lose their Self-government. I was offered any reinforcements I required, but asked only for horses, mules, and one battery of Horse Artillery.[1]

I no longer got all the telegrams from Pretoria, as the Resident communicated direct with the High Commissioner at Cape Town; but what made the Government uneasy was a strongly worded telegram sent by the Boers to Mr. Gladstone. I explained in a telegram to the Colonial Office that in my

[1] It should be remembered that the Boers at this time had no Artillery.

opinion the Boers fully intended to ratify, and that the aggressive telegram had been drafted by a Hollander, and the result showed that my surmise was correct. Doubtless it was difficult for the Government at Home to read between the lines of the information which they had received. I asked the Resident for his views, and in a cypher telegram he answered: "Impossible to predict course the Raad will resolve on; I doubt if Leaders know. Equally difficult to predict action in case of non-ratification, nothing allowed to be divulged; Raad sits in secret."

I did not believe the Boer Government would prosper, for, writing to my wife on the 31st of May, I said: "I cannot believe that the Boer Republic will last." And again on the 13th October I wrote to her: "I am very glad the English Government has answered the Boers in firm language. . . . In a few years, however, we shall have to take over the country."

This forecast would have been absolutely correct had it not been that the discovery of gold kept Mr. Kruger and his associates in power for eighteen years.

Although I anticipated the Convention would be ratified, I took precautions, and bought, in different parts of Natal, a number of oxen and a great quantity of mealies, at normal rates, without attracting attention.

I was satisfied with my preparations for secret service. As I wrote to Mr. Childers: "I ought to learn what goes on South of the Vaal; one man is entirely with us in heart, and I have two more I can buy. I had a Zulu in my service who brought me information from near Ulundi in 1879, and he was always accurate, although it is more difficult with the Boers."

I enjoyed on the 4th of November a long ride to Langabalele's location. I had been suffering from intestinal complaints for eight days, induced by overwork, and I thought, and as it proved correctly, that I should get better from change of air and exercise, so Slade and I left after lunch and rode to Weston on the Mooi River, 42 miles. Next day, leaving at 4.30 a.m., we covered 71 miles before two o'clock; I settled a land question,[1] overruling the decision given four

---

[1] Sir George Colley's predecessor had expressed dissatisfaction with the award which had been given on a disputed land case, but he was no horseman, and

years previously, and then rode 42 miles into Maritzburg by seven o'clock. It was a good day's work, 110 miles in $14\frac{1}{2}$ hours. My Aide-de-camp complained that he had to carry a chemist's shop for me, for besides a phial of medicine the doctor had made up for me, I had a bottle of essence of ginger and chlorodyne.

At the end of November I enjoyed another interesting ride by Rorke's Drift and Isandwhlana to the Ityatosi and back. I started Major Fraser, the Assistant Military Secretary, and the Aides-de-camp on the Saturday, and left with Sir Redvers Buller after church on Sunday, riding as far as Burrups, about 50 miles, and starting at three o'clock on Monday, crossing the Tugela, and afterwards riding up the Buffalo River, we reached Rorke's Drift, another 60 miles, in time for dinner. The heat was great, and the skin peeled off our noses and eyelids.

Next morning I conducted Sir Redvers over the battlefield of Isandwhlana, which he had never seen, and we had the story told by combatants who took part in the fights; Englishmen of the Natal Police, by Basutos, by friendly Zulus fighting on our side, and by two or three mounted officers of Cetewayo's army, which overwhelmed our forces. Their respective accounts tallied exactly; indeed, it seems as if uneducated men who cannot write are more accurate in their description of events than are the Western nations.

When Sir Redvers was quite satisfied that he knew all about the battle, he turned back, and went straight to Umsinga, I riding to the Ityatosi, where I had sent a photographer whom I had engaged to photograph the spot where the gallant Prince Imperial fell. This added another 50 miles to my journey beyond Rorke's Drift, where I dined on Monday night. Leaving after dinner, I joined Redvers Buller about 2 a.m., and rested for an hour at Umsinga, then, starting for Maritzburg, 80 miles distant, we arrived in time for dinner.

I had left the Sivewrights [1] in Government House, and

---

it was difficult to get to the spot on wheels. Sir George Colley equally doubted the propriety of the decision, and a quarter of an hour on the ground with a meeting of the contending parties left no doubt in my mind that the complaint of the Native was well founded.

[1] Now Sir James and Lady Sivewright.

found they were giving a small dinner party, not anticipating my return till the following evening; so telling the butler to lay an additional plate, I sat in the Governor's place as they entered the room, much to their astonishment.

On the 12th of December, at ten o'clock at night, while listening to a selection of Sacred music which the Colonel of the 21st Royal Scots Fusiliers had arranged that the band should perform for my pleasure, I got a telegram from Lord Kimberley, saying: "I shall have much satisfaction in recommending you for the appointment of Governor of Natal." I thought over it till six o'clock next morning, and then replied: "I appreciate highly the expression of your confidence, but must respectfully beg leave to decline."

I had ascertained some weeks earlier that the future Governor would not be permitted to command the troops, and decided not to accept if I got the offer, writing to my sister on 30/10/'81: "I propose to return through Egypt. That country must fall to us, or to France, or both, and it is as well I should have a look at it." The last week of my stay in the Colony showed plainly that the unfavourable impression regarding my conduct had died out, and indeed had been succeeded by a kindly sentiment for which I am still grateful.

Although the work had been unceasing, yet I had had the assistance of loyal and capable comrades. Sir Redvers Buller had taken all military details off my hands, while Major T. Fraser, R.E., afforded me the help of his fertile brain in Political matters. Captain Sandeman, the private secretary, had saved me from many mistakes as regards Natal affairs; while Lieutenant Slade, R.A., not only took all the trouble of entertaining upwards of two thousand guests in the three months off my hands, but gave me a slip of paper every Monday morning showing the numbers, and the cost per capita.

My visit to Isandwhlana was of great interest, the fall of the heroic Colonel Durnford, R.E., and the stand made by Natal policemen who stayed to die with him, in order to cover the retreat of the guns on the 22nd of January 1879, was the more touching in that he had spoken in terms of the conduct of the Police in the suppression of the Native out-

NATAL AND PART OF ZULULAND

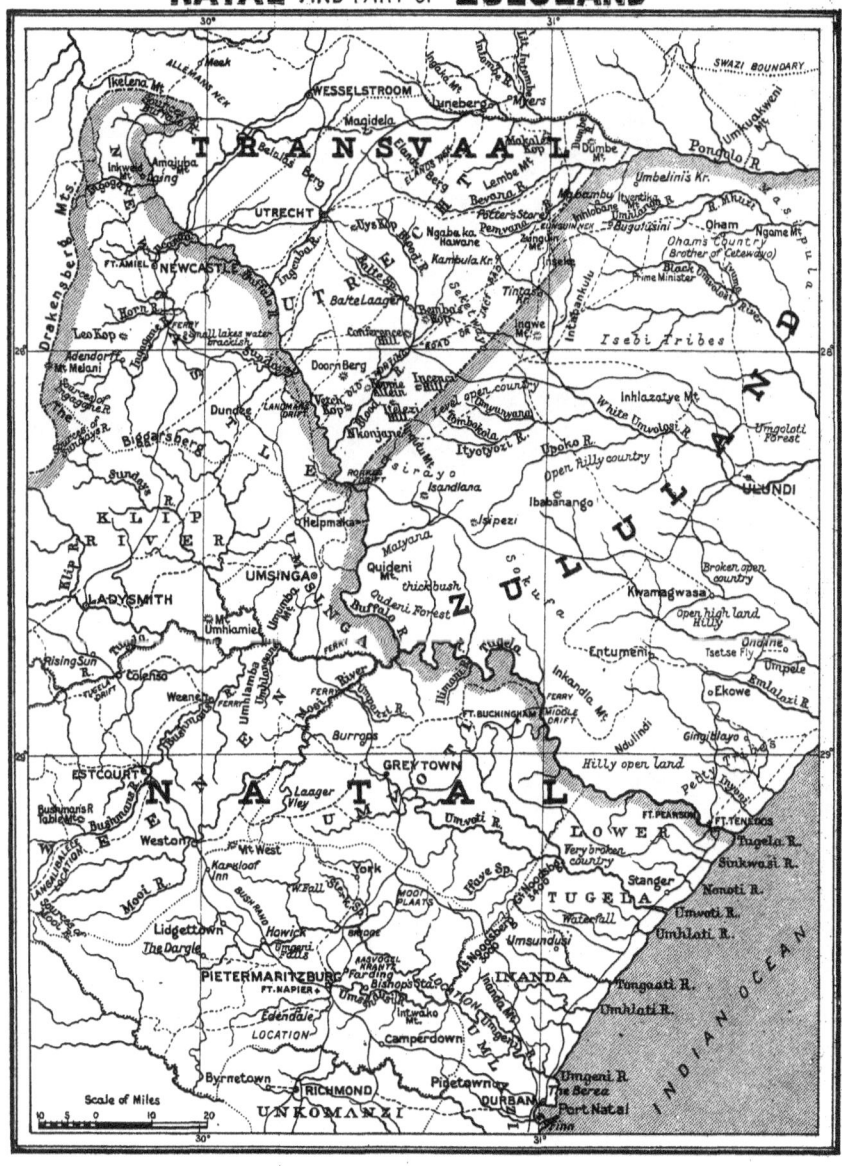

break in 1874, which had made him for some time unpopular in the Force.

I presented medals to a corps of Volunteers at Durban, many of whom had served in the war, and took the opportunity of speaking to the Colonists on the occasion of this parade,[1] which to some slight extent may explain the enthusiastic send-off I received at the end of December.

Kind friends, agreeing to forget the unpleasant memories following the disaster on the Majuba, vied with each other in offering me entertainments, the Burgesses of Durban presenting me with a beautiful vase and cups. The ladies said, "You may give him as many dinners as you like, but we must give him a Ball," and I went from one which followed the Farewell Dinner to me, direct on board a Union Steamship Company's vessel, which carried me to Lorenzo Marques, and there a few days later transhipped into another vessel, visiting Inhambane, Quillimane, Mozambique, and Zanzibar; we saw as much as was possible in a short time of Naples and Rome, and I resumed command at Chatham on the 14th February 1882.

[1] " Yet surely no greater proof of devoted steadiness was ever given than that shown by the Natal Carabiniers on the 22nd of January 1879. Imagine a gentle slope up which is storming a resistless, surging wave of encircling black bodies, which, though constantly smitten by leaden hail, breaks but to sweep on again with renewed force. Imagine a crowd of terrified non-combatants, and friendly Natives, flying through the already burning camp, and pressing on to the rapidly narrowing outlet over the fatal Nek.

"Then there comes on the scene a one-armed man, who, having slowly fallen back before the ever-increasing foe, is now determined to die. 'Save yourself, as for me I shall remain.' He thus dismisses the Staff officer, and H'Lubi's black soldiers, who vainly urge the great Chief to retreat with them.

"Recognising his commanding courage, around him gather some 20 similar spirits, who, nobly disdaining death, resolve to cover the retreat of the guns, or die with them.

"That melancholy field of Isandwhlana is a Record of what Colonists did, in Silence and Death, but none the less a living Record now and for ever. In the place where Durnford fell there was a heap of slain; the enemy lay thick about him, but your sons were as close, and the brave hearts of the best of your fighting men ceased to beat, in the effort to shelter their elected heroic leader. He himself was fully worthy of their devotion, and history will narrate how the ring of dead White men that encircled him, formed a halo round his, and their, renown."

CHAPTER XL

1882—CHATHAM AND ALEXANDRIA

Hospital Nurses—War Office denying my existence between December and February declines to issue even Half-Pay—Offered the Governorship of the Isle of Man—Cardinal Manning—Alexandria—A shell denudes a soldier of his trousers—Smith-Dorrien—Mr. Gladstone in Downing Street—Return to Egypt.

I WAS very happy at Chatham, being on good terms with all the officers, including the Medical officers, the senior of whom would not agree with me, however, as to the desirability of having female nurses to attend the soldiers, a reform which has happily since been carried into effect. He was one day arguing with me that Female nurses were entirely out of place in a Military Hospital, so I told him of a scene I had witnessed in the general Hospital under his charge only forty-eight hours earlier. I was passing through a ward after the Medical officers had left for lunch, and saw a soldier evidently on the confines of the next world refusing some food which an orderly taken out of the regiment was endeavouring to force on him. The man was too weak to speak, but the look of disgust on his face was so strong that I went up to the bed, and asked the orderly, " Why do you give him that black stuff from the inside of the chicken, when you have got half the breast, which he is more likely to fancy ? " The soldier said somewhat indignantly, " I was told to give him chicken, and I don't see it matters where he begins." Having told my story, I said, " Now, doctor, let us go to the Hospital, and see how he is." On arriving there we found the patient had died the previous evening.

I was engaged in a lengthy correspondence from March onward, with the Financial Authorities of the War Office. For the nine months I was Acting Governor and High Commissioner in South-East Africa I was paid at the rate of £5000 per annum, and although the Colonial Attorney-General advised me I was entitled to Half-Pay on my journey home, that is at the rate of £2500 a year,—the amount drawn from Colonial funds,—I drew nothing, for the Colonial Treasurer told me that as I had never been officially appointed, and was only Acting Governor, I should have troublesome correspondence with the Colony, and the Colonial Office later, if I drew it.

When I resumed the Command at Chatham I asked for my half-pay as a Major-General, from the 22nd December 1881 to the 13th February 1882; but the War Office alleged that as I was in receipt of a Civil salary I was not entitled to any ordinary pay, or to any allowance, on the termination of my Staff appointment. Weeks of correspondence ensued; I tried pleasant words, and then sarcasm, writing I would furnish a certificate from a clergyman that I was alive from the 22nd December to the 13th February, which would entitle me to half-pay in any case, but in vain. I then appealed to Lord Kimberley, and pointed out that as he had expressed satisfaction with my services, I hoped he would point out to the Treasury that I should not be treated as if I had been dead for two months.

His Lordship replied it was impossible for him to do anything except ask the War Office to accord me the most liberal treatment, which he did; nevertheless, there was no result until Mr. Childers helped me on my appealing personally to him. This I was too shy to do, until shortly before Sir Garnet Wolseley's victory at Tel-el-Kebir, in the following September, when an opportunity occurred.[1]

I had many reasons to be grateful to Her Most Gracious Majesty the Queen, who invested me shortly after my arrival

---

[1] The Secretary of State for War telegraphed to me, a small number of soldiers would be sent to strengthen the position in front of Alexandria, about which the Cabinet was apprehensive, and ended with the request, I would mention anything in which I desired help, officially or unofficially; this gave me an opportunity. I replied to the following effect:—"I am greatly obliged for your letter and telegram. I believe there is very little chance of the Egyptians attacking us, but if they do I am confident of defeating them. As a personal request, could you persuade your Department that I was alive from the 22nd December last to the 14th February, which has hitherto been denied, and I have been refused Half-Pay for that period."

I wrote also fully to a similar effect, adding, "I am ashamed to trouble you on a personal matter, but I am more ashamed of the War Office's interminable delays."

with the Grand Cross of St. Michael and St. George, and I went during the following week to stay at Sandhurst, where the Staff College students arranged a Drag hunt over my favourite line, beginning with the two flights of rails in East Hampstead Park. Captain George Gough,[1] 10th Hussars, mounted me on his best horse, which had won the Point to Point race in 1881, and would have probably repeated its victory in 1882, but that the horse Gough rode fell at the rails, and my friend broke a collar bone, so could not get into a saddle.

In the following week I had a kind letter [2] from Sir Vernon Harcourt, offering me the post of Governor of the Isle of Man. I was driving with Her Imperial Majesty the Empress Eugénie, when calling at my club for letters I received the offer, and with her permission read the letter. I had great difficulty in explaining to Her Majesty where the Isle of Man was situated, until I told her in my voluble, but badly pronounced French, it was the Island where the cats had no tails, when she at once understood.

The next few months at Chatham gave me opportunities of seeing many men in whom I was interested, Cardinal Manning coming twice to stay at Government House. He

Mr. Childers was prompt, and long before he got my letter, had a telegram sent to me, "Amount claimed paid to your account at Cox's."

Later, I told Mr. Childers I had addressed his office three times without any result, and without his help I should never have got it, unless, perhaps, my refusal to pay some stoppage accruing in January 1882, on the grounds that I could not pay something out of nothing, brought the case to the notice of a higher placed civilian than he who at that time generally decided such questions, even in the case of claims made by Generals.

[1] *Vide* p. 176.
[2] From the Secretary of State for the Home Department to Sir Evelyn Wood :—

"LONDON, 16*th March* 1882.

"SIR,—Though I have not the honour of your personal acquaintance, the great esteem and admiration which I entertain for the service rendered by you in the course of recent events in South Africa induce me to make to you a proposal for which I have received the sanction of the Commander-in-Chief, and the Secretary of State for War.

"The post of Governor of the Isle of Man is vacant, and if it were agreeable to you, I should be happy to submit your name to the Queen to fill that office. I should not have thought of proposing to so distinguished a soldier as yourself a civil office if I had not ascertained from the Military authorities that the temporary discharge of its duties would form no impediment in the future to your military career.

"Of course, if any considerable command offered itself to you, you would be at liberty to accept it, to cancel it, and rejoin the Government when you pleased.

"(Signed) W. V. HARCOURT."

received a very large number of soldiers of the Royal Irish into the Temperance League, and was out on the "Lines," from immediately after dinner till 2 a.m., watching Siege operations. Major Duncan, who later on commanded the Artillery of the Egyptian Army, and was subsequently Member of Parliament for Finsbury, was mounting heavy guns to open fire at daylight, and the glacis, which was honeycombed from the result of previous excavations, being treacherous, one gun slipped into a deep hole. As the scheme supposed him to be close to the enemy, the work of extricating it, which took five hours, had to be carried on in absolute silence. In spite of the fact that His Eminence's dinner, although he sat out as usual our succession of courses, consisted of some weak tea and two slices of bread and butter, he showed the most unflagging interest in the work, and did not return to Government House until I coaxed him back under the plea that I myself was tired.

On the 4th August I embarked in command of the 4th Brigade of the Expeditionary force on board the steamship *Catalonia*, Her Majesty coming on board to say good-bye to us. She embraced my wife, and was very gracious to me. She had honoured me with a long private interview in July, when I was commanded to Windsor, and treated me with a condescension for the memory of which I shall be ever grateful.

We landed at Alexandria on the 15th August, and went out to Ramleh. I took up my quarters in a convent school, which had prior to the bombardment been vacated by the nuns, and there remained for a day or two until another empty house became available.

Four days later I was a witness of an incident which is so remarkable that most people will have difficulty in believing the story. During the afternoon of the 19th of August, in accordance with orders received from the Divisional General, I made a demonstration with two battalions towards the enemy's lines at Kafr Dowar. I took two companies only within effective range, and few casualties occurred. We had extended the two companies at six paces between men, and were advancing, when the Egyptians getting the range dropped several shell just short, and over the line. One shell fell about 60 yards to my left, and apparently struck down a soldier of the 1st Berkshire Regiment. I saw the flash immediately in front of his feet, and the man fell headlong. One or two men near him wavered, but on my speaking to them they resumed their places and moved steadily on.

When retiring an hour or so later, we repassed opposite the spot. I was then riding on the bank of the Mahmoudieh Canal, and said to Captain Hemphill, the Adjutant, "Send a stretcher and four men to bring in your man's body." He replied, "The man is in the Ranks, he was not much hurt." " But I saw him struck by a shell; he was killed." "No; he is in the Ranks." "I should like to see him." "Well, you must look at him only in front, sir!" When I overtook the company to which the man belonged I asked for him, and a titter went round, as the man halting, faced me. He had all his clothes on in front, but the shell had burst immediately at his feet, and the flash of the explosion had burnt off the back of his socks, the whole of the back of his trousers, and the skirt of his serge up to the waistbelt; so that from heels to belt he was absolutely naked. He was bleeding from burns on the more protuberant parts up to the waist, but was not permanently injured.

A day or two afterwards, when we were advancing to carry out a similar operation designed to give the Arabists an idea that Sir Garnet meant to make his attack there, the Egyptians fired many shell at us, $5\frac{1}{2}$ inches in diameter, and 15 inches in length. One of these which failed to explode is now in my house, but another fell immediately in front of a section of Fours which was following me, and exploded. Putting up my hand to save my eyes from stones, I turned my face, and looked into the eyes of a young officer of the Berkshire, who delighted me by his naïve avowal. I asked, "A little nervous?" "Very much so indeed, sir;" but he did not show it in his bearing.

When Sir Garnet Wolseley took three Brigades away to Ismailia to attack Arabi at Tel-el-Kebir, I was left to defend a front $5\frac{1}{2}$ miles long, and on a Staff officer pointing out to our Chief that he was taking away every mounted soldier, he observed, "It does not matter, Evelyn Wood is sure to raise some more." This I did, but under some difficulties, for my Divisional General would not without authority from Headquarters sanction the purchase of any saddlery.

In the Derbyshire Regiment then under my command in the City of Alexandria was Lieutenant Smith-Dorrien.[1] By my orders he put fifty saddles together in a shop, and ransacked the Khedive's stables, which had indeed already been drawn on by various Staff officers. Within half an hour of the Divisional General embarking, Smith-Dorrien had collected 15 men, increased in a few days to 30. Many of them had never ridden, but before sundown a section defiled past me at Ramleh, 12 ponies, 2 mules, and a donkey; a somewhat motley detachment, and many of them held on to the saddle, but they proceeded 5 miles farther to the front, and managed to shoot an Egyptian officer that evening, and in five days killed or wounded 12 of the enemy, as they admitted. Three days later Smith-Dorrien had pushed back the Egyptian outposts, and we were not again troubled by the Bedouins looting the houses in Ramleh, as they had done the week before the other Brigade of the Division to which I belonged, embarked.[2]

It was necessary for me to cut down a large grove of Date trees, but I sent for the owner, and paid him the sum awarded by an Arbitrator, himself an Egyptian. It transpired that the owner was delighted, for as every female tree (and it is only the female which bears fruit) paid a yearly tax, the owner got his money based on the number of years before the trees would again bear fruit, and till then had no tax to pay.

Sir Garnet Wolseley, in sending instructions on the 5th of September, to attract the attention of the Egyptians in my front, wrote very kindly, "Your being detained at Alexandria is a sad blow to me, and I know it will be to you." He asked me to send some one into Arabi's lines, and find out the position of his troops. This I did by the help of our Resident, Sir Edward Malet, and furnished Sir Garnet

---

[1] Now Lieutenant-General H. L. Smith-Dorrien, commanding the Quetta District.

[2] I took the opportunity which Mr. Childers had given me of corresponding with him direct to tell this story, and to urge for an increased expenditure in the training of Mounted Infantry. I pointed out also that in spite of my remonstrances, we had only a Brigade Signaller, and thus when the Divisional Signalling Officer moved off with the General, the 4th Brigade was left without any signalling apparatus, as lamps, heliographs, were all taken away. The sailors put an electric light on the top of a fort on the extreme left of our position, which lit up at night the most vulnerable portion of the approach to the city.

Wolseley with information which he told me later was absolutely accurate.

I telegraphed to him on the 8th of September with reference to the orders I was "not to risk a man," that I proposed to attack three regiments at Mandara, a few miles out from Ramleh, encamped on the spot where Abercromby was killed in 1801. There were 3000 at Kafr Dowar, and I urged that I should be allowed to attack the Mandara Force, to draw the enemy from Kafr Dowar, explaining that I could carry the Mandara position at daylight, and get back to Ramleh by twelve o'clock. He telegraphed to me on the 10th and 11th, "Act on the defensive only, risk nothing."

The Cabinet was anxious at this time, regarding the six battalions as insufficient to defend the frontage of 55 miles, and promised a reinforcement in a fortnight. I replied to Mr. Childers, I did not expect the Egyptians would attack, but if they did so I was confident of defeating them. I could, indeed, have defended it against a force of Egyptians of eight or ten times our numbers ; and after a week's labour we opened on the 13th, the day of Sir Garnet's victory at Tel-el-Kebir, the seawall, and thus in a week, had the war continued, a lake would have covered the south, or open front of the city, rendering it secure against Assault.

I was at Chatham again early in November, and on the 8th dined with Mr. Gladstone, in Downing Street, and had an enjoyable evening, in spite of an adverse opinion on his Irish Land Bill, which, however, I gave only on his repeated demand.

The arrangements about going in to dinner were peculiar. In a large party there were only six ladies, and Mr. Gladstone did not take either of them in to the dining-room. Lord Hartington took Mrs. Gladstone, and our host followed his guests from the room in which we assembled. As I was one of the juniors I went to the foot of the table, and Mr. Gladstone followed me, apparently intending to sit next to me, but a Naval officer slipped in between us, and to our host's evident annoyance insisted in talking about what he did in the Egyptian Expedition, from which several of us, including Sir John Adye, who was on my left, had just returned. Mr. Gladstone indicated he wanted to hear nothing more of Egypt, and then turning the conversation asked me to describe the appearance of John Dunn. From this subject we got accidently on the derivations of words, and when he had mentioned one or two French words in ordinary use in Scotland, I asked him if he had ever noticed the use in Cumberland of the German word "Gerade," pronounced "grade." He was greatly interested, and asked how I came across it. I told him that in 1862 being near Penrith with a Woolwich cadet who was fishing, he asked a lad who had shown him a trout pool in a stream with great success, to show him another. It was eight o'clock, and the child replied, "No, I must go grade home." I made him repeat the word two or three times, until he became angry, thinking I was laughing at him, and then he changed the word, saying, "I must just go straight home." I have never had a more delightful table companion than Mr. Gladstone, and he himself was so eager in telling me about the derivations of various words that he overlooked his dinner.

I was shooting with Redvers Buller at Castle Rising on the 29th November, when I had a flattering letter from Lord Granville,[1] saying that Mr. Gladstone wished me to go out and recreate the Egyptian Army. This was the more complimentary on his part, as I had disagreed with him strongly about his Irish policy.

I went to London, and after a discussion by telegraph with Lord Dufferin, who wished to give me only half the salary I was willing to accept, went out on my own terms. When I reached Cairo, Lord Dufferin told me that although he had used the name of the Egyptian Government, it was he who had tried to get me at a small salary, and three months later he was good enough to say I was cheap at any price.

Chinese Gordon wrote on the 8th of December, when sending me a present of a gold-laced coat which the late Khedive gave to him, "I am *so truly glad* you are going out. For go you will. Remember you are creating there a British contingent." In a P.S. he urged I should be very careful in

---

[1] Lord Granville to Sir Evelyn Wood:—
"FOREIGN OFFICE, 28*th November* 1882.

"It is most important to get the best possible man to be the first of the English officers in the Egyptian service. Everything depends upon it. Should you be willing that I should tell Dufferin you would be available for the post . . .—Yours sincerely, GRANVILLE."

my choice of a Native writer, about which I will later narrate something which happened in 1884.[1]

Just before Christmas I was back again in Cairo, and taking steps to raise the Egyptian Army, which had been disbanded after Tel-el-Kebir.

[1] *Vide* p. 163.

CHAPTER XLI

1883—SIRDAR

I receive £200,000 to create an Army—First Ceremonial Parade in ten weeks—Lord Dufferin's recognition of work—Cholera—Three Britons administer Egypt—Devotion to duty shown by British Officers—Chinese Gordon—Roubi Tewhari—Turks Mutiny—Two shot—Determined conduct of Major Grant.

MY first week in Cairo was spent in conferences with His Highness the Khedive, Lord Dufferin, the principal Ministers of the Khedive who had interests in the Army, and with Sir Auckland Colvin, the Financial adviser of the Government.

As regards the creation of an Army I had an absolutely free hand, being informed by Lord Dufferin that I might do anything I liked, provided I did not spend more than £200,000. This sum, however, was to include the pay of officers, Europeans and Turks, or Egyptians, and the pay and rations of the men, but not the upkeep of barracks and hospital arrangements, which were provided by other Departments. I was told to select uniforms, and was later given a sum to buy Field artillery, and to replace the Remington rifle, by the pattern in use in the British Army.

I had put the conscription arrangements in motion immediately on my arrival, and within a fortnight got the first recruits, and had set the officers to work in creating and training the Force which has since proved to be a satisfactory instrument for war. I had obtained the services of 25 officers, of whom the following have risen in the Army:—Major Fraser, Royal Engineers,[1] Chief Staff officer; Captain Slade,[2] as Aide-de-Camp, replacing him on arrival by Stuart Wortley,[3] when Slade went to work

---

[1] Now Major-General Sir Thomas Fraser, K.C.B.
[2] Major-General F. Slade, C.B.
[3] Colonel the Honourable E. Stuart Wortley, D.S.O.

under Fraser. Somewhat later I got Lieutenant Wingate,[1] Royal Artillery; Major Grenfell[2] commanded a brigade of four battalions, each of which had three British officers. The first battalion was organised and commanded by Captain Chermside;[3] the 2nd Battalion by Captain Holled Smith;[4] the 3rd Battalion by Captain Parr;[5] the 4th, by Major Wynne.[6] Major Duncan[7] commanded the Artillery, the English Batteries of which were commanded by Lieutenant Wodehouse,[8] Lieutenant Rundle,[9] and somewhat later by Lieutenant Parsons.[10] Captain Kitchener[11] was second in command of the Cavalry Regiment. Captains H. S. Smith-Dorrien[12] and Archibald Hunter[13] joined later.

There was an Infantry Brigade under a Turkish General, Schudi Pasha. There were no Engineers, and no Departmental Corps.

The men conscripted were in physique superior to any European army, and their aptitude for the perfunctory parts of drill was remarkable. Their progress was indeed so rapid that the Khedive's guard at the Abdin Palace was taken over from British troops on the 14th February. Two days later, on parade of all troops then available, I returned £9 which had been given to a doctor to induce him to say a recruit was unfit for the service, and awarded the recruit twenty-one days' imprisonment for offering bribes.

On the 31st March we had our first parade, before the Khedive, Lord Dufferin, all the Ministers, and a large crowd, including all the European residents in Cairo. The cavalry were not fit to do more than "keep the ground," which was

---

[1] Major-General Sir F. R. Wingate, K.C.B., K.C.M.G., D.S.O., Sirdar.
[2] General the Right Honourable Lord Grenfell, G.C.B., G.C.M.G.
[3] Major-General Sir H. C. Chermside, G.C.M.G., C.B., Late Governor of Queensland.
[4] Major-General Sir C. Holled Smith, K.C.M.G., C.B.
[5] Major-General Hallam Parr, C.B.
[6] Lieutenant-General A. Wynne, C.B.
[7] Colonel-Duncan, later M.P. for Finsbury.
[8] Lieutenant-General J. H. Wodehouse, C.B., C.M.G.
[9] Lieutenant-General Sir Leslie Rundle, K.C.B.
[10] Major-General Sir C. Parsons, K.C.M.G.
[11] General Lord Kitchener, G.C.B., Commander-in-Chief in India.
[12] Lieutenant-General H. S. Smith-Dorrien, C.B., D.S.O.
[13] Lieutenant-General Sir Archibald Hunter, K.C.B., D.S.O.

done by some of the men who had learned enough to remain on their horses. The artillery had made most progress, but that Arm was the best before Arabi's rebellion, and we had kept several of the officers, and some of the non-commissioned officers came back voluntarily; moreover, the men were conscripted in Upper Egypt, and all such are more virile than the Delta Fellaheen. I showed eight battalions, and four batteries after six weeks' instruction, and they marched past in the stereotyped Aldershot fashion.

Schudi Pasha, the Egyptian Brigadier, had been educated in Berlin, and as Major Grenfell knew some German, it happened that the few orders I, as Commander of the Force, had to give on the ceremonial parade were spoken in the one language common to my Brigadiers, *i.e.* German; Schudi giving his words in Arabic; Grenfell, in English; and the four English Commanders in Turkish, as was the custom in the Egyptian Army. This I endeavoured to alter, but the Arabic language does not lend itself to the sharp monosyllables, which are most suitable for getting men to move with clock-like regularity.

Major Wynne not only compiled a Clothing warrant and Signalling manual, but also took in hand our Drill book, and Lieutenant Mantle, Royal Engineers, who was an accomplished Arabic scholar, put as much of it as I thought necessary into Arabic. By a strange coincidence, in 1887, Wynne, then in the War Office, followed my precedent and reduced the English Drill book by cutting out many superfluous exercises, which were appropriate to the movements practised before rifles were used. The Code Napoleon put into Arabic did not deal with some crimes common in the East, and so the Army Discipline Act of 1881, with the Khedive's name substituted for our Queen's, became in Arabic, our penal Code.

Lord Dufferin supported me most thoroughly, but while fully satisfied, warned me before he left, early in May, that I was working the officers too hard, and this was probably accurate.[1] Before his lordship departed he asked me to hand

[1] Lord Dufferin to Sir Evelyn Wood:—

"CAIRO, 1st *May* 1883.

"Before quitting Egypt I cannot help expressing to you in the warmest terms I can command my appreciation of the extraordinary energy you have exhibited in the creation of the Egyptian Army.

"Though not a military man, I am quite capable of understanding the in-back £10,000 in the first instance, and then another £10,000, but this latter sum I gave up provisionally on the understanding that I could reclaim it if necessary. I did not do so, spending thus in my first year only £180,000.

Colonel Hicks, who arrived at Cairo from India in January, had gone to Khartoum, and the following June, having telegraphed for reinforcements, the Ministers collected soldiers who had served in and prior to the Egyptian outbreak in 1882, and I was directed by the Premier, Cherif Pasha, to inspect them, and pass for service only such as I considered fit. Out of the first thousand I felt bound to reject over six hundred, and those who were not rejected, being aware that few Egyptians ever returned from Khartoum, were most unwilling to go, two men actually putting lime into their eyes to destroy their sight while on parade. These poor creatures who preferred life without eyesight in the Delta to probable death in the Sudan, were the fathers and uncles of those whom we were to teach to take a pride in themselves, and in the Army.

I limited the term of service, and gave every soldier a furlough as soon as he was reported to be efficient. When the first contingent of 2000 men received railway passes to their villages, I was assured by the Cairenes that few would return, but every man returned punctually. I introduced a postal order system, and the soldiers remitted home a portion of their pay, 2½d. a day. Later, when Hallam Parr asked for six soldiers to go with him to the Sudan, his whole battalion stepped forward.

We drilled five days a week, for the Moslems kept Friday as their Day of Rest, and I insisted on Sunday being kept as such. My action was based on the firm conviction formed in India, twenty years earlier, from my intimate knowledge of natives, that, putting one's own feelings aside, it is an error

numerable difficulties you have had to encounter. I am sure it will be a satisfaction to you to know that the success of your efforts is recognised by everyone, by the Khedive, by his Ministers, and by the Egyptian colony, as well as by Her Majesty's Government. The justice, the humanity, and the consideration with which you have treated your men have already changed the point of view from which the Native regards Military service, and all your countrymen are proud to think of the effect your character and conduct have produced upon all who have come into contact with you.—Yours sincerely, DUFFERIN."

to allow any soldiers to believe that their officers are without Religion.

I worked from daylight to 5 p.m. every week-day, when I played polo three times a week, and on the other days lawn tennis, one hour a day being devoted to the study of the Arabic language. Being an interpreter in Hindustani the characters presented no difficulty, but my desire to learn Arabic grammatically was damped when I saw there were seven hundred irregular conjugations.

I kept myself by regular exercise in tolerable health, but in June slight attacks of fever became more frequent, and His Highness the Khedive gave me leave to proceed to England for two months. In the middle of July I left for Suez, to catch a homeward-bound steamer; Grenfell and the officers commanding units saw me off, and out of mistaken kindness forbore to mention there had been a case of cholera in the barracks at Abbassieh the previous night. When I got to Zagazig the stationmaster told me there were several cases in Cairo, so I telegraphed to the Khedive, that I should not be out of the canal for three days, and trusted he would recall me if the cholera became Epidemic in the army, adding that whether he telegraphed or not, if I were not satisfied, I should return from Port Said. I was intercepted, however, by a launch sent after me, shortly after we passed Ismailia, and finding a special train waiting for me, reached Cairo twenty-four hours after leaving it.

The Khedive and his Ministers went to Alexandria, and Sir Edward Malet, Valentine Baker Pasha, and I practically ruled Egypt during the Epidemic. Strong measures were necessary, for some of the Egyptian authorities had established a cholera camp on the Nile, immediately above the intake of the Cairo waterworks, and it was difficult to induce adequate sanitary arrangements amongst a people who are by religion, and by inclination, Fatalists. The losses in the army were not very great, and they had the inestimable advantage of attaching the Fellaheen soldiery to the British officer. The Egyptian officer, except in some few instances, did not show to advantage.

His Highness the Khedive returned from Alexandria without his Ministers when the cholera became serious, and calling at my house at six o'clock in the morning, asked me to take him over the hospitals, which we had organised under Captain Rogers[1] of the Army Medical Department. The Khedive, whatever he felt, behaved well, but the senior Egyptian officers would not go near the hospitals, much less the patients, except with a surrounding of drugs, supposed to be prophylactics, and an Egyptian resented my rebuke for his sending a soldier still alive to the mortuary, saying, " He will be dead in a few minutes."

The British officer not only nursed the cholera-stricken patients day and night, performing every menial service, but in many cases washed the corpses prior to interment. Lieutenant Chamley Turner, in spite of having only slight colloquial knowledge of the language, so endeared himself to the stricken men of his camel Company that several of them when dying threw their arms round his neck. He must have infused some of his spirit into his men, for General Brackenbury wrote, dated 4.2.85, " The Egyptian Company is doing invaluable service."

When the Epidemic was nearly over, Turner[2] contracted the disease, and I had him brought to my house, where he soon recovered under the skilled attention of Dr. Rogers and the careful nursing of Walkinshaw.

From the cholera time, on, the Fellaheen soldier trusted the British Officer.[3]

By the middle of August the cholera had died out, and I went to England for two months, keeping up my study of Arabic on the voyage, assisted by Mrs. Watson, the wife of an officer whom I had got out as Surveyor-General, or Chief

---

[1] Now Colonel Sir John Rogers, K.C.B.

[2] He had shown remarkable courage at Tokar, Eastern Sudan, and was drowned later in the Nile.

[3] Extract: Sir E. Malet to Earl Granville :—

"CAIRO, 11*th August* 1883.

"I cannot forward Sir Evelyn's report on the cholera Epidemic among the Egyptian troops at Cairo, without adding a word to record the high admiration which the conduct of the English officers towards their men has elicited. Sir Evelyn Wood and his Staff, and all the officers, have worked night and day at the measures necessary to ward off and mitigate the disease, and their efforts have met with an almost unhoped-for success. Beyond the immediate benefit of the saving of life which they have obtained, an example has been given of Self-devotion which may have lasting consequences for good in the promotion of respect and regard of the men towards the officers."

business man. His wife knew the language well, although mainly self-taught.

Her Majesty the Queen was graciously pleased to command me to stay at Balmoral, and took much interest in the Egyptian army. I visited Lord Granville at Walmer, at his request, on my way back to Egypt, for the question was then constantly discussed as to whether the British Garrison could be withdrawn. I undertook to maintain order with the eight Egyptian battalions only as far as the internal peace of the country was concerned, but probably all the British troops would have been withdrawn had not the events at Khartoum in the following year enforced on us the permanent occupation.

In the summer of 1883 I was directed to ask the Turkish Pasha who had been serving at Khartoum if he would return there as Governor; and his observations in refusing—on Englishmen putting Turks in posts of danger—were so unpleasant that I offered Nubar Pasha to go up myself. This he declined, and then having made the offer, I told him I thought the decision was wise, as I was doing good work in Cairo, where several of the Egyptian officers knew me, and in Khartoum I should only be as any other officer.

In the third week of November we heard rumours, afterwards confirmed, of the annihilation of 10,000 men under Hicks Pasha, near El Obeid. Early in the month, and just before Christmas, Osman Digna, a powerful Slave dealer in the Eastern Sudan, routed Baker Pasha at El Teb on the Red Sea, killing two-thirds of his Force of Constabulary, composed of old soldiers discharged from the Army in 1882.

I was vilified in the British Press for not having sent rifles to Suakin when they were demanded by Baker Pasha, in order that he might arm " Friendlies," but I had nothing to do with the decision, which was taken by the Egyptian Government and the Consul-General in Council, and I merely obeyed orders in sending the telegram; but in fact there were at the time 2000 stand of rifles in store at Suakin. I took no notice of these attacks, which had been, as I was told later by one of my traducers who fell fighting bravely at Abu Klea, made for Political purposes. But when Sir Stafford Northcote, in moving a vote of censure on the Government, doubtless in perfect good faith, made several mis-statements: (*a*) That Sir

Evelyn Wood was answerable for Hicks Pasha's army. (*b*) That Sir Evelyn Wood refused to send the newly raised army to Khartoum, stating that he could not do so, as the British Government contemplated withdrawing from Egypt, and other such erroneous allegations, I wrote a letter, through the Foreign Office, which was published later in the Press: (*a*) That I had nothing at the time to do with the troops in the Sudan. (*b*) That I had never given Hicks Pasha any such information as alleged, for indeed I did not know the intention of the Government. I further explained that my only intervention in Sudan affairs was, at the request of Colonel Hicks, to induce the Finance Department in Cairo to send him money; while I at the same time, unasked, expressed to the War Minister the strongest opinion against the contemplated advance into Kordofan, where later the Pasha and his 10,000 men were annihilated.

The situation in the Sudan having become worse, Gordon Pasha offered to go up to extricate the garrisons. He telegraphed decidedly that he would not pass through Cairo, travelling to Khartoum via Suakin and Berber, and on the 23rd January the Resident sent me to Port Said, to induce him to go up the Nile after paying his respects to His Highness the Khedive.

My friend Captain Briscoe, commanding the mail steamer which brought Gordon from Brindisi, on my going on board bet me that I should fail to get Gordon to go through Cairo; but he did not know his character as well as I did, and Briscoe lost the bet.

Gordon had telegraphed to Colonel Evelyn Baring[1] that he wished to have Roubi Tewhari, a blind ex-clerk sent to him, and that a certain officer should be promoted to the rank of Colonel, and sent to him. Our Consul-General told me to arrange it, but I exclaimed that, though I could find the ex-clerk, I scarcely liked to ask the Khedive not only to take the Captain out of prison, for he had been an ardent Arabist and was still undergoing punishment, but at the same time to make him a Colonel. His Highness, however, was good enough to release him, and we let the question of his promotion stand over.

[1] Now Lord Cromer.

When I explained to Gordon that it was undesirable that he should go to Khartoum as the Khedive's Representative without seeing him, he at once agreed to go to Cairo with me. During our journey in the train he told me an interesting story.[1] Pointing to Roubi Tewhari, who sat in the saloon carriage with us, he said: "You see that man? He was my confidential clerk in Darfour. I trusted him implicitly, and believed in his honesty. One day I was told on authority I could not doubt that he had been levying fines, and receiving large sums of money—in one case £3000, which as he alleged went into my pocket: taxed with this wickedness, he admitted it with tears, and I said to him: "You villain, go back to El Obeid." Tewhari replied : " Have mercy on me; I have lost one eye in your service, and if you send me to that hot dusty place the other eye will suffer." "Whether it suffers or not, you shall go there as a punishment for your conduct."

Gordon taking £300, in notes of £10, out of his pocket said : " This is the only money I have in the world, and my sister found some of it for me, but I am going to give ten of these notes to Tewhari," and crossing over the carriage he put the notes into the blind man's hand. Gordon's Arabic, although intelligible, was not fluent, and it was not for a considerable time that Tewhari understood his former master's generosity, and the value of the paper money.

We reached Cairo at 9.30, p.m., and after dinner called on the Consul-General, with whom we sat till the early hours of the morning, returning again after breakfast. Gordon had accepted the task of evacuating the garrisons of the Sudan without financial aid, but eventually agreed to receive £100,000, of which he left £60,000 at Berber, and this I fear to some extent precipitated the tragedy enacted a year later; for the Mudir of Berber coveted the money and played Gordon false.

Early next day Roubi Tewhari, the blind man, sent to me an Arabic-speaking English officer, who had been with Gordon at Khartoum in 1874. The gist of Tewhari's petition was as follows: "I behaved badly to Gordon Pasha many years ago, and he banished me to El Obeid, where I lost my remaining eye. He has now given me more money than I can spend in my life, and I am going to Mecca, where I shall

[1] *Vide* page 154.

pray for his welfare in this world and in the next, until I die. Gordon Pasha is bent on having Zebehr sent up to Khartoum with him. Gordon's trustful nature will certainly undo him, and I implore everyone who loves Gordon as I do, not to allow Zebehr to go to Khartoum while Gordon is there. Whatever Gordon may say, do not let Zebehr go to Khartoum with Gordon. Send Gordon, or Zebehr, but not the two at the same time."

I do not know what influence, if any, this honest heartfelt request, passed on by me to Sir Evelyn Baring, made on the British Cabinet, but Tewhari's advice coincided with that of Sir Henry Gordon, Charles's brother. Zebehr remained in Cairo, in spite of the continuous carping in the Press at the decision of Government.

We spent all the next day at the Resident's house, where Gordon and Zebehr had animated and dramatic interviews. In 1879 a Court-Martial, assembled by Gordon's orders, had condemned Zebehr, who was then in Cairo litigating with a former Governor-General, to death. As a result of the facts brought out by the Court-Martial, Gordon confiscated Zebehr's property.

Now, in 1884, Zebehr accused Gordon of causing the death of his son Suleiman, and alleged that the confiscation was equally unjust. Gordon was in Abyssinia when Suleiman was executed, after a sentence of a Court-Martial approved by Gessi Pasha, Governor-General of the Sudan, in pursuance of instructions issued by Gordon, while he was Governor-General, that if found guilty Suleiman was to be executed.

I drove Gordon after dinner to the station on the Nile. On leaving the dining-room he said good-bye to Lady Wood, going upstairs to kiss my children, who were in bed. As he left the house he took off his evening-coat, and handing it to Walkinshaw, said: "I should like you to keep this, for I shall never wear an evening-coat again." A month later, however, in thanking officially an officer who was returning to Cairo, Gordon wrote: "There is not the least chance of any danger being now incurred in Khartoum,—a place as safe as Kensington Park."

At the Consul-General's request I now took charge of the Sudan Bureau, and became his Staff officer for Political affairs of the Red Sea Littoral to Massowah, which made my work heavy. Rising at daylight, I generally saw some military work at Abbassieh or elsewhere, and waited on Nubar Pasha at 9 a.m., always visiting the Consul-General, and often the General in Command of British troops, on my way to the War Office, where I remained till about four o'clock, when I played Polo or Tennis till night fell.

A Division of British troops under Sir Gerald Graham was sent to Suakin in February, and, after defeating Osman Digna at El Teb and Tamai, was recalled at the end of March, a Force of all Arms of the Egyptian Army holding Suakin.

The former Egyptian Army had suffered continuous defeats, accompanied either with annihilation or heavy loss, from 1875–6, when 11,000 were destroyed in Abyssinia. I consistently [1] urged that until the recollection of these disasters had been at least partially effaced by a victory, the Fellaheen soldier should not be allowed to fight without a

[1] Telegram—Evelyn Wood to Gordon Pasha, Khartoum :—
"*April 19th*, 1884.

(Extract): "Fifthly: I would give anything to be allowed to go up to Khartoum by river with British and Egyptian troops when the Nile rises, but I fear I may not be so fortunate as to get the chance, and, I gather from your telegrams in March, you think Egyptians are useless. I think that, considering about two-thirds have four months' service, and one-third three months only, they would do fairly well with British troops, or in fighting defensive actions. I could not recommend they should take the field without British support."

The gradual restoration of confidence, coupled with the brilliant example of the Sudanese Battalions, so encouraged the Fellaheen that General Sir Herbert Kitchener wrote to me: "Cairo, *17th February* 1888.—I hope my wound will soon be healed up. The Egyptian troops with me behaved splendidly, and were quite steady under fire, which was pretty hot at one time. If I had had more of them I could have cleared out the Dervishes. The Irregulars got quite out of hand."

Ten years later there were some remarkable instances of the change effected in the spirit of the Fellaheen.

On the 9th April 1898, Captain Hickman, with two troops of Cavalry, intercepted, near the Southern end of the Second Cataract (Wadi Halfa), a raiding party of Dervishes, mostly mounted on horses and camels, under the command of Emir Wad Rahma, driving off a number of looted cattle. Hickman charged home in the centre, his men fighting hand to hand, killing all except two horsemen, who escaped, and eight prisoners whose lives were spared. The Emir resisted with desperate courage, until a trooper, dismounting, literally jumped on and slew him.

Half a Battalion 16th Regiment, 300 men (Fellaheen), in September 1898, in a force under Colonel Parsons, near Gedareff, repeated the manœuvre for which the 28th Gloucester Regiment wears a double fore and hind peak to its head-dress, and alone successfully resisted a determined simultaneous attack in Front and Rear. As the Dervishes came on the Rear Rank faced about, and both attacks were repulsed.

backing of British troops. This was eventually approved, but not until after my retirement from the Command.

Early in 1884 I began to raise a battalion of Turks, mainly enlisted in Anatolia. They were paid five times the amount of the Fellaheen conscripts, and promised to fight any number of the Mahdi's soldiers.

When, however, the first Company was ordered up the Nile it mutinied, stopping the train by firing at the enginedriver, and made off in various directions. Major Grant,[1] 4th Hussars, who was in command of the Cadre battalion, riding to where the train had been held up, accompanied by one Egyptian policeman, came on seven of the mutineers in a serai or public Rest-house. Grant dismounting outside the enclosure, found the seven men cooking, their rifles piled in the courtyard. As he called to them to surrender and lie down, the ringleader fired at Grant, while the other men rushed towards their arms. Grant shot at and wounded the ringleader and another, which so cowed the other five that they obeyed his order to lie down, and Grant stood over them until the Sergeant, having tied up the two horses, came in and carried away their rifles, later assisting to bind the prisoners.

The ringleaders were tried by a general Court-Martial, presided over by a Turkish General, assisted by English officers, and seven mutineers were sentenced to death. I examined the cases carefully, with a view of carrying out the sentences only in such cases as appeared to be absolutely necessary, and at once eliminated from the condemned soldiers a youth, seventeen years of age, whose father had fired at Major Grant. I saw the condemned men, and was satisfied in my own mind that one of them was practically unaccountable for his actions; and eventually, after a consultation with the members of the Court-Martial, decided that two only should suffer death.

Lieutenant-General Sir Frederick Stephenson,[2] knowing that all the trained soldiers for the Egyptian Army were at

[1] Now General Grant, C.B.
[2] I heard later, in reply to various inquiries from Pall Mall as to whether I had not been unduly severe, he replied that he had the fullest confidence in my sense of justice.

Suakin, or on the Nile, the Depôt Companies in Cairo, consisting of men who had just been conscripted, kindly offered me assistance, but I determined to make the Egyptian recruits carry out the execution.

I asked for precedents in the Egyptian Army, and was told that at the last Military execution, the feet of the men condemned being tied, they were ordered to stand up at 400 yards distance, and a line of soldiers advanced on them firing, with the shocking results that can be readily understood. I had recently read the trial of a Neapolitan soldier, Misdea, who was shot while sitting in a chair, and arranged the execution on similar lines. The previous evening I sent the lad of seventeen away to a guard-room of the British Army of Occupation, as I did not wish him to hear the volley which was to kill his father, but, as will be seen later, my sympathetic consideration was unnecessary.

When I rode out next morning and met the procession marching to the place of execution, which was an incomplete barrack at Abbassieh, I was nearly ill from nervousness, but on arriving at the actual spot, when I had to give orders, the feeling passed off, the scene affecting me no more than any ordinary duty. Ten Egyptian recruit soldiers being told off for each of the condemned Turks, advanced close behind them, and at the word of command the mutineers ceased to exist.

I had some trouble after the sentence became known, for the Prime Minister sent for me, and said there was considerable feeling about Turks being executed by order of Christians. I pointed out that a Turkish General had presided over the Court-Martial, when the Minister said: " Well, do what you like; only, do not ask me or the Khedive to approve of it."

A day later he called on me to say that the Persian Minister claimed one of the condemned men, and wished to know what answer was to be given to him. I said: " Excellency, tell him ' Bukra '[1] (to-morrow)." And when that morrow came I wrote a note saying that the Persian Minister could now claim the man's body. I was then assured that it was a matter of no consequence.

[1] The invariable answer in the East, where nobody does anything to-day that can be left till to-morrow.

A few hours after the execution I sent for the son of the ringleader, and told him that his punishment had been commuted to imprisonment, but as he was so young, and it would distress him to serve under officers who had shot his father, I gave him £5 and told him to go back to Anatolia. The youth reappeared three days later, and said he much preferred to serve on; indeed, he thought less of the execution than I did.

The mutiny of the Turks was followed by that of two battalions which had been raised by Zebehr in the Delta for Baker Pasha, and some of these were condemned to death. I doubted their guilty intentions, although there was no doubt as to their overt acts, and commuted their sentence to service in the Eastern Sudan. I visited the men at their request a few days later, when the interpreter said: "They say, in olden times when soldiers went away for a long time, as is to be our case, they always had an advance of pay,—may we please have it?" This confirmed my impression that they had very little idea of how we regarded their conduct.

CHAPTER XLII

1884-5—THE SUDAN

Good work of British Officers—A cheery adviser—Arthur Wynne's determination—Father Brindle—Life in the Gakdul Desert—Walkinshaw's devotion—Fortitude of Mounted Infantry—Aden camel men—General Dormer's cheery nature—I am invalided.

IN the middle of August I followed the Egyptian troops up the Nile, where most of them had been since February, the balance of trained soldiers being at Suakin. At that place they came under the direct command of General Freemantle, who wrote to me in the most eulogistic terms of the work they had done, and on their steadiness on outpost duty. Colonel Duncan had got excellent work out of those on the Nile; they had fortified Korosko, Assuan, and Philæ. Here again I prefer to quote the words of the British officers, who certainly were not prepossessed in favour of the Fellaheen soldiery. Major Clarke, an officer sent from India, to act as Director of Railways, wrote officially: "The amount of work done on the railway by the 4th Battalion Egyptian Army (Colonel Wynne)[1] is simply prodigious." Lord Charles Beresford,[2] who was acting as Director of work on the Cataracts, wrote: "The way in which the 2nd Battalion (Smith's)[3] works the portage, carrying the whalers over the rocks for a thousand yards, is marvellous." It was somewhat galling for the British officers serving in the Egyptian Army to read in the Press that the sailors were carrying the whalers,

---

[1] Some officers, seeing little chance of promotion to be gained by serving in the Egyptian Army, got employment on the British Army Staff. I offered Colonel Wynne such a post, but he declined, saying: "I have a definite Command, and feel bound to hold it until the Expedition returns Northwards."

[2] Now Admiral Commander-in-Chief, Mediterranean.

[3] Now Major-General Sir Holled Smith, K.C.B.

for they never had any opportunity of doing so, and 609 out of 700 were carried by the 2nd Battalion Egyptian Army round the First Cataract.

Lord Wolseley, nominated to command the Gordon Relief Expedition while still on the sea, wrote me a very flattering letter asking me to accept the position of General of the Line of Communications, saying: "It is a most difficult, arduous, and responsible task, which I hope you will accept, as I feel sure that you will do it with credit to yourself and greatly to the advantage of the Service, and there is no doubt that on the manner in which this duty is performed will depend the success of the undertaking."

Long before I received my former Chief's kind letter he telegraphed its purport to me, and I, accepting his offer within ten minutes, he telegraphed again: "Your telegram has relieved my mind of a great trouble. Can you put some of your men on to the railway?" I replied: "You can confidently reckon on my cheerfully carrying out any duty you assign to me." On receipt of his letter on the 25th September I telegraphed: "Am taking every precaution to accelerate the transport by water, paying premiums for quick passages North of Halfa, and South of that place I have an Egyptian non-commissioned officer travelling in every native vessel.[1] I have got every man, except a guard of three per battalion, on railway work or portages." Lord Wolseley annexed the horses of the Egyptian Cavalry Regiment, and with reference to that order I, while expressing the pain it caused our officers, added, "but you may have the fullest confidence we shall all do our best to make the expedition a success." The one great factor of the good work done was the Arabic-speaking British officers, and their power of influencing the men.

Lord Wolseley, in appointing me General of the Line of Communications, reversed the previous decision of the War Minister who replied to my application for service at Suakin, when Sir Gerald Graham went there in January 1884, that, being in the Egyptian army, I could not be employed in command of British troops. As I then pointed out to the Commander-in-Chief, had I realised these conditions in 1882 I

---

[1] I had purchased every Native cargo vessel working on the Nile, north of Merowi.

should never have accepted Lord Granville's offer of the task of raising an Egyptian Army.

Early in September I disagreed with a gifted Naval officer who had charge of the Naval transport on the subject of putting steamers through the Second Cataract. He declared there was considerable risk for the steamers, and some for the crew, and demurred to my order that he should try it. We referred the point to the British General in Cairo, and to the Admiral, who replied that the officer was to "do his best to carry out my wishes, bearing in mind that, after stating his professional opinion, Sir Evelyn Wood was to be wholly responsible for what might happen to either steamers, officers, or men." Captain Lord Charles Beresford [1] was a much more cheery adviser. When I asked: "Will she go through?" said, "What sort of a hawser?" "Big steel." "How many darkies?" "Any number up to six thousand." "Well, sir, she must go through, or leave her bottom in it." The ship with several others went through the Cataract, in spite of all predictions to the contrary, but it is fair to observe that both paddle wheels were simultaneously on the rocks on either side, and when they reached the still waters up stream of the Cataract there was very little paddle wheel left intact.

Lord Wolseley and the Head Quarter Staff arrived at Halfa on the 5th October, stayed the greater part of a month, and then preceded me to Dongola. I worked from daylight to sunset throughout this month passing supplies, and later troops, up the river, storing 42,000 British rations at Dongola, before any Europeans went South of Halfa.

As General officer commanding on the Lines of Communication, it was my privilege to entertain a great number of the stream of officers who passed through Wadi Halfa. I was riding one evening, before the Camel battery under Captain Norton left for the Southward, and was so surprised to observe an officer turn away his head as I passed that I rode back to ascertain the reason; he had one eye bandaged, and saying he was suffering from slight ophthalmia, admitted he had turned away lest I, seeing his state, might prevent his going on with

---

[1] Now Admiral Lord Charles Beresford, G.C.B., Commander-in-Chief of the Mediterranean Fleet.

the battery. I reassured him by saying I was too sympathetic to think of stopping anyone from going to fight. He was mortally wounded at Abu Klea on the 19th January 1885. The militant spirit Lieutenant Guthrie showed was amusingly illustrated later by one of the gunners in the battery. When the square at Abu Klea was penetrated by the Dervishes, one of them attempted to spear a gunner who was in the act of ramming home a charge. The Briton brained the Sudanee, but the rammer head split on the man's hard skull. Next day the gunner was sent for; mistaking the reason, and knowing from experience soldiers are charged for Government property they break, he led off: "Please, sir, I'm very sorry I broke the rammer, but I never thought the nigger's head could be so hard. I'll pay for the rammer so as to hear no more of the case."

Before I left Wadi Halfa for the front Lord Wolseley entrusted to me for decision, as an Arbitrator, a claim by a contractor for services rendered, amounting to £42,000. The claimant, a public-spirited man of business, admitted some rebate should be made, as owing to change of plans his servants had done less than either party had contemplated, but suggested about £6000 would be a reasonable sum. I urged the Principal to come up himself for a personal interview, but he alleged pressure of work would not allow of his doing so, and he and the Commander-in-Chief, for the War Office, accepted my award of £29,000.

We had taken many camels off the Supply duties in order to assist Colonel Wynne's Egyptian battalion in carrying the frame of the *Lotus*, a Stern wheeler, which we desired to put together and launch above the Cataract at Semneh. The beams of steel being very heavy, were troublesome in transport, for if the two camels on which they were placed rose at different moments, the girders either slipped backwards or forwards, occasionally fracturing a camel's legs. All the riveters of the "Black Watch" and "Gordon Highlanders" were employed for a month in putting the *Lotus* together; she was ready when I passed, and instructed the Naval officer in charge to proceed.

Half a mile in front was an ugly belt of rocks, which extended, indeed, for 80 miles south of Wadi Halfa, and from a look in the Naval officer's face I turned back and said: "Now, while I should regret the loss of the steamer, please understand I would prefer she should lie at the bottom rather than you did not try to get through." "Yes, I understand." "Would you like to have it in writing?" "No, I understand you accept all responsibility."

Nevertheless, as I travelled up the Nile, at each successive telegraph station I received telegrams more and more pessimistic from the officer commanding the *Lotus*, and eventually he declined the task. Colonel Wynne,[1] who was the Station Staff-officer on the Line of Communication, telegraphed at the same time: "I have seen the Naval officer's opinion, and while I agree there is danger, request permission to order the Bluejackets and Voyageurs off the steamer, and let me take her through hauled by Egyptian soldiers." This he did; the *Lotus* proved to be worth her weight in gold to us in bringing down stream wounded and sick soldiers.[2]

When I was riding up the Nile the Consul-General in Cairo asked me my wishes about retaining command of the Egyptian Army, assuming that reductions then contemplated were carried out; and I replied, on the 10th December, that I wished to remain until Khartoum was taken, but afterwards not to remain on any terms.

Father Brindle[3] was travelling up in the boats of the Royal Irish, and I had determined, if it were possible, to overtake him and give him a Christmas dinner. We crossed to the left bank of the Nile, where the whalers moored, and were waiting, when the leading boat of the Irish appeared, the Reverend Father pulling stroke oar. His features were burnt by the sun, and, like his hands, were covered with blisters, as he stepped out of the boat stiff with the fatigue of pulling against the fast-running stream. Said I: "Father, why are you working like that?" "Oh, to encourage them." "Any result?" "Very little." The fact being, that the ordinary human creature was not endowed with the same energy and devotion

---

[1] Now commanding at Colchester.

[2] Captain Lord Charles Beresford, to chief of Staff, 10th December 1884: "Colonel Wynne's organisation here is perfect. I suggest he be made Captain of Cataracts. . . . Do not see any chance of a block here if all is left to Wynne."

[3] Now Roman Catholic Bishop of Nottingham.

as was my friend. Nevertheless the battalion won Lord Wolseley's prize of £100 for the best time, from Wadi Halfa to Korti, and smallest loss of Supplies.

Father Brindle was doubtless the most popular man in the Expedition. His own flock naturally loved him, and he was respected by everyone, from Bugler to Lord Wolseley, who more than once tried to get him knighted. He had a pony which he never rode, it being used to carry foot-sore men in turn. Preaching one day in the desert during Lent, he said: " Now, my men, I cannot ask you here on Service to abstain, but you might do something which would be pleasing to the Almighty, and will gratify me,—abstain from the use of bad language." Looking into the upturned faces, he thought from their sympathetic expression he had effected some good. When the parade was dismissed he stood for a few minutes speaking to some officers, and ten minutes later, walking behind two of his recent congregation, who, talking eagerly did not notice his footsteps on the soft sand, he overheard one say: " Bill, that was a bloody fine sermon the Father gave us."

When Lord Wolseley heard at Korti that General Sir Herbert Stewart was dangerously wounded he sent Sir Redvers Buller across the Bayuda Desert to replace him, and I became Chief of the Staff, General Grenfell replacing me on the Line of Communication. A few days later Lord Wolseley heard that Gordon had been killed at Khartoum; and the accounts he received from the troops on the Nile at Metemmeh being unsatisfactory, he despatched me as his Representative, with instructions, after consulting with Buller, to order a retirement if it seemed to be necessary.

I started within an hour, although I was in pain, for two days previously I had sat down in a fold-up chair with my finger between the joints, crushing the top so that it was in a jelly-like condition. The arm was in a sling, and it is difficult to get on a camel, which puts its head back and tries to take a piece out of your leg as you mount, if you have only one hand. I reached Gakdul, however, on the 18th February, to find that Sir Redvers and his column were then returning from Abu Klea.

There was no longer any hope of further offensive operations. Although 2200 camels had crossed the desert on the first journey, the Heavy Cavalry Regiment had now only 22 riding and 10 baggage camels. The Light Cavalry Regiment was 100 short, and the transport animals had all died from overwork.

Buller went on to rejoin Lord Wolseley on the Nile, while I remained at Gakdul until sunset on the 3rd March, clearing out the sick and wounded, then ammunition, and last of all stores.[1] We remained until the whole of the water in the big pools had been exhausted, and had men 30 feet down in wells, bailing up water in pannikins, to give the friendly Arabs who were carrying the stores as much time as possible.

The third day I was in the bivouac, for there were no tents except for the wounded. I went to a Station Hospital to have my finger dressed, which was necessary three times a day, as the smell from it was so unpleasant. The Medical Officer in charge was doubtless as much overworked as I was, and said shortly: "I tell you what it is, sir, if you were a soldier I should say, 'Sit down, my man, and I will pull out that finger-nail.'" "I am a soldier." "Yes, but you are a General." When he had dressed the finger I went back to my tree and sent for Doctor Conolly, a friend, and telling him what had passed, asked: "Please advise me, will this nail ever reunite?" "No, it never can, as it is crushed down to the root." "How do you pull it out?" "Slit the nail down the centre, and then take hold of one half with a pair of forceps, and pull." This I did, but when the first half came out I asked for some stimulant, and then I said: "Now please, I will look away while you take out the other half."[2]

The valley in which the wells were situated was shut in. Two of the regiments, for want of ordinary precautions, let a few Arabs drive off their slaughter oxen. The work

[1] Lord Wolseley to Sir Evelyn Wood: "Remain to see the desert posts cleared out yourself, an operation requiring wise calculation and a good military head. I have every confidence in your doing this difficult job well and quickly."

[2] I was advised by one of the first surgeons in London, whom I consulted on my return, that I should never get another nail, but Mr. Bader, the oculist, who was a warm personal friend of mine, discredited this opinion, and said if I kept the finger plastered up long enough a new nail would grow, and he was right.

of supervising a retirement is always depressing, and this, with the anxiety of getting some 2000 men across a waterless desert of 100 miles, told on my health and temper.

The discipline of some regiments was not satisfactory. Wine had been taken out to Metemmeh, which was wrong, as the men had no beer or spirits, and when Colonel Gough[1] and I rode round the bivouac lines after the troops had moved off to the point of Assembly we found two corps had left some ball ammunition on the ground. Near at hand were camels, one carrying mess kit, another wine-cases. We saw the loads exchanged and the camels started, the wine remaining for the Dervishes. Perhaps I felt the more angry as I had been there three weeks without wine or stimulant of any sort, but anyhow my temper was irritable, and ten minutes later I used offensive, improper language to an officer who made a stupid mistake in forming up his men on parade. Ashamed of my bad language, I turned away and saw Father Brindle, with a pained look in his face. Next day when I was feeling much happier he came up behind me, and putting his arm on my shoulder, said: "I hope your poor brain is somewhat rested?" The hope was justified, for I had induced the camel owners to carry double loads, relieving me of anxiety about ammunition. I had also heard from Lord Wolseley, who was arranging at Korti for further operations in the autumn: "When we advance finally you may count on being one of the Generals to have a command."

We marched from 5 till 11 p.m. in a hollow square, for there were a few Arabs about, when we lay down for three hours. It was very hot in the day, and my baggage camel with blankets not being available, I found it difficult to sleep from the cold, although probably the temperature was not really low as it seemed to me, wearing serge weighing only 3 lbs. I was lying with my knees drawn up for the sake of warmth when I felt a grateful weight on my shoulders, and my first inclination with the increased warmth was to sleep, but with an effort I sat up and saw Walkinshaw fifty yards away, walking up and down in his shirt sleeves, having put his serge over me.

[1] *Vide* page 148. The same officer.

The return to Korti was painful; the men who, intent on saving Gordon, had marched with elastic step, heads up, and shoulders back, were no longer the same soldiers. Depressed by the sense of failure, they straggled, and the bonds of discipline being relaxed, some gave in while still capable of exertion.

They had, however, been severely tried; roused an hour before dawn, with the thermometer at that hour always above 60°, they had pulled or tracked whaleboats for a month 420 miles, against a rapidly flowing river, under a burning sun, and many were nearly bootless.[1]

The discipline of the Mounted Infantry sections, who acted throughout as Rear guard, remained perfect. No men fell out on the line of march, though their camels had been taken from them to carry ammunition. During a halt, I having remained behind the Column to encourage stragglers to persevere, strolled round the Rear guard position. All except the sentries were asleep, and I counted rather more than two-thirds who were marching without boots, some wearing socks, and some strips of cloth. The sound principle of Lord Wolseley's proposal, vetoed by the Commander-in-Chief in 1873 for the Ashantee Expedition, was thoroughly shown in this, and in the second Expedition to Ashantee in 1896, when sections of selected men represented different battalions. The Regimental feeling was thus strongly evoked, and the Sections vied with each other in maintaining the reputation of their Corps. Behind the Mounted Infantry sections, Major French,[2] 19th Hussars, with about 20 of his men, followed in Rear of all, and was always alert, bright, and cheerful.

I rejoined Lord Wolseley at Korti on the 14th March, and three days later was ordered to take two Squadrons of the 19th Hussars and bring back by force the Aden camel men. They had been enlisted without sufficient forethought, on a six months' engagement, which had long since expired, and the General in command of "the Nile column" had coaxed them

---

[1] We had boots sent out to the desert, but vanity causes the Briton to wear at home boots a size too small for him, and the men with swollen feet could not get on those they would have worn in England.

[2] Now Lieutenant-General Sir J. D. French, G.C.V.O., K.C.B., K.C.M.G.

into remaining overtime by promising they should be discharged on their return to Korti. When they found the promise was not redeemed, leaving their camels tethered, they marched off in a body down the river. I ordered the Squadrons to parade at daylight on the 18th, and, accompanied by Lieutenant Wingate, rode after the fugitives, overtaking most of them before night fell on the 17th March.

I explained the situation, and the impossibility of their reaching Aden against the will of the Government: next day they returned, and by offering them enhanced terms they agreed to remain until I could get some Sudanees to feed and care for the camels.

On New Year's day, 1885, I had received from the Sheiks of the Korosko Desert a telegraphic greeting, for which they paid, as they also did for one which they despatched to Lady Wood in England. On my return to Korti they sent me another message, and in honour of my being back safely on the Nile they killed a camel, a peculiar compliment. I heard afterwards that they were nervous for my safety while I was at Gakdul, for they had an exaggerated opinion of the power of the Mahdi.

Lord Wolseley and the Headquarters Staff went down stream from Korti on the 24th March, and having cleared up the camp, I followed next day. From a mistake in the execution of some orders I was obliged to ride 70 miles in the hot sun, and thus brought on a recurrence of diarrhœa, from which I had previously suffered from the 23rd of February to the 9th of March, and which clung to me so persistently that I was never free from pain and inconvenience until I got on board a ship in the Suez Canal on my way to England. Throughout March the doctors urged me to go down the river, but anticipating an Autumn campaign, and with the promise of a command, I evaded compliance till May, when the doctors became more insistent, and I less capable of resistance.

My health improved at Debbeh, where I commanded about 6400 men, spread out on the bank of the Nile from Old Dongola to Hamdab. The men were employed in hutting themselves, and the work was certainly beneficial in the trying climate. It was generally cool, for the Sudan, from 3 a.m. to 6 a.m., but occasionally even at that hour the thermometer stood at 77°. From 10 a.m. to 4 p.m. daily, unless there happened to be a dust storm to add to our discomfort, there was as a rule not a breath of air, and even lizards and flies clustered under camel saddles to avoid the sun.

While two soldiers were working together one of them grumbled at the intensity of the heat, and was rebuked by his comrade, saying, " What is the use of your grousing? Don't you know there is only a bit of brown paper between us and hell?" The grumbler retorted, "And I expect that bit of paper is scorched." The Nile, always a rest for our parched eyes, at the end of March showed half a mile of mud between the banks, and little more than 100 yards of water opposite to my tent.

The soldiers had been on half rations of groceries for some weeks, and now we ran out of sugar. Officers scrambled for a 1-lb. tin of cocoa and milk at six shillings, while invalided officers sent down the river sold alcohol at thirty shillings a bottle.

The spirits of the troops had recovered from the depressing effect of the failure to save Gordon, and, in spite of all discomforts, remained good as a rule, though the difference of feeling in the camps varied according to the temperament of the general in command. Major the Honourable J. Dormer [1] wrote to me from Tani on the 16th of April, " Everyone here is cheery and contented, there is no grumbling." This, however, was primarily due to his own buoyant spirits. Two Sheiks rode into the General's camp with a message from the Mahdi, exhorting him and his followers to submit, and thus save their bodies in this world, and their souls in the next, by embracing the Mohammedan faith. The Sheik talked of the wondrous powers of the Mahdi, and when Dormer differed with him, said, " Well, can you do the marvellous things the Mahdi performs, such as praying for rain and ensure its falling?" Dormer, like all of us, knew that the Mahdi only prayed for rain when his barometer was falling, and having himself but one eye, he turned his back to the Sheiks, and taking out his glass eye he threw it up in the air and caught it, saying, " Can your Mahdi do that?" The Sheiks turned and ran without another word.

[1] Died from the effect of a bite from a panther while in command of the Madras Army.

On the 31st March I handed over the command of the Egyptian Army to Sir Francis Grenfell, who became Sirdar. I had overworked myself for two and a half years, spending £1600 of my capital, and missed all chance of joining in the fights near Suakin in 1884. His Highness the Khedive wrote me some very gracious letters, and sent me the Cordon of the Medjidie, but he could not forget how Arabi and the Egyptian soldiers had treated him in 1882, and never trusted the Fellaheen soldiery again. During my two and a half years' command he never gave them a word of praise.

I greatly admired the ability of our Consul-General, Sir Evelyn Baring,[1] a part of whose work I had shared, and was gratified by the feeling that my esteem for him was reciprocated by that singularly undemonstrative Briton.

The Commander-in-Chief, on the motion of the Secretary of State for the Colonies, was pleased to record his approbation of my efforts in endeavouring to create an Egyptian Army. The real pleasure to me was the expression of regard I received from the band of officers who came under my command in January 1883. As I wrote in my farewell order: 'He believes no body of officers have ever worked with more unremitting devotion.'

Lord Wolseley's opinion of our work during the campaign was favourable.[2]

---

[1] He wrote to me, Cairo, 18th March 1885: "You will be able to carry away the conviction that you did all that mortal man could do to make an army out of very indifferent material. I shall never forget all the support and assistance you gave me during a period of very great difficulty. . . ." And as Lord Cromer, 5th October 1892: "I do not want to go to India; if, however, I were to go I should prefer you to be Commander-in-Chief to anyone else."

[2] Extract from despatch, sent by Lord Wolseley to the Secretary of State for War:—

"CAIRO, 15th June 1885.

"Major-General Sir Evelyn Wood, V.C., G.C.M.G., K.C.B., was the General of Communications, and brought the utmost zeal to bear upon the arduous and difficult duties of that position. Our line of communications by rail, river, and desert, from Alexandria to Gubat, was about 1500 miles in length. The responsibility of supervising it was great, but, thanks to Sir E. Wood's ability and energy, and to the efficient support he received from the large staff of officers under his command, the army operating in the front was well fed and provided with all it required. The officers and men of the Egyptian army, under General Wood's immediate orders, worked along this line with indefatigable earnestness, and with the best possible results to the welfare of the Expedition."

I was disappointed when the Gazette for the Nile Expedition came out, less for myself than for those who had worked so hard while under my command, and I appealed to Lord Wolseley in their behalf, who replied on the 27th August, " I could not get my way,—the most notable omission from the list being yourself."

In spite of my being temporarily better early in May, Surgeon-General Lithgow sent me down the Nile on the 6th. As I passed Korosko the Ababdehs handed me a sword which the Sheiks then in Cairo had left for me, and a silver-mounted riding stick for Lady Wood, and they came to see me off the day I left the capital.

Lord Wolseley had expressed astonishment on my declining his offer of the Frontier command, but on seeing my thin body, and haggard face, was so startled that he tried to send me off to England the day I reached Cairo. This I earnestly represented was not necessary, as it was important that I should spend a few days in order to settle matters at the Egyptian War Office.

CHAPTER XLIII

1885-6-7-8—COLCHESTER DISTRICT

The Land League—Mr. Wrench—Life at Colchester—Useless Sentries—Reforms in Canteens—Nett profit trebled in twelve months—3rd Class shots—An unusual Inspection—My last lie—Visit to Corunna—Albuera.

I REACHED London on the 19th of June, lighter in body than I had been for many years, and I did not recover entirely from intestinal troubles till late in the year. I was no sooner home than I had some interesting correspondence with Mr. Wrench, my brother-in-law's agent at Clones in the north of Ireland. Since I assumed supervision of the estate in 1867, we had lived on amicable terms with the tenants, but in 1880 the Land League had formed branches in the north of Ireland, and most of the Clones tenantry joined the League, in 1885-6.

One farmer quarrelled with the League agents, who ordered his labourers to leave him, and the tenant appealed to Mr. Wrench for permission to hire the pig-carriers, who on the weekly market day carried pigs from the carts to the weighbridge, earning enough to enable them to remain idle for the rest of the week. Mr. Wrench observed, "I don't care what the men do, but you cannot have them on market day," and they worked for the former Land Leaguer. The local agent now wrote a demand to Mr. Wrench to dismiss the men from the pig-carrying job, which being referred to me was summarily refused. The League ordered that no pig buyer should go to Clones market, and as it was not only a question of principle, but also of the tolls of the market, worth £300 a year, we issued a notice that we would buy all pigs at a fair rate which were not sold on market days. As trouble was anticipated,

Colonel E. Saunderson, M.P., and some of his friends attended the next market, to support Mr. Wrench, but the Boycott was carried out without violence.

Mr. Wrench endeavoured to obtain buyers from Belfast, Drogheda, Newry, and other towns, but the League was too firmly established to enable him to succeed, and on the 23rd October I received the following telegram:—" Sending you 642 pigs next week—Wrench."

This was handed to me on my way to the War Office, and taking it to the City, I obtained the names of three respectable pig salesmen. Going to one shop in Smithfield, I asked, "What can you do for me, about 600 pigs on Tuesday next?" The man said, "Are they 'Lights' or 'Heavies'?" Now I knew something about Light and Heavy cavalry, but the term as regards pigs was unfathomable, and like Tittlebat Titmouse,[1] I said, "Little of both." The salesman looked me over, and contemptuously declined to quote a price, and so going farther down to another firm I repeated the question, only putting it, "What can you get me for 'Lights,' and what for 'Heavies'?" and having obtained an answer, I went outside, and telegraphed it to Wrench, adding, "Have you tried at Londonderry?"

Londonderry bought all our pigs, and after six months' quarrel the Land League giving in, rescinded their notice about the carriers, my brother-in-law's whole loss in the transaction being something less than a hundred pounds.

I took over the Command of the Eastern District from General White on the 31st March, and spent therein three very happy years. As soon as I had finished the inspection of the Regulars, and ten Militia, and all the Volunteer Battalions in the district, I turned my attention to "Long distance rides" for the Cavalry, and to initiating the practice of Night marches for the Infantry, beginning by training Officers and Sergeants, and the progress in the Army is shown by the fact that now brigades march many miles by compass bearings without difficulty, whereas, when I began at Colchester, the units became excited, and lost their way, in crossing diagonally the Abbey Field, the parade ground, of a few hundred yards in extent. Both officers and men took

[1] Warren's *Ten Thousand a Year*.

much interest in their work, the Artillery binding their gun-wheels with straw, to deaden the sound.

Most soldiers know the story of a sentry posted in the garden of the Kremlin at Moscow, over a plant in which the Empress Catherine was interested. The plant died in the winter, but the sentry post was maintained for over a hundred years. I believe, however, many of my comrades did not realise until the Boer War, the absurdities to be seen in our garrisons. It was so easy under most Generals to get a sentry posted; few even thought of removing a guard!

The day I assumed command at Colchester a sentry "Presented Arms" to me at the office. "What does he do here?" "Oh, sir, he is your sentry." "Send him away; I don't want him." Next day I asked, "Why is he still here?" "Oh, he's sentry over Ordnance Stores, as well as over your office." There was a wall, 10 feet high, intervening between the office and the Stores, so I ordered the post to be placed within the enclosure. When on the third morning I found the man still at the office door, I posted him myself inside the enclosure, but the Ordnance officer, thinking the place was safer if it was kept locked, begged he might be taken away.

Some days later on visiting the huts, forming the Garrison Hospital, I found a sentry over a prisoners' ward. "Open the door." "Please, sir, it's locked." "Yes, open it." "I've got no key." "Then call the Sergeant of the guard; I want to see the prisoner." "Please, sir, there is no prisoner." I said to the Medical Officer accompanying me, "What folly!" "Oh, there was a prisoner, quite recently." An indiscreet Lance-Corporal, of the Army Hospital Corps, remarked, "There has been no prisoner for three months."

A perusal of the Crime statistics induced a visit to Harwich, where one company of Garrison Artillery had more prisoners than 700 other Artillery men, in the Eastern District. Harwich and Landguard were not responsible for this unpleasant fact, but Shotley Magazine Guard, a detachment of some 25 Gunners stationed on a promontory between the Stour and Orwell rivers. The Guard duties were not heavy, but there was absolutely no means of recreation for the men,

The nearest farm was 2000 yards distant, but a public-house stood just outside the fort.

I imagine that the prestige of the Master-General of the Ordnance, typified by the Duke of Wellington, had not then died out, for I was warned by my Staff not to interfere with a Magazine. I disregarded their friendly counsels; removed all the celibate Artillery men, leaving a Master Gunner and seven married men, one of whom had to sleep dressed in the guard-room as a watchman, and to touch a tell-tale clock thrice every night, at varying hours, as ordered by the Warrant officer. This system has answered well to the present time.

In the Summer-time the officer commanding a Militia Battalion complained to me that the officer commanding a Line Battalion managing the canteen[1] would not give him sufficient for his share of the profits. Both parties agreed to accept my decision, but the line officer on my saying, " Well, give him from twenty to thirty pounds," observed, " We don't make that in a quarter." " Then you do your work badly." " If you think, sir, you could do it better, you had better try." " Yes, and I give you notice now, that I will manage it personally through one of your officers, and non-commissioned officers, from the 1st October." I made various innovations, advertising for tenders for beer, and sending for two old soldiers out of each Company, who were supplied with bread and cheese, desired them to pronounce as to the merits of samples. They all asked whose beer it was they were drinking? but the officers, who handed it out through a trap door, said, by my direction, that they were to make a choice, without receiving such information. A local Brewer obtained and kept the contract for many years.

I published a Quarterly statement of accounts, which was hung up in the canteen, and eventually paid £600 for rather more than half of a bathing-place, 100 feet × 50, the War Office granting the remainder. During the Summer-time I borrowed one of the bands twice a week to play in the evenings outside the canteen, under a large awning, and encouraged the married families to occupy the chairs I had placed for

[1] Each unit taking it in turn for three months.

them. I entirely failed, however, to induce them to take the tea and coffee, which I persevered in providing, at somewhat less than cost price, for several weeks.

The year before I took over the Command the divisible profit was under £340, whereas after twelve months I divided £1400, and the next year £1540. This money was earned to the detriment of the small public-houses in the vicinity of the barracks. I made the canteen as far as possible like a respectable music saloon, allowing free choice of music, admitting even songs which I thought vulgar, if they were not of an immoral tendency. I replaced the old beer-stained barrack tables and forms by arm-chairs and marble-topped tables. The commanding officers assured me I did not know what I was doing, and that there would be no arm on a chair in three months' time. Nevertheless I persevered, although I admit I had some misgivings when I put two large glass mirrors, 9 feet by 6, to light up the room, which being partly underground was dark, as I thought it was possible some drunken soldier might throw a pewter pot at them. Nothing untoward occurred in my time, however, nor had there been a single breakage when I visited the canteen some eight years afterwards. It is more remarkable that one of my successors, General Burnett, ten years later made a somewhat greater profit out of two Battalions, the garrison having been temporarily reduced during the building of the barracks, and mainly by raising the tone of the Entertainment.

The Adjutant-General wrote, the Eastern District was a model, and the Canteen Regulations I had then drawn up, have with some improvements since been adopted for the Army.

The Adjutant-General, Lord Wolseley, not only supported me officially in my efforts to raise the tone of the Rank and File by trusting them, but his private correspondence also was a great encouragement. I mentioned to him I meant to persevere against the views of my commanding officers, and in reply he wrote: "Your letter: every word of it is after my own heart, I have always believed in trusting the British soldier."

I had much correspondence with him throughout 1886, '87, and '88, he putting me on many War Office Committees; one of these was to decide whether the magazine of the new rifle should be Permanent or Detachable; he himself was in favour of the latter, and was proportionately disappointed when I took him the report of the Committee, which, with one dissentient, was in favour of the permanent arrangement. He asked, "Who is the one wise man?" I said, "I am, sir." "Then why did not you say so?" "Well, I thought it would look as if I were conceited." "But you are quite right." "Yes, I think so." Two days later two of those who had voted for the permanent arrangement came round and asked to be allowed to withdraw their vote. Eventually difficulties of manufacture in the permanent system caused the better method, the detachable, to be adopted.

In 1877 the Military Secretary asked if I was willing to be considered for an appointment as Commandant-General in Australia. Although I was advised by my Aide-de-Camp, a Tasmanian born, that Federation was too far off to justify my hoping to succeed in amalgamating the forces, I answered I would go if selected, but for reasons unconnected with me, the idea at that time was not carried out.

I was working throughout 1887 and 1888 on the subject of diminishing the number of third-class shots in the Eastern District, corresponding with the School of Musketry at Hythe, and we effected some good, although the percentage of men useless with the Rifle remained high.

The new Drill book was handed over to me for report, and many of the antiquated movements formed the subject of somewhat heated discussion between those who held Lord Wolseley's views, which I was advocating, and the Old School. My opinions were summed up in a letter to his lordship, dated 8.8.87, "I hope, however, we may recognise now, all our Drill is for the more ready destruction of our enemies, with a minimum loss to ourselves, and that we prescribe formations accordingly."

I was frequently consulted on the vexed question of Chief of the Staff, or Adjutant-General, and Quartermaster-General, on which the Commander-in-Chief and Adjutant-General could not agree. The latter system was maintained in Peace for eighteen years longer, but was abandoned for warlike operations.[1]

[1] This discussion lasted from the time Sir Garnet Wolseley joined the Horse Guards Staff, after the Red River Expedition, till 1904, when a Chief of the General

Lord Wolseley employed me constantly throughout the three years I was at Colchester, with reference to his attempts to modernise the Army; and the work he gave me, coupled with a close inspection of every unit, Regulars and Auxiliary Forces, in the Eastern District, kept me fully employed.

An interesting duty which came to me in July 1888 was the selecting of positions to defend the approaches to London from the eastward. The Headquarters Staff were unable at first to accept my views, and came down three times, and on the last occasion with Lord Wolseley, and the result was that he confirmed my judgment.

My father had lived, much respected, for forty years in Essex; my elder brother, Charles Page Wood, farming his estate 10 miles distant, was often in Colchester on market days, and being very popular I had the advantage of the friendships they had made, when I wanted the use of private lands for the training of troops. The occupiers near the Barracks were very generous in allowing me to practise Outposts of all Arms, and I often had a long line, mostly on arable land, without serious complaint, though on one occasion a farmer aggrieved by officers riding over a crop, ignoring my rank, said, "If you do that again I'll tell Mr. Evelyn Wood of you."

I inspected the Infantry of the District as outposts by day and night, and on the first occasion had to find grave fault with the arrangements of a Battalion of which I had then, and have had ever since, the highest opinion. I began my inspection on the left of a line of 3 miles, the Piquet in front

---

staff was appointed. The Duke of Cambridge's opposition to any change was shared by many of his contemporaries. General Sir John Michel, who was singularly broad-minded, opposed it. In the 1872 Manœuvres, from my accident I was unable to ride until the last few days, so undertook the office work of both branches. One evening Sir John Michel was arguing the point against his two Senior Officers, Colonel A. Herbert[1] and Sir Garnet Wolseley, and as neither disputant would give way, Sir John, to terminate the discussion, said, "There is no overlapping of work where Staff officers are properly trained, as I'll show you.—Here's Wood who has done all our writing, we'll leave it to him. Tell me, Wood, have I ever in the last three weeks made a single mistake in addressing the Adjutant-General, when I should have written Quartermaster-General, or the reverse?" I owed much to Sir John, but had to speak the truth: "Sir, I cannot recall a single day when you have not made mistakes."

---

[1] Later, Sir Arthur Herbert, Quartermaster-General.

of which was badly placed. No. 7 Company was worse. On passing behind No. 6, a sentry who should have been standing motionless looking to his front, faced about and "Presented Arms" to me. Losing patience, I ordered the Battalion home, saw the officers in the orderly room, and expressed very decided opinions as to the want of instruction, indicated that morning. As I finished, saying, "Gentlemen, I will see you again when your Commanding officer says you are ready for inspection;" he observed, "It is just lunch time, sir, will you come in?" I did so, and my friendship with that Battalion has been uninterrupted ever since.

A few evenings later, a Subaltern of the Battalion dining with me alone, said, "We had such bad luck with you, General, last week, the Regiment has now been inspected for 150 years, and you are the first general who ever began on the left of the line, and we knew when the word was passed up that you had started there, that we should have an unhappy morning, for Bobby ——, our show captain,[1] was on the right with the most capable officers, and on the extreme left were the most inefficient. Now it generally happens that a general when he has seen half a long outpost line well posted, being satisfied, goes home, and we were calculating on a stereotyped inspection."

In the middle of July, after seeing some interesting Artillery practice on Dartmoor, I took my horses on to Exmoor, where Mr. Basset, the Master of the Devon and Somerset Staghounds, had a meet for my pleasure, and gave me a most enjoyable run.

Yielding to a warm invitation from Canon Bell, I went to Marlborough at the end of the month, for the double purpose of attending the breaking-up day and inspecting the Cadet companies. While the Head was giving out prizes, he asked, "Sir Evelyn, did you learn much Latin here?" "Not much, I'm afraid." "Perhaps Greek?" "I think less." "Then may I ask what you did learn?" "Oh, I'll tell you presently, as you say I have got to speak to the School."

When I got up, in the course of my speech I mentioned this fact, and said, "I promised to tell the Head, and you

[1] Now a General officer on the Staff.

at the same time. You are probably envious of those boys who have taken prizes. In your place I should have been, for I never took a prize during the five years I was at school, but I learned something, and within 20 feet of where I am now standing, in May 1851. The Reverend J. Biden was an ardent fisherman, and one afternoon when our task was Arithmetic, somewhat scamped in work in those days, we knew that 'Jacky' was anxious to get out to the banks of the Kennet. He gave me four Addition sums out of Colenso's Arithmetic, which he apparently copied out of the book. After allowing an interval of a quarter of an hour to elapse, I, taking the answers from the book, wrote them down, and went up, expecting to see a big 'R' across the slate, and an intimation that I might go. To my horror he looked over the sums saying, 'But you have fudged this?' 'No, sir.' 'But you have.' 'No, sir.' Now, if 'Jacky' had ordered me to 'Stand round,' I might have continued to tell lies till to-day; he said, however, 'I thought you were a brave little boy, and only cowards tell lies.' I say to you, Boys, whether you believe me or not, I have never told a lie since, and that lesson was worth more than all the learning acquired by all the prize-takers who have just now been up to this table."

I travelled Westward that evening, joining Sir John Pender, who took a party in the S.S. *Electra* to the Mediterranean for a trip, inducing Sir John to invite my friend, Colonel Ardagh,[1] for whom indeed he waited till 1 a.m. on the 2nd September, when we sailed for Corunna. I saw a great deal of Dean Bradley, who was a sympathetic companion, and Sir Robert Herbert, whose charming personality was well known. When we got into the Bay on the 3rd, I gave a lecture on Sir John Moore's battle, the scene of which we successfully visited next day, except that Dean Bradley had a bad fall from a donkey, which rolled over him. Our impression, which I imagine is that of everyone who has visited the Field, was that Moore did very well under unusually difficult circumstances.

We steamed round the coast of Portugal, waiting on the King at Lisbon, and my kind host being greatly distressed to find I had no medals, insisted on my wearing on my evening coat, which we put on at midday, for our Royal audience, a

---

[1] General Sir John Ardagh, K.C.B.

C.M.G. Next day Ardagh and I visited Torres Vedras, on which immensely strong position the works erected by Wellington are apparently much as they were at the time of their occupation, A.D. 1810.

The party now separated, Ardagh and I going by train to Badajos, whence we visited the field of Albuera.

The young Spanish officer sent to us as a guide at Badajos because he spoke a little French, was not aware that the British had successfully assaulted the place, his knowledge of the operations of the Sieges being confined to the attacks, and defence of the French and Spaniards. It will repay any soldier even now to visit Badajos, for it is easy to follow Napier's wonderful description of the Assault.

Probably all soldiers have heard the story, that Lord Beresford had ordered a retreat from Albuera when it was countermanded, and how the gallant charge of the Fusilier Brigade snatched victory from the French at the last moment. At Gibraltar, coming fresh from the battlefield, I asked General Sir Arthur Hardinge, the Governor, "Did your father ever talk to you of Albuera?" "Yes, very often." "Is it true that he was the Staff officer who countermanded Beresford's order to retreat?" "No, no one did so; but my father went to Beresford, and said, 'You have got, sir, a Court-martial on one hand, and a Peerage on the other,' and he replied slowly, 'I will try for the Peerage,' and himself gave the order to stop the retreat, and my father then ordered the Fusilier Brigade to advance."

When the ship reached Cadiz, on the 13th August, I received a telegram from my wife, to whom a friend had confided the information that Sir Archibald Alison was about to vacate the Aldershot command, to join the India Council. Lord Wolseley had told me on many occasions he intended to press for my appointment to that command, and at one time he imagined the chances of my getting it were at ten to one; later, my chances sank to even betting. I thought, in any case, it would be wise for me to return home, and obtained the assent of our kind host to my leaving the ship at Barcelona.

Nothing could exceed his generosity; he not only entertained us perfectly on board, but insisted on paying our expenses on shore, even to our washing bills, when we were at Granada, where I lingered for forty-eight hours to enjoy more fully the Alhambra. Ardagh and I returned from Barcelona, after a delightful trip, and I reached Colchester after an absence of three weeks.

When the Headquarters Staff returned to London after the holidays, there was a protracted discussion over the question of my succeeding Sir Archibald Alison at Aldershot. Lord Wolseley advocated it strenuously, as he expressly said, not for any regard for me, but because he thought I was more successful in instructing [1] Regiments than anyone else he knew. I was also, he thought, fit to take the Division abroad should it be necessary.

The Commander-in-Chief wished to appoint an office for much longer service, and after weeks of argument the matter was left to the decision of Mr. Stanhope, the Secretary of State. He sent for Sir Redvers Buller, who was Quartermaster-General, and asked for his views. Buller replied, " I have seen three disasters in my service, and they all came from want of instruction. Do you believe that Evelyn Wood is a good teacher ? " " Yes," said Mr. Stanhope, " I am told he is quite satisfactory in that respect." " Then I advise you to appoint him." Mr. Stanhope was kind enough to say to me, when telling me the story, " I am glad I did so."

---

[1] Lord Wolseley, when informing me privately the matter was settled, wrote: " And I hope you may be as successful in teaching soldiers at Aldershot as you have been at Colchester."

CHAPTER XLIV

1889—ALDERSHOT

£3000 borrowed for Installation—Rebuilding of Barracks in Company blocks—Names of Barracks—A troublesome inheritance of debt—Personal Staff—Lonsdale Hale—Henderson—Commander-in-Chief disapproves of Night Marches—The German Emperor—Mr. Stanhope.

ALTHOUGH I had some horses and sufficient furniture for the house hired by Government for the General of the Eastern District at Colchester, yet I had to borrow £3000 to instal myself at Aldershot, where I took over Command on the 1st January. I returned to Colchester twice for farewell festivities, which the Residents kindly insisted on offering me. I received not only in Essex but in East Anglia much hospitality during my Command.

On getting to my new station I had a conference on musketry, but there being a Divisional Inspector for Aldershot I had merely to indicate my wishes, and support him in trying to improve the shooting of the troops.

I knew the wretched accommodation provided for the troops, neither wind nor rain proof, having been quartered in the North and South Camps twenty years earlier. The contractor in 1855 had guaranteed the huts for thirteen years, so his work was good; but the annual upkeep amounted in the eighties to £7000, with a constantly increasing outlay, in spite of the fact that the barracks of three battalions in the North Camp had been rebuilt in brick, on the bungalow principle.

I strongly advocated the immediate reconstruction of the South Camp, and the rebuilding in brick for the units still hutted in the North Camp, but on a different system. I had been striving for years to get a fuller recognition of the Company system, the value of which had been impressed on

II.—13

me in 1867-8, when I lived as Brigade Major in the Lines of the 68th battalion (1st Durham Light Infantry). One morning about 4 a.m., the Assistant Adjutant-General and I having spent the night at Sandhurst College helping to extinguish a fire, were parting close to his hut, when he said, "Send three more companies over at once." "Yes, sir." "Which shall you send?" "68th." "Why, are they first for duty?" "Oh, I don't know, nor care, for I am tired; and if they go, I need not get up at 6.30. to ensure their breakfasts are sent over." When the battalion was leaving Aldershot, General Sir Alfred Horsford said: "Wood, the 68th is the best organised battalion I have ever known. Find out the reason." Instead of riding down to the station, I walked on in advance with the Quarter-Master, Mr. Sladen, and from him elicited the fact that the Company system had been started in the forties, and maintained ever since, which accounted for the smoothness of running in the battalion.

The Commanding officer's or Adjutant's battalion is good enough for Peace and Show, but is ill-adapted for emergencies, and breaks-down on service. The disadvantage of breaking up units, now generally admitted in the army, was so little understood even thirty years ago, that a common order was: "Send a strong squadron, or a strong company;" and in 1881 when I demurred to sending from Natal "a strong Company," at least 120, to the mouth of the St. John river, my brother General at Cape Town declined my alternative proposal to send one Company, about 90, or two Companies, about 180 strong; and as I would not give way, the dispute was telegraphed to the War Office, and the Adjutant-General, Lord Wolseley, approved of my action. I advocated, therefore, from experience that the new barracks to be built should be in Company blocks, and after some discussion this was approved. My recommendation that each barrack should in name commemorate a British victory, was approved only after repeated applications. I personally "sited" all barracks built in my time, at a cost of about £1,500,000. The Adjutant-General and Inspector-General of Fortifications, who came to criticise before approving, on their departure said frankly, "In London we did not like your scheme at all, but are now in complete agreement with your views." Later, when the Plans, Prices, and

Execution were questioned in the House of Commons, the Secretary of State appointed a committee of Civilian Architects and builders, who reported that the Royal Engineers had made good plans, the Contractors had done their part satisfactorily, and the country had obtained full value for its expenditure.

I inherited a troublesome task in the Officers' Club-house, which I found with an increasing debt, the liabilities standing at £1100, and my brother officers disagreed with my economically drastic proposals for meeting our liabilities, offering several impracticable suggestions; one, that we should borrow the money in the name of the Division. I asked the General officer who made this proposal if he would sign a paper as one of the guarantors of the debt, but this he absolutely declined! I then offered to put down £100 on the table as my share, if every officer in the Division would subscribe in proportion to his pay, based on my pay and contribution. The Seniors at once vetoed this suggestion, and my plans were eventually accepted, with the result that four years later all the liabilities had been met, and I handed a cash balance of over £1600 to my successor. This satisfactory result was mainly owing to the business-like aptitudes of my senior Aide-de-camp, Major C. Parsons,[1] Royal Artillery, who made a profit of £550 out of Subscription dances.

Like Major Parsons, my Cavalry Aides-de-camp were selected on military grounds; indeed I did not know personally either Captain Babington, 16th Lancers, or his successor, Captain H. D. Fanshawe, 19th Hussars, before they came to Aldershot.

Babington had been described to me as a keen soldier, and one of the best "across country" men in the Cavalry, and he fully merited the description. When he was obliged to rejoin his Regiment, on its departure for India, I invited Hew Fanshawe to succeed him on my personal Staff; I had noticed his singularly quiet but determined manner, and thorough knowledge of all Regimental details two years previously, when inspecting the Regiment of which he was Adjutant. He was, moreover, a thorough sportsman, and in spite of being badly off, hunted the Regimental pack of Staghounds while quartered

[1] Now Major-General Sir Charles Parsons, commanding at Halifax, Nova Scotia.

at Norwich, and was known to have got single-handed, in Arran, on 12th August 1888, 161 grouse with 200 cartridges. I never met a harder working officer, or one who understood better, stable management. His horses never refused their food, though I have known him rail them to Reading, ride 17 miles to meet the South Oxfordshire hounds, and return at night to Aldershot. Such practical sportsmen were of great assistance to me in the outdoor work which now engaged most of my time.

The system of umpiring at tactical exercises with Opposing forces was unsatisfactory, and it had the effect of stopping all initiative on the part of the cavalry. In one of our first exercises I came on a brigade halted near a small wood. I asked, "What is it; why are you stopping?" "There are Infantry in the wood." "How many?" "We don't know." "Then why don't you ascertain?" "If we go forward and ascertain, the Umpire will send us home." "Well, I shall do that now, if you stop here doing nothing." Then Sir Drury Lowe, who commanded the Cavalry brigade, and with whom I had had the pleasure of serving in India, and I set to work to improve matters. We took command of opposing forces, Cavalry against Infantry, and acted also as Umpires on terms of equality, and soon had the satisfaction of seeing an improvement.

The Gunners had been dominated by the result of imaginary Infantry fire, the effect of which was estimated by the results of target practice on known ranges, and insufficient consideration had been credited to the Artillery for the effect of their fire on the opposing Infantry. The Artillery were still practising drill in use during the Peninsula War; one of the favourite movements, and perhaps the most useless, being "Changing front, right, and left, on the centre sub-division." I found there were two standards of Efficiency, the Aldershot ideal, which may be described as smartness in turn-out, and mobility, Regimentally known as "First gun off"; and the Okehampton ideal, the motto for which was "Hit, Hit, Hit." I tried to combine the better points of the two systems. The General in command of the Artillery, who possessed a high sense of duty, was, however, best known in the Army from his desire to advance to decisive Ranges. He talked openly, as indeed he wrote, against the work at Okehampton, where, however, he had never seen his men practise.

On the other hand, a very clever officer, who had the ear of the Artillery authorities in Pall Mall, was engaged in editing a new drill book, already in type, the key-note of which was "Service conditions." It inculculated, however, too strongly, in my opinion, caution in order to avoid losses. I endeavoured to find a middle way between these opposing views, and to some extent succeeded, laying down the principle that our ideal should be the destruction of the enemy as cheaply as possible, but when necessary at all costs.

After my first Artillery tactical exercise I remarked to the officers assembled at the conference, that I had looked through the sights of ten guns in one position, and found seven of them laid in the air. The Artillery tactical days I initiated in 1890 induced greater attention being paid to the handling of brigades when coming into action, and enabled me to classify the individual skill of the Lieutenant-Colonels in command. No part of my instructional duties has given me so much pleasure as I got from working with the Artillery, from the zest and broad-minded spirit with which Gunners of all Ranks took up the new system. I do not know any compliment which has pleased me so much as that paid to me by the Council in 1892, in enrolling me an honorary member of the Institution of the Royal Artillery, in recognition of my efforts to improve the war training of the Arm. The letter offering me the distinction was couched in such appreciatory words as to enhance the value of the honour.

I saw each Infantry Brigade separately, and created some astonishment by the attention I demanded to exactitude in the Manual exercises and in parade movements. One General said to me, "We thought you did not care for such details." I replied, "I do not think battles are won by them, and want to do as little as possible of them; but what we do should be done as well, and with as much exactitude, as possible."

While I was at Colchester I got three selected captains in different Battalions to draw up a form of report of Company training, which I introduced at Aldershot, and on which 82 Captains reported at the end of the first and second years' training. They were practically unanimous in favour of it, suggesting only minor alterations; and eighteen months later the Adjutant-General wrote: "As the system of Company training introduced at Colchester and at Aldershot by you has proved so successful, I am directed to ask you to consider the larger question of training Battalions throughout the year at all other Stations."

I began in 1889 with Companies of Infantry, then in succession giving my attention to the instruction of Battalions and Brigades, and later, the handling of Forces of all Arms; and endeavoured to work out the most useful method of applying Cavalry combined with Mounted Infantry, both in Strategical and Tactical operations. In the latter I made a point of never criticising adversely anyone, of whatever rank, for having failed to carry out orders, if he had a sound reason for not doing so.

In my criticisms on Tactical operations I was greatly assisted by the friendly advice of an old comrade, Colonel Lonsdale Hale, a man of calm judgment and of great military knowledge. He had at his fingers' ends every incident of the Franco-Prussian War, both as regards the operations on the eastern frontier and those on the Loire. While he took an interest in all Arms, he paid particular attention to Artillery and Infantry, and attended nearly every Tactical operation I carried out, often accompanied by Colonel Henderson, whose early death has been eloquently lamented by Lord Roberts as a great loss to the Army. Hale discussed with me, verbally or on paper, every decision after it was given, unless it met his views; and this had the effect of improving materially the value of my judgment.

I had the satisfaction of introducing a more even scale of justice, for on joining the Division I found that in two brigades, only half a mile apart, soldiers tried by Court-Martial on the same day for identical offences received, the better character a year, and the worse character—a man with two previous convictions—eighty-four days' imprisonment with hard labour.

The Draft Season 1889-90 impressed all with the value of Lord Wolseley's scheme of Territorial Regiments. On one occasion, when a large draft of the Suffolk Regiment was on furlough pending embarkation for India, we received a telegram that the ship would be delayed for another fortnight, and letters were sent to every man postponing his return. I asked the Commanding officer, "Will they all come back?" "We are absolutely certain of all except two, who are doubtful." In effect all, including those two, returned punctually; and later, when the 1st Somerset Light Infantry embarked for Gibraltar, every man was present.

This battalion had fought under my command at Kambula, Zululand, and happened to be quartered within 400 yards of Government House, in the grounds of which could be seen any afternoon from ten to a dozen hares, for which the enclosure became a preserve, thus affording officers and men much amusement with the Foot beagles. Some of the hares were coursed with greyhounds in the early mornings, and I had reason to believe that men in the Somerset owned the dogs. Two privates, indeed, were seen in the grounds; but I had been on especially friendly terms with the battalion since 1879, and instead of having the men punished I sent a message through the Adjutant, to be passed on by the Sergeant-Major, that the General particularly wanted poachers kept out of the Government House grounds, and from that day no soldier trespassers gave any trouble.

I found, on taking over the command, a system in force of issuing "General" and "Special" ideas the previous day, so that the officers in command might have ample time to make up their minds, and to ask advice as to what should be done. This system I changed, warning combatants to be ready to march at a certain hour, and sending the Special Ideas to Squadrons, Batteries, and Companies in reasonable time for them to be explained to all concerned, so that they were ready before the operations began, which was generally two hours later.

I did not always succeed in my efforts to impart instruction; indeed I learnt accidentally from a young officer, in the third year of my command at Aldershot, that he had not seen any of the criticisms on which, after long days in the saddle, Colonel Hildyard [1] and I had spent several hours every night, often not going to bed till 2 a.m. On inquiry I ascertained that the Adjutant (for the commanding officer did not appear much in the transaction) had kept them carefully in his camp-bag, that

---

[1] Now Lieutenant-General Sir Henry Hildyard, Commanding Troops in South Africa.

they might be read to the troops on their return, when any interest evoked must have evaporated. Still we imparted some instruction.

I was fortunate in having to deal with polished gentlemen as my subordinates; but in addition, Brigadier-General Mansfield Clarke [1] was a man of experience, tact, and decision. I cannot recall having made any adverse remarks on the training of those under his command.

I corresponded with some of my contemporary, and earlier Staff College graduates, then commanding troops in India, and endeavoured to assimilate the best of the methods practised in India. I was Staff officer in 1867 to, I believe, the first Flying Column which left Aldershot, and when I sent out those in 1889, I tried to bring the instruction up to date.

For this purpose, during the ten days or fortnight that each of the three columns was in the field, I not only kept it mobilised from Monday morning to Saturday night, but also the troops remaining in Aldershot, as this gave me the power of attacking the columns, which moved around Aldershot in a circle on a radius of from one to two marches.

The constant state of readiness from Monday to Saturday interfered with Society engagements; but my comrades accepted the innovations in a soldier-like manner, and I was enabled to test the precautions taken by the columns to ensure security by day and night, by sending parties out to endeavour to effect surprises. I always accompanied the attackers as Umpire in chief. Mansfield Clarke was the only General who escaped being surprised in our first year's operations.

On the 22nd of July, after the conclusion of a parade of the Cavalry brigade, the Commander-in-Chief, in the presence of Commanding officers and Squadron leaders, animadverted strongly on my practising Night operations, of which he expressed strong disapproval; adding that he had never carried them out, and he especially disapproved of horses being employed, as it interfered with their rest.

The Chief on this occasion declined to come to lunch, and rode straight back to Farnborough Station. I sent my Aide-de-camp, Captain Babington, who was the finest horseman in

---

[1] Now General Sir C. Mansfield Clarke, Bart., Governor and Commander-in-Chief, Malta.

the Division, to Government House at speed, whence, carrying a basket on his arm, he produced at the station something in the shape of light refreshments for the Head Quarters Staff.

When we were alone, Major Parsons,[1] the senior Aide-de-camp, observed, " It is scarcely possible, sir, you heard everything the Commander-in-Chief said?" "Why?" and I repeated the Chief's words almost verbatim. " But when you saluted I could not see a muscle of your face move." I then described the scene I had witnessed some twenty years earlier on the same spot, when the Colonel of the " Wait-a-bits " gave us an object lesson in discipline (*vide* vol. i. pp. 235–236).

The Chief had been misled, as only one Squadron had been employed once, at night, for a raid ; but Cavalry often moved before dawn in order to operate at daylight.

The unpleasant affair reacted locally in my favour, for even those who disliked the increased work I was imposing, resented a General being rebuked in the presence of his subordinates. Nevertheless, I felt that my position was difficult, and wrote that evening to the Adjutant-General offering to resign the command. This he strongly discouraged, writing, " Pray go on as you are doing ; " and I did so. At a Ceremonial parade which followed soon afterwards, the Commander-in-Chief announced " He had never seen anything better," which praise was repeated practically at every succeeding inspection during my command. The Chief had previously apprehended novel tactics implied relaxation of discipline.

Without the practice of night marches, the Boer War would have lasted much longer than it did.[2]

Towards the end of July we started some night firing, practising the repelling of an assault on trenches, the men being instructed to fire at a tinkling bell, with an occasional electric flash on a target.

On the 7th August His Imperial Majesty the German Emperor reviewed the Division. He is bright, with a decided direct manner; a good horseman. His quick and very intelligent

---

[1] Now Major-General Sir Charles Parsons, K.C.B.

[2] Extract from a private letter to Sir Evelyn Wood from Brigadier-General Rimington, one of the most successful Light Cavalry Leaders, who commanded a mounted column in the Boer War, dated Heilbron, O.R.C., 5.8.01 : " Nearly all our work is done at night, and we have not yet made a night march without a fairly good result."

mind takes in every detail at a glance, and he possesses a marvellous memory. In speaking of our soldiers boxing, the Emperor asked, " How do you manage to prevent the men of a defeated boxer's regiment quarrelling in the canteens?" I said, "Your Majesty, nearly all Britons are true sportsmen by instinct, and accept the umpire's decision; moreover, the championship is an honour which never induces bad feeling."

He was galloping on the Fox Hills, overlooking Aldershot from the eastward, when he passed an Infantry soldier with pouches for carrying the ammunition up into the firing line, and stopped to examine the sack. As he restarted, he remarked on it in German, and on my replying, asked, "When and where did you learn your German?" "Oh, many years ago, sir." "Well, how have you kept it up?" "I go occasionally to shoot with a friend in the Rhein Pfalz. He has a large tract of forest."

Two years later I wished to go to the German manœuvres, and wrote to our Military Attache stating that His Majesty the Emperor had been kind enough to ask me in 1889 and 1890, when I was unable to avail myself of the honour, but I should like to go in 1891, as for personal reasons I wanted a change of scene. The Emperor replied, "Tell him I am not asking any officers this year; but I remember he has a shooting, or one of his friends has a shooting, in the Rhein Pfalz, and if he should be there in my country before the Manœuvres, I shall be delighted to send him an invitation."

The Emperor spoke very well in English at the lunch given by Command of Her Majesty the Queen, and after it was over the Princess of Wales preceded the Imperial cortege to the Saluting Base, on which the troops assembled while the Imperial party lunched. His Majesty the Emperor galloped at speed for half a mile, and reining in his horse gracefully immediately in front of the carriage of the Princess of Wales, saluted. All the attending Staff reined up in their places except one German Naval officer, whose horse careered on wildly, until hearing all those following stop, pulled up very suddenly, with the result that the officer described a circle in the air, and sat on the ground immediately in front of the Royal carriage.

When at the conclusion of the Review the Emperor was cantering back to the station, the same officer passed him at a gallop, and coming on some gorse bushes, the horse jumped them, with the result that the officer again fell. As the Emperor passed he observed to me, "By Jove, there's the Admiral overboard again."

His Majesty, in thanking me, proposed to give me a decoration, but I explained that we were not allowed to wear them,[1] and he sent me, as he did to Admiral Sir E. Commerell, a magnificent uniform sword, the hilt studded with diamonds. As I learnt later, the Emperor was really pleased, and one of his generals spoke frankly about the day's operations to a friend of mine, who wrote down briefly all he said. "Everything was much better than we expected. The Cavalry, though individually man and horse is excellent, do not ride in sufficiently close formation in the charge. The Artillery horses and equipment is the finest ever seen. The Infantry are well drilled, but their pace is too short."

There had been much perturbation in Pall Mall as to this visit, for on previous occasions the Aldershot Division had rehearsed all parades for Royalties, thus losing time which should have been spent in training for Field Service, which I invariably, during my command, declined to interrupt for any Spectacular parades. Lord Wolseley declining to interfere, contented himself by saying, "Trust the man on the spot," and carried his point, though with some difficulty.

I received a very kind letter from the Secretary of State, congratulating me on the "brilliant success." He added, "Personally I was also exceedingly gratified by the March past, because some had been croaking to me that it would be spoiled by the previous manœuvres."

In thanking Mr. Stanhope, I explained that "the operations were as realistic as they could be under the given conditions, —a fixed hour, the area to be confined to the vicinity of the lunch tent, and the March past to be fitted in before the Emperor's return, which necessitated the attacks being pre-arranged, and timed like 'turns' in a large music hall. It is true I designed the movements, but there my personal share ended; the five general officers carried out my ideas with

[1] This has since been changed.

perfect loyalty, accepting victory or defeat *cum æquo animo*, and it is to them and the Divisional Staff, the general success of the day is due."

I went on to praise the arrangements made by Colonel North Crealock,[1] the Assistant Quarter-Master-General, who received and despatched troops attending the Review from outside Aldershot, every unit of which was met by an Army Service Corps officer, de-trained, conducted to a Rest camp with all sanitary arrangements, supplied with food, re-entrained, and enabled to reach its permanent station within its scheduled time.

At the end of August, Lords Wolseley, Wantage, and Harris came down to see "Field firing" on Bisley Common, and with Sir Henry Brakenbury and myself were riding behind a Maxim gun, which was drawn by a mule, when, the stopper not being on, a bullet was accidentally fired, passing between our horses' legs. After I had rebuked the man in charge for his carelessness, his comrade made the quaint observation, "My, wasn't that dangerous; it might have shot the poor moke."

[1] He died when commanding a Division in India.

CHAPTER XLV

1889-90—REFORMS AT ALDERSHOT

Colonel Grattan's Reforms in purchase of Supplies—Divisional Staff Brigadiers—Decentralisation—Useless Sentries—Cooking Reforms—Colonel Burnett's system—Lord Wantage's help in Field Training—Stanley, the Explorer—Sir John Pender—Ober-Ammergau—Cavalry Manœuvres—Concession in soldiers' fares—Changes for Christmas-Day.

THE day I joined at Aldershot I saw the Generals, Commanding officers, and all the Staff officers in succession. I was struck by one face and voice, Colonel Grattan of the Army Service Corps, and desired him to wait until the Reception was over. I then said: "Colonel, I am puzzled, because listening to your voice, and watching your eyes, I seem to dream I knew you years ago, but have the impression that the man whom I befriended materially in his career had a one-syllable name; moreover, I have only known one Grattan in the Service, and you are not the man." He replied: "Your memory is quite accurate, Sir. I was once your clerk; you got me made in succession, Camp Quarter-Master Sergeant, Garrison Sergeant-Major, and eventually got me a commission as a Conductor in the Army Service Corps, which I am now commanding at this Station. I enlisted under the name of Smith, and reverted to my own name on being commissioned." Grattan enabled me to introduce many reforms, which without his aid would have been impossible.

During my period of Command the Army Service Corps establishment was greatly increased, the officers by volunteers from the Line. The Commanding officers not knowing that 10,000, or one-third of our Crimea army, died from want of adequate Departmental arrangements, did not appreciate the necessity of recommending only thoroughly good officers.

Colonel Grattan and I rejected in one year one-third of those sent as Probationers.

Soon after I assumed command the Forage contractors raised their prices. The contractor for hay demanded a large advance; and being financially assisted by others, bought all the available crop in the four counties adjoining Aldershot. I declined the terms, and going further afield, bought largely in the Eastern counties—over 3000 tons in Essex alone; and even with the heavy railway rates, reduced the original contract price by three shillings a ton.[1] We purchased in most cases the hay in stacks in 1889, which was difficult, as it required officers with much experience in judging quantity and quality, with the further disadvantage that we had no market for " outsides," which are generally worth about 15s. a ton to farmers, for stock. We did not buy in stacks in 1890, as the hay harvest was gathered in very wet weather; but I maintained the practice of the Army Service Corps buying the hay, as —affording practice for their duties in war; secondly, to abolish the demoralisation of subordinates generally attendant on the contract system[1]; and thirdly, on the ground of economy, by eliminating the middleman.

In order to teach Cavalry officers to judge oats, I bought everything on the London Corn Exchange, the Cavalry brigadier selecting his Representative, while Colonel Grattan nominated an officer of the Army Service Corps with a view to due economy being exercised. These officers, supplied with the latest *Corn Circular*, were instructed to note the quantities in the port of London; the anticipated arrivals, and the customs of the market. In the result we bought oats weighing nearly 40lbs. a bushel, all expenses being included, with a considerable saving on the contractor's charge for oats weighing 38lbs.

Colonel Grattan's next marked assistance to me was in helping Colonel Burnett,[2] Assistant Quarter-Master General, to defeat the tactics of the Meat contractors. At the end of

---

[1] The contractor became a Bankrupt.

[2] Lieutenant-General Sir James Yorke Scarlett told me in 1868, that to a committee in the early 60's on which he served, it was clearly shown that on one Station all non-commissioned officers and men on duty received various sums from the forage contractors, down to the orderly officer's batman, who received 1s. 6d. per diem.

[3] Now Lieutenant-General C. J. Burnett, C.B.

May 1901, the Firm which had undertaken to supply us with live meat till the 1st November, refused to fulfil the engagement, forfeiting the £100 deposit. The contract was then offered to all other tenderers at their own prices, but they refused to undertake it, and believing that there was a combination to force up the price, on Sunday afternoon the 30th May I sent Colonel Burnett, Colonel Grattan, and the Master butcher to Smithfield with £1700,[1] which they spent soon after daylight before our former contractors came on to the Market. The Government, all expenses included, and even with the difficulty of disposing of the offal, made a profit on the transaction, and we found another contractor at our previous rates.

I was very fortunate in the officers on the Divisional Staff. Colonel C. W. Robinson, Assistant Adjutant-General, who had a particular polished manner, which ordinarily concealed considerable force of character, was followed by Colonel Henry Hildyard,[2] who on going to be Commandant of the Staff College was succeeded by Colonel James Alleyne, considered, and with reason, to be the best Gunner in the Army. Soon after he joined I observed to some senior Artillery officers with whom I was on friendly terms, "Hitherto I have spoken to you with an uncertain voice, but now I have got James Alleyne behind me, you may expect much more decided criticism."

Lieutenant-Colonel Edward Hutton[3] had been training Mounted Infantry successfully before I took over command, and continued to do that work, and much other, throughout my time at Aldershot. I have often been congratulated on the efforts I made in training Mounted Infantry, but I had little to do with it except to give Hutton a free hand, and to support

[1] The War Office system of centralisation was shown markedly by a Paymaster's conduct in this case. I received several telegrams suggesting I should give way to the contractors' demands, rather than risk a failure of supply; and when I declined, I was asked if I was prepared to accept the full responsibility of feeding the Troops. I answered in the affirmative. On the 30th May, sending for a Paymaster, I ordered him to give me a cheque for £1700. He absolutely refused to do so, without War Office authority. However, when I told him to go away under arrest for disobedience, and to send me the next senior Paymaster, he wrote the cheque.

[2] Lieutenant-General Sir Henry Hildyard, K.C.B., Commander-in-Chief in South Africa.

[3] Now Major-General Sir Edward Hutton, K.C.B.

him with those who were senior to him. No work was too much for him, and it was he who reorganised the Aldershot Tactical Society, and Officers' Library, besides undertaking other useful work.

Mansfield Clarke [1] and Hildyard advised me on all Infantry matters, while Lieutenant-Colonel French [2] of the 19th Hussars, after he came to Aldershot, was a warm supporter of my efforts to improve the Cavalry. I was unable to obtain for him written authority to carry out the Squadron system in its entirety, but he did it, and with such decision as to disregard the claims of seniority for the command of Squadrons.

I endeavoured to follow Lord Bacon's recommendation, "Preserve the rights of inferior places, and think it more honour to direct in chief than to be busy in all," which might be expressed in the language of the twentieth century, "Do nothing yourself that you can make another man do."

My first principle in teaching was de-centralisation. I tried to pass the training from the Commanding officers, that is, the Adjutants and Sergeant-Majors, to Squadron and Company officers. The Battery Commanders did their own work in striving for mobility and smartness. I to some extent satisfied the Commanding officers by giving them twice a week, for two months, every man on their strength for parade, the Generals and Staff having to give up their grooms and servants, which sacrifice, good as it was for efficiency, did not add to my popularity. I caused Coal and all other Fatigues to be done in the afternoon, employing condemned waggons to carry the coal and firewood. After abolishing Divisional fatigues, I assembled later a committee of the five generals, who laid down the exact number of non-commissioned officers and men who should be excused parades ordered to be "as strong as possible."

At the end of 1889 we had made some progress in reducing the percentage of third-class shots, which fell during the year from 40–54 per centum to 13–28 per centum in Cavalry units; and in Infantry units from 25–32 per centum to 13–28 per centum. I was not, however, satisfied, and realising that we

---

[1] Sir C. Mansfield Clarke, Bart, G.C.B., now Governor and Commander-in-Chief at Malta.
[2] Now General Sir John French, K.C.B., commanding at Aldershot.

should never get the men to shoot fairly until we had more officers as experts, I asked the commandant at Hythe if he could not take some more classes. As this was impossible for want of accommodation, I, with the sanction of the Adjutant-General, started classes at Aldershot under Major Salmond, who had been an Instructor at Hythe. The Hythe Staff objected, alleging that the instruction could not be so thorough, and would not justify a Hythe certificate. This I met by arranging that their Staff should examine the candidates, and before the Aldershot classes were stopped we trained 118 gentlemen in the first duty of an Infantry officer.

When inspecting what was then the First Division, Telegraph Battalion, at Chobham in the summer, I saw the men lay an overhead wire of 2 miles 7 furlongs, and pass a message through it in forty-two minutes. When the same Battalion were employed with troops the result was not satisfactory, as the men being unaccustomed to work with men of other units, made bad mistakes, and communication even for a short distance was not maintained. This reflected no discredit on the Corps, as I learned incidentally that this was the first time they had ever been either inspected by a general in command, or had worked with troops, having previously done their annual course as a separate and detached Unit.

Up to July 1889, when a soldier was sent to hospital his dinner was cooked regimentally, and sent to him in a tin can, involving often a journey of over half a mile, with the result which can be imagined. With the concurrence of the doctors I carried out an experiment of the rations being drawn by the hospital authorities. Theoretically somebody had less one day and more next day, but practically the 500th part of a pound makes no difference in the messing arrangements, and the practice is now established.

In the Autumn I was asked, by the Commander-in-Chief's directions, if I wished to be considered for the Bombay Command.[1] The Adjutant-General, Viscount Wolseley, while unwilling to advise me, was clearly against my accepting, and so I respectfully declined.

---

[1] In discussing a possible successor to the Aldershot Command, he wrote, 6th October 1889 : " It would be a real calamity to the Army that you should leave it."

I found no difficulty in reducing the number of sentries, except in the Mounted branches, and over the Hospitals, where our Conservative instincts were amusingly illustrated by the objections of Commanding officers and doctors. To my suggestion that one sentry would do to watch the horses of X, Y, and Z batteries Artillery, it was said, "No; 'Y' stablemen will steal the tackle of 'X'." I retorted, "But 'X' will have its chance next night, and so the result will be identical"; and up to my leaving Aldershot, four years later, no damage had resulted from the more reasonable arrangement, the Cavalry saving two-fifths, Artillery and Royal Engineers two-thirds of the night sentries.

I did not make up my mind about watchmen for stables until I had learnt the practice in London, where I again sent Colonel Gratton, who went round the buildings of several London Companies using a great number of horses, with the result that he found one watchman overlooking any number, from 230 up to 800.

The Senior Medical officer protested that the removal of a sentry from the Hospital gate would be attended with the worst results. I could not agree with him, but ordered the Army Hospital Corps to find the guard for the sentry, with the result that in a week's time the sentry was taken off by the Doctors, and has never since been replaced.

Soldiers were still doing the work of the General Post Office, so I communicated with the Secretary, who not only put collecting boxes in all the lines, but delivered letters at a central selected place in each Battalion.

Early in 1890 the issue of the .303 rifle, with its greatly increased trajectory, rendered the ranges at Ash unsafe, and some action essential. The greater part of the shooting of the Infantry was then done at Pirbright, where detachments occupied in succession huts which were, if possible, worse than those which housed the Aldershot Division. The Royal Engineers undertook work of considerable magnitude, the working parties employed on the Western slopes of the Fox Hills moving 260,000 cubic yards of soil, and the result has been very satisfactory; for whereas in 1889 the Range practices were necessarily extended for four months, the accommodation then provided enabled, two years later, an increased strength of over 5000 to get through the course in thirty-one firing days, and the ranges, moreover, afforded facility for practice more like that occurring on service.

Before I joined, a Lecture had been given showing what might be done in improving the soldiers' meals, but no practical steps were taken until early in 1890, when I invited Colonel Burnett,[1] who had successfully tried in his Battalion what is now the Army system, to come to stay with me at Aldershot, and to give a Lecture. He demonstrated that the dripping alone in a Battalion of 1000 men is worth £200 per annum, and I became a warm supporter of his theories. One brigade took up the idea, and worked it successfully, becoming the pioneers to the rest of the Army.

I was attacked in an amusing weekly journal,[2] and derided as a mischievous busybody. Later, the Editor sent a Representative, who not only visited the School of Cookery, then at work under Lieutenant-Colonel Edward Hutton, but also questioned many of the Rank and File, and in the result, published a handsome apology, stating he believed the former assertions were based on information furnished by individuals interested in the bad old system.

The day after the German Emperor left Aldershot in 1889, I went to Churn, near Wantage, to inspect the Home Counties brigade, which had done well under Brigadier Lord Wantage, V.C., at the Review the day before, and I took the opportunity of riding over the Berkshire Downs, and discussing with the Brigadier the possibility of having some manœuvres for Cavalry in 1890. He met me with the greatest generosity, undertaking not to claim compensation for any damage done to his property, and he himself farmed on a large scale; moreover, as a considerate landlord, and as Lord-Lieutenant of the county, he had great influence, which was placed entirely at my disposal. No other landord ever helped me so much to improve the Field-training of our troops; no man ever showed me and my Staff such

---

[1] Now Lieutenant-General C. J. Burnett, C.B.

[2] As indeed I have often been, but may say now that its statements, and vkward questions, have enabled me, since I became a General, to check many idesirable practices.

consistent generous hospitality as did Robert Lloyd Lindsay, V.C., Lord Wantage.

In the Spring of 1890 I examined the ground more closely, and sent round officers, who visited 142 tenants; and later, I obtained War Office sanction to my holding the Manœuvres, provided every landowner and tenant consented to troops passing over his land.

Early in 1890, after a full discussion with the five general officers serving under me, I changed, with their concurrence, our method of criticising the work done in tactical operations. The evidence of those taking part, as well as that of the umpire staff, which afforded information likely to prove of value in the future, was collected, and sifted on the spot, as in 1889, but the narrative and decision of the Umpire-in-chief was published next day.

On the 1st May I received a telegram from Sir William MacKinnon, urging me to go up to town next evening to dine with him at a welcome home to Henry Stanley, the Explorer, on his return from the expedition to succour Emin Pasha. I had known Sir William for many years, having been introduced to him by our common friend Sir Bartle Frere, who observed to me, "You should know MacKinnon, he has given us £10,000 to open a road through Uganda to the Lakes." I having heard that MacKinnon's business aptitude had created the British India Steamship Company, observed jokingly, "You do not expect, Mr. MacKinnon, that £10,000 will pay a dividend?" He said quietly, "No, never to me; but there is a great pleasure in having made enough money to be able to do something for the sake of those who come after us." I had known Mr. Stanley since 1873, when he had dined with me on Christmas Day at Prahsu, the boundary between Fanti and Ashantiland, when already in bearing, he showed the determination which distinguished him later as one of the most intrepid explorers of the Victorian Age. I had dined with Sir William MacKinnon at a Farewell dinner he gave, on the 19th January 1887, to Stanley ere he set out, when he talked to me about the officers to be employed under him, and regretted he had not consulted me before they were nominated.

He disappeared for three years; and on his return, MacKinnon telegraphed to me to come to London and redeem my promise to attend his Welcome Home dinner. This I did; and on the evening of the 1st May he walked into the room holding out his hand as if we had only separated the previous day, observing, " I have often thought of you. Do you remember what you said when we parted?" "Oh, I told you about the officers." "Yes," said he; "but you put to me a remarkable question which has often been in my mind. 'So you are going to look for Emin, is he worth the journey?' That interrogation has often recurred to me in my months of wanderings on Emin's trail."

Early in June I took advantage of two columns being at the south end of Woolmer Forest to practise Infantry making a Frontal Attack on Artillery in position. The Artillery umpires thought the Infantry would have been repulsed, while the Infantry were of opinion they would have carried the guns, though with considerable loss. This opinion was shared by my friend Major Comte Pontavice De Heussy, the French Military Attaché, himself a Gunner. It is interesting to recall the advance in breadth of Military knowledge. When two years later the Garrison at Aldershot had changed, I tried the identical Attack, with the sole difference that I placed Infantry officers as umpires with the guns, while Artillery officers accompanied the attacking Infantry; on this occasion the Gunners thought that the Infantry had succeeded, while the Infantry umpires thought that the guns had decidedly repulsed the Infantry.

In June I had a note from my friend Sir John Pender, saying that his wife was writing a Magazine article concerning soldiers, and would like to come to Aldershot for a short visit. It happened that Colonel Crease, Royal Marine Artillery, was with me, trying some Smoke balls which were to be thrown down by skirmishers to hide the advance of thicker lines. This experiment was in itself exciting, and against my will Lady Pender overtaxed her strength by undertaking a 24-mile drive in the afternoon, to visit the Gordon Boys' Home, near Bagshot. I tried to prevent her going, urging that she should lie down, for I saw what was not apparent to others, that she was about to become seriously ill; but she persisted, and, to my deep regret, died a few days after her return to London.

During my Home Service I have practically never asked for leave of absence, contenting myself with sport available from my residence, but in July I asked for twelve days before the Cavalry Manœuvres. The Commanding officers required a few days in which they might exercise their units before proceeding to the manœuvre ground; and I was, moreover, although I did not anticipate the calamity which I was to suffer next year in losing my wife, anxious to give her the pleasure of attending the Passion Play at Ober-Ammergau, which is acted only once in ten years. I was just ten days out of office, and it is still a consoling recollection to me that I was able to afford my wife so much enjoyment. I do not think that she, or my daughter, although Catholics, appreciated the reverential representation of the simple-minded peasants more than I did as a Protestant. Indeed, the wonderful scenes appeal to every Christian, irrespective of his religious form of worship.

Soon after my return from Ober-Ammergau the Cavalry Division paraded, 3400 strong, prior to its marching to the Berkshire Downs, where I obtained permission from landlords and tenants to manœuvre over a tract of country 22 miles from east to west, with an average of $7\frac{1}{2}$ miles from north to south. Just before we were about to start I received a telegram from the farmers asking if the manœuvres might be postponed; so I proceeded to Ilsley on the Downs with my friend Colonel Sir Lumley Graham, who was then living at Arlington Manor, and arranged matters with the sheep farmers without any further postponement, which would have been unfortunate, as about the middle of September the weather in England generally breaks up. I had agreed to buy all articles in the district as far as it could produce them, on condition that for oats I was not to pay more than the London Corn Exchange price, plus freight, plus two shillings a quarter. One of my strong supporters, a tenant farmer, came to me a few days after the Cavalry had arrived at the camps of Concentration, and complained that his oats had been rejected. I had heard the story, and said, "Yes, my friend, but they were bought in Mark Lane by you, and I can tell you exactly what price you paid, and we never agreed to give you two shillings a quarter plus freight for acting as a Buyer." He said naïvely, "I never thought that your officers could tell the difference in oats."

The Cavalry learned much on the Downs, in reconnaissance work, and in the fitting of saddlery and equipment, which can only be tried under service conditions. After the last day's work, in which Colonel John French,[1] 19th Hussars, showed considerable tactical skill, I rode with the Divisional Staff into Aldershot direct, the Cavalry returning in two marches.

We tried some interesting experiments in training Infantry as cyclists, and ascertained that men who had never ridden before, required two months' training to make them fairly expert, and to harden their bodies. Men can ride carrying rifle and ammunition and equipment, and average 8 miles an hour when travelling as a company, and can easily make 20 miles a day when moving in large bodies. The Irish Rifles Detachment on returning to Holyhead travelled 70 miles the first day, and 50 next day, without difficulty.

I was able to help materially the Auxiliary Forces during my time at Aldershot. I established the principle that the Auxiliaries being at Aldershot for a short time only, the Regulars were to give way to them as regards the use of ranges, and use of ground for tactical purposes. The result was a large increase in the number of applications to attend, thirteen battalions of Militia coming in my second year, instead of six, and eventually the applications for Volunteer Corps to train at Aldershot had to be checked by one of my successors, as more wished to come than the ground could accommodate.

Many Commanding officers thanked me, I quote two. Lord Wantage wrote: "This has been the best week's big drill that I ever remember. . . . I can assure you that the Volunteer Forces greatly appreciate the marked interest you take in their welfare." And the other: "I am a volunteer of thirty-three years' service, and thank you extremely for the interest you have shown in the Force, in which there has been a great and marvellous advance, in drill and attention to details."

[1] Now the General commanding at Aldershot.

I had been trying for several years to interest Directors of Railways in a scheme I had propounded for soldiers when proceeding on furlough, to be granted a Return ticket at single fare, but had no success until the middle of October, when I called on Mr. W. P. Dawson, the Managing Director of the Railway Clearing House, at Euston. I explained to him the importance of the question from a Recruiting point of view, and mentioned that prior to the embarkation of the Devon Regiment for Foreign Service, only eighty men had gone on furlough from Aldershot to Exeter, the double fare being prohibitive. Both Mr. Dawson, and Sir Miles Fenton, managing Director of the South-Eastern, and Mr. Charles Scotter, Managing Director of the South-Western, received my suggestion in a generous spirit; and from the 1st December the boon was conceded to soldiers, not only on these lines, but throughout Great Britain. In the following year I obtained a similar concession from the steamboat companies plying round the United Kingdom.

When I left the Aldershot Staff, eleven years earlier, although there were few outward breaches of discipline, yet officers and men agreed that more alcoholic liquor was consumed at Christmas than was desirable; and now being in command I encouraged officers to send their men on furlough for a week at Christmas, with the result that from 1890 onwards, about half the garrison spent the day at home.

CHAPTER XLVI

1891-2-3—TRAINING OF TROOPS ON PRIVATE LANDS

Death of Lady Wood—Manœuvres in Hampshire—Public Schools' Camps at Aldershot—Improvement in War Training—Ian Hamilton—Lord Roberts—Sealed patterns, Army Stores.

ON the 11th May I lost my wife, with whom I had enjoyed uninterrupted happiness since our marriage and who for twenty-four years, next to God, had given me all her life. The most loving and tender of women, endowed with the highest principles of morality, her companionship raised the standard of thought of even an ordinary man, increasing his respect for womankind, while her infinite compassion rendered her a hopeful and encouraging beacon to the weakest of her sex. She was to me not only an affectionate wife, but also adviser and confidential secretary. My greatest abiding regret is that devotion to the Army gave me so little time with her, and with our children; in seven successive years, employment on Foreign Service allowed me only $14\frac{1}{2}$ months at home.

I had no suspicion of her being ill until one afternoon walking in the grounds of Government House she told me she felt an unpleasant fluttering in her heart; but we had suspected so little her dangerous state, that I had allowed her to walk up a steep hill in the previous June, when I particularly asked Lady Pender, whose face I was watching, to go up in the carriage.

In the month of November Lady Wood complained of eczema, and was in bed for a week; but she made so little of her ailments that I went almost daily to London to sit on a Drill Committee, engaged in revising a new book, and when I was not in London I spent the day in office with Sir Mansfield Clarke and Colonel Hildyard, on the same duty. Ten days later my wife was sufficiently recovered to go about and look at houses, as it became necessary for us to turn out of Government House, which required repairs.

Early in the year Her Majesty the Empress Eugénie, whose kindness to us had been unceasing, since the journey in 1880 to Zululand, took Lady Wood and my eldest daughter to St. Remo for a change of air, I remaining ignorant of her precarious state of health until I received a note, written by the direction of the Empress, calling me to the Riviera.

The doctor at St. Remo told me frankly he thought very badly of Lady Wood's state, and advised me to take her back to England. I telegraphed for Surgeon-Major Finlay, who knew my wife's constitution, and he kindly hurried to St. Remo, meeting us, however, only at Paris, as we had left the Riviera before he arrived. The journey was exceptionally painful to me; I had not ventured to tell my young daughter what I feared, and the doctor had warned me that if my wife died in the carriage, which was possible, I should conceal the fact until we reached Paris to avoid removal from the train. After a week's rest in Paris we got back to Aldershot. Ten days before Lady Wood died I offered to telegraph for our eldest son, who was with his Battalion, Devon Regiment, in Egypt. She replied, "Certainly not, I will not be so selfish; let him come home later, and escape the hot weather."

Nothing could be more touching than the gracious solicitude of Her Majesty the Queen, who offered to come to Aldershot to see Lady Wood before she died, and the sympathy of my comrades of all Ranks. Her Majesty sent me a beautifully expressed letter of compassion; in thanking her I wrote it was the more acceptable as to her might appropriately be applied the line, "Non ignara mali miseris succurrere disco."

Friends in both Churches, the Catholic Bishop of Westminster, the Dean of Westminster, and soldiers' wives sent condolences to me. Forty-six non-commissioned officers and privates, living in different parts of Scotland, wrote to me in memory of our service together in South Africa in 1878-9.

Lady Wood had indeed done much for her poorer brothers and sisters. She was ever engaged in works of Charity, irrespective of the religion of those she succoured; indeed, when at Colchester, she gave effective assistance to a lady of the Baptist persuasion, who managed a Soldiers' Home. My wife and daughter organised a series of weekly concerts in the Cambridge Hospital for convalescents, collecting sufficient money, mainly through our friend Lord Wantage, to buy a second-hand Grand piano, and they made a practice of spending one afternoon every week in the Hospital, inducing other ladies to do the same, so that every ward where there were female nurses, was visited by one or more ladies weekly. Lady and Miss Wood, with the aid of friends, supplied the Cambridge Hospital with invalid chairs, and many other such articles, not issued in those days by Government.

It was fortunate for me that at this particular time I was if possible more than usually engaged on Military duties. I was unable to sleep consecutively at night, and never after four in the morning, at which time, after leaving her for only an hour, I had been called to my wife's bedside to say goodbye. The day after the funeral, I supervised the training of an Infantry Brigade, and on the day following, the Cavalry, working consecutively eleven hours on the Drill book after my return to Government House. When I was not in London, and there were no troops training, after clearing my office table, I remained on horseback till sunset.

Throughout the Autumn of 1890, and during the Winter of 1890–91, I was looking for ground for manœuvres in North Hampshire, assisted by Captain Rycroft, 7th Dragoon Guards, with whose uncle I had been shipmate on H.M.S. *Queen*, and I had every assistance possible from the Rycroft family, and Mr. Portal, who not only gave me free use of his land, but assented to my using the meadows on his dairy farm for encampments. The Earl of Carnarvon was also most generous, allowing me to select as a camp for 6000 men, a field within 200 yards of where most of his pheasants were to be raised.

With landowners I had but little difficulty, but much of the land was let to shooting tenants who were non-resident in the county, and the objections of two I found it was impossible to overcome. Both gentlemen were courteous in the extreme; one, the Head of a firm of prosperous drapers in Knightsbridge, told me frankly that he worked hard for ten months in the year, and that no compensation for disturbance of game would make up to him for less sport; and eventually I had to give up my scheme, trying then for ground between Basingstoke and Alresford, and when unsuccessful there, looking over more lands between Stockbridge and Winchester In both areas, however, there was considerable trouble in finding camping-places anywhere except on arable land, and the scarcity of water was a well-nigh insuperable difficulty; eventually I had to come back to a tract which I had looked at in 1890, about 7 miles from east to west, and 5 from north to south, lying between Butser Hill, Droxford, and West Meon, Hambledon. The clergy in the district were at first much opposed to the idea of seeing soldiers in their parishes, but eventually they all withdrew their objections, and after the manœuvres wrote to me in enthusiastic terms of the good conduct of our men. A week before Lady Wood died she rallied so remarkably as to enable me to go down to West Meon for a day, and fix the sites for the camps which we occupied in August. The Force employed consisted of two complete Infantry divisions; that is, each had a brigade of Artillery and a Squadron of Cavalry.

The men carried thirty-eight pounds weight besides the clothes they wore, and learnt a good deal marching down, some regiments more than others; as may be gained from the fact that with equivalent numbers 73 men fell out in one Battalion, and two in another. We learned also a good deal as regards the kits of soldiers, which can be tested only on Service or Manœuvres. The harvest was late, but I did not venture to delay the concentration about West Meon and Butser Hill, for fear of the weather breaking, and so we had the unusual spectacle of troops which had been engaged in tactical operations in the forenoon, reaping and stooking corn in the evening.

Eight days before we intended to return to Aldershot the weather broke, and after persevering for four days, the last forty-eight hours in incessant and heavy rain, we abandoned our scheme, and marched home, the men retaining the utmost good-humour in spite of their having lived for two days in

1892] TRAINING OF TROOPS ON PRIVATE LANDS 221

camps which were ankle-deep in mud. At the conclusion of the manœuvres I reported, " In tactical skill officers of all Ranks have improved in a very great degree; but the improvement in military spirit, in eagerness to learn, and to submit cheerfully to great physical discomfort, is even more remarkable, and this spirit reacts naturally on the lower ranks."

Although I did not propose to use private land for purposes of instruction in 1892, I spent the previous autumn in looking round for fresh ground, but came reluctantly to the conclusion, which I put officially on record, that in counties where the sporting rights are leased to non-residents, manœuvres are in the present state of Public feeling in the United Kingdom impossible without an Act of Parliament.

Although the tactical training of infantry in 1892 was confined to Flying Columns moving on the Government grounds in the vicinity of Aldershot, and to the exercise of a Cavalry Division, yet the opportunity of gaining instruction was eagerly taken advantage of by the Auxiliary Forces. A Division composed of the 13th and 14th Militia Brigades, each of five Battalions, came out for a month's training in July, and in August 16,000 Volunteers came into camp. There had been, I gathered, some disinclination in previous years to join us, but the written expression of gratitude I received from officers commanding for the instruction afforded, indicated that the efforts of the Staff had been appreciated.

In 1889 the Public School Volunteer Cadet Companies came out for a week in Berkshire, with a total strength of about 200. The following year the numbers dropped to 160; but in 1891 we encamped about 440 at Bourley, 3 miles west of Aldershot town. Some masters had demurred to allowing their pupils to come, until I wrote a circular letter to the effect that having two sons in school Volunteer Corps, I should have no objection to their attending under arrangements I contemplated, when the difficulty was waived; and in 1892 we encamped about 600 in the grounds of Government House, Aldershot. My friend Colonel Davis, commanding 3rd Royal West Surrey Regiment, lending me large marquees, each capable of seating about 360 persons.

I did not anticipate that every schoolboy who joined a

Cadet Corps would become professional soldiers, but I urged all should fit themselves early in life for the command of Volunteers; and my hopes have been thoroughly justified at Aldershot, for the movement under my successors' fostering care has continued to increase in popularity.

In 1890 I lost in Pall Mall the strenuous support of the Adjutant-General, Lord Wolseley, who had taken over the Irish Command, where he was eagerly practising what he had preached from the War Office. He wrote frequently to me: "Send me copies of your Military Training: how you carry it out, and indeed everything new you have introduced."[1]— And again: "I want to carry out your Night Manœuvres: have sent to me the orders you are giving this year." Lord Wolseley was succeeded as Adjutant-General by Redvers Buller, a friend of many years' standing, whom I personally recommended for the Victoria Cross in Zululand, and he also supported my views; thus my difficulties were practically at an end.

Moreover, the spirit of the troops at Aldershot had changed materially since 1889. The younger officers of the Brigade of Guards were always open to consider new ideas. One of its greatest enthusiasts for war training was Colonel Lord Methuen, who on the 21st August wrote to me: "You have given us the best five weeks' soldiering we ever had, and your work must do us permanent good. To-morrow night we have Night operations."

The march of opinion, however, is still more remarkably shown in a letter from General Sir George Higginson,[2] who as a guest had spent a week in camp with the Guards Brigade to the south of Aldershot. He wrote to me on the 5th September: "My recent opportunity of seeing your work has convinced me that the changes you and your colleagues have made, are not only justified, but imperatively called for, by the

---

[1] On the 2nd October 1891 : "No man has in my time effected more useful Military work than you, and the Army is beginning to realise this as fully as I do."

[2] Such rigidity of movement was suitable to the smooth-bore musket, "Brown Bess," used in the Peninsular, armed with which our troops embarked for the East, in 1854, and which the 4th Division still carried at the Alma, as sufficient Minié rifles had not been issued to equip it. Unfortunately in the eighties all the Heads of the Army had not, like Higginson, appreciated the history of the Campaigns of 1866, 1870-71, and the bloody lessons around Plevna in 1877.

altered circumstances of modern warfare." This open-minded admission is the more remarkable, that Higginson was Adjutant of his battalion when, shoulder to shoulder, it took part in the brilliant and successful attack on the hill above the Alma River, and ever since had lived amongst men who inculcated and eulogised drill, which would enable battalions to "wheel like a wall and swing like a gate."

His Royal Highness the Duke of Connaught was also a warm supporter of modern ideas, and while serving on our drill committee, strenuously advocated more space in the ranks, and the delegation of control to section commanders.

Prior to the commencement of each drill season I recapitulated the most common mistakes made in the previous year, and thus to some extent avoided their repetition. At the end of the season, 1892, I drew up a paper relating to Artillery; it was my own compilation, but the technical part of it came either from Colonel James Alleyne, who was admittedly one of the best Field Artillery men in the Service, or from Colonel N. Walford, employed in the War Office, who was the most scientific Gunner I ever knew, and whose knowledge of the Arm was remarkable. From him I had the advantage of a frank criticism on every Artillery decision which I gave at Aldershot, for he paid me the compliment of differing from me whenever he thought I was in error.

I was corresponding with Colonel Ian Hamilton,[1] then in India, on Musketry questions, and I sent him my paper on Artillery, dated 24th September 1892, with the result that Lord Roberts circulated it to the Artillery in India, Ian Hamilton writing: "I don't think he has before received a paper on this subject which has so absolutely carried him along with it." Five years later, when I was Adjutant-General, I got Ian Hamilton home, to take over the School of Musketry at Hythe, from the conviction that to his effort was due the great improvement of our soldiers' rifle shooting in India.

I took advantage of a rest day in the Cavalry manœuvres of 1890 to ride over the Down land between Swindon and the River Kennet, and in the winter of 1892–93 I revisited the ground, and got permission from the Earl of Craven to

[1] Now Lieutenant-General Sir Ian Hamilton, K.C.B., Southern Command.

address all his tenants, and he gave me the free access to his estate, much of which was in his personal occupation. I obtained the use of 11 miles from east to west, with a mean of 5½ from north to south, on which some useful work was done. One day we practised a frontal attack, having 15,000 troops on the ground.

It is interesting to record that the Rector of Liddington, unsolicited by anyone, wrote that "in spite of his Rectory being practically surrounded by camps, neither he nor his family experienced even a shadow of inconvenience."

I reported that the mistakes made by the officers were fewer, and were more readily acknowledged at the discussions on the conclusion of each tactical exercise. I added, " These conferences have been very useful in the improvement of our battle training. These, however, are by no means the only advantages obtained for the Army; such manœuvres induce officers to study their profession more keenly than they otherwise would do, and the inhabitants of the districts visited have now, I am confident, an increased respect for the Army as a Training school for the nation." The cost of the manœuvres was £7200.

In the Spring I was asked to choose a course for the Divisional Point to Point races, and Captain Norton Legge,[1] on a somewhat indifferent horse, won the Light-weight race from his attention to the instructions, which I printed, and handed round to every rider, besides the verbal explanation. Mr. Harris of Westcourt, Finchampstead, who had always provided foxes for us in his covert near Hook Station, gave me the use of his land. I pointed out to the riders a church in the distance, telling them they had to pass by east and north to the west of the church, on rounding which they would see a balloon in the air, and if they rode straight for the church going out, and the balloon coming home, I would be answerable there would be no wire or unjumpable fences in the line. Legge, an excellent officer, rode absolutely straight, and consequently won.

The new Ranges at Aldershot enabled us to hold the Army Rifle meeting there, causing a great increase in Regi-

[1] Killed in the Boer War.

1893] TRAINING OF TROOPS ON PRIVATE LANDS 225

mental Rifle clubs. At the Annual meeting there were 2000 individual entries, and a large number of teams.

Besides the tactical exercises carried out against the Field columns, which as in 1889 marched round Aldershot using Government ground or commons, we had a useful practice for the first time in mobilising a Divisional ammunition column, which was made up to war strength by borrowing men and horses from Batteries. We learnt a great deal in the packing arrangements of the boxes, and in so marking them as to be recognisable at night, when on service much of the replenishing of ammunition columns has necessarily to be effected. All the Artillery officers showed great interest in this practice, which so far as I know had not been previously attempted.

In the last few months of my Command the Administrative Staff had a lesson from my ingrained habit of looking into details. A new form of lamp chimney had been for some time under trial, and all the reports were unanimous in its favour. A letter to this effect was put before me for signature by an officer, whom I asked, "Have you personally tried the chimnies?" "No, but the Reports are unanimous in its favour." "Well, I'll wait a day or two." "Please, sir, we've had one reminder already, and the Director of Contracts is anxious for a Report." I declined to be hurried, but invited the Staff officer to dine that evening. After dinner I said, "Come for a stroll," and we walked over to the nearest barracks, and asked some men sitting at the tables: "How do you like those lamp chimnies?" "Very well; we don't pay much for them." "Pay, to whom do you pay?" "To Messrs. T. White & Co." "What, for the hire?—where is the Government new pattern?" "Oh, sir, locked up in the Quartermaster's store; we can't use them, as so many break."

In my first year of command Mr. Garth's hounds drew all the Government woods blank. I sent for the Warders and informed them that if it occurred again they would all be changed round;—that is, those on the East would go to the West, and those in the North would go to the South of Aldershot. Lord Cork was kind enough to send me some cubs from his estate, and I kept them in a large enclosure with an artificial earth until they were old enough to work their way out. We seldom found less than a leash, but in my time never succeeded in killing one.

The days the cubs were delivered Major Burn Murdoch, Royal Dragoons, calling to see me about five o'clock, asked if he might speak to me. "Yes, you can talk to me while I am engaged in a sporting operation, and as you are also very fond of it, here you are, snip this one's ears." He said with much adroitness: "Certainly, General, if you hold him!" The Master, Mr. Garth of Haines Hill, who hunted the hounds for nearly half a century, wrote to me on my departure in the autumn from Aldershot: "I thank you for all you have done, which is a very great deal, while at Aldershot for the Fox hounds."

I left Aldershot for Pall Mall in October, having satisfied my two friends, Sir Redvers Buller and Viscount Wolseley, to whose advocacy I owed my appointment; Redvers Buller told me at the time, and repeated his pleasant remark when he went to command at Aldershot in 1897. Lord Wolseley wrote to me as follows: "You have not only taught men a great deal, but have managed to popularise the acquisition of military knowledge."

I wrote to the Adjutant-General in my final Report that "The success obtained was due to the excellent spirit prevailing in all Ranks, and to the careful and unceasing labours of the Staff of the Aldershot Division. These officers, by their knowledge, energy, and loyal assistance, have relieved me of all details of work, and have thus enabled me to devote my attention to the Field training and Tactical instruction of the troops"; and in a farewell order I recorded my thorough appreciation of the sustained zeal with which soldiers of all Ranks had seconded my efforts in preparing the Division for the duties of active Field Service.

CHAPTER XLVII

1893-6—QUARTERMASTER-GENERAL

Prime Warden, Fishmongers' Company—Archbishop Vaughan—Mr. John Ropes—Visit to Gibraltar—An economy of £2300 per annum—Visit to the Crimea—Reform for soldiers travelling to their homes—I make large saving of public monies—Mr. Arthur Balfour's good temper.

I BECAME Quartermaster-General to the Forces on the 9th October 1893, and two months later the Commander-in-Chief offered me the appointment of Governor of Malta, which I respectfully declined.

The years 1893-4 were fully occupied, for I undertook a certain amount of literature, which I got through by rising before daylight; and in June I became Prime Warden of the Fishmongers' Company, which I had joined as a Liveryman in 1874. His Royal Highness the Prince of Wales was graciously pleased to dine with the Company, in recognition of my assuming office. The Prime Warden is by custom and practice allowed to select guests at one of the annual dinners, and I chose a company of fox-hunters. Thirty-five masters of hounds, headed by the Duke of Beaufort, and upwards of 200 sportsmen, the oldest being Mr. J. Crozier, who hunted the Blencathra foxhounds for sixty-four years, dined with the Company.

Archbishop Vaughan, with whom I was on friendly terms, invited me to join a committee for the management of an establishment for preparing Catholic young gentlemen for the army, as neither the Catholic clergy nor the parents were satisfied with the liberty accorded, in most of the establishments in and about London, to a young man just emancipated from school. I declined at first, pointing out that although the Cardinal and my friends knew my views were liberal about religion, earnest Catholics might object to arrangements made by a Protestant. He retorted, however, that that was his concern, and urged me to help him. This I did, although I predicted that the scheme could not answer financially, as there were an insufficient number of Catholic candidates for the army, and my forecast proved later on to be accurate. With the exception of one, Lord Edmund Talbot, the Cardinal asked me to nominate the Committee, and I suggested Sir Arthur Herbert, who afforded the Cardinal much assistance, and generally agreed with my views as against those of the Religious, who were inclined to attempt inculcation of Religion, with more restriction on liberty than young men were willing to accept.

I made the acquaintance of Mr. Ropes, the historian, in July, and, in asking him to give me the pleasure of his company at dinner at the Army and Navy Club, I mentioned a somewhat remarkable circumstance. In the previous month I had gone with three friends—Dr. Norman Moore, of St. Bartholomew's; Mr. Witham, head of the firm of Witham, Roskell & Co., Solicitors; and Major May, Royal Artillery—over the field of Waterloo, and on leaving Brussels it transpired that each one of us had a copy of " Ropes' *Waterloo*."

Mr. Ropes dined with me, and must have enjoyed his evening, for I, liking early hours, excused myself at 12.30 a.m. the following morning, asking General Sir Frederick Maurice, who was a member of the Club, to take my place as host, and I learnt next day the two authors were still discussing Grouchy's proceedings after the battle of Ligny at 2 a.m. when the Club closed.

I had much correspondence in 1896[1] with Mr. Ropes, when I published books entitled *Cavalry at Waterloo*, and *Cavalry Achievements*.

In August Sir John Pender invited Lords Wolseley, Portsmouth, and Kelvin, Sir John Mowbray, Sir John Ardagh, Mr. Bayard, the American Ambassador, and me to join him in a visit to the Crimea,—I at Lord Wolseley's request acting as guide to the party over the battlefields. I described the trip,

---

[1] He wrote to me from Boston, U.S.: "These two books give descriptions which are realistic and modern. In my judgment, you are quite alone in this, and also in giving unbiassed descriptions of facts."

however, in *The Crimea, 1854-94*, and say nothing more about it, except that the Governor of Sevastopol and all the officers received us with the greatest courtesy.

Our Consul, Captain Murray, gave us a curious piece of information,—that the Artillery horses during the winter in the Crimea never left their stables even for exercise. I was back again at work in Pall Mall within a month, and early in November visited Gibraltar on duty.

The expenditure of hired transport on the Rock was greater than appeared essential, and finding no satisfactory result was obtainable from correspondence with the Governor, I went to consult him on the spot, taking out with me Colonel Grattan, who had done so much to help me in initiating reforms at Aldershot. On arrival I explained to His Excellency that I was confident he did not know what was going on, and asked him if he would like the assistance of Colonel Grattan as President of a committee of investigation. After some consideration he accepted my offer, and I enjoyed a very pleasant week as his guest, seeing the fortifications of the Rock, the country in its vicinity, and the Calpe hounds. The result of Colonel Grattan's researches was that a saving of £2300 a year was effected.

After my return from the Crimea I published some reminiscences in the *Fortnightly Review*, afterwards expanded into the book entitled *The Crimea, 1854-94*. I described my first fighting Chief, Captain (afterwards Sir) William Peel, and one of my friends, who was staying in a house in which Lord Peel was visiting, wrote on the 12th October: "The Speaker says the portrait of his brother, which you have given in the article (*Fortnightly*), is the best thing he has ever read; the description of his face and figure is lifelike."

All through 1894-5 I began work at daylight, doing most of my writing before breakfast, and visiting that year every barrack in the United Kingdom; and I made several journeys in search of Artillery practice grounds, visiting Church Stretton, in Shropshire, and many other places.

There had been much trouble with the drainage of the Portsmouth Barracks, which are just on high-water level, causing an acrimonious correspondence with the Municipal Authorities, which resulted in the War Office arranging with the Treasury to withhold the voluntary Treasury contribution paid in lieu of Rates. At the same time the Admiralty was pressing the War Office to surrender, for a consideration, the site of Anglesey Barracks, and a part of the ground on which the Military Hospital stood.

Money for a new Hospital, though allotted, had not been expended, on account of drainage difficulties; for although the Army Medical Department had accepted a site adjoining Hilsea Barracks, there is but little fall from the site, which is practically on the same level as Southsea Common. I pointed out this difficulty, and suggested the new Hospital should be built on the lower slopes of Portsdown Hill, a site which, so far as I know, is now universally approved. Although at first the Medical officers objected to my suggestion, that the site was too far from the Barracks, on my pointing out that an electric tram service passes the site many times daily it was agreed that the additional distance was of no importance.

At the end of 1894 I began work on a reform fraught with great advantages to soldiers, besides saving the country £10,000 or £12,000 a year.

Eight "long-voyage troopships," and H.M.S. *Assistance*, used between the Home Ports, were paid off in 1894, and the question arose whether she should be replaced by another Man-of-war. This doubt enabled us to reconsider the method of conveying the troops throughout the United Kingdom. We had contracts with twenty-one lines of Coasting steamers, and parties both large and small were sent by sea and by land even where it was possible to make the entire journey by rail, if the mixed journey was any cheaper than the direct route; thus soldiers were sent from York by rail to Hull, then thence by sea to London, and by rail to Aldershot.

There was covering authority that in very inclement weather soldiers might travel direct, but as weather at sea cannot be forecasted at an inland station, troops practically always travelled by the cheapest route. Moreover, delays ensued from steamers failing to keep time, and as a rule, there being only deck accommodation, the discomfort involved was so great that £4000 annually was paid by soldiers sent home from the Discharge Depôt at Gosport in order to travel direct. The whole sum paid by soldiers averaged, according to the Accountant-General, £15,000 a year, and this argument he adduced later as a reason against approving of my proposition.

Major Lawson,[1] one of my assistants, at my request worked up the subject, my primary object being to help the soldiers, and in 1895 I obtained permission to endeavour to arrange terms with the Railway Companies of Great Britain. The existing Statutory rates had never been revised since the Act of Parliament was passed in the inception of railways, and on the 11th of March I opened negotiations with Sir Charles Scotter, of the London and South-Western, and Mr. Harrison, of the London and North-Western Companies, which carried most of the military traffic. I undertook, if the Railway companies reduced their rates to what I thought fair, the War Office would abandon the Coast-wise routes, and send troops direct by Rail; and that if special rates were given for the movement of Mounted troops we would, when convenient, use Railways for them.

The managers received my representations favourably, and after obtaining certain statistics from our records, which I got placed at their disposal, I met a deputation of Railway gentlemen on the 14th January 1896. At this meeting I stated I had regarded the matter not as one for making a hard bargain, but as one of friendly arrangement, and that I would make no proposition which I could not as a Director acting for shareholders accept. A schedule of rates prepared by Major Lawson, R.E., was handed to the managers for consideration, and after Examination was practically accepted.

We had many meetings, all the preparation for which, with the necessary calculations, were made by Lawson, who instructed me, as a solicitor does Counsel, before going into court. There was a great advantage in talking to business men with acute minds, for after they saw my proposals would help them as well as the soldiers no difficulty arose. The Secretary for State backed me thoroughly, and the new procedure came into operation on the 1st July. We got concessions of rates for small numbers to the value of 11 per centum, and for numbers over 25, 50 per centum. When troops over

[1] Now Brigadier-General H. Lawson, C.B.

that number were temporarily moved from a permanent station to a Camp of exercise and back within three months, the charge was to be a single fare for the double journey. Mounted troops were carried at a rate which brought the cost somewhat cheaper than the billeting money of troops marching, saving the wear and tear of horse flesh. There was also an incidental gain, lessening Billeting, a custom disliked by soldiers as it is by publicans.

I was, however, more anxious to lessen the hardships of the soldier than to save money for the State. On discharge, or transfer to the Reserve, he could only get the fare to his selected place of residence if it was no farther than the place where he had been enlisted, having to pay any excess. Moreover, this question constantly entailed irritating queries; for as a soldier went away after serving between five and seven years as a general rule, the Adjutant had in every case been changed, and small mistakes involving only a question of 2s. and less caused correspondence extending over months. The difficulty of estimating the soldier's journey home was accentuated by the fact that it had to be calculated by the cheapest routes. With the new Rates we send a soldier free by rail to his selected place of residence. This put £15,000 per annum into the pockets of the soldiers, and saves an appreciable sum in salaries of clerks for correspondence.

I asked Lord Lansdowne to obtain from the Treasury £3000 per annum, undertaking to save £12,000 per annum in perpetuity, but the Financial representative on the Council, after I had completed my arrangements, suggested that the boon to the soldiers should not be granted until the £12,000 had been brought into account. To this Lord Lansdowne did not assent, and I had the satisfaction of saving on the rates alone £14,000 the first year, and I believe there is still an annual saving of over £10,000, in addition to the saving to the Navy Estimates in doing away with the Home Port Troopship.

I failed in the same matter in Ireland, being handicapped by the fact that the "Cheap Rates Act" does not apply to that country, nor do the conditions of military life in Ireland lend themselves to the use of Coastwise journeys.

It is strange that while we made the life of the soldier wretched by sending him by the cheapest and most uncomfortable route, for on board the steamer he had to provide his own provisions, his Rifle from Weedon, his coat from Pimlico were sent by rail, the Army Ordnance Department, being allowed to send their stores as they liked, while the expense was debited to the Department administered by the Quartermaster-General. When I ascertained this fact, in spite of considerable opposition which lasted many months, I got the system reversed, undertaking the stores should be in time, and making the Army Service Corps responsible for all duties formerly carried out by carriers.[1] We thus saved £8000 per annum in commissions, and succeeded in reducing freightage charges from £82,515 in 1893-4, about £10,000 annually till 1896-7, when I vacated the appointment, when they stood at £63,873.[2]

This was not, however, the limit of the economies effected, for the new Railway rates enabled us to save in land transport for manœuvres alone about £13,000 in 1896.[3]

While I tried to save money on estimates, I pressed for some Expenditure which I considered essential. Many writers on the Recruiting problem have dwelt on the deterrent effect, on Recruits of the better class, by the faulty arrangements for Night urinals in Barracks, which after " lights out " were in Cimmerian darkness. The Accountant-General opposed my proposal for Night lights, showing the initial outlay in the United Kingdom alone would amount to £3000, and the annual cost to £2000. When, however, at an Army Council, I described from personal experience with Naturalistic accuracy the state of a corner tub in a Barrack room or

[1] Parliamentary Debates—16th March 1896. Supply in Committee—Army Estimates 1897:—"The Quartermaster-General, Sir Evelyn Wood, has in the last two years produced an annual saving of £21,000, on a not very large vote, by systematising transport of stores." And again, 12th February 1897:—"Sir Evelyn Wood has succeeded in making arrangements to send soldiers by the shortest route, and to give the discharged soldier free conveyance to his selected place of residence."

[2] " Despite these concessions, by a most careful economy in conveyance of stores, etc., Sir Evelyn Wood shows a reduction on the vote apart from special services on the manœuvres. The Vote was £329,000 in 1895-6, £309,000 in 1896-7, and £281,000 in the present year. This is, I think, peculiarly satisfactory."

[3] Supply, 19th February 1897. Mr. Powell Williams, Financial Secretary, in reply said: " With regard to Land Transport, a sum of £13,000 had been saved under this head, owing to the Quartermaster-General having made satisfactory arrangements with the Railway Companies."

passage, in the early morning, Lord Lansdowne's sympathetic feeling for soldiers induced him to side with me, against his Financial advisers, and one great improvement was effected.

He backed my views also against two of my colleagues on the Army Board, who argued that my scheme for issuing Government horses to mounted officers was not required; both my colleagues were rich, and had not the power of putting themselves in sympathy into the position of poor officers. The concession was made for Cavalry at once; but as the Commander-in-Chief, on the advice of the Inspector-General of Cavalry, made it optional, the boon was, as I officially predicted, never accepted by a subaltern. For several years the only horses, taken over at the annual payment of £10, were issued to Captains, who could disregard Regimental feeling. The Boer War has since made us more sensible in many ways.

To Lord Lansdowne's appreciation of the requirements of land for training soldiers, the purchase of a block 15 by 5½ miles, on Salisbury Plain, is due. When he sent me to report on it, a ride of five hours in a blizzard which froze my moustache made me realise the accuracy of those who describe it as the coldest place in England.

Although I was working hard, I do not wish it to be understood that I was having no amusement.[1] I took my sixty-one days' leave in the hunting field, or shooting, keeping my horses at Ongar, in Essex, about twenty-five miles from London; and my brother-in-law, Sir Thomas Lennard, for whom I was still supervising the management of an estate in Ireland, kept up the shooting of his Belhus estate for my pleasure. It is worthy of remark that on the 28th November the beaters put out of an osier bed, only eighteen miles from the General Post Office, a buck, a fox, many pheasants, a covey of partridges, and some wild duck.

It was often alleged during the South African War that the Army Staff had made no provision for it, and had given little or no thought to the subject prior to the outbreak of war. I give therefore an extract from my journal: " 2nd January

[1] Extract from Diary: 10.1.96—Up at 4 a.m. Left St. Pancras by 1st train.

1896.—Worked in the office all day; nothing but work. Prepared a Division and a Brigade of Cavalry on paper." In the Autumn of 1896 I induced the General Officer commanding in South Africa, by private correspondence, to propose a form of contract for providing Army Transport, and got one of a Firm of contractors to come to the War Office, where we discussed a scheme, the acceptance of which I recommended. The Financial side of the office made many and various objections. I, however, so persistently urged the matter that the Secretary of State consulted the Secretary of State for the Colonies, but I was told no action need be taken. One of the reasons alleged against doing anything to provide for the emergency which arose three years later was that the Boers might hear what we were doing, to which I replied: "That would certainly make for Peace."

When I failed to get a transport contract, being apprehensive of the immobility of the garrison at Ladysmith, I recommended, in 1897, that a reserve of two months' food should be maintained constantly at that Station. This was also refused.[1]

On the 17th of April 1897 I begged the Commander-in-Chief to press for Regimental transport being provided for all units in South Africa, equal to carriage of ammunition, tents, baggage, and two days' rations, and again urged that the contract I had suggested should be made at once.

At the same time, foreseeing there must be delay in providing horse fittings for transports, about which I had been in constant communication with the Director of Transports, going on several occasions to Liverpool and other ports to look at different vessels, I urged but in vain an immediate expenditure of £25,000 to obviate the delay which, as I foresaw, occurred two years later. Lord Wolseley warmly supported these suggestions for outlay at the present time, in order to save larger sums in the future.

I wrote at the time to the Secretary of State: "No doubt we must fight the Boers unless they become more reasonable." I asked for £36,000 to replace horses we handed over to the

[1] See pp. 16, 17, *Official History of the War in South Africa*, 1899-1902. By Major-General Sir Frederick Maurice, K.C.B.

Chartered Company, and for Mounted Infantry, and urged that one company should be mounted in each Battalion in South Africa. I pointed out that we should require six mules for every seven men in the Field.

I learnt to cycle, which added greatly to my recreation, for after I was fairly proficient I cycled down to Aldershot or into Essex, about the same distance, on Saturday afternoons, returning for an eight o'clock breakfast on the Monday morning. Before I left London in 1901, I had cycled over 2000 miles in twelve months; but did not attain this facility without some adventures. The first, when I was learning, occurred from a collision with a hansom cab-horse, which was moving just out of a trot on the Edgeware Road at eight o'clock on a Sunday morning. Without any warning the driver turned his horse suddenly as I passed him at a short distance, and the horse's head struck my arm so violently, as I put it up to save my face, that the arm was marked by the animal's teeth, and I was thrown from the centre of the road to the far curbstone, leaving the cycle under the horse's feet, in the wheel of which they remained imprisoned until we got a blacksmith to cut the spokes away. The driver was greatly relieved when I told him he had better complete the job by driving me home, for, as he admitted, " I thought I had killed you."

When I was still in the learning stage, going past the Mansion House I collided with the shoulder of an omnibus horse, and the impact sent me under the fore-feet of another, for the busses were moving in two lines; the driver pulled up very smartly, and I escaped without even damaging a new cyclometer, my anxiety for which caused me to pick it up ere I scrambled from my perilous position.

This accident was my own fault, but the following curious one was not contributed to by me in any way. I was going eastwards one evening from Hyde Park Corner, intending to turn up Hamilton Place. The traffic being stopped, I was just moving the pedals, close in to a four-wheeled cab, when a driver of a hansom coming down fast looked over my head; the hansom's off-wheel, grazing my knee, took the cycle away from underneath me, carrying it seventy yards before the driver could pull up. Strange as it may seem, whereas on being touched I was facing eastwards, the result was to land me on my feet in the road facing westwards. The cabman admitted to the Commissioner of Police it was entirely his fault, and that he, not looking down, failed to see me.

On the 8th May I had the pleasure of meeting Mr. Arthur Balfour for the first time, at a Newspaper and Press Fund dinner, and was struck with the good humour in which he accepted a quick reply I gave him. I was speaking: "It is a common expression, gentlemen, that the Press has improved in the last fifty years, but we are all more tolerant. I recall the time when the leading club in London ceased to take in the leading newspaper because it disapproved of the letters of its War correspondent in the Crimea, who, by describing our untold miseries, saved the remnant of our army."

I hear acutely when there is a noise, and my speech being favourably received, my ears were unduly sensitive, so I heard Mr. Balfour say in a low, quiet inquiring voice: "Dear me, I wonder which club?" Putting up my hand so that all the room should not hear it, I replied, "Carlton," which name was received by a burst of laughter by those near, in which Mr. Balfour joined, but with a gesture to the shorthand writers I prevented it being reported.

I had the pleasure on the 26th June of seeing my youngest son win the Riding prize at Sandhurst. The second son won it in 1892, and I had hoped that the eldest one would have succeeded in carrying it off in 1890, but unfortunately he had a riding accident three months before the competition.

In the Spring of the year Sir Redvers Buller, the Adjutant-General, came into my office, which was nearly opposite his room, and, for him an unusual custom, told a story, in the course of which he said: "And then they all became silent and listened attentively." I interupted him by the line—

"Conticuere omnes, intentique ora tenebant.

And he capped it at once by repeating—

"Inde toro pater Aeneas sic orsus ab alto
Infandum, Regina, jubes renovare dolorem."

I observed: "You don't know what you are quoting." "Yes, I do; you quoted the first line of the second book of the

Aeneid, and I the second and third lines; and in the Virgil we used at Eton it is on the right-hand side of the page when you open the book."

This proof of memory is more remarkable than my own, as I had re-read Virgil in 1857 for pleasure, and in 1869 before being entered as a student for the Bar.

All through 1896-7 I was urging on my Political Masters the importance, for the solution of our Recruiting difficulty, of reserving for discharged sailors and soldiers, fully qualified educationally and by character, the first claim on all vacant appointments in the Public service.

Lord Lansdowne and Mr. Brodrick warmly supported my representations. The Post Office met our views to some extent, and other Departments to about half the vacancies.

CHAPTER XLVIII

1897-90—ADJUTANT-GENERAL

The Duke of Connaught's generous letter—A Dargai Piper at a Music Hall—Consecration of the Colours of Catholic battalions—Lord Chesham's Yeomanry—Major Milton—Influence of British Officers over Asiatics—I offer to serve under Buller—Strange requests—The Misses Keyser—Colonel Hay—300 guns added to the establishment—A heavy fall—An appreciation of our Infantry.

I WAS appointed Adjutant-General on the 1st October 1897, and received many kind letters of congratulation; one from His Royal Highness the Duke of Connaught gratified me much, for he wrote: "I am heartily glad to see your appointment, and rejoice that now we shall make progress in our War training."

On my first day in office I submitted a memorandum, which I had had printed in anticipation, to the Commander-in-Chief, pointing out the absolute inadequacy of our forces. For years we had been adding to our Possessions, and consequently to our Responsibilities, without any increase to the army. Lord Lansdowne accepted my proposal for raising a Chinese battalion for Wei-hai-wei, and one of Yaos for British Central Africa, but this was only a small local increase.

In the time of my predecessor Gibraltar and Malta had been treated as Home battalion stations in the Link system,—that is, recruits were posted to units in those garrisons, and the older soldiers were drafted to India and to such sub-tropical stations as were barred, by Medical regulations, to lads only eighteen years of age. Neither of these Mediterranean garrisons were satisfactory training schools, and I strongly urged a substantial increase in Infantry, writing: "The march of events does not foreshadow any diminution of British soldiers on the African Continent, I beg that 9000 more be added to the army." On the 3rd November Lord Wolseley, supporting my demands of the previous month, added 4000 men to my estimate of what was required.

All through the hunting season of 1897-8 I enjoyed occasional days' relaxation, keeping my horses as in previous years in a farm near the residence of my friend Mr. H. E. Jones of Ongar. I did not allow my favourite amusement, however, to interfere with duty, as may be seen from one entry in my diary: "27th January 1898—Hunted with the Union Hounds. Worked after dinner till midnight."

In the Spring of the year I conducted a Staff ride in Essex, with the General Idea which was followed in 1904.

Towards the end of May a piper who had been awarded the Victoria Cross for gallantry shown at Dargai was advertised to appear on the stage of the Alhambra. On the morning of the 28th, before going to Mr. Gladstone's funeral at Westminster Abbey, I saw Mr. Dundas Slater, the manager, and induced him to cancel the "turn" after that week. Mr. Slater behaved with the greatest consideration, and on my telling him we would be responsible for the man's salary for a week, amounting to £30, he said laughingly: "It is scarcely worth while, sir, to talk about that, when I have spent £300 in advertising him."

Earlier in the year my attention had been drawn to the hardship to battalions which were practically all Catholics in having their colours consecrated by Protestant clergy. The general officer in command in Ireland felt the incongruity, and asked, in the case of a West of Ireland Regiment, that the ceremony should be performed by a Roman Catholic priest. This was not thought desirable, and afterwards, indeed, the request was cancelled as the officers, who were nearly all Protestants, objected.

With the permission of the Secretary of State I took up the question with the Chaplain-General, who afforded me the most valuable assistance, drawing out a form of prayer for the consecration of Colours of all Denominations. I sent it to my friend Cardinal Vaughan, writing I would call in a week, at the end of which time he approved generally, and I sent a copy in print. Some of those about him objected to one or two expressions in the prayers which they thought would not be acceptable to Catholics, and those the Cardinal altered. They were, however, slight, and I had no difficulty in accepting them on the part of the Secretary of State; but as I pointed out to the Cardinal, the prayers submitted to him were taken literally from those in use in the reign of Henry VII., before England became Protestant.

In the following year, when I was still pursuing the matter, I crossed over to Ireland and saw the Primate, Cardinal Logue, and Archbishop Walsh, both of whom approving the copy, thanked me for my efforts in removing what was felt to be a grievance; and now the form of Consecration of Colours is printed as a War Office document, for the correct use of which the Senior officer present is responsible.

In the early summer I saw the Buckingham Yeomanry under the command of Colonel Lord Chesham. He showed 469 men on parade, who worked in a way which, considering the short training they had received, could only be described as wonderful.

In August I went to Salisbury Plain for ten days, hiring a farmhouse at Durrington, in which I lived while watching Cavalry manœuvres under General G. Luck, Inspector-General of Cavalry, who was working a Division of 2800 sabres. He thought that our regiments were wanting in uniformity of pace and cohesion, which opinion corresponded exactly with that expressed by the German officers nine years previously in the Aldershot review before the Emperor. This is not extraordinary, as we had never worked a Division as such before I obtained the gratuitous use of private ground in 1890.

After leaving Salisbury Plain I went on to Chilmark Rectory in Wiltshire, which I had hired for the Commander-in-Chief and his Staff, whence he supervised manœuvres between Army Corps commanded by H.R.H. The Duke of Connaught and General Sir Redvers Buller.

All through August the office work which was sent to me daily while away from Pall Mall was hard, practically all day on the 3rd and 4th of the month, for we were considering affairs in South Africa. It seemed to be certain that war must ensue unless Mr. Kruger abated his menacing tone.

In the forenoon, 8th September, Lord Lansdowne desired me not to leave the office, for I had told him I was going away for twenty-four hours to shoot in Essex, and at 4 o'clock he gave me the order to put four Battalions under orders for the Cape. This involved the moving of seven: three from England to the Mediterranean; three going on from the garrisons there; while one went direct from England to South Africa. Staff officers on the Continent are not troubled with considerations which have to be borne in mind by the Headquarters Staff of our little army, for when Battalions are ordered abroad, many questions arise other than War Service. Corps have to be selected which have been longest in England, and are due to go abroad in their regular rotation, the selection of course being tempered by the question of efficiency, which, speaking generally, may be taken as the efficiency of the Lieutenant-Colonel and Senior officers. Nevertheless, the seven Battalions were selected and placed under orders in forty-five minutes.

I had heard privately, as well as officially, from the Cape that while in certain regiments, such as the King's Royal Rifles, no difficulty had been experienced in utilising the ponies we had supplied for the training of a Company of each Battalion as Mounted Infantry, yet in some Corps no progress had been made owing to the officers' want of experience in equitation and in the management of horses. We sent out therefore, six weeks before mobilisation, Major Milton,[1] Yorkshire Light Infantry, and Captain E. M. FitzG. Wood,[2] Devonshire Regiment, who were known to be good horse-masters, to teach the Company officers, so that they might instruct their men.

On the 21st October I telegraphed to my second son, Lieutenant C. M. Wood, at Wei-hai-wei, whose battalion was on its way to the Cape, suggesting that he should ask for leave, and rejoin. He had been some time in the Chinese regiment, and had no difficulty in obtaining five months' leave of absence. On the 22nd, when he got authority from

---

[1] Major Milton was not only a clever instructor, but a first-class fighting man, who always carried his troops to the Front. The two companies under his command at Belmont, on the 10th November 1899, lost two officers killed and two wounded, and when he fell, showing a grand example, on the 11th December, the three companies under him, comprising 13 officers, had lost six killed and six wounded. Captain E. M. FitzG. Wood being the only surviving Duty officer who had served with Major Milton throughout the month's operations.

[2] My eldest son, now Major and D.S.O., Royal Dragoons.

his Commanding officer to go, he left within three hours, obtaining a passage on H.M.S. *Brisk*, commanded by Captain Bouchier Wrey, who had been attached to my Staff in Egypt in 1882, to Shanghai, where he caught a liner, and reaching his battalion after the action at Stormberg, became Adjutant, the offer of which had been telegraphed by the Commanding officer to him while he was on his journey.

The influence British officers obtain over soldiers of Eastern races is remarkable; his Chinese servant begged to be permitted to accompany him, and the senior Sergeant of his Company implored to be allowed to revert to Private, and go as his servant.

My third son, who had been invalided from the Tirah, where he had served with the 2nd Battalion, Scottish Rifles, passed fit by a Medical Board, was on his way to join the 1st Battalion in Natal, being sent out in a Transport with mules. The fact that my three sons were on Service was some consolation for my own intense disappointment in not being sent to South Africa, where in 1881 I had suffered as a Soldier for my loyal obedience to orders.

I had a pleasant dinner on the 24th October at the American Ambassador's, sitting next to Mr. Smalley, for many years *The Times'* Commissioner in America; but what I enjoyed most was a conversation with Mr. Arthur Balfour in a room by ourselves, when, at his request, I explained to him the salient features in the work of mobilisation, for his quickness in comprehending a complicated problem made him a delightful companion.

On the 7th November Her Majesty the Queen, at 11.30 a.m., signed the authority for the Secretary of State for War to send a force out to South Africa, and to call out the Reserves. I having previously obtained the permission of the Secretary of the General Post Office to clear the lines, passed on immediately the Royal authority, which was received at 11.45 a.m., and its receipt at Districts was notified within half an hour. In most of them, all the Posters summoning Reservists were out by 2 o'clock, that is, within two hours and a quarter of the Queen's authority having been received at the War Office.

Colonel Stopford,[1] who had worked hard on Mobilisation questions for years, came into my office radiant with the news of the prompt action taken in the Districts, adding, "and now I shall go away and buy old furniture." I asked, "What is the joke?" He said, "That is what Count von Moltke did after he had telegraphed in 1870, 'Mobilise.'"

All through the Autumn and Winter of 1899–1900 the work was heavy at the office, and especially for me,[2] as the Deputy Adjutant-General was changed three times, two of them going to South Africa.

When at 2 p.m. on the 31st December we heard of the disasters south of Ladysmith, I wrote to Lord Lansdowne offering to start that evening for South Africa to serve under Sir Redvers Buller.[3] Lord Roberts was, however, appointed as Commander-in-Chief. The additional bad news kept us in office from early morn till late in the evening, and then I had to work at home till nearly midnight.

I noted in my diary that excitable Pressmen imagined that regiments had been cut off, and indeed all sorts of misfortunes besides those which our troops suffered. I was occupied a considerable part of each day in assuaging the fears of ladies, whose fathers, brothers, or lovers were at the seat of War, and spent a good deal of private money in telegrams for news as to the safety of those loved ones, for the War Office covers only expenses of telegrams for casualties.

My duties were not confined absolutely to Military matters, and I had much correspondence with my friend Lord Wantage, the President of the Red Cross Society. He wrote to me on the 10th January: "The Red Cross has

---

[1] Major-General the Hon. Sir F. Stopford, K.C.M.G., C.B. commanding the Home District.

[2] The pressure may be gauged by the fact that whereas in other years I had taken for hunting purposes forty-six of the sixty days' leave granted to a Staff officer, yet with the same number of horses I took twelve days only that hunting season.

[3] I had previously, on hearing Redvers Buller had gone to Natal, telegraphed and written to him my anxiety to serve under and assist him in any way I could. In reply, he wrote: "Frere Camp, 27th December 1899.—Your telegram offering to come and serve under me was a very great compliment to me, and also a temptation. . . . I was twice on the point of telegraphing from Cape Town to ask that you might come out, and then I thought it was not fair to ask you to come and undertake a job that I in my heart thought only doubtfully possible."

anticipated all your requirements mentioned in your letter, except crutches, and these shall be attended to at once."

Some of the requests made to me by importunate ladies were peculiar; one was very angry with me because the War Office would not send out an establishment for curing, or destroying painlessly, horses. Another lady said she did not want her son to go to war, because he was only twenty-one. A third wished her son, who had just joined the army, transferred to a depôt and kept in England, or allowed to exchange to a regiment at home. I explained to her that if her craven request were granted, none of his associates would speak to him. On the other hand, another lady was angry with me because I had not time to see her former footman. He was getting 28s. a week, but wanted to give up his situation and join his two brothers, who were serving under General Gatacre.

Two friends of mine, Miss Agnes Keyser and her sister, gave up their house in Grosvenor Crescent for "Sick and Wounded Officers," who might have no relatives in London. Some of the most celebrated Physicians and Surgeons volunteered to attend any patients in the Hospital gratis, and the Misses Keyser provided everything, including trained nurses, free of all expense to patients. This, however, was not in any way the limit of their generosity, for when a friend of mine, who had lost a foot in action, was leaving the Hospital, Miss Agnes Keyser asked me if he was fairly well off, to which I replied, "No, he has very small means, but is going to stay for a time with a married sister." On learning which, Miss Agnes, who superintended the Hospital, sent with him a nurse who had been attending him at her own house.

As I was the means of introducing patients in the first instance, the correspondence connected therewith occupied an appreciable portion of my time. When, many months afterwards, one of my sons was returning to England, invalided on account of appendicitis, Miss Agnes Keyser said to Sir Frederick Treves, "I want you to do an operation for appendicitis." "Yes, any day you like next week; a hundred guineas. Will you fix the day now?" She answered, "No, I cannot, for my friend's son is on the sea." "Why, is he in the army?" "Yes, he is on his way from South Africa." "Then I revoke my offer to operate, and will do it only on my own terms." "Well, you shall have them, whatever they are." "I shall charge nothing for the operation. Your friend's son will pay only the expense in the Home where I wish him to be under nurses whom I have trained especially for the aftercure of that operation."

In 1897 I had taken up the question of Artillery, in which the British army was deficient[1] and by corresponding privately with the Commander-in-Chief in India, simultaneous efforts were made to obtain the much-required increase. Lord Lansdowne received favourably my application, which was strongly backed by the Commander-in-Chief, and the result, helped by the "War Fever," was that in 1899-1900 we created 7 Batteries of Horse and 48 Batteries of Field Artillery. Some of them were very short of officers and sergeants; indeed one Battery was raised, and commanded for several months by a Riding-master. The popularity of the war enabled us to fill them up without any difficulty as regards the Rank and File; indeed all of them were, after a few months, considerably over strength, but in many cases there was only one sergeant for 60 or 70 Gunners and Drivers.

Three years before the war, on my suggestion to the Commander-in-Chief, Colonel Owen Hay, Royal Artillery, was sent out to command at Ladysmith; and in January 1899, not foreseeing the war would break out so soon, to my subsequent great regret (although his services were invaluable at home), I wrote to ask him as a favour to come home to help in this augmentation of the Artillery, and it was he who really did all the Head Quarters work of it.

Colonel Hay had no sooner got the Artillery augmentation into working order, than I turned his attention to our Depôts. When the war broke out in South Africa the administration of the Horse and Field Artillery was centralised at Woolwich, where an officer had two depôts under him. This arrangement for the Field Artillery did not work well even in Peace, and after Mobilisation the depôt became unmanageable. In March 1900, 200 Recruits joined at Woolwich every week, many sleeping on the floors in passages.

Although the army order which authorised Colonel Hay's

---

[1] The British army had 2½ guns for 1000 sabres and bayonets. On the Continent, armies had 4 or 5 guns for 1000 men.

change was not introduced till August 1900, he had been at work at it for months, and had decentralised the Field Artillery. I then asked the Commander-in-Chief to allow him to return to South Africa, but he was unwilling to part with him, and Hay's soldierlike resignation was a lesson to all of us.

Six months later we had some difficulty, as the Financial side of the office endeavoured, when the war took a more favourable turn, to reduce the batteries to one section each. This might have been carried out if the Commander-in-Chief had not, in strenuously supporting my objections, concurred in my view that it would be better to disband half the Batteries than have cadres of two guns only. This would have indicated such vacillation that I doubt if any War minister could have carried a reduction at the time; but the question was solved by its being made clear to the Secretary of State that the establishment of two guns per Battery would not produce the Reserve men required on Mobilisation.

I foresaw the war would last longer than many of my friends realised. In November 1899 I told an anxious mother that she must anticipate that it would be a much longer business than anyone in London thought, and she repeated this to one of my colleagues, who replied, "Yes, I know he thinks so; but I cannot imagine why he holds that opinion. In my mind, I think it will be over in a few weeks."

With mistaken views of economy, our Administration had framed Regulations that farriers, having been taught at the Public expense, should re-engage, thus leaving very few in the Reserve. It was clear for a serious war, involving the purchase of thousands of animals, there would be insufficient Shoeing-smiths, and before the first demand was made I consulted Colonel Owen Hay and Colonel C. Crutchley,[1] the Recruiting officer in the office. He was not only throughly versed in the complicated problem of the labour market, but a pleasant colleague, never losing heart in the longest hours and most difficult circumstances.

To him and to Colonel Hay I suggested there must be

---

[1] He came under my notice in February 1885 at Gakdul, where he arrived on a camel from Abu Klea, with an amputated leg, and I have never forgotten his cheerful demeanour, with the prospect of another 100 miles' journey to the Nile, which I endeavoured to make as little painful as possible.

plenty of young blacksmiths in villages, who, if they were promised they would not be drilled as a part of their bargain, would be willing to go to South Africa on a one year's engagement, with a bounty of £10 and the chance of getting a medal. My forecast was correct, for we sent out over 700 in 1900 and 5 per centum in the two following years to replace wastage, the two colonels taking all the arrangements off my hands.

While the Press reviled the Secretary of State and all who were working under him, officers in South Africa expressed very different opinions, and I was warmly thanked by them.[1]

I found that the hours in office,[2] often from 9.30 a.m. till 6 p.m., and two hours after dinner, told on my health, and an old trouble—neuralgia of the nerves of the stomach—warned me that I could not go on affronting nature by working without some relaxation.

On the 22nd of January Lord Strathcona and Mount Royal came into my office and said in his gentle voice, "I should like to do something for our Country, and raise some Mounted men in Canada and send them to South Africa." I asked, "Do you know that our men are serving for about 1s. 6d. a day, and you would not get Canadians to go for that?" "Oh," he said, "there will be no difficulty about that. I shall make up any deficiency. What I want you to do is to write down everything that is necessary in the way of organisation." "One Squadron, two, or what?" "Anything you like." So I told him a Regiment of three Squadrons was the most suitable organisation, if money was no object. He replied, "No, no object. I should like to do the thing well, and I want the Mother country to pay them only what she is paying her own soldiers." It did not take me long, with Colonel Robb's[3] assistance, to sketch out the establishment required, and our only

[1] Letter from Major-General Sir George Marshall, K.C.B., general officer commanding the Artillery :—
"I thank you very sincerely for all the assistance you have given us in so promptly supplying all our heavy demands in the Artillery, in men and horses, since we came out. I can assure you that the feeling of Gunners is one of amazement and admiration at such a large force of Field Artillery being sent out so efficiently and promptly. We owe you much for all you did to make us Shoot, and improving our Tactical efficiency, and now when we succeed we give you the praise and gratitude."
[2] I put in 64 hours a week in office, besides what I did at home, making up the time after an occasional day's hunting, by working till after midnight.
[3] Now Brigadier-General.

point of difference was that Strathcona insisted, in his quiet way, on having a great number of clergy. Himself a Protestant, he desired to keep on good terms with the Catholic clergy, amongst whom he had many friends; and the number of clergy accompanying the Regiment was certainly redundant, in our point of view. Lord Strathcona paid nearly £500,000 for our Country.

On the 27th of the month I had a heavy fall when riding an impetuous horse with hounds.[1] We found at Skreen's Park, near Chelmsford; and being in pain from neuralgia of the stomach I was irritated by the animal's impatience, and let him go his own pace at the first fence. The horse over-jumping, hit his knee, and the next thing I remember was being crushed to the ground. Miss Jones,[2] who saw me fall, accompanied me back two or three miles, and borrowed a pony-chaise from a friendly farmer, by which I was conveyed to Ongar station. I arrived in London in considerable pain, but without being seriously injured; indeed, I attended office for a full day on the 29th. The horse had pressed me so deeply into the ground that a gold crucifix and locket of Lady Wood's, suspended from my neck, were driven so deeply into the ribs that the impression was plainly discernible fifteen months later. Two years later I consulted my friend, Dr. Moore, for a peculiar mark on the left temple, saying, "I have got a spot there

---

[1] I had ridden the horse for a year or so, my friend Colonel Tollner, who is the best judge I ever met, having purchased it for me at £30 out of the Woolwich Drag Hunt, where it had been ridden by a succession of Subalterns who desired to qualify for Horse Artillery. Hounds no sooner broke covert than the little horse, for he was small, invariably tried to travel faster than I wanted. In a run of thirty-five minutes he got away with me after every fence, until exhausted I left hounds, and I never controlled him until I covered bit and snaffle with gutta-percha, on which he would not close his teeth. The horse had never before given me a fall, although he had occasionally been very nearly down, for being unusually sagacious with all his high courage, he generally contrived to land on his feet. On one occasion, led by the ex-master of the Essex hounds, Mr. Loftus Arkwright, we were galloping to the west of Parndon Wood, near Harlow, and approached a gate which was locked and chained. My companions went a hundred yards down, and then pressed slowly through a hedge with high growers. This was impossible for me, without grave risk to my eyes, and so riding the horse up to the gate, I put his head over it, that he might see that the field bridge beyond was broken down, and covered over with faggots, and then taking him back fifty yards I let him go. The horse's usual habit at timber was to rise straight up in the air, but he was so clever that on this occasion, "spreading himself," he cleared the broken bridge by two feet.

[2] The best lady "on any horse" to hounds in the Essex Hunt.

which is growing larger. I must say it is fainter in colour every week." He replied, "You remember the horse crushed your face into the ground. It broke a vessel, the blood from which is now slowly dispersing."

I had a mass of private correspondence from South Africa, for not only had I my three sons there, but many officers who had served under me at Aldershot wrote to me in terms of indignation at the strictures passed by civilian writers on the Aldershot training. One officer, who criticised severely certain branches of the army, wrote in such sympathetic terms of the Infantry, to which he did not belong, that I reproduce his letter below.[1]

I got some ponies sent to Malta—enough to train men in every unit—and asked the Secretary of State to request India to train a Company in every Battalion at our expense. I urged also that a Company in every Battalion should be trained at all stations at Home and Abroad to act as Mounted Infantry.

---

[1] "What a magnificent production is the British Infantry soldier. I thought as he went by, tattered and torn, black and greasy, bearded and filthy, on the squares of Johannesburg and Pretoria, how much the British nation owes to him and the officers who made him. I shall never forget the scene at these two places for the remainder of my lifetime; it was worth all the hardships of this war to have been privileged to be present."

CHAPTER XLIX

ADJUTANT-GENERAL—*Continued*

Misunderstanding of Military matters—Forecast of change of Staff by a Charwoman—Antiquated Military Exercises abandoned—A change in Inspections at Sandhurst—Funeral of Her Majesty Queen Victoria—Offer to go to South Africa—Accepted, but not carried out—Lord Roberts approves certain reforms initiated by me—I leave Pall Mall, after eight years' work.

ALL through the war I was asked by my friends, "Why ever did you send out so-and-so; see how badly he is doing?" And again, "Why did you not make better plans?" The ignorance of the Public is the more comprehensible when we consider that in February the Under-Secretary of State stated, in the House of Commons, that the Divisional and Brigade Commanders were appointed on the recommendation of the Army Board. He had been misinformed, and his informant, on my remonstrance, admitted the error. I was never able, however, to tell my friends the truth, until asked to give evidence before Lord Elgin's Royal Commission of Inquiry into the War. I then stated, in reply to questions, the facts. The Order in Council under which the War Office was administered at the time, had placed the Heads of the great Departments in a position of quasi-independence of the Commander-in-Chief, by allowing them the privilege of dealing directly with the Secretary of State for War, at his option. The Commander-in-Chief, however, ordered me to address him on any matters which I desired to place before the Secretary of State, and therefore, although Lord Lansdowne minuted papers to me, he received them back through Lord Wolseley; I therefore had no independent position. In regard to plans, as Adjutant-General I never knew of one plan of Military operations. The expression frequently used by the Secretary of State in the House, "My Military Advisers," implied only the Commander-in-Chief and the Director-General of Military Intelligence.

Throughout the year I was asking for an increase in the Establishment of officers, showing we had in one case, one officer to pay 850 men, of whom half were at Hounslow and half at Aldershot. I was urging that the Establishments of Rank and File were insufficient to enable us to train our soldiers, for when we had taken out the best educated and most intelligent men in each company for Mounted Infantry, as signallers, for Regimental Transport, and servants, there were few left capable of acting as section or group leaders; there were too few officers and too few men.

In one of the papers I submitted to the Secretary of State I wrote: " I am certain that all officers who have been fighting in South Africa will agree that the want of training has been the direct cause of many of our heavy losses, and of some of our reverses." I explained that the Rank and File were as untrained as they were brave, and this from no fault of their own or of their officers, but because the British soldier was never given sufficient opportunity of practising his profession in the United Kingdom. I was engaged in another long correspondence with Cavalry Colonels, endeavouring to reduce the obligatory expenses of officers.

Lord Lansdowne went to the Foreign Office in November. I had worked under his direction for five years, and regarding him with genuine affection, shall always gratefully remember his sympathy in my disappointment in not being allowed to proceed to South Africa. If it were not so sad, the animadversion of the Press on his want of vigour as War Minister would have been comical. He added ten Line Battalions, one of Irish Guards, and 330 field guns to the Army.

When it was foreseen that Lord Lansdowne would leave the War Office there were many speculations as to his successor, and we were under the impression that Mr. George Wyndham was on the point of being nominated, before it was decided to send him to Ireland; and I got him to agree in anticipation to support my proposition that any pensioned private soldiers of good character should receive an increase at the age of sixty-five to make up a living income.

In the office it was universally believed that when Lord Wolseley's Command terminated, some of the Senior officers who had shared his many years of work in trying to render the Army fit for War would be removed, and this feeling was amusingly indicated by the conversation of two women who, when scrubbing the floors of the War Office, were overheard talking by General Laye, the Deputy Adjutant-General, as he went into his room one busy morning at nine o'clock. During the War a Restaurant had been started in the basement of the building, and I, finding the smell intolerable, had a glass air-shaft carried from the basement above the level of the Adjutant-General's room. One woman, looking up from her scrubbing and pointing to the carpenter's poles, asked, "Sally, what 'as they put up that ere scaffolding for?" The other replied, "Don't yer know? That's where the new lot's going to 'ang the old lot."

When it became evident that the class of Yeomanry who for patriotic reasons, went to South Africa at Army rates of pay was exhausted, the Secretary of State enlisted men at five shillings, many of whom, in the opinion of the General Officer Commanding at Aldershot, were no better in education or class than the average Cavalry recruit.

The General Commanding in South Africa telegraphed for more Mounted Infantry, and I then suggested that, the Boers having no longer any Artillery, it would be simpler to train our Artillery in South Africa to shoot with a rifle. I was not certain how the Gunners would like the idea, but the sense of duty is very high in the Corps, and the result was very satisfactory.

In the Autumn I addressed the Commander-in-Chief, pointing out that our drill-book contained many obsolete movements, and asking leave to curtail as useless for war our Manual Exercise, containing in slow time nearly fifty motions, which most of our Generals and many of our Commanding officers still cherished, as their predecessors had, since it was instituted in 1780. I stated the Chinese was the only other nation which had any exercise like it; that Germany and Austria were content with teaching the men three motions; and also that we continued to practise the bayonet exercise, all of which was more suitable for a Music Hall than for training men to fight. The Commander-in-Chief approved, and on the 1st December an order was issued forbidding the Manual and Bayonet exercises being performed at Inspections or at any other time, as Regimental or Battalion parade practices. The order was actually signed by myself as Adjutant-General, although it was issued on the day I became acting Commander-in-Chief, for Lord Wolseley gave up his office on the last day of November.

In my one month of command I was able to carry out one reform. It became part of my duty to inspect the academies at Woolwich and Sandhurst. At the former I endeavoured, with only slight success, to render the inspection more practical, but at Sandhurst the reform was drastic. For eighty years, since the College was established, the young officers had been inspected in marching past, and in performing the Manual and Bayonet exercises as a preparation for war. When I ordered an inspection of the cadets in a practical Outpost scheme, one officer Instructor intimated privately his intention of resigning, as he considered my demands on him were outside his duty. I sent back a message that his resignation would be accepted; heard nothing more of it, and saw an attack on a line of Outposts, for which I had set the scheme, very well carried out.

At the end of 1900 and the beginning of the new year, I was occupied in preparing papers for a Committee of Inquiry into the War Office system, of which Mr. Clinton Dawkins was Chairman. I advocated strongly before the Committee the transfer to General officers commanding Districts, the greater part of the Administrative and Financial part of the business then transacted at the War Office, in two carefully prepared memoranda, and supplemented my arguments by giving evidence at length before the Committee.

I was much impressed by Mr. Clinton Dawkins' quick apprehension of points in administration; but his manner was so quiet that, as I told him months later, when he asked me what I thought of his report, "Oh, I am delighted; but I was astonished when it came out, for I thought when I left your committee room that I had failed to make much impression on you, and you have practically endorsed nearly all my suggestions."

Lord Roberts returned to London on the 3rd of January,

when my brief command of the Army ceased. He took up at once the question of officers, by Lord Wolseley's directions, wearing uniform [1] at the War Office, on which an order I had drafted two years previously was and is still in print, but it has not yet been issued.

In the evening of the 22nd January Her Imperial Majesty the Queen died, and besides my personal grief, I realised I had lost a Patroness who since the Zulu war had treated me with the most gracious kindness.

The hours in the office for the next week were longer than ever, much unnecessary work being occasioned by different departments overlapping in their desire to have everything according to the King's Commands.

On the 2nd February, the day of the funeral, the morning was bitterly cold, and the Commander-in Chief, being doubtless anxious, left his hotel ten minutes before the Head Quarters Staff were ordered to be present to accompany him. There was then a wait of over an hour and a half at Victoria Station, and when at last the procession moved, on a wave of the Chief's

[1] On the following 2nd May I received an order that all officers attending the Royal Academy dinner were to appear in full dress uniform, so I duly passed it on to a General who I knew had received an invitation. Late in the afternoon I received a telegram cancelling the orders which had been issued to me, not only by the Adjutant-General but by the private secretary of the Commander-in-Chief. I was unable to communicate with my General, who was the only person in uniform, but was much less annoyed than most of us would have been, while I was amused at the excitement of a court official who highly disapproved of officers appearing as such at this function.

The dinner was to me very pleasant, as I sat between the Dean of Westminster and Mr. Ouless, the Royal Academician, who were both delightful companions. Mr. Ouless capped my story of the corporal recognising me as an officer by my bad language when I was lying wounded under the Redan in 1855, by telling us one of an artist, celebrated as etcher and author, who was walking one winter's day on Hampstead Heath, and passing near one of the ponds, which was frozen over, he saw a crowd collected round it watching a small dog, which having ventured on the ice, had fallen through into the water. The ice was just so strong it could not get out, and yet would not support its weight. The excited owner was shouting, "Half a crown for anyone who will save my dog." The artist plunged in, and having rescued the animal put it down on the edge of the pond and started running at top speed towards his house at Highgate. He heard a panting man behind him, but fearing rheumatism ran on to change his clothes, till the man caught him up, shouting, "Hi, hi," and as he reached him called out, "Here's your money." Mr. Ouless' friend being very cold and cross said, "Damn you! Damn your dog; damn your half-crown." The man touched his cap and said, "Beg your pardon, sir. I didn't know you was a gentleman."

baton, it was difficult to start immediately the head of the column, which was already to the north of Buckingham Palace. When we moved, it was nearly impossible to make the cream-coloured horses walk at the pace of Infantry marching "in Slow time," and I apprehend the Procession could not have satisfied His Majesty the King.

When the team, being hooked in to the made-up gun carriage, moved from Windsor Station the bands, which were immediately under the overhead passage then recently erected, clashed with such a reverberating noise that some of the horses threw themselves into the collar violently, and the carriage rocked ominously. Fortunately the off wheeler broke the swingletree, and as there was no other at hand the sailors drew the coffin up to St. George's Chapel,—perhaps a more appropriate manner of haulage than horses for a Naval monarch.

Some people assumed it was the fault of the Adjutant-General that there was no spare swingletree as there is on every gun service carriage, but I had no difficulty in producing correspondence showing that I had been instructed from Windsor Castle that the War Office need not interfere in the matter of the made-up gun carriage, which was to be supplied by the Carriage factory at Woolwich on requisition by the Lord Chamberlain.

On the 1st February the Military Secretary came into my office and asked if I was willing to go to South Africa and serve under Lord Kitchener. I took two hours for consideration, and then assented, mentioning verbally, I thought that for Service there was no question of dignity involved, although Kitchener was a Lieutenant when I had been some years a Major-General.[1]

---

[1] Copy of letter to the Military Secretary :—

"*1st February* 1901.

" MY DEAR GROVE,—I have thought over your query, 'If Lord Roberts invited you, would you go out to South Africa and serve under Lord Kitchener?' I do not think the fact that Kitchener joined me in 1883 as a Lieutenant, when I was raising the Egyptian Army, should influence my decision. If it is thought I can serve our Country by going out, I will willingly go, and serve under Kitchener on the following assumptions : (*a*) If I am not killed, I come back here if I so desire, and that my South Africa time is not deducted. This was done in Lord Wolseley's case. (*b*) That if Lord Kitchener becomes a casualty, no one junior to me shall come out to supersede me."

On the 7th February I was informed it had been settled I was not to go to South Africa, and although I was not allowed officially to see the telegram on which the decision was based, it came into my hands, and was to the effect (telegram from Lord Kitchener), " While he would be delighted to serve under Sir Evelyn Wood, if he were sent out, he felt he ought not to have him under his command." I could not thank him at the time, but did so eight months later.[1]

All through January we were discussing the organisation of Ammunition columns, and to my regret I failed to make my Superiors realise that such could not be formed, unless the officers were available. I was asked, " But surely you can get them somewhere ? " So far as I know, the matter is " still under consideration."

In the second week in February His Majesty intimated his intention of presenting medals to a Colonial Corps which was about to arrive in the Thames. The matter was not definitely settled, so I was unable to let the Commanding officer know the reason why I sent him a written request couched in polite terms for a nominal roll of all Ranks: I received back for answer a verbal message, " he had no time for such Red-tape nonsense." Eventually, however, I obtained the names from a courteous subordinate, and by keeping Colonel Crutchley and non-commissioned officers of the Guards sorting up to a late hour, the medals wanted for the parade next day were arranged by Squadrons on trays. When the decorated men had passed, there were a dozen or so who were indignant at not receiving medals, but I elicited from them that they had been on sick leave in England, and only joined the Corps as it marched into the garden of Buckingham Palace !

[1] Copy of letter to Lord Kitchener :—

" *1st October* 1901.

" MY DEAR KITCHENER,—As I am now out of office, I can unburden my mind on the subject on which I have long desired to write to you, but I did not feel justified in doing so when I was Adjutant-General. I saw a very generous telegram from you relative to the proposition that I should go to South Africa to serve under your orders. I do not suppose you would ever have thought I was doing anything to try and inconvenience you in any way, but I should like you to know from me that the suggestion that I should go out did not emanate from me in any way, as will be seen by the answer which I gave to Sir Coleridge Grove when the proposition was made. Please regard this as confidential between you and—Yours very sincerely,

"(Signed) EVELYN WOOD."

On the 22nd March the Secretary of State informed me that it had been decided to reduce the status of the Adjutant-General, and asked for my views. I had worked for many years with Mr. Brodrick, and being on terms of personal friendship I offered to resign at once, if it would render his position less troublesome. This offer he declined to accept, and eventually it was settled I should go to Salisbury when the Army Corps system, which had been explained in his speech in the House of Commons on the 9th March, was brought into operation. He stated that his object was to centralise responsibility in the districts, but decentralise administration, and he fulfilled his object eventually to a great extent.

On the 15th May the Commander-in-Chief motored round a part of Essex from the Thames to Epping, in order to study the tactical features of the country. As we passed three miles to the east of Ongar I stopped the car at Stondon Place, in order that Lord Roberts might leave a card on my young friend Maurice White,[1] Rifle Brigade, who after showing marked courage, and being slightly wounded on the 22nd December 1900, was shot through the spine four days later. He chanced to be at the gate in an invalid carriage wheeled by his elder brother, one of the hardest riders in the Essex Hunt, as we passed, and I presented the wounded lad to his Lordship, who spoke very kindly to him.

I had arranged with Lord Roberts, who was dining with the Speaker, that he should go up by train from Epping; but when he saw I meant to drive through the Forest for pleasure, he elected to accompany me. Between Woodford and Walthamstow we passed a light grocer's van; the man was not driving carefully, and after we had passed, the noise of the motor frightened the horse, which, swerving, collided with a lamp-post. The shafts parted, the horse broke away, and the man was pitched into the road, where he lay insensible, till running back I picked him up. While Lord Roberts with General Nicholson proceeded to London, I put the man, whose thigh was broken, into the car, and drove to a Hospital about a mile off. The Matron and nurses were sympathetic and anxious to help, but they assured me that every bed was occupied. A Committee of doctors was sitting at the time, and one of them coming out

---

[1] Three times mentioned in Despatches.

to see who was talking, I offering money, used Lord Roberts' name; but all in vain, the Doctor saying, " It is not a question of money; our sole objection is that there is absolutely no spare bed." Handing him my card, I asked where I could take the man, on which he said, " You are Essex, I see; we must try and do something for you. If you will have the man lifted out, I will clear a bed." This he did by taking one of the patients who could best bear moving up to a nurse's room, and putting the injured man in his place.

I was now seeing more of the Commander-in-Chief daily, for we had been strangers until he took over Command. Travelling about with him we interchanged ideas, and I realised the charm of the personality which has so agreeably affected most of those with whom he has worked in his long career. On the 21st May he wrote to the Secretary of State that he had intended to take up the revision of Confidential Reports on assuming Command, but found it had already been done.[1]

I accompanied him to the Aldershot Central Gymnasium in July, and he was so impressed with the training that he wrote to me next day urging we should do all in our power to develop the individual intelligence of the men, and no longer train them like machines. I had the satisfaction of informing him we had taken up the matter in October 1900, and what he saw at Aldershot was being carried out at every Infantry Depot, and that the Commanding officers were all in favour of the new system.

In July the Commander-in-Chief, impressed by the difficulty of training officers with small companies, considered whether it would not be better to have four companies instead of eight in a battalion. I was able at once to give him the history of the proposals which had been made during the last forty years. I did not mention, as was the case, that General Blumenthal, when he attended our Manœuvres in 1872, told a friend of mine that he envied us our small companies, and that the large companies in Germany were due only to the impossibility of finding adequate numbers of gentlemen to

---

[1] " It has been most carefully threshed out by the A.G. The proposed Reports seem to me to be all that can be desired, and I recommend their immediate adoption."

officer the Army. I pointed out that most of the advantages were obtainable from two companies being worked together for five months in the spring and summer. This arrangement has, moreover, the advantage of enabling Commanding officers to so associate them that the most capable officers are responsible for the two companies. Lord Roberts wrote to me next day: "Your note on four versus eight companies is unanswerable; I shall not move in the matter."

Somewhat later he was not able to agree with me at first in my views about Volunteer Field Artillery. He had seen the excellent work done by high-class mechanics sent out by the Vickers Company, and wished to create batteries of Volunteers. I had frequently put on paper that it was impracticable for Volunteers to give sufficient time to become efficient Field Artillery men, but the Secretary of State formed a Committee composed of the Financial Secretary, a Militia officer, and a civilian, to report on the subject, and they soon came to the same conclusion as I had done. Indeed, it is obvious, as we have the greatest difficulty in getting a limited number of Volunteers to go into camp for a fortnight, and as three months initial, with a month annual, training is essential for Artillery, the proposition is not feasible.

Before I left the Office I got a grant from the Treasury, the mere idea of which was received with ridicule when I first mentioned it in the War Office. I pointed out that the Staff College graduates in 1899–1900 had fed the Drag Hounds and paid the wages of the kennel huntsman, although on duty in South Africa, the period for which they would have remained at the College had the war not arisen. When the Establishment was closed, no more funds were available, and so at the conclusion of the War, or when it was in sight, and we were arranging to re-open the College, there were no Drag Hounds. Now the most gifted Staff officer is useless in the Field unless he is at home in the saddle, and there are many who go to the College who have never had an opportunity of riding across country and over fences until they follow the Drag Hounds. I put this clearly, and to the astonishment of the Secretary of State the £200 was granted, and handed over to an officer who was rejoining on the Tutorial staff. I had met him when I was looking at some tactical operations near Tidworth, and heard the story, which interested me much, as I knew the educational value of the Drag Hounds.

In July I heard the name of my successor, and I then asked if I might be told officially that I was to leave the War Office at the end of September, and eventually got a month's notice.

I was the more anxious to make certain because I had received a tempting offer from the Chairman and Directors of a property in South America to go over, and make a report on it, receiving an honorarium of £1000, and all expenses for myself and a secretary. I informed the Commander-in-Chief and the Secretary of State of the offer, bearing in mind the apprehensions of the War Office in 1880, who had deprived me of all pay, even half-pay of 11s. per diem, for the six months I was in South Africa with Her Imperial Majesty the Empress Eugénie. Anxious to avoid the Secretary of State being inconvenienced by any questions in Parliament, I suggested I should go on half-pay for two months, and take up my new work on the 1st January. Neither of my Superiors raised any objection, but on reflection I thought that any delay in initiating the working of the Army Corps Districts might weaken the arguments of the Secretary of State, in favour of what I still regard as being a sound system, so I reluctantly abandoned the idea, going straight from Pall Mall to Salisbury.

On the 3rd September my comrades in the Adjutant-General branch, both Civil and Military, gave me a Farewell Dinner, which induced a touching outburst of regret from those who knew how I had tried to do my duty during the War.

The Commander-in-Chief, who was away from London, wrote in kind terms thanking me for the help I had afforded him during the nine months of our association. He dwelt especially on the use I had been to him from my knowledge of War Office details, and intimate acquaintance with the various localities to which I had accompanied him on his tours of Inspection.

CHAPTER L

1901-2-3—SECOND ARMY CORPS DISTRICT

Salisbury Plain—A cycle ride in the dark—Plan of Tidworth Barracks—Colonel Grierson—his forecast of Russo-Japanese War—An enthusiastic Horse Artillery man—The Blackmore Vale—Netley Hospital—Faulty Administration—A prolific Dame—Yeomanry characteristics—Tipnor Magazine—Bulford Camp—Stables, new plan—Shooting 180 years ago—The Chaplain-General—Surgeon-General Evatt—Improvement in visual efficiency—The choice of an Aide-de-Camp—The King's gracious letter.

ON the 1st October I went to stay with friends at Andover, accompanied by my second son, Captain C. M. Wood, Northumberland Fusiliers, who had just returned from South America, where he had gone, intending to leave the Army, but after personal experience declined a well-paid business engagement. He was better educated than are most Army officers, having on leaving school studied with Messrs. Wren & Gurney for the India Civil Service. When about to present himself for Examination, the entrance age limit was raised from seventeen to nineteen, dating from April 1st, and his birthday being on the 2nd April, the change would have obliged him to wait from seventeen till he was twenty years of age. I hesitated as to the expense involved, and he was unwilling to wait, so on a few days' notice he passed into Sandhurst. His experience in Egypt, China, and in South Africa as Adjutant during the war had been valuable, and I offered him the post of Assistant Military Secretary, or Aide-de-Camp, warning him that he must not expect in the better paid post to hunt as often as I did, and he decided that hunting with me was better than the extra emoluments. This suited my convenience, for he not only hired houses and stabling, but managed all my disbursements, leaving me free to devote my time to my profession, and to as much amusement as I chose to take.

He and I cycled on the 1st October from Andover to Tidworth, then in the hands of contractors. I had previously pointed out to the Secretary of State the great delay which had occurred in commencing to build the barracks, because no precaution had been taken to arrange with the Midland Railway Company how much the contractor should pay for the use of the short line from Ludgershall to Tidworth over the line which was made for Government by and was still in the hands of the Midland Railway. This I got arranged, and on the 1st October the contractor's son had begun, having about a thousand men at work.

The sites for the barracks had been approved by officers in the War Office who evidently had not been to the spot with the plans in hands, for a Barracks to be called "Assaye" looked close into a hill, and all the Commanding officers' quarters had been thrown so far forward in front of the barracks that they could not have walked to Mess, and as their stables adjoined the quarters, the grooms would have had a distance varying from 800 to 1100 yards intervening between their rooms and the horses. I could not alter the position of the barracks, but I moved the Commanding officers' quarters back, and personally never approved of any site which I did not see on the ground.

I found the question of the Tidworth barracks so interesting that we stayed late, and were benighted while we had still 7 miles to cycle to Penton Lodge, where we were staying with Mr. and Lady Susan Sutton. I was in front, followed at some distance by my son, the wheel of whose cycle catching a big stone turned him over, the somersault being so complete that a box of matches fell out of his waistcoat pocket. Walkinshaw, who was a few hundred yards behind, must have passed close to him, but in the darkness, the lamp having been broken, was unaware of what had occurred, and I was just starting back, after reaching Penton Lodge, to look for my son, when he appeared, cut about the face, but not seriously hurt.

Mr. Sutton mounted us at four o'clock next morning for cub-hunting, and after another visit to Tidworth I started on a round of inspection of my extensive District. I knew Dover,

Portland, and Milford Haven, and had been stationed as a sailor at Portsmouth and Plymouth, so had some knowledge of the 2nd Army Corps District.

As it was necessary to hire a house in Salisbury as an office, I was obliged to request the Generals to carry on as before for a short time. My son acted as my Staff officer, besides taking charge of my domestic concerns, until Colonel Grierson [1] joined me at the end of October. I had had the pleasure of meeting him before, and renewed his acquaintance late one evening, when I found him sitting on an empty packing case of stationery in a fireless, carpetless room, lighted by a guttering candle fixed in a mound of grease on the mantelpiece. I named him Mark Tapley, for on that occasion, as in other trying circumstances, he showed the utmost good-humour, and talked as if he were sitting in a well-furnished office.

In the two years we worked together I cannot recall we ever had a difference of opinion, and I found his knowledge of Continental Armies of great assistance in organising the Army Corps.

Six months before the Russo-Japanese War broke out, Grierson, who knew both Armies, said to me in reply to a question, "Yes, sir, the Japanese will win all along the line. Why? Because, they are just as brave, are better instructed and equipped, and on the battlefield will be more numerous than the Russians."

When we got to work I found it was difficult to extract from the War Office any delegation of authority in spite of the earnest wishes of the Secretary of State. As an instance in point, I mention the case of a sergeant of the Army, serving with a Yeomanry Regiment, whose Colonel thinking badly of him, asked that he might be remanded to his Regiment. This I recommended, pointing out that although it might be necessary if his Regiment had been out of the District that I should refer the point to the War Office, yet as both the Cavalry and Yeomanry regiments were in my Command, I submitted it was a matter for my decision. This view was not accepted at the time, although it was later on approved, after indeed much correspondence. Lord Roberts, to whom I appealed, saw matters as I did, but it was many months before

[1] Now Major-General J. Grierson, C.B., C.M.G.

the schedule of questions which I suggested should be dealt with locally, was approved.

I asked the Secretary of State and the Commander-in-Chief to cut me off from the War Office for three months, except in important financial matters, suggesting that if I had done anything seriously wrong at the end of that time I should be removed. My intimacy with Mr. St. John Brodrick helped me considerably, as did his repeated desire that I was to endeavour to obtain "real Service efficiency as cheaply as possible."

I was interested when making a surprise inspection of Taunton Barracks to find a sergeant proceeding to the post-office, about 400 yards from the Barracks. I had imagined that the reforms I introduced at Aldershot in 1889-90 had spread, but was mistaken, as indeed I was in believing I had done away with Sunday cleaning-up work, for when I visited some Artillery stables after I had been more than a year in command of the Army Corps, one Sunday morning, I found a general sweep-up being carried out, and stopped it peremptorily.

When I went to Aldershot in 1867, Sunday was a show day in stables, which gave rise to a Horse Artillery man's curious request. A young soldier going up to his Commanding officer, said, "Please, sir, I want to change my religion." "What's up? What do you want to be?" "I want to be a Roman Catholic." "Priest been at you?" "No, sir; no priest." "Woman?" "No, sir." "Well, I shall not allow you to change your religion." "Please, sir, any man may be any religion he likes in the Army." "Yes, but I have got you noted as being a Church of England man, and I don't mean to allow you to change without giving me some reason." The man then admitted his real object. "Well, you see, sir, a Roman Catholic always goes to church at eight o'clock, and I think if I was a Roman, it would give me a better chance with my 'arness."

The feeling of pride in the Horse Artillery is great. Grierson had a very good servant whom he wished to get put on the Married roll. Going up to London, having a friend in the Office, he got the servant put on the Married roll in Field Artillery, there being no vacancy in the Horse, and on coming back, told the man, thinking he would be pleased, but received for answer, "I am much obliged to you, sir, but I beg leave to decline, as once 'orse Artillery always 'orse Artillery. I won't go into Field, even to be put on the Married roll."

The day after I arrived at Salisbury, doing inspections without any Staff officer, I sent my son to Sherborne, where he hired for me a lodging and stabling, which I used in the winter throughout my three years' Command. The north part of the Blackmoor Vale Hunt country is as near perfection as possible, and a more pleasant set of hunting gentlemen it would be impossible to imagine. Mr John Hargreaves, a son of an equally enthusiastic Master of Fox Hounds, whom I had known in my first days at Aldershot, "carried the horn" himself, and the first season I hunted with him, 1901-2, accounted for a hundred brace of foxes.

The first time I was stopped by frost, I went on from Sherborne to Falmouth, and thence to the Scilly Islands. We were caught in a gale, and the Admiralty yacht, which by the Admiral's kindness had been placed at my disposal, made bad weather, so after enjoying for a day or two the hospitality of Mr. Dorrien-Smith, whose brother, Smith-Dorrien, had served with me in the Egyptian Army, I came back by the passenger steamer to Penzance, and as the frost still held, went from Exeter to examine a Rifle range about which the Inspector-General of Fortifications had disagreed with the General officer commanding the Western District. When we left the train at Lydford, Dartmoor was coated with ice, and the horses had great difficulty in keeping their feet. Grierson, however, extolled cheerfully and continuously the merits of the fine fresh air on the moor, his circulation being, I imagine, much better than is mine.

Just before Christmas I made a Surprise Inspection of Netley Hospital, and saw much of which I could not approve. A battalion at Portsmouth furnished a half company of 53 young soldiers all under a year's service, and these men had only done two hours' drill during the last three months, being employed in every sort of menial work. At least twice a week, six of them were supposed to be weeding gardens. If they did anything at all, they must have made them as bare as the General at Aldershot did the Long Valley, which he found covered with heather in 1855.

The misuse of soldiers had in this instance one good effect, for it helped me to abolish the appointment of Commandant just then vacant, and to let the Doctors manage their Hospital. There were many objections raised to the company being taken away: the Government lighter which brought stores from Woolwich would be kept waiting for men to unload it; there would be no guard to take charge of the Army Medical Corps men if they got drunk; there would be no one to keep the patients who were allowed to go outdoors from straying into the adjoining villages, and there would be no one to keep civilians out of the Hospital grounds. It took me many months, but eventually I was allowed to hire two civilian policemen, who with a few military police did everything that was required, the Army Medical Corps being told that if some of their men got drunk, others would have to go on guard; while the window-cleaning and coal-carrying was done by taking on a few discharged old soldiers. The Infantry can never be adequately instructed for Service until the Army Council and Generals realise that Service efficiency must be put before local administration.

It was fortunate that I was at the Railway station when a party of invalids, discharged from Hospital, and out of the Service, were being sent off, some of them to travel as far as Edinburgh. They were without greatcoats or rugs of any description, the thermometer being at 30°. This was in accordance with existing Regulations. I sent them back, and had coats issued at once, Mr Brodrick supporting my unauthorised action.

In February some Militia occupied the Bulford hutments. A battalion of the Lincoln were fairly grown men, but there was another alongside of it the sight of which indicated we had come to the end of those who enlist voluntarily even in a war. I asked one lad, who was about fourteen, his age, and he said seventeen, which was obviously inaccurate.

I now lost the assistance of General Grierson for some months, as he was called to London to work in the office of the Quartermaster-General; but he came down at his own expense every Saturday afternoon, thus keeping in touch with the work by reading up on Sunday what had been done during the week. My friend Colonel S. Lomax, who was Adjutant of the

90th Light Infantry with me in 1878 in South Africa, joined as Staff officer, and although he had not been on the Staff, yet being a thoroughly good Regimental officer, was useful. He had been at the Staff College, so soon acquired the necessary knowledge of Staff duties.

I had lived in a house belonging to Lord Pembroke on first going to Salisbury for six months, but on the return of the tenant was persuaded by my son to go into another, called " The Island." It was surrounded by streams, which after rain came up flush with the surface of the ground. There was obviously no possibility of a cellar, but my son was quite correct in asserting the house would be dry, for there was not a damp room in it, and it stood in a charming old-world garden.

There were thirteen Yeomanry regiments in the Command, all of which I saw yearly. They varied in efficiency, but all Commanding officers had loyally accepted the new idea that the Yeomanry should use their horses as a means of locomotion, dismounting to fight.

As a general rule, if an imaginary north and south line is drawn on a map through Bath, the men of the Regiments to the west of it were generally farmers or their sons, riding their own horses. The amount allowed, £3, for the hire of a horse in the west gave ample margin, while in the east of my District there was considerable difficulty in obtaining the horses, which mostly came from Livery stable-keepers in London, or on the south coast of England.

I always inspected Yeomanry in practical work, and in the first two years I looked at every man individually, finding there was much room for improvement in the saddlery, and the way in which it was fitted. Some of my readers will think this is scarcely the duty of a General, but I did it with an object, for my inspection induced closer attention by the Squadron commanders, who had evidently in some cases inspected in a perfunctory manner in previous years.

The Regiments nearly all trained about the same time, and as the Commanding officers naturally wished to have a week or ten days' work before the inspection, I had to use two sets of horses and servants, and to travel day and night to get from Welshpool or Tenby, to say Lewes, and Shorncliffe. In my second year of Command I induced two or more Regiments to train together, and encamped with them a battery of Artillery.

I received many offers of hospitality, but was too much hurried to avail myself of them as a rule, but I spent a delightful twenty-four hours at Badminton, where there is a stately avenue, three miles long, which runs up to the house through the park, nearly ten miles in circumference.

The men of the Glamorganshire raised during the War were mainly clerks and mechanics. The Colonel, Wyndham Quinn, a good officer with a progressive mind, had taught his town-bred recruits a great deal in a limited time. The County had behaved liberally in equipping the Corps, and I found the men encamped in Margam Park, which was generously placed at their disposal by the owner, Miss Talbot. Immediately opposite to her dining-room windows there is a steep hill, for the oaks on which it is said the Admiralty, shortly before the invention of iron hulls for ships, offered her father £100,000, which he declined.

The most remarkable of the Yeomanry Regiments in the 2nd Army Corps was the North Devon. It was commanded by Lieutenant-Colonel Viscount Ebrington, who if he had not been a Peer of the Realm might have been a successful man of business, for all his arrangements indicated a mastery of finance. I stayed with him one or two days on Exmoor, twelve miles north of South Molton, where he had converted a disused public-house into a fairly comfortable abode. The table arrangements were remarkable in that the whole of our dinner came off the estate on the moor. The soup made from mutton bred on the estate; the fish—trout—from a stream immediately above the house; while the joint, poultry, and indeed everything except the sweet, was produced within a few hundred yards of where we were sitting.

Next morning, when we left my entertainer, he guided me for a dozen miles over the moor to a cross track, where we were met by the huntsman of the Devon and Somerset Stag Hounds, who piloted us another ten miles, until he put us on to a bridle path leading into Minehead, where the West Somerset were awaiting my inspection. The North Devon is the only Regiment I know in which, among the officers, were to be found eleven Masters, or ex-Masters of hounds.

The Montgomeryshire Yeomanry were quite different in appearance from any others in the Command. Many understood little, and spoke no English. They performed tactical operations, however, with intuitive skill. The officers were unusually efficient, and nearly all the men were small farmers. It was remarkable that while some of the Eastern Regiments paid 4s. 6d. for their messing, the Welsh were content to expend only 1s. 6d. or 2s. per diem for their food. Colonel Sir Watkin Wynne would be a remarkable man anywhere. Possessed of great determination, he generally had his way, and being a believer in the theory that horses did not catch cold in the open, he brought into camp in 1902 eleven of his hunters, which stood in a sea of mud at the picket post without injury.

Visiting the Military Hospital at Portsmouth, in order to decide a point between the Sister Services, as the Navy wished to annex a bit of the Military Hospital grounds, I found I had sufficient time to visit Tipnor Magazine, a strange out-of-the-world place, reminding one of Quilp's counting-house in *The Old Curiosity Shop*.[1] I had just succeeded in carrying out, after months of importunity, a change of system which I had inaugurated when I was Adjutant-General. For a month at a time, an officer, 2 sergeants, and 33 men were stationed at Tipnor to guard the magazine. There was nothing for the soldiers to do, and any man confined to a beat, and given a rifle and a bayonet which he must not use, is as inefficient a watchman as can be readily imagined. Perhaps some of my readers may remember the picture of the gutter boy making faces at a handsome Guardsman at Whitehall, who says to the urchin, " You go along out of that." The boy replies, " That's just what you can't do."

I got permission for the Metropolitan Police to take over charge of the Magazine in 1900, when the number of trained soldiers remaining in the country made it difficult to find any such guard. I had represented to the Chief Commissioner, my friend Sir Edward Bradford, it was a most important charge, and must be carefully watched. A few days afterwards, I met Sir Charles Howard, one of the Divisional Superintendents, who lived in the same street as I, and he told me with much

[1] By Charles Dickens.

amusement that having gone to Tipnor unannounced he found the officer and two sergeants were away, and a Lance Corporal was the only person of authority in the place. To my regret, the soldiers have been ordered to resume charge of the place, which would have been much more effectually watched by three or four Civil or Military policemen.

My next visit to Portsmouth was made to decide as to the necessity of having a sentry over a Magazine. I had taken off all the Divisional sentries except one over the General's house, as I did not wish to deprive him of the honour which he prized, but which I had given up on assuming command of the Aldershot Division.

The Commanding officer, whose judgment I generally accepted, judged it to be essential that a guard should be retained, as the Magazine contained ball ammunition. On visiting it, I found it was fairly protected by its natural position, and as the total amount of ammunition in it never exceeded £120 in value, I considered it was bad economy to employ a guard, which cost at least £300 per annum in pay, food, and clothing for the men, and removed it, without any unfortunate result up to the time of my leaving the Command.

Some of the sentries removed have already been replaced. I was sitting at dinner towards the close of my Command between Lord Roberts and General Sir Forestier Walker, and mentioned to his Lordship the previous week I had found a sentry whose primary duty was the protection of a Regimental pet ram, to ensure its not being teased by children. "What Regiment?" he asked. I said, "No, my lord; it is one of my children, and I cannot tell tales out of the family. But you can be satisfied the ram is being teased now; at all events, the sentry is not protecting it." I then told him I had recently seen a sentry at Plymouth, who, on my asking him his duties, answered, "I am to prevent anyone landing at the steps below me in plain clothes except Lord Morley and Lord Mount Edgcumbe." I said, "Do you know these lords?" "No," he said; "I don't know one lord from another." Sir Forestier said, "Why, is that sentry on? I took him off when I was in command." I said, "He has been put back, and I am trying to get him removed by fair words." Sir Forestier observed, "His orders were much better in my time; they ran, " I am not to allow anyone to bathe at these steps improperly dressed, except Lord Mount Edgcumbe."

In one of my visits to a southern fortress I had been assured £500 should be granted for iron rails for fencing, but on visiting the spot I found that more than the length of railing already existed, and by a slight alteration no addition was required. Similarly, £180 for a Drill Hall having been strongly recommended, I found on visiting the spot there was already a verandah not required for other purposes, 700 feet long by 10 feet wide, which fully answered the purpose.

I did not always succeed. For example, after a year's correspondence, I got the stabling for the Mounted Infantry at Bulford built in the form of a hollow square, the parade being in the centre. My object was to save sentries, and the angles where no stabling existed were closed by five-feet-high iron railings, with gates which swung on rollers. After the stables had been in use for six months, I found that my reasons not having been passed on, the gates were not closed at night, as I had intended, and the economy of sentries had not up to that time been effected.

I shocked some of the Army Corps Staff by my practice of inspecting the unsavoury places at the back of Barracks during my unexpected visitations. The notice I gave as a rule was to despatch a message to the Senior officer on arriving at the Barrack gate. I found much that was undesirable, but never anything to equal that in the Eastern District in 1886–87, where I found a Commanding officer who had occupied barracks for six months did not know whether his latrines were on the dry-earth or water-carriage system, nor where they were situated.

At the close of the hunting season 1901–2 I was staying at Melbury, Lord Ilchester's seat, which is remarkable for many objects of beauty, but in the Fox-hunter's point of view particularly so, in that there were twenty-two litters of cubs in the vicinity of the house. His Lordship, who kept also a pack of Deer Hounds, told me that his best recorded run was some years ago, in the month of June. After dinner, most of the party sat down to Bridge, and Lady Helen Stavordale, his Lordship's daughter-in-law, knowing my tastes, gave me an old game book in which the list of game shot at Melbury and its vicinity has been noted for 150 years. I was reading about A.D. 1726, where the daily bags of Lords Digby and Ilchester are recorded. It appears they considered two pheasants was a poor day's sport, but anything over eight was held to be satisfactory. There is a curious entry in 1726, " Lord Digby made a very fine shot, and killed a cock pheasant. This was difficult, as it was siting (*sic*) on a hedge." Sportsmen of the present day should remember that the firearms of their predecessors were very different from those now in use.

I had several agreeable visitors at Salisbury, one or two belonging to the Opposition in Parliament, who thought more highly of Mr. Brodrick's scheme of the three Army Corps before they left the district, but perhaps the most pleasant of all was the new Chaplain-General. He kept me up till past midnight talking, being most earnest and enthusiastic about religion, but with a remarkably broad mind. He was addressing a crowded audience in the evening, and was arguing that the Church of England was like the nave of a wheel, the spokes representing all the other branches. When the people were dispersing a coachman came up to him and said, " I liked your address very much, and especially the story about the wheel, but, excuse me, I am a coachman, and think you might well have added the tyre is the love of Christ which should bind us together." The Bishop said, " Thank you, I will use that next time."

In all my efforts for decentralisation I was backed by Mr. St. John Brodrick. He was never wearied of hearing from me, and sympathised with my efforts, often ineffectual, to relieve the offices in London of petty details. I pointed out that I was not permitted to authorise a tenant who rented a piece of beach at Portsmouth which was gravelled, to have it cemented, without referring it to the Inspector-General of Royal Engineers. Mr. Brodrick tried to help me also in my efforts to induce delegation of authority to local Engineer officers. I found in the Western district stairs leading down into an engine-room, on which the soldiers had to carry coal trays, with much difficulty owing to a sharp turn, avoidable if a hole had been cut in the ground, as you see in every London street; and when I disapproved, I was told officially that it

II.—18

was a type, and types must be followed. Similarly, every screen for shutting off a bath is made about 7 feet high, as if intended for a zenana. Mr. Brodrick endeavoured to assist me in all such points. After inspecting the new Barracks being erected, he wrote: " I congratulate you most heartily on the immense progress made on Salisbury Plain since you assumed command."

He is one of the few Cabinet Ministers I have met who realise the importance of having somebody at the head of troops who can be held responsible for seeing that they are prepared for war. Such an officer must exist to ensure that the ammunition columns, waggons, and equipment of every kind is complete; that the harness for the horses, and the vehicles are all in good order. There are numbers of officers who have a divided duty in these matters, but there should be one person to whom the Army Council can look, and who can be held responsible that the command is ready for War Service.

I was greatly assisted in my endeavours to improve the sanitary state of the barracks in the 2nd Army Corps district by the persevering efforts of the principal Medical officer, Surgeon-General G. J. Evatt, M.D., C.B., than whom I have never had a more enthusiastic sanitary assistant. He introduced great changes, incurring a certain amount of ill-will, as all eager reformers do. His visits to the kitchens of the officers' messes in the barracks of the district brought to the notice of the Commanding officers what I had long known, they were the dirtiest places in barracks, except perhaps the canteens. In few of the latter was there sufficient accommodation, with the result that the contractor's agent was reported in several instances to be "sleeping at the back of the grocery bar, with his head on a cheese and his feet in a butter bowl."

The Surgeon-General helped me to obtain a concession for the soldiers, for which I had striven many years in vain. Up to the time of my command at Salisbury the soldier never had more than two shirts; as one went to wash if he got wet, he had to sleep in it, or sleep naked, at his choice, but day and night one shirt at the wash, and one shirt on the man's body was the custom. With Evatt's assistance and his graphic accounts of the state of some Militia regiments, the Secretary of State gave way, and authorised a third shirt.

I had hoped that Evatt and I might serve on to get the men a sleeping suit, but the "guns having ceased to shoot," to paraphrase Mr. Kipling, there is now less consideration for the private soldier than is felt in War time.

My indefatigable Sanitary Inspector sympathised greatly with my desire to reduce the number of sentries, appreciating as a doctor the unfavourable effect of night duty on the health of the young soldier; and although I, personally preferring a hard bed, did not sympathise so thoroughly with a reform he advocated, yet I authorised in the command the abolition of the boards on which the soldier slept in the guard-room, which were replaced by bedsteads.

The Surgeon-General found out in one Hospital some reprehensible customs, such as the officer in charge signing his Diet Sheets for a week in advance, and this was in a district where the Ward master, after committing frauds of over £100 on Diet Sheets alone, had just committed suicide.

Surgeon-General Evatt tried to help me in another Reform, which may, I hope, be effected by my successors, for when I gave over the Southern Command in December 1903, my recommendations were "still under consideration."

When I was Quartermaster-General, a company of Garrison Artillery detained for Free Town, Sierra Leone, was quartered half at that Station, and half at Plymouth, ready to embark if required. My study of the Health statistics disclosed the fact, that of 16 men, the 1st Relief of the guns in a battery, at King Tom, situated at the head of a lagoon, 13 were continuously on the Sick Report. I got this detachment removed up to hills, whence they could still get to the battery quickly in case of need. In the nineties a complete Company was stationed at Sierra Leone for twelve months, and in June 1903, when I was inspecting a Company at Falmouth, which had returned four months previously, I was so perturbed by the look of the remains of malarial fever in the men's faces, that I demanded a history of their service on the West Coast. The Company disembarked at Free Town 93 men of unusually fine stature; lost 5 dead, 5 invalided, 1 sent home, and 1 deserter. Struck by the fact that no man died, or was invalided within the first six months of residence, I submitted that irrespective of dictates of humanity, we should exchange the men every six months, as a more economical arrangement.

The first year I went to Salisbury I gave a cup, with a view to improving the shooting of the Rank and File at unknown distances. Each of the Sub-Districts in the command sent a team of four, who were presumably the best in the corps, as they were ordered to have a preliminary Competition. The result was such as would, if known, encourage soldiers in their first battle. The ground on Salisbury Plain is certainly difficult, consisting of rolling plains without a tree or any mark to guide the eye, and consequently it is very difficult to estimate distances. The first team was composed of three very young soldiers and one veteran who wore spectacles and could not double 300 yards, which was a condition of the competition. Another team consisted of soldiers of about four months who had not done the "Trained Soldier's course" of musketry. The third, from the Devon Regiment, which won, had men of seven, eleven, and eighteen years' service. The targets were actually 2500, 1400, 800, and 340 yards distant. The judging, except at 2500 yards, was ludicrously erroneous, and when the targets jumped up like a "Jack in the box" at 340 yards, all the teams guessed 500 or 600. These targets were only the size of a man's chest, but those $1\frac{1}{2}$ miles off represented a quarter of a Battalion standing in column, and were a broad and deep mark, but in the result 1100 shots fired by the three teams gave only five hits. Although this was very unsatisfactory, it called attention to our faulty training, which I am glad to believe has since been rectified.

The result of the above competition induced me to consult the Surgeon-General, whom I told that when the targets jumped up close to the men, being visible only for forty seconds, many men did not see them until they were disappearing, and under his advice I initiated a system of improving the visual efficiency of the soldiers. It was taken up by Colonel S. Lomax, who was temporarily in command of a brigade, and the result gave satisfaction to everyone. The doctors tested every man separately in the first instance, and the company officers then endeavoured to improve the eyesight of all.

I mentioned the successful result of enabling the Army Service Corps to do their own work and eliminating the middleman as a forwarding agent of Stores,[1] but I was able, by bringing to the notice of the generals under me, to cause them to make considerable saving of public money; that in one Sub-District amounting to something over £2000 per annum.

I called for a return of all the boats in the Command belonging to Government, and also those hired, with a very curious result. It transpired that in one district a coxswain and crew had been paid, although from time immemorial no boat had existed. The oldest clerk in the office had never heard of the boat, nor was there any record of it, and to render the situation rather more comical moorings had been for years hired for that boat. This was explained later by the statement that the moorings were available for all boats, and they merely happened to be entered to that boat as a matter of account; but further inquiry whether any of the boats used the moorings, elicited a negative reply, and a further statement that the hiring of moorings had been discontinued. I said nothing more on the subject, on ascertaining that the general concerned made the economies I have stated above. In another great Naval port there was a similar case, and that was also terminated.

Perhaps the most interesting part of my duties consisted in the instruction and practice of Artillery. I took my Senior Aide-de-camp[2] without ever having seen him, from the recommendation of one of the best Senior officers of Garrison Artillery in the district, Colonel W. W. Smith, writing to him: " Will you please recommend me a Garrison Artillery-Aide-de-camp? He must be able to ride, and must have a good knowledge of, and be keen about his work." He named Major C. Buckle, D.S.O., who found for us the Rhyader Range after looking over many places in Cardiganshire and the adjoining counties. There were only two or three small houses on it which was essential to vacate. The range is quite safe for 12,000 yards, but it has its disadvantage, as have all such places, that it is isolated, and there is a steep climb up to the range of mountains.

I saw some of the Garrison Artillery at one of my inspec-

[1] See vol. ii. p. 233.
[2] Who was also Assistant Military Secretary.

tions fire at a target 3800 yards distant, travelling at 6 miles an hour. The first five shots were all on the target, and the sixth shot cut the connecting rope by which the steamer was towing it.

Early in the Spring of 1903 I read at breakfast in the *Times* that Sir George White had been made a Field Marshal by His Majesty the King, who was visiting Gibraltar, and when I got to the office I found the Army Corps Staff indignant, as Sir George was a colonel when I as a Major-General of four years' standing had got him brought out to Egypt for the Khartoum Expedition. I sent him a telegram congratulating him on his good fortune, and received a reply in a very short time, that he heard on the best authority I had received the same honour. In the afternoon I had a kind private letter from the Secretary of State announcing His Majesty's pleasure, to whom I wrote a letter of grateful thanks the same evening, and received the following gracious reply:—

H.M. ROYAL YACHT <i>VICTORIA AND ALBERT</i>,
MALTA, <i>April</i> 1903.

MY DEAR SIR EVELYN WOOD,—Many thanks for your kind letter. It has given me the greatest pleasure and satisfaction to promote you to the rank of Field Marshal, after the long and distinguished services you have rendered for the Crown and country.—Believe me, very sincerely yours,

EDWARD R.

INDEX

Ababdeh Arabs, ii. 181.
Abatis, i. 92.
Abbassieh, ii. 159, 165.
Abbaye, i. 261.
Abbey Field, Colchester, ii. 183.
Abdin Palace, ii. 156.
Abercromby, Sir Ralph, i. 29.
Aboukir, i. 29.
Abrakampa, i. 263, 272.
Abu-Hamed, i. 42.
Abu Klea, ii. 161, 172, 174, 247.
Abyssinia, i. 227.
Academy, Royal Military, Woolwich, ii. 75.
Accassi, King, Queen, i. 274.
Acting Governor, Natal, ii. 146.
Adelphi Hotel, i. 229.
Aden, camel men, ii. 177, 178.
Adjutant-General, ii. 107, 186, 194, 259.
,, appointment, ii. 239.
Administration, Faulty, ii. 262.
Administrator of Transvaal, ii. 71, 112.
Admiral "overboard again," ii. 203.
Advocate General Judge, i. 233.
Adye, Sir John, ii. 152.
Agamemnon, H.M.S., i. 27.
Agar, i. 149.
Agram, i. 213.
Ahmednagar, i. 136.
Aide-de-camp, ii. 187, 263.
Airey, Lord, i. 206.
Ajmir, i. 127, 158.
Akim, King, i. 263.
Albert, Prince Consort, i. 206.
Albuera, i. 250; ii. 182, 191.
Alcock, i. 291.
Alcohol, Abuse of, i. 113.
Aldershot, i. 221, 224, 229, 231, 232, 233, 236, 289, 290; ii. 35, 36, 65, 90, 192, 193, 205, 209, 215, 220, 221, 224, 225, 230, 241, 252, 265.

Aldershot, General Officer Commanding, ii. 253.
,, central gymnasium, ii. 259.
Alexandria, ii. 146, 147, 149, 151, 159.
Algebra, Todhunter's, i. 209.
Algiers, i. 11.
Alhambra, ii. 192, 240.
Ali Jaroor, i. 161.
Alice Holt, i. 244.
Alison, Sir Archibald, ii. 191, 192.
All Saints, i. 242.
Allan, Bridge of, i. 248.
Allen, Sergt., Death of, ii. 62, 66.
Alleyne, Colonel James, ii. 207, 223.
Allied Fleets, i. 18, 20.
Alma, "Brown Bess" at, ii. 222.
,, River, i. 31; ii. 223.
Amahwenkwee Regiment, ii. 81.
Amanquatsia, i. 269.
Amatolas, ii. 7, 9, 28, 85.
Amberg, Van, i. 24.
Ambiguous telegrams, The Cabinet's, ii. 114.
Amet, i. 160.
Ammunition Column, Divisional, ii. 225.
Anatolia Recruits, ii. 166.
Andoo, Quacoe, i. 263, 264, 285.
Andros, i. 17.
Annexation, Transvaal, ii. 107, 108, 109, 110.
Annual Army Rifle Meeting, ii. 224, 225.
Antiquated Military Exercises, ii. 251.
Arabi, The Egyptian, ii. 150.
Arabian Nights, i. 146.
Arabic language, ii. 157.
Arabists, ii. 150.
Arangabad, i. 124, 166, 167, 168.
Aravalli Range, i. 158.
Arbitrator in Egypt, ii. 172.
Ardagh, General Sir John, ii. 190, 191, 192, 228.
Arethusa, H.M.S., i. 21, 22.

INDEX

Arithmetic, ii. 190.
Arkwright, Loftus, M.F.H., ii. 249.
Arlington Manor, ii. 214.
Armistice, ii. 117.
Army Council, ii. 233.
,, Discipline, ii. 157.
,, Order, i. 199.
,, Service Corps, ii. 233.
Arnau, Marshal, i. 31.
Arroyo dos Molinos, i. 237.
Artillery, i. 153; ii. 196, 210, 246.
,, in South Africa, training to shoot with rifle, ii. 253.
Ascension, ii. 86.
Ascot, i. 225, 290.
Ashanti, i. 254, 273, 274, 285, 288.
,, Expedition, ii. 177.
Ashantiland, ii. 212.
Asia Minor, i. 18.
"Assaye" Barracks, ii. 263.
Asseerghur, i. 123, 125, 126, 127.
Assistance, H.M.S., ii. 230.
Assuan fortified, ii. 169.
Atalanta, H.M.S., i. 15.
Attorney, Cork, i. 13.
Attorney-General Holker, ii. 94.
Australia, Commandant-General, ii. 187.
Auxiliary Forces, School of Instruction, i. 254.
Aveley, Essex, ii. 86.
Ayr, i. 247.
Ayrshire, i. 120.

Baba Bhut, i. 194, 195.
Babington, Captain, A.D.C., ii. 195, 200.
Bacaland, ii. 3, 5.
Bacas, Chief of, ii. 5.
Bacon's (Lord), recommendation, ii. 208.
Badajos, i. 31; visited, ii. 191.
Bader, Mr., ii. 175.
Bailie's grave, i. 299, 300, 304, 309, 311, 312, 313, 314.
Baker Pasha, Valentine, ii. 159, 161, 168.
,, T. D., Colonel, i. 278, 280.
Balaklava, i. 25, 29, 33, 34, 35, 37, 60, 63, 64, 65.
Balfour, Right Hon. Arthur, ii. 227, 234, 243.
,, of Burleigh, i. 180.
Baljic, i. 26, 28.
Balmoral, Visit to, ii. 89, 161.

Baltazzi, the Misses, i. 99.
Balte Spruit, ii. 25, 26, 28, 29, 30, 43, 45, 70, 71.
Bansha, i. 111.
Banswarra, i. 148.
Baptist persuasion, Lady Wood helps, ii. 219.
Barber, Mr., i. 305.
Barbour, murder of, ii. 116, 124.
Barcelona visited, ii. 191, 192.
Bareli, Levy, i. 178.
Baring, Sir Evelyn, ii. 162, 164, 180.
Baroda, i. 148.
Barode, i. 152, 153, 154.
Barracks, names of, ii. 193.
Barsad, i. 194.
Bartolozzi, engraver, i. 4.
Barton, Captain, ii. 24, 25, 26, 30, 41, 52, 53, 54, 55, 69, 100.
,, Robert, i. 243.
Base in Natal, ii. 76.
Basingstoke (manœuvring ground), ii. 220.
Bassano, Marquis de, ii. 96.
Basset, Mr., ii. 189.
Bastei, i. 212, 213.
Bastion, Central, i. 36.
Basuto, i. 314.
Basutos, ii. 75, 143.
Bath, Order of the, ii. 85.
Bath, Somersetshire, ii. 268.
Battalion Scottish Rifles, ii. 243.
Battery, Black, i. 50.
Bautzen, i. 146.
"Bawabbas," ii. 141.
Bayard, Mr., Ambassador, ii. 228.
Bayuda Desert, ii. 174.
Bazaar, Master, i. 146.
Beaconsfield, Lord, i. 294; ii. 90, 91, 92.
Beagle, H.M.S., i. 62.
Beatson's Horse, i. 166, 170, 178, 181, 184, 203.
Beaufort, Fort, i. 295, 296, 298, 314, 315, 316; ii. 111.
Bedford, 3rd Bn., i. 245.
Beicos Bay, i. 18.
Belfast, Land League, ii. 95, 182.
Belhus, i. 228; ii. 88, 234.
Bell, Canon, ii. 189.
Bellerophon, H.M.S., i. 28, 55.
Belmont, Lieutenant Wood, ii. 242.
Bemba's Kop, ii. 60.

INDEX

Benson, Colonel, i. 145, 146.
Berber, ii. 162, 163.
Beresford, Bill, V.C., ii. 79.
,, Lord Charles, ii. 169, 171.
Berkshire Downs, ii. 211, 214.
Berkshire Regiment, 1st, ii. 149.
Berlin, Schudi Pasha, ii. 157.
Bersia, i. 135, 168, 169, 180, 185, 187, 190, 191.
Betul, i. 127.
Betwa, River, i. 136.
Beumbei, Hotel at, ii. 126, 136, 137.
Beyah, i. 258.
Bezeidenhout, ii. 106.
Bhopal, i. 127, 145, 187.
Biden, John, ii. 190.
Biggarsberg, ii. 108, 109, 112, 127.
Bigge, Lieutenant Arthur, ii. 5, 59, 95, 99, 100, 101.
Bikaneer, i. 158.
Bilko, i. 176.
Biora, i. 134, 164, 165.
Bishop's Stortford, i. 231.
Bishund Dhutt, i. 194, 195.
Black Battery, i. 50.
,, Sea, i. 18, 27.
,, Umvolosi, ii. 39.
"Black Watch," ii. 172.
Blackett, Sir William, i. 88.
Blackmore Vale, ii. 262, 266.
Blair, Lieutenant, i. 187.
Blake, Captain, R.M.L.T., i. 253, 287.
,,   ,,   R.N., i. 261.
Blake Stopper, i. 19.
Blandford, i. 104.
Blarney, i. 224.
Blenheim, ii. 215.
Blewitt, John, i. 77.
Blood River, ii. 9, 28, 29, 66, 98, 99, 100.
Blumenthal, General, ii. 259.
Boat, My, i. 12.
Boer flag at Heidelberg, ii. 122.
,, leaders, ii. 121.
,, Republic, ii. 142.
,, War, ii. 234.
Boers, ii. 43, 117, 235.
Bombay, i. 119, 120, 168.
,, Command of, offered, ii. 209.
,, Rifles, i. 159.
Bonny men, i. 262, 278.
,, Prince Charles, i. 262.

Bonny River, i. 262.
Booth, Sergeant, ii. 39.
Boots, too small, ii. 177.
Bosphorus, i. 17, 21, 58, 99.
Bosquet, General, i. 51.
Bothwell, Sergeant, i. 180.
Bowker, Mr., i. 305, 313, 314.
Boxer, Captain, i. 65.
Boys, brave or cowards, ii. 190.
Brabant, Captain, i. 297, 299, 304, 306, 308, 309, 310.
Brack, de, Colonel, i. 120.
Brackenbury, Captain, i. 259.
,, General Sir. Hews, ii. 160.
Bradford, E.R.C. Lieutenant, i. 142, 181, 187, 189, 190, 192, 195, 196, 197.
,, Sir Edward, ii. 270.
Bradley, Dean, ii. 190.
Bradshaw, Captain, ii. 45.
Brahman, i. 125.
Braintree, i. 4.
Bramshill, i. 222.
Brand, President, ii. 107, 111, 116, 119, 121, 128.
Brazils, i. 3.
Brewer for canteen, ii. 185.
Brigade, 4th, Egypt, ii. 149.
,, of Cavalry prepared on paper, ii. 235.
,, team of Guards, ii. 36.
Bright, Arthur, ii. 26, 62, 66.
Brighton, i. 221, 232.
Brindisi, ii. 162.
Brindle, Father, ii. 169, 173, 174.
Briscoe, Captain, ii. 162.
Brisk, H.M.S., ii. 242.
Britain, Great, i. 117.
Britannia, H.M.S., i. 25.
British India Steamship Company, ii. 212.
,, rations, 42,000 at Dongola, ii. 171.
Brixton, Plymouth, i. 1.
Brodrick, Mr., M.P., ii. 238, 258, 265, 273, 274.
Brooke, Sir Victor, i. 241.
"Brown Bess" at Alma, ii. 222.
,, General Sir George, i. 25, 31.
,, Trooper, V.C., ii. 53.
,, Trumpeter, i. 151.
Buckingham Palace, medal parade, ii. 257.

INDEX

Buckle, George, Private, R.M.L.I., i. 24.
„ Major C., ii. 277.
Buffalo Mountains, i. 302.
„ Poort, i. 300, 311.
„ Range, i. 297, 298, 299, 300.
„ River, i. 296, 300; ii. 19, 28, 29, 143.
Bugler, A brave, i. 66.
Bugler's opinion, ii. 93.
Bukra (to-morrow), ii. 167.
Bulford Camp, ii. 267.
Bulganac, i. 27, 30.
Buller, Redvers, Major, i. 296, 304, 318, 319, 320.
„ „ Colonel, i. 307.
„ „ Sir, i. 267.
„ „ V.C., ii. 1, 24, 26, 27, 30, 31, 41, 46, 47, 48, 49, 51, 52, 54, 59, 60, 63, 68, 70, 72, 74, 76, 80, 83, 84, 85, 99, 120, 130, 143, 144, 153, 174, 175, 198, 226, 237, 241, 244.
„ Sir Edward, ii. 95.
Bundelas, i. 127.
Burgers, troop of forty, ii. 31.
Burgesses, ii. 145.
Burgoyne, Sir John Fox, Field Marshal, i. 13, 253.
„ Hugh, i. 13, 62.
Burial service under fire, ii. 51.
Burke, Sergeant-Major, i. 42.
Burmadeen Singh, i. 172, 180, 184, 186, 193, 198.
Burnett, Captain C., i. 277.
„ Colonel, ii. 206, 207, 211.
„ General, ii. 186.
Burns Hill, i. 312, 315.
Burrups, Natal, ii. 143.
Burwanee, i. 147.
Butcher, Mr., M.P., ii. 123.
Butler, William, Major, i. 274.
„ „ Colonel, i. 294, 295.
Butser Hill, ii. 220.

Cabinet, ii. 92, 114, 164.
Cæsar's Camp, i. 242.
„ Commentaries, i. 240.
Cahir, i. 110, 111.
Cairo, ii. 154, 155, 159, 162, 181.

Calcutta, i. 197, 199, 201.
Calverley and Rorke, Colonists, ii. 41.
Camberley, i. 4.
Cambridge, Duke of, i. 246.
Camel men, Desert, ii. 178.
Cameronians, i. 249.
Campbell, Captain Ronald, ii. 37, 44, 47, 48, 49, 50, 51, 53, 56, 71, 89, 96, 99.
„ Colin, i. 63.
Canada, i. 207.
Canning, Lord, i. 183, 196.
Canrobert, General, i. 25.
Canteen regulations, ii. 186.
Canteens, Reforms in, ii. 182.
Cape Coast Castle, i. 260.
Cape of Good Hope, i. 4, 12.
Cape Matapan, i. 17.
Cape Smoke, i. 306.
Cape Tarkan, i. 29.
Cape Town, i. 118, 295, 317; ii. 97, 106, 108.
Captain, H.M.S., loss of, i. 15.
Carcases, 100 years old, i. 78.
Cardigan, Lord, i. 113.
Cardwell, Mr., M.P., i. 256.
Careenage Ravine, i. 37.
Carlton Club, ii. 237.
Carnarvon, Earl of, ii. 219.
Caroline, Queen, i. 25.
Castle Rising, ii. 153.
Castlereagh, Viscount, ii. 116.
Catalonia ss., ii. 149.
Cathcart, Sir George, General, i. 239, 297, 311.
Catherine, Empress, ii. 184.
Catholic Army candidates, ii. 228.
Catholic Emancipation, i. 203.
Cator, Susan, i. 108.
Cats (Manx) have no tails, ii. 148.
Cattle, The Royal Zulu Coronation white, ii. 80.
Cavalry, Heavy, tunics, ii. 35.
„ manœuvres, ii. 214.
„ Native, i. 137.
"Cave Canem," i. 208.
Cawdor Castle, ii. 88.
Cawdor, Lord, ii. 89.
Central India, i. 127.
Cetewayo, ii. 8, 9, 22, 28, 29, 30, 39, 41, 43, 47, 68, 73, 80, 97, 101, 143.
Chads, Captain, i. 7.

INDEX

283

Chaka, ii. 35.
Chambal River, i. 155, 157, 161.
Chambers, Colonel, i. 119.
Chancellor, the Lord, ii. 94.
Channel, i. 106.
Chaplain-General, ii. 240, 273.
Chartered Company, ii. 235.
Charteris, Captain, The Hon., i. 259.
Charwoman, A sagacious, ii. 251.
Chatham, ii. 95, 140, 145, 146, 152.
Chelmsford, Lord, ii. 27, 29, 43, 44, 46, 52, 58, 65, 67, 72, 73, 78, 80, 81, 83.
Chemmun Singh, i. 177, 180, 181.
Chenwassa, i. 161.
Chermside, Captain, ii. 156.
Cherry, Major, i. 317.
Chesham's (Lord) Yeomanry, ii. 239.
Chesney, Colonel C., i. 215.
Chicheeli, ii. 54, 55, 100.
Chief Justice, Natal, ii. 112.
Chifney Rush, i. 133.
Childers, Hugh, M.P., ii. 116, 133, 142, 147, 148, 151, 152.
Chilmark Rectory in Wiltshire, ii. 241.
China, ii. 262.
Chinese, ii. 253.
,, servant, ii. 243.
Chislehurst, ii. 75.
Chobham, Telegraph Battalion at, ii. 209.
Cholera, i. 26, 28, 76.
Christmas Day, soldiers' changes for, ii. 205, 216.
,, i. 17, 62, 201.
Chunda, i. 170.
Chuppra, i. 154.
Church Parade on service, ii. 50.
,, i. 211.
,, Wardens, i. 242.
Circassian chief, i. 66.
Clark, Major, ii. 167.
Clarke, Brigadier-General Mansfield, ii. 200, 208, 218.
,, General Sir Stanley, i. 101, 113, 120, 211.
Cleland, Colonel, i. 249, 250.
Clement, Reynold, i. 101, 113, 211.
Clery, Major, ii. 17, 25.
Climate of Crimea, i. 57, 58.
Clones, i. 217, 226, 227, 241.
,, Market, ii. 182.
Clowes, Lieutenant, i. 263.
Clyde, Lord, i. 63.

Coal fatigues, ii. 208.
Code, Napoleon, ii. 157.
Colbert, ii. 91.
Colchester, i. 289; ii. 184, 192, 193, 197.
Colebrooke, i. 241.
Colenso, ii. 114.
,, Bishop, ii. 39, 140, 141.
Colenso's Arithmetic, ii. 190.
College Staff, i. 207, 208, 233, 290.
,, Wellington, i. 292, 294.
Colley, Sir George, i. 294; ii. 106, 107, 108, 109, 110, 111, 112, 115, 118, 119, 142.
Collingwood, Lord, i. 12.
Colonial Office, ii. 53, 147.
,, forces, Command of, i. 321.
Colonists, tribute to, ii. 145.
Colony of Natal, ii. 144.
Colossa, Transkei, ii. 3.
Colvin, Sir Auckland, ii. 155.
Commandant Colonial Forces, i. 321.
,, Netley Hospital, ii. 267.
,, General, Cape Colony, ii. 121.
Commander, Our, ii. 13.
,, H.M.S. *Queen*, i. 32, 33.
Commander-in-Chief, disapproves of night marches, ii. 193.
,, i. 235; ii. 148, 201, 244, 247, 252, 253, 259.
Commanding Officers' Quarters at Tidworth, ii. 263.
Commerell, Sir John, i. 255.
,, Admiral, Sir E., ii. 203.
Commissariat, i. 126.
,, in 1879, ii. 74.
Commissary General, ii. 103.
Commission, The High, 1881, ii. 123.
Commodore, i. 32.
Company system, ii. 193.
,, training, ii. 198.
Complimentary Honours, ii. 88.
Connaught, Duke of, ii. 223, 239.
Conolly, Doctor, ii. 175.
Consort, Prince, i. 206.
Constantine, Fort, i. 25.
Constantinople, i. 18, 20.
Consul-General, Egypt, ii. 161, 162, 173.
Continental Staff Officers, duties of, ii. 242.
Contracts, Director of, ii. 225.

Cookery, School of, ii. 211.
Coomassie, i. 269, 277, 285, 286.
Cork, Lord, i. 112-117, 289; ii. 225.
Corn Circular, ii. 206.
Cornwall, i. 4.
Corunna, Visit to, ii. 182.
Cost of manœuvres, £7000, ii. 224.
Cotton, Dr., i. 7.
Council, Military education of, i. 290.
Couper, Mr., i. 199.
Court Martial, i. 17.
Cowling, Robert, i. 10.
Craven, Earl of, ii. 223.
Crealock, Colonel North, ii. 53, 204.
Crease, Colonel, ii. 213.
Cressing, i. 4.
Crime statistics, ii. 184.
Crimea, i. 22, 106, 251.
Croft, West, i. 2.
Cromer, Lord, ii. 180.
Cronje's treachery, ii. 123.
Cross, Victoria, i. 114.
Crozier, Mr. J., M.F.H., ii. 227.
Crutchley, Colonel C., ii. 247.
Cuffe, Surgeon-Major, ii. 25.
Cumberland dialect, ii. 153.
Curiosity Shop, The Old, ii. 270.
Curragh, i. 113, 115.
,, Kildare of, i. 219.
Cyclades, i. 17.
Cycle, Learnt to, ii. 236.
Cyclists, Training of, ii. 215.
Cyprus, Acquisition of, ii. 90.

Daily News, i. 46.
Dalhousie, Lord, i. 199.
Dalserf, Manse of, i. 289.
Dalyell, Lieutenant, i. 139, 210.
Daniel Lysons, Sir, i. 254, 293.
Daniels, R. N., i. 41, 42, 52, 62, 75, 84, 89, 96, 100, 114.
Danube, Mouth of, i. 28.
Darfour, ii. 163.
Dargai piper, ii. 239, 240.
Dartmoor, ii. 189, 266.
Date trees destroyed, ii. 151.
D'Autemarre, General, i. 97.
David, i. 139, 210.
Davis, Colonel, ii. 221.
Dawkins, Mr. Clinton, ii. 254.
Dawson, Mr., Clearing House, ii. 216.
"Day of Rest," ii. 158.

Debbeh, Command at, ii. 178.
Debe Flats, i. 300, 311.
Decentralisation, ii. 205.
Dehri, i. 191.
Dekham, i. 181.
Delagoa Bay, ii. 126, 135, 137.
Delissert, Mons., i. 203, 212.
Departmental arrangements on Service, ii. 205.
Deputy Adjutant-General, changed three times, ii. 244.
Derby, Transvaal, ii. 38.
Derby Dog, i. 212.
Dervishes, ii. 165.
D'Estrees, Gabrielle, ii. 91.
Destruction of our enemies, Drill for, ii. 187.
Detachable magazine rifle, ii. 186.
Devil's Pass, Inhlobane, ii. 99.
Devon and Somerset Stag Hounds, ii. 269.
Dewlish, i. 211.
Dewud, i. 148.
Dhokul Singh, i. 132, 139, 140, 143, 147.
Diamond Fields Light Horse, i. 311.
Diamond, H.M.S., i. 25, 41, 46, 47, 49, 66.
Dickens, Charles, ii. 126, 270.
Diet Sheets faulty, ii. 275.
Digby, Lord, ii. 273.
Digna, Osman, ii. 161.
Dihlí, i. 118, 119, 121, 199.
,, King of, i. 128.
Diogenes, i. 18.
Director of Contracts, ii. 225.
,, General of Military Intelligence, ii. 252.
,, ,, ,, Operations, ii. 252.
Dirks Uys, ii. 40.
Discharge Depôt at Gosport, ii. 231.
"Dissent, My," ii. 129.
Division, 2nd Zululand, ii. 45.
Divisional Ammunition Column, ii. 225.
,, Athletic Sports, Zululand, ii. 35.
,, Staff at Aldershot, ii. 207.
Dockyard, Turkish, i. 20.
Dogmersfield Park, i. 243.
Döhne, Kabousie Nek, i. 248.
Dongola, ii. 171.

INDEX 285

Dorchester, i. 211.
Dormer, General, The Hon. J., ii. 169.
Dorrien-Smith, ii. 266.
Douglas, Lieutenant, i. 32, 38, 39, 41, 42, 47, 72.
Dover, i. 288.
Doyle, Canon, i. 227.
Drag Hounds, ii. 260.
Drakensberg Mountains, ii. 109.
Dream, a premonitory, i. 217.
Dresden, i. 212, 213.
Drill Book, ii. 187, 219.
Drinking to excess, i. 13.
Dublin, i. 217.
Duchess of Kent, i. 2.
Dufferin, Lord, ii. 153, 155, 156, 157.
Duke of Kent, i. 2.
,, Wellington, i. 172.
Dukwana, i. 321.
Duncan, Adjutant, i. 163.
,, Major, ii. 149, 156, 169.
Dunn, John, White Zulu, ii. 136, 153.
Dunquah, i. 261.
Durban, ii. 74, 108, 137, 144.
Durham Light Infantry, ii. 194.
Durnford, Colonel, ii. 144, 145.
Durrington, ii. 241.
Dutchmen, ii. 22, 121.

Earlston, Kirkcudbright, i. 119.
East Hampstead Park, drag line, ii. 148.
East London, i. 296.
Eastman, i. 7.
Ebrington, Lieutenant-Colonel, Viscount, ii. 269.
Edgecumbe, Lord Mount, ii. 272.
Edgeware Road, accident in, ii. 236.
Edison's phonographic machine, "my voice like," ii. 141.
Edmonstone, Sir George, i. 199.
Eelmore Hill, i. 235, 236, 242, 243.
Egginassie, i. 274, 275.
Egypt, Charles Gordon's journey there, ii. 162.
Egyptian Army, raising of, ii. 149, 154, 180.
,, Officer, no value in epidemics, ii. 159.
,, soldiers, their good work, ii. 173.
El Obeid, annihilation near, ii. 161, 163.

El Teb, ii. 161, 165.
Elbe, i. 212.
Electra, Sir John Pender's yacht, ii. 173.
Elgin's (Lord) Royal Commission, ii. 251.
Elliott, Major, Murder of, ii. 116, 124, 127.
Elmina, i. 257, 258, 261, 262, 263, 267, 284.
Elsworthy, able seaman, i. 43, 44.
Ely, Lady, ii. 89.
Eman Khan, i. 194.
Emancipation, Catholic, i. 203.
Emin Pasha, " not worth the search," ii. 213.
Emir Wad Rahma killed, ii. 165.
Emperor, German, his visit, ii. 201, 203, 211, 241.
England, going to, when cholera broke out, ii. 159.
English horses, must be acclimatised, ii. 133.
Epidemic, ii. 159.
Epping, accident near, ii. 258.
Epsom, i. 290.
Esaughur, i. 135.
Essaman, i. 259.
Essevie, Quamina, i. 263, 264, 265, 278, 284.
Essex, Honours from county, ii. 88.
,, Hounds, ii. 249.
,, Hunt, a wounded sportsman, ii. 258.
,, Stag Hounds, i. 224.
Euclid, i. 204.
Eugénie, Empress, ii. 54, 95, 97, 103, 148, 218, 261.
Eupatoria, i. 27.
Eurasians, i. 165.
European Infantry, i. 129.
Eurydice, loss of, i. 15.
Evatt, Surgeon-General, ii. 262, 274, 275.
Everitt, saved by Redvers Buller, ii. 69.
Eversley, i. 210.
Examination, i. 7.
,, Tactics in, i. 291.
Expedition against Sekukuni negatived, ii. 73.
Eyre, Arthur, i. 248, 257, 263, 275, 276, 277, 278, 279; ii. 2.
,, Colonel, ii. 1.
,, Sir William, i. 248, 321.

Fairy, H.M.S., i. 16.
Faisoo, i. 270.
Faisowah, i. 269-270.
Faku, ii. 8, 12, 18, 97.
Fanshawe, Captain H. D., ii. 195.
Fanti, Christmas dinner in, ii. 212
Farewell dinners, ii. 145, 261.
Farewell, Sir George, i. 269-270.
Farnborough Grange, i. 245.
Farnborough Station, lunch sent to, ii. 200.
Farquharson's, Mr., Hounds, i. 104.
Father, My, ii. 188.
Fatigues lessened, ii. 208.
Federation, Colonies, Australia, ii. 187.
Fellaheen conscripts, ii. 166.
Fenton, Sir Miles, ii. 216.
Filter, Rev. Mr., ii. 8.
Finglas, Dublin, i. 219.
Fingoe's Kraal, ii. 19.
Fingoes, i. 298, 302, 304, 308, 311, 312, 313, 314, 319; ii. 3.
Finlay, Surgeon-Major, ii. 218.
Firebrand, H.M.S., i. 33, 34.
Firoz Shah, i. 148, 161, 168, 195.
"First gun off," ii. 196.
Fish River Bush, i. 321.
Fishmongers' Company, ii. 86, 227.
Fitzgerald, Lord, i. 203.
Flanders, soldiers' language in, i. 236.
Fleets, Allied, i. 18, 20.
"Flying Column," ii. 73, 74, 76, 80, 84.
Fog in Black Sea, i. 22.
Folkestone, arrival at, i. 109.
Fontainebleau, i. 109.
Forage contractors raise demands, ii. 206.
Fordham, George, i. 133.
Foreign Legion, i. 115.
,, Service, soldiers leaving for, ii. 217.
Forlorn Hope at Badajos, i. 31.
Forstchen, i. 214.
Fort Beaufort, i. 295, 316.
,, Constantine, i. 25.
,, Hare (Alice), i. 317.
Fortescue, Colonel, ii. 123.
Fowler, Private, ii. 50, 61.
Fox Hills, Rifle ranges move, ii. 210.
Fox, Private, my servant, ii. 15.
Fractious, i. 230.
Franco-Prussian War, Lonsdale Hale's knowledge of, ii. 198.

Frazer, Major, ii. 135, 143, 144, 155.
Frederick the Great, i. 212.
French, Major, ii. 177, 208, 215.
French at Staff College, i. 209.
Frere, Sir Bartle, ii. 4, 9, 11, 26, 39, 44, 52, 85, 86, 90, 91, 92, 97, 105, 106, 212.
Frontier Light Horse, ii. 1, 36, 69, 70.
Frost, Commandant, i. 304, 306, 308.
Fund Insurance Beatson's Horse, i. 185, 194, 199.
Furious, H.M.S., i. 31.
Furse, Captain, i. 270, 281.
Fusilier Brigade, i. 250.
Fyz Ali Khan Beatson's Horse, i. 194.

Gaikas, i. 297, 298, 299, 300, 301, 302, 304, 305, 306, 309, 310, 312, 313, 314, 317, 319, 320, 321; ii. 7, 65, 94.
Gakdul Desert, ii. 169, 174, 175, 247.
Gale, great, i. 53, 54, 55, 56, 57.
Galekas, i. 297, 298.
Garaispur, i. 145.
Garrison, Aldershot, changed, ii. 213.
,, Artillery at Portsmouth, ii. 36.
,, ,, Shotley, ii. 184.
,, Instruction, i. 289.
Garth's Hounds, ii. 225.
Gatling Gun, i. 273.
Gatlings, ii. 81.
Gedareff, ii. 165.
General Post Office, soldiers doing work of, ii. 210.
"Gerade," ii. 153.
German at Staff College, i. 209.
,, Emperor, ii. 201, 202, 203, 211.
,, Legion, i. 300.
Ghaut, Khandala, ii. 118.
Gibraltar, i. 116; ii. 199, 227, 239.
Gladstone, Mr., ii. 116, 119, 122, 140, 141, 146, 152, 153.
,, Mrs., ii. 152.
Glamorganshire Yeomanry, ii. 268.
Glasgow, i. 247.
Glassite, A, i. 295.
Glover, Sir John, i. 287.
Glyn, George, M.P., i. 253.
Gnonyama, Gaika chief, i. 298.
Golden Horn, ii. 18.
Goodenough, Major, i. 245.
Goodwood, i. 290.
,, Cup, i. 208.

INDEX

Goona, i. 165, 187, 190, 193, 194.
Gordon, Boys' Home, ii. 213.
,,   Chinese, ii. 153.
,,   Highlanders, ii. 172.
,,   Lieutenant, i. 266, 271.
,,   Pasha, ii. 162, 163, 164, 179.
,,   Relief Expedition, ii. 170.
,,   Sir Henry, ii. 164.
,,   Sir William, i. 119, 121, 122, 125, 126, 127, 131, 133, 138, 142, 151, 156, 162.
Gordon's Hill, Sevastopol, i. 51.
Gosport, Discharge Depôt at, ii. 231.
Gough, Captain The Hon. George, ii. 148, 176.
Government House, ii. 112, 143, 218, 219.
Governor of Natal, ii. 144.
Governors' Wives, i. 258.
Grace, Pilgrimage of, i. 239.
Graham, Sir Gerald, ii. 165, 170.
,,   Sir Lumley, ii. 214.
Grammar School, Marlborough, i. 5.
Granada, visit to, ii. 192.
Grand Cross of St. Michael and St. George, ii. 148.
Grange, Farnborough, i. 215.
Grant-Hope, Sir, General, i. 246.
Grant, Major, ii. 166.
,,   Sir Hope, ii. 24.
Granville, Lord, ii. 153, 160, 161.
Grattan, Colonel, ii. 203, 206, 210, 229.
Graves, Lieutenant, i. 73, 92.
Great Britain, i. 117.
Green, Charles, death of, i. 70.
Green & Co., Merchant Navy, i. 7.
Grenfell, Lord, ii. 1, 3, 5, 156, 157, 159, 174, 180.
Grierson, General, ii. 262, 264, 265, 267.
Grove, Colonel, offer to go to South Africa, ii. 256.
Gurdon, Sir Brampton, ii. 135.
Gwaliar, i. 125, 126, 132, 134, 153, 162, 165, 199.
Gwili-Gwili Mountains, i. 300, 304, 305, 306, 308, 310.

Hackett, Brevet Major, ii. 27, 61, 62, 63, 64, 65, 66.
,,   Major, i. 315.
Haidarabad, i. 124, 184, 185.
Hale, Colonel Lonsdale, ii. 193, 198.

Halfa, cataracts, ii. 171.
Hallett, A Bluejacket, i. 49.
Hamed-Abu, i. 42.
Hamilton, Lieutenant, General Sir Ian, ii. 135, 217, 223.
,,   N. B., i. 288.
Hamley, General Sir E., i. 74, 215.
Hampden and Eliot, Boers' examples, ii. 106.
Hampshire manœuvres, ii. 217.
Handel's Dead March, i. 301.
Harcourt, Sir Vernon, ii. 148.
Harding, Adjutant, death of, i. 140, 141.
Hardinge, General Sir Arthur, ii. 191.
,,   Lord, i. 100.
Hardy, Michael, i. 70, 71, 89, 96.
Hareston Manor, near Plymouth, i. 1.
Hargreaves, John, M.F.H., ii. 266.
Harman, George, Colonel, i. 291.
Harness, Major, R.A., i. 318.
Harris, Mr., of West Court, ii. 224.
Harrison, Mr., ii. 231.
Hartingdon, Lord, ii. 152.
Hartley Row, i. 292.
Harwich, Garrison Artillery at, ii. 184.
Haussas, i. 260, 261, 262, 263, 265, 266.
Hayden's coffins, i. 273.
Haydn's Dictionary, i. 204.
Haynes Mill, Perie Bush, i. 309, 311, 318.
Hay's, Colonel, soldier-like resignation, ii. 239, 246, 247.
Head-dress thrown away, Crimea, i. 29.
Headquarters, Staff, ii. 74, 255.
Health statistics, Sierra Leone, ii. 275.
Heavy Dragoon Guards, their tunics, ii. 35.
Heidelberg, i. 204, 212; ii. 114, 122, 123.
Helpmakaar, ii. 70, 98.
Hemphill, Captain, ii. 150.
Henderson, Mr.,Transvaal, ii. 14, 15, 17.
,,   Colonel, ii. 198.
Hennessy, Lieutenant, his personal combat, i. 200.
Herbert, Arthur, General, i. 246, 291.
,,   A., Colonel, his views on Staff, ii. 188.
,,   Sir Robert, ii. 190.
Heussy, de, Comte Pontavice, ii. 213.
Hewett, V.C., K.C.B., i. 50, 277.

Hickman, Captain, his charge, ii. 165.
Hicks, Colonel, his troops, death, ii. 158, 161, 162.
Higginson, General, Sir George, ii. 222.
High Commissioner, ii. 32, 53, 68.
Highlanders, i. 152, 156.
Hildyard, Colonel, ii. 199, 207, 218.
Himalayas, i. 199.
Hindustani, i. 118, 120, 202, 209.
,, interpreter in, ii. 159.
"Hit, Hit, Hit," ii. 196.
H'Lubi's black soldiers, their escape, ii. 145.
Hodson's Horse, i. 194, 199.
Holker, Sir John, ii. 94.
Holyhead, cycle ride to, ii. 215.
Home, Colonel, ii. 90.
,, Robert, Major, i. 246, 272, 273.
Hong Kong, i. 219.
Horned owls, i. 22.
Horse Artilleryman, pride, ii. 262.
,, Artillery only required, Transvaal, ii. 141.
,, Guards, i. 207.
,, Insurance Fund, Irregular Cavalry, i. 185, 194, 199.
Horsford, General Sir Alfred, ii. 27, 194.
,, Sir Alfred, i. 222, 233.
Hotham, Lieutenant, ii. 26.
Hottentots, i. 296.
Howard, Sir Charles, ii. 270.
Hudson, Dr., i. 219.
Hughenden Manor, visit to, ii. 88, 90.
Hughes, Mr., ii. 29, 44.
Hull, soldiers sent by, ii. 230.
Hungry Hill, i. 254.
Hunter, Sir Archibald, ii. 156.
Hussars, 8th, i. 137, 138, 143.
,, a patrol of, ii. 111.
Hutton, Lieutenant-Colonel Edward, ii. 207.
Hyde Park Corner, ii. 236.
Hythe, ii. 209.

Ibabanango, ii. 76.
Ilchester, Lord, ii. 272, 273.
Ilsley Downs, ii. 214.
Impetuous Horse, riding with hounds, ii. 249.
Incandu River, ii. 19, 117.
Inchanga Mountain, ii. 102.

Inconstant, H.M.S., i. 11.
India, Central, i. 127; ii. 133, 250.
Indore, i. 118.
Industrial Schools, ii. 135.
Infantry, European, i. 129.
,, as cyclists, ii. 215.
Ingagane River, ii. 19, 109, 117.
Ingogo River, ii. 107, 117.
Inhambane, ii. 145.
Inhlazatse, ii. 126.
Inhlazatze Mountain, ii. 102.
Inhlobane, ii. 31, 32, 43, 45, 46, 48, 58, 60, 63, 68, 84, 100, 135.
Inkerman, i. 50.
Inniskilling Dragoons, ii. 114.
Inspector General of Fortifications, ii. 194.
Instruction Garrison, i. 289.
Insurance Fund Horse, Native Cavalry, i. 185, 194, 199.
Intaba Indoda, i. 34, 300, 313.
Intombe River, ii. 38, 44, 46.
Ireland, journey to, ii. 241.
Irish Rifles, their long ride, ii. 215.
Irish Times at Turkeenagh, i. 227.
Isandwhlana, ii. 31, 60, 68, 80, 143, 144, 145.
Island of St. Vincent, i. 118.
"Island, Wilton, The," ii. 268.
Isle of Man Governorship, ii. 146, 148.
,, Wight, i. 9.
Ismailia, ii. 159.
Itilezi, ii. 75.
Ityatosi, ii. 54, 100, 102, 143.
Ityenteka Range Nek, ii. 30, 31, 54.
Ixopo, ii. 6.

"Jacky," my master, ii. 190.
Jalna, i. 124, 145.
Jalra Palun, i. 127, 148.
Jaora, i. 127, 148.
Jaroor Ali, i. 161.
"Jemmy" of the Fleet prison, ii. 126.
Jenkins, Mr., Pondoland, ii. 4.
,, Mrs., ii. 5, 6.
Jerusalem, i. 212.
Jervis, Captain, i. 110.
Jhansi, i. 127.
Jones, Miss, ii. 249.
,, Sir Harry, i. 69.
,, Hugh, Colonel, i. 206.
Jorissen, Mr., ii. 134.

INDEX

Joubert, Piet, ii. 22, 96, 105, 106, 107, 109, 114, 117, 119, 121.

Kabousie Nek, i. 304.
Kadi, i. 146.
„ Koi, i. 35.
Kaffraria, British, i. 296.
Kafirland, i. 298.
Kafirs, i. 313.
Kafr Dowar, ii. 149, 152.
Kala Sind River, i. 92.
Kalamita Bay, i. 27.
Kambula, ii. 36, 44, 50, 70, 72, 80, 81, 84, 85, 94, 96, 98, 99, 199.
Kamiesh Bay, i. 33, 44, 62.
Kanhpur, i. 127.
Kankroli, i. 160.
Katcha River, i. 27, 55.
Katra, i. 191.
Kavarna Bay, i. 21-23, 27.
Kazatch, i. 97.
Keate award, ii. 130.
Kei River, i. 304.
„ Road, ii. 1, 3.
Keiskama Hoek, i. 299, 301, 304.
Kelvin, Lord, ii. 228.
Kempt Mount, i. 301, 311, 321.
Kennet River, ii. 223.
Kensington Park, ii. 164.
Kent, Duke, Duchess of, i, 2.
Keyser, Miss Agnes, ii. 229, 245.
Khandala, i. 118.
Khandeish, i. 147.
Khartoum, ii. 158, 161, 162, 163, 164, 174, 278.
Khedive, ii. 155, 159, 160, 162.
Kilchipur, i. 149.
Kimberley, Lord, ii. 106, 107, 108, 109, 110, 115, 116, 118, 119, 120, 121, 123, 124, 125, 126, 127, 128, 144.
King, Tom, Sierra Leone, ii. 275.
„ William's Town, i. 248, 296, 305, 320; ii. 4, 36.
„ Lieutenant, i. 40, 41.
King's gracious letter, ii. 262, 278.
Kingsley, Rev. Charles, i. 210.
Kipling, Mr., ii. 265.
Kirkcudbright, i. 119, 205.
Kirki, i. 118, 121, 123, 124, 162, 165, 168.
Kitchener, Lord, ii. 156, 256, 257.
Knight, Major Lewis, i. 156, 157, 158.

II.—19

Koh-i-noor Battery, i. 39, 47.
Kokstadt, ii. 1, 4, 5, 6.
Kordofan, ii. 162.
Korosko, ii. 169, 178, 181.
Korti, ii. 174, 177, 178.
Kossoos, i. 262, 263.
Kota City, i. 155, 156.
Kreli, i. 321.
Kremlin, ii. 184.
Kruger, Mr., ii. 22, 96, 105, 110, 115, 117, 118, 119, 134, 142, 241.
Kwamagasa, ii. 98.

Laager at Utrecht, ii. 8, 34.
Ladysmith, ii. 108, 127, 244.
Lakanwas, i. 195.
Lakuni, Author's Zulu name, ii. 54, 84, 136.
Lalitpur, i. 136.
Lambart, Captain, ii. 124.
Lancaster Gun, i. 5, 61.
Lancers, 12th, i. 243.
„ 17th, i. 129, 131, 133, 138, 149, 150, 151, 152, 153, 159, 161, 162, 205; ii. 75.
Land League, Irish, ii. 182.
Landdrost, ii. 18, 25.
Landtman's Drift, ii. 76.
Langotis, i. 139.
Lang's Nek, ii. 7, 107, 121, 122, 130.
Lansdowne, Lord, ii. 232, 234, 238, 239, 241, 251, 252.
Lawson, Major, ii. 231.
„ Mr., A. and N. Co-op. Society, i. 285.
Laye, Captain, i. 319; ii. 63.
Leaders, Boer, ii. 142.
Leahy, Major, i. 246.
Leander, H.M.S., i. 66, 67, 70, 76.
Learmouth, Major, i. 118.
Lebombo Mountains, ii. 136.
Leet, Major, V.C., ii. 46, 54, 55.
Lefroy's Handbook, i. 135.
Legge, Captain Norton, ii. 224.
Legion, Foreign, i. 135.
Lendy, Captain, i. 203, 204, 208.
Lennard, Sir Thomas, i. 217, 228, 240, 286; ii. 86, 88, 234.
„ Lady, ii. 94.
Lewes, Yeomanry at, ii. 268.
Liddington, Rector of, ii. 224.
Lie, My last, ii. 190.

INDEX

Light Infantry, 13th, ii. 73, 79.
,, ,, 90th, i. 313, 321; ii. 31, 79, 84.
Lincoln and Bennett, i. 285.
,, Militia, ii. 267.
Lindsay, Robt. Lloyd, ii. 212.
"Lines," Kafr Dowar, ii. 142.
Lion King, i. 24.
Lisbon, i. 3.
,, King of, ii. 190.
Litany, i. 210.
Lithgow, Surgeon-General, ii. 181.
Lively, H.M.S., i. 3.
Liverpool, visit to, ii. 235.
Lloyd, Llewellyn, ii. 42, 44, 47, 48, 49, 50.
Logue, Cardinal, ii. 241.
Lomax, Colonel S., ii. 267, 286.
London Companies, watchmen over horses, ii. 210.
London Corn Exchange, ii. 206.
London, H.M.S., i. 27, 72.
London, soldiers sent by, ii. 230.
Londonderry, ii. 183.
Long distance rides instituted, ii. 183.
Long Hill, Aldershot, i. 243.
,, Valley, Aldershot, i. 225; ii. 266.
Lonsdale, Rupert, i. 299, 301, 305, 306, 307, 311, 313, 314, 315, 319, 320, 321.
Lord Mayor, i. 287.
Lorenzo Marques, stay at, ii. 145.
Lotiti, ii. 126, 136.
Lotus, stern whaler, ii. 172.
Low Church, a colonel, i. 242.
Lowe, Sir General Drury, ii. 196.
Luck, General G., ii. 241.
Lucknow, ii. 10.
Luneberg, ii. 8, 9, 10, 11, 12, 18, 34, 35, 38, 45, 46, 54, 70, 97.
Lushington, Sir Stephen, i. 33, 59, 60, 61, 72, 75, 97, 114, 120.
Lydford Rifle range, ii. 266.
Lyndenburg Garrison, ii. 106.
Lyons, Lord, i. 114.
Lysons, Lieutenant Harry, ii. 18, 19, 20, 26, 47, 48, 50, 51, 61, 76.
,, Sir Daniel, General, i. 254, 293.

Mabamba's Kraal, ii. 135.
Macaula, Baca Chief, ii. 4.
Mackenzie's Farm, i. 32.
Mackinnon, Sir William, ii. 212, 213.
Maclean, Commandant, i. 319.
Macleod, Colonel, i. 275, 280.
,, Norman, ii. 39.
Macomo, Tini, i. 298, 299, 314, 315.
McElnea, Tenant, i. 226.
McGregor, a Colonist, ii. 1.
McLeod, Captain, Political Agent, ii. 18.
,, Colonel, i. 275, 280.
McNaughten, Captain, death, i. 318, 319.
McPherson, Cluny, Colonel, i. 275.
Madeira, i. 297.
Madhoo, Singh, i. 178, 190, 193, 194.
Magazine at Shottey, ii. 185.
,, Rifles, Permanent or detachable, ii. 186.
Mahableshwar, i. 121.
Mahdi and his soldiers, ii. 166, 179.
Maidenhead, i. 205.
Major General, half pay as, 147.
Major White, 17th Lancers, i. 162.
Majuba, ii. 92, 145.
Makabalikile Ridge, i. 312, 315, 316.
Makulusi, ii. 2, 9, 31, 32, 42, 43, 63, 72.
Malakoff, i. 36, 39. 40, 42, 51, 61, 69, 72, 73, 82, 86.
Malet, Sir Edward, ii. 151, 159, 160.
Mallow, i. 224.
Malta, Home tour station, ii, 239.
,, to train Mounted Infantry, ii. 250.
Mamelon, i. 36, 39, 40, 51, 61, 78, 79, 80.
Mampon, i. 261.
Mandara, wish to attack, 154.
Manitoban, S.S., i. 284.
Manning, Cardinal, ii. 146, 148.
Manœuvres, Cavalry, ii. 223.
Manœuvres in Hampshire, ii. 217.
Mansion House, cycling accident at, ii. 236.
Mantle, Lieutenant, ii. 157.
Manual exercises, curtailed, ii. 253.
Manyoba, ii. 12, 38.
March, Captain, i. 52.
Margam Park, Yeomanry at, ii. 268.
Margate, leave for, i. 244.
Marines, i. 12.
Maritzburg, i. 321; ii. 6, 10, 23, 35, 38, 46, 72, 84, 85, 97, 102, 108, 111, 115, 135, 137, 143.

INDEX

Markham, Frank, i. 233.
Marlborough College, i. 7, 113, 204.
,, ,, speech day, ii. 189.
,, Duke of, i. 215.
,, Grammar School, i. 5.
Married Roll, Artillery, ii. 265, 266.
Marshal, Junot, i. 2.
Marshall, Sir George, ii. 248.
Martini-Henry Rifles, ii. 60.
Masipula, ii. 101.
Mason, Confederate Commissioner, i. 207.
Massowah, Red Sea Littoral, ii. 164.
Master Butcher, ii. 207.
Master General of the Ordnance, ii. 185.
Mat, Bastion du, i. 74.
Matapan, Cape, i. 17.
Mathematics, i. 208, 209, 231.
Mau, i. 122, 123, 125, 127, 147, 161, 162, 166.
Maude, Captain, ii. 14, 15, 16, 17, 18, 61, 63, 66, 71.
Mauldslie Castle, i. 149.
Maundsar, i. 149.
Maun Singh, i. 164, 165.
Maurice, General Sir Frederick, ii. 228.
Max Müller, Dr., i. 205.
May, Major, ii. 228.
Mayne, H. O., Major, i. 135, 165, 169, 188.
Mayne's Horse, i. 187, 191, 192.
Meade, Major, i. 164.
Meath Hospital, i. 219.
Mecca, ii. 163.
Mediterranean, moving three Battalions from England, ii. 242.
Meek's Farm. ii. 21.
Melampus, H.M.S., i. 12.
Melbury, ii. 272.
Melokazulu, ii. 28, 54, 99.
Menagerie, Nawab's, i. 148.
Metemmeh, ii. 176.
Methuen, Lord, ii. 222.
Metropolitan Police, ii. 270.
Michel, Sir John, i. 125, 135, 136, 141, 155, 162, 166, 169, 179, 202; ii. 188.
Michell, Charles, i. 3.
,, Frederick, i. 2, 11, 20, 25, 32. 56, 97, 98.
,, Sampson, i. 2, 3.
Midland Railway, Tidworth, ii. 263.

Mildmay, Sir Henry, i. 243.
Miles Hill, Aldershot, i. 243.
Miles—On the Horse's feet, i. 174.
Military Education, Council of, i. 290.
,, Exercises, antiquated, ii. 251.
,, Kraal, Transvaal, ii. 6.
,, Secretary, i. 295.
,, ,, offers Colonial appointment, ii. 187.
,, ,, My letter to, on Major Hackett, ii. 65.
Militia Battalion Canteen profits, ii. 185.
Mill Street, i. 224.
Milman, Dean, i. 206.
Milo, i. 17.
Milton, Major, ii. 239, 242.
Mirath, i. 199.
Misfortune, Land of, ii. 105.
Misunderstandings, "Land of," ii. 105.
Mkusi River, ii. 39.
Mnyamane, ii. 80, 100, 125.
Moltke, Count Von, ii. 244.
Monastery, St. George, i. 82.
Mongroulee, i. 135.
Montgomeryshire Yeomanry, ii. 270.
Mooi River, ii. 142.
Moore, Dr. Norman, i. 3; ii. 249.
,, Sir John, ii. 190.
Moorsom, Captain, i. 62.
Morar, i. 162.
Morris, Colonel, i. 120, 155, 190.
Morrogh, Leonard, i. 230.
Mortar Shell, i. 67.
Mortlake, i. 202.
Moslems, Sunday, ii. 158.
Mount Edgcumbe, i. 20.
,, Frere, ii. 3,
,, Wise, i. 10, 20.
Mounted Infantry, i. 251; ii. 177, 252.
Mowbray, Sir John, ii. 228.
Moysey, Major, ii. 18.
Mozambique, ii. 145.
Mullingar, i. 218.
Mulloob Khan, i. 190.
Munich, i. 214.
Murdoch, Burn, Major, ii. 226.
Murray, Captain, Consul, ii. 229,
,, Lindley, ii. 25.
,, Major, i. 200, 201.
Musooda, i. 158.

Mutiny, India, i. 118, 251.
Mutton Cove, i. 10.

Nakimoff, Admiral, i. 79.
Nana Sahib, i. 127.
Nantes, i. 4.
Napier, Robert of Magdala, i. 227.
,, Sir Charles, i. 216.
,, Sir Robert, i. 126.
,, William, Colonel, i. 216, 218, 219, 230.
,, W., General, i. 293.
Napier's Peninsula War, vol. vi. 391, i. 105.
Napoleon, i. 212.
,, Code, ii. 157.
Narbada, i. 125, 145, 147, 148.
Narsinghar, i. 162, 191, 194, 195, 196.
Natal, ii. 76, 100, 114, 123, 126, 136, 142.
,, Carabineers, ii. 145.
,, Government of Zulu reports to, ii. 68.
,, Governor of, ii. 95, 144, 194.
,, Police, ii. 143.
Native Cavalry Regiment, i. 137.
Naturalistic accuracy, ii. 233.
Naval Brigade, i. 35, 36, 37, 38, 39, 40, 41, 42, 43, 44, 45, 46, 47, 48, 49, 57, 58, 59, 60, 76.
,, Instructor, i. 20.
Nawab's Menagerie, i. 148.
Ned, Uncle, i. 108.
Negropont, i. 17.
Nek, Ityenteka, ii. 31.
Nenagh, i. 227.
Netley Hospital, ii. 262, 266.
Newbridge, i. 115, 116.
Newcastle, ii. 10, 20, 21, 44, 72, 98, 108, 111, 114, 115, 117, 121, 127.
Newdigate, General, ii. 73, 74, 79.
Newspaper and Press Fund dinner, ii. 237.
Ngaba Ka Hawane Mountain, ii. 33, 59.
Ngobamakosi Regiment, ii. 53, 54, 61, 62, 99.
Nicholson, Lieutenant, Death of, ii. 59.
,, General, ii. 258.
Niel, General, i. 62.
Night Lights, ii. 233.
,, Marches, ii. 183.
,, Manœuvres, ii. 222.

Nile, Cataracts on, ii. 173.
Ninetieth Light Infantry, i. 250, 286.
Nixon, Captain, i. 306.
Nkonjane Hill, Zululand, ii. 29.
Nodwengu Regiment, ii. 32.
Nolan, i. 123.
Nondweni River, ii. 76, 78.
North Devon Yeomanry, ii. 269.
Northcote, Sir Stafford, ii. 161.
Nubar Pasha, ii. 161.
"Number 20" in Pickwick, ii. 126.

Ober-Ammergau, ii. 205, 214.
Odessa, i. 21.
Officers' Club House, ii. 195.
Officers, increase in establishment of, ii. 252.
Ordah, i. 279.
Ordasu, i. 279, 280, 281.
Ordnance Stores, Aldershot, ii. 184.
Osborne House, command to, ii. 103.
,, Mr., ii. 100, 101.
Oscott, i. 104.
Osman Digna, ii. 161.
Otto Emil, Grammar, i. 205.
Ouchy, i. 212.
Ouless, Mr., ii. 255.
Owls, horned, i. 22.
Oxford, i. 205.

Paarde Kop, accident near, ii. 122.
Pachmarlie Hills, i. 147.
Pachor, i. 195.
Pack, Colonel, i. 116, 117.
Paget, Major, coolness in action, i. 151.
Paliso, interpreter, ii. 8, 16.
Palki Dak, i. 199.
Panmure, Lord, ii. 100.
Parbati River, i. 135, 177.
Parke, Colonel, i. 147, 148.
Parker, Dr., i. 219.
Parkes, Dr., i. 223.
Parndon Woods, Essex, ii. 249.
Parr, Hallam, Major-General, ii. 156, 158.
Parsons, Mr., i. 87.
,, Sir Charles, i. 195.
,, Sir C., Major-General, ii. 156, 165, 195.
Passages, Spain, i. 4.
Passion Play, ii. 214.
Patriotic Fund, i. 11.

INDEX

Patun Jalra, i. 127, 128.
Paulina Southwell, i. 250, 251.
Pavilion, Royal, i. 243.
Paymaster, ii. 207.
Peace and Show Soldiers, ii. 194.
Pearson, Colonel, ii. 85.
Peel, Sir Robert, i. 25.
,, Captain Sir William, ii. 229.
,, Sir William, i. 25, 41, 42, 43, 45, 46, 47, 49, 51, 52, 53, 59, 62, 65, 66, 71, 75, 78, 80, 84, 85, 86, 87, 88, 89, 92, 93, 100, 101, 114, 117.
Peerage, or Court-Martial, ii. 191.
Pélissier, General, i. 83, 97.
Pembroke, Lord, ii. 268.
Pemvane River, ii. 30.
Pender, Lady, ii. 217.
,, Sir John, ii. 205, 213, 228.
Pennyfather, General Sir John, i. 239.
Penrith, dialects, ii. 153.
Penton Lodge, ii. 263.
Penzance, ii. 266.
,, Lord, Commission, ii. 93.
Perie Bush, i. 308, 321 ; ii. 8.
Permanent, or Detachable magazine, ii. 186.
Perrier, Jouet champagne, ii. 5.
Perseverance, H.M.S., i. 99.
Persian Minister, ii. 167.
Perth City, i. 250, 251.
Perthshire, 73rd Regiment, i. 205, 248.
Philæ, ii. 169.
Pickwick repeated, ii. 126.
Pieter-Maritzburg, ii. 7, 94.
"Pig, The," i. 119, 137, 178.
Pilgrimage of Grace, i. 239.
Pimlico, coats from, ii. 233.
Pirbright, ii. 210.
Plevna, ii. 222.
Pluton, i. 55.
Plymouth, i. 7.
,, arrival at, ii. 86.
,, I knew, ii. 264.
"Pocket Hercules," i. 120.
,, Siphonia, ii. 75.
Political Agent for North Zululand, ii. 78.
Pollard, Lieutenant, R.N., i. 271.
Polo in Egypt, ii. 165.
Pondo Queen, ii. 4.
Pondos, ii. 4, 5.

Pongola River, ii. 14.
,, Valley, ii. 11.
Ponsonby, Sir Henry, i. 243.
Pontavice, Comte, de Heussy, ii. 213.
Pony, my, i. 99.
Poole, Lieutenant, killed, ii. 55.
Poona, i. 120, 121, 125, 168.
Port Admiral, i. 11.
Port Said, Home's scheme for a fort, ii. 90.
Portal, Mr., ii. 219.
Porter, Dr., i. 233.
Portland, ii. 264.
Portsea, i. 7.
Portsmouth, i. 7 ; ii. 264, 271.
,, Lord, Yachting, ii. 228.
,, Military Hospital at, ii. 270.
Portugal, i. 2.
Potchefstroom, ii. 106, 114, 117, 123.
Potter, Mr., ii. 47, 53, 72.
Potter's Store, ii. 9, 54.
Potton, deputation from, i. 101.
Prague, i. 214.
Prahsu, i. 272, 273 ; ii. 212.
Premier, dominant will of, ii. 115.
"Present Arms," i. 245.
Pretoria, ii. 43, 70, 114, 123, 126, 128, 129, 132, 134, 141.
Pretorius, Andries, ii. 21, 22, 33, 122.
Prime Minister, Egypt, ii. 167.
Prince Consort, i. 292.
,, Imperial, ii. 72, 74, 79, 86, 102, 143.
,, of Wales, ii. 227.
Prince Regent, H.M.S., i. 16.
,, S.S., loss of, i. 55.
"Private Affairs," leave for, i. 244.
Prospect Camp, ii. 107, 110, 111, 112, 116, 122.
,, Mount, ii. 107, 108, 119.
Public Schools' camp at Aldershot, ii. 217.
,, Volunteer Cadet Companies, ii. 221.
Purtabghar, i. 148.
Pym, Boer model, ii. 106.

Quarries, i. 85, 86, 94.
Queen, H.M.S., i. 8, 9, 16, 20, 21, 27, 31, 44, 55, 58, 60, 62, 293 ; ii. 219.
Queen Victoria, Her Majesty, i. 16, 239, 242, 243, 293.

INDEX

Queenstown, i. 13, 304.
Quillimane, ii. 145.
Quinn, Wyndham, Colonel, ii. 269.

Raad Volks, ii. 141, 142.
Raaf Colonist, ii. 58.
Rabula Heights, i. 304, 306, 313.
Raglan, Lord, i. 27. 100.
,, his horses lost, i. 30, 50, 51, 62, 63, 65, 69, 80, 83, 86, 87, 88, 97, 98, 100.
Railway Clearing House, Euston, ii. 216.
Rajghur, i. 129, 146.
Ramleh, Egypt, ii. 151, 152.
Randall, Trooper, saved by Redvers Buller, ii. 69.
Ranston, i. 253.
Rao Sahib, i. 127, 168, 193, 194.
Rawson, Private, i. 255.
Reading, i. 225.
Rectory at Liddington, ii. 224.
Red Cross Society, ii. 244.
,, River Expedition, ii. 187.
,, Sea Littoral, and Massowah, ii. 164.
Redan, i. 36, 39, 40, 42, 71, 86, 96.
Redding Point, i. 20.
Redhill, i. 232.
Refugees from Zululand, ii. 41, 43.
Regiment, 80th, ii. 70.
Regimental transport, ii. 6, 35.
Religion, Horse Artillery man wishes to change, ii. 265.
Rennie, Captain, V.C., i. 248.
Resident in Pretoria, ii. 142.
,, in Zululand, offer to be, ii. 29.
Restaurant opened at War Office, ii. 253.
Rest-house in Delta, ii. 166.
Retrocession of Transvaal, ii. 134.
Rheims, Colbert born at, ii. 91.
Rhein Pfalz, ii. 202.
Rhyader Range, ii. 277.
Richmond, Lieutenant, i. 258, 262, 270, 271.
Ridge, Lieutenant, i. 46.
Righi, i. 24.
Rimington, Brigadier General, ii. 201.
Rivenhall, i. 231.
Robb, Colonel, ii. 248.
Roberts, Lord, ii. 115, 198, 217, 223, 244, 254, 256, 258, 259, 264, 271.
Robinson, Colonel C. W., Aldershot, ii. 207.

Robinson, Sir Hercules, ii. 106, 118, 127, 130.
,, Sir John, i. 46.
Rogers, Doctor, ii. 166.
,, Major, V.C., i. 288.
Ronald Campbell, The Hon. Mrs., ii. 96.
Ropes, Mr. John, Historian, ii. 227, 228.
Rorke, Mr., ii. 41.
Rorke's Drift, ii. 29, 71, 143.
Rose, Sir Hugh, i. 119, 124, 126, 196, 200, 201, 222.
Rosse, Shakespeare, ii. 87.
Roubi Tewhari, Gordon's Secretary, ii. 162, 163, 164
Round robin, i. 185.
Royal Coronation White cattle, ii. 80.
,, Engineers, night sentries, ii. 210.
,, Kraal, Zulu, ii. 32.
,, Scots Fusiliers, 21st, ii. 144.
Rudolph, Mr., ii. 10, 73, 98, 136.
Rugeley, i. 254.
Rundle, Lieutenant H. M. L., ii. 81, 156.
Russell, Baker, i. 272.
,, Sir William, i. 63.
Russell's Regiment, i. 273, 274.
Russia, War scare, ii. 92.
Russo-Japanese War, ii. 264.
Rustenberg, ii. 117, 134.
Rustum, Ali Khan, i. 194, 195.
Rutlam, i. 147.

Sagar, i. 119, 124, 136.
St. George's Chapel, sailors drew Queen's coffin up to, ii. 256.
St. Helen's, i. 16; ii. 86.
St. John River, ii. 137.
St. Paul's Cathedral, i. 207.
St. Remo, ii. 218.
St. Thomas' Hospital, i. 108.
St. Vincent, Island of, i. 118.
Salisbury Plain, ii. 241, 262, 275, 276.
,, settled I should go to, ii. 258.
Salmond, Major, ii. 209.
Saltmarshe, Lieutenant, Death of, i. 316, 317.
Saltmarshe, ii. 66.
Sampson, H.M.S., i. 30.
Sanctuary, Mr., mate, i. 32, 38, 48.
Sandeman, Captain, ii. 144.
Sandhurst, Change in inspection at, ii. 251.

INDEX

Sandhurst College, i. 37, 166, 289; ii. 194, 254, 262.
Sandilli, i. 248, 297, 298, 308, 314, 320, 321.
Sandilli's Krantz, i. 300.
Sandy, i. 101.
San Stefano, ii. 92.
Sardinian Army, i. 75, 76.
Sarthal, i. 149.
Saunderson, Colonel E., M.P., ii. 183.
Scarlett, Hon. Sir James Yorke, i. 222, 243; ii. 206.
School of Cookery, ii. 211.
Schudi Pasha, ii. 156, 157.
Scindia, i. 164.
Scindia's Treasury. i. 126.
Scotland, ii. 153.
Scott, Dr., ii. 96.
Scotter, Sir Charles, ii. 216, 231.
Scutari, i. 101, 107, 108, 110, 241.
Seagrove, Messrs. W. E., i. 102.
Seamen Gunners, i. 12.
Seaton, Lord, i. 115, 116.
Secretary of General Post Office, ii. 210.
,, of State for War, ii. 148, 253.
Sehore, i. 119, 124, 149.
Seketwayo, ii. 29.
Sekukuni, ii. 22, 73, 83, 132.
Self-Government, Kruger's aims, ii. 105.
Sentries, ii. 182.
Sergeant Smith, i. 317.
Sevastopol, i. 25, 32, 33, 50, 51, 55, 100, 110, 117.
Sewell's Yard, i. 230.
Seyolo, i. 308, 311, 312, 313, 315, 316, 318, 321.
Shah Firoz, i. 193.
Shakespeare, quotation from, ii. 95.
,, Sir Richard, i. 192.
Shamsabad, i. 175, 187, 190.
Shaporah, i. 158.
Shephard, John, i. 66.
Shepstone, Sir Theophilus, i. 295; ii. 24, 26, 101.
Sherborne, hired lodgings at, ii. 266.
Shorncliffe, i. 289.
Shotley Magazine Guard, ii. 184.
Sick Report, ii. 275.
Sierra Leone, Company stationed at, ii. 275.
,, ,, men, ii. 83.
Signal Midshipman, i. 32.

"Silence and Death," Colonist's heroism, ii. 145.
Silidar System, i. 128.
Silver, Sergeant, i. 128.
Simferopol, i. 100.
Simmonds, Able Seaman, i. 49.
Simoom, H.M.S., i. 266, 267.
Sindhara, i. 168, 177, 174, 180, 193.
Sindwaha, i. 136.
Sinope, i. 18.
Sipri Column, i. 137.
Sirayo, ii. 28, 31, 80, 98, 99, 100.
Sirayo's son, ii. 54.
Sironj, i. 162, 187, 190.
Sitapur, i. 199.
Sivewrights, ii. 143.
Siwani, i. 311.
Siward, Shakespeare, ii. 86.
Skene, Mr., i. 167.
Skreens Park near Chelmsford, hunting at, ii. 249.
Slade, Lieutenant, ii. 59, 95, 99, 135, 137, 144, 155.
Sladen, Mr., ii. 194.
Slater, Mr. Dundas, ii. 240.
Slidell, i. 207.
Smidt, Boer General, ii. 122, 123.
Smith, Colonel, W. W. R.G.A., ii. 277.
,, Dr., i. 107.
,, Lieutenant, ii. 61, 66.
,, Percy, Captain, i. 107, 110.
,, Sir Holled, General, ii. 156.
Smith's Battalion, ii. 169.
Smith-Dorrien, Lieutenant H. S., ii. 146, 151, 156, 266.
Smithfield pig market, ii. 183.
Sobuza's Kraal, ii. 100, 102.
Somerset, General, i. 151, 158.
,, Light Infantry, 1st, ii. 199.
Soosneer, i. 128.
Sound, Plymouth, i. 20.
Southampton, i. 223.
,, Empress leaves, ii. 95.
South Africa, deprived of pay while there with the Empress, ii. 261.
,, ,, offer to go to, ii. 251.
South America, offer to go to, ii. 261.
Southwell, Paulina, i. 211, 225, 226.
,, Viscount, i. 202, 203, 205, 210, 237.
Spain, i. 4.
Spartan, H.M.S., i. 12.

INDEX

Spectacular parades, ii. 203.
Spider, journey in, ii. 21, 98.
Spithead, i. 20.
Spy, a, i. 130.
Staff College, i. 290 ; ii. 148.
,, ,, Graduates kept up drag hounds, ii. 260.
Staff Rides in Essex, ii. 240.
Stafford Northcote, M.P., ii. 116.
Standerton, ii. 123.
Stanhope, Hon. Edward, ii. 90, 192.
Stanley, Private, i. 108.
,, the Explorer, ii, 205, 212.
State Attorney, Transvaal, ii. 134.
Stavodale, Lady Helen, ii. 272.
Steele, Sir Thomas, i. 97.
Steeplechase course, i. 243.
Stephenson, Sir Frederick, General, ii. 166.
Stevens, Captain, i. 316, 317 ; ii. 66.
Stewart, Sir Herbert, ii. 174.
Stirling Castle, i. 247, 251.
Stockbridge, ii. 220.
Stondon Place, near Ongar, called at with Lord Roberts, ii. 258.
Stonyhurst, i. 104.
Stopford, General Sir Fred., ii. 243.
Stormberg, action at, ii. 243.
Stour and Orwell Rivers, confluence of, ii. 184.
Strathcona and Mount Royal, Lord, ii. 248, 249.
Streatfield, Frank, i. 302, 306, 311, 313, 315.
Stringer, Private, ii. 15, 17.
Strong, Lieutenant, ii. 62.
Stuart-Smith, Captain, i. 317, 318.
Suakin, ii. 161, 162, 165, 167.
Sudan, ii. 158, 162, 163.
,, Bureau, ii. 164.
Suffolk Regiment, ii. 198.
Sujnaur River, i. 142.
Suleiman, son of Zebehr, ii. 164.
Sully, a great Minister, ii. 91.
Sunbury, i. 203, 204, 212.
Supplies, ii. 7.
Surgeon General, consulted *re* visual efficiency of soldiers, ii. 276.
Surveyor-General, ii. 160.
Sutah, i. 269.
Sutton, Mr., and Lady Susan, ii. 263.
Suzerainty, British, ii. 118.

Swallow, H.M.S., i. 62.
Swazi States, ii. 108.
Swazis, ii. 11, 43, 46, 76.
Swinburne-Henry carbine, ii. 61.
Swiss, Colbert a, ii. 91.
Switzerland Saxon, i. 212, 214.
Syllabus, garrison instruction of, i. 289.
Sylvester, John Henry, Dr., i. 174.
Symonds, Sir William, i. 21.
Syrian coast, i. 25.

Tactics, Examiner in, i. 291.
Tagus River, 2.
Talbot, Lord Edmund, M.P., ii. 228.
,, Miss, ii. 269.
Tamai, action at, ii. 165.
Tantia Topi, i. 126, 127, 129, 134, 135, 136, 145, 147, 148, 150, 152, 158, 165, 182.
Tantia's Cavalry, i. 138.
Tapley, Mark, named Colonel Grierson, ii. 264.
Tarkan, Cape, i. 29.
Tattersall's, i. 225.
Taunton Barracks, inspection of, ii. 265.
Tchernaya River, i. 31, 33, 75.
Tchorgoum, i. 75.
Tchungwassa, ii. 3.
Telegraph Battalion, ii. 209.
Tel-el-Kebir, i. 215 ; ii. 147, 152, 154.
Tell-tale clock, ii. 185.
Temperance League, ii. 148.
Tennyson, Lord, i. 49.
Terrible, H.M.S., i. 22.
"The Pig," i. 119, 137.
Therapia, i. 20, 99.
Thesiger, General, the Hon. F., i. 295, 296, 297, 298, 309, 318, 322 ; ii. 4, 6, 7, 9, 92.
Thionville, i. 247.
Thirteenth Light Dragoons, i. 100.
Thurlow, Captain, ii. 63.
Tidworth Barracks, ii. 262, 263.
,, tactical operations, ii. 260.
Tiger, H.M.S., i. 22.
Tinta's Kraal, ii. 30, 100.
Tipnor Magazine, ii. 262, 270, 271.
Tittlebat Titmouse, ii. 183.
Todleben, General, i. 74, 97.
To-morrow "Bukra," ii. 167.
Tontea, The, i. 177, 182, 195.
Torbay, i. 16.

INDEX 297

Torres Vedras, ii. 191.
Totnes, i. 11.
Toulouse, i. 3.
Townspeople of Utrecht, ii. 25.
Toynbee, Mr., i. 202.
Tractir Bridge, i. 76.
Trader, in Zululand, ii. 70.
Trafalgar, H.M.S., i. 26.
Transkei District, i. 311.
,, Fingoes, i. 312, 313.
Transport officers, ii. 76.
Transvaal, ii. 22, 29, 71, 96, 115, 118, 128, 134, 136.
Travers, Colonel, i. 198.
Treasury, ii. 147, 260.
,, Lords of, ii. 230.
,, Scindia's, i. 126.
Tremayne, Captain and Brevet-Major, i. 103, 104, 113, 169.
Tremlett, Major, ii. 59.
Treves, Sir Frederick, operation by, ii. 245.
Triumvirate, ii. 126, 129.
Truce, flag of, i. 66.
Truro, i. 3.
Tufnell, Captain, i. 237.
Tugela River, ii. 143.
,, Valley, ii. 98.
Turkey, i. 18, 107.
Turner, Lieutenant Chamley, ii. 160.
Tutu Bush, i. 311, 313, 315.
,, Plateau, i. 315, 316.
Tweezle Down, i. 225.

Udaipur, i. 148.
Udloko Regiment, ii. 32, 81.
Uhamu, ii. 39, 41, 45, 58, 72, 100.
Ujjain, i. 149.
Ulundi, ii. 9, 15, 23, 39, 42, 45, 47, 55, 72, 80, 97, 101, 102, 142.
Umbandeen, ii. 122, 137.
Umbeline, ii. 18, 30, 46, 76, 84, 98.
Umbonambi, ii. 60.
Umcityu Regiment, ii. 54, 62, 80.
Umfundisweeni, ii. 4.
Umjeid Ali, i. 128.
Umkandampenvu, ii. 62.
Umpanda, ii. 47.
Umpanda's Prime Minister, ii. 101.
Umquikela, ii. 4, 5, 6.
Umsebe, ii. 30.
Umsinga, ii. 143.

Umtonga, Cetewayo's half brother, ii. 47, 51.
Umvolosi, ii. 30, 33, 42, 80.
Umvunyana River, ii. 74.
Umzila, ii. 133.
Undi Regiment, ii. 63.
Union Steamship Company's vessel, ii. 145.
United Service Institute, i. 253.
Upland, the, i. 34, 37, 50, 51, 54.
Urinals, night, ii. 233.
Usibebu, ii. 81, 125, 135.
Utrecht, ii. 7, 18, 23, 26, 36, 43, 58, 71, 72, 74, 98, 127.
,, Landdrost, ii. 43.
Uys, Mynheer Swart Dirks, ii. 14, 40.
,, Piet, ii. 10, 31, 33, 35, 36, 40, 42, 47, 52, 58, 72.

"Vagabond," i. 219, 231.
Van Amberg, i. 24.
Varna, i. 21, 26.
Vauban, i. 21.
Vaughan, Archbishop, ii. 227, 240.
,, Captain, ii. 44.
Vengeance, H.M.S., i. 30.
Venter's Drift, ii. 33.
Verner, Colonel Willoughby, ii. 93.
Vernon, John, i. 241.
Vesuvius, H.M.S., i. 30.
Veterinary Amateur, i. 173.
Viceroy, i. 167.
Vickers Company, mechanics sent out by, ii. 260.
Victoria and Albert, H.M.S., i. 30.
Victoria Cross, i. 47, 196; ii. 55, 69, 79, 99, 222.
,, Hill, i. 97.
,, Queen, ii. 89, 108, 147, 149, 218, 243, 254.
,, Ridge, i. 36.
Victory, H.M.S., i. 8.
Villiers, Sir Henry de, ii. 118, 124, 126.
Virgil, i. 7, 113, 240.
,, re-read, ii. 238.
Vivian, Colonel, i. 104.
Volksraad, ii. 70.
Volunteer Forces, ii. 215.
Volunteers at Durban, ii. 145.
Von Linsingen, i. 315.
Voyageurs, ii. 173.
Vryheid, ii. 42, 46, 58.

INDEX

Waddington, Mr., ii. 90.
Waddy's Company, 13th Light Infantry, ii. 63.
Wadi Halfa, ii. 171, 172.
"Wait-a-bits" nickname, ii. 201.
"Wait for the waggon," ii. 79.
Wakkerstroom, ii. 23, 43, 110, 111.
Walford, N., Colonel, ii. 223.
Walker, Sir Forestier, General, ii. 271.
Walkinshaw, ii. 15, 50, 71, 85, 96, 114, 122, 160, 169.
Walmer, ii. 161.
Walsh, Archbishop, ii. 241.
Wantage, Lord, ii. 205, 211, 212, 215.
Warden, Prime, Fishmongers' Company, ii. 227.
"War Fever," ii. 246.
"War-game," i. 296; ii. 4, 19, 20.
War Minister, ii. 103.
War Office, denies my existence, ii. 147.
War training, improvement, ii. 217.
Warren, Captain, i. 311.
Waterkloof, i. 315.
Waterloo, i. 172.
  ,, Place, i. 13.
Watson, Mrs., ii. 160.
Weedon, rifle from, ii. 233.
Weenen, ii. 10.
Wei-hai-wei, ii. 239.
Welch, Stephen, i. 77.
Wellington, i. 115.
  ,, College, i. 292.
  ,, Duke of, i. 25, 172; ii. 115.
Wesselstroom, ii. 14, 24, 43, 73, 127.
West Coast, i. 287.
Western, Great, i. 109.
West Meon, Hants, ii. 220.
Westminster, Catholic Bishop of, ii. 218.
  ,, Dean of, ii. 218, 255.
Weston, ride to, ii. 142.
"Westward Ho," i. 210.
Wetherall, G. Adjutant-General, i. 103.
Wheeler, Sir Hugh, i. 127.
White, General, my predecessor, ii. 183.
  ,, Major, i. 162.
  ,, Maurice, called on with Lord Roberts, ii. 258.
  ,, Messrs. T., & Co., i. 240, 253, 292, 293.
  ,, Sir George, made Field-Marshal, ii. 278.
  ,, Umvolosi, ii. 28, 46, 80.

White's lanterns, ii. 15.
Wight, Isle of, i. 9.
Wilayati, i. 127, 138, 139, 140.
Wilkes, Captain, i. 207.
Wilkinson, Messrs., i. 120.
William the Conqueror, i. 239.
Williams, Mr. Powell, M.P., ii. 233.
  ,, Lieutenant, ii. 53, 72.
Wilson's (Captain) Company, ii. 30.
Wimbledon, i. 237.
Winchester, i. 4.
  ,, Bishop of, i. 240.
Windsor, commanded to, ii. 149.
Wingate, Lieutenant, ii. 156, 178.
Witham, i. 232.
  ,, Mr., ii. 228.
W. Napier, General, i. 293.
Wodehouse, Lieutenant-General J. H., ii. 156.
Wolff, Sir Drummond, ii. 91.
Wolseley, Lord, i. 255, 257, 258, 259, 272, 273, 280, 281, 284, 294, 295; ii. 79, 81, 82, 90, 93, 106, 112, 147, 150, 151, 152, 170, 171, 174, 175, 176, 177, 178, 181, 186, 187, 188, 191, 192, 194, 203, 209, 222, 226, 228, 235, 240, 251, 255, 256.
Wood, Benjamin, M.P., i. 4.
  ,, C. M., Lieutenant, at Wei-hai-wei and Andover, ii. 242, 262.
  ,, Charles Page, ii. 188.
  ,, Cornet, i. 103.
  ,, Evelyn, Brigadier-General, ii. 82, 83, 89, 93, 110, 114, 119, 122, 132, 148, 150, 160, 162, 171, 180, 201, 223.
  ,, ,, Colonel, i. 310, 322; ii. 11, 23, 27, 32, 71.
  ,, ,, Fitz-G., i. 285.
  ,, ,, Lieutenant-Colonel, i. 264, 277. 285.
  ,, ,, General, i. 307.
  ,, Lady, ii. 62, 96, 103, 119, 178, 181, 217, 218.
  ,, Matthew, Lord Mayor, i. 287.
  ,, Messrs., i. 114.
  ,, Midshipman, i. 38, 41, 42, 55, 71, 75.
  ,, Rev. Sir John Page, i. 96.
  ,, Sir Francis, i. 221.
  ,, ,, William Page, i. 107.

INDEX

Wood's Column, i. 304.
,, Irregulars, ii. 46, 47, 58, 67, 68, 71, 81, 82, 83, 98.
,, Regiment, i. 261, 273, 274, 276, 277.
Woodford and Walthamstow, accident to grocer's van while motoring near, ii. 258.
Woodgate, Captain E. R. P., ii. 6, 16, 18, 25, 26, 27, 30, 40, 62.
,, Lieutenant, i. 270, 271, 274, 276, 290.
Woolmer Forest, i. 244; ii. 213.
Woolwich, i. 3.
,, Artillery centralised at, ii. 246.
,, Government lighter kept waiting, 267.
Woolwich, Royal Military Academy, ii. 75, 254.
,, and Sandhurst, inspect academies, ii. 254.
Woronzow Road, i. 37, 39, 50, 77.
Wortley Stuart, Major, ii. 155.
Wren and Gurney, Captain Wood studied with, for India Civil Service, ii. 267.
Wrench, Hon. F., i. 241; ii. 182.

Wrey, Captain Bourchier, Commander of H.M.S. *Brisk*, ii. 243.
Wynne, Sir Watkin, Colonel, ii. 270.
,, Major, ii. 156, 157, 169, 173.
Wynne's Egyptian Battalion, ii. 172.

Yaos, raising battalion of, ii. 239.
Yeomanry, Bucks, 249 men on parade, ii. 241.
Yeomanry characteristics, ii. 262.
Youatt, on the Horse, i. 174.
Young, Daniel, i. 41.

Zabanga, ii. 102.
Zagazig, ii. 159.
Zanyorkwee, Ravine, i. 313.
,, River, i. 314.
Zanzibar, ii. 145.
Zebehr, ii. 164, 168.
Zirapur, i. 149.
Zobell, Herr, i. 202, 222.
Zouaves, i. 20, 79.
Zulu Campaign, ii. 7, 8, 33, 51.
Zululand, ii. 28, 81, 85, 100, 108, 140.
Zulus, i. 298; ii. 10, 32.
Zunguin Mountain, ii. 30, 31, 40, 42, 53, 54, 58, 68.
,, Nek, ii. 51, 52.

www.ingramcontent.com/pod-product-compliance
Lightning Source LLC
Chambersburg PA
CBHW021755220426
43662CB00006B/68